Muhammad's Military Expeditions

ADVANCED PRAISE FOR IBRAHIM'S *MUHAMMAD'S MILITARY EXPEDITIONS*

"This book is an ambitious, and much needed, survey of the earliest Muslim accounts of the Medinan period of Muhammad's prophetic mission and their major themes. Prof. Ibrahim offers the reader and scholar an indispensable map of this early genre of Arabic historical writing dedicated to the last decade of Muhammad's life and provides an important critical analysis of both the earliest accounts and their modern reception in the Arabic-speaking world. I recommend this work wholeheartedly."

—Sean W. Anthony, Professor of Near Eastern and South Asian Languages and Cultures, The Ohio State University

"In this meticulous work of scholarship, Ayman Ibrahim shows how medieval Muslim historians presented the birth of Islam as an exceptionally violent story. This is a troubling legacy that every thinking Muslim must come to terms with, and they could be helped by another insight from this remarkable book: Muslim historiography had its own earthly reasons for hyperbole, and the historical truth may be quite different."

—Mustafa Akyol, author of *Reopening Muslim Minds: A Return to Reason, Freedom, and Tolerance*

"In this comprehensive and meticulously researched book Ayman Ibrahim delves deep into the multifaceted and intricate tapestry of Muhammad's *maghāzī*, shedding light on the complexities of Muslim historiographical traditions. Ibrahim's approach, marked by scholarly precision and critical analysis, brings to the forefront a vivid portrayal of how medieval Muslim narrators shaped and conveyed the image of Muhammad as a divinely guided commander-in-chief. The book does not just dissect historical accounts; it disentangles the layers of storytelling, revealing how these narratives evolved, transformed, and were meticulously crafted to suit varying sociopolitical, sectarian, and religious contexts. It illuminates the centrality of the *maghāzī* in Muslim thought, highlighting their theological implications and their role in interpreting Islam's scripture. With a blend of Arabic Muslim sources, secondary studies, and insights from non-Muslim scholarship, this book serves as an invaluable contribution, providing a nuanced understanding of the complexities and challenges inherent in Islamic historiography. The author's meticulous dissection of various *maghāzī* accounts throughout the chapters underscores the complex nature of these narratives, leaving readers with a profound appreciation for the depth and complexity of medieval Muslim thought surrounding Muhammad's military career."

—Uriel Simonsohn, Head of the Haifa Laboratory for Religious Studies, University of Haifa

"The most thorough, wide-ranging, and well-informed study of Muhammad's military expeditions available in English today. Ibrahim's methodology and arguments will spur fruitful debate among readers. There is no question, however, that everyone interested in Muhammad's life story, the status of warfare in early Islam, and the construction of the Islamic tradition will benefit from his exploration of these delicate and important issues."

—Luke Yarbrough, Professor of early and medieval Islamic history and thought at UCLA

"In this pathbreaking new book, Ayman Ibrahim makes available to a broader audience the many memories that the Islamic tradition has kept of Muhammad's military campaigns. As such, it offers an essential supplement to other collections of Muhammad's biographical traditions that focus more on presenting him as a prophet and religious teacher. Here we learn how Muhammad's followers remembered his martial leadership of the early community in a way that is both critical and true to the sources. On the whole, this book marks a significant contribution to the study of the historical Muhammad and the memory of Muhammad in the Islamic tradition, focusing on aspects of his career that are not always given the attention that they merit."

—Stephen J. Shoemaker, Professor and Ira E. Gaston Fellow in Christian Studies, Department of Religious Studies, University of Oregon

"This is a magnificent and thorough survey of the literary aspects of Muhammad's conquests. Such is the breadth of primary and secondary source material adduced in Ibrahim's work, that it makes other works on the subject redundant. However, this work does not even suffice with historiographic discussion, but places the events described and analyzed within their social, religious, and even legal contexts. An absolutely vital contribution to the study of early Islamic history, the life of Muhammad, and even to contemporary Arabic-language perceptions and assessments of the prophetic era. This will be the go-to volume on the subject for the foreseeable future."

—David B. Cook, Professor of Religion at Rice University

Muhammad's Military Expeditions

A Critical Reading in Original Muslim Sources

AYMAN S. IBRAHIM

OXFORD
UNIVERSITY PRESS

OXFORD
UNIVERSITY PRESS

Oxford University Press is a department of the University of Oxford. It furthers the University's objective of excellence in research, scholarship, and education by publishing worldwide. Oxford is a registered trade mark of Oxford University Press in the UK and certain other countries.

Published in the United States of America by Oxford University Press
198 Madison Avenue, New York, NY 10016, United States of America.

Library of Congress Cataloging-in-Publication Data
Names: Ibrahim, Ayman S., 1973– author.
Title: Muhammad's military expeditions : a critical reading in original Muslim sources / by Ayman S. Ibrahim.
Description: 1. | New York : Oxford University Press, 2024. | Includes index.
Identifiers: LCCN 2024004677 (print) | LCCN 2024004678 (ebook) |
ISBN 9780197769171 (hardback) | ISBN 9780197769195 (epub)
Subjects: LCSH: Muḥammad, Prophet, -632—Military leadership. |
Muhḥammad, Prophet, -632—Campaigns. |
Muhḥammad, Prophet, -632—Biography—History and criticism.
Classification: LCC BP77.7 .I285 2024 (print) | LCC BP77.7 (ebook) |
DDC 297.6/3—dc23/eng/20240217
LC record available at https://lccn.loc.gov/2024004677
LC ebook record available at https://lccn.loc.gov/2024004678

DOI: 10.1093/oso/9780197769171.001.0001

The manufacturer's authorised representative in the EU for product safety is Oxford University Press España S.A. of El Parque Empresarial San Fernando de Henares, Avenida de Castilla, 2 – 28830 Madrid (www.oup.es/en or product.safety@oup.com). OUP España S.A. also acts as importer into Spain of products made by the manufacturer.

To the loving memory of my father, who did not complete his high school education, yet always encouraged me to read, study, and write. Without his support I would not be where I am now.

To my mother who loves me unconditionally and cherishes everything I write, even before reading it.

To my sisters whom I deeply admire for their perseverance and strength and who genuinely care for me.

And to my loving and caring wife who is undoubtedly my most valuable treasure and with whom I cherish every moment I live.

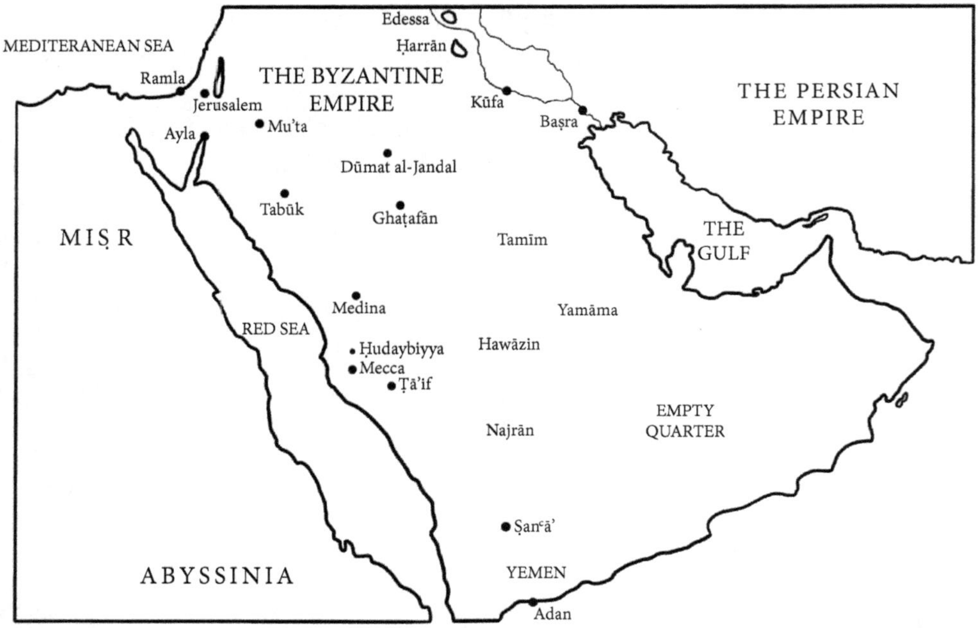

Seventh - Century Arabia
According To Muslim Historiography

Contents

Acknowledgments xi
Glossary of Key Terms xiii
Muhammad's Major Maghāzī *as Reported by Ibn Jarīr al-Ṭabarī (d. 310/923)* xv

1. Muhammad's Expeditions: Introduction 1
   Classical Muslims on Muhammad's Expeditions 4
   Modern and Contemporary Muslims on Muhammad's Expeditions 11
   Non-Muslim Interactions with Muhammad's *Maghāzī* 24
   The *Maghāzī* as Historiography: Methodology and Approach 46
   Structure of the Book 57
2. Muhammad's Early Expeditions: The Strategic *Maghāzī* before the Battle of Badr 60
   The Incursion of Ḥamza ibn ᶜAbd al-Muṭṭalib (1/623) 62
   The Incursion of ᶜUbayda ibn al-Ḥārith (1/623) 70
   The Incursion of Saᶜd ibn Abī Waqqāṣ (1/623) 76
   The Earliest Four Raids Led by Muhammad (1–2/623–624) 79
   The Incursion of ᶜAbdullāh ibn Jaḥsh to Nakhla (2/624) 90
3. Muhammad's Confrontations with Meccan Pagans: The Battles of Badr and Uḥud 103
   The Battle of Badr (2/624) 104
   The Battle of Uḥud (3/625) 121
4. Muhammad's Triumph over the Meccans 138
   The Battle of the Trench (5/627) 139
   The Raid of the Ḥudaybiyya (6/628) 154
   The Conquest of Mecca (8/630) 178
5. Muhammad's Confrontations with the Jews 198
   The Raid against Banū Qaynuqāᶜ (2/624) 202
   The Raid against Banū al-Naḍīr (4/625) 215
   The Raid against Banū Qurayẓa (5/627) 225
   The Raids to Khaybar and Fadak (7/628) 238
6. The King of Arabia: Raiding the Bedouins 247
   The Incursion to Banū Jadhīma (8/630) 248

The Battle of Ḥunayn (8/630) 254
The Raid to al-Ṭā'if (8/630) 269

7. Muhammad's Expeditions to Byzantine Frontiers 280
The Raid to Mu'ta (8/629) 281
The Raid to Tabūk (9/631) 299
Usāma's Incursion to Syria (11/632) 316

Concluding Remarks: Which Muhammad? Whose *Maghāzī*? 323

About the Author 333
Works Cited 335
Index 373

Acknowledgments

My interest in the topic of Muhammad's military expeditions began in 2010, when I was working on my first PhD. I began piling up numerous Arabic primary sources that detail fascinating aspects of the topic, and I located ample Arabic Muslim scholarly studies that engage and interpret it. Fortunately, I also had countless discussions on the topic with outstanding Western scholars. This propelled me to begin writing this book in 2021.

During the initial stages, I benefited enormously from the incredible wisdom and critical remarks of David B. Cook, Fred M. Donner, Gabriel S. Reynolds, Uriel Simonsohn, and Luke B. Yarbrough. These scholars read portions of this book and kindly offered their observations and valuable insights. Each of them taught me something along the way. I am very thankful for each of them. Then, during the final stages of writing this book, I became friends with two outstanding thinkers. The first is Stephen Shoemaker. His ideas constantly encouraged me to think about the Muhammad of history and the one of traditions. I am grateful for his continued support and our growing friendship. The second is Mustafa Akyol. I had wonderful conversations with him about the topic and have always appreciated his unique approach to and interpretations of Islam. He generously commended my work, especially as he read my methodology and the chapter on the Jews. I am grateful for this edifying friendship.

In all my writings, Jack Tannous is somewhere behind the scenes. His knowledgeable insights and intriguing ideas inspire me and always open new horizons of research. Once he begins talking—or texting—about a topic, I just stay still and listen, knowing there is enormous opportunity and great wisdom flowing in. I am honored to call him a friend.

In 2021, when I began the conversation with Oxford University Press about this book, Cynthia Read believed in the project and its importance. She encouraged me to proceed and was thrilled about another book for me with OUP. Then, as she moved on to retirement, she gave the baton to the outstanding, professional, and supportive Theodore Calderara. He led the process marvelously, assisting the work along the way until it came to fruition. He also believed in the project and supported it enthusiastically. I am genuinely thankful for Cynthia and Theodore and their wonderful team.

I am greatly indebted to my supervisors and colleagues at Southern Seminary. I could not ask for a better community. They constantly support my work and inspire me to write more. Every book I publish is a result of their continued encouragement. I am also full of gratitude for my students at Southern and my staff at the Jenkins Center. They help me think about Islam and its traditional accounts. Their questions and passion to study are a source of inspiration to me. On my team at the Jenkins Center, I am particularly thankful for Tracy Martin, who reads and edits my work. If there is anything eloquent or beautiful in my sentences, it is probably because of her talent and skill. I am very grateful for her work. Thanks also to the meticulous and thorough Torey Teer who proofread and edited the first four chapters in their initial stage. Special thanks to the Office of Communications at Southern Seminary, especially to Kelsie Marques, who designed the map of the Arabian Peninsula at the beginning of the book.

Finally, I am eternally grateful to my wife for her loving and exceptional support. I could never do anything of this enormous importance without her constant belief in me. To her, all my love and gratitude.

And, to all, I say *shukran*, *alf shukr*.

Glossary of Key Terms

ᶜAbbāsids: They overthrew the Umayyads in ca. 133/750. They trace their lineage back to al-ᶜAbbās ibn ᶜAbd al-Muṭṭalib (d. 32/653), the uncle of Muhammad from the other branch of the Hāshim's family. The ᶜAbbāsids claimed that the imamate was only in their family, either by *wirātha* (inheritance) from Muhammad or by *waṣiyya* (bequest) from ᶜAlī and his grandson Abū Hāshim. Cf. ***ᶜAlids*** and ***Hāshimites***.

Ahl al-ḥadīth: The *ḥadīth* scholars, who were also known as *aṣḥāb al-ḥadīth* or the *ḥadīth* party, identifying them as the adherents of Muhammad's traditions. They revered the *ḥadīth*, and elevated it as the second authority in Islam, only second to the Qur'ān. They grew in power in the early ᶜAbbāsid period and became the major opposition against the caliphal authority during the *miḥna*. Cf. ***traditionists***, ***ᶜulamā'***, and ***muḥaddithūn***.

ᶜAlids: The descendants of ᶜAlī, who claim the imamate in his descendants alone. Today, they represent broad Shīᶜism and include several groups, such as the Imāmīs, Ismāᶜīlīs, and Zaydīs. Cf. ***Shīᶜism***, ***Saba'iyya***, and ***ᶜAbbāsids***.

Anṣār: The locals of Medina known as the supporters of Muhammad. They believed his message and helped him and his followers after their emigration from Mecca. Cf. *muhājirūn* and *hijra*.

Futūḥ: These are the military conquests conducted by the Arab commanders after Muhammad's death during the caliphate period. The term also refers to the written traditions (*futūḥ* literature) that deal with the military expeditions. This Arabic term describes the conquests as acts of "opening" and liberating the conquered lands.

Ḥadīth: This is a report of a saying, teaching, or deed attributed to a religious figure, particularly the Prophet Muhammad. Its plural form is *aḥādīth*, which are brought together in sets by various Muslim compilers.

Hāshimites: This refers to the Hāshimite family, the wide family of Muhammad, which includes both ᶜAlids and ᶜAbbāsids. The Hāshimites claim that the imamate is in all Hāshim descendants, both ᶜAlids and ᶜAbbāsids.

Hijra: This refers to the emigration of Muhammad and his followers from Mecca to Medina. It took place in the year 622 in the Julian calendar, which was later adopted by the second Caliph ᶜUmar as the starting year of the Muslim lunar calendar, known as Hijri dating.

Maghāzī: This term refers to the raids, incursions, or expeditions organized, led, or commissioned by Muhammad after he emigrated from Mecca to Medina. It also refers to Muhammad's life generally. This term was later developed to *sīra* (biography). The noun *maghāzī* is plural of *maghzā*. Its verbal form is *ghazā*, which means to invade.

***Muḥaddithūn* (sg. *muḥaddith*)**: The transmitters or scholars of *ḥadīth*; experts in traditions, and thus traditionists.

Muhājirūn: These are the Meccan emigrant Believers, who were the earliest to believe in Muhammad's message. Under the hostile persecution of the pagan Meccans, they were forced to leave their homes and emigrate with Muhammad to Medina, in the event called the *hijra*.

***Munāfiqūn* (sg. *Munāfiq*)**: The term refers to "lukewarm Believers" or "uncommitted Muslims," yet commonly translated as "hypocrites."

***Mushrikūn* (sg. *Mushrik*)**: The term is best translated as "associaters," those associating partners with Allah. It is commonly understood as polytheists.

Shīᶜism: A vision within Islam which claims that Muhammad's family is the only source for political leadership and religious guidance. The religio-political leaders are called Imāms. Shīᶜism in the early Islamic period is better understood as a political movement of the supporters of ᶜAlī. The commonly understood religious Shīᶜite veneration—advocating that *ahl al-bayt* (Muhammad's Household) is the source of leadership (imamate)—did not develop until later.

Sīra: This means "biography," especially when linked to Muhammad. Linguistically, the word refers to behavior, deeds, and conduct.

***Ṭabaqāt* (sg. *Ṭabaqa*)**: Classes or generations of the Believers.

Tafsīr: The word means "explanation" and refers to a commentary on the Qur'ān, or more generally the branch of Qur'ānic exegesis within the Islamic sciences.

Ta'rīkh: The term refers to historiography, which is writing about the past. It is the literary genre that represents what Muslims believe to have happened in their *tārīkh* (past).

Traditionalists: The term throughout this study usually refers to Muslims adopting a traditional and mostly conservative approach toward Islamic origins. When used in relation to non-Muslim authors, it refers to scholars who are likely to view the sources' reliability positively.

Traditionists: Scholars and transmitters of Muslim traditions. See ***muḥaddithūn***.

Muhammad's Major *Maghāzī* as Reported by Ibn Jarīr al-Ṭabarī (d. 310/923)

The *Hijrī* Year 1 (622–623)
The incursion led by Ḥamza
The incursion led by ᶜUbayada
The incursion led by Saᶜd ibn Abī Waqqāṣ
Muhammad's raid to al-Abwā' and other minor expeditions

The *Hijrī* Year 2 (623–624)
The Incursion of ᶜAbdullāh ibn Jaḥsh to Nakhla
The Battle of Badr
The raid against the Jews of Banū Qaynuqāᶜ
The raid of al-Sawīq

The *Hijrī* Year 3 (624–625)
The assassination of Kaᶜb ibn al-Ashraf the Jew
The raid to al-Qarada
The assassination of Abū Rāfiᶜ the Jew
The Battle of Uḥud
The raid to Ḥamrā' al-Asad

The *Hijrī* Year 4 (625–626)
The raid to al-Rajīᶜ
The raid to Bi'r Maᶜūna, against Najd
The raid against the Jews of Banū al-Naḍīr
The Expedition of Dhāt al-Riqāᶜ
The Expedition of al-Sawīq (or Badr al-Mawᶜid)

The *Hijrī* Year 5 (626–627)
The raid to Dūmat al-Jandal
The Battle of the Trench, or the Confederates
The raid against the Jews of Banū Qurayẓa

The *Hijrī* Year 6 (627–628)
The raid against the Banū Liḥyān
The raid to Dhū Qarad
The raid against Banū al-Muṣṭaliq (al-Muraysiᶜ)
The raid and treaty of the Ḥudaybiyya

The *Hijrī* Year 7 (628–629)
The raid against the Jews of Khaybar
The raid against the Jews of Fadak
The raid to Wādī al-Qurā

The *Hijrī* Year 8 (629–630)
The incursion against the Banū al-Mulawwiḥ
The incursion against Dhāt al-Salāsil
The incursion of al-Khabaṭ (tree leaves)
Minor Incursions (e.g., Ibn Abī Ḥadrad and Abū Qatāda)
The raid to Mu'ta
The Conquest of Mecca
The incursion of Khālid ibn al-Walīd to Banū Jadhīma
The Battle of Ḥunayn (targeting Hawāzin)
The siege of al-Ṭā'if (targeting Thaqīf)

The *Hijrī* Year 9 (630–631)
The raid to Tabūk

The *Hijrī* Year 11 (632–633)
Usāma's Incursion to Syria

1

Muhammad's Expeditions: Introduction

> In early Islam, Muslims never fought except in self-defense or to push away those opposing the Islamic proclamation by using charitable preaching.—ᶜAbbās Maḥmūd al-ᶜAqqād (1889–1964)

> Islam is truth, and everything else is false—that which Islam prescribed, be it jihad or else, is truth that does not require apology or justification. We do not adjust Islam and its history to the taste of people and their intellectual ideologies in any given age.—Akram Ḍiyā' al-ᶜUmarī (1942–)

> Muslims used warfare only in self-defense.—Abubakr Asadulla (1970–)

> In fact, expecting from Muhammad a perfect universal wisdom, totally unbound from his time and culture, would not be consistent with Qur'anic theology.—Turkish Muslim modernist Mustafa Akyol (1972–)[1]

This is a historiographical study concerned with the fascinating and multifaceted historical accounts, written by classical Muslims, of the life and career of their prophet, Muhammad. This book focuses on the last ten years of his life when he reportedly resided in Medina, after being forced by pagan Meccans to emigrate from his hometown, Mecca, to Medina.[2] Muslim traditions describe those ten years as significantly pivotal in the history of the

[1] ᶜAqqād, *Mā yuqāl*, 168; ᶜUmarī, *Mujtamaᶜ*, 22–23; Asadulla, *Islam*, 53; Akyol, *Islam*, 59. In this study, bibliographical references are presented in abbreviated form (author and the first few words of the title). See Works Cited for publishers and publication places and dates.

[2] For secondary studies on Muhammad's life and career, see the valuable Arabic studies of Akram Ḍiyā'al-ᶜUmarī, *al-Sīra al-nabawiyya*; ᶜUmarī, *al-Risāla wa-l-rasūl*; Birayk Abū Māyla, *al-Sarāyā wa-l-buᶜūth*; Abū Māyla, *Ghazwat*; Haykal, *Ḥayāt Muḥammad*; Haykal, *Fī manzil*; Khalīl ᶜAbd al-Karīm, *Quraysh: Min al-qabīla ilā al-dawla al-markaziyya*; ᶜAbd al-Karīm, *Mujtamaᶜ Yathrib*; Sayyid Maḥmūd al-Qimanī, *al-Ḥizb al-hāshimī wa ta'sīs al-dawla al-islāmiyya*; Qimanī, *Ḥurūb dawlat al-rasūl*; Aḥmad Ibrāhīm al-Sharīf, *al-Dawla al-islāmiyya*; Sharīf, *Makka wa-l-Madīna*; Ṭāhā Ḥusayn, *ᶜAlā hāmish al-sīra*; ᶜAbbās Maḥmūd al-ᶜAqqād, *ᶜAbqariyyat Muḥammad*; Maᶜrūf al-Ruṣāfī, *Kitāb al-shakhṣiyya al-Muḥammadiyya*; Muḥammad ibn ᶜAbd al-Wahhāb, *Mukhtaṣar sīrat al-Rasūl*. For secondary studies in English, see Ibrahim, *Stated*, 66–119; Buhl et al., "Muḥammad," *EI*[2], 7:360ff.;

Muhammad's Military Expeditions. Ayman S. Ibrahim, Oxford University Press. © Oxford University Press 2024.
DOI: 10.1093/oso/9780197769171.003.0001

Muslim community. They *represent* a remarkable portrayal of Muhammad's success not only in reconciling many Arab tribes under his leadership, as they embraced his religious message, but also in becoming the most powerful leader in Arabia.[3] In particular, this study focuses on the various ways early Muslim historians described Muhammad's military campaigns.[4] Scholars and students of Arabic Muslim literature are now truly fortunate—as compared to previous generations—to have access to ample Muslim primary sources, many of which are in scholarly critical editions and some of which have been translated into English.[5] The question remains: why should we study Muhammad's military activities?

From the earliest generations of Islam, Muslims cherished and circulated numerous traditions about Muhammad's expeditions, calling them *maghāzī rasūl Allāh* (the expeditions of Allah's messenger).[6] These *maghāzī* (expeditions), as described in the Muslim sources, were military campaigns led or commissioned by Muhammad. They transformed the Muslim community, rapidly and decisively, from an inferior and vulnerable community in Mecca for thirteen years to a strong and dominant one in Medina under Muhammad's leadership during the last ten years of his life. Muslims in Mecca were reportedly identified as *al-mustaḍᶜafūn* (weak, downtrodden,

Brockopp, ed., *Cambridge Companion*; Margoliouth, *Mohammed*; Margoliouth, *Mohammedanism*; Rodinson, *Muhammad: Prophet of Islam*; Watt, *Muḥammad at Mecca*; Watt, *Muḥammad at Medina*; Watt, *Muḥammad: Prophet and Statesman*; Michael Cook, *Muhammad*, 12–24; Andrae, *Mohammed: The Man and His Faith*; Gabriel, *Muhammad*; Bennett, *In Search of Muhammad*; Lings, *Muhammad*; Ali Dashti, *Twenty-Three Years*. For a recent study on the sources of Muhammad's life, see Anthony, *Muḥammad*, 83–101.

3 The word "represent" is intentional. I discuss source problems later in this chapter; however, here, see Robinson, *Empire and Elites*, viii, where he argues that our sources provide a "representation rather than record," as Muslim historians "wrote well after the events they describe." See Hawting, "Review," 126–129, where he argues, "It is difficult to see how anyone could expect to recover real facts about Muḥammad's life from the sort of traditions and reports examined here" (127). See also Rubin, *Eye*, 1–3, where he treats the Muslim accounts as reflecting "the self-image of medieval Islamic society" (3), not Muhammad's time, and examines these texts "for the sake of the stories recorded in them, not for the sake of the events described in these stories" (1). Rippin writes, "The actual 'history' in the sense of 'what really happened' has become totally subsumed within later interpretation and is virtually, if not totally, inextricable from it," as "the records we have are the existential records of the thought and faith of later generations." Rippin, "Literary," 156; also Rippin, "Function," 1–20.

4 For a recent study on Muhammad's *maghāzī*, see Ibrahim, *Stated*, 66–119, where I focus on the "stated" motivations for the Medinan military campaigns.

5 On the scholarly breakthrough in editing and translating numerous Arabic Muslim primary sources, see the comments of Abdel Haleem, professor of Islamic studies at the School of Oriental and African Studies, University of London, in his foreword to the 2014 edition of Maᶜmar ibn Rāshid and ᶜAbd al-Razzāq al-Ṣanᶜānī, *The Expeditions: An Early Biography of Muhammad*, xi.

6 See, for instance, Ibn Saᶜd, *Ṭabaqāt*, 2:3; Khalīfa, *Ta'rīkh*, 1:57–65; Ibn Ḥabīb, *Muḥabbar*, 127; Wāqidī, *Maghāzī*, 7; Ibn Hishām, *Sīra*, 1:598; Fasawī, *Maᶜrifa*, 1:508; Ibn al-Kalbī, *Nasab*, 1:347; Yaᶜqūbī, *Ta'rīkh*, 2:45; Kharkūshī, *Sharaf*, 3:7–10; Suhaylī, *Rawḍ*, 5:99; Kalāᶜī, *Iktifā'*, 1:586.

or oppressed).[7] In Medina, through strategic and successful *maghāzī*, Muhammad's community controlled all of the region of West Arabia, known as the Hijaz, to the extent that by his death in 11/632, some identified him the "King of the Hijaz."[8]

The Arabic Muslim literature on Muhammad's *maghāzī* is bountiful. Since this book focuses on Muhammad's *maghāzī*, a survey of this literature is important not only to establish the centrality of the topic in Islamic thought but also to relay the uniqueness and contribution of this book. To that end, in this chapter, I first explore that which classical Muslim narrators wrote on Muhammad's *maghāzī* and the ways they used the accounts to reflect Allah's support for Muhammad and the believers. In the second section, I examine discussions by modern and contemporary Muslims, relaying how they interpret the accounts of the *maghāzī*.[9] In particular, I discuss their articulation of the motivations and results of Muhammad's military campaigns. The first two sections of this chapter thus establish the centrality of the *maghāzī*, as a literary genre, as well as its importance among Muslims, past and present. In the third section, I take the discussion to non-Muslim scholarship. I explore briefly early views by non-Muslims on Muhammad and his career before I focus on works and arguments of key Western scholars from the nineteenth century until our present day. This section leads smoothly to the fourth section of this chapter, in which I explain my approach to Islamic historiography, highlighting the source problems. I discuss how these problems should give pause to any historian due to the internal and external textual challenges. In the fifth and final section, I survey the major sources on Muhammad's *maghāzī*, particularly those used in this study. Then I discuss the structure of the book, detailing the suggested categorizations of Muhammad's *maghāzī* as examined in the subsequent chapters.

[7] The term *mustaḍʿafūn* appears in the Qur'ān (Q 4:97; 8:26). For primary sources on it, see Muqātil, *Tafsīr*, 2:87–108; Ṭabarī, *Jāmiʿ*, 9:110 (on being vulnerable and weak at Mecca), 13:476–478; Zamakhsharī, *Kashshāf*, 2:211; Rāzī, *Mafātiḥ*, 15:474; Qurṭubī, *Jāmiʿ*, 7:394; Bayḍāwī, *Anwār*, 3:56. For secondary studies, see Rahemtulla, *Qur'an*, 20–24, 273; Esack, "In Search," 78–97 (esp. 81).

[8] Ibn Hishām, *Sīra*, 2:336; Ṭabarī, *Ta'rīkh*, 1576, 1582; Yaʿqūbī, *Ta'rīkh*, 2:56; Zuhrī, *Maghāzī*, 161–162. In Bayhaqī, *Dalā'il*, 4:230–232, it is rendered "the king of Yathrib."

[9] It is true that academics differ on periodization. For valuable discussions, see Donner, "Periodization," 20–36; Borrut, "Vanishing," 37–68; Morony, "Bayn," 247–251; Goitein, "Plea," 224–228. In this study, the classical period stretches from Islam's origins to the fifteenth century. While some scholars do not make a distinction between "contemporary" and "modern," I use the terms to describe living writers and the deceased modern ones of the sixteenth to twentieth centuries, respectively.

Classical Muslims on Muhammad's Expeditions

In classical Islamic sources, Muslim narrators marvel at Muhammad's *maghāzī*. They list them, specify their targets, describe their eventful details in the battleground, and emphasize their tremendous success. They also describe miracles performed by Muhammad during these battles.[10] For these writers, Muhammad's *maghāzī* reflect Islam's hegemony and Allah's favor on his community against pagans and non-Muslims who rejected his message.[11] In one of the earliest extant Muslim commentaries on the Qur'ān, Muqātil ibn Sulaymān (d. 150/767)—in his interpretation of *sūrat Muḥammad* (Q 47)—explains that Muslims marched on raids not for their own sake but because Allah taught them *kayfa yaṣnaᶜūn bi-l-kuffār* (how to deal with the unbelievers) in battles.[12] For Muqātil, Allah was guiding the Muslims to fight *al-mushrikūn ḥaythu wajadūhum* (the polytheists—or better, associaters—wherever they find them) until they forsake *al-shirk* (the sin of associating partners with Allah).[13] Muhammad's expeditions, says Muqātil, aimed at fighting *ḥattā lā yakūn fī al-ᶜArab mushrik* (in order that there be no associater among the Arabs).[14] Many classical Muslim *mufassirūn* (Qur'ān

[10] For Muhammad's miracles during the Battle of Badr, see Ibn Hishām, *Sīra*, 1:633; Suhaylī, *Rawḍ*, 5:86; Bayhaqī, *Dalā'il*, 3:61, 78; Ibn Saᶜd, *Ṭabaqāt*, 2:14–15; ᶜAbd al-Jabbār, *Tathbīt*, 2:403ff. For miracles during the Battle of the Trench, see Ibn Hishām, *Sīra*, 2:217ff.; Ibn Hishām, *Life*, 451–452; Ṭabarī, *Ta'rīkh*, 1468ff. In several verses, the Qur'ān explicitly highlights that Muhammad's only "miracle" was the revelation of the Qur'ān (Q 6:37; 11:12; 13:7; 17:59; 28:48; 29:50–51). Later Muslims, however, claim that Muhammad did actually perform physical miracles. See ᶜAbd al-Jabbār, *Tathbīt*, 1:58. For critical Muslim views of the "supernatural elements" in Muhammad's life, see the discussion of the Moroccan historian Jābrī, *Mawāqif*, 49–50, and that of the Egyptian Muslim historian Qimanī, *Ḥurūb*, 2:253. See also the critical views of Djait, *Waḥy*, 79–80, where he argues that later traditions of the miracles contradict the Qur'ān. For modern Muslims discussing the invention of traditions for religious and political reasons, see Abū Rayya, *Aḍwā'*, 85–92; ᶜAbd al-Raḥmān, *Judhūr*, 7–9; ᶜAbd al-Raḥmān, *al-Tārīkh*; ᶜAlawī, *Maḥaṭṭāt*, 19–20. Cf. Brown, *Misquoting*, 216–222; Brown, "Did," 259–285. For a recent discussion on Muhammad's miracles, see Ibrahim, *Stated*, 90–91; Ibrahim, *Concise Guide to the Quran*, 119–122 (hereafter cited as Ibrahim, *Quran*, 119–122).

[11] On the theme of "hegemony" in Islamic traditions, see Donner, *Narratives*, 144ff. In the same vein, Albrecht Noth discusses topoi serving "to Glorify Former Times," including the "Summons to Islam" theme. Noth/Conrad, *Early*, 146–165. See Ibrahim, *Conversion*, 89–92, 130–134, 213–215.

[12] Muqātil, *Tafsīr*, 4:44; also 2:104. On Muqātil and his *tafsīr* (commentary), see Plessner and Rippin, "Muḳātil b. Sulaymān," *EI*², 7:508–509; Sirry, "Muqātil," 51–82; Reynolds, *Subtext*, 27–28, 200–229. For a primary source on Muqātil, see Ibn Khallikān, *Wafayāt*, 5:256; Dāwūdī, *Ṭabaqāt*, 2:330–331.

[13] Concerning the term *mushrikūn* (sg. *mushrik*), Hawting convincingly argues that it refers to associaters who were in fact "as bad as idolaters" because they were weak in their monotheism. Hawting, *Idea*, 1, 62, 67; also Crone, "Religion," 151–200, where she argues that "the *mushrikūn* believed in the same Biblical God as the messenger and that their lesser beings, indiscriminately called gods and angels, functioned much like (dead) saints in later Islam and Christianity."

[14] Muqātil, *Tafsīr*, 4:44.

commentators) shared Muqātil's interpretations.[15] Although Muqātil's work is not a historiographical one, he reflects on historical episodes and emphasizes Muhammad's *maghāzī*, specifying their motivations, goals, and results.[16] The matter is even more evident in historical writings achieved under the ᶜAbbāsids.[17]

A few decades after Muqātil, the Muslim historian Ibn ᶜUmar al-Wāqidī (d. 207/823)—under the instruction of the ᶜAbbāsid caliph—devoted an entire historical work to Muhammad's military campaigns, titling it *Kitāb al-maghāzī* (the Book of Expeditions).[18] While some Muslim authors reportedly wrote *maghāzī* works before al-Wāqidī, none of these works has reached us.[19] For centuries, *Kitāb al-maghāzī* has been celebrated by Muslims as an early authoritative account of Muhammad's military campaigns in which al-Wāqidī lists many of Muhammad's expeditions—some having a large number of warriors and others being limited in scope and results.[20] From al-Wāqidī's

[15] For some examples of similar classical interpreters, see Ṭabarī, *Jāmiᶜ*, 3:272; 22:153–155; Zamakhsharī, *Kashshāf*, 4:334; 9:28ff.; 4:317ff.; Rāzī, *Mafātīḥ*, 28:38–53; Qurṭubī, *Jāmiᶜ*, 16:225–229; Bayḍāwī, *Anwār*, 5:119–120. Some modern Muslim commentators follow similar interpretations. See Riḍā, *Manār*, 10:73ff.; Shaᶜrāwī, *Khawāṭirī*, 16:9847.

[16] On historical reports found in nonhistoriographical works, see Ibrahim, *Conversion*, 19.

[17] See Robinson, *Historiography*, 39, where he writes of "the explosive growth of historical narrative in the eighth and early ninth centuries." On the genesis and growth of historiographical documentation in Islam, see Muṣṭafā, *Ta'rīkh*, 74ff.; Dūrī, *Baḥth*, 15–70; Petersen, *ᶜAlī*, 19–20, et passim. See Suyūṭī, *Ta'rīkh*, 194. For history writing under the Umayyads, see Ibn al-Nadīm, *Fihrist*, 81, 91; Masᶜūdī, *Tanbīh*, 1:93. For secondary studies, see Muṣṭafā, *Ta'rīkh*, 1:66–67, 1:80–83; Borrut, *Entre*, ch. 1 (esp. pp. 37–40); also Ibrahim, *Conversion*, 23, where I argue, "Islamic historiography is not only written but also *rewritten*."

[18] On al-Wāqidī, his religious and political inclinations, as well as his *Maghāzī*, see the discussion in Ibrahim, *Conversion*, 110–116. Some Muslims distrusted him as a narrator. Jūzjānī, *Aḥwāl*, 1:228; ᶜAqīlī, *Ḍuᶜafā'*, 4:107; Ibn Khallikān, *Wafayāt*, 4:348; Dāraquṭnī, *Ḍuᶜafā'*, 3:130; Rāzī, *Jarḥ*, 8:20–21; Ishbīlī, *Fahrasat*, 1:200; Dhahabī, *Mīzān*, 3:662ff.; Dhahabī, *Tadhkirat*, 1:254; Ibn Abī Yaᶜlā, *Ṭabaqāt*, 1:203; Ibn al-Ṣalāḥ, *Maᶜrifat*, 378–379, 396–398; Ibn al-ᶜImād, *Shadharāt*, 1:19–20. For secondary studies, see Sezgin, *Ta'rīkh*, 1:2:100–106; Muṣṭafā, *Ta'rīkh*, 1:67, 1:163ff.; Ziriklī, *Aᶜlām*, 6:311–312; Kaḥḥāla, *Muᶜjam*, 11:95–96; Dūrī, *Rise*, 37–38. Al-Wāqidī is considered Shīᶜite by many. See Ibn al-Nadīm, *Fihrist*, 98; Ṭūsī, *Fihrist*, 3; Brockelmann, *Ta'rīkh*, 3:16; Brockelmann, *History*, 1:123.

[19] According to Muslim sources, we know that Ibn Shihāb al-Zuhrī (d. 124/741) and Mūsā ibn ᶜUqba (d. 135/752 or 141/758), both of whom served under the Umayyads, had works on the *maghāzī*. See the detailed discussion in Ibrahim, *Conversion*, 41–54. On al-Zuhrī and Mūsā, see Ishbīlī, *Fahrasat*, 198; Khalīfa, *Ṭabaqāt*, 1:464; Yāqūt, *Muᶜjam*, 3:1201–1204; Ibn al-Muᶜtazz, *Ṭabaqāt*, 69; Jumaḥī, *Ṭabaqāt*, 1:48; Dhahabī, *Siyar*, 5:326–350 (on Zuhrī) and 1:41ff. (on Mūsā); Dhahabī, *Tadhkirat*, 1:83–85; Nawawī, *Tahdhīb*, 2:118. For secondary studies, see Sezgin, *Ta'rīkh*, 1:2:74–79 (on al-Zuhrī) and 1:2:84–86 (on Mūsā); Muṣṭafā, *Ta'rīkh*, 1:87; Ed., "Mūsā B. Uḳba al-Asadī," *EI²*, 7:644; Ziriklī, *Aᶜlām*, 7:97. As mentioned earlier, history writing existed under the Umayyads, but the corpus did not reach us. On the problematic nature of determining the authorship of historical writing, particularly *sīra* and *maghāzī* works, see Görke, "Authorship," in *Concepts*, ed. Behzadi and Hämeen-Anttila, 63ff.

[20] Al-Wāqidī precisely lists seventy-four expeditions. See Watt, *Muḥammad*, 2, where he reflects on the number of Muhammad's warriors in the early *maghāzī*, suggesting that some of the numbers are exaggerated. For studies on the exaggeration in some Muslim traditions, see Ḥusayn, *Fī al-shiᶜr*, 84; Ḥusayn, *Shaykhān*, 34–35; ᶜAbd al-Raḥmān, *Judhūr*, 7–9; ᶜAlawī, *Maḥaṭṭāt*, 19–20; Qimanī, *Ḥurūb*, 2:239. For exaggerations in numbers given in non-Muslim sources, see Hoyland, *Seeing*, 186.

work, we learn how Muhammad led or commissioned these *maghāzī*, as al-Wāqidī repeatedly describes him as a divinely guided commander who *ghazā* (raided) and *aghār* (assaulted, attacked) various locations, tribes, or clans.[21] For al-Wāqidī and other classical Muslim writers, Muhammad's life was identified as a series of *maghāzī*.[22]

In the same vein, al-Wāqidī's contemporary ᶜAbd al-Malik ibn Hishām (d. 218/833) produced the important recension of Muhammad's *Sīra* (Biography) based on an earlier copy that was reportedly composed a half century earlier by the renowned Muslim traditionist Muḥammad ibn Isḥāq (d. 151/761).[23] In the *Sīra*, we read that Muhammad was forced, by the unbelieving Meccan pagans, to emigrate from his hometown Mecca to Medina—an event known as the *hijra*. At Medina, Muhammad consolidated power by reconciling rival clans and establishing a strong community of people who reportedly believed he was a prophet and leader. From Medina, Muhammad's community successfully launched many military expeditions against various non-Muslims.[24] According to Ibn Hishām, during a ten-year period in Medina, Muhammad led twenty-seven military campaigns *bi-nafsihi* (by himself) and commissioned thirty-eight other raids, assigning them to his faithful soldiers—although these numbers differ significantly in other traditions.[25]

[21] Wāqidī, *Maghāzī*, 11 and 103 (*ghazā* at Badr), 684 (*ghazā* Khaybar), 1022 (*ghazā* Tabūk), 407 (*aghār* against Banū al-Muṣṭaliq), 534 (*aghār* on the tribe of Qurṭā'), et passim. Cf. Ibn Shabba, *Ta'rīkh*, 1:187, 1:318, 2:438, 3:832. See the use of the term *ghazā* by renowned traditionist Dāraquṭnī, *Mu'talif*, 1:164, 1:368.

[22] The Iraqi Muslim historian Dūrī writes, "The earliest studies of the Prophet's life were also referred to as the *maghāzī*." See Dūrī, *Rise*, 24, 76 n. 1. See Nöldeke, *History*, 320, where he states, "The interest in the life of the Prophet first centred on the military campaigns." Hinds, *Studies*, 188; Ibrahim, *Stated*, 34.

[23] For a critical discussion on Ibn Isḥāq, Ibn Hishām, and the *Sīra*, see Ibrahim, *Conversion*, 121–128; Horovitz, *Earliest*, 80–87; also Ibn al-ᶜImād, *Shadharāt*, 1:18–19; Muṣṭafā, *Ta'rīkh*, 1:67; Jones, "Ibn Isḥāḳ," *EI*², 3:810–811; Watt, "Ibn Hishām," *EI*², 3:800; Lecker, "Muḥammad ibn Isḥāq," 36; Lecker, "Notes," 246; Amīn, *Ḍuḥā*, 2:319–360; Djait, *Tārīkhiyyat*, 214–220. On the *Sīra*, see Brockelmann, *History*, 1:122–123; also Brockelmann, *Ta'rīkh*, 3:10 (on Ibn Isḥāq) and 3:12–13 (on Ibn Hishām). For primary references on Ibn Isḥāq, see Ibn al-Nadīm, *Fihrist*, 92; ᶜIjlī, *Ta'rīkh*, 400; Ibn Ḥibbān, *Mashāhīr*, 1:213 (died in A.H. 154); Ibn Khallikān, *Wafayāt*, 4:276; Jurjānī, *Kāmil*, 7:254ff.; Ibn Shāhīn, *Ta'rīkh*, 1:199; Ibn Ḥajar, *Taqrīb*, 1:467; Ishbīlī, *Fahrasat*, 1:200; Ibn al-Ṣalāḥ, *Maᶜrifat*, 100, 300, 323, 334; Dhahabī, *Mīzān*, 3:468ff.; Dhahabī, *Tadhkirat*, 1:130–131. For Shīᶜite perspectives, see Ṭūsī, *Rijāl*, 277 (entry # 3998); Barqī, *Rijāl*, 10, 20; Ḥillī, *Khulāṣat*, 363. According to Dūrī, Ibn Shihāb al-Zuhrī is the earliest to transform the term *maghāzī* to *sīra* in relation to the life of Muhammad. Dūrī, *Rise*, 27.

[24] Allah's command to commence "jihad" and "fighting" came in Medina. See Ibn Hishām, *Sīra*, 1:590. See also Ibn Hishām, *Life*, 280, where it reads, "Then the apostle prepared for war in pursuance of God's command to fight his enemies and to fight those polytheists who were near at hand whom God commanded him to fight. This was thirteen years after his call." See ᶜUmarī, *Sīra*, 337ff.

[25] Ibn Hishām repeatedly refers to Muhammad as *ghazā bi-nafsihi* (raided by himself): see *Sīra*, 2:43 (Banū Sulaym); 2:203 (Najd); 2:289 (Banū al-Muṣṭaliq). On the different numbers of the military campaigns, see ᶜAbd al-Razzāq, *Muṣannaf*, 5:294; Masᶜūdī, *Murūj*, 2:222. Ibn Hishām, *Sīra*,

Numerous classical Muslim historians came after al-Wāqidī and Ibn Hishām.[26] They referred to or wrote extensively on the *maghāzī*. Muḥammad ibn Saᶜd (d. 230/844) indicates the number of Muhammad's *maghāzī* and details many of their events.[27] Yaḥyā ibn Maᶜīn (d. 233/847) refers to Muslims who proudly participated in over ten expeditions with Muhammad.[28] Khalīfa ibn Khayyāṭ (d. 240/854) lists several of Muhammad's *maghāzī*, mentions Muslims who participated in them, and details their events.[29] Muṣᶜab ibn ᶜAbdullāh al-Zubayrī (d. 236/851) highlights Muslim companions whom Muhammad assigned to protect Medina while he went for the *maghāzī*.[30] Ibn Ḥabīb al-Baghdādī (d. 245/895) refers to Muhammad's expedition to the Jewish settlement of Khaybar and specifies the name of a Muslim man whom Muhammad entrusted to manage Medina in his absence.[31] Abū al-Qāsim ibn ᶜAbd al-Ḥakam (d. 257/871), though discussing the conquest of Egypt after Muhammad's death, mentions Muhammad's *maghāzī*.[32] ᶜUmar ibn Shabba (d. 262/875) writes of several of Muhammad's *maghāzī*.[33] Ibn Qutayba al-Dīnawarī (d. 276/889) provides a list of *maghāzī* and details aspects of the battles of Badr and Uḥud.[34] Yaᶜqūb al-Fasawī (d. 277/890)

2:608–609. Fasawī, *Maᶜārif*, 3:261 (Muhammad led eighteen or twenty-four raids). See Aṣbahānī, *Akhlāq*, 1:454, where he states that Muhammad led twenty-one expeditions by himself. See also Kharkūshī, *Sharaf*, 3:9, where he states that Muhammad reportedly led nineteen or twenty-one expeditions. See Bayhaqī, *Dalā'il*, 3:126, where the number given is nineteen expeditions, which is similar to the number given by Dhahabī, *Ta'rīkh*, 2:710 (although in 2:714, the number given is forty-three). Compare with Ibn ᶜAbd al-Barr, *Durar*, 95ff.; Ibn Qudāma, *Mughnī*, 2:143. Still, relying on Ibn Hishām's *Sīra*, several classical Muslims claim that Muhammad actually led twenty-seven expeditions. See Ibn Saᶜd, *Ṭabaqāt*, 2:3; Suhaylī, *Rawḍ*, 7:520; Kalāᶜī, *Iktifā'*, 1:569; Maqdisī, *Bad'*, 4:180. See Ibn Taymiyya, *Minhāj*, 4:77–80, where he claims that Muhammad led twenty-seven expeditions and commissioned fifty-six incursions. See the discussion of Abū Māyla, *Sarāyā*, 57ff., where he lists the various numbers offered by classical Muslims concerning the *maghāzī*.

26 See, for instance, Khalīfa, *Ta'rīkh*, 1:57–65; Ibn Ḥabīb, *Muḥabbar*, 1:127; Ibn Qutayba, *Maᶜārif*, 1:152; Fasawī, *Maᶜrifa*, 3:261; Maqdisī, *Bad'*, 4:180–182; Balādhurī, *Futūḥ*, 23–101; Abū Zurᶜa, *Ta'rīkh*, 1:166; Ṭabarī, *History*, vols. 7–9 (on the raids in Medina); Kalāᶜī, *Iktifā'*, 2:3ff.

27 Ibn Saᶜd, *Ṭabaqāt*, 2:3–60. On Ibn Saᶜd's *Ṭabaqāt*, see Lucas, *Constructive*, 290–297; also Ibrahim, *Conversion*, 180–181.

28 Yaḥyā ibn Maᶜīn, *Ta'rīkh*, 3:149. On Ibn Maᶜīn and his *Ta'rīkh*, see Lucas, *Constructive*, 298–301; also Ibrahim, *Conversion*, 181–182.

29 Khalīfa, *Ṭabaqāt*, 128, 182; Khalīfa, *Ta'rīkh*, 1:57ff. On Khālīfa's religious and political inclinations, see Ibrahim, *Conversion*, 183–185. For Khalīfa and his works, see Andersson, *Early*, 45ff. Khalīfa ibn Khayyāṭ was a notorious opponent of Muᶜtazilism. Wakīᶜ, *Akhbār*, 2:175; see Muṣṭafā, *Ta'rīkh*, 1:234–236.

30 Zubayrī, *Nasab*, 101, 265.

31 Ibn Ḥabīb, *Muḥabbar*, 127.

32 Ibn ᶜAbd al-Ḥakam, *Futūḥ*, 145–146 (Khandaq), 214 (Tabūk), 287 and 294 (Badr). Shīrāzī, *Ṭabaqāt*, 1:151.

33 Ibn Shabba, *Ta'rīkh*, 1:80 (Abwā'), 1:80–82, 187 (Khaybar), 1:82, 163 (Tabūk), 1:301 (Dhāt al-Salāsil), 1:318 (Banū al-Muṣṭaliq), 1:356 (Badr), 2:440 (Dhū Qird), 2:452 (Khandaq). He also provides a list of the *maghāzī* in 2:438 and discusses the incursion of Nakhla in 2:472.

34 Ibn Qutayba, *Maᶜārif*, 152–158 (Badr), 158ff. (Uḥud).

refers to the birth and death dates of some Muslims with respect to specific *maghāzī* of Muhammad.[35] Ibn Yaḥyā al-Balādhurī (d. ca. 279/892), in his work *Futūḥ al-Buldān* (Conquests of the Lands), systematically lists the raids of Muhammad followed by the conquests of his successors.[36] Al-Balādhurī also writes of various *maghāzī* in his *Ansāb al-Ashrāf*.[37] Ibn Abī Khaythama (d. 279/892) lists many raids led by Muhammad and incursions commissioned by him.[38] Abū Zurʿa al-Dimashqī (d. 281/894) writes of the Battle of Badr and of Muhammad's conquest of Mecca.[39] Similarly, classical Shīʿite historians marvel at Muhammad's successful campaigns, by referring to them and detailing their events. Abū Ḥanīfa Dīnawarī (d. ca. 282/895) and Ibn Wāḍiḥ al-Yaʿqūbī (d. 284/897 or 292/905) are clear examples.[40] Finally, Ibn Jarīr al-Ṭabarī's (d. 310/923), in his magnum opus on the history of Islam, not only writes repeatedly of Muhammad's *maghāzī* but also provides various versions of the battles.[41] Certainly, al-Ṭabarī's "work marked a significant turning point in Muslim historical writing, as it designed a major 'historiographical filter' and 'a distorting [historical] prism,' which created a historiographical 'orthodoxy' during an 'intense period of canonization.'"[42] Many classical historians who came after al-Ṭabarī simply followed his narratives on the *maghāzī*: "His accounts became the decisive corpus of historical reports on early Islam."[43] Chase Robinson calls al-Ṭabarī's *Ta'rīkh* "the definitive record of the first three centuries of Islam," "the *ne plus ultra* of Islamic historical writing," and concludes, "In several respects, al-Tabari can be said to mark the end of the beginning of Islamic historiography."[44]

[35] Fasawī, *Maʿrifa*, 1:237, 303, 3:256ff. (Badr and Uḥud), 1:337, 358, 369, 394, 398 (Tabūk), 1:384, 2:387 (Ḥunayn). He also specifies the number of the *maghāzī* in 3:261–262.

[36] Balādhurī, *Futūḥ*, 2–49; Balādhurī, *Origins*, 15–77.

[37] Balādhurī, *Ansāb*, 1:142 (Ṭā'if), 1:348 (Banū Ḥayyān), 1:368 (Tabūk).

[38] Ibn Abī Khaythama, *Ta'rīkh (Part 3)*, 1:378–387; see also 2:5ff.

[39] Abū Zurʿa, *Ta'rīkh*, 1:163–166. Abū Zurʿa was a close friend of Aḥmad ibn Ḥanbal and is reported to have been influenced greatly by him. Dhahabī, *Siyar*, 13:65; Ibn Abī Yaʿlā, *Ṭabaqāt*, 1:199–200; Rāzī, *Jarḥ*, 1:328, 5:324–326; Mizzī, *Tahdhīb*, 19:89–104.

[40] Dīnawarī, *Akhbār*, 20; Yaʿqūbī, *Ta'rīkh*, 35–70.

[41] See Ṭabarī, *Ta'rīkh*, 1265ff.; Ṭabarī, *History*, 7:10ff.

[42] Ibrahim, *Conversion*, 3. On the impact of al-Ṭabarī's *Ta'rīkh*, see Borrut, *Entre*, 103–107, where, he concludes, "Pratiquement tous les développements suivants offriraient nombre d'interprétations nouvelles, mais le squelette historiographique n'était plus appelé à se transformer . . . peu importait les réinterprétations successives, puisque l'on avait déterminé le cadre d'un passé autorisé dans lequel elles étaient appelées à se couler" (108). See also Muṣṭafā, *Ta'rīkh*, 1:253–264 (esp. 264); Shoshan, *Poetics*, 61–107; Keaney, "Remembering," 13; Rosenthal, *Historiography*, 63; Gilliot, *Exégèse*, 8, 207, 277; Judd, *Religious*, 143ff.; Donner, *Narratives*, 127–128.

[43] Ibrahim, *Conversion*, 4. See also Muṣṭafā, *Ta'rīkh*, 1:261; Dūrī, *Baḥth*, 154; Robinson, "Local," 521–536; Rosenthal, *Historiography*, 139ff.

[44] Robinson, "Islamic Historical," in *Oxford*, ed. Foot and Robinson, 239–240. Robinson writes, "In subsequent centuries, universal historians would draw regularly and copiously upon al-Tabari's work for material on early Islam" (240). See also Robinson, "Local," 521–536. See also the remarks of

This brief list of classical Muslim historians suggests the importance and centrality of the literary topic of the *maghāzī* among medieval Muslims. Indeed, these historians cherished the memory of Muhammad's *maghāzī*. Once the literary topic of the *maghāzī* was introduced in early historical writings, it began to circulate and evolve as the "historical memory" of the faithful was developing.[45] In their articulation of the topic, Muslim historians categorized the military activities based on their number of warriors and the scope of their military goals. If Muhammad himself led the campaign, historians called it *ghazwa* (raid or expedition, pl. *ghazawāt*) or *maghzā* (campaign, pl. *maghāzī*). If he merely commissioned it without being present as its chief commander, they labeled it *sariyya* (incursion, pl. *sarāyā*), *baᶜtha* (task force or mission, pl. *baᶜathāt*), or *liwā'* (literally "a banner," referring to a small army dispatched by Muhammad to spy on the enemy, pl. *alwiya* or *alwiyāt*).[46] The *ghazwa* is thus larger in its size and goal when compared to the *sariyya*, *baᶜtha*, or *liwā'*.[47] Still, we should note, the terms are not distinctly defined, as historians sometimes used *ghazwa* and *sariyya* interchangeably.[48] Furthermore, Muslim historians employed a unique term to describe what they viewed as Muhammad's greatest military achievements: *fatḥ* (conquest, literally [great] opening, pl. *futūḥ*).[49] The term *fatḥ* is particularly used for the expedition of the Ḥudaybiyya (6/627) and that of Mecca (8/629), which is called by some *fatḥ al-futūḥ* (the conquest of the conquests, or the greatest conquest).[50] The significance of the term *fatḥ* is evident in that it was later

Rosenthal, *Historiography*, 139ff. The impact of al-Ṭabarī's *Ta'rīkh* on historical writing is evident in the conclusion of ᶜAbd al-ᶜAzīz al-Durī, who states, "It was al-Ṭabarī who established in final form the ḥadīth scholars' approach to the writing of history." Dūrī, *Baḥth*, 154; see also Dūrī, *Rise*, 159. See also Khalidi, *Arabic*, 73–74; Shoshan, *Poetics*, 109ff.

[45] On the development of historical memory, see Savant, *New*, 3ff.; Spiegel, "Memory," 149–162; Clanchy, *From Memory*, ch. 9; Robinson, *Historiography*, 172–177; Geary, *Phantoms*, 111–122; Hirschler, *Written*; Innes, "Memory."

[46] For *sariyya*, see Ibn Manẓūr, *Lisān*, 14:381–383, where he claims that *sariyya* is a noun based on the notion that the warriors march secretly at night and differentiates it from *ghazwa* in that *sariyya* includes no more than four hundred warriors. See also Fīrūzābādī, *Qāmūs*, 664, 949, 1016. For *liwā'* as a limited military force, see Ibn Manẓūr, *Lisān*, 15:266; Wāqidī, *Maghāzī*, 10–13; Yaᶜqūbī, *Ta'rīkh*, 2:44–45; also Ibn Saᶜd, *Ṭabaqāt*, 2:6. See Wehr, *Dictionary*, 65 (*baᶜtha*), 673 (*ghazwa*). On *sariyya*, see Lane, *Arabic-English Lexicon*, 2:1366. See also Abū Māyla, *Sarāyā*, 54–55.

[47] For a secondary study, see Haykal, *Ḥayāt*, 255–257; Ibrahim, *Stated*, 101–102.

[48] A good example is the raid to Mu'ta. It is labeled *ghazwa*, although Muhammad did not lead it. See Khalīfa, *Ta'rīkh*, 86; Ṭabarī, *Ta'rīkh*, 1614; Masᶜūdī, *Tanbīh*, 1:230. See the explanation in al-Masᶜūdī, *Tanbīh*, 1:242, where he suggests that Muhammad led many *maghāzī*, during which he also commissioned *sarāyā*; see also Ḥalabī, *Insān*, 3:213. See Abū Māyla, *Sarāyā*, 54.

[49] On the term *fatḥ* and its ideological meaning, see Donner, *Narratives*, 174; Hinds, *Studies*, 199–231; Lewis, *Political*, 93–94; Ibrahim, *Stated*, 36; Donner, "Arabic *Fatḥ*," 1–14.

[50] The Ḥudaybiyya (6/627) is called a *ghazwa* (raid), *fatḥ* (conquest), and *ṣulḥ* (treaty). Ibn Hishām, *Sīra*, 2:308ff.; Dhahabī, *Ta'rīkh*, 2:397 (it was *aᶜẓam al-futūḥ*, i.e., the greatest conquest). See

used by Muslim historians to refer to the great conquests accomplished by Muhammad's successors.[51] Not only did classical historians differentiate between the terms used for the military campaigns, but they also went to great lengths to emphasize Allah as the orchestrator of all military successes. When Muslims won, it was due to Allah's intervention; when defeated, we are told, it was because they disobeyed Allah and Muhammad.[52] After all, one should acknowledge that classical Muslim historians were not merely reporting past events.[53] They served as religious writers, traditionists, who sought to depict the deity at work in supporting Muhammad and his believing community.[54] They articulated the success of Muhammad's *maghāzī* as an affirmation of the truth of Islam's message and Muhammad's mission.[55]

also Watt, "al-Ḥudaybiya" *EI*², 3:539. For the conquest of Mecca as *fatḥ*, see Ṭabarī, *Ta'rīkh*, 1618–1621 (esp. 1621); Ibn Hishām, *Sīra*, 1:490; 2:389ff.; Ibn Ḥishām, *Life*, 542; Dhahabī, *Ta'rīkh*, 2:521ff. For secondary studies, see Ibrahim, *Stated*, 96ff.; Qimanī, *Ḥurūb*, 2:330.

[51] On the Arab conquests, see Donner, *Early Islamic*; Kaegi, *Byzantium*; Kennedy, *Great*; Kennedy, *Prophet*; Hoyland, *God's Path*; Ibrahim, *Stated*. Donner questions the use of the Arabic term *futūḥ* as conquests; see Donner, "Arabic *Fatḥ*," 1–14, where he argues, "The rigid translation as 'conquest' is therefore potentially misleading."

[52] See the comparison between the Battle of Badr (Muslims won) and that of Uḥud (Muslims were defeated) in Ibrahim, *Stated*, 73–85. For examples of classical accounts of Allah's intervention in battles for the Muslims, see, for instance, Kalāʿī, *Iktifā'*, 1:388, and 1:317, where he states that through Muhammad's raids, *aʿazza Allāhu al-īmān wa-l-mu'minīn* (Allah strengthened the faith and the believers). See Ibn Hishām, *Sīra*, 1:633, which states that Allah's angels wore turbans in battles to support the Muslims (at the Battle of Badr, we are told, the turbans were white, while at the battle of Ḥunayn, they were red). See also Ṭabarī, *Ta'rīkh*, 1328; Suhaylī, *Rawḍ*, 5:86; Bayhaqī, *Dalā'il*, 3:61, 78. See Ibn Saʿd, *Ṭabaqāt*, 1:338, and 2:11, which states that angels rode horses to bring victory to Muslims; ʿAbd al-Jabbār, *Tathbīt*, 2:403ff. Of course, the theme of a defeated community of believers when they disobeyed divine commands is also found in biblical accounts, including Joshua 7, where the Israelites disobeyed the divine instructions and were defeated by the people of Ai. For similar instances where Islamic traditions seem to adopt biblical narratives, see Donner, "Historical," in *Companion*, ed. McAuliffe, 34ff., where he writes on the "biblical tropes." See Ibrahim, *Stated*, 91, where I explain similarities between Muslim traditions and biblical narratives; also Qimanī, *Ḥurūb*, 2:253.

[53] I explain this point more in a following section on approaches to Islamic historiography, but here, see Robinson, *Empire*, viii, where he rightly concludes that Muslim sources provide a "representation rather than record," as the historians "wrote well after the events they describe." See also Robinson, *Historiography*, 38, where he observes that Muslims "were not simply taking liberties with texts: they were generating the texts themselves." Similarly, Rippin writes, "The actual 'history' in the sense of 'what really happened' has become totally subsumed within later interpretation and is virtually, if not totally, inextricable from it," as "[t]he records we have are the existential records of the thought and faith of later generations." Rippin, "Literary," 156.

[54] See Ibrahim, *Conversion*, 167, where I conclude, "It is evident that Muslim historians serve as religious scholars who establish a dogmatic precedent." See also Ibrahim, *Stated*, 161; Hoyland, *God's Path*, 42. On Muslim scholars as religiously driven writers, see Crone, *Medieval*, 88; van Ess, *Theology*, 4:616; Judd, *Religious*, 52–61. For medieval historians as *muḥaddithūn* (traditionists, i.e., scholars of the *ḥadīth*), see Crone, *Medieval*, 125ff.; Crone and Hinds, *God's Caliph*, 92–97; Ibrahim, *Conversion*, 172–173; Watt, *Islamic*, 34.

[55] Ibrahim, *Stated*, 1–14.

This survey of classical Muslim historians and their emphases on Muhammad's *maghāzī* demonstrates that the topic is not only crucial to Muslims but also central to Islamic historiography in general and to Muhammad's life and career in particular. The earliest documentation of Islam's origins has Muhammad's *maghāzī* at its core, portrayed with awe and admiration. It is plausible to deduce that when Muslims sought to *represent* Muhammad's career, they formed a memory designed largely around his successful military campaigns. Thus, I argue that any rigorous study of early Islam has to dwell significantly on the reported *maghāzī* during the last ten years of Muhammad's life. Just as Muhammad's *maghāzī* have been fundamental and central to classical Muslims in their documentation of Islam's origins, so also the topic is highly meaningful and significant to modern and contemporary Muslims, especially in their interpretations of Muhammad's prophetic mission and the emergence of Islam. To this subject we now turn.

Modern and Contemporary Muslims on Muhammad's Expeditions

Like classical Muslim historians, modern and contemporary Muslim thinkers marvel at and cherish Muhammad's *maghāzī*. While they largely view them as effective campaigns and consequential incursions, they do not stop at merely retelling them—they analyze, explain, and interpret their motivations, contexts, and results. For many Muslim thinkers, these *maghāzī* served as the strong foundation of the early Islamic state centered at Medina.[56] Still, these Muslims generally differ in their approaches to and interpretations of the *maghāzī*. Some adopt a traditional apologetic approach, claiming that the *maghāzī* were mainly defensive and driven by the

[56] The term "Islamic State" is used by Muslim and non-Muslim scholars alike. Muslim thinkers speak of *al-dawla al-islāmiyya* (Islamic State). See, for instance, Sharīf, *Makka*, 561; also Qimanī, *Ḥurūb*, 2:190–191, where he argues that after the *hijra*, Muhammad's goal was to abolish the rule of the elites of Mecca by establishing *dawlat al-rasūl fī Yathrib* (the Messenger's State at Yathrib [Medina]) (191). Like al-Qimanī, ᶜAbd al-Karīm argues that the Medinan Islamic State was formed at the expense of the Meccan tribe of the Quraysh. See ᶜAbd al-Karīm, *Quraysh*, 387. See Abū Māyla, *Ghazwat*, 1:207, where he explicitly uses the term "Islamic State" to refer to Muhammad's Medinan community; also Abū Māyla, *Sarāyā*, 1:101, 1:128, 1:141, et passim. Similarly, non-Muslim scholars use the term "Islamic State"; see Donner, "Introduction," in *Expansion*, ed. Donner, xv, et passim; Donner, "Formation," 283–296. However, Donner recently shed some doubts on the usage of the term, calling it anachronistic. See Donner, "Talking," 1–23. See Hoyland's recent discussion of Donner's views, "Reflections," 113–140.

Muslim warriors' zeal to proclaim Islam.[57] Others—usually progressive and modernist thinkers—contextualize the *maghāzī*, view them as a part of a historical reality of the Arabian raids of the past, and present them as driven by political and socioeconomic gains, aimed at accumulating possessions and consolidating military power.[58] The two groups are not monolithic, and they do overlap. Some examples of both groups should make the point.

In his famous study of Muhammad's life and expeditions, modern Muslim historian Muḥammad Ḥusayn Haykal (1888–1956), former minister of education in Egypt, explains that "Islam is jihad for the sake of peace" and that Muhammad's *maghāzī* were *fī sabīl al-salām* (for the sake of peace). Their goals, says Haykal, were to defend Medina and "to proclaim Allah's message to the people completely."[59] Haykal views Muhammad's raids as a way of spreading Islam to non-Muslims, specifically to Meccan pagans and Medinan Jews. Knowing how his arguments might bring criticism against Islam, depicting it as a religion spread by the sword, Haykal is careful to distance Muhammad from any hint of delight in wars, and argues that Muhammad loathed *al-qitāl* (fighting) and preferred peace *ṭūl ḥayātih* (all his life). For Haykal, Muhammad only raided for "defending freedom, and protecting the religion and its tenets."[60] In his analysis of the Muslim defeat at the Battle of Uḥud, Haykal insists that the Muslims were seeking to defend *al-ᶜaqīda* (the Islamic dogma, creed), *al-īmān* (the faith), and *al-dīn* (the religion or the law) of Allah as well to secure *al-waṭan* (their homeland) and its *maṣāliḥ* (interests).[61] Undoubtedly, Haykal's claims reflect his traditional approach to interpreting Islam's origins.[62] His arguments highlight the common

[57] For the "traditional" approach to the *maghāzī*, with various examples, see Ibrahim, *Stated*, 1–14. For the crisis of Islamic studies in Muslim nations, see Ḥanafī, *Turāth*, 69–105, where he tackles the common traditional apologetic approach adopted by Muslim researchers, who often study traditions through a religious lens that lacks any significant critical assessments.

[58] For a detailed discussion on the various Muslim interpretations of the motivations for the *maghāzī*, see Ibrahim, *Stated*, 1–19. See also the valuable discussion of Donner, *Early Islamic Conquests*, 3–9, where he studies various non-Muslim arguments that attempt to interpret the reasons for and goals of the Muslim campaigns after Muhammad's death. Although his focus is on the period immediately after Muhammad's *maghāzī*, there is little doubt about the continuity between Muhammad's raids and his successors' conquests. See Donner, "Introduction," in *Expansion*, ed. Donner, xiii–xlii; Donner, "Formation," 283–296.

[59] Haykal, *Fī manzil*, 427–428, 430; also Ibrahim, *Stated*, 6–7. On the works and thought of Muḥammad Ḥusayn Haykal, see Smith, *Muhammad Husayn*. For Haykal's biography, see Smith, *Islam*. Compare with different Muslim views advanced by ᶜAbd al-Karīm, *Qur'ān*, 1:72.

[60] Haykal, *Ḥayāt*, 235–236. For another Muslim defense that Islam did not spread by the sword, see Ṣaᶜīdī, *Dirāsāt*, 111–116.

[61] Haykal, *Ḥayāt*, 305. Similarly, see Khaṭṭāb, *Rasūl*, 40–41.

[62] Some Muslim thinkers critiqued Haykal's views on the *maghāzī* and Islamic history in general. See ᶜAbd al-Karīm, *Qur'ān*, 1:72, where he writes a negative analysis of Haykal's work *Ḥayat Muḥammad*.

traditional Muslim interpretations of the motivations for Muhammad's *maghāzī*.[63]

Haykal's treatment of the *maghāzī* is shared by other modern Muslims. His contemporary ᶜAbbās Maḥmūd al-ᶜAqqād (1889–1964) writes an apologetic study, titled *Mā yuqāl ᶜan al-Islām* (*What They Say about Islam*), in which he refutes charges leveled against Islam. He explains the Islamic jihad in its connection with waging wars and insists that military activities were an act of religious devotion "to spread *ādāb al-ᶜaqīda al-islāmiyya* (the ethics of the Islamic tenets), aiming to offer justice, tolerance, and protection for the poor."[64] "In early Islam," says al-ᶜAqqād, "Muslims never fought except in self-defense or to push away those opposing the Islamic proclamation by using charitable preaching."[65] With this blanket statement, al-ᶜAqqād hopes to dismiss accusations against his religion without conducting any reasonable study of the various reported expeditions that could be understood as offensive, not defensive. In another book, titled *ᶜAbqariyyat Muḥammad* (*The Genius of Muhammad*), al-ᶜAqqād studies Muhammad's life and career. In examining Muhammad's *maghāzī*, al-ᶜAqqād praises "Muhammad's military genius," insists that Islam was never *dīn qitāl* (a religion of fighting), and argues that the military campaigns were *ḥurūb difāᶜ* (defensive wars).[66] For al-ᶜAqqād, Islam succeeded not because of any military attacks but mainly because of the divinely "obligatory calling achieved by a successful messenger."[67]

Like Haykal and al-ᶜAqqād, Ṭāhā Ḥusayn (1889–1973)—best known as "the dean of Arabic literature"—studies the historical context of Muhammad's *maghāzī* and argues that non-Muslims waited eagerly for Muhammad's advent. They welcomed his message, as it was *hudā wa-nūr* (guidance and light) for them, because they encountered Allah's "heavenly power," which released them from the tyranny of their unbelieving rulers. For Ḥusayn, Muhammad's *maghāzī* were an essential part of a prophetic mission seeking to free humankind.[68] While Ḥusayn has been known for his critical evaluation of Islam's

[63] See the critical assessment of various *maghāzī* in Ibrahim, *Stated*, 66–119; see also the valuable Arabic studies of Qimanī, *Ḥurūb*, 1:38–40; ᶜAbd al-Karīm, *Shadwu*, 1:71, 2:193.

[64] See ᶜAqqād, *Mā yuqāl*, 168–172 (quote from 172); also Ibrahim, *Stated*, 2. For a moderate Muslim interpretation that fighting in Islam is for the sake of protecting *al-daᶜwa* (the Islamic preaching), not to force non-Muslims to accept the religion, see Ṣaᶜīdī, *Ḥurriyya*, 86–91.

[65] ᶜAqqād, *Mā yuqāl*, 168; also Ibrahim, *Stated*, 66.

[66] ᶜAqqād, *ᶜAbqariyyat Muḥammad*, 28–30; also Ibrahim, *Stated*, 177.

[67] ᶜAqqād, *ᶜAbqariyyat Muḥammad*, 28.

[68] See Ḥusayn, *ᶜAlā*, 2:15. See also his treatment of the Arab Muslim conquests after Muhammad's death in Ḥusayn, *Shaykhān*, 172.

history, his arguments about the *maghāzī* seem to follow a largely traditional interpretation.[69]

In the same vein, the well-known Indian Muslim author Ṣafī al-Raḥmān al-Mubārakpūrī (1943–2006) studies Muhammad's *maghāzī* and argues that they were for the "Muslims to gain freedom to live peacefully and spread Islam without restrictions."[70] Muhammad's *maghāzī*, says Mubārakpūrī, were never offensive in nature.[71] Mubārakpūrī seems to have been influenced by the Indian-Pakistani Muslim thinker Sayyid Abū al-Aᶜlā Mawdūdī (1903–1979). Mawdūdī is known to have been a fundamentalist thinker who opposed what he viewed as Western values infiltrating Islamic societies. In his famous study of jihad, Mawdūdī defends Muslim military activities as a religious duty that had nothing to do with *al-sayf wa-l-qitāl* (sword and fighting) unless executed defensively. These *maghāzī*, says Mawdūdī, were *fī sabīl Allāh* (for Allah's cause) and not comparable by any means to the non-Muslim wars that were for the sake of fulfilling the "despicable lust, wicked desires, and reprehensible ambitions" of their warriors.[72] Like Mubārakpūrī and Mawdūdī, contemporary Saudi scholar ᶜAbdullāh ibn Aḥmad al-Qādirī (1937–)—in his lengthy PhD dissertation *al-Jihād fī sabīl Allāh: Ḥaqīqatuh wa-ghāyatuh* (*Jihad in Allah's path: Its reality and purpose*)—takes the traditional argument one step further. He presents Muhammad's raids not only as defensive expeditions but also as a religious *farḍ* (duty or obligation).[73] For al-Qādirī, the *maghāzī* were *jihād fī sabīl Allāh* (jihad for Allah's cause) motivated by several factors, including the power of faith among Muslims, the knowledge of the great rewards awaiting the *mujāhidūn* (the strivers in

[69] Indeed, Ḥusayn is known for his critical reading of Islam's origins, as evidenced in his controversial book *Fī al-shiᶜr al-jāhilī* (On Pre-Islamic Poetry), published in Egypt in 1926. In it, Ḥusayn sheds doubts on various traditional Muslim beliefs related to the Qur'ān, rejects the exaggeration of exalting Muhammad and his tribe, and concludes that Muhammad might have gained assistance from pagan poets in forming the Qur'ān. See Ḥusayn, *Fī al-shiᶜr*, 19–24, 38, 82–84, 94. The book drew severe criticism of Ḥusayn and some accused him of apostasy. In what appears as yielding to the pressure, Ḥusayn published several books studying early Islam, usually adopting a traditional conventional approach. See Ibrahim, *Stated*, 26. For a study on Ḥusayn's legal case in Egyptian courts and the accusations posed against him by various Muslims, see Shalabī, *Muḥākamat*, 55ff.

[70] See Mubārakpūrī, *Rawḍat*, 97. He argues, "War is a way of bringing victory to the oppressed and suppression to the oppressor; it is a way to extend security and peace on earth, and a means to establish justice, rescue the weak from the clutches of the strong, and release people from worshipping *al-ᶜibād* (servants, i.e., human beings) in order to worship Allah, moving them from the injustice of the [other] religions to the justice of Islam" (187).

[71] Mubārakpūrī, *Rawḍat*, 187. See Ibrahim, *Stated*, 3–4, where al-Mubārakpūrī's arguments concerning *qitāl* (fighting) are analyzed.

[72] Mawdūdī, *Jihād*, 2–5. On Mawdūdī, his education, and thought, see Nasr, *Mawdudi*, 9–140; see also, "Sayyid Abu'l-A'la Maududi," in *Princeton Readings*, ed. Zaman, 79–106. See also Jackson, *Mawlana*, 7–177; Hartung, *System*, 11–98, 209–212. See the discussion in Ibrahim, *Stated*, 3.

[73] Qādirī, *Jihād*, 1:49–50, 109.

jihad), the affirmation of Islam's truth, the desire to destroy all falsehoods, and the realization that non-Muslims will always continue to fight Allah's *awliyā'* (friends, i.e., Muslims).[74]

One can trace a common trend among some Muslims who not only cherish Muhammad's *maghāzī* but also insist on interpreting them as religious expeditions without any hint of nonreligious motives or goals. This is evident in important arguments voiced by the renowned Iraqi Muslim historian Akram Ḍiyā' al-ᶜUmarī (1942–).[75] He studies Muhammad's *maghāzī* in several books and views them as jihad for Allah's cause, and defines the term "jihad" as *al-qitāl fī sabīl Allāh* (fighting for Allah's cause).[76] For al-ᶜUmarī, Allah did not prescribe jihad when Muhammad was in Mecca; thus, there were no military expeditions during Muhammad's early prophetic career. When Muslims emigrated from Mecca to Medina, says al-ᶜUmarī, Allah *sharraᶜ al-jihād* (prescribed jihad) and then *amara al-muslimūn bi-l-qitāl* (commanded the Muslims to fight).[77] In describing the motivations of the *maghāzī*, al-ᶜUmarī believes that Muhammad's expeditions at the beginning were for defending the Muslims and Islam, but later Muslims were given *al-amr bi-qitāl al-mushrikīn wa-ibtidā'ihim bihi* (the [divine] command to fight the associaters and to initiate the fighting) in order to "establish and spread the Islamic belief."[78] In describing his views on Muhammad's *maghāzī*, al-ᶜUmarī insists on rejecting any apologetic approach to interpreting the expeditions. While some contemporary Muslims may attempt to contextualize the *maghāzī* by arguing that they should be understood apart from the sword associated with the coercive proclamation of faith, al-ᶜUmarī unequivocally rejects these attempts. He criticizes some of his fellow Muslim historians when they attempt *tabrīr* (to justify or provide reasons for) the expeditions by using *al-uslūb al-iᶜtidhārī* (an apologetic rhetoric).[79] For al-ᶜUmarī, the right

74 Qādirī, *Jihād*, 1:540–570.

75 Professor Akram al-ᶜUmarī, born in Iraq in 1942, graduated with a BSc and an MA in Baghdad University, then obtained his PhD in Islamic history at Ain Shams University in Cairo in 1974. He taught at the Islamic University of Medina as a historian of Islam from 1976 to 1995. He is known as an expert in Arabic manuscripts and a scholar of Muhammad's sound traditions, especially those related to his *Sīra* (biography). He recently taught at the University of Qatar as a Sharia professor. He is a prominent historian of Islamic history with about two dozen books published.

76 ᶜUmarī, *Sīra*, 337; see also 22–23.

77 ᶜUmarī, *Sīra*, 337. Like ᶜUmarī, see Khaṭṭāb, *Rasūl*, 39–40. In one of the earliest accounts we have on the *maghāzī*, we are told that after Muslims emigrated from Mecca to Medina, "The Messenger of God received the command to wage war soon thereafter in several verses of the Qur'an." Maᶜmar, *Expeditions*, 51.

78 ᶜUmarī, *Sīra*, 338.

79 ᶜUmarī, *Mujtamaᶜ*, 22.

interpretation of the *maghāzī* is not *difāᶜiyyan tabrīriyyan* (apologetic and explanatory) but based on the "conviction that Islam is truth, and everything else is false—that which Islam prescribed, be it jihad or else, is truth that does not require apology or justification."[80] Indeed, al-ᶜUmarī repeats his interpretation of the *maghāzī* in some of his other studies.[81] His interpretations are a clear example of a traditional conservative approach to Islam's origins in general and to Muhammad's military campaigns in particular.

Al-ᶜUmarī's interpretations are influential, and such influence is evident in the work of his student, the Saudi thinker Birayk Abū Māyla, who argues—in his 1996 PhD dissertation—that Muhammad's *maghāzī* sought to spread Islam in Arabia by proclaiming the *daᶜwa* (Islamic preaching) in regions where pagan polytheism existed.[82] In another work, Abū Māyla asserts that Muhammad sent out his military campaigns because Allah prescribed the jihad against the associaters and all of the enemies—the goal was to get people out of the darkness of ignorance and into the light of faith and belief.[83] Like al-ᶜUmarī and Abū Māyla, Lebanese Muslim historian Muḥammad Suhayl Ṭaqqūsh (1955–) argues that Muhammad was never satisfied with being silent or quiet or with resting but was always concerned with "the spread of Islam," as evidenced in the case of his campaigns to Yemen, where it was necessary to march to "defend his religion."[84] Like Ṭaqqūsh, Libyan Muslim scholar ᶜAlī Muḥammad al-Ṣallābī (1963–) adopts a similar approach, arguing that Muhammad's *maghāzī* targeted *al-mushrikūn* (the polytheists, associaters) and aimed at *tamkīn al-dīn* (strengthening or consolidating the religion).[85] For al-Ṣallābī, the *maghāzī* were a religious

[80] ᶜUmarī, *Mujtamaᶜ*, 22–23. He continues, "We do not adjust Islam and its history to the taste of people and their intellectual ideologies in any given age" (23). In his study of Muhammad's expedition of Banū Qurayẓa, al-ᶜUmarī acknowledges that some fellow Muslim historians attempt to deny that it took place because of the reported killing of Jewish men and the enslavement of their children and women; however, al-ᶜUmarī argues that the account is truthful and that the incident took place, as he questions these apologetic attempts by Muslims who try to defend Islam, although they should not do so.

[81] See, for instance, ᶜUmarī, *Risāla*, 123–137; ᶜUmarī, *ᶜAṣr*, 73–74.

[82] Abū Māyla, *Sarāyā*, 238, 248. Birayk Abū Māyla is a faculty member at the Islamic University of Medina. This study was his master's thesis written under the supervision of Akram al-ᶜUmarī, who also supervised his PhD dissertation on the Battle of Mu'ta. For a smiliar opinion, see Khaṭṭāb, *Rasūl*, 40–41.

[83] Abū Māyla, *Ghazwat*, 13; see also 18, 214–215, 228–229, 251, 398, 493, 500–501, et passim.

[84] Ṭaqqūsh, *Ta'rīkh*, 47; see also 152, where he states that the goal of Muhammad's campaigns was *nashr al-islām* (the spread of Islam).

[85] Ṣallābī, *Sīra*, 355; see also the larger discussion in 355–365. Al-Ṣallābī is a Libyan Muslim historian. He self-identifies as a Salafī Sunnī. He studied Islam in Saudi Arabia, Sudan, and Qatar. He lived in Yemen for a while, then moved to Qatar in order to study under the renowned Islamist Yūsuf al-Qaraḍāwī (1926–2022).

duty as jihad for Allah's cause aimed at fulfilling several goals, including the protection of Islam's tenets, the prevention of all evils in the non-Muslim lands, *irhāb al-kuffār wa-ikhzā'uhum wa-idhlāluhum* (terrorizing, shaming, and humiliating the unbelievers), and "the establishment of Allah's rule and Islam's system on earth."[86]

The above-mentioned examples demonstrate that the traditional Muslim views and interpretations of Muhammad's *maghāzī* are common among modern and contemporary Muslims. However, they are by no means adopted unanimously.[87] Kuwaiti American Muslim scholar Khaled Abou El Fadl (1963–), distinguished professor in Islamic law at the UCLA School of Law, treats these traditional views as a product of the "puritans" within Islam.[88] His use of the term is undoubtedly negative.[89] Abou El Fadl acknowledges that the Qur'ān presents mixed messages about violence and tolerance, but he argues that it can be better understood through contextual interpretations (i.e., by understanding the historical contexts of the text) rather than by insisting on the literal reading and application.[90] Indeed, the problem is that if one views the *maghāzī* of Muhammad as *prescriptive*—rather than *descriptive*—accounts, then the result may be consequential for the world. Abou El Fadl's arguments are not an exception in our day. A number of Muslim thinkers—both in the West and in the heartland of Islam—argue for nonliteral interpretations for the reasons for and applications of the *maghāzī*. Rather than adopting and advocating for religious literal interpretations, these thinkers view the expeditions through social, tribal, political, and economic lenses. By so doing, these scholars both reject literal classical interpretations and attempt to dissociate the spread of the religion from the launching of military campaigns.[91] This is

[86] Ṣallābī, *Sīra*, 358–361.

[87] For examples of similar traditional arguments adopted by classical, modern, and contemporary Muslims, see Ibrahim, *Stated*, 1–9.

[88] Abou El Fadl, *Great*, 5–6, et passim.

[89] On labeling them as "puritans," see Akyol, *Reopening*, xxvi, where they are defined as "a wide range of Salafis, Islamists, and rigid conservatives—who act as the defenders of the Islamic orthodoxy against modern liberal values."

[90] See Abou El Fadl, "Place," 3–26. See also Abou El Fadl's arguments concerning what he identifies as the "unreasonable interpretations and the authoritative" in Abou El Fadl, *Speaking*, ch. 4. See also Abou El Fadl, *Rebellion*, where he examines how Muslim jurists restructured competing doctrines by developing creative responses to religious matters in order to establish sophisticated claims on the crucial topic of rebellion (62ff.).

[91] For a modern Muslim approach to tradition, see Ḥanafī, *Turāth*, 176–180, especially his critical arguments on dealing with the *ḥadīth* and *sīra* on 178–179; also Ḥanafī, *Min*, 3:19–21. See the conclusion of Ibrahim, *Stated*, 236–240, where I examine numerous Arabic Muslim sources and argue, "It is

evident in the writings of Egyptian Muslim historian Khalīl ᶜAbd al-Karīm (1930–2002).[92] He treats Muhammad's *maghāzī*—and the Muslim conquests after his death—as a continuation of the pre-Islamic customs of Arab raids and incursions. For ᶜAbd al-Karīm, Islam, as a religion, did not change much in the Arabs' tribal customs of raiding against each other.[93] He argues that Muhammad's *maghāzī* were neither for spreading Islam nor protecting the Muslim lands. While he acknowledges the Qur'ān as a heavenly message, ᶜAbd al-Karīm calls the early Muslims *al-ghuzāt al-ᶜArab* (Arab invaders), identifying them as seeking *al-amwāl* (the wealth and possessions) of the conquered lands.[94] ᶜAbd al-Karīm dismisses traditional Muslim arguments that portray the military campaigns as means for religious proclamation. He rejects conventional claims that the military campaigns served as a means for worshipping Allah. He quotes Muslim primary sources that demonstrate horrific actions done by Muslim warriors during the expeditions—including *qatl, saby, taḥrīq, hadm, istiṣfā' al-amwāl* (killing, taking people captive, burning, destroying, and plundering possessions).[95] ᶜAbd al-Karīm does not treat the *maghāzī* texts as prescriptive. He does not believe that the warriors were seeking to proclaim Islam. For him, the Muslim warriors were lustful for wealth because they were poor Arab nomads. He criticizes their reported deeds—including the murder of conquered people after they surrendered or the enslavement of women and children—and wonders, "How could such deeds be considered as actions for the sake of guiding the conquered people to worship Allah?"[96]

essential to distinguish between the expansion of an empire and the conversion of conquered peoples to the faith of the conquerors" (236). I conclude, "This traditional interpretive hypothesis as to what motivated the raids and conquests is not the only thoughtful Muslim option" (237).

[92] Khalīl ᶜAbd al-Karīm (1928–2002) was born in Aswan, Egypt. He received a law degree and practiced law his entire life. He began his career as a devoted member of the Muslim Brotherhood group. Later, he realized many problems in the ideology and practice of the group and abandoned it. He became well known for defending the Muslim scholar Naṣr Ḥāmid Abū Zayd when Islamists accused him of apostasy. ᶜAbd al-Karīm became known for his writings on early Islam, especially with many books on Muhammad's life and career. His books include *The Yathrib Community before Islam*, *The Historical Roots for the Islamic Sharīᶜa*, and *The Quraysh: From a Tribe to the Central State*.

[93] ᶜAbd al-Karīm, *Shadwu*, 1:71; ᶜAbd al-Karīm, *Mujtamaᶜ*, 79ff. On incursions and wars among the Arabs before Islam, see ᶜAlī, *Mufaṣṣal*, 10:5–140; also 7:142–414.

[94] ᶜAbd al-Karīm, *Shadwu*, 1:71.

[95] ᶜAbd al-Karīm, *Shadwu*, 2:182–193 (quote from 193).

[96] ᶜAbd al-Karīm, *Shadwu*, 2:193. He also wonders whether people converted to Islam voluntarily or compulsorily, as he believes that the practical action for any man faced by an army is to "convert" to save his life and family (2:182). See Ibrahim, *Stated*, 178.

Like ᶜAbd al-Karīm, Egyptian Muslim scholar Sayyid Maḥmūd al-Qimanī (1947–2022) does not adopt a traditional approach.[97] This is evident in that he titles his study of Muhammad's raids *Ḥurūb dawlat al-rasūl* (*the wars of the Apostle's state*). Al-Qimanī describes the *maghāzī* as wars of a state growing in power at the expense of the Meccans and other non-Muslims, but he does not argue for viewing the raids as self-defense campaigns or as raids for spreading Islam. Instead, he views the *maghāzī* as a continuation of pre-Islamic tribal raids aiming to secure wealth and dominance among the Arabs. He argues that the *maghāzī* were a part of the fight for power among the families within the Quraysh and that Muhammad's raids sought to accomplish his great-grandfather Quṣayy's dream of achieving a unified power over various clans.[98] Al-Qimanī views Muhammad's *maghāzī* as "a call for a national unity under the leadership of a prophet, [who is] the founder of one central state."[99] It is apparent that he does not adopt traditional approaches to understanding the *maghāzī*. This is evident in al-Qimanī's arguments that the victories of the Muslims in the *maghāzī* were not due to Allah's support but because Muhammad was a shrewd warrior who was able to make treaties and break alliances when needed.[100] In clear disagreement with traditional claims, al-Qimanī is willing to question Muhammad's actions during the raids. He describes Muhammad as a mere human with no divine support who needed advice from skilled warriors, and he indicates that Muhammad, at times, employed lying and deception to achieve his goals.[101] Unlike traditional interpretations, al-Qimanī does not seem to seek to justify Muhammad's actions as prophetic. Thus, it appears that ᶜAbd al-Karīm and al-Qimanī attempt to distance Islam as a religious message from the military expansion of conquering armies.

[97] Sayyid al-Qimanī is an Egyptian Muslim thinker who holds a doctorate in sociology of religion from the United States. His critics identify him as a liberal rationalist, and some accuse him of *kufr* (unbelief). In his writings, he criticizes religious fundamentalism and political Islam. He wrote many studies on early Islam, including *The Wars of the Prophet's State* and *The Hashemite Party and the Establishment of the Islamic State*.

[98] Qimanī, *Ḥurūb*, 2:185–191; see also Qimanī, *Ḥizb*, 51–61. For another modern Muslim perspective that armed jihad and *qitāl* (fighting) are only for self-defense in Islam, see Ḥanafī, *Yamīn*, 5–41, especially 7–9.

[99] Qimanī, *Ḥizb*, 8; see also 73–76, where he explains the dream of tribal dominance among Muhammad's family, and 79–83, where he studies the role of Muhammad's great-grandfather Quṣayy ibn Kilāb. On Quṣayy, see Ṭabarī, *Ta'rīkh*, 1093–1094; Ṭabarī, *History*, 6:19–21; Ibn Hishām, *Life*, 52–53. See the study of Peters, *Muhammad*, 16–30.

[100] Qimanī, *Ḥurūb*, 1:38–40.

[101] Qimanī, *Ḥurūb*, 1:59–60 (Muhammad's limitations) and 61–62 (Muhammad's lies). See also Ibrahim, *Stated*, 77.

Like ᶜAbd al-Karīm and al-Qimanī, Turkish author and self-described Muslim modernist Mustafa Akyol (1972–) employs a similar approach. In his opposition to any coercion in religion, Akyol advocates reading Islamic texts as descriptive, not prescriptive. In reading ancient texts such as those of Muhammad's *maghāzī*, says Akyol, it is best to *reinterpret* them through historicism because religious texts are a product of specific social, cultural, and political features.[102] In discussing what he views as "controversial aspects of Muhammad," Akyol argues that "expecting from Muhammad a perfect universal wisdom, totally unbound from his time and culture, would not be consistent with Qur'anic theology."[103] This claim undoubtedly is in dissonance with traditional Muslim interpretations. For Akyol, Muslims need to distance themselves from rigid traditionalism. They should reinterpret the Quran and Islamic sources by focusing on the divine intent in the context of the work's initial production. This approach is evident in his recent book, where, as the title indicates, he argues for "reopening Muslim minds" through "a return to reason, freedom, and tolerance" by rejecting "an interpretation of Islam that is, by modern standards, authoritarian and intolerant."[104] Akyol continues to advocate for the reinterpretation of Muslim texts, emphasizing an approach to a "contextual" and "interactive" Scripture in Islam and exhorting Muslims to support various—even competing—interpretations.[105] The interpretations, says Akyol, "can be helped greatly by a historical and comparative perspective" rather than a literal reading and application of ancient Muslim traditions.[106] Overall, Akyol views his book as "an intervention into this big crisis of Islam," namely, the literal interpretation and application of the Islamic sources.[107] Thus, it appears that for Akyol, the *maghāzī* texts are to be viewed as descriptive, not prescriptive; they should be understood against the backdrop of their historical reality and interpreted in ways that fit today's norms of reason, freedom, and tolerance.

While Akyol seems careful to maintain a balance between the sacred Muslim text and its interpretation, some modernist Muslim thinkers can take a *significantly* sharp critical approach to Islamic history, including its reports

[102] See Akyol, *Islam*, 58–59, where he details his views on Muhammad's actions and how it is best to view them through "historicity" and "historicism." The term "historicism" is also used by the Muslim scholar Fadel, "Is Historicism," 131–76.

[103] Akyol, *Islam*, 59.

[104] Akyol, *Reopening*, xxiv.

[105] See in particular the epilogue in Akyol, *Reopening*, 231–234.

[106] Akyol, *Reopening*, 157–180.

[107] Akyol, *Reopening*, xxvi.

on Muhammad's *maghāzī*. The Tunisian Muslim historian Hichem Djait (1935–2021) views Muhammad and his followers as forming a *dawla* (state) that *innamā buniyat ᶜalā al-ḥarb, ᶜala tashkīl quwwat tadakhkhul* (was indeed built on war, by establishing an aggressive intervention force).[108] Djait—like al-Qimanī—is willing to critique some of Muhammad's actions during the expeditions. In analyzing Muhammad's expedition against the Jews of Banū Qurayẓa, Djait goes against conventional Muslim claims, refusing to justify actions attributed to Muhammad. Djait calls Muhammad's decision of beheading hundreds of Jewish men a *majzara* (butchery) and argues that this raid inaugurated "a truly violent *dawla* (state)" where violence—as Arabs had never seen before—became a frequently applied practice.[109] Djait contextualizes Islam's origins. While some may apologetically argue that the execution of Jewish men during this expedition was acceptable as a part of war rules, Djait disagrees and argues that the punishment, particularly against women and children, was unusual among the Arabs.[110] Although Djait places early Islam in its historical context, he is unwilling to shy away from questioning some deeds of early Muslims. While some Muslims may attempt to deny that this expedition had ever occurred due to its apparent violence against the Jews,[111] Djait does not appear to follow that course.

This survey of modern and contemporary Muslim arguments concerning Muhammad's *maghāzī* leads to at least two major observations. First, while classical Muslims portrayed the *maghāzī* and their accomplishments as both

[108] See Djait, *Fitna*, 26–28. Djait was born in Tunis in 1935 into a family known for its roots in Islamic learning. In his university years, he was exposed to Western culture and education. He traveled to France, where he studied history and received a master's degree in 1962. He then pursued his PhD, focusing on Islamic history at the Sorbonne University in Paris. He received his doctorate in 1981. He wrote many daring books, especially his analysis of Muhammad's *Sīra* in three volumes, in which he applied Western approaches and scientific analyses. He was well known for his criticism of political Islam. See Ibrahim, *Stated*, 117.

[109] Djait, *Fitna*, 28. See also his views on the massacre of Banū Qurayẓa in his latest book *Masīrat Muḥammad*, 132–138, and see 9–10, where speaks of the *maghāzī* in the Medinan period as launching "the fighting Islam." For Djait, Muhammad's time at Medina was *marḥalat ḥurūb wa-aᶜmāl ᶜunfiyya* (a period of wars and violent actions) (9).

[110] Djait, *Fitna*, 28. Djait's arguments are echoed in those of the Muslim author ᶜAbd al-Raḥmān, *Judhūr*, 148ff., who interprets the expedition as a tactical raid initiated by Muhammad to suppress the might of the Jews. See the non-Muslim views of Kister, "Massacre," 61–96; see Watt, "The Condemnation," in his *Early Islam*, 1–11 (previously published as an article in 1952 with *Muslim World*).

[111] See the study of the Muslim apologist Arafat, "New Light," 100–107. He rejects the incident entirely, viewing it as a myth that was placed by evildoers in Islamic sources. Arafat concludes, "So then the real source of this unacceptable story of slaughter was the descendants of the Jews of Medina, from whom Ibn Isḥāq took these 'odd tales.' For doing so Ibn Isḥāq was severely criticized by other scholars and historians and was called by Malik an impostor" (106). Compare Arafat's conclusions with the similar approach but slightly different arguments of Mubārakpūrī, *Rawḍat*, 130–131; Mubārakpūrī, *al-Raḥīq*, 314.

a sign of divine intervention and as a proof of Islam's hegemony, modern and contemporary Muslims did not stop at a mere retelling of the narratives but interpreted various aspects of the *maghāzī* by explaining their motivations, analyzing their goals, and assessing their results. If Muslim primary sources present accounts of Muhammad's *maghāzī*, then later Muslims—in their secondary studies—needed to communicate these narratives to an audience of different generations and contexts and, more importantly, to an audience with different social, religious, and political questions. This resulted in developing, and sometimes competing, interpretations. After all, these interpretations seem to have been largely a response to the religious debates, cultural concerns, and sociopolitical requirements of the day.

Second, among modern and contemporary Muslims, there seems to be roughly three major views of Muhammad's *maghāzī* in their relation to our day. The first reflects a traditional reading of Islam's texts, the second focuses on contextualizing the campaigns as a historical reality with current theological lessons, while the third condemns them altogether as being a part of tribal and political advancement and not as being an authoritative precedent that Muslims should emulate. The three views are not completely distinct—they sometimes overlap. In the traditional view, Muslim scholars tend to follow the letter of the historical account, viewing the military campaigns as a religious duty of jihad for Allah's cause to proclaim Islam. Scholars adopting this view tend to articulate the *maghāzī* as a part of a broader religious commitment to liberating non-Muslim lands—from the darkness of unbelief—by spreading Islam. This commitment, for them, is valid and appropriate for all times and places. In this view, the *maghāzī* are fundamentally led by pious and religiously devoted commanders as a sign of religious piety. In rejecting this literal reading and application of the *maghāzī* accounts, other Muslim scholars treat the campaigns as descriptive, not prescriptive, by advancing a contextualized historical evaluation. For these scholars, the *maghāzī* texts should be read in their historical contexts. In this reading, mainly theological lessons—rather than a blind literal application of an ancient text—are to be gleaned in our day. In this view, Muhammad should not be expected to have had an unlimited knowledge and wisdom apart from his time and context—he was a limited human who lived as a part of a historical reality of his day and who is cherished and supported by the Qur'ān. If this second view attempts to navigate ways to reconcile the ancient texts with modern realities through historicism and contextualization, the third view seems willing to outright condemn the military campaigns as having had nothing particularly religious about them. While this view acknowledges the historical contexts of the raids, it undermines any claims for religious motivations for the *maghāzī*. This third view treats the *maghāzī* as a part of a pre-Islamic system and insists on dissociating the faith from the sword in both the past and the present. In this view, even military commanders—including Muhammad—were not always unquestionable or blameless in their actions. They were not pious proselytizers but mere humans seeking wealth and dominion.[112]

There is one final remark that we should add to the two abovementioned major observations regarding the survey of modern and contemporary Muslim literature on the *maghāzī*—a remark that is central to the unique contribution and major aim of this book. The secondary studies presented in the survey are all by Muslim scholars, and all but two are in Arabic.[113] There is a wealth of Arabic Muslim secondary studies on Muhammad's *maghāzī*. It is obvious that discussions of this topic are vivid and rich among Arab Muslims in the heartland of Islam, but there are few detailed secondary studies on this topic in the English-speaking world. This deficiency is why this book is important. By relying on original Arabic Muslim sources, this study seeks to accomplish two goals: (1) to emphasize how classical Muslims, in different times and generations, have cherished, treated, and portrayed particular aspects of Muhammad's *maghāzī*, and (2) to provide students and scholars of Islam a unique means of access to Arabic primary sources on the topic that would otherwise be inaccessible. In addition to relying on original Arabic Muslim sources, this book interacts with ample Arabic Muslim studies on the topic and analyzes their findings and arguments with the hope of making these valuable studies—and their arguments and findings—accessible to the English-speaking world.

However, non-Muslim Western scholars have also contributed to the study of Muhammad's *maghāzī*. These scholars do not approach the topic with religious reverence and dogmatic devotion as Muslims often do. The non-Muslim arguments often tackle the *maghāzī* from nonreligious angles, thus expanding and advancing the understanding of the historiographic reports. In the following section, I explore key studies on Muhammad's *maghāzī* by Western scholars, particularly from the nineteenth century until the present

[112] Ibrahim, *Stated*, 155–156.

[113] All of the authors are Arabs, except Akyol Turkish. All wrote in Arabic, except Akyol and Abu El Fadl, who wrote in English.

day, which demonstrates once more the importance and significant contribution of the current study.

Non-Muslim Interactions with Muhammad's *Maghāzī*

When assessing Muhammad's *maghāzī* critically, non-Muslim thinkers do not usually adopt the sensitivity embraced by the Muslim community. While Muslim historians generally tend to view Muhammad's *maghāzī* and their success as a reflection of the religious fervor of the early Muslims and as a demonstration of divine support to Muhammad as a prophet, non-Muslim scholars seek to interpret these military expeditions in other ways—often through a nonreligious lens. This is evident in ample non-Muslim texts that, from the earliest centuries of Islam, do not shy away from treating Muhammad and his message critically. These texts depict Muhammad not only as a religious revivalist, a preacher of monotheism, or a false prophet led by the devil, but also as a warlord who initiated military incursions, as well as a lawgiver king.[114] In his examination of numerous Medieval Syriac and Arabic Christian texts, Sidney H. Griffith concludes, "It was not uncommon in Christian/Muslim debate texts in Syriac and Arabic from the early Islamic period for the question to arise about what status the Christian was prepared to accord to Muḥammad as a prophet, and to the Qur'ān as an inspired scripture. For the most part the answer was that, at best, Muḥammad was a little less than a prophet, and the Qur'ān not quite a book of divine revelation."[115] Similarly, in his survey of the various images of Muhammad as imagined and advanced in Europe between the twelfth and twentieth centuries, John Tolan writes that, for the most part, Muhammad was viewed as either an idol worshipped by the Arabs or a deceiving heretic who sought to lead

[114] See the examination and analysis of Christian texts from the first century of Islam by Hoyland, "Earliest," 276–295. See Ibrahim, "Review," 1–18, especially 4, where I write, "In the first Hijri century, non-Muslim sources depict Muḥammad not only as a monotheist revivalist and trader, but also as a conquest initiator, king, lawgiver, and false prophet." See Shoemaker, *Apocalypse*, 183, where he rightly concludes, "The image of Muhammad as an often brutal warlord is ensconced in his traditional biographies—there is simply no avoiding this fact."

[115] Griffith, "The Qur'an," 203–233. See also Samir, "Earliest," 57–114; Beaumont, ed., *Arab Christians*; Wilde, *Approaches*. For examples of Arabic-speaking Christians interacting with Islam, Muhammad, and the Qur'ān, see Ibrahim, ed., *Medieval Encounters*, where ten medieval Christian thinkers provide views on Muhammad and his message. See also the example of the thirteenth-century debate text between Monk Jurjī and Muslim jurists in the emir's court, translated and introduced in Ibrahim and Hackenburg, *In Search of the True Religion*.

Arab Christians astray from Christianity.[116] Indeed, since the earliest years of Islam, non-Muslims have generally been intrigued by Islam's prophet—his message, character, and deeds, including his raids.[117] These non-Muslim thinkers have arguably viewed Muhammad in various ways, but for the most part negatively.

However, there was a significant breakthrough by the nineteenth century, as many Arabic manuscripts on Islam's origins were discovered.[118] The discovery resulted in the publication of a number of important sources on Islam's history.[119] This provided a wealth of research material for non-Muslim scholars, especially in the West. They began to interact with narratives on Muhammad's life and provided a variety of arguments that go beyond religious sentiment and conventional interpretation. While their focus has been to a large extent on Muhammad's life in general, a few scholars treated his *maghāzī* as well. Although in this study my aim is to engage Muslim works on Muhammad's *maghāzī*, it is important to explore the major non-Muslim Western arguments on the topic as well. In this section, I highlight the works and arguments of key Western scholars from the nineteenth century until our present day.[120] Since only a few of these non-Muslim scholars had exclusively focused on Muhammad's *maghāzī*, in this survey I expand the scope to highlight their scholarly approach to the Muslim sources, interpretation of Islam as a religion, and views of Muhammad and his deeds.

Some of the earliest Western studies that interact with materials on Muhammad resemble a mere retelling of the then-newly discovered Muslim

[116] Tolan, *Faces*, 1–19, especially 2. Tolan's goal is not to compile a chronicle of negative hostility against Muhammad, but instead to survey the various images of Muhammad as imagined and advanced in Europe between the twelfth and twentieth centuries. See the Muslim perspective of Buaben, *Image*. See also the volume by Gruber and Shalem, eds., *Image of the Prophet*.

[117] See the Christian critique of Muhammad's *maghāzī* by ᶜAbd al-Masīḥ al-Kindī and al-Wāḍiḥ ibn Rajā' in *Medieval*, ed. Ibrahim, chapters 3 and 10, by Takawi and Bertaina, respectively.

[118] Conrad writes, "Untold thousands of manuscripts survived from the medieval period, and through the nineteenth century Arabic manuscripts continued to flow into Europe in large numbers." Conrad, "Introduction," in Horovitz's *Earliest*, ed. Conrad, xvii. Cf. See Fück, *Die Arabischen*, 189–191.

[119] See Goldziher, *Mohammed*, where, in the introduction of this book, Morris Jastrow writes, "Through the publication during the past fifty years of a large number of Arabic sources for the study of Mohammedanism, before that accessible only in the manuscript collections of European libraries, our knowledge of the origin and course of Islam, and more particularly of the development of Islamic theology in the various countries to which the religion spread, has been greatly extended" (vii).

[120] See Tolan, *Faces*, 16, where he sets the aim of his work: "Restoring the variety, ambivalence, and complexity of European views of Muhammad and Islam is one of my principal goals in this book." Tolan concludes, "For over a thousand years, Europeans have been writing, thinking, talking, and arguing about the prophet of Islam. Much of what they have to say is negative, but much is ambivalent or praiseful" (16).

narratives, often by paraphrasing the sources.[121] German-Jewish Gustav Weil (1808–1889) was one of the earliest scholars to write on early Islam.[122] He studied Arabic, Persian, and Turkish, and wrote extensively on Islam's origins, often relying on manuscripts and unpublished works.[123] Although he did not write precisely on Muhammad's *maghāzī*, he was clearly interested in the sources of Islam, especially the Qur'ān and Muhammad's *sīra*. Among Weil's many works, three stand out as relevant to our discussion: an innovative biography of Muhammad, *Mohammed der Prophet*; a critical study of the Qur'ān, *Historisch-kritische Einleitung in den Koran*; and a five-volume history of the Caliphate, *Geschichte der Chalifen*.[124] In his interaction with Arabic Muslim sources, Weil adopted a sanguine approach, as he largely viewed the sources as containing reliable material.[125] He treated them as reliable records sketching the history of Islam.[126] Indeed, since the nineteenth century, Western scholarship on the emergence of Islam "has accepted the general outlines of the picture of 'what happened' conveyed to us by traditional Islamic sources"—with the exception of the skeptical and revisionist studies of the 1960s and 1970s.[127] In discussing Muhammad's life, Weil managed to both praise and criticize Islam's prophet: "Mohamed set a shining example to his people. Apart from his weakness for the fair sex, his character was pure and stainless."[128] Weil's statement reflects that he was less critical of the reliability of the Muslim accounts, treating them as largely factual. Weil did not view Muhammad as a divinely guided prophet, but instead identified him as a religious reformer.[129] Lawrence I. Conrad argues that Weil's "aim was not to dismiss or disparage, but rather to treat Muḥammad as

[121] Donner calls this the "descriptive approach." Donner, *Narratives*, 8.

[122] Conrad argues that Weil was "perhaps *the* central figure" in advancing new methodologies in nineteenth-century Orientalism. Conrad, "Introduction," in Horovitz's *Earliest*, xiv. Johnston-Bloom provides reasons for such a designation. Johnston-Bloom, "Oriental," 39. See also the outstanding observations of Dunlop, "Some Remarks," in *Historians*, ed. Lewis and Holt, 326–327; also Tolan, *Faces*, 210–231.

[123] Johnston-Bloom, "Jews," 49–59; also Johnston-Bloom, "Oriental," 45–125, where the author focuses on Weil, while tracing the phenomenon of German-Jewish Orientalism from mid-nineteenth century onward. See also Tolan, *Faces*, ch. 8.

[124] See Weil, *Mohammed*; Weil, *Historisch-kritische*; and Weil, *Geschichte*.

[125] For a discussion on the various approaches to Islamic sources, including sanguine and skeptical, see Ibrahim, *Conversion*, 20–24; Donner, *Narratives*, 4ff., 112–122, 203–208; Humphreys, *Islamic*, 69–91; Robinson, *Historiography*, 8–17; Robinson, "Study." See also the following section in this chapter.

[126] Johnston-Bloom, "Oriental," 35.

[127] Donner, "Introduction," in *Expansion*, ed. Donner, xiv.

[128] Weil, *History*, 27.

[129] See Johnston-Bloom, "Gustav," in *Modern*, ed. Fraisse, 95–119. Tolan, *Faces*, 14; Johnston-Bloom, "Oriental," 45–125.

a personality who had played an enormous role in history and thus deserved serious historical attention."[130] Some argue that Weil's positive depiction of Muhammad as a reformer is one of the earliest positive depictions in Europe of Islam's prophet.[131] By portraying Muhammad as a religious reformer, Weil was arguably calling Muslims to seek reformation in order to embrace modernity.[132] This depiction of Muhammad as a reformer was also advanced by Abraham Geiger (1810–1874), who was also a Jew and a fellow student with Weil at Heidelberg.[133] Unlike Weil, however, Geiger did not write extensively on Islam, with the exception of his well-known 1833 essay, *Was hat Mohammed aus dem Judentume aufgenommen?*, in which he discussed that which Muhammad adopted from Judaism.[134] For Geiger, Muhammad was not a divinely guided prophet, but he was not a deceptive religious leader either. Like Weil, Geiger viewed Muhammad as a reformer, but, unlike Weil, Geiger believed that Muhammad was highly influenced by Judaism and that he was convinced of the truthfulness of the religious message he preached among the Arabs. Muhammad's message, says Geiger, brought concepts and values proclaimed earlier in the biblical text to the pagan Arabs.[135] While Weil and Geiger did not study Muhammad's *maghāzī* in any significant depth, it is clear that they were both interested in the life of Muhammad and his message as a field of research. Indeed, neither viewed Muhammad as a divinely guided prophet, but they both thought of him positively, depicting him as a religious reformer of some sort. Their views and arguments were undoubtedly shaped by the social, cultural, and political necessities of their time. John Tolan rightly observes that the views of these non-Muslim scholars were "inevitably linked to social and intellectual upheavals in Europe around them,

[130] Conrad, "Introduction," in Horovitz's *The Earliest*, ed. Conrad, xv.

[131] Johnston-Bloom, "Gustav," 107, where she argues, "Though his access to sources was limited and though he was not as methodologically sophisticated as later generations of orientalists, Weil's attempt to produce a historically accurate biography of Muhammad did mean that he developed a relatively positive picture of Muhammad."

[132] See Johnston-Bloom, "Oriental," 9. See also Weil, "Introduction," 112–113, where he argues, "In order to push itself to the heights of European civilization, it seems probable that [Islam] must go the same way as reformed Judaism, both in sundering tradition from revelation and in making a distinction in the sacred word between eternal truth and laws and precepts which are called out only by temporary external circumstances, and are suited only to a certain period and people."

[133] Tolan, *Faces*, 215; also Tolan, "Prophet," 256–279. See Rippin's comments on Geiger's arguments on Muhammad at Rippin, "Foreword," in Wansbrough, *Qur'ānic*, ix–x.

[134] See Geiger, *Judaism and Islam*. In his comments on Geiger's article, Tolan writes that Geiger "was twenty-three when he published his essay, and he would then leave aside scholarship on Islam, concentrating his academic efforts on the relations between Judaism and Christianity." Tolan, *Faces*, 213.

[135] See Geiger, *Judaism*, 26–30; also Tolan, *Faces*, 212.

notably in their own Jewish communities."[136] Thus, while Weil attempted to re-create Muhammad's biography, Geiger was interested chiefly in the Jewish influence on Islam's prophet and Scripture.

Not only modern Jews but Western Christians also interacted with the growing number of materials discovered and printed on Muhammad's life. Austrian physician Aloys Sprenger (1813–1893) was Roman Catholic. In 1832 he joined the University of Vienna where he studied philosophy and medicine, but showed clear fascination with oriental languages. In his mid-twenties, he moved to London and later to British India, where he spent most of his career as secretary of the Asiatic Society of Calcutta, devoting time and energy to examining Arabic Muslim manuscripts. His extensive research produced many works. Most importantly for our purposes, he wrote an introductory study on Muhammad's biography, titled *The Life of Mohammad*, which he later expanded to a larger work in German.[137] His work was ambitious, as Conrad observes, but it included some inaccurate information.[138] Still, we should acknowledge that these were some of the earliest steps taken by Western scholars in their attempt to unlocking the mysteries of a growing body of Arabic Muslim manuscripts. Sprenger attempted to be critical of the sources, without any particular method of analyzing the reports.[139] In the same generation, Scottish-born Sir William Muir (1819–1905) has been known as a Christian highly devoted to the mission work in India. Serving with the Indian Civil Service, he also dedicated his time to examining Arabic Muslim manuscripts.[140] This resulted in his first major academic work, which was focused on Muhammad's *Sīra*, titled *The Life of Mahomet: From Original Sources*. It was published in four volumes between 1858 and 1865.[141] Muir is known to have pioneered relying on original Muslim sources in Arabic, including Ibn Hishām's *Sīra*, al-Ṭabarī's *Ta'rīkh*, and Ibn Saᶜd's *Ṭabaqāt*, in addition to the Qur'ān.[142] Moreover, unlike earlier scholars, he appears to

[136] Tolan, *Faces*, 210. For the fluidity and complexity of religious and social spheres, see Barth, "Introduction," in *Ethnic*, ed. Barth, 9–38; Payne, "Christianity," ch. 1; Berger, *Sacred*, 51.

[137] Sprenger, *Life of Mohammad*.

[138] Conrad, "Introduction," in Horovitz's *Earliest*, ed. Conrad, xv–xvi.

[139] See, for instance, Sprenger, *Life*, 8, where he writes, "Yet we should be under a great mistake, were we blindly to believe Mohammadan authors, who state, that, not only all the Arabs, but even the Persians performed pilgrimage to Makkah."

[140] For his life and accomplishments, see Lyall, "Sir William," 875–879. For a Muslim perspective on Muir, see Buaben, *Image*, 42, where he criticizes Muir's emphasis on "the falsity of Muhammad's prophethood, faking of revelations to justify evil acts, violence, sexuality, immorality and the like."

[141] Published in London with Smith, Elder, and Co. See Kerr, "Muir, William," in *Biographical*, ed. Anderson, 478–479.

[142] Lyall, "Sir William," 876.

have treated the sources *somewhat* critically, mainly by questioning their authenticity. This is evident in how he begins his work on Muhammad's life with a lengthy and thorough commentary on the reliability of the Muslim sources.[143] He argues that Muslim narratives include three categories of accounts: legendary or mythical (like the story of the divine light cleansing Muhammad's heart), traditional (because of the oral transmission and the time gap between the events and the recorded reports), and "also some elements of *History*, because there are contemporary records of undoubted authenticity, to which we can still refer."[144] Granted, he distinguished between the three without any particular method, but merely based on his preferences or personal judgment. Still, this critical assessment of the Muslim sources was remarkable for its time, although he ultimately adopted the traditional Muslim narratives and retold the *Sīra* as attributed to Ibn Hishām.[145]

Unlike Weil and Geiger, Muir does not view Muhammad in any positive sense. He treats the reports of Muhammad's revelations through the angel Gabriel as a "deceptive process, [which] led to the high blasphemy of forging the name of God."[146] Muir does not hesitate to criticize Muhammad as having been deceived by the devil in the incident of the Satanic Verses.[147] In discussing Muhammad's *maghāzī*, Muir devotes two entire volumes (vols. 3–4) to examining Muslim traditions on the expeditions. He views the sword as a means to silence the unbelievers and claims that Muhammad always used hostilities against those of whom he did not approve.[148] For Muir, "The thoughts of [Muhammad], indeed, from the day of his flight [i.e., the *hijra*] were not thoughts of peace. He had threatened that condign vengeance should overtake the enemies of his Revelation—a vengeance not postponed to a future life, but immediate and overwhelming even in the present world."[149] The *maghāzī* as found in Islamic sources, says Muir, are evidence of Muhammad's "cruelty toward" his enemies.[150] Muir devotes an entire chapter to criticizing Muhammad and questioning his actions.[151]

[143] Muir, *Life*, 1:i–cv. Muir's entire first chapter of more than one hundred pages is about the sources and their reliability. See Conrad, "Introduction," in Horovitz's *Earliest*, ed. Conrad, xvi.

[144] Muir, *Life*, 1:i–ii.

[145] See Watt, *Muḥammad: Prophet and Statesman*, 244, where he writes of Muir's work as "following in detail the standard Muslim accounts, though not uncritically."

[146] Muir, *Life*, 2:75.

[147] Muir, *Life*, 2:149–160. See also Muir's criticism of Muhammad's many marriages after Khadīja's death at 2:208 and 3:14.

[148] Muir, *Life*, 3:63ff.

[149] Muir, *Life*, 3:63.

[150] Muir, *Life*, 4:307–308.

[151] See Muir, *Life*, 4:302–324.

These negative views of Muhammad extend to Muhammad's message, the Qur'ān. For Muir, the Qur'ān was an invented message that borrowed from Judaism, Christianity, and other pagan tales.[152] In treating the Qur'ān, Muir endeavored to link the text to Muhammad's *Sīra*, attempting to establish a chronological order of its verses—this arguably proved helpful for future scholars.[153] In his works, Muir states his indebtedness to various earlier scholars, including Weil and others.[154] In particular, Muir emphasizes that he wrote *The Life of Mahomet* "at the insistence" of his friend, German Pietist missionary Karl Gottlieb Pfander (1803–1865), and identifies him as a well-known "Christian apologist in the controversy with the Muhammadans."[155]

Pfander is an important Christian apologist who interacted with Islamic narratives on Muhammad, mainly to critique Islam's claims and advance the Christian gospel. While he seems to have indeed influenced Muir's decision to write his four volumes on Muhammad's biography, Pfander did not write much. His major contribution is undoubtedly *Mīzān al-ḥaqq* (The Balance of Truth), although he also wrote *Miftāḥ al-asrār* (The Key of Mysteries) and *Ṭarīq al-ḥayāt* (The Way of Life). While none of these works focus explicitly on Muhammad's life and deeds, they reflect Pfander's method of using original Muslim sources to criticize Islam's figures and doctrines. In his *Mīzān al-ḥaqq*, Pfander devotes a section for the "Personal Character of Mohammad," in which he aims "to examine whether the personal character and conduct of Mohammad show him to have been a true prophet, or the contrary."[156] In his analysis of the Muslim sources, Pfander is skeptical of their reliability. He identifies external (related to the time of documentation) and internal (related to literary contradictions) problems in Muslim sources. He questions the authenticity of the sources, based on the fact that the "persons who collected and compiled the traditions, had not themselves seen and heard any of the circumstances; but, one or two hundred years after Mohammad's death, gathered up the stories which were then current, and, rejecting those which they did not consider true, incorporated the others in their works."[157] He

[152] Muir, *Life*, 2:308.

[153] See, for instance, Muir, *Life*, 2:135ff., where he links various passages in the Qur'ān to the stories he discusses in Muhammad's biography.

[154] Lyall, "Sir William," 876.

[155] Muir, *Life*, 1:iii. On Pfander, see Nickel, "Karl Gottlieb Pfander," *CMR*, vol. 23, forthcoming; also Bennett, "Legacy," 76–81. See also Powell, *Muslims*, 132–157.

[156] See C. G. Pfander, *Mīzān al-Ḥaqq*, 105. For a detailed study on the work, see Nickel, "Mīzān al-Ḥaqq," *CMR*, vol. 23, forthcoming. I am grateful for Gordon Nickel for sharing his forthcoming articles with me.

[157] Pfander, *Mīzān*, 111. On this, see the observation of Roohi, "Muḥammad's Disruptive," 40–80, where he argues, "The wide chasm of a century or so that separated Muḥammad's biographers and

also argues, "Many of the traditions are at variance with one another."[158] He follows styles adopted by Muslim writers, yet uses the Qur'ān and Muslim sources to demonstrate what he identified as weaknesses and imperfections in Islam and Muhammad's actions. Relying on stories from Muhammad's *Sīra*, Pfander criticizes Islam's prophet regarding lusting after his adopted son's wife, questions his morality in allowing Muslims to fight during the sacred month, and critiques Muhammad's beheading of seven hundred men from the Jews of Banū Qurayẓa.[159] Pfander saw Muhammad as a man "full of sensual desires," who "had no idea of inward purity" and "was bitter and revengeful towards his enemies."[160] In treating Muhammad's *maghāzī*, Pfander contrasts the spread of Christianity and Islam. He emphasizes that Christ's apostles only preached the gospel peacefully and endured persecution and martyrdom without waging wars against nonbelievers, while Muslim warriors launched military campaigns, subjugating non-Muslims by the sword and forcing them to accept Islam.[161] Thus, although Pfander questions the reliability of the Muslim sources, he uses them to question Islam and its founder.

But Pfander's arguments did not go unchallenged. They energized Muslim scholars to respond, which created back-and-forth disputations, both in person and in writing. A few years after Pfander published his *Mīzān al-ḥaqq* (1866), Muslim scholar and apologist Moulavi Chirágh Ali (1844–1895) published response to Christian charges, titled *A Critical Exposition of the Popular "Jihad."*[162] The subtitle of the book is relatively lengthy but revealing: *Showing That All the Wars of Mohammad Were Defensive; and That Aggressive War, or Compulsory Conversion, Is Not Allowed in the Koran.* Additionally, in the title page, Ali indicates the inclusion of "Appendices Proving That the Word 'Jihad' Does Not Exegetically Mean 'Warfare,' and That Slavery Is Not Sanctioned by the Prophet of Islam." It is clear how Ali's

the events they describe, along with their politico-sectarian agendas, have made the *sīra* an accumulation of topoi deployed to glorifying or apologetic ends, or, at times, simply to fill a void" (73).

158 Pfander, *Mīzān*, 114.

159 Pfander, *Mīzān*, 119–120.

160 Pfander, *Mīzān*, 117, 118, respectively.

161 See Pfander's section titled "The Manner through Which Islamism Was Spread," in *Mīzān*, 125–134, where he concludes his critique of Islam and Muhammad's raids with a full presentation of the Christian gospel, calling his readers to repent from their sins and accept Christ as savior (133–134). Gordon Nickel identifies *Mīzān al-ḥaqq* as "a Christian appeal to Muslim readers to accept the authenticity of the Bible, to read it, and to consider its teachings." See Nickel, "Mīzān al-Ḥaqq," *CMR*.

162 On Moulavi Chirágh Ali and his works, see Khalidi, "Muslim," in *Just Wars*, ed. Hashmi, 305–323. See also Hardy, *Muslims*, 112–113.

work aims at refuting Christian accusations against Islam and its founder. Ali was considered a modernist Muslim who sought to present Islam and the Qur'ān in modern interpretations, although, as Peter Hardy observes, Ali's arguments resonated more with educated Muslims who were willing to integrate in modern multireligious contexts.[163] In defending Muhammad and his *maghāzī*, Chirágh Ali argues that the Qur'ān does not incite violence and the verses that call Muslims to wage jihad and fighting are not prescriptive nor obligatory for all times and places. Ali insists that Muhammad's wars were all defensive: "Mohammad and his followers had every sanction, under the natural and international law, then and there to wage war against their persecutors with the object of removing the (*fitnah*) persecution and obtaining their civil rights of freedom and religious liberty in their native city."[164] Ali's modern reinterpretation of Islam appears in his bold assertion, "The Mohammadan Common Law is by no means divine or superhuman. It mostly consists of uncertain traditions, Arabian usages and customs, some frivolous and fortuitous analogical deductions from the Koran, and a multitudinous array of casuistical sophistry of the canonical legists."[165] He argues that Islamic common law "has not been held sacred or unchangeable by enlightened Mohammadans of any Moslem country and in any age since its compilation in the fourth century of the Hejira."[166] This appears in remarkable dissonance with traditional and conventional Muslim arguments.

The works of Pfander and Ali reflect the vivid dynamic interaction between Christians and Muslims—particularly in British India—toward the end of the nineteenth century. There was not only a growing theological conversation between Muslims and non-Muslims but also a modernized version of Islam being formed.[167] This is evident in how Ali was a colleague and supporter of Sir Sayyid Ahmad Khan, who identified Islam as "a religion of progress"[168] and promoted not only Western education for Muslims

[163] See Hardy, *Muslims*, 112–113, where he writes that Ali's "arguments for the reinterpretation of Islam were more likely to appeal to Muslims who had already opted for a modern education."

[164] Ali, *Critical*, ii.

[165] Ali, *Critical*, 159–160.

[166] Ali, *Critical*, 160.

[167] Speaking on the growing dialogue between Christians and Muslims in British India and particularly using the example of Pfander's *Mīzān*, Gordon Nickel observes, "The *Mīzān al-ḥaqq* turned out to be one of the best examples of a type of Christian-Muslim engagement that takes seriously the truth or falsehood of religious claims, including the central beliefs of the partner, while inviting the partner to a friendly, respectful, and reasonable conversation." Nickel, "Mīzān al-Ḥaqq," *CMR*; Hardy, *Muslims*, 78.

[168] See the discussion of Hardy, *Muslims*, 94ff.

but also political cooperation and collaboration with the British.[169] During that time, there seems to have been diligent enthusiasm among non-Muslim scholars to make many Muslim primary Arabic sources available in print.

Austrian scholar Alfred von Kremer (1828–1889) was interested in geography and ethnographic research, as well as in Arabic Muslim original sources. Among his many works, one stands relevant to our discussion. In 1855 von Kremer published a critical edition of the most important Muslim accounts on Muhammad's expeditions, al-Wāqidī's *Kitāb al-maghāzī*. He compared seven manuscripts and created an Arabic edition published in Calcutta by Baptist Mission Press. This was a remarkable achievement, as it served as the first scholarly edition of the earliest accounts of Muhammad's *maghāzī*. In his introduction to the critical edition, von Kremer shows awareness of several Muslim primary sources, evaluates their reliability by questioning their late date of documentation, and identifies the importance of Wāqidī's *Kitāb al-maghāzī*.[170] Because of his interest in social and cultural matters, von Kremer studied the history of Islam against the backdrop of the Arab culture with all of its sectarian, sociopolitical, economic, and intellectual aspects. He opened the gate wide for more scholars to work on critical editions of Muslim primary sources. Among these scholars, the Dutch scholar Michael Jan de Goeje (1836–1909) stands out.[171] Being proficient in Arabic from an early age and having studied at the University of Oxford, de Goeje successfully edited numerous Arabic primary sources, including most importantly al-Balādhurī's *Kitāb futūḥ al-buldān* and al-Ṭabarī's *Ta'rīkh*. He also edited works on Muslim geography, such as al-Iṣṭakhrī's *Kitāb al-masālik wa-l-mamālik*. Even today, de Goeje's works are respected and still used by scholars. Around the same time, German biblical scholar Julius Wellhausen (1844–1918) showed interest in studying Islam, although he began as a researcher in biblical material. His interest in Muhammad's *maghāzī* was evident in that he—like von Kremer before him—worked on an abridged translation of al-Wāqidī's *Kitāb al-maghāzī* and published it in 1882, emphasizing Muhammad's raids during the Medinan period. Notably, Wellhausen viewed religion as

169 See Hardy, *Muslims*, 78. On Sir Sayyid Ahmad Khan, see the important dissertation by Begum, "Educational."

170 See Kremer, "Introduction," in al-Wāqidī's *Kitāb al-maghāzī*, 4.

171 On de Goeje, see Engberts, *Scholarly*, 25–32, 39–42, 49–51, 178–182, 184–186.

an essential factor in building the Muslim state.[172] For him, Muhammad's *maghāzī* cannot be voided from the religious aspect of the growing Muslim community.[173]

Wellhausen's works represent a period of scholarly attempts to question the reliability of Muslim traditions, thus pioneering modern skeptical scholarship. Wellhausen was a Protestant and arguably applied principles of biblical higher criticism to Islam's origins and traditions.[174] His critical arguments were joined and expanded significantly by the Hungarian Ignaz Goldziher (1850–1921). Many consider Goldziher the founder of the modern study of Islam and its texts.[175] While he did not focus on Muhammad's *maghāzī*, he championed skepticism of traditions in general, and the *ḥadīth* in particular. Since the *maghāzī* reports consist mainly of *ḥadīth* traditions, Goldziher's works shed doubts on the authenticity of the entire corpus.[176] He "demonstrated convincingly that many traditions that Muslims treat as sound and authentic are simply invented statements aimed at supporting political or religious agendas."[177] Goldziher's skepticism appears clearly when he argues, "It is not surprising that, among the hotly debated controversial issues of Islam, whether political or doctrinal, there is not one in which the champions of the various views are unable to cite a number of traditions."[178] Goldziher demonstrated that opposing traditions are often supported by a strong *isnād* (chain of informants) linking them directly to Muhammad and his immediate companions: "Anything which appears desirable to pious men was given by them a corroborating support reaching back to the Prophet. This could easily be done in a generation in which the Companions, who were represented as the intermediaries of the Prophet's words, were no longer

[172] See Wellhausen, *Medina*, 4:1–64; Wellhausen, *Reste Arabischen*, 234. See the explanation of Donner, *Early*, 294. On Julius Wellhausen, see Becker, "Julius," 95–99; Rahlfs, "Verzeichnis," in *Studien zur semitischen*, ed. Marti, 351–368. See also the works of Smend, *Julius Wellhausen*; Smend, "Julius," in *From Astruc*, ed. Smend, 91–102; also the recently published Smend et al., eds., *Julius Wellhausen*, 818–837. For biography and works, see also the entry by Ludmila Hanisch, "Wellhausen," in *EIR*.

[173] Wellhausen, *Reste arabischen*, 228–235; Wellhausen, *Das arabische*, ch. 1, especially 3–5. *Das arabische* was translated by Margaret Weir as *The Arab Kingdom and Its Fall*, see especially 5–6. On Wellhausen, see Badawī, *Mawsūʿat*, 408–410.

[174] van Ess, "From Wellhausen," in *Islamic*, ed. Kerr, 27–51, especially 40–43.

[175] Fück, *Die Arabischen*, 226–233; Conrad, "Introduction," in Josef Horovitz's *The Earliest*, xix. Simon, *Ignać*, 13ff. On Goldziher, see the recent study by Turán, *Ignaz*, 1–99, where Turán studies Goldziher's complex religious and historical contexts.

[176] Donner, *Narratives*, 13–14.

[177] Ibrahim, *Concise Guide to the Life of Muhammad*, 16 (hereafter cited as Ibrahim, *Muhammad*, 16).

[178] Goldziher, *Muslim*, 2:44.

alive."[179] Goldziher opened the gate wide for others to follow with similar skepticism in other fields of Islamic studies.[180]

During the same generation, Dutch scholar Christiaan Snouck Hurgronje (1857–1936), who was de Goeje's student, showed a significant interest in the history of Islam and Muhammad.[181] Snouck Hurgronje completed his PhD in Semitic languages in 1880 under de Goeje's supervision and wrote his dissertation, titled *Het Mekkaansche feest*, on the history of the Islamic rituals of the *ḥajj* (pilgrimage).[182] Like many Western scholars before him, Snouck Hurgronje did not view Muhammad favorably. For him, Muhammad continued pagan worship and customs and integrated them into Islamic rituals.[183] Snouck Hurgronje viewed Muhammad as a sensual, lustful man who could not control his sexual desires.[184] Snouck Hurgronje did not treat Muhammad's *maghāzī* directly; however, he viewed the raids as a part of the political and religious development of Muhammad's career and identified Muhammad as a "military commander of his theocratic state."[185] He viewed Muslims as imitators of Muhammad's example "when they represented fighting for Allah's cause as the most enviable occupation."[186] For Snouck Hurgronje, "But for the military success of the first khalifs [successors] Islam would never have become a universal religion."[187] Contemporary to Snouck Hurgronje, Josef Horovitz (1874–1931) was born in Germany to Orthodox Jewish parents of Hungarian descent. Influenced by Eduard Sachau (1845–1930), Horovitz showed interest in Islamic historiography, particularly in Ibn Saᶜd's *Ṭabaqāt* and Wāqidī's *Maghāzī*. In his relatively short PhD dissertation, Horovitz evaluated the life of al-Wāqidī and his work (mainly one manuscript of his *Maghāzī*), highlighting in particular the sectarian inclinations of al-Wāqidī. Horovitz assisted Sachau in editing Ibn Saᶜd's *Ṭabaqāt*, which served—along with al-Ṭabarī's *Taʾrīkh*, edited by de Goeje at Leiden in ca. 1904—to enhance the understanding of Islamic

179 Goldziher, *Muslim*, 2:42.

180 Berg, *Development*, 8–16; Berg, "Implications," 3–22; Berg, "Competing," in *Methods*, ed. Berg, 259–263. Donner, "Introduction," in *Expansion*, ed. Donner, xxviii–xxxi; Donner, *Narratives*, 20–31.

181 See Engberts, *Scholarly*, 14, 27.

182 He was twenty-three years old when he completed his doctorate. See the valuable thesis of Carvalho, "Christiaan," 27.

183 See Snouck Hurgronje, *Mekka*, chs. 1–2. His interest in Islam and Mecca was deep, to the extent that he faked conversion to Islam to be able to witness the pilgrimage in Mecca. See Carvalho, "Christiaan," 40–59.

184 Snouck Hurgronje, *Mekka*, 50.

185 Snouck Hurgronje, *Mohammedanism*, 86.

186 Snouck Hurgronje, *Mohammedanism*, 88.

187 Snouck Hurgronje, *Mohammedanism*, 88.

sources and advance scholarship on early Islam. Relying on material from Ibn Saᶜd's *Ṭabaqāt*, Horovitz produced a study titled *The Earliest Biographies of the Prophet and Their Authors.*[188] In this study, Horovitz examined thirteen early Muslim authorities on *maghāzī*, such as ᶜUrwa ibn al-Zubayr, Wahb ibn Munabbih, and al-Zuhrī of the Umayyad era, and al-Wāqidī and Ibn Saᶜd who wrote under the ᶜAbbāsids. Horovitz did his best to work with the few early sources available to him from the first part of the century. One of the most important contributions by Horovitz is his attention to the sectarian inclinations and political sympathies of the classical authors.[189] Still, we should note, most of the studies in that generation resembled a general extraction of data from the discovered manuscripts without any substantial or rigorous critical analysis.[190]

The works and arguments of von Kremer, de Goeje, Wellhausen, Goldziher, and Snouck Hurgronje represent a growing non-Muslim scholarly interest in studying, analyzing, and evaluating Islamic historiographical works in the second part of the nineteenth century. This scholarly interest continued well into the twentieth century and grew rapidly, resulting in more analyses of sources and arguments concerning Muhammad's character and deeds. Snouck Hurgronje's German colleague Carl Heinrich Becker (1876–1933) studied the military expansion of Muhammad and his successors and argued that it is better to view these military activities as driven by lust for power and economic gain than as religiously motivated incursions.[191] Here Becker deviated from earlier assumptions on the Muslim military activities voiced by earlier scholars, including Wellhausen. Becker's diluting the religion—as the driving force behind the Muslim raids and conquests—can be viewed as a response to his social and political contexts, in which he was—in various

[188] Horovitz, *Earliest.*

[189] Horovitz, *Earliest*, 40–124, especially 22–23, 63, et passim.

[190] In commenting on Horovitz's work and those in his generation, Conrad concludes, "But important as these works were at the time, they suffered from a common weakness in that they simply collected information about separate individuals. The data was not critiqued to any significant extent, and little attempt was made to extract from it any overall picture of the development of early Islamic historical writing about the Prophet Muḥammad or to raise and resolve historiographical issues." Conrad, "Introduction," in Horovitz's *Earliest*, xxiii.

[191] See Becker, "Expansion" in *Cambridge*, ed. Gwatkin et al., 329–364. See Donner, *Early*, 4–5, where he explains Becker's arguments on the military Muslim activities as "stimulated by the promise of wealth and of land in the conquered domains" (4). Donner argues that "Becker was of the opinion, however, that the first conquests were essentially accidental, and that it was only after these decisive early victories that the further Islamic conquests became regular, planned operations" (4); Ibrahim, *Stated*, 42. On the friendship between Snouck Hurgronje and Becker, see Engberts, *Scholarly*, 14, 27; on the disputes between them, see Engberts, "Orientalists," in *Scholarly*, ed. Engberts and Paul, 172–192.

writings—admiring and praising the growing strong ties between Germany and the Ottoman Empire.[192]

Unlike Becker, some scholars during the same time did not dilute the religious aspect of the military activities of early Islam. They viewed religion as an essential part of the expansion of the Muslim community. Belgian scholar Henri Lammens (1862–1937) was a Jesuit missionary who taught in Rome and Beirut and spent most of his life in the Middle East. He was interested in the history of Islam, particularly the early period. He did not view Muhammad and his deeds—that includes the *maghāzī*—favorably.[193] Building on earlier scholarship, Lammens was skeptical of the reliability and authenticity of Muslim traditions. In 1910 he argued skeptically that Muhammad's biography was created to interpret and make sense of the ambiguous Qur'ān.[194] In his study of the Muslim military expansion, Lammens viewed the religious motivation as essential in the military expansion; however, he also argued for the superiority of the Arabs on the battlefields and for their love for raids.[195] Here, Lammens combined religious and nonreligious factors as motivations for the Muslim military activities.

Lammens' generation witnessed other remarkable scholars on Islam, including British scholar David Samuel Margoliouth (1858–1940) and Italian prince Leone Caetani (1869–1935). The two arguably viewed Muhammad's life from differing angles, as the former was *somewhat* more positive in his views than the latter. Born to a Jewish father who converted to Christianity, Margoliouth served briefly as a priest in the Church of England and was professor of Arabic at the University of Oxford from 1889 to 1937.[196] Three of his works discuss important aspects of Muhammad's life: *Mohammed and the Rise of Islam* (1905), *The Early Development of Mohammedanism* (1914), and to a lesser extent *The Relations between Arabs and Israelites prior to the Rise of Islam* (1924).[197] Margoliouth appears to have decided to view Muhammad and interpret his actions—for the most part—positively.

192 Engberts, *Scholarly*, 191.

193 Lammens, *Islam*, 24–36.

194 See Lammens, "Qoran," 25–51; Lammens, "Age," in *Quest*, ed. Ibn Warraq, 188–217; also Jarrar, "Exegetical," in *Oxford*, ed. Abdel Haleem and Mustafa Shah, 621. Particularly, Lammens viewed the *Sīra* as a product of Muslim exegetes to explain ambiguity in the Qur'ān. See Lammens, "L'Age," 209–250. See also Reynolds, *Qur'ān*, 9, where he writes, "Henri Lammens argues that the biography of Muḥammad is not something that the Islamic community remembered, but rather something that Muslim exegetes developed in order to explain the Qur'ān."

195 Lammens, *Le berceau*, 176–177. See the discussion on Lammens in Donner, *Early*, 4.

196 Shelley, "David S. Margoliouth," in *CMR*, vol. 17, forthcoming.

197 For the life and works of Margoliouth, see Buaben, *Image*, 49ff.

He states his goal of studying the *Sīra* with a clearly defined approach "to do justice to [Muhammad's] intellectual ability and to observe towards him the respectful attitude which his greatness deserves."[198] Yet he insists that his book "does not aim at being either an apology or an indictment."[199] In defining his approach, he critiques both the sympathizers who present mainly the "superiority" of Muhammad as well as the antagonists who highlight only his "inferiority."[200] Margoliouth declares he adopts neither of these approaches. Rather, he claims that he seeks to present a reading of Islamic sources that is "absolutely free" of religious bias.[201] With this ambitious goal, Margoliouth calls Muhammad a "hero," although he does not idealize him.[202] Unlike those earlier scholars who demonized Muhammad, Margoliouth writes positively on Muhammad whenever a chance occurs: "the Prophet shared to the full the misery of his followers," and "as he refused to employ the Alms for his private needs, he had no source of revenue."[203] Of course, here Margoliouth is not only positive in his interpretation, but also appears to take the Muslim accounts at face value, believing them to be accurate documentations of that which occurred.[204] He relies on Muslim accounts from the *ḥadīth*, *tafsīr*, *trājim*, and *ṭabaqāt*, but with the slightest skepticism, although he views Muhammad as a main contributor to the laws of Islam.[205] But Margoliouth is also willing to criticize Muhammad and his actions. Not ready to affirm Muhammad's prophethood, Margoliouth rather claims that Muhammad seized an opportunity to declare himself a prophet among the Arabs.[206] Margoliouth also questions Muhammad's sexual behaviors and marriages, portraying him as an opportunistic man who waits a "moment

[198] Margoliouth, *Mohammed*, vii.
[199] Margoliouth, *Mohammed*, vii.
[200] Margoliouth, *Mohammed*, vii.
[201] Margoliouth, *Mohammed*, vii.
[202] We should note that it was not uncommon in that era—the Romantic period, from the late eighteenth to the mid-ninteenth centuries—for Europeans to be interested in heroes. See, for instance, Carlyle, *On Heroes*, 65–120, where he treats Muhammad under the title "The Hero as Prophet." Carlyle was a Scottish historian and philosopher. His book is a collection of six lectures he gave a year earlier on heroic leaders. I am grateful for Gabriel Reynolds for this reference.
[203] Margoliouth, *Mohammed*, 236.
[204] He also adopts positive views on the Qur'ān and its canonization, claiming it traces back to Muhammad's time and that the text is genuine—although it needed a supplement since it did not include a complete guide to Islamic life. Margoliouth, *Early*, 1–34 (on the Qur'ān), and 230–258 (on historical writings). His trust in the sources and their descriptions appears in his important article Margoliouth, "Muhammad," 8:871–880, especially 878, where he writes, "No European apologist for Muhammad seems to have possessed any proper acquaintance with the Arabic sources."
[205] Margoliouth, *Mohammed*, iv–ix.
[206] Margoliouth, *Mohammed*, 73.

before putting any plan into execution."[207] In treating Muhammad's *maghāzī*, Margoliouth, again, does not advance substantial skepticism toward the Muslim accounts, interacting with the sources as if they describe factual actions truly performed by Muhammad and his followers. For Margoliouth, Muhammad's *maghāzī* traditions must be factual because they portray him negatively.[208] These *maghāzī*, says Margoliouth, reflect Muhammad's pursuit of revenge against his enemies, through "despatching assassins" and making "display of force" in his raids.[209] Still, many of Margoliouth's interpretations of Muhammad's actions are positive. We should note that Margoliouth's positive interpretations are arguably one of the earliest scholarly precursors of the "irenic approach" in Islamic studies, as explained by Charles Adams and Andrew Rippin. The approach reflects "the greater appreciation of Islamic religiousness and the fostering of a new attitude toward it."[210] As Rippin observes, this approach "has led to the unfortunate result of a reluctance on the part of many scholars to follow all the way through with their insights and results."[211]

This irenic approach is clearly not shared by Italian prince Leone Caetani (1869–1935). He is known as a remarkable historian on early Islam, especially because of his significant ten-volume *Annali dell'Islam*. The book is foundational, thorough, and meticulous, as he relies heavily and masterfully on original Arabic Muslim sources.[212] Unlike Margoliouth, Caetani is skeptical of Muslim traditions. He follows the skeptical approach of Goldziher and refers to him as "the greatest historian and critic of Islam, Ignaz Goldziher."[213] For Caetani, Muslim traditions are largely forgeries—at times, he appears to delight in highlighting inconsistencies and contradictions in Islam's texts.[214] For him, Ibn Isḥāq forged the *Sīra* and various elements in

207 Margoliouth, *Mohammed*, 177. He claims, "Moslem mind had by this time been somewhat tainted by licentiousness, whence any meeting between persons of different sex gave rise to sinister rumours" (341).

208 See Margoliouth, "Muhammad," 8:878. On this claim, see Shoemaker, *Apocalypse*, 183.

209 Margoliouth, *Mohammed*, 311.

210 Rippin, "Literary," 159.

211 Rippin, "Literary," 159. See also Nickel, " 'Our Friendly Strife,' " in *CMR*, 15:255–280, especially 276. Michael Cook contrasts Islam and Christianity and writes of Islamic political notions and activities supported by Muslim sources, "These ideas are not notably eirenic, and to anyone brought up on the New Testament they will seem very alien. In the face of persecution, Jesus neither resisted nor emigrated. . . . If Christians want to be political activists, they cannot in good faith take their values from the life of their founder." Cook, *Muhammad*, 57–58.

212 See Ahmad, "Leone," 203–216.

213 Caetani, *Annali*, 1:29.

214 He observes a tradition on the renowned Muslim narrator Abū Hurayra and describes him as excessively joking. See Caetani, *Annali*, 1:52–54.

Muhammad's *maghāzī*.[215] He questions the plausibility of Muhammad's campaign to Mu'ta against the Byzantines—and calls it an outright fabrication.[216] However, in his treatment of events, sometimes he appears selective in what to accept or reject from the traditional Muslim narrative.[217] In his *Annali*, Caetani devotes the first volumes to Muhammad's career. Questioning Muhammad's morality, Caetani considers him to be a false prophet and chiefly anti-Christian.[218] On the positive side, Caetani views Muhammad as a revivalist who reformed the Arabs.[219] He examines Muhammad's *maghāzī* and the subsequent conquests and views these military activities as a momentous migration of "uncivilized" Bedouins in pursuit of materialistic gain and dominance, diluting the weight of the religious fervor and zeal of the commanders as a driving force for the expansion, thus agreeing with Becker and disagreeing with Wellhausen.[220] It could be argued that Caetani's negative views of Islam and Muhammad's deeds and morality are likely a product of his social and political context—his upbringing in Rome within the prominent and wealthy Caetani family.

Like Caetani, Swedish scholar Tor Julius Efraim Andræ (1885–1947) did not generally view Muhammad favorably. Andræ was trained as a Lutheran clergyman and later became a bishop. He also served as religious history professor at Stockholm University.[221] In his important work *Muhammed: Hans liv och hans tro* (Stockholm, 1930)—translated into English as *Muḥammad: The Man and his Faith* (1936)—he attempts to unlock the psychological character of Muhammad and the process of Muhammad's reception of the alleged divine message.[222] Andræ pays attention to Muhammad's context and examines his inner struggles, pursuit of power, self-consciousness, and even arrogance.[223] Andræ was skeptical of Muslim sources, most likely as he studied for a time under Goldziher.[224] For Andræ, Muhammad was not

215 Caetani, *Annali*, 1:34, 1:194. He also critiques the *ḥadīth* narrators (e.g., Bukhārī), calling them dishonest (1:40–41). For a modern study on Bukhārī and its textual problems, see Aylāl, *Ṣaḥīḥ*.

216 Caetani, *Annali*, 2:409–413.

217 For instance, he accepts the accounts of Muhammad's ancestors like Quṣayy. Caetani, *Annali*, 1:81–83. However, he rejects the accounts of the Year of the Elephant and its connection with the Qur'ān (1:123–125), as well as Muhammad's journey to Syria to meet Monk Baḥīrā (1:160–161).

218 In the first few pages of the book, Caetani describes Islam as a harmful instrument to Christianity on various levels. Caetani, *Annali*, 1:5, 1:49–51. See his comments about Muhammad marrying the Jewess Ṣafiyya (*Annali*, 2:34–35).

219 Caetani, *Annali*, 1:7–9.

220 See Caetani, *Annali*, 1:2–4, et passim in vols. 1–2; see Donner, *Early*, 4–5.

221 On his life and work, see the important work of Widengren, *Tor Andrae*.

222 Andræ, *Muḥammad*, 31–52.

223 Andræ, *Muḥammad*, 167.

224 Andræ viewed aspects of Muhammad's life as legends created by later Muslims. See Andræ, *Die Person Muhammads*, 26ff., where he examines "Die propheten legend."

original or genuine and did not receive any unique revelation. Rather, he was influenced by Christianity and Judaism and borrowed much of earlier traditions through his interaction with religious missionaries.[225] He writes, "Mohammed received from the Nestorians of Persia the impressions which decisively influenced his personal religious message."[226] In some instances, Andræ attempts to be charitable in his treatment of Muhammad, as evidenced in his examination of the incident of the Satanic Verses, where Andræ suggests that Muhammad did not believe Allah had daughters, but accepted that the goddesses could be sought for intercession.[227] Thus, Andræ follows the arguments of Geiger and Muir and argues that Muhammad relied on earlier religions to establish his claims for prophethood.

Scottish scholar Sir Hamilton Alexander Roskeen Gibb (1895–1971) served at the School of Oriental and African Studies at the University of London, Oxford University, and Harvard University.[228] From an early age, he was interested in Islamic studies and historiography, as evidenced in his 1922 MA thesis (University of London) on the Muslim conquest of Transoxiana. In 1930 he succeeded Sir Thomas Arnold as both the chair of Arabic at the University of London and as the British editor of the *Encyclopaedia of Islam*. In 1937 Gibb succeeded Margoliouth as Laudian Professor of Arabic at Oxford. Gibb wrote extensively on Islam and contributed many articles to the *Encyclopaedia of Islam* in its original and revised editions. Among his books, two stand with importance in our discussion: *Modern Trends in Islam* (1947) and *Mohammedanism: An Historical Survey* (1949)—which was later retitled as *Islam: An Historical Survey* (1980). In these two books, Gibb attempts to present Islam in a postwar context in a noticeably balanced way. He is decidedly positive in valuing aspects of Islam, acknowledging that "the practice of every religion to some extent falls short of its own highest ideals," and argues that "Islam is an autonomous expression of religious thought and experience, which must be viewed in and through itself and its own principles and standards."[229] In portraying Islam in Western academia, Gibb argues that, contrary to general opinion, Islam did not stand still since the medieval times—it is in a changing state, and clearly swinging between a transcendental and a pantheist conception of the divine. For him, those

[225] See Andræ, *Muḥammad*, 53–93, especially 87, where he discusses the influence of "Syrian Christianity" on Islam.
[226] Andræ, *Muḥammad*, 90.
[227] Andræ, *Muḥammad*, 21–22.
[228] See Shaw, "Bibliography," in *Arabic*, ed. Makdisi, 1–20; also Lambton, "Obituary," 338–345.
[229] Gibb, *Mohammedanism*, vii.

who view Islam as a static and "unreformed" entity from the thirteenth century are missing the point. He observes that "modernism" in Islam has been running under the surface.[230] Arguably, Gibb shows sympathy to the faith and its followers, but clearly avoids joining the camps of sympathizers—who seem fascinated at anything non-Western—which flourished in postwar context. He cherished elements in Islamic civilization, with a keen interest in establishing a balance between the study of medieval Islam and contemporary Muslim thought.

Gibb's sanguine approach to Islam and appreciation of various elements in Muslim civilization can be traced in scholars of the following generation such as English professor of Middle Eastern studies Albert Habib Hourani (1915–1993), Scottish Islamicist William Montgomery Watt (1909–2006), and French Marxist sociologist and historian Maxime Rodinson (1915–2004). Born and raised in England to Lebanese parents, Hourani's interest was mainly in the modern period, but he wrote *A History of the Arab Peoples*, in which he treated the early Islamic society and traced the development of Islamic institutions.[231] Watt and Rodinson wrote on Islamic history. Their works and arguments have been influential, placing them as two of the important Islamicists of the twentieth century.

Watt was influenced by Gibb and called him "the doyen of Islamic studies in the English-speaking world," and undoubtedly embraced Gibb's positive attitude to Islam.[232] This is one reason why Watt sought to correct what he viewed as the prevailing negative approaches to Islam in Europe. He writes that, "Because Europe was reacting against Islam it belittled the influence of Saracens and exaggerated its dependence on its Greek and Roman heritage. So today an important task for us is to correct this false emphasis and to acknowledge fully our debt to the Arab and Islamic world."[233] This is reflected in Watt's views of Muhammad and the Qur'ān, as he identified the former as one of the greatest humans who ever lived and treated the latter as an inspired text—though not infallible.[234] His positive reading of Muhammad's life appears in his admission, "From an early date I held that Muhammad

[230] Gibb, *Modern*, ch. 2.

[231] See Sluglett and Farouk-Sluglett, "Albert," 139–141.

[232] Watt finished his classics degree at Edinburgh University in 1929 and began his PhD in 1933. His thesis was rejected without revision, so he again started a PhD in 1938 and finished it in 1943, examining "Predestination and Free Will in Islam." For his life and work, see the excellent chapter by his student Hillenbrand, "William," in *Life*, ed. Hillenbrand, 3–14.

[233] Watt, *Influence*, 84.

[234] See Hillenbrand, "William," 3–14.

must have been sincere. It is unthinkable that a great world religion should have been based on imposture or falsehood."[235] Arguably, Watt was conscious of how Muslims viewed his words. Many Muslim thinkers valued Watt's views on Islam and in particular on Muhammad, although some Muslims still viewed him as less sympathetic toward Islam than Gibb was.[236] According to his student Carole Hillenbrand, Watt believed that Muhammad was a true prophet and wished that Christians would accept his prophethood.[237] In one of his arguments, he claims that Islam is Abrahamic and thus linked with Christianity and Judaism.[238] Watt's view here is arguably shared by Maxime Rodinson (1915–2004), who studies Islam from a sociological lens and argues that "Muḥammad really did experience sensory phenomena translated into words and phrases and that he interpreted them as messages from the Supreme Being."[239] Unlike Watt, however, Rodinson does not view the Qur'ān as inspired. He writes, "It is evident that I do not believe that the Koran is the book of Allah."[240] Thus, while Watt and Rodinson share some positive views on Muhammad, they deviate on the Qur'ān. Both adopt a sanguine interpretation of Islam and its prophet, albeit relying on different methodologies. It appears they were decidedly positive—and, to some extent, not relativistic—in their portrayal of Muhammad. Moreover, Watt and Rodinson share another important feature in their study of Islam. In their positivist readings of its texts, they were *not* overly skeptical of the reliability of the Muslim sources. They largely accepted the traditional Muslim narrative, although they, at times, offered critical arguments, especially concerning possible embellishments and exaggerations in Muslim accounts.[241]

In the middle part of the twentieth century, a notable scholar emerged: Marshall Goodwin Simms Hodgson (1922–1968). He was one of the major scholars of Islamic civilization of the past century and served as

235 Hillenbrand, "William," 11.

236 See Siddiqi, "Review," 446–450, especially 446, where he claims, "Most of the books written by Prof. Watt on Islam and the life of the holy prophet of Islam show him to be not too much sympathetic to Islam." See also Hillenbrand, "William," 13, where she speaks of Muslim scholar Mahmoud Ayoub's views of Watt.

237 Hillenbrand, "William," 14.

238 Watt, *Muḥammad: Prophet and Statesman*, 55; Hillenbrand, "William," 11.

239 Rodinson, *Mohammad*, 218. The book was first published in French as *Mahomet* by Club français du livre in 1961. Rodinson was born into a Jewish family in France, and throughout his career he was known as a Marxist historian.

240 Rodinson, *Mohammad*, 218.

241 See, for example, Watt, *Muḥammad*, 24 (hereafter cited as Watt, *Muḥammad*, 24); also his critique of traditions on Muhammad's prophethood at Watt, *Muḥammad: Prophet and Statesman*, 2. See Rodinson, *Mohammad*, 110 (Bilāl), 135 (Abū Lahab), 180 and 211 (Muslim traditions exaggerated accounts).

professor of history and social thought at the University of Chicago. He was also known as a Christian pacifist—a fact that might have led to his negative views of Muhammad, particularly as an initiator of military campaigns. In his important magnum opus, *The Venture of Islam*, Hodgson evaluates Muhammad's *maghāzī* as recounted in Muslim sources and argues: "It is not just a Christian squeamishness, I think, that points to Muhammad's military measures as a central problem in his prophethood."[242] It appears that Hodgson is ready to evaluate Muhammad's life in moral terms, and largely through his Christian lens.[243] Indeed, Hodgson presents his views on Muhammad with a negative commentary, although he is also aware of the shortcomings of Muslim sources as he writes, "though what I have to say about Muhammad is largely conjecture, yet it can be responsibly offered."[244] Still, Hodgson seems to have had hopes in the text of the Qur'ān as a source for Muhammad's life. He claims, "We can rely on the text of the Qur'ān itself as direct evidence [for the life of Muhammad]."[245] Despite his obvious skepticism of the sources, it appears that Hodgson continued the scholarly trend of his day of largely accepting the traditional narrative as true.

However, in the decade following Hodgson's sudden death in 1968, the almost universal trust in Islam's traditional narrative was beginning to crack among scholars. There was a growing trend of skepticism in dealing with Islam's origin and the Muslim traditional narrative.[246] This trend is indebted to the arguments of revisionist scholar John Wansbrough (1928–2002).[247] Wansbrough was not concerned with a new portrayal of Muhammad but rather with the traditional Muslim narrative about him and the claims of the early canonization of the Qur'ān. He applied the principles of biblical studies and the skeptical approach to Christian origins on the texts of Islam.[248] While the skeptical approach can definitely trace back to the work

242 See Hodgson, *Venture*, 1:186.

243 In his comments on Hodgson's critique of Muhammad, Richard C. Martin writes, "The difference between Hodgson and many of his Western Islamicist critics is that Hodgson dared to believe that moral issues do not disappear when a scholar takes up the study of a civilization other than his or her own." Martin, "Religious," in *Just War*, ed. Kelsay and Johnson, 108. Martin wished for Hodgson's critics to "direct their refutations toward his argument and not his religious background."

244 Hodgson, *Venture*, 1:161. In his examination of the age of the caliphate, he states, "Generalizations in this period cannot expect to be better than educated guesses" (2:373).

245 Hodgson, *Venture*, 1:160. This point in particular was criticized by John Wansbrough. See Wansbrough, "Review," 169–170.

246 Donner argues that the revisionist arguments began to emerge in the 1960s and 1970s. See Donner, "Introduction," in *Expansion*, ed. Donner, xiv. Still, Wansbrough and his arguments served as a paradigm shift.

247 Berg considers Wansbrough as "one of the most prominent 'revisionists' or 'skeptics.'" See Berg, "Preface," in *Method*, ed. Berg, x; Berg, "Implications," 3–22.

248 See Stewart, "Wansbrough," in *Qur'ānic Studies Today*, ed. Neuwirth and Sells, 18–19.

of Goldziher, Wansbrough's works consolidated the approach and drove it forward. He questioned the common scholarly acceptance of the Muslim tradition. For him, Islam's accounts are religiously driven. They do not reflect a recorded history but rather a collective interpretation of events by later Muslims.[249] Wansbrough argued that the Qur'ān took centuries to canonize, and the *tafsīr* traditions and Muhammad's *Sīra* were forged to explain it.[250] Wansbrough's work influenced other scholars including Patricia Crone (1945–2015), Michael Cook (1940–), and Andrew Rippin (1950–2016).[251] Scholars began to explore new sources to interpret Islam's origins and to evaluate the portrayal of Muhammad. Crone and Cook—and later Robert Hoyland (1966–)—explored non-Muslim sources to sketch Islam's origins.[252] This trend grew in remarkable ways and gained momentum with the publication of recent studies reflecting the revisionist skeptical approach to Islamic origins. However, the growth was not unchallenged.[253] It resulted in a growing schism between two scholarly approaches in Islamic studies, that is, sanguine (traditional) and revisionist (skeptical).[254] It also resulted in

[249] Wansbrough, *Qur'ānic*, 12, 58; Wansbrough, *Sectarian*, ix, 118–119, 147; Wansbrough, "Res," in *Method*, ed. Berg, 10–19; Rippin, "Literary," 155–156; Howard-Johnston, *Witnesses*, 355ff.; Sfar, *Search*, 40–48.

[250] Donner explains that Wansbrough argued that the accounts of the *Sīra* "do not represent an independent body of information that might be used to understand the text of the Qur'ān, but rather were fabricated precisely to explain various verses of the Qur'ān." Donner, "Historical," in *Cambridge*, ed. McAuliffe, 33. According to Chase Robinson, Wansbrough "pushed the closure of the Qur'ānic text into the late second/eighth or early third/ninth centuries." See Robinson, "Reconstructing," in *Method*, ed. Berg, 132. For scholars who disagree with Wansbrough's conclusion on the Qur'ān's closure, see Sinai, *Qur'an*, 40–77; Sinai, *Rain-Giver*, 1ff.; Stewart, "Wansbrough," in *Qur'ānic*, ed. Neuwirth and Sells, 18–19; Motzki, "Alternative," in *Cambridge*, ed. McAuliffe, 59ff.

[251] See the important Foreword of Andrew Rippin to the work of Wansbrough. Rippin, "Foreword," in Wansbrough, *Qur'ānic Studies*, ix–xx, in which Rippin explains the major arguments of Wansbrough.

[252] See the controversial work by Crone and Cook, *Hagarism*, 8; also the arguments of Cook, *Muhammad*, 75–76. See the important studies Hoyland, *Seeing*; also his *God's Path*.

[253] See, for instance, the important studies of Donner, *Early Islamic*; also Donner, "From Believers," 9–53; and Donner, *Muhammad*. See also the critical evaluation of Donner's argument on early Islam by Jack Tannous, "Review," 126–141; also Sinai, "The Unknown," 49ff.; Hoyland, "Review," 573–576. Like Donner, see Schoeler, Motzki, and Görke, "First," 2–59. Cf. Shoemaker, "In Search," 257–344. See also the scholarly debate between Donner and Hoyland in the articles Donner, "Review," 134–140; Hoyland, "Reflections," 113–140.

[254] While I provide a survey in the following section, see here briefly Ibrahim, *Stated*, 11–12; also Ibrahim, *Conversion*, 19–25. Some scholars reject both groups. Schoeler argues for a middle ground between skeptics and traditionalists in treating the *Sīra*. He is convinced that neither "the extensive trust in Muslim transmission" nor "the total rejection of the traditional material" is successful, and asserts that "a middle way must be found," and "The correctness of this middle way will arise, it is hoped, from the compilation and evaluation of a corpus of traditions that are attributed by Islamic transmission to the earliest historical researcher (collector of historical reports), from ʿUrwah b. al-Zubayr." Schoeler, "Foundations," in *Method*, ed. Berg, 22. Rippin questions the plausibility of a middle ground. Rippin, "Literary," 156.

more studies on Muhammad, especially in recent years (e.g., Fred Donner's *Muhammad and the Believers*, Hoyland's *In God's Path*, and Sean Anthony's *Muhammad and the Empires of Faith*).[255] This scholarly division is important to explore as it is foundational to describing my approach to studying Muhammad's *maghāzī* in this study. Thus, I highlight the two approaches in the following section.

This brief (and incomplete) survey of non-Muslim Western scholarship interacting with Muslim sources in general and Muhammad's life and *maghāzī* in particular is sufficient to demonstrate the general disagreement surrounding Muhammad and his life among non-Muslim scholars. The disagreement traces back to the earliest years of Islam, and it grew rapidly with modern scholarship since the nineteenth century. In the following section, in addition to explaining the two major scholarly approaches to Islamic historiography, I draw attention to the unique contribution of this study and its importance to the growing literature on Muhammad's *maghāzī*.

The *Maghāzī* as Historiography: Methodology and Approach

Muhammad's *maghāzī*, as a literary topic, is a central topic in Islamic historiography. Reports of the *maghāzī* appear extensively in early Islamic sources, both historiographical (e.g., *maghāzī*, *sīra*, *ta'rīkh*, *futūḥ*, *ṭabaqāt*) and nonhistoriographical (e.g., *tafsīr*, *adab*, *ḥadīth*, *ᶜulūm al-Qur'ān*, *fiqh*, *maᶜājim*, *masālik al-buldān*).[256] In this book, I focus on the *maghāzī* reports as found in historiographical sources—a historiographical work is one that is *primarily* concerned with representing and narrating past events. While

[255] See, for instance, two recent studies. Juan Cole published a revisionist fanciful tale of Muhammad as only a prophet of peace, by selectively elevating and discarding primary sources to enforce his claims. Cole, *Muhammad.* See my critical review, "Review," 1–18. Unlike Cole's selectivity with the sources, Sean Anthony, in a more rigorous research, focuses on the *sīra-maghāzī* traditions, alongside other Muslim and non-Muslim sources, to reconstruct a historical portrayal of Muhammad. See Anthony, *Muhammad.* Still, Anthony's study received some critical views. See Powers, "Review," 244–267.

[256] In this section, I rely on the discussion in Ibrahim, *Conversion*, 20–24. For references on the *maghāzī* in nonhistoriographical sources, see Muqātil, *Tafsīr*, 1:144–147 (the Battle of Badr); 1:101, 106 (the raid to Khaybar); ᶜAbd al-Razzāq, *Muṣannaf*, 1:191 (Tabūk), 3:302 (report of many raids), 5:361 (Banū al-Naḍīr); Bukhārī, *Ṣaḥīḥ*, 1:125, 2:15, 2:77, 3:88, et passim; also Ibn Ḥajar, *Fatḥ*, 2:438, 3:63. For a primary source evaluating the importance of al-Bukhārī's *Ṣaḥīḥ*, see Ibn al-Ṣalāḥ, *Maᶜrifat*, 16–29. See Görke, "Relationship," 171–185, where he argues that "*maghāzī* and *ḥadīth* emerged as separate fields; each influenced the other but they preserved their distinctive features."

historical reports, such as those of the *maghāzī*, may indeed be found in nonhistoriographical sources, I rely primarily on historiographical works in my investigation. They are numerous, and the historical reports we find in nonhistoriographical works largely appear in historiographical ones. In defining history and historiography, I follow the helpful criteria offered by Franz Rosenthal and Chase Robinson. The term "history" refers "both to the process of historical development and to the description of that process," and "historiography" (*ta'rīkh*) "means one thing: *writing about the past*."[257]

In order to articulate my approach to Islamic historiography, I should begin by explaining that the scholarly study of Islamic historiography can be roughly divided into two major camps: revisionists (or skeptics) and traditionalists (or sanguine, or positivists).[258] These two camps are not monolithic, as the approaches and arguments of each author may still differ. The dividing line between the two is chiefly a result of their competing views concerning how to deal with the textual problems of the Muslim sources. In these sources, scholars observe, we find that "chronological discrepancies and obscurities abound, as do flat contradictions in the meaning of events or even, less frequently, on their fundamental course."[259] The two camps view these problems differently, hence the existence of two major scholarly approaches.

[257] Rosenthal, *Historiography*, 10; also Spiegel, "History" 59–86. On history and historiography, see the valuable Arabic studies by Dūrī, *Baḥth*, which was translated as *The Rise of Historical Writing among the Arabs* by Conrad; also Muṣṭafā, *Ta'rīkh*. See the English studies of Petersen, *ʿAlī*; Humphreys, *Islamic*; Khalidi, *Arabic*; Khalidi, *Islamic*; Donner, *Narratives*; Robinson, *Historiography*.

[258] See the discussion of the two scholarly approaches in Ibrahim, *Stated*, 10–14; Ibrahim, *Conversion*, 20–24; Berg, "Competing," in *Method*, ed. Berg, 259–261. For these approaches in relation to Islamic historiography, see Donner, "Introduction," in *Expansion*, ed. Donner, xxvii–xxxi; Donner, *Narratives*, 5ff.; Kennedy, *Prophet*, 347ff.; Hoyland, *God's Path*, 231ff. Arguably, these labels are sometimes unhelpful. See Conrad, "Heraclius," 151 n. 188. The revisionist approach is highly influenced by Wansbrough, who is considered by some to be "one of the most prominent 'revisionists' or 'skeptics.'" See Berg, "Preface," in *Method*, ed. Berg, x; Berg, "Implications," 3–22. See Wansbrough's main works, *Qur'ānic*, 43, and *Sectarian*, 20, 49, especially Andrew Rippin's helpful remarks in the introduction to the expanded edition of the former (published in 2004). Donner writes that Wansbrough argued that the *sīra* accounts "do not represent an independent body of information that might be used to understand the text of the Qur'ān, but rather were fabricated precisely to explain various verses of the Qur'ān." Donner, "Historical," in *Companion*, ed. McAuliffe, 33. For examples of the sanguine approach, see Schoeler, "Foundations," in *Method*, ed. Berg, 22; also Görke and Schoeler, "Reconstructing," 209–220. See the fierce debate between Shoemaker (skeptical approach) on the one hand and Schoeler, Motzki, and Görke on the other. Shoemaker, "In Search," 257–344; Görke, Motzki, and Schoeler, "First," 2–59. For the development of scholarly works on Islamic origins, see Daniel, *Islam*, 294–301.

[259] Donner, *Narratives*, 4–5. On the different ways these two approaches deal with the problems of the sources, see Humphreys, *Islamic*, 69–91; Donner, *Narratives*, 112–122, 203–208; Robinson, *Historiography*, 8–17; Robinson, "Study," 209. The Tunisian scholar Nājiya al-Wurayyimī traces some contradictions in the *Sīra* and early *tafsīr*. See Wurayyimī, *Fī al-I'tilāf*, 35ff.; Cf. Anthony, *Muḥammad*, 83–101.

Revisionist scholars do not usually trust the reliability of the Muslim sources, while traditionalists—despite being critical of the sources, as all scholars should be—view reliability differently. In their sanguine approach, traditionalists commonly argue that a "kernel" of reliable reports is in the sources despite their apparent textual problems: the "kernel" is "a core of genuine collective memory."[260] While they recognize the sources' internal and external problems, they believe that, through diligent analysis, one can reconstruct the historical events, at least in a rough outline. Indeed, for traditionalist scholars, "despite the fact that there is virtually no extant written material from the first two centuries of Islam, the later collections of the third and fourth centuries contain an accurate record of the past."[261]

For instance, Ira Lapidus adopts a sanguine approach to Muslim historiography and criticizes "the radical skeptical approach," claiming that it "is based on a misunderstanding of the transmission of knowledge in late antiquity and the early Islamic era."[262] In rejecting skepticism toward the sources, Lapidus concludes that "the rich, vivid, and extensive materials in the early Arab-Muslim histories were not invented in a later period. Although the Arabic literary tradition was indeed shaped by the later eras in which it was compiled and edited, it embodies an historical recollection of the Arabian milieu and of Muhammad that preserves a core of genuine collective memory."[263] Lapidus' approach is echoed in a study by the German scholar Tilman Nagel (1942–), who believes in the existence of historically reliable material in Muslim historiography, particularly in the accounts of Muhammad's life; still, he affirms that later Muslims forged a legendary portrayal of Muhammad that differs from the historical one.[264] Nagel is an example of scholars who are not only critical of the Muslim sources and their reliability but also have apparent hopes in the historical accounts and that which they present.[265] Like Lapidus, Nagel openly criticizes the skeptical approach and particularly the arguments of Wansbrough.[266] "It is clear," as one

[260] See Lapidus, *History*, 24. For "historical memory," see Spiegel, "Memory," 149–162; Clanchy, *From Memory*, ch. 9; Robinson, *Historiography*, 172–177; Geary, *Phantoms*, 111–122; Hirschler, *Written*; Innes, "Memory."

[261] For source criticism, see Danto, *Historical*, 12, 63; McDowell, *Historical*, 3–15, 54ff. See also Berg, "Competing," in *Methods*, ed. Berg, 259; Berg, *Development*, ch. 1.

[262] Lapidus, *History*, 23.

[263] Lapidus, *History*, 24.

[264] Nagel, *Mohammed*, ch. 8.

[265] For Nagel, the historical Muhammad merely desired to advance his clan's dominion over the local Meccans. Nagel, *Mohammed*, 178ff.

[266] See Nagel, *Mohammed*, 643–833. See also Nagel's other work, *Allahs Liebling*, 15–133, where he reiterates his arguments concerning the legendary Muhammad in contrast to the one of history, describing the former as the "imagined" Muhammad and the latter as the "above-historical" one.

scholar observes, "that Nagel believes that the events described in Muslim accounts actually occurred, although he concedes that the memory of the Muslims had shaped their documentation against the backdrop of later cultural and social contexts."[267]

But this positivism is largely rejected by revisionists. Andrew Rippin (1950–2016) skeptically questions this positivism, affirming that "the real problem here is that even if one admits the existence of such a 'kernel' of history, is it ever possible to identify and extract that information?"[268] Patricia Crone (1945–2015), a prominent skeptical scholar, states that whether "one approaches Islamic historiography from the angle of the religious or the tribal tradition, its overall character thus remains the same: the bulk of it is debris of an obliterated past."[269] Her skepticism is also apparent in another work, where she argues, "The entire tradition is tendentious, its aim being the elaboration of an Arabian *Heilgeschichte*, and this tendentiousness has shaped the facts as we have them, not merely added some partisan statements we can deduct."[270] Crone's comments are echoed in Chase Robinson's assertion that the Muslim writers "were not simply taking liberties with texts: they were generating the texts themselves."[271]

Still, this skepticism is not only found among Western and non-Muslim scholars. We can trace it in the works of modern and contemporary self-identified Muslim scholars. The Tunisian Muslim historian Hichem Djait (1935–2021) does not *fully* trust Muslim traditions. For him, the Qur'ān is the only foundational book in understanding Muhammad's history, while Muslim traditions—such as the accounts of the *Sīra*—are merely *taṣawwur islāmī* (Islamic projection, or opinion) of later generations of historians who wrote what they thought to have happened.[272] Djait discusses the story of Muhammad's first meeting with the angel Gabriel and argues that it should be learned from the Qur'ān and not from later traditions, which

Rudolf Sellheim distinguishes between three kinds of material in Muhammad's *sīra*, including mythical legends on Muhammad and ᶜAbbāsid propaganda against the Umayyads. Sellheim, "Prophet," 53–73 and 49–53, respectively. See also Wansbrough, *Qur'ānic*, 58.

267 Ibrahim, *Conversion*, 21 n. 75.
268 Rippin, "Literary," 156; also Rippin, "Function," 1–20.
269 Crone, *Slaves*, 10.
270 Crone, *Meccan*, 230. Another example of Crone's skeptical orientation toward the traditional accounts of Islamic origins is her "How Did the Qur'ānic Pagans Make a Living?," 387–399; see also Crone, "Pagan," 140ff.
271 Robinson, *Historiography*, 38.
272 Djait, *Waḥy*, 35–42 (esp. 41); see also 90–91, where he studies traditions about how Muhammad acted in crazy manners and argues that "one cannot rely on the *Sīra* accounts at all" (90).

for Djait are tendentious.[273] In another work, Djait argues that we cannot rely on the *Sīra, illā qalīlan* (except a little), as most reports are suspicious, although the *Sīra* "sometimes presents precious material."[274] It is clear that Djait is selective in that which he accepts from Muslim traditions and that which he rejects, with no particular method rather than what he believes to be matching the Qur'ān.[275] A similar approach can be traced in the historical study of the Tunisian scholar Salwā Balḥāj Ṣāliḥ. She examines the life of Khadīja, Muhammad's first wife, as represented in Islamic historiography. Ṣāliḥ affirms that she does not trust the specifics in the Muslim traditions, only the general outline.[276] She believes that Islamic historiography should be approached with a cautious attitude, as we should not accept the unreasonable accounts.[277] With the examples of Djait and Ṣāliḥ, we can trace the skeptical approach in some Muslim writings, although it is still uncommon.

With these two scholarly camps in mind, I describe my approach to Islamic historiography via three major points. First, Islamic historiography is better viewed as a representation of the time of documentation than of the period it allegedly describes. Like Robinson, I believe that our sources provide a "representation rather than record," as the historians were authors "who wrote well after the events they describe."[278] Because of the source problems, I am convinced that historiographical accounts do not describe that which actually happened but that which classical Muslim historians, at best, believed to have occurred or, at worst, sought to convey to their audience about past generations.[279] My point is echoed in a statement by Gerald Hawting, who—in

[273] Djait, *Waḥy*, 90–91.

[274] Djait, *Tārīkhiyyat*, 28–29.

[275] For example, he rejects the historicity of Waraqa ibn Nawfal because it does not fit the Qur'ān in his estimation. Djait, *Tārīkhiyyat*, 152ff. However, Djait believes that some historical episodes—such as the Raid to Banū Qurayẓa—represent true events. Djait, *Fitna*, 28. We know of Waraqa and Banū Qurayẓa from the same pool of traditions, and Djait's methodology is at best selective. He also rejects the historicity of Khadīja. Djait, *Tārīkhiyyat*, 150. Similarly, Djait rejects the historical tradition of Muhammad's encounter with the angel Gabriel in Ghār Ḥirā' (the Cave of Hira) because, Djait claims, it was not referenced in the Qur'ān. See Djait, *Waḥy*, 33–45. Still, Djait is a respected scholar who attempts to understand Islam through scientific methods and modern perspectives. See Djait, *Waḥy*, 8, where he argues that "Islam, as any other religion, is naturally always developing."

[276] Ṣāliḥ, *Daththirīnī*, 11. See also the comments of Djait in his foreword to Ṣāliḥ's book, 5.

[277] Like Djait, Ṣāliḥ is selective about what to accept and what to reject of the Muslim sources, without a clear methodology. Ṣāliḥ, *Daththirīnī*, 15–20.

[278] Robinson, *Empire*, viii. See a similar approach adopted by Rubin, *Eye*, 1–3, where he argues that the Muslim accounts reflect "the self-image of medieval Islamic society" (3). Rubin studies these texts "for the sake of the stories recorded in them, not for the sake of the events described in these stories" (1). This is commonly described as a "literary" approach. See also Hawting, "Review," 126–129. See Roohi, "Muḥammad's Disruptive," 40–80.

[279] See the skeptical comments on historiography in Ibrahim, *Conversion*, 20–24; also Petersen, *ʿAlī*, 11–20; Khalidi, *Images*, 151–280; Gottfried, "Imagined," 97–111; Wansbrough, *Sectarian*, ix, 118–19; Wansbrough, "Res," in *Method*, ed. Berg, 10–19; Rippin, "Literary," 155–156; Genette,

commenting on Muhammad's *Sīra*—asserts, "It is difficult to see how anyone could expect to recover real facts about Muḥammad's life from the sort of traditions and reports examined here."[280] Thus, the *maghāzī*, as historical narratives, are better viewed as a product of the time of documentation rather than as a precise description of past events. These accounts present a religious history as authors sought to depict it to their audience in the generations after Muhammad's time.[281]

Second, Islamic historiography, including its accounts of Muhammad's *maghāzī*, conveys not only depictions of the past but also—and perhaps more so—the political, religious, and social debates of the historians.[282] Like Erling Petersen, I believe that "the traditionist never relinquishes his right to personal political or religious commitment to the subject he deals with" and that "the formation of the historical tradition consists above all in reflections of the political and religious conflicts of its own age."[283] Consider a few revealing examples from classical Muslim historians. According to traditions, Ibn Shihāb al-Zuhrī (d. 124/742)—who was probably the earliest forerunner to write on Muhammad's *maghāzī*—complained that the Umayyad rulers "forced" him and other Muslims to "fabricate historical accounts."[284] This

Narrative, 25–31; Hoyland, "History," 16ff.; Gilliot, "Récit," 277–289; Prince, "Surveying," in *What Is Narratology?*, ed. Kindt and Müller, 1–16.

280 Hawting, "Review," 126–129 (quote from 127). Rippin argues that from a "salvation history" standpoint, "The actual 'history' in the sense of 'what really happened' has become totally subsumed within later interpretation and is virtually, if not totally, inextricable from it"; in other words, "The records we have are the existential records of the thought and faith of later generations." Rippin, "Literary," 156.

281 See Roohi, "Muḥammad's Disruptive," 40–80. Robinson rightly argues that Muslim historians—of al-Balādhurī's time—were *authors* rather than compilers of reports—they "impressed their vision upon the material" by "breaking them up, by rephrasing, supplementing and composing anew." Robinson, *Historiography*, 35–36. Donner, *Narratives*, 127ff.; Hodgson, "Two Pre-Modern," in *Towards*, ed. Nef, 53–69. See also Ibrahim, *Conversion*, 194.

282 For the influence of religious and sociopolitical contexts on historical accounts, see the discussion in Ibrahim, *Conversion*, 35–55, 107–130, 169–199; see also Hoyland, "Arabic," 211–233, where he traces how the early ᶜAbbāsids adapted history to their cultural and political requirements. Robinson states, "The rise of the historiographic tradition, whether or not it was triggered by caliphal patronage, was a deeply political process." Robinson, *Historiography*, 40. On historians' manipulation of reports, see Savant, *New*, 13; Wellhausen, *Arab*, xi–xii; Borrut, *Entre*, 37–40; Hoyland, *Seeing*, 35; Robinson, *Empire*, ch. 1; Petersen, *ᶜAlī*, 17, 50; Anthony, *Muhammad*, 129ff.; ᶜAlawī, *Maḥaṭṭāt*, 19–20.

283 See Petersen, *ᶜAlī*, 17 and 50, respectively.

284 As for al-Zuhrī, the quote is reported by Ibn Saᶜd, *Ṭabaqāt*, 2:334. On the political influence on historical writing, see Borrut, "Vanishing," in which he discusses the ᶜAbbāsids' influence on creating and erasing the past; see also Anthony, *Muhammad*, 129ff. See Décobert, *Le mendiant*, 34, where he states, "Une sédimentation est reparable." See also Borrut, *Entre*, 17, 37; Donner, *Narratives*, 276–282. On al-Zuhrī's statement, see Schoeler, *Écrire*, 55; Martinez-Gros, *L'idéologie*, 20–21. On attributing false traditions to previous authorities for legitimization, see Yāqūt, *Muᶜjam*, 3:1201–1204; Ibn al-Muᶜtazz, *Ṭabaqāt*, 69; Jumaḥī, *Ṭabaqāt*, 1:48.

is likely one reason why the renowned Muslim historian Ibn Khaldūn (d. 808/1406) emphasized the complex relationship between the sword (of the Muslim ruler) and the pen (of the history writers).[285] In the same vein, we also know that traditions were created in response to religious debates. This is evidenced in an early pro-ᶜAlid tradition, where "Muᶜāwiya summoned the reciters and judges of Syria, gave them money, and sent them all over Syria narrating false reports and fabricating historical accounts."[286] Whether Muᶜāwiya's reported action has actually occurred is not certain; however, the report reflects how anti-Umayyad authors formed traditions for sectarian purposes.[287] This also appears in a *maghāzī* report attributed to Ibn ᶜUmar al-Wāqidī (d. ca. 207/823), who was known for his Shīᶜite and pro-ᶜAbbāsid leaning.[288] In describing Muhammad's conquest of Mecca, al-Wāqidī depicts ᶜAlī ibn Abī Ṭālib—the major Shīᶜite imam—as leading a majestic procession of Muslim warriors following Muhammad, while he (i.e., al-Wāqidī) describes Abū Sufyān—the Umayyad leader—as a reluctant and cowardly Muslim.[289] When compared to reports of the same event by pro-Umayyad

[285] See Ibn Khaldūn, *Muqaddima*, 1:318, where he observes that the pen and the sword *kilāhumā āla li-ṣāḥib al-dawla* (both are a tool [in the hands] of the ruler). Cf. Māwardī, *Aḥkām*, 297. On Ibn Khaldūn's thought, see Jābrī, *Fikr*, 243–280; Jābrī, *Naḥn*, 261ff.; Wurayyimī, *Ḥafriyyāt*, 15–34. See ᶜAẓma, *Turāth*, 129–145, where he responds to al-Jābrī's views; see also ᶜAẓma, *Ibn Khaldūn*, ch. 2.

[286] Sulaym ibn Qays, *Kitāb Sulaym*, 279. On Sulaym and his religious and political views, see Ibrahim, *Conversion*, 35–41; Djebli, "Sulaym b. Kays," *EI*², 9:818–819; Ziriklī, *Aᶜlām*, 3:119; Baḥr al-ᶜUlūm, *Fawā'id*, 2:96. See also Amir-Moezzi, *Silent*, 13–22; Modarressi, *Tradition*, 82–83; Dakake, "Writing," 186ff.; Dakake, "Loyalty," 346ff. For primary sources on Sulyam, see Najāshī, *Rijāl*, 8 (entry #4); Ṭūsī, *Fihrist*, 81; Ṭūsī, *Ikhtiyār*, 99–100; Ṣadūq, *Kitāb man lā*, 4:189; Masᶜūdī, *Tanbīh*, 1:198–199; Ibn al-Ghaḍā'irī, *Rijāl*, 63–64; Ḥillī, *Khulāṣat*, 223–224; Anonymous, *Akhbār*, 45. For a negative Shīᶜite view of *Kitāb Sulaym*, see Mufīd, *Taṣḥīḥ*, 149–150. See also Amīnī, *Ghadīr*, 2:106. See ᶜUmarī, *Buḥūth*, 12–40, where he discusses how narrators forged accounts to advance their "political, sectarian, or personal" desires. Cf. Subḥānī, *Kulliyyāt*, 25–28.

[287] For the anti-Umayyad pro-ᶜAlid inclinations during the Umayyad period, see Donner, "Umayyad," 187, where he states, "A powerful stream of anti-Umayyad rhetoric had begun to circulate already during the years of their rule among groups who opposed them, especially the supporters of their ᶜAlid rivals." See also Mu'nis, *Tanqiyat*, 53ff.; Borrut, *Entre*, 6, 8–9. On the anti-Umayyad "pious opposition," see Watt, *Muḥammad*, 73–75, 348–353. For Muslim studies on Muᶜāwiya and his character, see ᶜAqqād, *Muᶜāwiya*, 17–88; Khuḍarī, *Dawla al-umawiyya*, 424–452; Ṣallābī, *Dawla al-umawiyya*, 1:28ff.; Ṣallābī, *ᶜAṣr al-dawlatayn*, 12–20. For a contemporary defense of Muᶜāwiya, see the study of the Egyptian scholar Ṣaqr, *Muᶜāwiya*, 157ff. For a non-Muslim study, see Humphreys, *Muᶜawiya*. See also Keshk, *Historian's Muᶜāwiya*; Keshk, "When Did," 31–42.

[288] On al-Wāqidī and his religio-political views, see Ibrahim, *Conversion*, 110–116; Robinson, *Historiography*, 86, 88, 97, and generally chs. 9–10; Khalidi, *Arabic*, 17ff.; Partner, "New," in *Classical*, ed. Breisach, 11; Dūrī, *Rise*, 37–38; Donner, *Narratives*, 168, 215, 265; Rosenthal, *Historiography*, 31; Sezgin, *Ta'rīkh*, 1:2:100–106; Muṣṭafā, *Ta'rīkh*, 1:67, 1:163ff.; Ziriklī, *Aᶜlām*, 6:311–312; Kaḥḥāla, *Muᶜjam*, 11:95–96. For primary references, see Ibn Qutayba, *Maᶜārif*, 518; Ibn Saᶜd, *Ṭabaqāt*, 5:493ff.; Khaṭīb, *Ta'rīkh*, 4:5–6; Ibn Maᶜīn, *Ta'rīkh*, 3:160; Ibn Ḥajar, *Lisān*, 7:521; Samᶜānī, *Ansāb*, 13:271–272; Dhahabī, *Ta'rīkh*, 14:362; Dāraquṭnī, *Ḍuᶜafā'*, 3:103.

[289] Wāqidī, *Maghāzī*, 814–823. See the contrasting portrayal of the two figures in Ibrahim, *Conversion*, 157–158. On Abū Sufyān as a leader of Muhammad's tribe Quraysh, see Mu'nis, *Ta'rīkh*, 344–347.

historians, the depiction is different, as ᶜAlī is not significantly elevated and Abū Sufyān not humiliated or placed in a dark light.[290] It is a plausible scholarly argument that medieval Muslim texts were significantly influenced by their contexts.[291] Petersen rightly argues that writing history "left a wide margin for tendentious presentation."[292] Thus, it is better to view Islamic historiography—including the accounts of Muhammad's *maghāzī*—as a reflection of the "historical memory" of the believers and as an evolving description of the time of documentation rather than as "a precise account of the past."[293]

Third, historical accounts, such as those of the *maghāzī*, are not only written but also *rewritten*.[294] While the genesis of Islamic historiography is to be credited to the Umayyad era, its growth was accomplished under the ᶜAbbāsids, the Umayyad's rivals.[295] While the earliest *maghāzī* works are arguably attributed to Umayyad-era historians, like Ibn Shihāb al-Zuhrī (d. 124/741) and Mūsā ibn ᶜUqba (d. 135/752 or 141/758), none of their complete works has reached us, except in quotes in later sources.[296] Robinson

[290] See the pro-Umayyad portrayals in Zuhrī, *Maghāzī*, 66; Mūsā ibn ᶜUqba, *Maghāzī*, 269–273. On the Umayyad inclination of al-Zuhrī and Mūsā, see Ibrahim, *Conversion*, 41–54; Ibn ᶜAsākir, *Taʾrīkh*, 42:227–228; Thaqafī, *Ghārāt*, 395–396; Ibn Ḥibbān, *Majrūḥīn*, 1:258.

[291] Robinson, *Historiography*, 13, 38; Petersen, *ᶜAlī*, 17; Crone, *Meccan*, 230.

[292] Petersen, *ᶜAlī*, 18.

[293] Ibrahim, *Conversion*, 23. Sarah Savant writes on the memory formation and the ways through which communities create new memories. See Savant, *New*, 3ff., where she argues, "Conversion to Islam led Iranians to recall their past in new ways and to accumulate new memories about their history" (3). See also Clanchy, *From Memory*, ch. 9; Robinson, *Historiography*, 172–177; Geary, *Phantoms*, 111–122. Roohi, "Muḥammad's Disruptive," 74–76.

[294] Geary, in studying European society in the tenth–eleventh centuries, argues that there was a large amount of "creative forgetting" from both individuals and communities as they readjusted their sense of connection to their past by creating new memories more useful to their present, using a process of transmission, adaptation, and suppression. See his work *Phantoms of Remembrance* and his article "Oblivion between Orality and Textuality in the Tenth Century," in *Medieval*, ed. Althoff and Geary, 111-122 (esp. 111). See also Borrut, *Entre*, 80; Savant, *New*, 3.

[295] See Ibn al-Nadīm, *Fihrist*, 81, 91, where he identifies Umayyad figures who wrote history; see also Masᶜūdī, *Tanbīh*, 1:93. For secondary studies, see Muṣṭafā, *Taʾrīkh*, 1:66–67, 1:80–83; Dūrī, *Baḥth*, 15ff.; Borrut, *Entre*, ch. 1, especially 37–40, where he writes of Muᶜāwiya's attention to historical writing. Borrut provides various examples of history writing in Umayyad Syria and analyzes the possible layers of historical writing and the scrupulous work of transmission. Robinson believes history writing began as early as the rise of Islam itself. Robinson, *Historiography*, 14. See also Ibrahim, *Stated*, 24–65; Donner, "Umayyad," 187–211; Wellhausen, *Arab*, xv; Ḍayf, *ᶜAṣr*, 126.

[296] See Ibrahim, *Conversion*, 45, where I write, "It is commonly accepted that there are no available sources directly written by al-Zuhrī, as his accounts survive only in later sources." See Robinson, *Historiography*, 25; Schoeler, *Charakter*, 32ff.; Schoeler, *Biography*, 23–26; Schoeler, *Oral*. See the discussion on the Umayyad-era historians Ibn Shihāb al-Zuhrī (d. 124/741) and Mūsā ibn ᶜUqba (d. 135/752 or 141/758) in Ibrahim, *Conversion*, 41–54. Huart, *History*, 61, 236, 303 (on al-Zuhrī) and 175 (on Mūsā). See Schacht, "On Mūsā," 288–300, where he treats Mūsā's accounts as fiction (291–292), with which Schoeler disagrees. Schoeler, "Mūsā," 92–94. Compare Schoeler's argument with the opposite view of Juynboll, *Muslim*, 158. For scholarly discussions on the problem of early accounts quoted in later works, see Borrut, *Entre*, 57–58; Landau-Tasseron, "On the Reconstruction," 47; Conrad, "Recovering," 258–263. For examples of scholars who attempt to compile lost texts by

calls this feature the "gobbling up" phenomenon, which he defines as "the integration of monographic works into composite and often very large compilations."[297] This phenomenon, Robinson observes, "is a crucial feature of ninth- and tenth-century tradition, and goes some way towards explaining why so much of tradition's earlier layers have fallen away" and "why we are left with what al-Balādhurī and al-Ṭabarī preserved of al-Madā'inī's work, rather than al-Madā'inī's work itself, and with what Ibn Isḥāq-Ibn Hishām preserved of al-Zuhrī's work, rather than al-Zuhrī's work itself."[298] This is one reason why earlier works tended to be shorter and more concise than later works. If al-Zuhrī reportedly wrote a short work on the *maghāzī*, then al-Wāqidī produced a significantly larger account, expounding upon and explaining the same material. Historians tended to add literary features in order to elaborate on earlier accounts as they responded to concerns of their day.[299] Still, we should note that while the ᶜAbbāsid-era historians have significantly shaped historical depictions, the Umayyad voice is not completely absent.[300] Therefore, I argue that Islamic historiography reached us through "a variety of literary filters," "dictated by a host of sectarian and political considerations which result in a series of historiographical layers."[301] "Classical Muslim historians," I argue, "relied on a shared pool of memory, but utilized it selectively and manipulated the records to promote their views."[302] This is evident in a study by Sarah Savant, who examines the role of memory and the way it is revised or even erased. She rightly observes that "[a]s a tradition accumulates weight and authority, it shapes collective agreements about the past, thereby creating memories."[303] I am convinced that Islamic historiography reflects a likely distorted description of past events. Historical narratives of Muhammad's *maghāzī* do not necessarily describe past activities and precise military campaigns. Instead, they reveal a picture more

using quotes found in later works, see Guillaume, "Note," 1–4; also Lindstedt, "Al-Madā'inī," 65–150, where he aims to reconstruct the "skeleton" of al-Madā'inī's *Kitāb al-dawla* by utilizing "later quotations of it." See also the discussion in Ibrahim, *Conversion*, 52–55.

297 Robinson, *Historiography*, 34.

298 Robinson, *Historiography*, 34–35.

299 See Donner, *Narratives*, 66, where he examines al-Zuhrī as a source for al-Wāqidī. Donner demonstrates how Muslim historians relied on each other and how later works incorporate "numerous reports" from earlier sources in order to shape an "unbroken narrative" (258).

300 See Hibri, "Redemption," 241ff., where he studies pro-Umayyad accounts that survived ᶜAbbāsid censorship. See also Petersen, *ᶜAlī*, 109ff.; Borrut, *Entre*, ch. 1.

301 Ibrahim, *Conversion*, 23; also Borrut, *Entre*, 59–60, 80; Savant, *New*, 13–14. Noth/Conrad, *Early*, 17; Borrut, *Entre*, 35; Robinson, "Conquest," 38; Mourad, "On Early," 588.

302 Ibrahim, *Conversion*, 246.

303 Savant, *New*, 4.

suitable for the time of documentation—a picture colored by a host of dynamic cultural, religious, and political concerns of the Muslim historians and their ideologies and opinions.[304] I believe that classical Muslim narrators designed the *maghāzī* stories to communicate a religious lesson, social significance, and political disposition. These traditions were fashioned to serve as an ideological homily, advancing theological instructions for Muslims and non-Muslims in later generations.

These three above-mentioned points describe my approach to Islamic historiography in general as well as my understanding of the narratives of Muhammad's *maghāzī*. Without a doubt, topics related to Muhammad and his career can be controversial. As a result of contemporary political discourse, some scholars avoid these topics entirely.[305] However, I argue that the topic of Muhammad's *maghāzī* should not be viewed as controversial for at least two reasons.

First, we should distinguish between Muhammad as a prophet and Muhammad as a tribal leader.[306] Conflating these two major roles creates confusion, which results in equating the spread of a religious message with military activities. This is incorrect and misleading. I argue in another study that they "must be viewed within the framework of military expansion, rather than religious proclamation."[307] When Muhammad reportedly commissioned raids and expeditions, he was following a common pattern

[304] Ibrahim, *Conversion*, 24. Thus, I follow the method of Robinson, *Empire*, viii, where he chooses "to marry history and historiography," which acknowledges simultaneously the problematic nature of the Muslim sources as well as the historians' explicit goals in their disposition. See also Spiegel, "Task," 1–15; Spiegel, "Political," 314–325.

[305] See the remarkable comments on this reality by Hoyland, *God's Path*, 232, where he argues that "the massively increased public profile of Islam since [the 1970s–'80s] has made many academics, who are usually left-leaning liberals, shy of criticizing Islam and this has favored the traditionalist approach while pushing skeptics/revisionists to become more extreme." Similarly, Nickel observes, "The need for accurate information about Islam has grown since 9/11. However, because they fear for life and career, many qualified scholars have balked at sharing what they know." Nickel, "Scholarship," 219–231, especially 219–220.

[306] Djait argues that Muhammad began as an ascetic—a great inspirer, a dreamer, a true possessor of a vision—but later transformed into a *rajul siyāsī ʿaqlānī bi-shaklin khāriq* (political man, with an unmatched intellectual power). Djait, *Masīrat*, 172–173. On the various images of Muhammad, see Khalidi, *Images*, 151–280, where he examines how Muslim narrators constructed accounts of Muhammad's life in order to address different purposes by portraying him in different images, including a hero, model mystic, liberator, and canonical prophet, among others. See Ibrahim, *Muhammad*, 35–41; also Tolan, *Faces*, where he studies various depictions of Muhammad through the Reformation and up to the present day. For Muhammad as a figure of history and cultural memory, see Anthony, *Muhammad*, 7–17.

[307] See Ibrahim, *Stated*, 236–240 (esp. 237). In describing Muslim authors who argue for a traditional reading of the *maghāzī* as aiming to proclaim Islam, I argue, "Those authors eventually hurt the image of Islam by linking political dominion to religious proclamation" (237).

shared by all tribal leaders in seventh-century Arabia.[308] These raids were a part of securing power, resources, and dominion in a tribal setting rather than a tool to advance religion and seek converts. Muslim commanders were not proselytizers.[309] More important, we should also distinguish the Muhammad of history from the Muhammad of tradition.[310] Very little is known about the historical Muhammad from contemporary or near-contemporary sources, but the Muhammad of Muslim traditions is portrayed by later Muslims in much detail. I view the Muhammad of tradition as distinct from the historical Muhammad and as "a figure whom the Muslim historians chose to present to their audience for religious and political reasons."[311] While I am highly skeptical of the reliability and accuracy of the traditional Muslim accounts, here I study the portrayal of Muhammad given in the sources of Islam. While I am uncertain that Muhammad's raids and expeditions actually occurred as described in the sourcebooks of Islam, in this study I examine the Muhammad of the Muslim tradition, although I understand that the historical Muhammad might have differed significantly from his portrayal by later Muslim traditionists.

The second reason the topic of Muhammad's expeditions should not be controversial is that they are a significant part of his canonical biography written and taught by Muslims throughout the past twelve centuries or so. For Muslims, the *maghāzī* narratives are not myths or despicable charges claimed by haters of Islam, but rather are a significant part of the self-description of the earliest Muslim community about Islam's prophet. When Muslims began writing Muhammad's life and career in the eighth and ninth centuries, they openly labeled Muhammad's life using the Arabic term *maghāzī*, which literally describes a series of military expeditions for the purposes of fighting and plundering. The genre of the *maghāzī* thus refers to the memory, created by

[308] See ᶜAbd al-Karīm, *Mujtamaᶜ*, 21ff., where he studies Muslim primary sources and argues that Muslims during Muhammad's time did not change many of their tribal customs after accepting Islam, *illā bi-nisba ḍa'īla* (except just a little) (27). See also Abd al-Karīm, *Judhūr*, 109–110.

[309] See Ibrahim, *Stated*, 163, where I argue, "The traditional interpretations insist that the early Arab conquerors were religious heroes akin to exceptionally pious ascetics, carrying the banner of their new religion to proselytize the conquered peoples. This fanciful portrayal is not supported by most of the early Muslim accounts, although they were written by sympathetic authors" (237). However, it is true that many classical and modern religious enthusiasts insist that Muhammad launched raids to spread Islam. See Ibrahim, *Stated*, 66–119, 236–240.

[310] See Hagen, "Imagined," 97–111. In another study, I identify at least three different Muhammads: "the one in popular and cultural Islam, that of the Muslim traditions, and finally the Muhammad of history." See Ibrahim, *Muhammad*, 35, where I argue that we "can label these three Muhammads the legendary, the traditional, and the historical." In this study, I focus on the Muhammad of the Muslim tradition.

[311] Ibrahim, *Muhammad*, 38.

later Muslim narrators, to highlight the deeds of the earliest Muslim warriors under Muhammad's leadership as they engaged in warring and plundering. Muslims, past and present, acknowledge the heroic success of Muhammad as a tribal leader and view this as evidence of divine support of him over his enemies. Consider the wealth of Arabic Muslim secondary studies on the *maghāzī* that we explored in a previous section: the discussion of the topic among Muslims is vivid and rich, with various competing interpretations and claims. Scholars and students in the West should engage in this vibrant discussion, learning from and contributing to it. I believe that there is need for a modern study that details Muhammad's expeditions as found in Muslim primary sources, emphasizing them as a series of tribal incursions rather than religious missions. This is the unique contribution of this study.

Structure of the Book

In the following chapters, I focus on classical Islamic historiographical works that describe the *maghāzī* that Muhammad led or commissioned during his ten years in Medina. While I consult numerous Arabic Muslim sources, my emphasis will be largely on the earliest sources, including works on the *maghāzī*, *sīra*, *futūḥ*, *ṭabaqāt*, *ta'rīkh*, and others. Among the major historiographical works used in this study, I rely on *Kitāb al-maghāzī* by Ibn ᶜUmar al-Wāqidī (d. ca. 207/823), *al-Sīra al-nabawiyya* by Ibn Hishām (d. 218/833), *Futūḥ al-buldān* by Ibn Yaḥyā al-Balādhurī (d. *ca.* 279/892), the Shīᶜite *Ta'rīkh* by Ibn Wāḍiḥ al-Yaᶜqūbī (d. 284/897 or 292/905), and the magnum opus *Ta'rīkh* by Ibn Jarīr al-Ṭabarī (d. 310/923).[312] For comparison, I also incorporate earlier reports on the *maghāzī* attributed to Ibn Shihāb al-Zuhrī (d. 124/741) and Mūsā ibn ᶜUqba (d. 135/752 or 141/758).[313] In addition, I refer to traditions from the *ḥadīth*, *shamā'il*, *ansāb*, and other early works.

[312] On these Muslim historians, their works, and secondary studies on them, see Ibrahim, *Conversion*, 110–116 (al-Wāqidī), 121–128 (Ibn Isḥāq and Ibn Hishām), 192–194 (al-Balādhurī), 197–199 (al-Yaᶜqūbī), and 3–5 (al-Ṭabarī).

[313] See Muḥammad ibn Shihāb al-Zuhrī, *al-Maghāzī al-nabawiyya*; al-Zuhrī, *Marwiyyāt al-imām al-Zuhrī fī al-maghāzī*; see also the scholarly critical edition and translation of al-Zuhrī's *Maghāzī*, Maᶜmar ibn Rāshid and ᶜAbd al-Razzāq al-Ṣanᶜānī, *The Expeditions: An Early Biography of Muhammad*. On this translation, see Lecker, "Review," 854–857. As for Mūsā ibn ᶜUqba, see his *Aḥādīth muntakhaba min maghāzī Mūsā ibn ᶜUqba* as well as his *al-Maghāzī*. On al-Zuhrī and Mūsā, their works, the textual problems in their accounts, and various secondary studies on their works, see Ibrahim, *Conversion*, 41–49 (al-Zuhrī), 49–55 (Mūsā ibn ᶜUqba); see also Motzki, "Der *Fiqh*," 1–44; Schacht, "On Mūsā," 288–300; Schoeler, "Mūsā b. ᶜUqba's *Maghāzī*," 67–97.

In matters related to the Qur'ān, I consult *Asbāb al-nuzūl* and many works on *Tafsīr*. In this study, I focus on the last decade of Muhammad's life with a particular emphasis on his *maghāzī*—their reported motivations, goals, and results—as depicted by the earliest Muslim narrators. Relying on numerous original Arabic Muslim sources, this book examines the beginnings of the Muslim community at Medina and analyzes how these reported military campaigns served not only as the establishment of the Muslim stronghold at Medina but also as the launching pad for the great Arab Muslim conquests led by Muhammad's successors after his death. Throughout the book, I interact with many Arabic Muslim secondary studies on the *maghāzī*. My hope is to highlight the various strands of Muslim thought on the topic, especially as I compare them with recent non-Muslim Western arguments. Each chapter begins with an examination of the primary Muslim accounts on the *maghāzī*, followed by critical observations on the accounts. The truth is that many in the English-speaking world can hardly access a detailed account of Muhammad's military expeditions in a modern English study based on the numerous Arabic Muslim accounts. Herein lies the main contribution of this study.

In chapter 2, I devote the discussion to the earliest *maghāzī* that reportedly took place after the *hijra* (emigration) and before the great Battle of Badr. These early *maghāzī*—eight in number—largely targeted the pagans of Mecca and their caravan trades. Muhammad led four of them in person, while he entrusted the commandership of the other four to a quartet of his faithful companions. These campaigns served as precursors to later confrontations, which empowered and elevated the Muslim community in Medina as a major power in Arabia.

In chapter 3 and chapter 4, I examine the most important battles between the Medinan Muslims and the Meccan pagans. While there were many confrontations, I focus on five in particular: the Battle of Badr, the Battle of Uḥud, the Battle of the Trench, the Battle (and treaty) of Ḥudaybiyya, and the conquest of Mecca.[314] Chapter 3 studies Badr and Uḥud, while chapter 4 examines the other three. These battles covered a span of about six

[314] My choice of the "important" battles is not arbitrary. I rely on the concise historiographical work of Ibn Wāḍiḥ Yaʿqūbī, where he details the most important episodes of Islamic history. See Yaʿqūbī, *Ta'rīkh*, 45–63. On al-Yaʿqūbī and his works, see Yāqūt al-Ḥamawī, *Muʿjam*, 2:557; al-Maqrīzī, *Mawāʿiẓ*, 2:107; Ibn Taghrībirdī, *Nujūm*, 2:40–41. For secondary studies, see Millward, "A Study of Al-Yaʿqūbī"; Millward, "Adaptation," 329–344; Ibrahim, *Conversion*, 197ff.; Brockelmann, "Al-Yaʿqūbī," *EI*², 11:257–258; Dūrī, *Rise*, 66; Petersen, *ʿAlī*, 169; Donner, *Narratives*, 134; Khalidi, *Arabic*, 120ff.; Robinson, *Historiography*, 36, 76, 98, 136–137.

years, from the year 2/624 to 8/629, during which the Muslims reportedly won all battles except at Uḥud.[315] Still, the conquest of Mecca was not necessarily a real battle but arguably a negotiated surrender of the pagans of Mecca to the victorious Muhammad, with the pagans declaring him the ultimate ruler of Mecca and all of the Hijaz. Within the course of these battles, there were other military activities targeting other non-Muslims that are covered in other chapters.

In chapter 5, the discussion centers on Muhammad's confrontations with the Jews of Medina and its surroundings. I begin by exploring the accounts of the Jewish communities at Medina and the reported growing tensions between the Muslims and the Jews, as evidenced in the escalating friction between Muhammad and individual Jews as well as their three major Jewish tribes: Banū Qaynuqāᶜ, Banū al-Naḍīr, and Banū Qurayẓa. This tension reportedly led to three major expeditions, which ultimately resulted in the expulsion of the Jews from Medina. These three expeditions were followed by two more, the Raid to Khaybar and the Raid to Fadak, which targeted two Jewish settlements on the outskirts of Medina, ensuring the elimination of any Jewish threat against the Muslims in Medina.

In chapter 6, I study the elevation of Muhammad as "the King of Arabia" after his victory over various Arab Bedouins. The focus is on the incursion to Banū Jadhīma, the Battle of Ḥunayn, and the raid to al-Ṭā'if. I then discuss the reports of many Arabs who came to offer him their loyalty, as they accepted Islam in the year known in Muslim traditions as the Year of Delegations.

I devote attention in chapter 7 to some final expeditions, where Muhammad allegedly targeted Christians in the Byzantine frontiers. The focus is on the Battle of Mu'ta, the Battle of Tabūk, and Muhammad's final instructions—before his sudden death—for Usama's expedition against the Byzantines. I highlight the reports of the battles as well as the Muslims' reported reasons for challenging the Byzantines in Northern Arabia. In chapter 8, I conclude the study with final remarks on Muhammad's *maghāzī* as historiography.

[315] Muslim traditions depict an early victory of the Muslims who turned to defeat—due to their disobedience of Muhammad's commands—by the Muslim archers who rushed to seize the spoils. See Ṭabarī, *Ta'rīkh*, 1400; Kalāᶜī, *Iktifā'*, 1:370ff. (esp, 1:377); Bayhaqī, *Dalā'il*, 3:309. See the discussion of the initial victory in Ibrahim, *Stated*, 80–85.

2

Muhammad's Early Expeditions

The Strategic *Maghāzī* before the Battle of Badr

The purpose of fighting is not for the Muslims to enjoy the pleasure of superiority, but rather that the religion of truth must become plainly above all the others, and that the law of justice and the word of piety should become superior above all falsehood, injustice, and immorality.—The renowned Shīᶜite Qur'ān commentator Muḥammad Ḥusayn al-Ṭabāṭabā'ī (1904–1981)

Muhammad's *maghāzī* were jihad and fighting *fī sabīl Allāh* (for Allah's cause). Allah did not prescribe jihad in Mecca. After they emigrated from Mecca to Medina, Allah prescribed jihad and commanded them to fight. The [divine] command was to fight the polytheists and initiating the fighting, in order to establish and spread the Islamic belief.[1]—Professor Akram Ḍiyā' al-ᶜUmarī (1942–), the Islamic University of Medina and the University of Qatar

According to Muslim historiography, Muhammad began to receive divine revelations in 610 in a cave in Mecca, after which he began preaching Islam to the Meccan pagans. His preaching was reportedly faced with rejection and hostility from the Meccans, especially from his tribe the Quraysh.[2] He and the few who believed in his message were vulnerable to severe persecution from the unbelieving Meccans. Muhammad was divinely commanded

[1] Ṭabāṭabā'ī, *Mīzān*, 9:246; ᶜUmarī, *Sīra*, 337–338.

[2] For Muhammad's tribe, the Quraysh, see Watt, "Ḳuraysh," *EI*², 5:434–435; Rubin, "Quraysh," *EQ*, 4:329–333; Ṣaᶜīdī, *Tārīkh*, 42–47. For its history, see the valuable Arabic study by Mu'nis, *Ta'rīkh*, 13–83 (historically), and 85–232 (politically, socially, and economically). See also ᶜAlī, *Mufaṣṣal*, 7:18–30; ᶜAbd al-Karīm, *Quraysh*. See Kister, "Mecca," 113–163. See also Ibrahim, *Concise Guide to Islam*, 27–28 (hereafter cited as, Ibrahim, *Islam*, 27–28). For a primary source that reports the virtue and excellence of the Quraysh as an Arabian tribe, see Ibn Qutayba, *Faḍl*, 38–39. For another primary source aiming at stressing the excellence of the Arabs, see Jāḥiẓ, *Bayān*, 2:5ff. On al-Jāḥiẓ, see van Ess, *Theology*, 3:503.

Muhammad's Military Expeditions. Ayman S. Ibrahim, Oxford University Press. © Oxford University Press 2024.
DOI: 10.1093/oso/9780197769171.003.0002

to persevere and endure persecution and was reportedly prohibited from fighting his persecutors.[3] After almost thirteen years of preaching in Mecca, particularly in 622, the divine command came to Muhammad to emigrate from Mecca to Medina—a significant event that served as a turning point for the Muslims, known in Islamic historiography as the *hijra* (emigration).[4]

Not only was Muhammad welcomed at Medina, where he had some family relatives, but, we are told, he was also able to reconcile various Arab groups, despite their enmity toward each other.[5] By unifying and uniting them, he was able to establish a stronghold centered at Medina against any possible outside attack. He reportedly assumed a unique role as the leader of the unified Arab clans. A few months later, Muhammad's military campaigns began, which targeted Meccan pagans and their Arab allies. Traditions reveal that the campaigns began due to a divine command, in which Allah prescribed jihad—fighting in Allah's path.[6] Muhammad's first great victory over the Meccan pagans occurred at the Battle of Badr in the second year after the *hijra*; however, before Badr, there were reportedly several initial campaigns.[7] He led some of these campaigns in person (known as *ghazawāt*, i.e., raids, sg. *ghazwa*) and commissioned others (identified as *sarāyā*, i.e., incursions, platoons, or expeditions, sg. *sariyya*) to his faithful companions to lead as commanders. These initial expeditions are the focus of this chapter.

While Muslim traditions, at times, provide competing reports regarding the number and details of the military campaigns, we can largely assert that based on most traditions, the earliest campaigns included at least four *maghāzī* (raids) and four *sarāyā* (incursions). The initial *maghāzī* that Muhammad led were al-Abwā', Bawāṭ, the early Badr, and al-ᶜUshayra—all of which are named after the target location of the raid. As for the early *sarāyā* that he commissioned, they are identified by their commanders whom Muhammad appointed and sent: Ḥamza ibn ᶜAbd al-Muṭṭalib, ᶜUbayda ibn al-Ḥārith, Saᶜd ibn Abī Waqqāṣ, and ᶜAbdullāh ibn Jaḥsh. All

[3] ᶜUmarī, *Sīra*, 337.

[4] See Ibn Hishām, *Sīra*, 1:480ff.; Khalīfa, *Ta'rīkh*, 1:50 (on how it marked the beginning of the Islamic calendar); Khalīfa, *Ṭabaqāt*, 1:40 (on the two emigrations); Ibn Ḥibbān, *Sīra*, 1:72 (on the first *hijra*, as compared to that to Medina), and 1:127 (the *hijra* to Medina); Kharkūshī, *Sharaf*, 2:349ff.; Yaᶜqūbī, *Ta'rīkh*, 2:39–41; Ibn ᶜAbd al-Barr, *Durar*, 1:75ff.

[5] On reconciling various rivals in Medina, see Ṣallābī, *Sīra*, 312–323; ᶜUmarī, *Sīra*, 240–249.

[6] See Kalāᶜī, *Iktifā'*, 1:317, where Allah commanded Muhammad to initiate jihad and fight against his enemies. For a summary of this early period, see Cook, *Understanding*, 5–8. Muhammad's death date is disputed. See Shoemaker, *Death*, 1–16, where he rightly observes that while various traditions claim that his death was in Medina in 632, other sources—both Muslim and non-Muslim—claim that he was alive and led expeditions in 634–635.

[7] For a Muslim study of these early incursions, see Ṣallābī, *Sīra*, 361–375.

of these campaigns took place less than two years after the *hijra* but before the great Battle of Badr.[8] These eight initial campaigns serve as the early combats that led to the great victory at Badr and thus are important to study.[9]

This chapter's goal is to investigate the historiographical accounts of these early battles and to provide critical observations on their narratives. While I am largely skeptical as to whether these battles occurred in the first place, I examine these accounts to reveal what Muslim historians narrated about the earliest military campaigns led or commissioned by Muhammad. This chapter studies these accounts not as history in the sense of what actually happened, but rather as "religious history"—a tradition advanced by the Muslim community in its presentation of Islam's origins and representation of Muhammad's career. While the following analysis of the historical accounts may appear as rather detailed, this should in no way suggest that I trust the historicity of these military campaigns. I believe these accounts are a reflection of the social, political, and religious contexts of the time of their writing, not that of Muhammad's. My goal is to detail what the Muslim sources reveal about Muhammad's early expeditions and their goals and motivations, then to offer critical observations on the multifaceted ways in which Muslim historians sought to present these events. In examining these initial campaigns, as is the case in each chapter, we follow two major steps. First, we begin with a discussion of the primary sources, investigating what the earliest available Muslim literature—including *maghāzī*, *sīra*, and *ta'rīkh*—reveals about these military campaigns. Second, we analyze the accounts of the campaigns with an emphasis on their stated motivations, goals, and results. The analysis interacts with Muslim and non-Muslim secondary literature in order to shed light on various interpretations offered by different scholars.

The Incursion of Ḥamza ibn ᶜAbd al-Muṭṭalib (1/623)

Seven months after the *hijra*, Muhammad sent Ḥamza ibn ᶜAbd al-Muṭṭalib as a commander on a *sariyya*.[10] Ḥamza was an early convert to

[8] See Yaᶜqūbī, *Ta'rīkh*, 2:45, where he begins with Badr and ignores all the earlier expeditions.

[9] On the location of Badr, see the encyclopedic work by Bakrī, *Muᶜjam*, 1:231–232.

[10] This was Ramaḍān, the ninth month of the first lunar year of the *hijra*, about March 623. Ṭabarī, *History*, 7:10; Ṭabarī, *Ta'rīkh*, 1265; Wāqidī, *Maghāzī*, 9ff.; Wāqidī, *Life*, 6; Khalīfa, *Ta'rīkh*, 1:62; Ibn

Islam.[11] He was both an uncle and a milk-brother of Muhammad—only four years older than him.[12] Ḥamza was called Asad Allāh (Allah's lion); he fought bravely in many battles, including the Battle of Badr (2/624), and was killed at the Battle of Uḥud (3/625).[13] Traditions claim that Ḥamza was *aᶜazz Quraysh wa ashadduhā shakīma* (the mightiest of the Quraysh and its most stubborn and unyielding [person]).[14] The literary choice of Ḥamza ibn ᶜAbd al-Muṭṭalib as the commander of this early raid is better viewed as a reflection of the tendency of the ᶜAbbasid-era historians to elevate members of Muhammad's tribe, the Quraysh, and particularly his Hāshimite family, which includes both ᶜAlids and ᶜAbbāsids.[15] As I explained in an earlier publication, early Muslim historiographical accounts "not only reflect sectarian concerns and political debates among early Muslims but also emphasize the religious and sociopolitical agendas of the historians, highlighting how they use literary features to advance their competing opinions. Religious and political disputes influence historiographical accounts."[16] Ḥamza, as a literary figure, is presented as a devoted commander—courageous, astute, and willing to lead under Muhammad's instructions. This portrayal advances the prestige, pride, and devotion associated with figures deemed important for the ᶜAbbāsid claims of legitimacy, thus their rule and power.[17] The

Kathīr, *Bidāya*, 3:234ff. For secondary Muslim studies, see Jamīlī, *Ghazawāt*, 20; Abū Māyla, *Sarāyā*, 84; Haykal, *Ḥayāt*, 255; Khaṭṭāb, *Rasūl*, 86–88.

[11] On Ḥamza's conversion to Islam, see Ibn Qāniᶜ, *Muᶜjam*, 1:187; Ibn al-Athīr, *Kāmil*, 1:678; Dhahabī, *Ta'rīkh*, 1:171; Ibn Kathīr, *Bidāya*, 3:33.

[12] On Ḥamza, see Ibn Saᶜd, *Ṭabaqāt*, 1:88, 2:32, and the entry at 3:5–12; Khalīfa, *Ṭabaqāt*, 620–636; Abū Nuᶜaym al-Iṣfahānī, *Maᶜrifat*, 1:133; Masᶜūdī, *Tanbīh*, 1:200; Maqdisī, *Bad'*, 5:98; Ibn ᶜAbd al-Barr, *Istīᶜāb*, 1:369–370; Ibn al-Athīr, *Usd*, 2:67ff.; Dhahabī, *Siyar*, 1:171–184; Balādhurī, *Ansāb*, 4:282ff.; Samᶜānī, *Ansāb*, 13:289.

[13] Ḥamza's killer converted to Islam and was later a fighter in Muhammad's army. Samᶜānī, *Ansāb*, 13:289.

[14] Jawzī, *Muntaẓim*, 2:385.

[15] The ᶜAlids and ᶜAbbāsids are cousins. For the initial ᶜAlid support of the ᶜAbbāsids in their revolution against the Umayyads, see Masᶜūdī, *Murūj*, 3:212ff.; Ḍayf, *ᶜAṣr*, 9–13; Rifāᶜī, *ᶜAṣr*, 1:82ff.; Dūrī, *ᶜAṣr*, 36–41. On the ᶜAlids, see Bernheimer, *ᶜAlids*, 1–12. For the history of Shīᶜat ᶜAlī, see Dabashi, *Shiᶜism*, 47ff., 103ff.; Enayat, *Modern*, 18ff.; Halm, *Shīᶜism*, 1–27, and 154ff.; Hodgson, "How," 1–13. In his study of historiographical accounts, Hibri writes of "the political, cultural, and religious interests of the ᶜAbbāsid period, especially between 750 and 861, in projecting a certain type of historical representation on the earlier period of Islamic history." Hibri, *Parable*, xi. Hibri interprets historiographical writing—particularly those on the ᶜAbbāsid caliphs—as attempts "to provide commentary on a certain political, religious, social, or cultural issue that may have derived from a real and controversial historical episode." Hibri, *Reinterpreting*, 13.

[16] Ibrahim, *Conversion*, 6–7. I also contend that historiographical reports "carry and promote the religious inclinations and sociopolitical tendencies of the historians" (7).

[17] Indeed, the early ᶜAbbāsid era was "decisive in enforcing ᶜAbbāsid claims of legitimacy (pro-ᶜAbbāsid orthodoxy); it was a period of significant growth in historical and traditional writings." Ibrahim, *Conversion*, 239. See also Hibri, "Redemption," 241–242, where he analyzes pro-Umayyad reports that survived ᶜAbbāsid hostility; Hibri, *Parable*, 25, where he rightly observes that "Balādhurī

rationale goes, the members of the family of Hāshim—which includes the ᶜAbbāsids—were devoted to Islam and supportive of Muhammad from the early beginnings of his career. In contrast, Umayyad figures appear in various ᶜAbbāsid-era accounts as weak Muslims or enemies of Muhammad who delayed before accepting Islam (although some pro-Umayyad reports have permeated these accounts).[18]

The expedition of Ḥamza is identified by many narrators as the first *sariyya* in Islam, although some dispute this report.[19] Al-Wāqidī reports that, under Ḥamza's leadership, the expedition included thirty Muslim warriors—fifteen from the Meccan emigrants (known as *muhājirūn*) and fifteen from the Medinan supporters (*anṣār*); however, al-Ṭabarī and other historians insist that they were all from the former.[20] This discrepancy between reports is important to note, as it reinforces the scholarly contention that classical Muslim historians adjusted narratives over time to address their contexts and the varying requirements of their times. While the early report of al-Wāqidī elevated both groups of Muslims—Meccans and Medinans—as participants in Muhammad's first commissioned incursion, this was not corroborated by other historians who instead appear to have tweaked the story to magnify the role of the Muslim *muhājirūn* of Muhammad's tribe. These Muslim narrators seem to have relied on a shared pool of memory, but they used it selectively to narrativize their accounts.[21] Here, it is not difficult to notice that ᶜAbbāsid-era historians—through their accounts—attempt to marginalize the role played by the Medinan Muslims—known as the *anṣār* (helpers or supporters)—in early Islam.[22] Although the *anṣār* were an essential part

compiled an even more extensive volume about the Umayyads in his work *Ansāb al-Ashrāf*, even though he wrote with ᶜAbbāsid patronage"; Petersen, *ᶜAlī*, 109ff.; Borrut, *Entre*, ch. 1.

[18] On pro-Umayyad reports permeating ᶜAbbāsid-era accounts, see Ibrahim, *Conversion*, 223–227.

[19] ᶜAbd al-Barr, *Istīᶜāb*, 1:369–370. Ibn Isḥāq and Ibn Hishām write that the first expedition was to Waddān, which is also called al-Abwā'. Ibn Hishām, *Life*, 281–282, 659. Ḥamza's expedition is also called *liwā'*, i.e., banner. Ṭabarī, *History*, 7:10; Ṭabarī, *Ta'rīkh*, 1265; Wāqidī, *Maghāzī*, 9.

[20] Wāqidī, *Maghāzī*, 9ff.; cf. Maqdisī, *Bad'*, 4:181. The report that all of the men were from the Meccan emigrants is found in Khalīfa, *Ta'rīkh*, 1:62; Ṭabarī, *History*, 7:10; Ṭabarī, *Ta'rīkh*, 1265; Masᶜūdī, *Tanbīh*, 1:200; Jawzī, *Muntaẓim*, 3:80; Ibn Kathīr, *Bidāya*, 3:234.

[21] Savant, *New*, 13. Noth/Conrad, *Early*, 17; Borrut, *Entre*, 35; Robinson, "Conquest," 38; Mourad, "On Early," 588; Ibrahim, *Conversion*, 16–17. See also Lassner, *Islamic*, 25, where he demonstrates the various ways a Muslim narrative changed over time. On narratives and narrativizing, see Sizgorich, "Narrative," 9–11; Spiegel, "Form," 43–53; Abbott, *Cambridge*; White, "Value"; Prince, "Surveying Narratology," in *What Is Narratology?*, ed. Kindt and Müller, 1–16. See Spiegel, "Revising," 1–19, where she explores "the various forces that may help to explain the ongoing historiographical phenomenon of revision."

[22] Most accounts indicate that the *anṣār*, in the Second ᶜAqba Pledge, promised to support Muhammad only within Medina. This might offer a reason that he did not rely on them in earlier

of the early Muslim community who sustained and protected Muhammad and the Meccan Muslims,[23] there seems to have been diligent attempts by the Muslim traditionists to elevate the status and position of the *muhājirūn* (Meccan emigrants) over those who accepted Islam in Medina. This led some scholars to argue that Muhammad's Medinan state was primarily a successful move to advance the dominion and rule of the Quraysh—particularly its notable aristocrats—at the expense of the various Medinan groups of the time.[24] This argument has some support if we accept the general outline of Muslim historiography, in which the incident of the *saqīfa*, for example, resulted in the appointment of Abū Bakr—a notable Meccan aristocrat—as caliph on the day of Muhammad's death.[25] In this incident, the *anṣār* demanded to be a part of the leadership among Muslims, relaying their crucial role in supporting Muhammad and his nascent community.[26] However, the request was viciously denied by the *muhājirūn*—particularly the aristocrats of the Quraysh, including Abū Bakr and ᶜUmar, who became the first two caliphs in Islam.[27]

According to traditions, Muhammad learned of a Meccan caravan traveling with merchandise from al-Shām (Greater Syria) to Mecca. He thus commanded Ḥamza to march to *yaᶜtariḍ* (intercept, obstruct, or block) the caravan.[28] This background—as a literary picture—is similar to the context

incursions. See ᶜUmarī, *Sīra*, 358. On the ᶜAqaba Pledge, see Ibn Hishām, *Sīra*, 1:441–467; Dhahabī, *Ta'rīkh*, 1:300.

[23] See the valuable comments of ᶜAbd al-Karīm, *Quraysh*, 186 and 267–274, where he explains the crucial role played by the *anṣār* (mainly composed of the two major Medinan tribes, the Aws and the Khazraj) in supporting Muhammad and his Meccan *muhājirūn* (emigrants, all from the Quraysh). For some traditions praising the *anṣār*, see Bukhārī, *Ṣaḥīḥ*, 1:12; 5:33; 8:17.

[24] See the valuable works of ᶜAbd al-Karīm, *Quraysh*, 377–392, and also Qimanī, *Ḥizb*, 51ff. This argument may have support in Ibn Hishām, *Sīra*, 2:406–407, which highlights that the conquest of Mecca was still viewed by Muhammad as establishing the Quraysh's rule. Similarly, after the conquest of Mecca, Muhammad gave incentives to people from the Quraysh, while the *anṣār* were reportedly left uncompensated and they complained. See Ibn Kathīr, *Sīra*, 3:676; Ḥalabī, *Insān*, 3:175; also Bukhārī, *Ṣaḥīḥ*, 5:30. Furthermore, in the Year of Delegations, many non-Muslims came to submit to Muhammad's leadership in Arabia. This submission is better viewed as a political one, rather than as a religious acceptance of faith. Ibrahim, *Stated*, 156.

[25] For a detailed analysis of major historical accounts of the *sqīfa*, see Ibrahim, *Stated*, 127–130.

[26] The Medinan *anṣār* offered, "Let us have a leader from among ourselves, and you a leader from among yourselves." Ṭabarī, *History*, 10:3. The chief of the Khazraj (part of the *anṣār*) Saᶜd ibn ᶜUbāda was mysteriously murdered. See the discussion in Ibrahim, *Stated*, 129; ᶜAbd al-Karīm, *Quraysh*, 277.

[27] See Ṭabarī, *History*, 9:186.4. Compare Ṭabarī, *History*, 9:194 and 10:8. For some critical comments on how the *anṣār* were dismissed and harassed, according to traditions, see Ibrahim, *Muhammad*, 105–107.

[28] For the importance of these caravans to the Meccans, see Donner, "Mecca's Food," 263–265, where he argues, "Mecca was unable to produce the basic foodstuffs required to support its growing population on the eve of Islam. The city relied on the outside world not only for the transit trade

within which the great Battle of Badr was reportedly initiated a few months later. This is instructive, as classical Muslim historians—unlike today's scholars—did not seem to object to this depiction of Muhammad as a war initiator.[29] After all, the Muslim military incursions are often depicted in historiographical accounts as a continuation of the tribal custom of fights to seize possessions, secure spoils, and defeat enemies.[30] The two groups—the Muslims and the Meccans—met at Sīf al-Baḥr.[31] The number of the Meccans was reportedly ten times more than that of the Muslims. They were 300 under the leadership of the infamous Abū Jahl—a ruthless Meccan leader who had been known as the most hostile opponent of Muhammad since he began preaching.[32] There are two important remarks concerning the number of soldiers in the two camps. First, while the number of the unbelievers of Mecca is given here as 300, it is significantly different in earlier reports: In a report attributed to Ibn Shihāb al-Zuhrī (d. 124/742), Abū Jahl had 130—not 300—Meccan men with him.[33] Numbers appear to be *authored*, not *recorded*. While a *presumably* early report places the number at 130, later historians found it more appealing to raise the number in order to amplify the results of the raid.[34] This is another common literary feature in Islamic historiography—historians seem to favor the embellishment of earlier accounts by forging further literary dimensions to establish a more persuasive picture in their minds and to their audience.[35] Second, the discrepancy

which gave rise to its prosperity, but also for the staples needed to sustain life itself. It was a prosperity as precarious as it was brilliant." Regarding al-Shām, this is not today's Syria. The term Bilād al-Shām often refers to Greater Syria, which encompasses areas of today's Lebanon, Syria, Palestine, Egypt, and even sometimes Greece. See Ibn al-Faqīh, *Mukhtaṣar*, 91–93; Yaʿqūbī, *Buldān*, 160ff.; Iṣṭakhrī, *Masālik*, 55ff.; Yaqūt, *Muʿjam*, 3:311–315. See also Webb, "Pre-Islamic al-Shām," 135–164; Hitti, *History of Syria*, 3; Hitti, *Syria*, 1.

29 See the comments of Hoyland, "Earliest," 276–295; Shoemaker, *Apocalypse*, 182–183.

30 Hoyland, *God's Path*, 56ff.

31 This this why the expedition is called the *sariyya* of Ḥamza to Sīf al-Baḥr. For references on Sīf al-Baḥr, see Ibn al-Faqīh, *Buldān*, 437; Bakrī, *Masālik*, 2:651; Bakrī, *Muʿjam*, 1:236, 3:771; Yaqut, *Muʿjam*, 2:70. For a secondary study, see Shurrāb, *Maʿālim*, 204. The location is rendered Sayf al-Baḥr in several traditions. See Ṭabarī, *Ta'rīkh*, 1265; Ibn Saʿd, *Ṭabaqāt*, 2:4, 3:6; Khalīfa, *Ta'rīkh*, 1:62.

32 Khalīfa, *Ta'rīkh*, 1:62. On Abū Jahl, see Ibn Ḥabīb, *Muḥabbar*, 1:161, 176; Ibn Ḥabīb, *Munammaq*, 1:389; Balādhurī, *Ansāb*, 1:125ff.; Masʿūdī, *Tanbīh*, 1:200; Jawzī, *Muntaẓim*, 3:115ff. (on his death). See also ʿAlī, *Mufaṣṣal*, 7:105; Ziriklī, *Aʿlām*, 5:87.

33 See Dhahabī, *Siyar*, *sīra* 1:297, where he provides al-Zuhrī's report and other accounts.

34 See Shoemaker, *Creating*, 98, where he demonstrates that these numbers are highly exaggerated and explains that Mecca "was a very small village with only a few hundred inhabitants, perhaps around five hundred or so, with around 130 free adult men."

35 For how ʿAbbāsid-era historians embellished accounts, see Berg, "ʿAbbāsid," 13ff.; Ibrahim, *Conversion*, 215–229. See also Donner, *Narratives*, 145, where he contends that historians "continued to develop the material by reorganizing, recombining, or reinterpreting it, and (occasionally) by introducing completely new concerns." See similar arguments in Watt, "al-ʿAbbās," *EI*², 1:8–9; Petersen, *ʿAlī*, 88, 119; Ahmed, *Religious*, 13, 35, 64 n. 280, 108, 135; also Crone, *Nativist*, 88.

between the number of Muslim soldiers and that of the unbelievers of Mecca represents a reoccurring literary theme, advanced by storytellers to amplify the Muslim victory and establish a claim for divine support to the believers.[36] Arguably, Muslim historians serve not only as storytellers but also as religious narrators—each historian adds to or removes from the literary pieces created by another.[37]

Abū Jahl's real name was reportedly ᶜAmr ibn Hishām. The term "Abū Jahl" is a derogatory epithet, meaning "the source (or father) of ignorance or folly," reportedly given to ᶜAmr by Muhammad or Allah himself instead of his respectful and reputable name Abū al-Ḥakam (the father of wisdom).[38] Abū Jahl was of Muhammad's tribe, the Quraysh, but from the family of Makhzūm. In despising him, Muhammad reportedly called him "the pharaoh of this nation."[39] Some traditions claim there was an old enmity between Ḥamza and Abū Jahl, indicating that possible bloodshed was imminent.[40] However, when the two groups came face to face and began preparations for fighting, Majdī ibn ᶜAmr, a *ḥalīf* (an ally and friend) of both parties, sought to prevent the conflict. He negotiated between Ḥamza and Abū Jahl until both departed ways, the former to Medina and the latter to Mecca.[41] Thus, there was no fighting between the parties. When Ḥamza returned to Medina, he spoke with Muhammad about the result of the expedition and how Majdī intervened between the parties. Muhammad reportedly commended Majdi's actions and was kind to him and his people.[42]

There are two critical observations on the historical narrative of the reported incursion of Ḥamza ibn ᶜAbd al-Muṭṭalib. First, Abū Jahl is better

[36] Robert Hoyland writes on these "erratic" numbers in Muslim historiography. Hoyland, *God's Path*, 42. The Qur'ān seems to marvel at how "too often a small group overcame a large one by Allah's permission" (Q 2:249).

[37] Patricia Crone argues, "It is obvious that if one storyteller should happen to mention a raid, the next storyteller would know the date of this raid, while the third would know everything that an audience might wish to hear about it." Crone, *Meccan*, 224. Similarly, Wellhausen states, "The accounts are sifted, edited, and blended together by [later narrators]." Wellhausen, *Arab*, xii.

[38] Balādhurī, *Ansāb*, 1:125. Some report that Allah, not Muhammad, gave ᶜAmr the epithet "Abū Jahl." See Balādhurī, *Ansāb*, 1:298, 10:174; Ibn ᶜAsākir, *Ta'rīkh*, 11:500, 41:51, 66:309–310; also Andalusī, *Nashwat*, 1:360–361. He was known as Abū al-Ḥakam because of his wisdom, to the extent that he joined the elites of the Quraysh when he was twenty-five years old. Ziriklī, *Aᶜlām*, 5:87; ᶜAlī, *Mufaṣṣal*, 9:235; Ḥalabī, *Insān*, 2:34.

[39] Balādhurī, *Ansāb*, 1:298, 10:174.

[40] Jawzī, *Muntaẓim*, 2:384–385; Ibn Ḥabīb, *Munammaq*, 1:340; Ibn al-Athīr, *Kāmil*, 1:678.

[41] Ibn Saᶜd, *Ṭabaqāt*, 2:4; Ibn Ḥibbān, *Thiqāt*, 1:143.

[42] Wāqidī, *Maghāzī*, 10; Wāqidī, *Life*, 7. Muhammad reportedly admitted Majdī's "righteous deeds."

viewed as a literary theme rather than an actual historical figure. There are diligent attempts by Muslim traditionists to forge a portrayal—with several literary layers—in order to advance relevant Islamic claims. Not only is Abū Jahl depicted as a pharaoh and as Allah's enemy, but he is also identified by a derogatory epithet to advance Islam's claims that only people of folly and ignorance refuse the religion proclaimed by Muhammad. In this narrative, one encounters a stark literary comparison between the camp of Muhammad—particularly Ḥamza—and that of Abū Jahl, which is centered on light and darkness, truth and falsehood. Ḥamza is depicted as "Allah's lion," while Abū Jahl is presented as a man of folly. Much in these representations aims to advance religious claims of Islam's superiority, highlighting the newly born united community of Muhammad as the replacement of the old disjointed Arabian tribal system. It is rather obvious that Muslim historiographical accounts reflect hagiographical reports with a sharp emphasis on pious companions serving the Muslims under Muhammad's leadership.[43] However, the depiction of Abū Jahl, as created and shaped by Muslim historians, is starkly unrealistic in many ways, which highlights its fanciful nature and tendentiousness.[44] Consider one literary element in Abū Jahl's character as designed by Muslim traditionists, namely, the portrayal of his death. While he did not die in Ḥamza's incursion, he was reportedly killed about a year later in the Battle of Badr. We are told that three Muslim warriors courageously murdered him, but he mysteriously emerged from his tomb, presumably to fight again, before some other Muslims kicked him back in; Muhammad then prophesied that Abū Jahl would continue to be assaulted in such a way until the Day of Judgment.[45] This portrayal was not illogical for classical storytellers, who were not mainly concerned with logical constructs but with religiously driven depictions. The unrealistic portrayal of Abū Jahl's character reflects an undeniable feature of early Islamic historiography: religious sympathies of Muslim historians shape literary accounts.[46] Muslim writers were not merely narrating past events, but *authoring* and *embellishing*

[43] See Hibri, *Parable*, 9, where he argues, "Historical accounts, it therefore often seems, belonged to an earlier (or different) climate of parabolic narration, which as mentioned earlier continued the tradition of biblical storytelling with a different focus, on the lives of the companions."

[44] See Crone, *Meccan*, 230, where she argues, "The entire tradition is tendentious, its aim being the elaboration of an Arabian *Heilgeschichte*, and this tendentiousness has shaped the facts as we have them, not merely added some partisan statements we can deduct." See also Crone, *Slaves*, 10. Cf. Ibrahim, *Conversion*, 245–247.

[45] See Ibn Hishām, *Sīra*, 1:634–636, 1:710–711; Ṭabarī, *Ta'rīkh*, 1329–1331; Bayhaqī, *Dalā'il*, 3:89–90.

[46] Ibrahim, *Conversion*, 35.

the narratives themselves.[47] This reiterates a major premise of this study: the historiographical accounts are representations, not records, of the past.[48]

Second, as a narrative, Ḥamza's expedition does not appear to be an incursion but more of a tribal skirmish. We know from Muslim historiography that the Muslims and the Meccan pagans fought major battles as well as skirmished continually, and this is one such skirmish. Based on Muslim traditions, this *sariyya* was initiated by Muhammad. It was his attempt to inform the Meccans of the new rules of the game: Muslims are ready to combat. If we hypothetically accept the representation of Muslim traditions, it does not seem plausible that the Muslims actually sought a real fight, as they were outnumbered greatly. Instead, the *sariyya* was a proactive and provocative action to let the Meccans realize the growing power of the Muslim community centered at Medina. The skirmish seems to have accomplished its initial results. While one cannot be certain if the combat had actually occurred, the narrative as advanced in Muslim traditions suggests that Muhammad and the Muslims clearly targeted the Meccans and their caravans, seeking to establish the presence of the Muslims at the center of the tribal balance of power.

We should also note that the *sariyya* itself—and the presence of a negotiator who stopped the fight between the two parties—was not an unfamiliar episode in Arabia. It was a regular part of the life of the Arabs.[49] Only now, the Muslims were reportedly *not* fighting for their tribes or clans but, as the tradition claims, for Allah and in his path: "Their devotion to the newly founded *umma* [Muslim community] replaced and surpassed their earlier tribal loyalties."[50] This represents a reoccurring historiographical theme: portraying the Muslim raids as fighting *fī sabīl Allāh* (in Allah's path).[51] The theme transforms a pre-Islamic tribal understanding of raiding into a new ideological disposition, which colors the act of marching into battle with religious meaning. Nonetheless, this historiographical theme—soldiers fighting *fī sabīl Allāh*—is better viewed as a later creation, more suitable for

47 Robinson, *Historiography*, 38. See Décobert, *Le Mendiant*, 34; ᶜAlawī, *Maḥaṭṭāt*, 19–20.

48 See Robinson, *Empire*, viii.

49 On pre-Islamic raids among the Arabs, see ᶜAlī, *Mufaṣṣal*, 10:5–140; 7:142–414.

50 Ibrahim, *Stated*, 239 and 151. See also ᶜAbd al-Karīm, *Judhūr*, 7, 132.

51 For the theme of *fī sabīl Allāh* in the Qur'ān and early historiographical accounts, see Ibrahim, *Stated*, 197–212, especially 211–212. For various themes in Muslim historiography, see Ibrahim, *Conversion*, 35–229. On detecting historical themes, see Noth/Conrad, *Early*, 26–61; Donner, *Narratives*, 141ff.; Robinson, *Historiography*, 18, 95–98; and Cook, *Martyrdom*, 4, 55, 124, 157. For the issue of "themes" in Muslim literature in general, see Goitein, *Studies*, 11, 32; Rosenthal, *Man*, 11ff.; Rosenthal, *Historiography*, 114; Renard, ed., *Islamic*.

the age of caliphal conquests.[52] Since tribal raids were common among the Arabs in seventh-century Arabia, warriors were not necessarily in need of support to continue marauding other tribes. They were accustomed to such a practice as it was often the case among the Bedouins.[53] In later generations, when more soldiers were needed for further military expansions, a layer of religious appeal was created: fighting for Allah provides better rewards—not only spoils, as often had been the case in tribal raids, but also an appealing reward in the afterlife. This may reflect one reason for the creation and development of historical narratives centered on the heroism and bravery of Muslim warriors who fought for Allah's cause. They serve as precedents for later Muslims to emulate.

The Incursion of ᶜUbayda ibn al-Ḥārith (1/623)

One month after Ḥamza returned to Medina, Muhammad dispatched another *sariyya*, entrusting to ᶜUbayda ibn al-Ḥārith commandership over it and sixty Muslims—all of whom were from the *muhājirūn* (Muslim emigrants) from the Quraysh.[54] This narrative suggests that Muslims had gained momentum and that their determination to fight the Meccan pagans grew. It also reiterates once more a literary claim indicating that Muhammad *initially* did not trust the loyalty of the Medinan *anṣār*—who pledged to

[52] See Ibrahim, *Stated*, 71–72, where I conclude that "if the Muslim soldiers die in battle, they are guaranteed *al-shahāda* (martyrdom). If they win, they are promised at least four kinds of economic gain." See also Ibn Hishām, *Sīra*, 1:602–603 (for the reward of martyrdom). On the various kinds of spoils gained by Muslim warriors, see Yaḥyā ibn Ādam, *Kharāj*, 58–61, 82; Ibn Zanjawayh, *Amwāl*, 477ff.; Ibn Qudāma, *Mughnī*, 6:453ff. See also Ibn Sallām, *Amwāl*, 87–96, 132–145, 301–311, where he explains a kind of spoils labeled *al-fay'*; as for distinguishing between *ghanīma* and *fay'*, see 342–349. He also identifies the *salb* (snatching property after murdering a warrior), see 403–408. An English translation of Ibn Sallām's *Kitāb al-amwāl* is now available as *The Book of Revenue*. See *al-fay'* in ch. 2 (17–24) and ch. 7 (211–239), the *salb* (295–304). For secondary studies on these kinds of spoils, see ᶜAbd al-Karīm, *Shadwu*, 1:75–77; Kister, "Land," 273. See also Ibn ᶜAbd al-Ḥakam al-Miṣrī, *Sīrat*, 1:83–84, although Luke Yarbrough presents some reservations regarding the work's reliability and authenticity. Yarbrough, "Did ᶜUmar," in *Christians*, ed. Borrut and Donner, 175–176.

[53] Relying on non-Arabic and non-Muslim sources, Hoyland argues that Arabs were fond of raiding and aspired to conquer and control neighboring lands. Hoyland, *God's Path*, 31–65, especially 56.

[54] This was Shawwāl, the tenth month in the first lunar year of the *hijra*, about April 623. On this *sariyya*, see Ṭabarī, *History*, 7:10; Ṭabarī, *Ta'rīkh*, 1265; Wāqidī, *Maghāzī*, 10–11; Wāqidī, *Life*, 7; Ibn Saᶜd, *Ṭabaqāt*, 2:4; Ibn Hishām, *Sīra*, 1:591; Masᶜūdī, *Tanbīh*, 1:201; Suhaylī, *Rawḍ*, 5:38; Ḥalabī, *Insān*, 3:215; Jawzī, *Muntaẓim*, 3:80; Ibn Kathīr, *al-Bidāya*, 3:234. On ᶜUbayda, see Ibn ᶜAbd al-Barr, *Istīᶜāb*, 3:1020; Abū Nuᶜaym al-Iṣfahānī, *Maᶜrifat*, 4:1914. See Jamīlī, *Ghazawāt*, 21; Abū Māyla, *Sarāyā*, 89.

support him only within the city—and preferred to rely on the Meccan *muhājirūn*.[55] This account should not be understood to preserve the factual record of a historical incident, but rather as a literary composition with a religious disposition appropriate to the time of documentation.[56] From a critical standpoint, the sole reliance on Meccan Muslims is better viewed as a literary embellishment established later by traditionists who sought to magnify the status and prestige of Muhammad's tribe, the Quraysh, from which the Meccan *muhājirūn* came.[57] The rationale is that the Muslim *muhājirūn* (essentially Qurashites) bore the hardships with Muhammad from the start and thus deserve leadership and commandership. This literary thread weaves smoothly into other narratives that highlight the Meccan *muhājirūn* as those deserving to succeed Muhammad.[58]

The narrative gives a reason for Muhammad's choice of the commander of the *sariyya*: ᶜUbayda was an early convert to Islam—which, in Muslim traditions, suggests devotion and loyalty. He was ten years older than Muhammad.[59] According to traditions, the goal of the *sariyya* was to march to a valley named Rābigh in order for the Muslim army to *yaᶜtariḍ* (intercept or block) another major Meccan leader, Abū Sufyān ibn Ḥarb, who reportedly had two hundred people with him.[60] Targeting Abū Sufyān was a strategic action by the Muslims because he was one of the *sādat* (notables) of the

55 On the limitation of the support promised by the Medinan *anṣār*, see Ibn Hishām, *Sīra*, 1:441–467. See the explanation of ᶜUmarī, *Sīra*, 358.

56 On "fiction and history," see the comments of Hoyland, "History," 16ff.; Gilliot, "Récit," 277–289; Roohi, "Muḥammad's Disruptive," 40–80; Genette, *Narrative*, 25–31. In his analysis of historiographical accounts, Hibri concludes, "The story preserved in the early Islamic narratives was neither real in its details nor intended to be factual." Hibri, *Parable*, 237. See Petersen, *ᶜAlī*, 50, where he argues, "The formation of the historical tradition consists above all in reflections of the political and religious conflicts of its own age." Robinson states, "The rise of the historiographic tradition, whether or not it was triggered by caliphal patronage, was a deeply political process." Robinson, *Historiography*, 40. See also ᶜAlawī, *Maḥaṭṭāt*, 19–20; Hoyland, *Seeing*, 35.

57 See the two valuable Arabic studies ᶜAbd al-Karīm, *Quraysh*, 52–54; Qimanī, *Ḥizb*, 89–105.

58 See Petersen, *ᶜAlī*, 17, where he argues, "The traditionist never relinquishes his right to personal political or religious commitment to the subject he deals with."

59 On ᶜUbayda, see Abū Nuᶜaym al-Iṣfahānī, *Maᶜrifat*, 4:1914; Ibn ᶜAbd al-Barr, *Istīᶜāb*, 3:1020; Ibn al-Athīr, *Usd*, 3:547; Dhahabī, *Siyar*, 1:256ff. See also Ziriklī, *Aᶜlām*, 4:198. For contradicting reports on the expedition, see Ṭabarī, *History*, 7:13. For the prestigious status of being an early convert, see Ibrahim, *Conversion*, 57–62, 143–150. Concerning being early in conversion to Islam, Rosenthal observes, "The question: Who was first [to convert]? was soon asked in connexion with every conceivable subject and always answered, though often in a rather fanciful manner." Rosenthal, "Awā'il," *EI*², 1:758. See Lang, "*Awā'il*."

60 Some medieval Muslims place this *sariyya* as the first in Islam. Ibn Hishām, *Sīra, 1:591*; Suhaylī, *Rawḍ*, 5:38; Ibn ᶜAbd al-Barr, *Istīᶜāb*, 1:43. On Rābigh and its location, see Bakrī, *Muᶜjam*, 2:625; Zamakhsharī, *jibāl*, 161; Hamadānī, *Amākin*, 453; Yāqūt, *Muᶜjam*, 1:405, 3:11; Maqrīzī, *Mawāᶜiẓ*, 1:33; Samhūdī, *Wafā'*, 4:78; Balādī, *Muᶜjam*, 287.

Quraysh.[61] He was also known as *sayyid* (the master) of the family of ᶜAbd Shams—the cousins of Muhammad's family, Banū Hāshim. The two families reportedly had generational conflicts.[62] Abū Sufyān here is better viewed as a literary portrayal, precisely designed to establish clear ᶜAbbāsid propaganda against the Umayyads.[63] Since Abū Sufyān was a major Umayyad notable, the ᶜAbbāsid-era historians—who controlled the historical orthodoxy—sought to portray him negatively, depicting the Umayyads as enemies of Muhammad and thus as weak Muslims.[64] The list of Abū Sufyān's unfavorable literary characteristics in ᶜAbbāsid-era accounts is long: The tradition presents him as a hostile opponent of Muhammad who rejected Islam for two decades and persecuted many Muslims. Abū Sufyān did not convert to Islam, we are told, until he realized that Muhammad's victory over the Meccans was imminent, immediately before the conquest of Mecca (8/629).[65] This portrays him and his Umayyad clan unfavorably. Some traditions even emphasize that he only converted after he received incentives from Muhammad.[66] To further emphasize his unbelief and wickedness, ᶜAbbasid-era historians insist that Abū Sufyān was part of a plot to kill Muhammad before he emigrated from Mecca.[67] Based on these negative literary features, the rationale goes, fighting

[61] For primary sources on Abū Sufyān, see Khalīfa, *Ta'rīkh*, 1:166; Khalīfa, *Ṭabaqāt*, 39; Ibn Qutayba, *Maᶜārif*, 73–74, 136, 344–345; Fasawī, *Maᶜrifa*, 3:167; Dhahabī, *Ta'rīkh*, 3:368ff.; Dhahabī, *Siyar*, 2:105ff.; Ibn Abī Ḥātim, *Jurh*, 4:426; Ibn ᶜAbd al-Barr, *Istīᶜāb*, 2:714; Ibn ᶜAsākir, *Ta'rīkh*, 23:421ff.; Ibn al-Athīr, *Usd*, 3:9; Ibn Hajar, *Iṣāba*, 3:332. For secondary studies on Abū Sufyān, see Watt, "Abū Sufyān," *EI²*, 1:151; ᶜAlī, *Mufaṣṣal*, 7:110ff.; Mu'nis, *Ta'rīkh*, 344–347; Dangar, *Career*; Gabriel, *Muhammad*, 169–170; Humphreys, *Muᶜawiya*, 31; Lecker, *Dustūr*, 104; Keshk, "Depiction," ch. 1; Keshk, *Historian's Muᶜāwiya*.

[62] For the conflict between the families of ᶜAbd Shams and Hāshim, see Maqrīzī, *Nizāᶜ*, 37–59; also Ibrahim, *Islam*, 31–37.

[63] See Ḥusayn, *Shaykhān*, 34–35, where he writes of exaggerated historical accounts established by ᶜAbbāsid-era historians against the Umayyads. See Hibri, *Parable*, 3ff.

[64] On ᶜAbbāsid propaganda against the Umayyads, see Sellheim, "Prophet," 33–91; Hoyland, "Arabic," 211–233, as he argues that the early ᶜAbbāsids shaped history to their cultural and political requirements. See also Ibrahim, *Conversion*, 71–76, where a pre-ᶜAbbāsid account of Abū Sufyān's conversion is examined, suggesting that the ᶜAbbasid-era historians sought to rework historical portrayals for their political and religious goals. For how the ᶜAbbāsid-era historians controlled the knowledge of the past, see Borrut, *Entre*, 37–40, 103–107; Muṣṭafā, *Ta'rīkh*, 1:253–264; Shoshan, *Poetics*, 61–107; Rosenthal, "Review," 537–538.

[65] Khalīfa, *Ṭabaqāt*, 39; Ibn Qutayba, *Maᶜārif*, 73–74, 136, 344–345; Fasawī, *Maᶜrifa*, 3:167; Dhahabī, *Ta'rīkh*, 3:368ff.; Dhahabī, *Siyar*, 2:105ff.

[66] See Ed., "al-Mu'allafa Ḳulūbuhum," *EI²*, 7:254; Watt, *Muḥammad*, 73–75, 348–353; Ibn Hishām, *Life*, 594–595; Ibn Hishām, *Sīra*, 2:492–493; Wāqidī, *Maghāzī*, 3:939. On this term, see also Bearman et al., *Islamic School*, 128–129. Franz Rosenthal calls *al-mu'allafa qulūbuhum* the sympathizers of Muhammad. See Rosenthal, *Man*, 404–405. We should emphasize that traditions about Abū Sufyān come from the ᶜAbbāsid-era historians who rivaled the Umayyads, from whom Abū Sufyān descended. See the discussion in Ibrahim, *Conversion*, 157–158.

[67] Ṭabarī, *History*, 6:140; Ṭabarī, *Ta'rīkh*, 1230. It is worth noting that the same charge—of plotting to kill Muhammad—was stated against Abū Jahl. See Ibn Hishām, *Sīra*, 1:482.

Abū Sufyān was justified and even commanded. He was reportedly a wealthy and powerful merchant among the Meccans, and was known for leading frequent caravan trades between Greater Syria and Mecca.[68] Consequently, the account of ᶜUbayda's incursion aims to relay that targeting Abū Sufyān—in one of his caravan trades—was a great opportunity and significant humiliation against the Meccan unbelievers, especially their notable elites. This tradition is formed to describe a great opportunity for Muhammad and the Muslims to gain revenge against the pagans. By dispatching a *sariyya* against Abū Sufyān (like the earlier one against Abū Jahl), the Muslims were establishing a strong presence in front of the Meccans and were provoking them.[69] After all, Abū Jahl and Abū Sufyān—who were targeted in the first two incursions—were among the elites and most powerful of the Quraysh tribe.[70]

In this *sariyya*, sixty Muslims, we are told, faced two hundred pagans.[71] Among the sixty Muslims, there was a skillful warrior named Saᶜd ibn Abī Waqqāṣ. He was a faithful convert to Islam and a skillful archer.[72] He was one of the earliest converts to Islam, which reflects his devotion and commitment to the faith.[73] The accounts of ᶜUbayda's incursions introduce Saᶜd, who was entrusted by Muhammad to command the following incursion. Saᶜd's fame came to the forefront of Muslim traditions based on a report that he "was the first who aimed an arrow for Islam."[74] This statement demonstrates his bravery and willingness to serve under Muhammad's leadership and for the causes of Islam. Because of his service to Islam, we are

68 See Watt, "Abū Sufyān," *EI*², 1:151. Abū Sufyān was also the father of Muᶜāwiya, who later became the first caliph of the Umayyad Dynasty. These caravans were essential for sustaining life in Mecca, as the people who resided there relied on outside goods for their livelihood. Donner, "Mecca's Food," 263–265.

69 See Watt, *Muḥammad*, 3, where he discusses the early raids led or commissioned by Muhammad and states, "In all this we may see a deliberate intention on Muhammad's part to provoke the Meccans."

70 They were reportedly members of the ruling aristocrats of Mecca. ᶜAbd al-Karīm, *Quraysh*, 107–137; Qimanī, *Ḥizb*, 51–54.

71 On the hyperbolic numbers of soldiers in Muslim historiography, see Hoyland, *God's Path*, 42. Cf. Shoemaker, *Creating*, 98.

72 For primary sources on Saᶜd ibn Abī Waqqāṣ, see Abū Nuᶜaym al-Iṣfahānī, *Maᶜrifat*, 1:180; Ibn Qāniᶜ, *Muᶜjam*, 1:247; Ibn Qutayba, *Maᶜārif*, 1:241; Fasawī, *Maᶜrifa*, 1:279; Maqdisī, *Bad'*, 5:84; Isfahānī, *Maqātil*, 1:60; Dhahabī, *Ta'rīkh*, 4:212ff.; Dhahabī, *Tadhkirat*, 1:21–22; Dhahabī, *Siyar*, 1:92ff.; Ibn Saᶜd, *Ṭabaqāt*, 3:101ff.; ᶜIjlī, *Ta'rīkh*, 180; Ibn ᶜAbd al-Barr, *Istīᶜāb*, 2:606ff.; Ibn ᶜAsākir, *Ta'rīkh*, 20:280–373; Ibn al-Athīr, *Usd*, 2:452ff.; Ṣafadī, *Wāfī*, 15:90–91; Ibn Ḥajar, *Iṣāba*, 3:61ff.; Ibn Hajar, *Tahdhīb*, 3:483. For a secondary reference, see also Ziriklī, *Aᶜlām*, 3:87.

73 Some traditions claim Saᶜd was one of the three earliest converts. Dhahabī, *Ta'rīkh*, 4:212ff.; Maqdisī, *Bad'*, 5:84.

74 Wāqidī, *Life*, 7.

told, Saᶜd was one among ten men whom Muhammad promised would be in Paradise.[75] These ten, not surprisingly, were all from the Quraysh, which reflects a literary claim in ample Muslim traditions—designed by ᶜAbbāsid-era historians, mostly from the *aṣḥāb al-ḥadīth* (traditionists)—which praises and elevates Muhammad's family and tribe.[76] Of course, this tradition is rejected by Shīᶜites, who largely oppose Sunnī traditions.[77] In the same vein, the traditions of this *sariyya* depict Saᶜd as a major warrior, to the extent that his fame exceeds that of commander ᶜUbayda. In one tradition, Saᶜd is reported to have "protected the Muslims from the associaters [i.e., Meccan polytheists]" in this *sariyya*.[78] He had twenty arrows in his quiver and threw them at the Meccans, and they all reportedly succeeded in hitting Meccan targets, both men and animals.[79] Here the narrative drives a stark comparison to advance a religious philosophy. It contrasts two Meccan Qurashites: a faithful Muslim who is promised Paradise due to his bravery in battle, and an unbelieving Umayyad who—despite his wealth, status, and prestige—lacks insight and prudence since he does not see the truthfulness of Muhammad's mission. Muslim historians fashioned this narrative to convey that Muslims will win—in this life and in the afterlife—when they remain faithful to Islam and obedient to Muhammad's commands.[80] Moreover, the contrasting literary picture between Abū Sufyān and Saᶜd seeks to elevate Muhammad's companions as representatives of the faith. Just as older generations of Jews and Christians had prophets and apostles who served as defenders and proclaimers of their respective faiths, the rationale goes, Muslims also

[75] Wensinck, "al-ᶜAshara al-Mubashshara," *EI²*, 1:693. Ibn Qutayba, *Maᶜārif*, 1:241; Fasawī, *Maᶜrifa*, 1:279.

[76] On *ahl al-Ḥadīth* or *aṣḥāb al-ḥadīth* (traditionists, the Hadīth party, or the adherents of traditions), see Crone, *Medieval*, 125; Ibrahim, *Conversion*, 172–179; Ḥammāmī, *Islām*, 55ff.; Abū Zayd, *Imām*, 37ff. In describing the crucial role played by the traditionists to forge traditions under the ᶜAbbāsids, Hibri writes, "The scene of the leading companions engaged in bitter civil war barely two decades after Muḥammad's death posed a moral dilemma to orthodox writers of the ninth century, who generally sought to look on the Prophet's companions with unquestioning reverence as supporters of the early message." Hibri, *Parable*, 8. On the ᶜAbbāsid tendency to praise Muhammad's family (Hāshim) and tribe (Quraysh), see Qimanī, *Ḥizb*, 51ff., and ᶜAbd al-Karīm, *Quraysh*, 377–392, respectively. For a classical praise of *aṣḥāb al-ḥadīth*, see Khaṭīb, *Sharaf*, 22ff. and 55ff., where he praises them and claims that Muhammad foretold of their esteem and status. See also similar praises by Kabīr, *Shiᶜār*. For a classical Shīᶜite view on *aṣḥāb al-ḥadīth*, see Ibn Shādhān, *Īḍāḥ*, 7–44.

[77] The ten names include the Shīᶜite Imam ᶜAlī. See Sulaym ibn Qays, *Kitāb Sulaym*, 188, where ᶜAlī prophesies that nine of the ten are destined to hell, maintaining that he is the only one in the list to be promised paradise. See the discussion of Kohlberg, *In Praise*, 67.

[78] Dhahabī, *Taʾrīkh*, 4:212.

[79] Wāqidī, *Life*, 7. Ibn Saᶜd, *Ṭabaqāt*, 3:103; Ibn ᶜAbd al-Barr, *Istīᶜāb*, 2:607.

[80] See Hibri, *Parable*, 16, where he compares historical accounts and writes on religious philosophy.

have their own champions of faith who bravely served as commanders in Muhammad's camp.[81]

Still, the narrative highlights that there were only injuries, no deaths. It appears that like the previous *sariyya* of Ḥamza, this one was also a skirmish, for it was limited in scope. The Muslim historian al-Wāqidī reports, "They did not draw swords nor stand in line for battle other than for this shooting and skirmish."[82] Some Muslim historians consider this *sariyya* the first in Islam, not the second, perhaps because it only had a small amount of combat in the form of throwing arrows.[83] Again, these internal discrepancies between historical accounts force modern historians to pause: not only do the accounts appear in disarray and disunity, but also the reconstruction of a clear and coherent overall narrative is impossible if we rely on the Arabic Muslim sources.[84] Additionally, the critical evaluation of the reports of this *sariyya* yields similar conclusions to those we derived from the previous one led by Ḥamza. These incursion reports are literary representations designed by traditionists to elevate major Qurashite companions (ᶜUbayda and Saᶜd).

In the accounts of this *sariyya*, we encounter another attempt initiated by the Muslims to establish their presence against the Meccans who forced them to emigrate about a year earlier. Contrary to modern Muslim apologetic claims that all Muslim raids were launched in self-defense, this narrative indicates otherwise.[85] Now the Muslims, we are invited to believe, are growing in power and waiting for the right time to attack the Meccans. Nonetheless, the Muslims are outnumbered, and there is no real fight. The targets are Meccan leaders—so far, Abū Jahl and Abū Sufyān—and their people. While the Muslim traditions call this a *sariyya*, it appears to be more of a tribal skirmish or a limited provocation. More importantly, the *sariyya* traditions introduce the heroic actions of Muslim companions of

[81] See Hibri, *Parable*, 8, where he contrasts biblical prophets to Muhammad's companions.

[82] Wāqidī, *Life*, 7.

[83] See Ibn Hishām, *Sīra*, 1:591, where he considers this *sariyya* as the first in Islam; also Ibn ᶜAbd al-Barr, *Istīᶜāb*, 3:1020; Ibn al-Athīr, *Usd*, 3:547; Dhahabī, *Siyar*, 1:256ff. Al-Wāqidī counts it as the second. Wāqidī, *Life*, 7. See the study of Abū Māyla, *Sarāyā*, 84ff., and his conclusions in 304, where he relies on various *maghāzī* accounts to prove that the *sariyya* of Ḥamza was the first, not that of ᶜUbayda.

[84] See Crone, *Slaves*, 13, where she writes of the work of Muslim historians as a task that is "strikingly devoid of overall unity." Donner writes of the "internal complexities" in our sources, and argues they give "pause to the serious researchers." See Donner, *Narratives*, 4; also Robinson, *Historiography*, 19–20. Hugh Kennedy concludes that the "nature of the sources has also discouraged historians from trying to give a bold and clear narrative of these world-shaking events [of the conquests]." Kennedy, *Conquests*, 4. Cf. Danto, *Historical*, 12, 63.

[85] See Ali, *Critical*. For some Muslim scholars who argue the raids were all in self-defense, see Ibrahim, *Stated*, 1–5.

Muhammad. In this incident, we encounter Saᶜd ibn Abī Waqqāṣ, who is depicted as a faithful Muslim fighter who was the first to throw an arrow for Islam. This report reflects a tendency among classical historians to paint a religiously colored picture of an expedition, not only portraying Allah at work for the hegemony of Islam, but also depicting the warriors as serving the divine and the religion in their military combat.[86] Because of the outstanding reported achievement of Saᶜd ibn Abī Waqqāṣ in this *sariyya*, one month later, Muhammad reportedly entrusted to him commandership over the next incursion.

The Incursion of Saᶜd ibn Abī Waqqāṣ (1/623)

A month after ᶜUbayda's incursion (i.e., in the ninth month after the *hijra*), Muslims were reportedly ready to initiate a third incursion to declare their presence as a meaningful power in the land.[87] Thus, in three months, they initiated one incursion a month. The target of the latest one was also the Quraysh tribe, who expelled the Muslims from Mecca about nine months earlier. We should note that the traditions appear to convey that Muhammad was not primarily targeting the people of the Quraysh themselves, but precisely its notable aristocrats who openly opposed him. He wanted to hurt their livelihood and prestige, and sought to establish his leadership in contrast to theirs. Some Muslim scholars argue that Muhammad desired to elevate the Quraysh and expand its rule, but only with himself as the ruler.[88] As plausible as this line of thought can be, we should note that these scholars seem to trust the reliability of the Muslim accounts and treat them as factual information.[89] From a critical standpoint, it might be more plausible to argue that medieval historians—especially under the ᶜAbbāsids—designed tales to establish Muhammad's gradual victory over his own tribe. These tales aim to answer social, sectarian, and political questions that were of concern to the

[86] For the historiographical theme of hegemony, see Donner, *Narratives*, 144; Ibrahim, *Conversion*, 91.

[87] This occurred in Dhū al-Qiᶜda, the eleventh month of the first lunar year of the *hijra*.

[88] Two Muslim scholars adopt this argument. See Qimanī, *Ḥizb*, 51ff.; ᶜAbd al-Karīm, *Quraysh*, 377–392.

[89] Some accounts indicate that Muhammad did indeed target the notables of the Quraysh. For instance, according to al-Ṭabarī, Muhammad and the Muslims treated the dead notables of Mecca, after a battle, in a humiliating way, by throwing their bodies in *al-qalīb* (a garbage hole). Ṭabarī, *Ta'rīkh*, 1331. See also Qimanī, *Ḥizb*, 121.

Muslim community at the time of documentation.[90] Nonetheless, while this is the picture painted in the Muslim tradition, it appears plausible to assume that the conflict was not *primarily* religious, but instead mainly tribal over resources and dominion.[91]

In this incursion, Muhammad entrusted the now-famed warrior Saᶜd ibn Abī Waqqāṣ to lead, probably because of his reported courage and heroism in the previous incursion.[92] Muhammad reportedly said, "O Saᶜd, march now until you reach [the location named] al-Kharrār, because a caravan of the Quraysh will pass by it."[93] Al-Kharrār was a valley with water wells, adjacent to the famed location Khumm.[94] In obedience to Muhammad's instructions, Saᶜd took twenty or twenty-one Muslims and departed on foot, seeking to reach al-Kharrār in order to fight the Meccans. To surprise the Meccans, we are told, Saᶜd and his soldiers traveled by night and hid by day for five days. When they arrived at al-Kharrār, they realized that the Meccans and their caravan had just left the location a day earlier. Traditions claim that Saᶜd sought to chase the Meccans anyway, but he then remembered that Muhammad commanded him not to go beyond al-Kharrār and Saᶜd promised to heed the command. Arguably, such reports aim to paint an image of piety and heroism. As we mentioned earlier, Muslim historians served as religious authors who sought to instill a portrayal of Allah at work with and through the Muslim warriors. Still, the narrative indicates there was no confrontation between the Muslims and the Meccans. Saᶜd's *sariyya*—although labeled an "incursion" in Muslim traditions—did not actually involve any fighting.

The accounts of Saᶜd's *sariyya* reemphasize an important decision reportedly made by Muhammad concerning his Muslim soldiers. Up to this point, he only relied on Meccan Muslims (known as *muhājirūn*) in expeditions. Whenever he sent out a *sariyya*, we are told, the army was composed of only

90 Crone, *Slaves*, 230; also Hoyland, "History," 16ff., where he studies the issues of "fiction and history," examining the scholarly debate among historians between "how the past was" and "how it was represented." Genette, *Narrative*, 25–31. In studying conversion to Islam as a historiographical theme, I argue, "Early Islamic depictions of conversion not only reflect the diverse nature of the phenomenon and its varied perceptions, but also cast light on the religious debates, social concerns, political orientations, and ideological agendas of early Muslim historians." Ibrahim, *Conversion*, 2.

91 See ᶜAbd al-Karīm, *Quraysh*, 294; Ibrahim, *Stated*, 236–240.

92 Ṭabarī, *History*, 7:11; Ṭabarī, *Taʾrīkh*, 1266; Wāqidī, *Maghāzī*, 11; Wāqidī, *Life*, 7.

93 Wāqidī, *Maghāzī*, 11.

94 See Bakrī, *Muᶜjam*, 2:492, 2:510, where he claims that some say that al-Kkarrār is actually the Pond of Khumm; Hamadānī, *Amākin*, 1:399, where he indicates that Kharrār is near Juḥfa, which was ten miles from Rābigh, the location of the previous incursion led by ᶜUbayda; Yaqūt, *Muᶜjam*, 2:350. See also Jamīlī, *Ghazawāt*, 22.

Meccans, not anyone from the Medinan *anṣār* (supporters) who protected him "in their land alone."[95] For classical Muslim historians, it appears, the repetition of literary claims is not redundant—it drives important political positions and affirms religious dispositions. In my estimation, drawing straightforward connections between historical accounts and events that may have occurred centuries earlier is problematic, especially in the absence of independent documentation. These accounts are better viewed as metaphorical stories with religious meanings.

Nonetheless, if we accept the Muslim claim that Muhammad did not rely on the *anṣār* in the early beginnings, we may deduce, from a logical standpoint, that he was not yet certain of their loyalty. It is plausible to argue that he knew the Meccan companions and trusted them greatly; this was not yet the case with the Medinan Muslims. The Meccan Muslims were reportedly Muhammad's people who suffered persecution with him for years and who endured the hardship of emigrating with him from their homes to a new land. It appears possible that Muhammad waited until he established a stronger bond with the Medinan Muslims, who were capable enough to protect Medina, as it had their homes and wealth. He needed time to ensure the Medinans' loyalty before he entrusted them with commandership of expeditions. Still, more importantly, the literary theme of the marginalization of the Medinan *anṣār* and the elevation of the status and participation of Meccan *muhājirūn* appears tendentious. Here we witness again attempts by classical Muslim historians to stress ᶜAbbāsid dispositions for legitimization.[96] The historiographical accounts seek to point out that Meccan Muslims—because of their devotion and commitment—were faithful Muslims who could be trusted for rule and spiritual guidance of the Muslims.

But there is more to consider about the historical accounts of the incursions' narratives. If the tradition of these early incursions—Saᶜd's incursion and those of the two earlier ones—is to be roughly accepted, there are six important observations to state. First, at this point, it was nine months after the *hijra*, and the Muslims had already tried three times to hurt the caravan

95 Wāqidī, *Life*, 7–8. However, as we have already encountered, this claim is factually contradicted by earlier reports stating that the earliest *sariyya*—led by Ḥamza—involved both. Wāqidī, *Maghāzī*, 9ff.; cf. Maqdisī, *Bad'*, 4:181. The report that all of the men were from the Meccan emigrants is found in Ṭabarī, *History*, 7:10; Ṭabarī, *Ta'rīkh*, 1265; Masᶜūdī, *Tanbīh*, 1:200; Jawzī, *Muntaẓim*, 3:80; Ibn Kathīr, *Bidāya*, 3:234.

96 See Hibri, *Parable*, 24, where he writes of "the invention of an ᶜAbbāsid messianic image" through "a relation of cooperation and sympathy between the ᶜAbbāsid court and the 'ᶜulamā' [religious scholars]." See also Ibrahim, *Conversion*, 169–179.

trades of the Meccans. These early incursions appear to have served mainly as skirmishes. They aimed to humiliate the Meccan notables who led the caravan trades and who forced the Muslims to leave their homes nine months earlier.[97] Second, the locations targeted by these incursions were strategically chosen. All three locations—Sīf al-Baḥr, Rābigh, and Kharrār—are near the trade routes reportedly adjacent to the Red Sea. This reflects the tactical steps taken by Muhammad and the Muslims to combat the Meccans. Third, up to this point, there was no major clash between the Meccan pagans and the Muslims—no true fight occurred, nor were any deaths reported on either side. Fourth, the frequency of the incursions—once a month—invites us to believe that the Muslims were serious about sending a message to the Meccans and all of the Arabs in the land: There was a new powerful, united, and well-organized community in Medina under the leadership of Muhammad. Fifth, contrary to traditional Muslim arguments, the reports of these early incursions do not state that any proclamation of Islam took place. While traditional interpretations advanced by some Muslim scholars tend to depict the military incursions as aiming to proclaim Islam to nonbelievers, this is not supported by textual evidence we possess. The traditions reveal a sequence of tribal platoons aiming to seize possessions and declare dominion. They paint a picture of incursions initiated by the Muslims to declare that there was an emerging and growing power in the land and that it was not going away soon. Sixth, the three incursions were commissioned to faithful Muslim commanders chosen carefully by Muhammad. He did not participate in any of them. However, after these three incursions created a new reality in western Arabia, it was now a suitable time for Muhammad to lead an expedition in person.

The Earliest Four Raids Led by Muhammad (1–2/623–624)

Three months after Saᶜd's incursion, Muhammad reportedly *ghazā* (raided or invaded) the village named al-Abwā'. Muslim narrators call it the expedition of al-Abwā' and treat it as the first raid Muhammad led in person after he moved to Medina eleven months earlier.[98] It reportedly occurred in the

[97] See the discussion of Qimanī, *Ḥurūb*, 1:51.

[98] Khalīfa, *Ta'rīkh*, 1:56; Ibn Saᶜd, *Ṭabaqāt*, 2:5; Ibn Ḥibbān, *Thiqāt*, 1:145; Ṭabarī, *History*, 7:11; Ṭabarī, *Ta'rīkh*, 1266; Wāqidī, *Maghāzī*, 11–12; Wāqidī, *Life*, 8; Ibn Kathīr, *Sīra*, 2:352. See Ibn Hishām, *Sīra*, 1:591, where he claims that the raid was before the incursion of ᶜUbayda, in contradiction to the reports by al-Wāqidī and al-Ṭabarī. On the raid to al-Abwā', see also Bayhaqī, *Dalā'il*,

Muslim month of Ṣafar.[99] Muhammad's goal, we are told, was to *yaᶜtariḍ* (intercept or block) the Quraysh's caravan.[100] This is the same stated goal as that of the earlier incursions. This goal is not surprising, as it rightly presents these military activities as a continuation of the pre-Islamic tribal Bedouin raids.[101] While some may seek to depict the Muslim raids as different from the common raiding practices among seventh-century Arabs, the Muslim sources do not support such a claim. Here, al-Ṭabarī reports that Muhammad "went out on a raid as far as Waddān, searching for Quraysh and [other Arabs]."[102] While he reportedly could not find any from the Quraysh at that time, he successfully made a treaty with the Arabs of Banū Ḍamrah, ensuring an alliance of friendship and protection with them.[103] The goal was that "they would not increase forces or help any one against him."[104] These reports depict Muhammad as a shrewd commander who was able to use opportune chances and make deals to achieve strategic goals. This is one reason why Muslim thinker Sayyid al-Qimanī argued that Muhammad was acting strategically and tactically, not religiously and divinely.[105] While Muslim narrators wrote as religious scholars, their reports still convey that "the early expeditions were part of a broader picture of tribal alliances and political tactics."[106] As a reported narrative, this treaty was a strategic action by Muhammad, but his goal of finding the notables of the Quraysh was not fulfilled, so he "returned to Medina without any fighting."[107] Still, Muslim

3:10; Ibn ᶜAbd al-Barr, *Durar*, 1:95; Suhaylī, *Rawḍ*, 5:36; Kalāᶜī, *Iktifā'*, 1:317; Dhahabī, *Ta'rīkh*, 2:45; Dhahabī, *Siyar*, *sīra* 1:297; Ṣafadī, *Wāfī*, 1:82. See Jamīlī, *Ghazawāt*, 22–24.

99 This Ṣafar is actually in the second year of the *hijra* because the emigration reportedly occurred in the month of Rabīᶜ al-awwal, the third month in the lunar Muslim calendar. See Ṭabarī, *History*, 7:12.

100 Wāqidī, *Maghāzī*, 12; Wāqidī, *Life*, 8.

101 On the common tribal incursions in the 620s, see Hoyland, *God's Path*, 56ff.

102 Ṭabarī, *History*, 7:12; Ṭabarī, *Ta'rīkh*, 1266. On Waddān, see Zamakhsharī, *Jibāl*, 1:317; Yāqūt, *Muᶜjam*, 5:365, where he states that Waddān is eight miles from al-Abwā'. On al-Abwā', see Iṣṭakhrī, *Masālik*, 22; Bakrī, *Muᶜjam*, 1:102; Zamakhsharī, *jibāl*, 1:161; Hamadānī, *Amākin*, 1:231, 1:453; Yāqūt, *Muᶜjam*, 1:79; Samhūdī, *Wafā'*, 4:163; Balādī, *Muᶜjam*, 332.

103 Ṭabarī, *History*, 7:12; Ṭabarī, *Ta'rīkh*, 1266.

104 Wāqidī, *Life*, 8.

105 Qimanī, *Ḥurūb*, 1:38–40.

106 Ibrahim, *Stated*, 71. On Muslim historians as religious authors, see Hoyland, *God's Path*, 42 and 231ff., where he argues, "Their purpose in writing was to show the workings of God, not the machinations of man" (42). In a previous publication I argue, "Islamic historiography is not only reports of the past, but also, and perhaps more so, a collective representation of the political, religious, and social contexts and realities of its authors." Ibrahim, *Stated*, 33. See also Ibrahim, *Conversion*, 167 and 232, where I conclude, "It is evident that Muslim historians serve as religious scholars who establish a dogmatic precedent" (167).

107 Ṭabarī, *History*, 7:12; Ṭabarī, *Ta'rīkh*, 1266.

traditions treat this raid as Muhammad's first expedition that he led in person.[108]

Two months after al-Abwā', Muhammad *ghazā* (raided) Buwāṭ. This was reportedly his second raid in person.[109] According to traditions, this raid was also to intercept an important caravan of the Quraysh. The caravan had an abundance of wealth—"two thousand five hundred camels."[110] Here, this account furthers a religious dilemma: Classical Muslim historians do not shy away from depicting Muhammad as a highwayman who seeks to intercept caravans and seize their possessions. While this image of Muhammad is often discouraged and vehemently rejected by modern and contemporary Muslim apologists, classical historians did not find it odd to present Muhammad in this way.[111] The reason may simply be that the concerns of classical Muslim historians differed from those of modern times—each presents a specific Muhammad whose character answers the questions posed by the immediate religious, social, and political contexts.[112] Classical traditionists viewed the image of a warrior as a better fit for the promotion of the hegemony of Islam and for establishing its claims of supremacy and superiority, while modern apologists—both Muslim and non-Muslim—prefer a more desirable picture for our day: a mosaic image of both a victorious commander and peaceful proselytizer. Modern thinkers must contend with classical accounts that portray a different Muhammad than the one they purport to depict.[113] Indeed, apologetic studies are largely occupied with tweaking ancient reports to argue in defense of Muhammad's use of violence, whereas Arabic Muslim classical sources seem to marvel at Muhammad's victories as a warrior and ignore preoccupation with defending his use of violence.

In the narratives of this raid to Buwāṭ, we are told that the Meccan caravan had the notable Meccan chief Umayya ibn Khalaf as its leader, along

[108] See, for instance, Ibn ᶜAbd al-Barr, *Durar*, 1:95; Suhaylī, *Rawḍ*, 5:36; Kalāᶜī, *Iktifā'*, 1:317; Dhahabī, *Ta'rīkh*, 2:45; Ṣafadī, *Wāfī*, 1:82.

[109] This was in Rabīᶜ al-awwal, only thirteen months after the *hijra*. Wāqidī, *Life*, 8; Ṭabarī, *History*, 7:13; Ṭabarī, *Ta'rīkh*, 1268.

[110] Wāqidī, *Life*, 8.

[111] For a discussion on the competing views among classical, modern, and contemporary Muslims, see Ibrahim, *Stated*, 1–8. See Shoemaker, *Apocalypse*, 183, where he rightly concludes, "The image of Muhammad as an often brutal warlord is ensconced in his traditional biographies—there is simply no avoiding this fact."

[112] Ibrahim, *Conversion*, ch. 1.

[113] See Margoliouth, "Muhammad," 871–880, especially 878, where he writes, "No European apologist for Muhammad seems to have possessed any proper acquaintance with the Arabic sources." On the various "Muhammads," legendary, traditional, and historical, see Ibrahim, *Muhammad*, 35–41.

with a hundred men of the Quraysh.[114] Like Abū Jahl and Abū Sufyān, who were the targets of earlier incursions, Umayya was reportedly another notable elite of the Quraysh who was hostile to Muhammad and the Muslims and persecuted many while they were still in Mecca before they emigrated. It appears that this was a suitable opportunity for the Muslims to raid the Meccan caravan and attack Umayya. This tradition reinforces the comments made earlier—that Muhammad seems to have targeted the chief aristocrats of the Quraysh of Mecca instead of the whole tribe. After all, the Quraysh was his tribe and encompassed his people and relatives. This argument relies on various traditions to establish that Muhammad, from the start, desired to expand the rule of the Quraysh in Arabia, only this time he sought to ensure it was under his sole leadership.[115] Nonetheless, the traditions are ambiguous regarding what actually occurred during this raid. There seems to have been no significant encounter, combat, or even result. While this is considered the second raid led by Muhammad, traditions indicate that he *rajaᶜ wa-lam yalqa kaydan* (returned [to Medina] and there was no fighting).[116] It is logical to assume that the Meccans had learned of the Muslims' planned interception—which allowed them to elude them and escape.[117]

In the same month, Muhammad reportedly led his third raid against the non-Muslims. The storytellers seem to emphasize determination and purposefulness on the part of Muhammad and the Muslims. The target of this raid was not a group of Meccans but only one man of the Quraysh: Kurz ibn Jābir al-Fihrī.[118] He was reportedly from the notable elites of the Meccan pagans.[119] Traditions allege that Kurz assaulted "the pasturing cattle of Medina."[120] In response, Muhammad "went out in pursuit of him and reached a valley called Safawān in the region of Badr, but Kurz eluded him and was not caught."[121] This appears to have been a punitive raid. Again here,

114 On Umayya ibn Khalaf, see Ibn Ḥabīb, *Muḥabbar*, 1:160; Ibn al-Athīr, *Kāmil*, 1:666–669; Ibn Kathīr, *Bidāya*, 3:301–302; ᶜAlī, *Mufaṣṣal*, 7:125, 7:261; Ziriklī, *Aᶜlām*, 2:22.

115 For this argument, see ᶜAbd al-Karīm, *Quraysh*, 377–392; Qimanī, *Ḥizb*, 51ff. Cf. Ibn Hishām, *Sīra*, 2:406–407; Wāqidī, *Maghāzī*, 2:811; Khalīfa, *Ta'rīkh*, 1:104; Ibn Kathīr, *Sīra*, 3:676; Ḥalabī, *Insān*, 3:175; also Bukhārī, *Ṣaḥīḥ*, 5:30. Ibrahim, *Stated*, 156; Sharīf, *Makka*, 533.

116 Wāqidī, *Life*, 8.

117 See the comments of ᶜAlī, *Mufaṣṣal*, 7:261; 14:40.

118 On Kurz ibn Jābir al-Fihrī, see Ibn Saᶜd, *Ṭabaqāt*, 2:6; Ibn Hibbān, *Thiqāt*, 1:147; Zubayrī, *Nasab*, 1:445; Balādhurī, *Ansāb*, 1:287, 11:60; Ibn ᶜAbd al-Barr, *Istīᶜāb*, 3:1310; Ibn al-Athīr, *Usd*, 4:443; Dhahabī, *Siyar*, *sīra* 1:299; Ibn ᶜAsākir, *Ta'rīkh*, 4:233; Ṣafadī, *Wāfī*, 1:82; Ibn Ḥajar, *Iṣāba*, 5:434. Watt, *Muḥammad*, 4.

119 Ibn Ḥajar, *Iṣāba*, 5:434.

120 Wāqidī, *Maghāzī*, 12; Wāqidī, *Life*, 8.

121 Ṭabarī, *History*, 7:14.

Muhammad did not seem to achieve any significant results.[122] However, since Muhammad ended his pursuit when he reached the valley of Badr, Muslim traditions identify this as a raid and call it *Badr al-ūlā* (First Badr), in contrast to the great Battle of Badr, which reportedly occurred a few months later. Some call it the raid of Safawān.[123] Although Kurz was not caught and no possessions were seized, traditions still consider the incident a raid led by Muhammad.[124]

From a critical standpoint, one may wonder at the relevance and significance of such an account, especially as it does not appear to be a raid, but rather a chasing activity. One may even question why Muslim historians included this pursuit and chase as an important raid in the record of Muhammad's military career. For a modern reader, the account seems completely irrelevant, especially as it states that no goals were accomplished and no fighting occurred. However, this line of reasoning is suitable for a contemporary skeptical mind that may doubt the reliability of the entire narrative and dismiss its details. As for classical Muslim historians, the matter was different. They wanted to design stories—no matter how similar they were to each other—that portrayed Muhammad as a superior commander in the Arabian context—a fighter, in the battlefield, driven by religious zeal and supported by divine favor. This is a religious design, not a reference for actual events.[125] This multifaceted literary portrayal advances religious claims of Muslim hegemony by marveling at a military commander who is unyielding, unafraid, and unstoppable. For classical traditionists, the listing of several comparable raids was not redundant; after all, they were religious storytellers, not meticulous scribes of past events.[126] Nevertheless, we should note that, while the Muslim community—past and present—may trust and adopt these narratives as religious facts, there is no independent evidence that these raids—allegedly led by Muhammad—actually occurred. Yet one

[122] See the discussion of Watt, *Muḥammad*, 2.

[123] Ḥalabī, *Insān*, 2:169, 2:177; Khalīfa, *Ta'rīkh*, 1:57.

[124] Watt writes, "The one early expedition which was not against the Meccans, that against Kurz al-Fihrī, illustrates the dangers against which he had to be constantly on guard; it was an attempt to punish a freebooter of the neighbouring region for stealing some of the Medinan pasturing camels." Watt, *Muḥammad*, 4. It is worth making clear that, unlike skeptical scholars, Watt treats Muslim traditions, to a large extent, as records of Islam's origins.

[125] In his study of historiographical accounts of the divisions among Muslims under the Rāshidūn Caliphate, Hibri writes, "This portrayal of a clear division between a perfect age and a phase of decline is, however, more a form of religious representation than one of actual historical fact, even if some elements of the story may be real." Hibri, *Parable*, 4–5. On the Rāshidūn, see Ṣaᶜīdī, *Tārīkh*, 157–199; Ṣaᶜīdī, *Siyāsa*, 31–215.

[126] See Hoyland, *God's Path*, 42; Hibri, *Parable*, 9.

can definitely concede that these narratives were important for the medieval Muslims to design as religious tales, in order to establish the image they desired for their prophet and his nascent community.

Three months after Muhammad's expedition of First Badr (also called Safawān), he reportedly led a fourth expedition, which was sixteen months after the *hijra*.[127] Muslim traditions reveal its stated motivation: Muhammad received news that the Quraysh had prepared a large caravan leaving Mecca to Greater Syria. This caravan had an abundance of the Quraysh's wealth and possessions.[128] Upon hearing the news, Muhammad reportedly selected 150 of his best warriors (although some reports claim he chose 200) and marched to intercept the Meccan caravan. The Muslims traveled through valleys until they reached al-ᶜUshayra. This is why this raid is traditionally called *ghazwat Dhū al-ᶜUshayra*. The Muslims waited at al-ᶜUshayra for about a month in hopes that the Quraysh's caravan would pass by. But it never did. Still, the tradition claims that Muhammad was able to cut "a treaty of friendship" with some Arabs, "the Banū Mudlij and their confederates."[129] Banū Mudlij were the Arab inhabitants of al-ᶜUshayra and its vicinities.[130] This alliance was indeed tactical, as Muhammad consolidated his tribal support with Banū Mudlij, just as he had done earlier with Banū Ḍamrah. Here we witness again how Muslim historical reports portray Muhammad as a shrewd leader, capable of discerning the right timing for creating alliances even with those who did not believe his presumed religious message.[131] However, it is clear that he did not succeed in intercepting the Quraysh's caravan, as it reportedly left days earlier.[132] Al-Ṭabarī observes that Muhammad "went back to Medina without any fighting."[133] Although he was unable to catch the Quraysh on their way from Mecca to Greater Syria, Muhammad was still determined to attack their caravan, and he successfully did so a few months

[127] Ibn Hishām, *Sīra*, 1:595; Suhaylī, *Rawḍ*, 5:47–49; Al-Ṭabarī provides a slightly different sequence than that of al-Wāqidī. Ṭabarī, *History*, 7:14–17. Wāqidī, *Maghāzī*, 12; Wāqidī, *Life*, 8.

[128] Ḥalabī, *Insān*, 2:175.

[129] Ṭabarī, *History*, 7:14.

[130] On Banū Mudlij, see Balādhurī, *Ansāb*, 1:287, 11:134ff.; Ibn Ḥazm, *Jamharat*, 1:187, 465. See the studies of ᶜAlī, *Mufaṣṣal*, 2:51, 7:265–267 (on their location and treatment of Muhammad), 8:123 and 12:350 (on what they were known for); also Kaḥḥāla, *Muᶜjam qabā'il*, 5:368.

[131] See Qimanī, *Ḥurūb*, 1:38–40; Ibrahim, *Stated*, 4.

[132] Samhūdī, *Wafā'*, 1:213, 4:116.

[133] Ṭabarī, *History*, 7:14. Ibn Hishām, *Sīra*, 1:596. This is the expedition when Muhammad named ᶜAlī as Abū Ṭurāb, meaning "the dusty one" or "the father of dust"—a name that is reportedly most loved by ᶜAlī. See Ṭabarī, *History*, 7:14–17; Ibn Hishām, *Sīra*, 1:599. The Umayyads used this name to criticize ᶜAlī and degrade him. See Goldziher, *Muslim*, 1:117; Nasr, *Shiᶜism*, 39.

later, as he caught them on their way back from Greater Syria to Mecca, in the well-known Battle of Badr.[134]

The abovementioned four raids, according to traditions, are Muhammad's earliest expeditions that he led in person. The accounts of these raids among ample sources are largely comparable—with minor discrepancies. In concluding the examination of these early raids, we can make seven critical observations regarding their narratives.

First, these four raids are a natural development of the preceding confrontations. Before these raids, Muhammad had already commissioned at least three incursions—led by his trusted companions—that served as skirmishes, demonstrating the growing power of the Muslim community at Medina. They provoked the Meccans and served as initial combats.[135] The accounts of these four raids depict Muhammad as taking the lead, after he reportedly sent his companions as commanders in earlier incursions. He is now the chief commander against the Meccans. Still, the examination of the accounts sheds some doubt about the scope and results of these early raids—namely their limited scope and lack of significant results.

Second, these four raids had one target: the Meccan tribe of the Quraysh and its caravan trades. This was true with the exception of the raid of First Badr, in which Muhammad raided against one Qurashite man, Kurz. The raid appears to have been a punitive attack against a lone assailant—from a region neighboring Medina—who had reportedly attempted to steal some cattle. Still, it is important to mention that Kurz was a notable from the Quraysh. For Muhammad, in this early stage, the target had always been the Quraysh and their wealth, particularly their trading caravans. This target was the same not only for the raids Muhammad led but also for the earlier incursions he commissioned. Traditions indicate that Muhammad initiated the raids precisely to *yaʿtariḍ* (intercept) the caravans of the tribe of the Quraysh. The accounts—all are somewhat comparable, though they present various expeditions—drive the same point: Muhammad wanted to hurt the Quraysh. This was Muhammad's tribe. It included his people and even many of his relatives. He reportedly targeted them as a response to their forcing him to leave Mecca a few months earlier. They had now become his enemies. These raids—as literary tales—appear to have been a form of natural and expected

134 Jamīlī, *Ghazawāt*, 24–25.

135 Watt titles his discussion of the early raids and incursions "The Provocation of Quraysh." See Watt, *Muḥammad*, 1ff., where he explains that "they are excellent illustrations of Muḥammad's attitude towards the Meccans shortly after his departure from their city" (2).

revenge.[136] Muhammad and his community were keen to capture and hurt the Meccan caravans; they perhaps even considered raiding the Meccans as a reward for the Muslims. Medieval Muslim historians *display* a specific picture: In a little over a year, a great deal had changed. At Mecca, Muhammad and his small community were inferior, weak, and often persecuted—but not anymore. Now, under his leadership, they consolidated power and created some tribal alliances in Medina and its vicinities.

Third, whether Muhammad led a campaign or commissioned it, there seems to be another goal in the larger scheme of these expeditions: to humiliate Meccan leaders and notables.[137] In the traditions narrating these early campaigns, we hear of major Meccan notables, including Abū Jahl, Abū Sufyān, and Umayya ibn Khalaf. These notables were major Meccan aristocrats, who were clearly humiliated and shamed by the attack on their caravans. Each of them was joined by many Meccans in any given caravan, sometimes as many as two hundred men.[138] Combatting or confronting these men in front of other Meccans was likely meant to dishonor the Meccan elites. It was a message of humiliation, declaring that those who were once weak and inferior at Mecca are no longer so. This picture of humiliation and shame is precisely what the Muslim historians sought to advance. It is a religious metaphor: unbelievers are unwise to reject Muhammad and should be shamed and humiliated. Although no Meccan was severely hurt or wounded in these early confrontations, the historical reports suggest that it became clear to the Meccans that the balance of power was changing: They would have to watch out for the Muslims' intercepting their trade journeys from now on.

Fourth, while the raids had certain goals, they did not seem to have achieved major results. While traditions portray Muhammad as leading these early raids, taking control and advancing in regions around Medina, a closer look at the narratives reveals no significant results. Most of these raids—and even the earlier commissioned incursions—ended with no fighting and no spoils of war seized by the Muslims.[139] These confrontations

[136] See Haykal, *Ḥayāt*, 261, where he argues that the Muslims had the right to revenge because the Quraysh prevented them from taking their possessions as they emigrated from Mecca to Medina. See the discussion of ᶜAbd al-Karīm, *Qurʾān*, 1:91–92, where he argues that the early raids and incursions were a part of the tribal revenge practiced by the Arabs, both before and after Islam.

[137] Qimanī, *Ḥurūb*, 1:51.

[138] These numbers are given by Muslim traditions, scholars view them as exaggerated figures. See Ibrahim, *Stated*, 182; Hoyland, *God's Path*, 42; Watt, *Muḥammad*, 2–3.

[139] See Watt, *Muḥammad*, 2, where he writes of these early expeditions: "They are of slight importance, in that nothing seemed to happen, but they are excellent illustrations of Muḥammad's attitude towards the Meccans shortly after his departure from their city."

were limited skirmishes. Even when Muhammad chased one man, nothing was accomplished by this raid. Perhaps the most important accomplishment for Muhammad and the Muslims was that they were reportedly able to establish friendship treaties with Arab tribes such as Banū Mudlij and Banū Ḍamrah. This is evidenced in the accounts of the expedition of Dhū al-ᶜUshayra. While Muhammad reportedly aimed to target a Meccan caravan that presumably had an abundance of the Quraysh's wealth and possessions, nothing was seized or accomplished. Later raids, as we shall see, would demonstrate greater results for the Muslims. It appears that these early raids—if we hypothetically accept the traditional stories—were an attempt to show power, cut treaties, and control regions in western Arabia, particularly near Medina.

Fifth, geographically, the four raids led by Muhammad covered a relatively large area in the southwestern regions of Medina, including areas adjacent to the Red Sea. The aim was to control trade routes, making them unsafe for the Meccan caravans, and particularly to hurt the Quraysh's usually safe journeys that were reportedly established and conducted based on the so-called *īlāf* Quraysh. The *īlāf* traditionally refers to economic treaties or understandings that the Quraysh reportedly established with powerful Arabs and non-Arabs inhabiting the areas around the routes—the goal was for the caravan trade routes to be safe and protected in both the summer and winter.[140] Based on this *īlāf*, traditions reveal, the Quraysh had had safe and protected journeys, before Islam, in the summer and winter. Now, the Muslim narratives suggest, these journeys had become unsafe because of Muhammad's expeditions. Consider the strategic locations Muhammad targeted. His first raid, al-Abwā', targeted a village a little over one hundred miles southwest of Medina, in a place relatively close to the Red Sea. His raid to Badr reached a place also about one hundred miles southwest of Medina. Badr is about seventy miles northwest of al-Abwā'. As for his raid to ᶜUshayra, it was only fifty miles south

140 The term *īlāf* is mentioned in the Qur'ān (Q 106) and in many traditions, describing economic treaties for safe caravan trades. On *īlāf* Quraysh, see Ed., "Īlāf," *EI²*, 3:1093; Rubin, "Ilāf," *EQ*, 2:489–490. See also Jāḥiẓ, *Rasā'il*, 3:47; Rāzī, *Mafātiḥ*, 32:294–296. For secondary studies, see ᶜAlī, *Mufaṣṣal*, 7:67–69; Taqqūsh, *Ta'rīkh*, 82–90, and especially 428ff.; Mu'nis, *Ta'rīkh*, 119ff., where he explains that the *īlāf* began from the time of Muhammad's grandfather, Hāshim, who skillfully established protection agreements with strong notable Arabs, who gave him the *īlāf*, committing to secure the trade routes between Mecca and Greater Syria. A similar argument is adopted by ᶜAbd al-Karīm, who credits the *īlāf* agreements to Hāshim. See ᶜAbd al-Karīm, *Quraysh*, 52–54; Qimanī, *Ḥizb*, 89–105. See also Qimanī, *Ḥurūb*, 1:11–49, where he argues that the Muslims sought to intercept the Meccans by destroying the safety of the *īlāf* routes. See also the important studies of Crone, *Meccan*, 109–132; Kister, "Mecca," 113–163; Rubin, "Quraysh," 1–31. For the importance of these caravans for the Meccan supplies, see Donner, "Mecca's Food," 263–265.

of Medina. The examination of these locations suggests that Muhammad aimed to control the areas west, southwest, and south of Medina in order to ensure dominion over the trade route adjacent to the Red Sea and thus to gain an upper hand in attacking the Meccans.[141] The geographical targets were strategic. It appears that the Muslim historians who designed these narratives sought to, once again, reemphasize Muhammad's image as a shrewd and skillful commander who outsmarted the Meccan pagans. However, this pristine image is hard to believe. The narratives depict the Meccan pagans as naïve and less prudent, although the same traditions highlight that they were aged tribal leaders who allegedly established good reputations, strong ties, and tactical alliances with other tribes. We are even told—by the same traditions—that the *īlāf* of the Quraysh included deals with the superpowers of the day—the Byzantine and Persian Empires. Now, within two years and with few skirmishes, we are invited to believe that Muhammad cut treaties with Arab tribes while the Meccan pagans were stumbling and struggling to maintain the source of livelihood that they had held for generations. The picture painted by the narrators contains obvious gaps and, as Crone observes, is "strikingly devoid of overall unity."[142]

Sixth, the tradition portrays Muhammad's *maghāzī* as having two major dimensions: one political and the other religious.[143] While the narratives depict tribal campaigns supported by spying, schemes, and tactics, we are told that the raids were only launched after Allah *sharra*[c] (prescribed) jihad and fighting in his path or for his cause.[144] Arguably, classical Muslim historians

141 See Watt, *Muḥammad*, 2, where he writes, "The geographical situation lent itself to this. Caravans from Mecca to Syria had to pass between Medina and the coast."

142 See the critical remarks of Crone, *Slaves*, 13. Thus, Hibri concludes, "The story preserved in the early Islamic narratives was neither real in its details nor intended to be factual." Hibri, *Parable*, 237. However, we should note, Hibri does not agree with Crone regarding the "overall unity." Donner agrees with Hibri and argues that "the extensive reports about the rāshidūn caliphs found in the Islamic historiographical tradition are largely shaped by later—in particular, Abbasid period—narrators who succeeded in creating a coherent, unified story that frequently included allegories and other kinds of parallels." Donner, "Review," 570. Hibri argues in a different study that "these texts do form a cohesive array of narratives that were meant to be read in a specific way, even when that way is in itself indeterminate." Hibri, *Reinterpreting*, 15. See Andræ, *Die Person*, 26ff., where he examines "Die propheten legende"; also Rubin, *Eye*, 3.

143 Watt observes, "The phenomenal expansion was primarily a political expansion, and was based on the two concepts of razzia and federation together with a third that may be called military aristocracy." Watt, "Islamic Conceptions," 147.

144 See Haykal, *Ḥayāt*, 261, where he argues that Allah prescribed fighting with the goal of defending the faith and preventing the Muslims from being forced to abandon it by the Quraysh. See Ibrahim, *Stated*, 43, where I conclude my study of various accounts of the raids led by Muhammad and assert, "Muhammad appeared as a social and religious leader, declaring Islam as a religious unifying power among the Arabs." I also add, "Muhammad's religious proclamation and his role as a tribal leader have created a social, religious, and political integration, which resulted in the establishment of a unique, strong, and unified Muslim *umma*" (43). Similarly, Fred Donner concludes, "The appearance

write as traditionists—scholars of *ḥadīth* traditions—and emphasize both elements in their narration by depicting Allah at play for the advancement of the Muslim community.[145] The picture suggests that the Muslims in Muhammad's community have gained a new and stronger loyalty. Islam unified them, under the leadership of Muhammad, and created a strong bond between them that surpassed any previous tribal loyalty.[146] In their previous lives before Islam, they used to fight for their own tribes and clans. Now, after Islam, they fight for Allah and his cause.

Seventh, in modern and contemporary literature, the traditional Muslim interpretation tends to portray Muhammad's *maghāzī* as both expeditions for proclaiming Islam to non-Muslims and campaigns for self-defense. We explored many examples of this approach in chapter 1. Based on the accounts of Muhammad's earliest four raids, this traditional interpretation does not ring true. Concerning the proclamation of Islam to non-Muslims, there is no evidence in the Muslim sources that Muhammad or the Muslims sought to proclaim Islam to the Meccans. That which we find in the literature is mainly one incursion leading to another, skirmishes followed by tribal treaties, and sporadic assaults with no significant results. No religious proclamation is stated in any of these *maghāzī* accounts, whether before, during, or after the raid. It appears that the claim—that the raids were for the proclamation of Islam—is just that.[147] Furthermore, the narratives do not support the traditional claim that these raids were for self-defense. Instead, they reveal that Muhammad and the believers sought to intercept the Meccan caravans once they heard news of them. The caravans did not initiate assaults against the Muslims in Medina; it was the other way around.[148] The Muslims marched from Medina, seeking regions where the Meccan caravan routes were known, and waited in hopes of intercepting the caravans of the Quraysh and thus obtaining its possessions and wealth. This is the scenario offered

of the unifying ideology of Islam, coupled with the skillful use of both traditional and novel means of political consolidation, resulted in the emergence under Muḥammad and Abū Bakr of a new state that was able to organize and dominate more effectively than ever before the different tribal groups of the Arabian peninsula." Donner, *Conquests*, 251.

145 See Ibrahim, *Conversion*, 28, 83, 246, where I write, "Classical Muslim historians served as religious writers. They wanted to emphasize Allah at work in the Muslim community, and to display the unique qualities of Muhammad and his message, the Qur'ān" (246); also Ibrahim, *Stated*, 4.

146 Ibrahim, *Stated*, 103; Qimanī, *Ḥurūb*, 1:37.

147 See Ibrahim, *Stated*, 66–119.

148 Watt discusses these early raids and asserts, "The chief point to notice is that the Muslims took the offensive." Watt, *Muḥammad*, 2.

by the Muslim traditions about Muhammad's early raids. Of course, we still read of an incident of a pagan Qurashite man who assaulted pasturing cattle in Medina. However, his assault was not to attack the Muslims in Medina but to steal livestock. Although traditions insist on portraying this as one of Muhammad's raids, it is more plausible to view it as a random incident, especially if we consider the larger context of Muhammad's early raids and commissioned incursions, which clearly targeted the Quraysh of Mecca and their caravans.

The Incursion of ᶜAbdullāh ibn Jaḥsh to Nakhla (2/624)

One month after his expedition to Dhū al-ᶜUshayra, Muhammad dispatched his fourth incursion, entrusting it to one of his reliable companions, ᶜAbdullāh ibn Jaḥsh. ᶜAbdullāh was the son of Muhammad's aunt and an early convert to Islam.[149] These two characteristics—being a relative to Muhammad and an early convert to Islam—suggest his strong connection with Islam's prophet; however, classical historians also emphasize that ᶜAbdullāh was from the Umayyad branch of the Quraysh and that he was particularly *ḥalīf* (an ally) to the Umayyads of Banū ᶜAbd Shams.[150] This literary detail—ᶜAbdullāh's alliance to the Umayyads—will prove crucial shortly when we analyze the way ᶜAbbāsid-era historians shaped the story. This incursion reportedly occurred seventeen months after Muhammad's *hijra*.[151] We are now in the second year after he emigrated from Mecca to

[149] On ᶜAbdullāh Ibn Jaḥsh, see Ibn Saᶜd, *Ṭabaqāt* 2:7, 3:65 (he was a relative to Muhammad); Ibn Hishām, *Sīra*, 1:324, 1:499 (on ᶜAbdullāh's enmity with the Meccan Abū Sufyān), and 1:602–603 (on the incursion); Muqātil, *Tafsīr*, 1:184; Ibn Ḥibbān, *Thiqāt*, 1:148–149; Balādhurī, *Ansāb*, 1:199 (Muhammad's relative), also 1:371–372, 11:190; Iṣfahānī, *Ḥilyat*, 1:108–109; Bayhaqī, *Dalā'il*, 3:17–20 and 3:159 (ᶜAbdullāh died at Uḥud); Khalīfa, *Ta'rīkh*, 1:63–68; Ibn Ḥabīb, *Muḥabbar*, 1:86–87; Masᶜūdī, *Tanbīh*, 1:203; Maqdisī, *Bad'*, 4:182–183; Ibn al-Athīr, *Kāmil*, 2:10–12; Ibn al-Athīr, *Usd*, 3:194; Ibn ᶜAbd al-Barr, *Istīᶜāb*, 1:43, 3:877–879; Ibn ᶜAsākir, *Ta'rīkh*, 29:356–359; Dhahabī, *Ta'rīkh*, 2:48–49; Ibn Hajar, *Iṣāba*, 4:32–33. See also Ziriklī, *Aᶜlām*, 4:76; Andrae, *Mohammed*, 140–143. See also the Arabic studies Qimanī, *Ḥurūb*, 1:40–41; Jamīlī, *Ghazawāt*, 25–27; Haykal, *Ḥayāt*, 261–264; Sharīf, *Makka*, 424–425; Khaṭṭāb, *Rasūl*, 91–92; Shams al-Dīn, *Majmūᶜ*, 137–138; Khaṭṭāb, *Rasūl*, 92–94. For a critical Muslim approach to this incursion, see ᶜAbd al-Karīm, *Qur'ān*, 1:102–106.

[150] Khalīfa, *Ta'rīkh*, 1:68; Muqātil, *Tafsīr*, 1:184–186; Ibn Ḥabīb, *Muḥabbar*, 1:172; Fasawī, *Maᶜrifa*, 1:306; Ṭabarī, *Jāmiᶜ*, 4:303; Zamakhsharī, *Kashshāf*, 1:259; Dhahabī, *Ta'rīkh*, 2:200; Ibn ᶜAbd al-Barr, *Istīᶜāb*, 3:877; Ibn al-Athīr, *Usd*, 3:90; Ibn Hajar, *Iṣāba*, 4:31. We should note, Abū Sufyān is also identified as *ḥalīf* of ᶜAbd Shams. Ibn Saᶜd, *Ṭabaqāt*, 2:50. This demonstrates the significance of identifying a person as "an ally" to the Umayyads in Muslim historiography.

[151] See Watt, *Muḥammad*, 2, where he states, "Of the seventy-four expeditions listed by al-Wāqidī seven are assigned to the first eighteen months after the Hijrah." According to al-Ṭabarī, Muhammad initially assigned Abū ᶜUbayda to be the leader of this incursion, but he *bakā ṣabāba* (cried of

Medina. During this short period in Medina, Muslim traditions claim that Muhammad successfully dispatched four incursions and led four raids. This incursion was important on several levels and served as a precursor for the subsequent great Battle of Badr.[152] The incursion amplified the enmity between the Muslims and the Meccans because there were actual deaths among the Meccans and the Muslims were able to take some of the Meccans' possessions as well as seize their caravan and all of its goods. Moreover, the attack was reportedly accomplished during *al-shahr al-ḥarām* (a sacred, protected month), Rajab, during which Arabs were supposed to refrain from shedding blood or attacking anyone. This makes it a unique incursion; thus, a study of its details is important.

Like the previous incursions and raids of the prior year, the stated goal of this incursion was clear: The Muslims aimed to *yaᶜtariḍ* (intercept) the Quraysh's caravan. Muhammad appears to have practiced more secrecy in dispatching this incursion.[153] He reportedly instructed ᶜAbdullāh ibn Jaḥsh to gather some men and journey eastward, not westward or southwestward as in previous campaigns.[154] Muhammad also handed ᶜAbdullāh a sealed letter and instructed him, "I have appointed you over this group. Proceed until you have traveled for two nights, then unfold my letter and do as it says."[155] ᶜAbdullāh reportedly followed Muhammad's instructions to the letter. Here the story seems to advance a religious disposition: Muhammad was willing to rely on people who were known as allies to the Umayyad family as long as they were committed Muslims.

Two days into the journey, ᶜAbdullāh opened the sealed letter and found Muhammad's instructions: "March until you come to the valley of Nakhla—in Allah's name and with His blessings—but do not oblige any of your companions to march with you. Proceed, heeding my command with those who follow you, until you reach Nakhla's valley and, from there, *taraṣṣad*

love and affection) to Muhammad, as he did not want to be separated from him, at which time Muhammad assigned ᶜAbdullāh as the leader. Ṭabarī, *Tafsīr*, 4:307.

152 See the comments of Ṭabarī, *Taʾrīkh*, 1285; Ṭabarī, *History*, 7:29. We examine the Battle of Badr in the next chapter. Here, briefly, see Watt, "Badr," *EI*², 1:867–868. See also Qimanī, *Ḥurūb*, 1:40–41, where he explains how this incursion was important strategically for the next great Battle of Badr. See Yaᶜqūbī, *Taʾrīkh*, 2:45–47, where he labels it *Waqᶜat Badr al-ᶜuẓmā* (the greatest battle of Badr), indicating its importance and significance.

153 See Khaṭṭāb, *Rasūl*, 94.

154 According to al-Ṭabarī, Muhammad instructed the men to journey toward a place between Mecca and al-Ṭāʾif. Ṭabarī, *Tafsīr*, 4:302.

155 Wāqidī, *Life*, 9.

(watch attentively for) the caravan of the Quraysh."[156] Muhammad's two actions—ordering the men to journey eastward and giving the instructions in a sealed letter—appear to have been aimed at avoiding the possibility of spies who could inform the Meccans of the plan for the incursion.[157] Consequently, ᶜAbdullāh summoned his companions and, in fulfilling Muhammad's commands, told them, "I will not compel any of you—whoever of you desires martyrdom, let him proceed according to the messenger's command, and whoever wants to return, let him do so now."[158] There were reportedly twelve (or eight, or thirteen) Muslim soldiers with ᶜAbdullāh—all from the Meccan emigrants and none from the Medinan supporters of Muhammad, perhaps as he was not yet fully confident of the loyalty of the Medinan people.[159] (Here we encounter similar literary features, as we did earlier, that dilute the role of the Medinan *anṣār*, elevate the role of the Meccan *muhājirūn*, and praise the companions of Muhammad as carriers and fulfillers of Islam's commands and mission.) The men responded, "We will obey and listen to Allah, his messenger, and you. March, by Allah's blessing, wherever you wish."[160]

This unanimous agreement and total support settled the matter, and the men marched forward until they reached a valley called Nakhla.[161] This is why the incursion is called the *sariyya* of Nakhla, or the *sariyya* of ᶜAbdullāh ibn Jaḥsh. Of course, the unanimous willingness of the men to march for

[156] Wāqidī, *Maghāzī*, 13–14; Wāqidī, *Life*, 9; Ṭabarī, *History*, 7:18ff.; Watt, *Muḥammad*, 2, where he observes, "The idea in these expeditions, as in most of the fighting of the desert Arabs, was doubtless to catch the opponents at a disadvantage by ambushing them." For a Muslim perspective on the secrecy of the incursion and how Muhammad was strategic to use a sealed letter, see Abū Māyla, *Sarāyā*, 102.

[157] Watt, *Muḥammad*, 5–9.

[158] Wāqidī, *Maghāzī*, 14. Ṭabarī, *History*, 7:18ff. Faizer, the translator of Wāqidī's *Maghāzī*, inaccurately renders *al-shahāda* as "to be witness" instead of "martyrdom." This rendition does not fit the context, nor does it echo other Muslim accounts of the incursion. See Wāqidī, *Life*, 9.

[159] See Ibn Hishām, *Sīra*, 1:601; Ibn Ḥibbān, *Thiqāt*, 1:148–149. On how Muhammad relied only on Meccan *muhājirūn* (emigrants) and not on Medinan *anṣār* (helpers) in the early expeditions, see also Masᶜūdī, *Tanbīh*, 1:200; Jawzī, *Muntaẓim*, 3:80; Ibn Kathīr, *Bidāya*, 3:234. The number of the men, according to various reports, was eight, twelve, or thirteen. See Wāqidī, *Maghāzī*, 19, where he gives the three figures and states that he supports the number eight. For narrators who suggest that the number of men was eight, see Ibn Hishām, *Sīra*, 1:601; Ṭabarī, *History*, 7:18; Ṭabarī, *Tafsīr*, 4:302; Masᶜūdī, *Tanbīh*, 1:203; Bayhaqī, *Dalā'il*, 3:20; Maqdisī, *Bad'*, 4:182; Ibn ᶜAbd al-Barr, *Durar*, 1:99; Suhaylī, *Rawḍ*, 5:52; Kalāᶜī, *Iktifā'*, 1:321; Ḥalabī, *Insān*, 3:218; Dhahabī, *Siyar*, *sīra* 1:299. See also the study of Abū Māyla, *Sarāyā*, 95.

[160] Wāqidī, *Maghāzī*, 14.

[161] On Nakhla and its location, see Hamdānī, *Ṣifat*, 1:71–75; Zamakhsharī, *Jibāl*, 1:219; Hamadānī, *Amākin*, 1:760; Yāqūt, *Muᶜjam*, 1:78, 1:375, 1:414, where the exact location of Nakhla is uncertain, but we are told that it was "a night journey from Mecca." See also Samhūdī, *Wafā'*, 1:213, 4:29; Balādī, *Muᶜjam*, 317. According to al-Ṭabarī, Nakhla was a place between Mecca and al-Ṭā'if. Ṭabarī, *Tafsīr*, 4:302. See also Abū Māyla, *Sarāyā*, 96; Andrae, *Mohammed*, 18, 141, 185.

intercepting the caravan is depicted in Muslim traditions as a sign of how the men were devoted to the cause of Islam. Still, we are told, two of the Muslims had to stay behind, as they had lost their camel and had to attempt to find it.[162] Al-Ṭabarī provides some traditions that shed doubt on the true motives of these two men, depicting them as not truly serious about joining the group and suggesting that they were not devoted to the Muslim cause.[163] From a critical standpoint, this unanimous agreement among the soldiers to march to the battlefield is better viewed as a literary construction—reflecting a theme of devotion serving as a religious lesson—rather than documentation of a factual occurrence on a battlefield. Also, the negative depiction of the two men who deserted the warriors is better understood as a designed theological warning, advanced by storytellers, aiming to contrast them with the heroes who marched to fight Allah's enemies in obedience to Muhammad's commands. The story is meant to convey a clear lesson: If Muslims follow Muhammad's commands and strive to remain committed to fighting Allah's enemies, the community will flourish and accomplish its greatest destiny. Still, the incursion narrative, in its literary descriptions, promotes more important lessons.

At Nakhla, as the Muslims were laying in wait, a caravan of the Quraysh approached their location. It had raisins, leather, wine, and other merchandise.[164] In addition to the abundance of goods, the caravan had four Meccan men: ᶜAmr ibn al-Ḥaḍramī and three of the notables of the Meccan clan of Makhzūm: ᶜUthmān ibn ᶜAbdullāh ibn al-Mughīra, his brother Nawfal ibn ᶜAbdullāh ibn al-Mughīra, and al-Ḥakam ibn Kaysān.[165] According to Muslim traditions, when these notables in the caravan saw the Muslims, their hearts melted in fear, for they were uncertain of the intentions of the Muslim men.[166] Still, they calmed each other, as they thought there was no

162 These two Muslims were later caught by the Meccans. See Ṭabarī, *Ta'rīkh*, 1274; Ṭabarī, *History*, 7:19. See the study of Khaṭṭāb, *Rasūl*, 91–92.

163 Ṭabarī, *Ta'rīkh*, 1278; Ṭabarī, *History*, 7:22.

164 Ṭabarī, *History*, 7:19; Wāqidī, *Maghāzī*, 16.

165 Ṭabarī, *History*, 7:19; Wāqidī, *Maghāzī*, 14. On Banū Makhzūm, see Zubayrī, *Nasab*, 1:299–300; Ibn Saᶜd, *Ṭabaqāt*, 4:101; Khalīfa, *Tabaqāt*, 1:51–55, 483–486; Yaqūt, *Muᶜjam*, 856, 1291; Samᶜānī, *Ansāb*, 12:136. See also ᶜAlī, *Mufaṣṣal*, 2:160 (on Banū Makhzūm's classification among the Arabs); 7:26 (on their clan within the Quraysh); 7:58 (on their opposition to Muhammad's family); 7:91 (on their being from the notables of Mecca); 7:105 (one of Banū Makhzūm's aristocrats was Abū Jahl, one of Muhammad's major opponents); 7:83, 7:114, and 14:130 (on their influence, possessions, and wealth); 7:339, 8:163, and 17:146 (on their pride and haughtiness); 8:72 and 9:250 (on Khālid ibn al-Walād's being one of them); also Ziriklī, *Aᶜlām*, 5:195. On the Quraysh and its clans, see Masᶜūdī, *Murūj*, 212ff.

166 Ṭabarī, *History*, 7:19; Wāqidī, *Maghāzī*, 14.

danger from the Muslims, and said, *naḥnu fī shahrin ḥarām* (we are in a sacred, protected month).[167] Among the Arabs, there were four special months in any given year. They are called *al-ashhur al-ḥurum* (sacred or protected months, sg. *al-shahr al-ḥarām*), during which attacking and raiding were forbidden.[168]

With the abundant merchandise and the presence of the notables in the caravan, this was a great opportunity for the Muslims to accomplish the goals of the incursion; however, there was the apparent problem of the sacred month (it was the last day of the sacred month of Rajab).[169] No Arab was supposed to fight on that day.[170] Both the Meccans and the Muslims appear to have realized this custom. If it were one day later, then the matter would have been different, because following Rajab was the month of Shaᶜbān, which was not a sacred month. Since Rajab was one of the protected months, the Muslims were in a tough spot. If, on the one hand, they attacked the caravan and killed any of its people, then they would have violated the sacred month. But if, on the other hand, they waited and let the Meccans travel for one day, then they would leave quickly and enter the Meccan territory, which was considered a sacred one where fighting was not allowed.[171]

The narratives claim that the Muslim companions of ᶜAbdullāh voiced different opinions regarding attacking the Meccans and began to offer competing claims about that day.[172] "We do not know whether this day is in the protected month or not," one of the Muslim soldiers declared, while

167 Wāqidī, *Maghāzī*, 14; Wāqidī, *Life*, 9.

168 On *al-ashhur al-ḥurum* (sacred or protected months), see Rāzī, *Mukhtār*, 145; Ibn Manẓūr, *Lisān*, 3:211, 12:121; Ibn ᶜAbd Rabbih, *ᶜIqd*, 6:103. See also Muqātil, *Tafsīr*, 1:448, 2:135ff., 2:157; Ṭabarī, *Jāmiᶜ*, 4:312–315, where the prohibition of fighting is abrogated; Zamakhsharī, *Kashshāf*, 2:243–247; Ibn Ḥajar, *Fatḥī*, 1:134, 8:91, 325. See also ᶜAlī, *Mufaṣṣal*, 10:52, where he explains the sanctity of these months among the Arabs. See also Ibrahim, *Stated*, 72; Ibn Ḥazm, *Muḥallā*, 10:206, 11:153. The Qur'ān mentions that the protected months are four, but it does not specify them. See *sūrat al-Tawba* (Q 9:36) and *sūrat al-Baqara* (Q 2:194). However, the tradition specifies them. See Bukhārī, *Ṣaḥīḥ*, 2:176–177, 4:107, 5:177, 6:66, 7:100, 8:15, 9:133.

169 See the discussion of Watt, *Muḥammad*, 5–9; also Ibrahim, *Stated*, 72–73, where I write, "The violation of the sacred month's sanctity displayed the general defilement of the tribal system—a system which protected the trading roads against murdering, kidnapping, and stealing." See also Qimanī, *Ḥizb*, 153, where he observes that Muslims violated the sacred month by killing, stealing, and taking people captives.

170 In a Muslim tradition, we are told that once the month of Rajab came, Arabs used to cease raids. They named the month *munaṣṣil al-asinna* (the iron remover), as they used to remove the iron parts of every spear and arrow, throwing them away to declare that no raids were expected. See Bukhārī, *Ṣaḥīḥ*, 5:171. According to al-Ṭabarī, some Arabs called the month of Rajab *al-shahr al-aṣamm* (the deaf month) because no sound of fighting or swords existed during it. Ṭabarī, *Jāmiᶜ*, 4:300.

171 Ṭabarī, *History*, 7:19; Wāqidī, *Maghāzī*, 14. See also Wāqidī, *Life*, 9, where the problem is rendered, "If you [O Muslims] delay about [the Meccans] today, they will enter the sanctuary and will be protected, and if you attack them now, it is in the sacred month."

172 See Wāqidī, *Maghāzī*, 14, where he provides several contradicting reports.

others insisted that it "was the first day of Shaᶜbān" already, so fighting was allowed.[173] Still, some in the Muslim camp were reluctant and spoke to each other, "We do not know this day except that it is in the protected month, and we do not think that you should violate it for what you desire."[174] In this dispute, nonetheless, there was eventually a winning voice. We are told that "those who desired the things of the world emerged victorious."[175] This meant that the Muslims decided to attack the Meccans despite the sacred month. This literary detail—that ᶜAbdullāh and the warriors preferred the worldly matters—is meant to depict the preferences of the commander of the incursion negatively. Al-Ṭabarī observes that the Muslims "plucked up courage and agreed to kill as many of [the Meccans] as they could and to seize what they had with them."[176] The attack targeted the caravan, its merchandise, and the four notables in it: ᶜAmr was killed by an arrow from a Muslim soldier, while ᶜUthmān and al-Ḥakam surrendered and were taken captive. As for Nawfal (ᶜUthmān's brother), he was able to escape and fled to Mecca.

Thus, the traditions indicate, ᶜAmr ibn al-Ḥaḍramī was the first pagan to be killed in the escalating fight between the Muslims and the Meccans.[177] While ᶜAbdullāh ibn Jaḥsh wanted to behead al-Ḥakam after taking him captive, the companions were of the thought to keep him alive in order to bring him to Muhammad.[178] This is another literary detail—fashioned by ᶜAbbāsid-era historians—that arguably portrays an ally of the Umayyad family (ᶜAbdullāh) as more concerned with matters of this world than fulfilling honorable commitments. The result of this incursion was that ᶜAbdullāh ibn Jaḥsh successfully seized the caravan and took the two captives back to Medina so as to present them to Muhammad.[179] In the Medina-Mecca combat, this "was the first booty taken by the companions of Muḥammad."[180] Still, overall, the literary accounts drive a lesson of heroism and devotion to Islam on the part of the Muslims, as well as a precedent ascribing legitimacy to the act of seizing possessions from unbelievers

[173] Wāqidī, *Life*, 9.
[174] Wāqidī, *Life*, 9.
[175] Wāqidī, *Life*, 9.
[176] Ṭabarī, *History*, 7:19.
[177] On ᶜAmr ibn al-Ḥaḍramī, see Dhahabī, *Ta'rīkh*, 2:50; ᶜAlī, *Mufaṣṣal*, 15:128.
[178] Wāqidī, *Maghāzī*, 15. Eventually, al-Ḥakam accepted Islam after meeting Muhammad, and thus he was spared. On al-Ḥakam, see Ibn ᶜAbd al-Barr, *Istīᶜāb*, 1:355.
[179] Ṭabarī, *History*, 7:19.
[180] Ṭabarī, *History*, 7:22. See also Ibn Ḥabīb, *Muḥabbar*, 1:86.

whenever a believer is able.[181] ᶜAbdullāh ibn Jaḥsh, we are told, divided the booty, setting aside a fifth for Muhammad and the rest for the soldiers.[182] Overall, it appears that ᶜAbdullāh was convinced of the great accomplishment of the incursion. He also assured his companions that the portion of the booty that he designated for Muhammad was the right amount.[183]

Nonetheless, when ᶜAbdullāh and his companions arrived back in Medina, a surprise awaited them. Muhammad was not happy about what they did, as they violated the sacred month. He rebuked the men, saying, "I did not order you to fight in the sacred month," then he "impounded the caravan and the two captives and refused to take anything of it."[184] Moreover, he reproved ᶜAbdullāh in front of the companions: "You have done what you were not commanded to do, and have fought in the sacred month when you were not commanded to fight."[185] This literary detail is better viewed as a later ᶜAbbāsid claim that is unfavorable toward Umayyad figures, portraying them as displeasing to Muhammad although he trusted them with commandership. Unsurprisingly, the Meccans, too, were reportedly furious. They said, "Muḥammad and his companions have violated the sacred month and shed blood in it, have seized property in it and taken men captive in it."[186] For them, these actions were a great offense.[187] The traditions depict Muhammad as aggravated and infuriated about the matter; Allah comforted him and the Muslims, however, by revealing a verse from the Qur'ān about the sacred months: "They ask you concerning fighting in the sacred month. Respond, fighting in it is indeed a grave transgression. However, the prevention of access to Allah's path, disbelieving in him, and prohibiting access to the Sacred Mosque are graver. Sedition is worse than slaughter. They will not cease fighting you until they turn you back from your religion if they

181 Muqātil, *Tafsīr*, 1:184–186; Ṭabarī, *Jāmiᶜ*, 4:303; Zamakhsharī, *Kashshāf*, 1:259.

182 Wāqidī, *Maghāzī*, 17. Al-Wāqidī observes that in pre-Islamic Arabia, army leaders used to receive a fourth of the booty, not a fifth.

183 ᶜAbdullāh's decision regarding the fifth for Muhammad was done before Allah prescribed the amount as a divine order later. See Ṭabarī, *History*, 7:20, where he states, "This was before God made (surrendering) a fifth of booty taken a duty." See Masᶜūdī, *Tanbīh*, 1:203. On the fifth as a portion given to Muhammad, see Ibn Zanjawayh, *Amwāl*, 90–99, 676–679; also Ibn Sallām al-Khuzāᶜī, *Amwāl*, 14, 382–387. See also the Qur'ān in *sūrat al-Anfāl* (Q 8:41). On the divine designation of the fifth of the spoils for Muhammad, see Muqātil, *Tafsīr*, 2:116; Ṭabarī, *Jāmiᶜ*, 13:546–557; Rāzī, *Mafātiḥ*, 15:484–485; Qurṭubī, *Jāmiᶜ*, 8:1–21.

184 Ṭabarī, *History*, 7:20. See the explanation of the Muslim historian Sharīf, *Makka*, 424, where he argues that ᶜAbdullāh and his companions acted on their own, in disobedience to Muhammad. The author concludes that this incursion was not supposed to be a fighting campaign, because "Muhammad never initiated an offensive raid" (425).

185 Ṭabarī, *History*, 7:20.

186 Ṭabarī, *History*, 7:20.

187 See ᶜAlī, *Mufaṣṣal*, 10:52, 11:223, 14:49, and especially 16:94–95.

can" (Q 2:217).[188] This literary report clearly links historiographical narratives with the Qur'ān and reflects the exegetical nature of various traditions. The verse serves as a divine acknowledgment that fighting in the sacred month was indeed a grave offense, but the actions of the Meccans against the Muslims, as the verse indicates, were graver and worse offenses.[189] The classical narrators design a historical account to exegete a verse from the Qur'ān.

The verse comforted the Muslims, as it relieved them of the guilt and fear associated with violating the sacred month.[190] Al-Ṭabarī observes that Allah revealed this verse not only to comfort the Muslims but also "in rebuke of the Meccans."[191] With the revelation of this verse, we are told, Muhammad was comforted, and he then decided to take "possession of the caravan and the two prisoners."[192] As for the Meccan captives, the Quraysh reportedly wanted to pay Muhammad to ransom them, but he rejected their offer and demanded the release of his two companions who were being held captive by the Meccans.[193] When the Meccans yielded and sent him the men, Muhammad released the captives and accepted the ransom payment.[194] As for the sacred months, al-Wāqidī reports that Muhammad observed them until Allah revealed *sūrat al-Tawba* (Q 9).[195] Even though he was initially rebuked, based on his leadership in this incursion and what he accomplished, ᶜAbdullāh was given the honorable title *amīr al-mu'minūn* (the Commander of the Believers).[196]

The incursion of ᶜAbdullāh ibn Jaḥsh to Nakhla was a turning point in the Meccan-Medinan combat for at least five reasons. First, the incursion's accounts—as we find in Muslim traditions—reflect that it was the first serious clash between the Muslims and the Meccans in which three new

188 See the discussions of the Muslim scholars Sharīf, *Makka*, 445; Abū Māyla, *Sarāyā*, 100. Both scholars argue that Allah's revelation of the verse was in response to the severe propaganda driven by the Quraysh against the Muslims for the violation of the sacred month.

189 For classical Muslim interpretations of this verse, see Muqātil, *Tafsīr*, 1:184ff.; Ṭabarī, *Jāmiᶜ*, 4:299ff.; Zamakhsharī, *Kashshāf*, 2:211; Rāzī, *Mafātiḥ*, 6:387–389; Qurṭubī, *Jāmiᶜ*, 3:44ff. See Rippin, "Function," 1–20.

190 Haykal, *Ḥayāt*, 263.

191 Ṭabarī, *History*, 7:22; Ṭabarī, *Ta'rīkh*, 1278.

192 Ṭabarī, *History*, 7:20.

193 These were the two men who reportedly ended up staying behind in order to try to find a straying camel. See Ṭabarī, *Ta'rīkh*, 1274; Ṭabarī, *History*, 7:19. They ended up being seized by the Quraysh and were later released in exchange for the Meccan war prisoners. Ṭabarī, *Ta'rīkh*, 1276; Ṭabarī, *History*, 7:21. See Khaṭṭāb, *Rasūl*, 92.

194 Ṭabarī, History, 7:20–21; Wāqidī, *Maghāzī*, 17; Wāqidī, *Life*, 10.

195 Wāqidī, *Maghāzī*, 18; Wāqidī, *Life*, 11.

196 Wāqidī, *Maghāzī*, 19; Wāqidī, *Life*, 11. On this honorific title given to ᶜAbdullāh, see Masᶜūdī, *Tanbīh*, 1:203; Ibn Hajar, *Iṣāba*, 4:32–33.

developments occurred: a Meccan man was killed, two others were taken captive, and a caravan with all of its goods was seized. As argued earlier, this outline should be viewed as a story with a religious message, rather than as documentation of a factual encounter. As a narrative, this incursion changed the balance of power between the Muslims and the Meccans. Now it is obvious that vengeance would escalate and more confrontations would follow. Moreover, from a tactical and military perspective, this was the first successful campaign launched by the Muslims against the Quraysh. It reportedly achieved political and economic results for the growing Muslim community at Medina. This success is probably indebted, at least in part, to the way Muhammad acted in secrecy. He not only sent the warriors via an unexpected route but also concealed news of the incursion, making it known only to his commander through a sealed letter.[197] In all earlier campaigns—whether he led in person or commissioned his companions—the pagan Meccans seem to have gained knowledge of the attack and avoided it.[198] However, from a critical perspective, these literary stories are designed to serve later Muslims who seek religious advice, especially as they aim to imitate the paramount precedent of Muhammad and his earliest companions. In the same vein, up to this point, as we explained earlier, Muhammad relied on *muhājirūn* (Meccan emigrants) as his warriors. He did not begin to rely on the *anṣār* (Medinan supporters) until the Battle of Badr.[199] Based on the understanding that these accounts were designed by later historians under the ᶜAbbāsids, we can assume that a diligent attempt to elevate the value and status of the Meccan Muslims was at play.

Second, the traditions of this incursion highlight that the loyalty of the Muslims appears to have now clearly changed. In the past, they raided in support of their tribes and clans and served the causes of their Meccan people. Now, their loyalty and devotion were both directed to Muhammad and given to Allah's religion. This literary thread is clear throughout the narratives of the early incursions in general. One reads accounts of Muslim soldiers who were ready to fight with no limitations or restrictions and who were even willing, eager, and ready for martyrdom. This is also reflected in the way they were willing to fight during a sacred month, violating the customs of the

[197] Watt, *Muḥammad*, 5–6; also Khaṭṭāb, *Rasūl*, 94; Abū Māyla, *Sarāyā*, 101–102.

[198] See the explanation of Abū Māyla, *Sarāyā*, 102.

[199] See Ibn Hishām, *Sīra*, 1:601; Ibn Ḥibbān, *Thiqāt*, 1:148–149; Ṭabarī, *History*, 7:10; Ṭabarī, *Ta'rīkh*, 1265; Masᶜūdī, *Tanbīh*, 1:200; Jawzī, *Muntaẓim*, 3:80; Ibn Kathīr, *Bidāya*, 3:234. In the early period, Muhammad relied on the Medinan Muslims to protect him only "in their land." Wāqidī, *Life*, 7–8.

day.[200] While the sacred month was an Arabian custom, now their loyalty to Islam—we are invited to believe—was superior.[201] Later Muslim memory, it seems, relied on Muhammad's idealized image and looked back on this *sariyya* to seize an opportunity for a doctrinal message: No matter what tribal commitments or social bonds a Muslim may have, nothing matches or even compares to the devotion and loyalty to Allah and Muhammad, or to giving oneself in battle for martyrdom. Arguably, a lesson of that sort was needed in the age of caliphal expansion, as it exhorted Bedouins to march for wars and give their lives for a higher cause.

Third, the accounts of this incursion indicate that the Muslims were serious about escalating the conflict with the Quraysh. While there are various competing accounts centered on the sacred month and whether it was legitimate to attack the Meccans in it, we should note that Muhammad reportedly commissioned and dispatched the Muslims while knowing it was the month of Rajab, a sacred month.[202] This indicates that Muhammad and the Muslims were adamant about provoking the Meccans.[203] Even the Muslim traditions highlight that Rajab was known as a month when the Arabs put down their weapons, removing the iron parts of their spears and arrows.[204] Instead of putting down their weapons, the Muslims reportedly planned and prepared to intercept a Meccan caravan and ended up killing one Meccan, taking two others captive, and seizing the caravan and its goods. Undoubtedly, one of the possible rationales Muslims may assert was that their cause was legitimate after they were forced to leave their homes in Mecca a year earlier.[205] The logic goes like this: We were expelled from our homes, so now we are not abiding by the tribal rules anymore, not even the Arab custom of preserving the sacred months.

[200] For a contemporary Muslim justification of the violation of the sacred month, see Abū Māyla, *Sarāyā*, 99.

[201] According to al-Ṭabarī, Muhammad is reported to have said in one of his expeditions that *maḥā al-islām al-ᶜuhūd* (Islam erased the treaties [or covenants]). Ṭabarī, *Taʾrīkh*, 1450; Ṭabarī, *History*, 7:158, where it is rendered "Islam has wiped out the old covenants." See Ibrahim, *Stated*, 89.

[202] Ibn Hishām, *Sīra*, 1:601. Some reports place the dispatching of this incursion one month earlier. Ṭabarī, *History*, 7:22.

[203] See Watt, *Muḥammad*, 4, where he studies the early incursions and states, "In all this we may see a deliberate intention on Muhammad's part to provoke the Meccans."

[204] See Bukhārī, *Ṣaḥīḥ*, 5:171; Ṭabarī, *Jāmiᶜ*, 4:300.

[205] This justification is given by several Muslim scholars, including Abū Māyla, *Sarāyā*, 100; Sharīf, *Makka*, 445; Jamīlī, *Ghazawāt*, 26; Khaṭṭāb, *Rasūl*, 92. For a different Muslim perspective, see ᶜAbd al-Karīm, *Qurʾān*, 1:102, where he argues that the lust for possessions was the driving force among the companions.

Fourth, while most Muslim accounts claim that this incursion was fulfilled on the last day of Rajab, al-Ṭabarī provides a drastically different report. He writes that some narrators have actually timed the incursion a month earlier: "Some say it was on the first night of Rajab, and some say it was on the last night of Jumādā [which precedes Rajab] and that the Muslims sheathed their swords when Rajab began."[206] This report is unique, and other Muslim historians have echoed al-Ṭabarī's claim.[207] If this claim is true in any sense, then it is plausible to conclude that the reported dispute among the Muslim warriors—concerning whether they should launch an attack on the last day of Rajab—was an embellishment added later to make the incident look better.[208] If al-Ṭabarī's report is to be accepted, then it suggests that Muslims were purposeful from the start, plotting, intercepting, and attacking the Meccans and their caravan. They had no regard for sacred or protected months. It appears that Muslim historians, in later generations, have resorted to adding some literary features in order to justify the attack. Among these literary features, one may argue, are the confusion about whether the date was in Rajab or already the first day of the following month, Shaᶜbān, as well as the fury of the Muslims and Muhammad in the face of ᶜAbdullāh and the companions upon their return to Medina. An earlier memory seems to have needed adjustments. By creating contradictory reports, any specific particularity is dispersed. Still, we should note that a mere agreement between ample traditions does not make them correct, factual, or reliable.

Fifth, the incursion's accounts commence a recurring pattern that we can trace in Muslim historiography: actions of the believers receive justification and legitimacy through divine revelations.[209] In this incursion, we are told that while the Muslims were aggravated about the violation of the sacred month, Allah revealed the verse (Q 2:217) to comfort the Muslims and rebuke the Meccans.[210] This is a repeated pattern in Islamic traditions. The Muslim author Khalīl ᶜAbd al-Karīm examines various incidents in Muslim

[206] Ṭabarī, *History*, 7:22; Ṭabarī, *Ta'rīkh*, 1278.
[207] See, for instance, Ibn ᶜAbd al-Barr, *Istīᶜāb*, 1:43.
[208] For embellishment in historical writing, see Berg, "ᶜAbbāsid," 13–38; Ibrahim, *Conversion*, 218ff.
[209] See the discussion of ᶜAbd al-Karīm, *Qur'ān*, 1:33–34. In analyzing verses of the Qur'ān, he argues that some verses were revealed to fulfill Muhammad's desires (1:45–155), and others were proclaimed to meet the lustful needs of his *ṣaḥāba* (companions) (1:231–244).
[210] See the justification given by the Muslim scholar Abū Māyla, *Sarāyā*, 100, where he argues that Allah came right on time to comfort the Muslims, because the Meccan pagans and the Medinan Jews were harassing the Muslims about violating the sacred month. For a Muslim argument on how the Medinan Jews were a threat to Muslims, see Sharīf, *Makka*, 433.

historiography and explains how specific verses of the Qur'ān were revealed precisely to fulfill the personal quests and needs of Muhammad, while other verses were revealed to meet the desires of his companions.[211] ᶜAbd al-Karīm studies the incursion of ᶜAbdullāh ibn Jaḥsh to Nakhla as an example of how Allah revealed verses *taḥqīqan li-raghbat al-qā'id* (in fulfillment of the desire of the leader, i.e., Muhammad).[212] Like ᶜAbd al-Karīm, Watt studies this incursion and writes of the violation of the sacred month by the Muslims, arguing that "eventually a revelation justified their action."[213] This pattern can be traced in other episodes in Islamic historiography.[214] While the pattern may indeed reflect the diligent attempts of Muslim historians to establish legitimacy for specific actions and certain incidents, it may also support the scholarly contention that some historical reports were designed to interpret passages in Islam's Scripture. In examining historiographical narratives from Muhammad's *Sīra*, Fred Donner asserts, "There is evidence to support the contention that some reports in the *sīra* literature are of dubious validity and may, in fact, have originated in the need to invent a supported historical context for exegetical readings of particular verses [of the Qur'ān]."[215] He also refers to John Wansbrough, who argued that the traditional accounts of the *sīra* "do not represent an independent body of information that might be used to understand the text of the Qur'ān, but rather were fabricated precisely to explain various verses of the Qur'ān."[216] Indeed, classical Muslim historiographers have arguably served as religious authors and aimed to

211 ᶜAbd al-Karīm, *Qur'ān*, 1:33–34, 1:45–155 (revelations to fulfill Muhammad's own desires), 1:231–244 (verses to meet the needs of the companions). See also Ibrahim, *Stated*, 26. It is understood that ᶜAbd al-Karīm's treatment of the Qur'ān is in total disharmony with traditional Muslim approaches.

212 See ᶜAbd al-Karīm, *Qur'ān*, 1:102.

213 Watt, *Muḥammad*, 5.

214 See Powers, *Zayd*, 34–39, where he studies the revelation of a verse of the Qur'ān in response to "Muḥammad's reaction to Zaynab [as] formulated in the language of human passion and sexual desire" (34) and examines it as a "divine intervention" for the sake of Muhammad. On the same incident, see ᶜAbd al-Karīm, *Qur'ān*, 1:55–62, where he argues that the revelation of the verse of *sūrat al-Aḥzāb* (Q 33:37) "fulfilled the desire of Muhammad" (62). See the recent study of Görke, "Between," 31–63, where he "shows how societal change and different ideologies influenced the interpretation of the story." See also the feminist analysis of the same incident by the Muslim writer ᶜĀ'isha ᶜAbd al-Raḥmān, *Nisā'*, 153–172, where she writes of "a divorce by divine command" in order for a woman, Zaynab, to leave her husband and be given to Muhammad as a wife.

215 Donner, "Historical," in *Cambridge*, ed. McAuliffe, 34. Cf. Cook, *Commanding*, 13–30.

216 See Donner, "Historical," in *Cambridge*, ed. McAuliffe, 33. Donner also concludes, "This comfortable replication of the Islamic tradition's own view of Islamic origins would be perfectly acceptable if it could withstand critical scrutiny." Donner, *Narratives*, 8. For another scholarly example, see Beck, *Evolution*, 1–41, where he studies the historiographical narrative of the Year of the Elephant in its relation to attempts by Muslims to interpret *sūrat al-Fīl* (Q 105) as a difficult passage in the Qur'ān.

emphasize Allah at play to support Muhammad and prosper the Muslim community.

The incursion of ᶜAbdullāh ibn Jaḥsh to Nakhla was a significant development in the Meccan-Medinan struggle. It was arguably the first military success of the Muslims, as they killed one Meccan, took two captives, and seized the Meccan caravan with all of its possessions. Despite its reported violation of the sacred month, this incursion and its results were made legitimate by a divine revelation. The victory seems to have encouraged the Muslims to be bolder and more ready for further confrontations.[217] As the Meccans were reportedly trying to deal with their huge embarrassment and anger, the Muslims were getting ready to intercept another Meccan caravan in what became known as the great Battle of Badr, in which the Muslims reportedly accomplished a huge victory, with Allah's support and intervention.

[217] In explaining the significance of this incursion, al-Ṭabarī writes, "This incident had provoked (a state of) war between the Messenger of God and Quraysh and was the beginning of the fighting in which they inflicted casualties upon one another." Ṭabarī, *History*, 7:29; Ṭabarī, *Ta'rīkh*, 1285.

3

Muhammad's Confrontations with Meccan Pagans

The Battles of Badr and Uḥud

The mark of the angels was turbans that dropped to their shoulders, green, yellow, and red, of light. The wool was in the forelocks of their horses."—Ibn ᶜUmar al-Wāqidī reports the angels appearing to aid the Muslims at the battle of Badr

The Messenger of God's lower lateral incisor was broken, his lip was split, and he was wounded on the cheeks and on the forehead at the roots of his hair.[1]—Ibn Jarīr al-Ṭabarī reports Muhammad's injury after the Muslim defeat at the battle of Uḥud

After Muhammad's early expeditions against the Meccans, the time had come for his first momentous victory at the Battle of Badr. While there were reportedly many confrontations between the Muslims and the Meccan pagans, in this chapter and the next we focus on the five most significant raids: the Battle of Badr, the Battle of Uḥud, the Battle of the Trench, the Battle (and treaty) of Ḥudaybiyya, and the conquest of Mecca.[2] Muhammad led the Muslims in all of them. Muslims achieved a great victory at Badr (2/624) but incurred a humiliating defeat at Uḥud (3/625) to the extent that Muhammad was injured and almost died. The Battle of the Trench (or al-Khandaq), also known as the Battle of the Confederates (or al-Aḥzāb), reportedly took place

[1] Wāqidī, *Life*, 39; Ṭabarī, *History*, 7:120.

[2] Some of the other raids include al-Sawīq (2/624), al-Qarada (3/624), Ḥamrā' al-Asad (3/625), Badr al-Mawᶜid (4/625), and others. These were reportedly important raids, but their significance is not by any means comparable to the major five discussed in these two chapters. Some classical historians do not even mention these minor battles. For example, see the list of Muhammad's raids included by Ibn Ḥabīb, *Muḥabbar*; Khalīfa, *Ta'rīkh*; Yaᶜqūbī, *Ta'rīkh*. For the Mecca-Medina combat, see Sharīf, *Makka*, 433–495.

Muhammad's Military Expeditions. Ayman S. Ibrahim, Oxford University Press. © Oxford University Press 2024.
DOI: 10.1093/oso/9780197769171.003.0003

in 5/627, when the Muslims successfully defeated the Meccans and their allies. The Battle of the Ḥudaybiyya (6/628), though often described as a successful Muslim raid, was actually a strategic treaty, through which the Muslims secured a period of less tension with the Meccans that provided time and space for the Muslims to secure Medina and focus on other enemies. Finally, the conquest of Mecca (8/630) was identified as the greatest of conquests, although it was more of a negotiated surrender of the Meccans to the victorious Muhammad, elevating him as the major leader of the Hijaz. In addition to discussing these five raids, I also highlight various minor raids, in order to examine the development of the Medinan-Meccan combat. In this chapter, we focus on Badr and Uḥud, leaving al-Khandaq, Ḥudaybiyya, and the conquest of Mecca to the following chapter. I do not treat these accounts as a factual record of battles that took place in seventh-century Arabia. Rather, I view them as representations of what Muslim historians narrated about Muhammad's military raids. These *maghāzī* are better viewed as meaningful tales designed by religious scholars to provide Muslims—who lived many generations after the presumed time of the battles—with religious lessons and sociopolitical orientations.

The Battle of Badr (2/624)

Muslim traditions establish the context of how the Battle of Badr started. Labeling it "the greater battle of Badr," al-Ṭabarī writes that it took place between Muhammad and "the unbelievers of Quraysh" in the month of Ramaḍān of the year 2 after the *hijra*.[3] According to al-Wāqidī, Muhammad "watched for the [Meccan] caravan returning from al-Shām [Greater Syria]" and sent some of his companions "to seek information about the caravan."[4] According to al-Masʿūdī, the goods of this caravan were the *sabab* (reason)

[3] Muslim traditions provide different dates, including the seventeenth, eighteenth, or twenty-first of Ramaḍān in the second *hijrī* year, which falls in March 624. See Ṭabarī, *Ta'rīkh*, 1282; Ṭabarī, *History*, 7:26. For Muslim secondary studies on the battle, see Hamidullah, *Battlefields*, 35–73; Ṣallābī, *Sīra*, 391ff.; ʿUmarī, *Sīra*, 354–377. For non-Muslim discussions on Badr, see Watt, *Muḥammad*, 10–14; Ibrahim, *Stated*, 73–79; Ṣaʿīdī, *Tārīkh*, 90–101; Ṣaʿīdī, *Dirāsāt*, 131–135.

[4] Wāqidī, *Maghāzī*, 19; Wāqidī, *Life*, 11. Bilād al-Shām in Muslim historiography refers to Greater Syria, which encompasses areas of today's Lebanon, Syria, Palestine, Egypt, and even sometimes Greece. See Ibn al-Faqīh, *Mukhtaṣar*, 91–93; Yaʿqūbī, *Buldān*, 160ff.; Iṣṭakhrī, *Masālik*, 55ff.; Yaqūt, *Muʿjam*, 3:311–315. See also Webb, "Pre-Islamic al-Shām," 135–164; Hitti, *History of Syria*, 3; Hitti, *Syria*, 1.

for launching this raid.[5] Ibn Hishām explains the backdrop of how the raid began: "The messenger of Allah heard that Abū Sufyān ibn Ḥarb was returning from al-Shām with a huge caravan of the Quraysh that contained *amwāl wa-tijāra min tijāratihim* (money and items they had acquired through their trade), accompanied by some thirty or forty men of the Quraysh."[6] Abū Sufyān was one of the *sādat* (notables) of the Quraysh and a major opponent of Muhammad.[7] He appeared as the central figure in an earlier incursion discussed in the previous chapter; we highlighted how the ᶜAbbāsid-era historians seem to have designed his portrayal—as a major Umayyad notable—to depict the Umayyad rivals as weak Muslims who remained in enmity to Islam for a long time. The narrative supports a religious claim for legitimacy: The Umayyads had fought Muhammad and his family, thus their dominion deserved to be uprooted and replaced by the pious and devoted relatives of Muhammad (the ᶜAbbāsids). Here, too, the narrative advances an important point: the enemies should be fought unceasingly.

We are told that, for the Muslims, "The only object of their expedition at the time was Abū Sufyān and his companions."[8] Al-Ṭabarī describes the caravan and its wealth and indicates that "Abū Sufyan b. Ḥarb came from Syria at the head of nearly seventy horsemen from all the clans of Quraysh. They had been trading in Syria and they all came together with their money and their merchandise."[9] This was a great opportunity for the Muslims, as Ibn Hishām writes that Muhammad summoned the companions and said,

[5] Masᶜūdī, *Tanbīh*, 203. On al-Masᶜūdī, see ᶜAẓmah, *Masᶜūdī*. Similarly, al-Wāqidī affirms that the Muslims "had set out for the caravan." Wāqidī, *Maghāzī*, 21; Wāqidī, *Life*, 12. Al-Ṭabarī writes that Muslims "did not suppose that there would be a great battle." Ṭabarī, *Ta'rīkh*, 1285; Ṭabarī, *History*, 7:29.

[6] See Ibn Hishām, *Sīra*, 1:606; Ibn Hishām, *Life*, 289. See also Wāqidī, *Maghāzī*, 27 (the caravan contained all that the Quraysh owned); Mūsā ibn ᶜUqba, *Maghāzī*, 122–124; Abū Zurᶜa, *Ta'rīkh*, 162–167; Yaᶜqūbī, *Ta'rīkh*, 2:45. Al-Ṭabarī indicates that the Quraysh had *amwālahum wa-tijāratahum* (their possessions and merchandise). Ṭabarī, *Ta'rīkh*, 1285; Ṭabarī, *History*, 7:29.

[7] Abū Sufyān was also the leader of an earlier expedition, the incursion of ᶜUbayda ibn al-Ḥārith, which we discussed in the previous chapter. On Abū Sufyān, see Khalīfa, *Ta'rīkh*, 1:166; Khalīfa, *Ṭabaqāt*, 39; Ibn Qutayba, *Maᶜārif*, 73–74, 136, 344–345; Fasawī, *Maᶜrifa*, 3:167; Dhahabī, *Ta'rīkh*, 3:368ff.; Dhahabī, *Siyar*, 2:105ff.; Ibn Abī Ḥātim, *Jurh*, 4:426; Ibn ᶜAbd al-Barr, *Istīᶜāb*, 2:714; Ibn ᶜAsākir, *Ta'rīkh*, 23:421ff.; Ibn al-Athīr, *Usd*, 3:9; Ibn Hajar, *Iṣāba*, 3:332. For secondary studies, see Watt, "Abū Sufyān," *EI²*, 1:151; ᶜAlī, *Mufaṣṣal*, 7:110ff.; Dangar, *Career*. The enmity between Muhammad and Abū Sufyān reportedly goes back to the conflict between the Hāshimites and the Umayyads. See Maqrīzī, *Nizāᶜ*, 37–59. See also Hibri, *Abbasid*, 28ff., where he explores "The Roots of Umayyad-Hashimite Rivalry."

[8] Ṭabarī, *Ta'rīkh*, 1286; Ṭabarī, *History*, 7:30.

[9] Ṭabarī, *Ta'rīkh*, 1285; Ṭabarī, *History*, 7:29. Unlike camels, horses are not *normally* suitable for crossing deserts. See Crone, *Slaves*, 22–23, where she writes, "Ecologically, the deprivation of the desert is extreme: sheep and goats can be reared only along the edges, but in the interior only camels can subsist." She also states, "Horses in the desert are as great a luxury as tomatoes in the Negev" (220).

"This is the caravan of the Quraysh, containing their properties *fa-khrujū ilayhā laᶜall Allāh yanfulukumūh* (so, march out to raid it, hopefully Allah would give it to you as spoils)."[10] The caravan reportedly had a thousand camels and was worth fifty thousand dinars.[11] To exhort the Muslims, Muhammad emphasized *mā maᶜahum min al-amwāl* (that which [the Meccans] possessed of wealth) and *qillat ᶜadadihim* (their scarce number of people).[12] He declared, "Here Mecca has flung its dearest flesh and blood to you."[13] The focus on the abundance of wealth in the caravan—as a literary report—deserves close attention. Classical narrators appear to be overly occupied with the abundance of wealth that Muhammad and the Muslims were seeking to seize. These storytellers were not, for instance, describing the religious proclamation of Islam or the defense of Muslim lands against Qurashite attackers as the reason for the raid. Rather, for classical narrators, a portrayal of believers who were driven by vengeance to seize an abundance of wealth was a satisfactory justification for launching the attack. Undoubtedly, this portrayal may not fit into the religious discourse of modern times—but it appeased the medieval generations as a religious exhortation in times of conquest.

However, according to various traditions, many Muslims showed reluctance to march for the attack. Muhammad kept "commanding them and urging them and increasing their desire regarding the reward that was to come," but they held him back, as they "hated his going out raiding and there were many words of dispute about it."[14] Among these Muslims, many were reportedly confused, as they "thought that [an] apostle of Allah will not create a war."[15] Others were concerned, as they believed that a messenger

[10] Ibn Hishām, *Sīra*, 1:606–607; Ibn Hishām, *Life*, 289. See also Ṭabarī, *Ta'rīkh*, 1285, 1292; Mūsā ibn ᶜUqba, *Maghāzī*, 122; Ibn Qutayba, *Maᶜārif*, 152–158; Kalāᶜī, *Iktifā'*, 1:324. According to Wāqidī, *Life*, 12, Muhammad said, "This caravan of the Quraysh holds their wealth, and perhaps God will grant it to you as plunder."

[11] Wāqidī, *Maghāzī*, 200; Wāqidī, *Life*, 100. Watt, *Muḥammad*, 10.

[12] Ṭabarī, *Ta'rīkh*, 1285; Ṭabarī, *History*, 7:29. Traditions provide contradicting numbers for the warriors. For example, Ibn Qutayba states that the pagans were 950, while the Muslims were a little over 300. See Ibn Qutayba, *Maᶜārif*, 152; Masᶜūdī, *Tanbīh*, 203–205; cf. Ṭabarī, *Ta'rīkh*, 1296–1297. In a unique report, al-Kharkūshī states that Abū Sufyān had 90 men with him in the caravan. Kharkūshī, *Sharaf*, 3:11. Other reports state the number was "some thirty or forty men of the Quraysh." Ibn Hishām, *Life*, 289; Wāqidī, *Maghāzī*, 27.

[13] Ṭabarī, *Ta'rīkh*, 1305; Ṭabarī, *History*, 7:44. See also Ibn Hishām, *Sīra*, 1:617, where it reads, "This is Mecca *qad alqat ilaykum aflādh kabidihā* (have given you her precious life, literally 'her inner, and most valuable, liver')." Wāqidī, *Maghāzī*, 53.

[14] Wāqidī, *Life*, 31, 12, respectively. See Wāqidī, *Maghāzī*, 58 and 20.

[15] Ibn Hishām, *Sīra*, 1:607; Ibn Hishām, *Life*, 289. Perhaps the reluctance was also due to the notion that these Muslims would have to fight their own Meccan relatives. See Dhahabī, *Ta'rīkh*, 2:50ff. See a similar account in Kalāᶜī, *Iktifā'*, 1:324. About relatives fighting each other, see also Ṭabarī, *Ta'rīkh*, 1290; Ṭabarī, *History*, 7:33.

of Allah "would not take any booty."[16] These literary details are important. While many Muslims—past and present—may have sought to portray Muhammad as a prophet marching into battles to proclaim Islam, these literary descriptions demonstrate otherwise.[17] They reflect that Muhammad—at least in this battle—was not launching this battle as Allah's prophet, but as a tribal leader seeking resources and power. Just as the case would be in our day, Muslim warriors—we are told—frowned upon the notion of a prophet initiating war or plundering; however, Muhammad is depicted as an astute warrior who seems to have realized he could not let this chance be lost. While we cannot be certain of the historicity of these details, this picture obviously appealed to ᶜAbbāsid-era historians, despite creating challenges for later generations.

Still, some Muslims were swift and hastened to join the expedition.[18] Traditions indicate that spies, from both sides, were everywhere.[19] When Abū Sufyān heard of the Muslim preparation to attack his caravan, he strongly desired to avoid the fight: he changed his caravan route to head home, sent a message to the Meccans, and sought reinforcements.[20] The Meccans were reportedly greatly concerned about the imminent attack, fearing for their merchandise and people and diligently attempting to thwart the scheme.[21] The Muslims, on the other hand, appeared to have realized the strategic opportunity laying before them to humiliate the Meccans, seize the caravan, and accomplish a significant victory.[22] While Abū Sufyān was reportedly able to take a different route, traveling adjacent to the Red Sea and thus avoiding the Muslims, the precursors of the battle had already started, because the Meccan elites reportedly prepared enforcements, sending them to aid the caravan and face the Muslims. The reinforcements raised the number of

[16] See Ṭabarī, *Ta'rīkh*, 1292; Ṭabarī, *History*, 7:35. See ᶜUmarī, *Sīra*, 357–358.

[17] Still, see the Sunnī Muslim view of Ṣallābī, *Ghazawāt*, 92, where he claims that the Meccan pagans attempted "to destroy Islam" and spent ample resources to prevent people from accepting the religion.

[18] Wāqidī, *Maghāzī*, 20; Wāqidī, *Life*, 12, where we read that "Some men were even prepared to draw lots against their fathers" in order to join the raid. See also Ṭabarī, *Ta'rīkh*, 1286–1288.

[19] Wāqidī, *Maghāzī*, 19–20; Wāqidī, *Life*, 12. Ibn Hishām, *Sīra*, 1:617–618; Kalāᶜī, *Iktifā'*, 1:324.

[20] See Ṭabarī, *Ta'rīkh*, 1285; Yaᶜqūbī, *Ta'rīkh*, 2:45; Mūsā ibn ᶜUqba, *Maghāzī*, 123 (seeking reinforcement); Ibn Hishām, *Sīra*, 1:618–619. On the reinforcement, see Watt, *Muḥammad*, 10.

[21] According to Ṭabarī, *History*, 7:35, "Abū Sufyān had been seeking information and questioning the riders whom he met as he approached Hijāz, being fearful for his people's wealth." Wāqidī, *Maghāzī*, 19–20.

[22] Wāqidī, *Maghāzī*, 20. Al-Ṭabarī writes it this way: "This is the caravan of Quraysh, containing their wealth; so go out against it, and it is to be hoped that God will give it to you as booty." Ṭabarī, *History*, 7:35.

the pagan Meccans to one thousand or a little less.[23] The story here appears to aim to amplify both the hegemony of Islam and Muslims and the cowardice of Abū Sufyān and the pagans. However, the portrayal appears significantly exaggerated, as it is hard to believe that in less than two years, the astute Meccan elites—who had accumulated power, reputation, and experience for years—floundered and fled from a small group of men whom they forced into exile months earlier. We can trace a *perplexing* and *unconvincing* shift in Muhammad's depiction between Mecca and Medina: At Mecca, he was vulnerable, persecuted, and mainly preaching Islam to his people and relatives. Then suddenly we are invited to believe that, once he emigrated to Medina, he became a tribal leader among the inhabitants of Medina who had lived and flourished in the city for generations; they welcomed him, and he promptly became their commander. At Mecca, he was known as *zāhid* (an ascetic), uninterested in worldly possessions or matters and mainly concerned with preaching to his own people. Then, the tradition indicates, Muhammad rapidly became an astute warrior—an interceptor of caravans for the purpose of seizing wealth from other Arabs, thus destroying their livelihood. This sudden change in his portrayal seems at best unconvincing and at worst tendentious. It encourages skepticism toward the sources' reliability and validity and reemphasizes the contention that these tales *represent* ideological preferences rather than factual encounters.

In preparation for the attack, "The Prophet marched forward and spent the night near Badr."[24] The location of Badr was a well of water.[25] Muhammad and his companions reached Badr early and stationed themselves near the water well in order to lay in wait for the Meccans—an act that provided them the element of surprise, as Muhammad affirmed, "This is where you will fight."[26] The number of Muslims was a little over three hundred,[27] which was

[23] The Meccan elites were reportedly led by Abū Jahl, one of the most hostile enemies of Muhammad. Ṭabarī, *Ta'rīkh*, 1285; Ṭabarī, *History*, 7:29, 7:33; Ibn Qutayba, *Maᶜārif*, 152; Masᶜūdī, *Tanbīh*, 203–205; Dhahabī, *Ta'rīkh*, 2:78. See Jamīlī, *Ghazawāt*, 1:28; Ṣallābī, *Sīra*, 394; ᶜUmarī, *Sīra*, 356–357. Watt, *Muḥammad*, 10.

[24] Ṭabarī, *Ta'rīkh*, 1286; Ṭabarī, *History*, 7:30.

[25] On Badr and its location in Arabia, see Hamdānī, *Ṣifat*, 1:185; Hamadānī, *Amākin*, 111 (a famous place of water located between Mecca and Medina); Bakrī, *Muᶜjam*, 1:231–232 (it is a water well); Zamakhsharī, *Jibāl*, 185; Yāqūt, *Muᶜjam*, 1:357–358; Samhūdī, *Wafā'*, 4:26; Balādī, *Muᶜjam*, 41–42.

[26] Ṭabarī, *Ta'rīkh*, 1288; also Ṭabarī, *History*, 7:31, where it reads, the Meccans "found that the Prophet had reached Badr before them and occupied it."

[27] See Wāqidī, *Maghāzī*, 23 (precisely 305, although 8 Muslims withdrew before the battle started), 319; Wāqidī, *Life*, 154; Ṭabarī, *Ta'rīkh*, 1269–1299; Ṭabarī, *History*, 7:38–40; Yaᶜqūbī, *Ta'rīkh*, 2:46; Bayhaqī, *Dalā'il*, 3:36–37; Ibn ᶜAbd al-Barr, *al-Durar*, 1:105; Ibn Qutayba, *Maᶜārif*, 1:152 (the Meccans were 950); Masᶜūdī, *Tanbīh*, 1:204; Dhahabī, *Ta'rīkh*, 2:78. See Jamīlī, *Ghazawāt*, 1:28; also ᶜUmarī, *Sīra*, 354, where he writes that about one-third of the group was from the *muhājirūn* (Meccan emigrants), while the rest were from the *anṣār* (Medinan supporters). Note that the *anṣār*,

the largest number of warriors they could gather up to this point.[28] In what proved to be strategic in the battle, Ḥubāb ibn al-Mundhir, a Medinan Muslim and companion of Muhammad, gave him two pieces of advice. Ḥubāb asked Muhammad whether the location he chose was determined by a divine revelation or a human choice. When Muhammad declared that the choice was not divine but "a matter of judgment, tactics and stratagem," Ḥubāb told Muhammad, "This is not the proper position for you."[29] Accordingly, the Muslims moved a little toward a higher hill to control the Meccans from a stronger location.[30] This literary detail is crucial, as it demonstrates Muhammad's human limitations. It reflects that his supposed prophetic abilities did not serve him in this situation. He is here as a tribal leader, not a preaching prophet. Even though Muslim historians served as religious scholars, their portrayals of Muhammad, at times, fail to ascribe him prophetic abilities and instead allow for other humans—like Ḥubāb in this tale—to outsmart him and provide him needed counsel.[31] Moreover, Ḥubāb advised Muhammad to contaminate all of the water wells—except one, from which the Muslims would drink—in order to leave the Meccans at a great disadvantage with no water: "We will fight the enemy [the Meccans] and have water to drink while they do not."[32] This was reportedly strategic and exhausted the Meccans.[33] The higher location and the contamination of water were significant steps toward the Muslim victory. These literary details highlight major *natural* advantages for the Muslim camp. Furthermore, on the night of the battle, there was reportedly a heavy rainfall that made it difficult for the Quraysh "to set off" when the battle

in the Second ᶜAqba Pledge, reportedly promised to support Muhammad only within Medina. This is likely why he did not rely on them in earlier incursions. Now they are a major actor in the battles. See ᶜUmarī, *Sīra*, 358. On the number of Muslims being the highest in contrast to earlier incursions, see Watt, *Muḥammad*, 10–11.

28 Still the number is arguably exaggerated. See Shoemaker, *Creating*, 98.

29 Ṭabarī, *Taʾrīkh*, 1309; Ṭabarī, *History*, 7:47; Wāqidī, *Maghāzī*, 53. For a secondary study on this advice, see Ṣallābī, *Sīra*, 397. On Ḥubāb and his strategic advice to Muhammad, see Ibn Saᶜd, *Ṭabaqāt*, 2:114 (he was from the Khazraj clan in Medina), 3:135 (he resisted Abū Bakr's appointment as caliph), 3:427 (his strategic advice of contaminating the water); Ibn Ḥibbān, *Thiqāt*, 1:161–162 (his advising Muhammad to change the location and contaminate the water); Dāraquṭnī, *Muʾtalif*, 1:475; Abū Nuᶜaym al-Iṣfahānī, *Maᶜrifat*, 2:867 (he was thirty-three years old at Badr); Ibn ᶜAbd al-Barr, *Istīᶜāb*, 1:316 (the Angel Gabriel told Muhammad to listen to Ḥubāb); Khaṭīb, *Taʾrīkh*, 16:263; Ibn al-Athīr, *Usd*, 1:665; Ṣafadī, *Wāfī*, 14:35; Balādhurī, *Ansāb*, 1:590. See also Ziriklī, *Aᶜlām*, 2:163; ᶜAbd al-Raḥmān, *Judhūr*, 97.

30 Ṭabarī, *Taʾrīkh*, 1308; Ṭabarī, *History*, 7:47.

31 Later Muslim traditionists began to censor accounts that depicted Muhammad as having limitations or weaknesses. See Ahmed, *Before*, 268–269; Ahmed, "Satanic Verses," *EQ*, 4:531ff.

32 Ṭabarī, *History*, 7:47; Ṭabarī, *Taʾrīkh*, 1309.

33 See the natural factors for the Muslim victory as discussed in Ibrahim, *Stated*, 77–78. Muhammad reportedly commended Ḥubāb, saying, "You have given judicious advice." Ṭabarī, *History*, 7:47.

started.[34] While the rainfall may appear to some as an act of nature, Muslim historians attribute it to Allah's intervention: "God had sent rain, and the wadi-bed [where the Quraysh camped] was soft."[35] The classical narrative is shaped by indications of both divine elements and natural advantages in support of the Muslims. Immediately before the battle started, the Meccans were reportedly about one thousand warriors (i.e., three times more than the Muslim forces).[36] Nonetheless, in an unrealistic claim, the Meccans—we are told—realized their great disadvantage, and some advised their fellows to withdraw; they were terrified and described the Muslims as "people who are determined to fight to the death."[37] We are told that Muhammad's battle cry was *yā manṣūr amit amit* (O victorious, kill, kill).[38] Here we encounter once more what appear as exaggerated literary devices aiming to depict the Meccans—despite their surpassing number of soldiers—as weak and cowardly, thus magnifying Muslim courage and reflecting divine favor. These devices serve as religious lessons for the faithful.

The fighting started with individual *mubārazāt* (fencing), followed by the use of *nibāl* (bows), then the two armies clashed.[39] In summarizing the battle and the Muslims' victory, al-Ṭabarī writes, "The Meccan force and the Prophet met and God gave victory to His Messenger, shamed the leaders of the unbelievers, and satisfied the Muslims' thirst for revenge on them."[40] This "was the first raid in which God strengthened Islam and humbled the disbelievers."[41] Here is an excellent example of how Muslim storytellers—mostly scholars of *ḥadīth*—served as religious narrators, authoring stories for ideological purposes. No matter what may have caused the victory, we are invited to believe that Allah intervened and the Muslims won.

Since the historians basically *formed* their own narratives, we encounter various literary contradictions in the accounts. Some traditions

34 Ṭabarī, *History*, 7:47; Ṭabarī, *Ta'rīkh*, 1308; Wāqidī, *Maghāzī*, 51–54.

35 Ṭabarī, *Ta'rīkh*, 1308; Ṭabarī, *History*, 7:47. On the effect of the rainfall, see Ṣallābī, *Sīra*, 403.

36 In describing the number of the Meccans in the battle, al-Ṭabarī states, "There are between nine hundred and a thousand of them," or in another report, "The force of Quraysh on that day was, in fact, nine hundred and fifty." See Ṭabarī, *Ta'rīkh*, 1287–1288; Ṭabarī, *History*, 7:31. Similarly, see Yaᶜqūbī, *Ta'rīkh*, 2:45.

37 Ṭabarī, *Ta'rīkh*, 1290; Ṭabarī, *History*, 7:33. Wāqidī, *Maghāzī*, 37.

38 Wāqidī, *Maghāzī*, 72; Wāqidī, *Life*, 37. According to Ibn Hishām, this was the same slogan in two other battles, Khaybar and Banū al-Muṣṭaliq. Ibn Hishām, *Sīra*, 2:294, 2:333. Other Muslims used the same slogan in later battles. See Isfahānī, *Maqātil*, 1:133–134. Dhahabī, *Ta'rīkh*, 5:413.

39 Ṭabarī, *History*, 7:52–61. See ᶜUmarī, *Sīra*, 363. According to Watt, "There seems to have been a series of single combats between champions, the normal prelude to Arab set battles." Watt, *Muḥammad*, 12.

40 Ṭabarī, *History*, 7:32; Ṭabarī, *Ta'rīkh*, 1288.

41 Wāqidī, *Life*, 13; Wāqidī, *Maghāzī*, 21.

to the Muslims. Although the Muslims in the battle presumably killed many of the notable Meccans, the narrators redirect our thinking—it was not the Muslims, but instead Allah, who killed the Meccan chiefs. Much in these stories is not meant to record "what actually happened," but to present the storytellers' opinions, thoughts, and beliefs for later generations.[59]

Concerning the booty at Badr, some narrators highlight that there was little besides the wealth of the caravan, which made the Muslims quarrel among themselves, until Allah revealed a Qur'ānic verse to settle the matter.[60] Still, Muhammad, based on a divine revelation, "received the fifth from the first plunder of Badr."[61] Before any of the booty was apportioned, there was a *ṣafiyy min al-ghanīma* (a specific portion of it) given to Muhammad.[62] As for the remaining part, Muhammad divided it equally between the soldiers who participated at Badr.[63] In describing the spoils, al-Wāqidī writes, "When the plunder was collected, there were camels, leather mats, and clothing included."[64] It is not surprising that the narratives place considerable emphasis on *seizing* and *distributing* the spoils after the battle. Despite the traditional tendency to portray these raids as fighting *fī sabīl Allāh* (in Allah's path), we should not forget that these Muslims were reportedly tribal warriors who previously launched attacks against other Bedouins and often sought to seize possessions and wealth.[65] It is only now, we are invited to believe, that they possess a higher cause. However, from a critical perspective, their belief in Islam had merely added a religious dimension to their raiding practices—without bringing them to a stop. They previously fought in order to obtain spoils and seize captives, but now they march for the same raids and seek the same gains while claiming to do so for Allah and his apostle. This added a theological layer: if they die, they become martyrs who are promised Paradise, with all that a Bedouin man desires. Islam, here, appears to serve as a glue that unifies the soldiers in contrast to their old loyalties.

59 Rippin, "Literary," 156.

60 Wāqidī, *Maghāzī*, 98; Wāqidī, *Life*, 50. According to al-Ṭabarī, a Muslim solider reported that *Sūrat al-anfāl* (Q 8) "was revealed concerning us, the participants in the battle of Badr, when we disagreed about the booty and became very bad-tempered about it. God removed it from our hands and handed it over to his Messenger, and the Messenger of God divided it equally among the Muslims. In this matter there can be seen fear of God, obedience to his Messenger, and the settling of differences." Ṭabarī, *History*, 7:64; Ṭabarī, *Ta'rīkh*, 1334.

61 Wāqidī, *Life*, 50; Wāqidī, *Maghāzī*, 99.

62 Wāqidī, *Maghāzī*, 103; Wāqidī, *Life*, 52.

63 Watt, *Muḥammad*, 12.

64 Wāqidī, *Life*, 51; Wāqidī, *Maghāzī*, 100.

65 For the practice of raiding among the Arabs before Islam, see Hoyland, *God's Path*, 56ff.; ᶜAlī, *Mufaṣṣal*, 10:5–140; 7:142–414.

The killed and the captives at Badr were plenty. According to traditions, there were only fourteen "martyrs" among the Muslims.[66] As for the unbelievers of Mecca, we are told that the Muslims "killed seventy of them and took seventy of them captive."[67] While the numbers appear greatly exaggerated, especially if we consider the claim that the Meccans were triple the size of the Muslims, the narrators emphasize a religious disposition: only the Muslims who are killed are identified as "martyrs"—the others are merely murdered. This literary dimension idealizes believers over nonbelievers. The killed and the captives among the Meccans were for the most part relatives of the Muslims—"fathers, sons, brothers, uncles, and sons of uncles."[68] Some may be appalled at how Muslims were willing to kill their own relatives. However, we should reemphasize that these are merely fashioned tales, not factual records, designed by narrators for religious and political purposes. In a sense, one lesson for later Muslims to glean might be that the new commitment of the Muslims had replaced their earlier loyalty. This is explained in a statement by a Muslim solider who declared, *qaṭaᶜa al-islām al-ᶜuhūd* (Islam broke [my previous] covenants).[69] This was evident in the reported treatment of the dead and the captives among the Meccans—a topic discussed in detail in many traditions. Regarding the dead, we are told that the dead Meccans were thrown in *al-qalīb* (a deep well used as a garbage hole) based on Muhammad's instructions.[70] This treatment, as a literary device, may appear inhumane to modern eyes, but the narratives seem to contrast the value and worth of the believing soldiers to that of the unbelieving pagans. The contrast aims to provide a figurative image: The Muslim soldiers were Allah's warriors. They were divine instruments, designated to bring punishment on unbelievers who openly rejected Muhammad and his message.

As for the prisoners, there was a disagreement among the Muslims as to what they should do with them. The narratives advance crucial literary

[66] Ṭabarī, *Ta'rīkh*, 1358; Ṭabarī, *History*, 7:83. Wāqidī, *Maghāzī*, 102; Wāqidī, *Life*, 52. Yaᶜqūbī, *Ta'rīkh*, 2:46.

[67] Ṭabarī, *Ta'rīkh*, 1290, 1354; Ṭabarī, *History*, 7:34, 81. Ibn Hishām, *Sīra*, 1:714. Yaᶜqūbī, *Ta'rīkh*, 2:46.

[68] Wāqidī, *Maghāzī*, 108; Wāqidī, *Life*, 54. Abū Bakr reportedly told Muhammad, "These people are cousins, fellow clansmen and nephews." Ṭabarī, *History*, 7:81; Ṭabarī, *Ta'rīkh*, 1355.

[69] Wāqidī, *Maghāzī*, 107; Wāqidī, *Life*, 54. The same statement was given by Muhammad when he expelled Banū al-Naḍīr from Medina, as he reportedly declared, *maḥā al-Islām al-ᶜuhūd* (Islam erased the covenants). Ṭabarī, *Ta'rīkh*, 1450. Al-Wāqidī provides a similar report—attributed to Muhammad—in the expedition to Banū Qaynuqāᶜ (*Maghāzī*, 179) and in the one to Banū al-Naḍīr (*Maghāzī*, 375).

[70] Ṭabarī, *Ta'rīkh*, 1331; Ṭabarī, *History*, 7:62. See Ibrahim, *Stated*, 78–79. See the competing comments on *al-qalīb* by the Muslim scholars Qimanī, *Ḥizb*, 121; Haykal, *Ḥayāt*, 280.

elements for the ᶜAbbāsid claims of legitimacy. A companion of Muhammad insisted on killing the prisoners and declared, "This was the first defeat inflicted by God on the polytheists, and killing the prisoners would have been more pleasing to me than sparing them."[71] ᶜUmar ibn al-Khaṭṭāb also urged the killing of the captives.[72] Muhammad was reluctant to follow this opinion because he realized that some of his relatives were prisoners. We are told that a Medinan man captured Muhammad's paternal uncle al-ᶜAbbās and brought him to Muhammad.[73] This account arguably caused embarrassment for the ᶜAbbāsids, as al-ᶜAbbās is a significantly important figure to them: he serves as their progenitor. The ᶜAbbāsid-era narrators had to adjust the narrative.[74] As I argued in a previous publication, "This picture—of a late convert, a prisoner at Badr, and a ransomed captive—portrays him negatively. This depiction was unacceptable within a pro-ᶜAbbāsid paradigm. Consequently, the ᶜAbbāsid-era writers had to rehabilitate al-ᶜAbbās's image by adjusting his conversion anecdote through the addition or suppression of literary features."[75] The examination of various accounts of al-ᶜAbbās and his participation at Badr suggests that Umayyad narrators were not largely concerned with his portrayal; they placed him as a late convert, an unbeliever who fought against the Muslims at Badr and was taken captive. However, the early ᶜAbbāsid-era historians "developed an excuse for al-ᶜAbbās's late conversion," and later historians "complemented this depiction in ways which served the ᶜAbbāsid ideology."[76] Here, once again, we find that Muslim narrators were *authors* who shaped their stories to advance their religious inclinations and sociopolitical sympathies. This is evident in how Muhammad reportedly

[71] Ṭabarī, *Ta'rīkh*, 1323; Ṭabarī, *History*, 7:56. In another report, a companion told Muhammad, "It is the first battle in which we encounter the polytheists. I would love for Allah to humiliate them, and that they would be massacred." Wāqidī, *Life*, 53; Wāqidī, *Maghāzī*, 106.

[72] Wāqidī, *Maghāzī*, 105; Wāqidī, *Life*, 53. ᶜUmar was reportedly strongly demanding the killing of the captives. He asked Muhammad, "What are you waiting for? Cut off their heads and God will put them down with Islam, and humiliate the people of polytheism. They are the enemies of God. They did not believe in you, and they fought you and exiled you!" Wāqidī, *Life*, 55.

[73] Ṭabarī, *Ta'rīkh*, 1290; Ṭabarī, *History*, 7:34. Compare with a positive report on al-ᶜAbbās in Yaᶜqūbī, *Ta'rīkh*, 2:45–46. This matter is of a high importance in Islamic historiography, as the portrayal of al-ᶜAbbās was crucial to the ᶜAbbāsids, under whom these accounts were documented. See Ibrahim, *Conversion*, 218–223. Berg writes, "What is clear is that [al- ᶜAbbās's participation at Badr] was a source of embarrassment and several ᶜAbbāsid era historians made a concerted effort to mitigate or obviate that embarrassment." Berg, "ᶜAbbāsid," 13–38 (quote from 36); Sellheim, "Prophet," 49–73; Wansbrough, *Qur'ānic*, 58. For primary sources on al-ᶜAbbās, see Balādhurī, *Ansāb*, 4:1–22; Ibn Saᶜd, *Ṭabaqāt*, 4:3ff.; Khalīfa, *Ta'rīkh*, 1:86, 168; Khalīfa, *Ṭabaqāt*, 29; Ibn Qutayba, *Maᶜārif*, 374; Fasawī, *Maᶜrifa*, 1:493ff.; Dhahabī, *Ta'rīkh*, 3:373ff.; Dhahabī, *Siyar*, 2:78ff.; Ibn ᶜAbd al-Barr, *Istīᶜāb*, 2:810ff.; Ibn ᶜAsākir, *Ta'rīkh*, 26:273ff.; Ibn al-Athīr, *Usd*, 3:163; Ibn Hajar, *Iṣāba*, 3:511.

[74] See the discussion at Hibri, *Parable*, 8.

[75] Ibrahim, *Conversion*, 218. See Brown, *Muhammad*, 87. Watt, "al-ᶜAbbās," *EI*², 1:9.

[76] Ibrahim, *Conversion*, 218.

provided an excuse for some of his family members, and stated, "I know that some of the Banū Hāshim and others have been forced to march against us against their will."[77] Some Muslims were of the opinion to accept a ransom for the captives, while others insisted on cutting off their heads.[78] Of course, killing prisoners would have a negative financial incentive: the captor would not gain any ransom money.[79] Eventually, Muhammad reportedly instructed different treatments of the captives—some were pardoned, some were freed in return for a ransom, and others were killed.[80] For the Muslim storytellers, these differences in treatment seem to convey a religious lesson: this is not partiality but wisdom from the leader who sees things with discernment and in a fuller way. Al-Ṭabarī reports that as a result of the Muslim victory, some Arabs embraced Islam, as they realized the growing power of the Muslim community.[81] In this report, al-Ṭabarī is a religious traditionist par excellence—he never relinquishes his right to bring forth his religious sentiment to the tale he is designing.[82] We are also told that the people of the Quraysh were in total shock and complete disarray after their severe humiliation. Abū Sufyān reportedly forbade mourning and wailing over the dead people until the Meccans could exact their revenge.[83]

Such, at least, is the general tradition of the Battle of Badr given by major historiographical sources. Since Badr was reportedly the first major victory for the Muslims, it is understandable that there are ample reports about it. In analyzing Muslim accounts, I offer four critical observations regarding the reported Muslim victory.

First, while we cannot place too much confidence in the details of the Battle of Badr as given in historiographical accounts, we can say that the literary accounts paint a remarkable victory for the Muslims. The narratives portray

[77] Ṭabarī, *Ta'rīkh*, 1323; Ṭabarī, *History*, 7:56. See ᶜUmarī, *Sīra*, 367.

[78] Ṭabarī, *Ta'rīkh*, 1355; Ṭabarī, *History*, 7:81. ᶜUmar wanted each captive to be killed by the captive's brother. He suggested that Muhammad "should hand Ḥamzah's brother over to him so that he can cut off his head, and that [Muhammad] should hand over ᶜAqīl to ᶜAlī (his brother) so that he can cut off his head." Traditions highlight that the Angel Gabriel gave the Muslims "a choice regarding the captives: between cutting off their heads or taking a ransom from them." Wāqidī, *Life*, 54; Wāqidī, *Maghāzī*, 107.

[79] Watt, *Muḥammad*, 13.

[80] Ṭabarī, *Ta'rīkh*, 1354–1359; Ṭabarī, *History*, 7:80–85. For the various ways the prisoners were treated, see Watt, *Muḥammad*, 13. In particular, Muhammad instructed the killing of two captives: ᶜUqba ibn Abī Muᶜayṭ and al-Naḍr ibn al-Ḥārith. Ṭabarī, *Ta'rīkh*, 1336; Ṭabarī, *History*, 7:65–66. See ᶜUmarī, *Sīra*, 370. Watt comments, "One or two of the prisoners were treated with the harshness and ferocity which were probably not unusual among the Arabs of that age." Watt, *Muḥammad*, 12.

[81] See the conversion examples of Abū al-ᶜĀṣ and ᶜUmayr ibn Wahb. Ṭabarī, *Ta'rīkh*, 1350–1354.

[82] See Petersen, *ᶜAlī*, 17.

[83] Watt, *Muḥammad*, 19.

Muhammad as having had the lead in planning and obtaining news about the enemy. He succeeded in surprising the Meccans and thus had a tactical advantage.[84] The location that the Muslims chose for stationing—thanks to Ḥubāb's suggestion—gave them a huge element of surprise against the Meccans.[85] This location offered the Muslims another advantage: they were at the top of a hill, and because the ground was muddy due to heavy overnight rain, the Meccans were "not able to march on it."[86] We should also note that in addition to these *natural* reasons, the Meccans were reportedly in disarray. The Meccan aristocrat Abū Jahl was the leading figure in preparing the reinforcements to assist Abū Sufyān. While the reinforcements *initially* consisted of about 950 Meccans, it appears that many of them—especially those from Muhammad's family of Banū Hāshim—were not wholeheartedly with Abū Sufyān against Muhammad.[87] This literary detail might provide a reason why Muhammad was reportedly reluctant to execute some captives—they included some of his immediate relatives. In fact, some sources describe hundreds of them withdrawing immediately before marching to Badr.[88] This was the opposite case among the Muslims, who were reportedly unified and enthusiastic about the prospect of getting revenge and securing the caravan. Thus, the entire narrative, which insists on a divinely given triumph, suggests various natural reasons for the inevitable victory of the Muslims. This is probably what some scholars identify—in their critique of the random work of the narrators—as a product that is "strikingly devoid of overall unity."[89]

Second, Muslim historians seem to have insisted on depicting the victory in supernatural and metaphysical terms. After all, these historians served as authors of religious traditions.[90] They interpolate literary features of huge miracles and many angels serving the Muslims in the battle, to portray

84 Watt, *Muḥammad*, 11.

85 Watt, *Muḥammad*, 12.

86 Ibrahim, *Stated*, 77–78. See Ṭabarī, *Ta'rīkh*, 1308. See also Wāqidī, *Maghāzī*, 54, 132; Ibn Hishām, *Sīra*, 1:620; Bayhaqī, *Dalā'il*, 3:35; Suhaylī, *Rawḍ*, 5:77; Kalāʿī, *Iktifā'*, 1:330; Ibn Kathīr, *Sīra*, 2:400; Ḥalabī, *Insān*, 2:211; Ibn al-Athīr, *Kāmil*, 2:17.

87 See Ṭabarī, *Ta'rīkh*, 1308; Ṭabarī, *Ta'rīkh*, 7:46, where it states of these Meccans, "Your sympathies are with Muḥammad." See also the comments of Watt, *Muḥammad*, 13.

88 See Ṭabarī, *Ta'rīkh*, 1307; Wāqidī, *Maghāzī*, 54; Ibn ʿAbd al-Barr, *Durar*, 1:105; Suhaylī, *Rawḍ*, 5:76; Kalāʿī, *Iktifā'*, 1:330; Watt, *Muḥammad*, 11.

89 Crone, *Slaves*, 13.

90 See Ibrahim, *Conversion*, 83, 167, 246; Ibrahim, *Stated*, 4, 161; Hoyland, *God's Path*, 42. On Muslim scholars as religiously driven writers, see Crone, *Medieval*, 88; van Ess, *Theology*, 4:616; Judd, *Religious Scholars*, 52– 61. For medieval historians as religious traditionists (i.e., scholars of the *ḥadīth*), see Crone, *Medieval*, 125ff.; Crone and Hinds, *God's Caliph*, 92–97; Ibrahim, *Conversion*, 172–173; Watt, *Islamic*, 34.

the victory as an event isolated from the natural course of life.[91] For these historians, the victory could have not been without angels wearing turbans and surrounding Muhammad or archangels appearing in the sky and slaughtering the unbelieving Meccans. The victory, we are invited to believe, could have never been without Allah's sending rains at night or without Muhammad's throwing dust against the Meccans in order to cause them to lose their sight.[92] One possible problem with this supernatural element is that it does not appear to have helped the Muslims one year later, when they were reportedly defeated at the Battle of Uḥud by the same Meccan enemy. At Uḥud, Muhammad was reportedly severely wounded and almost died, but there were no angels, miracles, or other metaphysical support.[93] But the historians' insistence on Muhammad's miracles creates a deeper problem, as it appears to be in dissonance with the Qur'ān. In several verses, Islam's Scripture explicitly states that Muhammad's only "miracle" was the revelation of the Qur'ān.[94] Although the Qur'ān presents a Muhammad who was divinely given one miracle, later historians—who engaged Jews and Christians in religious debates—did not find this sufficient.[95] The narrators appear to have been under pressure to detail proofs for Muhammad's prophethood. They desired a specific portrayal of Muhammad who performed wonders and was supported by metaphysical signs—so they designed one.[96] Not only at the Battle of Badr, but also in a following battle at the Trench, the tradition lists numerous miracles performed by Muhammad, and the similarities with biblical accounts can hardly be overlooked.[97]

Third, while the traditional Muslim approach of explaining the motivations for the *maghāzī* often tends to depict them as self-defense campaigns aimed at proclaiming Islam, the extant accounts of Badr do not seem to support this line of reasoning.[98] We are told that in the lead-up to the battle, the Muslims

[91] See Ibrahim, *Stated*, 76.

[92] Historians report, "Allah killed a great number of the Quraysh's mighty men and took many captives of their elites." Ibn Hishām, *Sīra*, 1:628; Bayhaqī, *Dalā'il*, 2:578; Ṭabarī, *Ta'rīkh*, 1322. See the discussion in Ibrahim, *Stated*, 76.

[93] For Muhammad's injury at Uḥud, see Wāqidī, *Maghāzī*, 237, 295; Ṭabarī, *Ta'rīkh*, 1408–1409; Ṭabarī, *History*, 7:120, 123–125, where it states that Muhammad "washed the blood from his face and poured the water over his head, saying, 'May God's anger be intense against those who have bloodied the face of His Prophet'" (124). See also Kharkūshī, *Sharaf*, 3:32; Bayhaqī, *Dalā'il*, 3:270; Suhaylī, *Rawḍ*, 6:58; Kalāᶜī, *Iktifā'*, 1:380; Ibn Kathīr, *Sīra*, 3:47; Ḥalabī, *Insān*, 2:310, 320.

[94] See Q 6:37; 11:12; 13:7; 17:59; 28:48; 29:50–51. See Ibrahim, *Quran*, 119–122.

[95] See ᶜAbd al-Jabbār, *Tathbīt*, 1:58ff.

[96] See Ibrahim, *Muhammad*, 24–25, 69–70; Ibrahim, *Quran*, 119–122.

[97] See the comments on the similarities with biblical miracles at Ibrahim, *Stated*, 90–91.

[98] For a detailed study on the stated motivations of Badr, see Ibrahim, *Stated*, 66–118.

precisely targeted Abū Sufyān, the caravan, and the Meccan Quraysh. The stated reason for the Muslims' targeting the Meccans is reportedly the wealth they possessed in the caravan as well as the scarce number of people in it. Classical narratives clearly depict the Muslims as forcing the Meccans to the battlefield.[99] Abū Sufyān diligently sought to avoid the fight, choosing a different route and sending messengers to the Meccan aristocrats in order to obtain assistance and reinforcements. These reports do not reflect a Muslim campaign for self-defense. This image appealed to medieval storytellers. As for proclaiming Islam as a reason for the battle, the Muslim traditions can hardly paint that picture. We read of strategic spying, individuals fencing, warriors with bows and swords, two armies clashing, and the massacring of some and the taking captive of others—a picture of tribal incursion. No proclamation of a religious message is stated. In reality, it should not be expected, yet the traditional approach—often adopted by apologists and polemicists—insists on portraying battles in such a way.[100] Even the classical Muslim historians—who wrote to demonstrate that Allah was at work for the Muslims—did not seek to depict a religious proclamation as a motive for the battle. The literary story displays a successful tribal raid, one in which the raiders sought possessions and dominion. This is evident in the Muslims' reported treatment of the Meccans whom they killed (i.e., throwing them in a deep well) and held captive (i.e., freeing some, killing some, and ransoming others). We read of Muslim warriors seeking spoils, complaining about their quantities, and disagreeing over portions—there are no stated conversations about their plans to lead pagans to Islam. The reports reflect tribal measures, not religious proclamation.

Fourth, the accounts of Badr should be viewed as a product of their time of documentation. We only know about the battle from Muslim narratives written over a century after Muhammad's death. No eyewitness nor contemporary sources reveal anything about a battle between Muslims and Meccan Quraysh in seventh-century Arabia. While the majority of today's Muslims may believe that the Battle of Badr actually occurred and that it revealed Allah's support of the Muslims and the newly established religion, there should be doubts about the narratives from a scholarly perspective. In a sense, apart from religious devotion and a trust in the Muslim sources,

99 Watt observes, the Quraysh "was apparently placed in a position in which it could not avoid fighting, though the conditions were unfavourable." Watt, *Muḥammad*, 12.

100 Mubārakpūrī, *Raḥīq*, 319, 397, 405; Abū Māyla, *Sarāyā*, 239; Abū Māyla, *Ghazwat*, 13, 18; Ṣallābī, *Ghazawāt*, 7–8; ᶜUmarī, *Mujtamaᶜ*, 22–23.

one cannot be certain that Muhammad led such a battle. The Muslim historical accounts fit and reflect a later period in Islam in which the caliphs were seeking a religious legitimization for their military expansion. They needed to create a religious memory, advancing fighting as jihad for Allah's cause and highlighting both its earthly and heavenly rewards. Of course, this picture is problematic for obvious reasons: In examining the accounts of this battle, one can hardly deny that they do not depict Islam and Muhammad in a good light.[101] It is no surprise that, from the earliest days of Islam's encounter with other religions, many critics of Islam used this picture to critique Islam and Muhammad.[102] Accounts of Badr describe a man seeking revenge, instructing the killing of prisoners of war, and diligently seeking to rob others. We read reports of how Muslims slaughtered many Meccan notables, to the extent that the blood shed reportedly reached the "armpit of ᶜAlī."[103] With this amount of bloodshed, one may wonder how this report can reflect a battle for a religious cause.[104]

In my estimation, none of these accounts should be trusted as factual. Instead of adopting them as historical facts, one surely hopes, believers should consider distancing the religion and its founder from the shedding of blood in military combats by rejecting the authenticity of these accounts. Even if we argue that these actions were *somewhat* a part of the overall life of seventh-century Arabia, the idea of a divinely guided prophet holding a sword against his relatives is highly problematic, especially once we attempt to legitimize it in religious terms.[105] This line of reasoning was even problematic in the seventh century, as evidenced in some non-Muslim sources.[106] When religious enthusiasts insist on linking Islam and Muhammad to

[101] See Shoemaker, *Apocalypse*, 183; also Roohi, "Muḥammad's Disruptive," 40–80, where he rightly observes, "Far from being a reliable source for the history of seventh-century Arabia, the *sīra* represents the needs and concerns of eighth- and ninth-century Islamic society" (73).

[102] See the valuable chapters in the edited volume by Ibrahim, ed., *Medieval Encounters*, especially chs. 3, 4, 10. See also Ibrahim and Hackenburg, *In Search*, 106ff.

[103] Bayhaqī, *Dalāʾil*, 3:55. For the brutality of the treatment of the Meccan notables, see Ṭabarī, *Taʾrīkh*, 1302. See Watt, "Islamic," 147.

[104] Muslim scholar ᶜAbd al-Karīm criticizes actions of Muslim soldiers—including the murder of people or the enslavement of women and children—and wonders, "How could such deeds be considered as actions for the sake of guiding the conquered people to worship Allah?" ᶜAbd al-Karīm, *Shadwu*, 2:193.

[105] For tribal raids in the 620s, see Hoyland, *God's Path*, 56ff.

[106] This same idea was criticized in the Greek work *Doctrina Jacobi*, which tells of "the prophet who has appeared with the Saracens," identifying him in negative terms: "He is false, for the prophets do not come armed with a sword." See Hoyland, *Seeing*, 55. Hoyland argues that *Doctrina* was "purportedly composed in Africa in July 634." If this is true, then the reference of *Doctrina* is one of the earliest reports of unrest in Arabia contemporaneous with Muhammad's career. See also Hoyland, "Earliest," 276–295; O'Sullivan, "Anti-Jewish," 49–68.

massacres and taking people captives, they actually hurt Islam's image. This is one reason why progressive and modernist Muslims often argue that these accounts should be viewed as *descriptive*, not *prescriptive*, and understood within their historical context.[107]

The accounts of the Battle of Badr claim a huge success for the Muslims. The attack represented a tactical success. The Muslims not only humiliated the Meccans but also exacted revenge against those who forced them to emigrate over a year earlier. Through the spoils of combat and the ransom money received for some of the captives, the Muslims acquired enough resources to support the newly growing Muslim community at Medina. With this victory, the Muslims established themselves as a significant power in Arabia. Of course, the Quraysh would not be silent until they obtained revenge. It would take them about a year before they would reportedly defeat the Muslims in the major next expedition, the Battle of Uḥud.

The Battle of Uḥud (3/625)

One year after Badr, according to traditions, the Meccans exacted their revenge against the Muslims at the Battle of Uḥud; however, within this year, there were four minor raids led by Muhammad and one he commissioned that was led by his adopted son, Zayd.[108] Indeed, "After his success at Badr," as Watt observes, "Muḥammad must have realized that he was committed to 'total war' with the Meccans."[109] There exists no clear agreement in Muslim traditions about the scope and goals of these minor expeditions; their list is Qarqarat al-Kudr, al-Sawīq, Dhū Amarr, Baḥrān, and al-Qarada. The Muslim narrators place considerable emphasis on the frequency of raids Muhammad led or commissioned, thus creating a theme of hegemony and dominance.[110] Repeatedly, they depict Muhammad as a

[107] See Abou El Fadl, *Great*, 5–6 et passim; Abou El Fadl, *Speaking*, ch. 4; Akyol, *Islam*, 58–59; Akyol, *Reopening*, 157–180.

[108] For a Muslim study of these minor expeditions, see ᶜUmarī, *Sīra*, 374–376. For a non-Muslim study, see Watt, *Muḥammad*, 21ff. On Zayd, see Powers, *Zayd*; also Chapter 7 in this study.

[109] Watt, *Muḥammad*, 21, where he speaks of the Meccans and how "their prosperity depended to a great extent on their prestige, and in order to maintain their position they must in no uncertain fashion retrieve what they had lost at Badr, in addition to loosening Muḥammad's hold on their route to the north."

[110] On historiographical themes, see Noth/Conrad, *Early*, 26–61, and Donner, *Narratives*, 141ff. On detecting these themes, see Noth/Conrad (109ff.) and Donner (141–142); also Ibrahim, *Conversion*, 5–7.

master warrior, relentless out of obedience to Allah, leading one raid after another, constantly subduing enemies, seizing spoils, and advancing dominion.[111] The theme reflects a religious philosophy, clearly highlighting how Muslim narrators *devised* and *cherished* a memory of a divinely guided prophet succeeding in a battle. Their representations often switch between describing major battles and recounting minor ones. Shortly after Badr, we are told, Muhammad led the expedition to Qarqarat al-Kudr.[112] It did not target the Meccan Quraysh, but two of its allies, Banū Sulaym and Ghaṭafān.[113] Qarqarat al-Kudr was a water-well location controlled by Banū Sulaym. Muhammad reportedly led two hundred Muslims and came to Qarqarat al-Kudr, only to find that all of the people had fled, leaving their camels behind.[114] The Muslims seized the camels and remained for three days near the well, then returned to Medina.[115] Much of the narrative is a construction of a certain memory—created by classical historians—which narrated military expeditions and theft as chief components of Muhammad's career.

Soon after Qarqarat al-Kudr, the expedition of al-Sawīq was a minor confrontation between the Muslims and the Meccans.[116] We are told that after the defeat at Badr, Abū Sufyān forbade himself from any hint of rejoicing until he had gained revenge against the Muslims.[117] He then led two hundred Meccans, seeking to attack the outskirts of Medina in what appears to have been an attempt by the Meccans to save face after their defeat at

[111] The theme can be detected by the frequently repeated terms *wa-ghazā* (and he raided, or invaded) and *wa-baᶜatha* (and he commissioned, or sent out troops). For the theme of hegemony in Muslim historiography, see Ibrahim, *Conversion*, 6–7, 89–93; also Donner, *Narratives*, 174–182.

[112] Ibn Saᶜd, *Ṭabaqāt*, 2:23 (occurred twenty-three months after the *hijra*); Ibn Hishām, *Sīra*, 2:45; Bayhaqī, *Dalā'il*, 3:165; Ibn ᶜAbd al-Barr, *Durar*, 1:140; Suhaylī, *Rawḍ*, 5:270; Kalāᶜī, *Iktifā'*, 1:364.

[113] Ṭabarī, *Ta'rīkh*, 1363; Ṭabarī, *History*, 7:88 (Muhammad "led an expedition to Qarqarat al-Kudr when he heard that the Banū Sulaym and Ghaṭafān were gathering"). The confusion in Muslim traditions concerning the details and the dates of these expeditions is evident in how al-Ṭabarī and al-Wāqidī switch the order of al-Sawīq and Qarqarat al-Kudr. See Wāqidī, *Maghāzī*, 181; Wāqidī, *Life*, 90–91. Compare with Ibn Hishām, *Sīra*, 2:44. On the discrepancies in dates in traditions, see Jones, "Chronology," 279–280. For dating events in Muslim historiography, particularly in the *Sīra*, see Conrad, "Abraha," 225–40; Donner, *Narratives*, 5–7. Note that Banū Sulaym and Ghaṭafān would later help the Meccans in the battle of al-Khandaq, known as the siege of Medina. Watt, *Muḥammad*, 17.

[114] See Ibn Saᶜd, *Ṭabaqāt*, 2:23, which reports that five hundred camels were looted by the two hundred Muslims—Muhammad took one hundred, and the rest were divided among the Muslim warriors.

[115] Ṭabarī, *Ta'rīkh*, 1363; Ṭabarī, *History*, 7:88.

[116] Khalīfa, *Ta'rīkh*, 1:59; Ibn Saᶜd, *Ṭabaqāt*, 2:22 (occurred twenty-two months after the *hijra*); Ṭabarī, *Ta'rīkh*, 1365; Ṭabarī, *History*, 7:89–91; Ibn Hishām, *Sīra*, 2:44; Bayhaqī, *Dalā'il*, 3:164; Ibn ᶜAbd al-Barr, *Durar*, 1:139; Suhaylī, *Rawḍ*, 5:271; Kalāᶜī, *Iktifā'*, 1:364.

[117] See the comments in Watt, *Muḥammad*, 19.

Badr.[118] Muslim traditions claim that Abū Sufyān conspired with some Jews in Medina and killed two people before fleeing in haste and returning to Mecca.[119] In their hastening, the Meccans left *al-sawīq* (their flour-based meal provisions) behind to travel faster.[120] When the Muslims chased the Meccans, they could not catch them; however, they were able to collect *al-sawīq* as loot.[121] Here we encounter once more the negative depiction of the Meccans—particularly the Umayyad figure of Abū Sufyān—as weak, cowardly, and terrified of the Muslims. The exaggeration is stark if we consider how the tradition portrays them as mighty and powerful when they were persecuting the Muslims two years earlier. A month later, Muhammad led another expedition to Dhū Amarr in order to face Ghaṭafān for a second time, but no fighting occurred, as the people of Ghaṭafān fled.[122] Similarly, after Dhū Amarr, Muhammad gathered three hundred Muslims and led an expedition to Baḥrān, which is located on the trade route between Mecca and Syria; however, like the previous expedition, no fighting occurred.[123] The expeditions to Dhū Amarr and Baḥrān did not reportedly target the Meccan Quraysh but served as terrifying military activities meant to intimidate the Meccans' allies. These four minor expeditions were reportedly executed by Muhammad within six months after Badr. One can hardly miss the alleged frequency, which reemphasizes the theme of Muslim hegemony. These traditions are better viewed as religious fictions than as records of military encounters. The narratives fashion a specific memory of Muhammad, designed by medieval historians who chose to emphasize their prophet as a serial raider, caravan interceptor, and property seizer.

Then Muhammad learned of a Meccan caravan full of silver and merchandise, led by Abū Sufyān and journeying through the Najd route, which was a different route chosen by the Meccans to evade the Muslims. Here the narrative brings back the negatively depicted figure Abū Sufyān and highlights the contrasts between him and Muhammad. Abū Sufyān appears as an

[118] See Watt, *Muḥammad*, 21, where he argues that Abū Sufyān's "primary aims were doubtless to restore confidence among the Meccans and to show the world that the day of Quraysh was not yet over."

[119] See Ibn Saᶜd, *Ṭabaqāt*, 2:22–23, where he reports that some Jews did not cooperate with Abū Sufyān, while others did.

[120] Some traditions, with an apparent anti-Jewish disposition, refer to Abū Sufyān drinking wine with some Jews and murdering two Muslim men. See Yaᶜqūbī, *Taʾrīkh*, 2:68–70.

[121] This is the reason for the name given to the expedition in the tradition. See Ibn Saᶜd, *Ṭabaqāt*, 2:23; Yaᶜqūbī, *Taʾrīkh*, 2:68.

[122] Khalīfa, *Taʾrīkh*, 1:65; Ibn Hishām, *Sīra*, 2:46; Bayhaqī, *Dalāʾil*, 3:167 (it is also called the expedition to Ghaṭafān); Ibn ᶜAbd al-Barr, *Durar*, 1:140; Suhaylī, *Rawḍ*, 5:274. See Yaᶜqūbī, *Taʾrīkh*, 2:68–70, where he lists the expeditions that did not involve fighting.

[123] Khalīfa, *Taʾrīkh*, 1:65.

unbelieving coward, while Muhammad is a courageous leader. Of course, the literary hint against the Umayyad family—as represented by their major elite, Abū Sufyān—is at the center of the story.[124] Muhammad commissioned his adopted son, Zayd ibn Ḥāritha, to march with a hundred Muslims to intercept the caravan; thus, some call it the *sarriya* (incursion) of Zayd.[125] Much in this tradition aims to display two frequent claims in the *maghāzī* literature: it advances anti-Umayyad rhetoric and reiterates Muhammad's close reliance upon trusted companions, largely from the Banū Hāshim and the Quraysh, who served as carriers of his directives and fulfillers of his commands.[126] Tayeb el-Hibri makes a valuable comparison between the disciples of pre-Islamic prophets and the companions of Muhammad, and argues that historiographical accounts serve as parabolic narrations that "continued the tradition of biblical storytelling with a different focus, on the lives of the companions."[127] Indeed, these narratives are more like religious lessons than historical records. Additionally, this tradition reinforces the cherished Muslim portrayal of Muhammad's unceasing attempts to intercept the Meccan caravans, to hurt the Quraysh's livelihood and humiliate her notable elites.[128] We are told that the Muslims caught the Meccans by surprise at a water-well location called al-Qarada. The Muslims reportedly seized the entire caravan, including thirty thousand silver dirhams, while the Meccans fled in humiliation.[129] This literary detail invites the reader to believe that the Muslims—through Muhammad's *maghāzī* and under his leadership—are consolidating power and accumulating resources. Moreover, this expedition was the last straw for the Meccans and led to the second momentous confrontation between the Muslims and the Meccans at the Battle of Uḥud.

Many Muslim accounts represent the Battle of Uḥud as a culmination of these earlier raids and, particularly, as revenge against the Muslims for their harsh treatment of the Meccans in Badr.[130] Uḥud was a result of the growing Meccan-Medinan tension. It also reflects a calculated step by the

[124] See the discussion on the evolving image of Abū Sufyān in early Muslim historiography in Ibrahim, *Conversion*, 71–75.

[125] Ibn Saᶜd, *Ṭabaqāt*, 2:27–28 (occurred twenty-eight months after the *hijra*); Ibn Hishām, *Sīra*, 2:50; Ṭabarī, *Ta'rīkh*, 1374; Ṭabarī, *History*, 7: 98–99. This was the first incursion led by Zayd ibn Ḥāritha. Zayd led six *sarāyā*. See Wāqidī, *Maghāzī*, 553, 555, 564; Ibn Kathīr, *Bidāya*, 4:203–204. On Zayd, see Powers, *Zayd*, ch. 1; also Powers, *Muhammad*, 24–34.

[126] See ᶜAbd al-Karīm, *Quraysh*, 377–392; Qimanī, *Ḥizb*, 51ff. Cf. Ibn Hishām, *Sīra*, 2:406–407; Ibn Kathīr, *Sīra*, 3:676; Ḥalabī, *Insān*, 3:175; also Bukhārī, *Ṣaḥīḥ*, 5:30.

[127] Hibri, *Parable*, 9.

[128] Crone, "How Did," 387–399; Crone, "Pagan," 140ff.

[129] Ibn Saᶜd, *Ṭabaqāt*, 2:27–28 (occurred twenty-eight months after the *hijra*).

[130] Ṭabarī, *Ta'rīkh*, 1383–1384; Wāqidī, *Maghāzī*, 199–200. For Muslim secondary studies on the battle, see Hamidullah, *Battlefields*, 75–114; Ṣallābī, *Sīra*, 470ff.; ᶜUmarī, *Sīra*, 378–397; Haykal,

Meccans—who planned adequately and collected enough resources—to exact revenge against the Muslims after the defeat at Badr.[131] Al-Ṭabarī reveals the motivation for the Battle of Uḥud, saying, "What provoked the expedition to Uḥud by the polytheists of Quraysh against the Messenger of God was the battle of Badr and the killing of those nobles and chiefs of Quraysh who were killed there."[132] The literary detail that identifies the Meccans as polytheists establishes an ideological disposition, displaying the fight in religious terms. According to traditions, at Uḥud, the Muslims were seven hundred warriors led by Muhammad, while the Meccans were three thousand led by Abū Sufyān. Once again, we encounter what appears as an exaggerated detail to highlight the great Muslim disadvantage to amplify the victory.[133] The Meccans reportedly included the shrewd and skillful commander Khālid ibn al-Wālīd.[134] They also brought women to *yuḥarriḍū* (boost the morale of) the warriors.[135] The presence of a shrewd commander and of available women for the polytheists creates a more compelling picture to emphasize the disadvantage of the Muslim camp. We are even told that the Muslims initially numbered one thousand, but about one-third of them decided not to march to war following the advice of the Muslim companion ᶜAbdullāh ibn Ubayy ibn Salūl, who was consequently identified in traditions as a *munāfiq* (hypocrite, or lukewarm Muslim).[136] Those who joined ᶜAbdullāh were also identified as hypocrites, although they were earlier identified in the traditions as devout Muslims. This literary detail is important, as it reflects how the narrators shaped their narrative to communicate to the Muslims that withdrawing from a battle is tantamount to hypocrisy and religious

Ḥayāt, 298–299. For non-Muslim discussions on Uḥud, see Watt, *Muḥammad*, 21–29; Ibrahim, *Stated*, 73–79.

[131] ᶜUmarī, *Sīra*, 378–398.

[132] Ṭabarī, *History*, 7:105; Ṭabarī, *Ta'rīkh*, 1383.

[133] For a valuable discussion on the possible numbers of the residents of Mecca and Medina in seventh-century Arabia, see Shoemaker, *Creating*, 98–113. On exaggerated historical accounts, see ᶜAbd al-Raḥmān, *Judhūr*, 7–9; Sawwāḥ, *Usṭūra*, 103; Sawwāḥ, *Dīn*, 55–56; Ūzūn, *Jināyat*, 13–30; Ūzūn, *Laffaq*.

[134] Wāqidī, *Maghāzī*, 220; Ibn Hishām, *Sīra*, 2:86. On Khālid, see the Muslim study of ᶜAqqād, *ᶜAbqariyyat Khālid*, 11–60.

[135] Ṭabarī, *Ta'rīkh*, 1385–1386 and 1400; see also Wāqidī, *Maghāzī*, 206; Wāqidī, *Life*, 110, where it states, "The women of the polytheists led the rows of polytheists, striking their large drums and tambourines," and "whenever a [Meccan] man turned away, they goaded him and reminded him of their dead at Badr."

[136] Ṭabarī, *Ta'rīkh*, 1361; Ṭabarī, *History*, 7:86. Yaᶜqūbī, *Ta'rīkh*, 2:49; Kalāᶜī, *Iktifā'*, 2:89; Suhaylī, *Rawḍ*, 5:302. The term *munāfiqūn* is better rendered "lukewarm Believers" or "uncommitted Muslims" rather than simply "hypocrites." Donner uses it in this sense in his *Early*, 68; Donner, *Muhammad*, 43, 59, 160, 161; also Cook, *Understanding*, 8, 138.

cowardice. This lesson was arguably needed during an age of conquests. The stigma is amplified if we consider the Qur'ān's portrayal of the hypocrites and their damnation in the lowest depths of the hellfire (Q 4:145).[137]

Still, the narrators relay unexpected reports about the rest of the Muslims. Al-Wāqidī observes that not all Muslims in Muhammad's camp were in harmony concerning participating at Uḥud—some of them, including Muhammad himself, "hated" marching to this battle.[138] In fact, Muhammad received a divine dream (labeled in some reports as a vision), instructing him to stay in Medina to be protected, as marching to Uḥud would be perilous and result in many Muslims killed.[139] In the dream, Muhammad was wearing powerful and secure armor, but his sword broke and he saw many cows slaughtered. He understood the dream as a divine warning not to leave Medina. In interpreting the dream, Muhammad reportedly said that his strong armor was the protection he had in Medina, his broken sword was a warning he would be injured, and the slaughtered cows were a sign of many casualties among the Muslims.[140] These reports add spectacular complexity to a seemingly monochromatic narrative. While they come from the same tradition, these accounts seem to cast doubt on the claim that the Muslims were in harmony even before the so-called hypocrites withdrew—after all, Muhammad received a divine warning against marching to the battle. From a critical standpoint, the complex narrative with its competing reports demonstrates the failure of Muslim narrators—despite their diligent attempts—to create a unified harmonious tradition. In their attempts to create a portrayal that places significant blame on the so-called hypocrites who left the Muslim camp, other reports—in the same tradition—manage to sneak in and depict a more complex picture with competing literary details. While classical Muslim narrators appear to have relied on a common pool of memory, they cherry-picked from competing narratives; this resulted in a less unified image than one may have hoped.[141] Additionally, the existence of competing reports in the same tradition reflects different attitudes

[137] Many other verses convey the same about the hypocrites (Q 3:167; 4:61; 4:138; 9:67–68; 33:73; 48:6; 57:13). See Muqātil, *Tafsīr*, 1:329, 1:417; Ṭabarī, *Jāmiᶜ*, 9:337; Zamakhsharī, *Kashshāf*, 1:54, 1:57.

[138] Ibn Hishām, *Sīra*, 2:63. Wāqidī, *Maghāzī*, 213–214.

[139] Yaᶜqūbī, *Ta'rīkh*, 2:47; Both Wāqidī, *Maghāzī*, 209 and Ibn Hishām, *Sīra*, 2:62 (treat it as a vision, not a dream); Bayhaqī, *Dalā'il*, 3:163.

[140] For the details of the dream and its interpretation by Muhammad, see Ṭabarī, *Ta'rīkh*, 1387; Ṭabarī, *History*, 7:108; also Yaᶜqūbī, *Ta'rīkh*, 2:47; Wāqidī, *Maghāzī*, 209; Wāqidī, *Maghāzī*, 104; Ibn Hishām, *Sīra*, 2:62; Ibn Hishām, *Life*, 371; Bayhaqī, *Dalā'il*, 3:163.

[141] On the shared pool of memory, see Savant, *New*, 13; Noth/Conrad, *Early*, 17; Borrut, *Entre*, 35; Robinson, "Conquest," 38; Mourad, "On Early," 588. For examples of scholars who claim that

of the storytellers in various times, and explains how a memory is *adjusted* depending on the narrator and the time of writing. Surprisingly, despite the dream, Muhammad followed the opinion of some companions anyway and decided to march to fight the Meccans at Uḥud.[142] In justifying his decision, one day before the battle started, Muhammad reportedly wore *la'matah* (his full armor) and declared, "It is not appropriate for a prophet, once he puts on his armor, to lay down unless he fights."[143] Thus, he marched to Uḥud.

The two armies gathered in the areas surrounding Mount Uḥud.[144] Al-Ṭabarī reports that the Muslims initially won over the Meccans, as Allah fulfilled his promises by granting the believers a great victory. The Muslims, we are invited to believe, "slew" the Meccans with their swords—the defeat of the Meccans was certain and starkly apparent.[145] The literary details of this initial Muslim victory appear to be embellishments by the Muslim narrators who could not relinquish their religious commitments.[146] An outright Muslim defeat, the rationale goes, would not fit into the picture of a community supported by the divine. Soon after, in spite of this reported early victory, things changed dramatically. Some Muslim archers reportedly left their assigned positions to secure the spoils after the Meccans fled.[147] Initially, Muhammad commanded the archers, saying, "If you see us victorious over them, do not leave your position, and if you see them victorious

the Muslim narrators succeeded in composing a unified narrative, see Hibri, *Parable*, 237; Donner, "Review," 570. For the opposite argument, see Crone, *Meccan*, 117, 224, 230; Crone, *Slaves*, 13.

142 See Wāqidī, *Life*, 106, where it states that these Muslims spoke to Muhammad of the rewards of the battle: "It is one of the two good results. Either martyrdom or plunder and victory in killing them," to which Muhammad responded, "Indeed I fear defeat." See Wāqidī, *Maghāzī*, 213.

143 Ibn Hishām, *Sīra*, 2:63; Ibn Hishām, *Life*, 372. See also a slightly different report in Wāqidī, *Maghāzī*, 214; also Wāqidī, *Life*, 106, where it reads, "It is not appropriate for a prophet once he puts on his cuirass to then put it down until God judges between him and his enemies." See Ibn Ḥibbān, *Sīra*, 1:220; Kharkūshī, *Sharaf*, 3:21; Bayhaqī, *Dalā'il*, 3:226; Suhaylī, *Rawḍ*, 5:302; Kalāʿī, *Iktifā'*, 1:372; Ibn Kathīr, *Sīra*, 3:26; Ḥalabī, *Insān*, 2:299. See Sharīf, *Makka*, 354; also Watt, *Muḥammad*, 21, where he renders it, "once a prophet has put on armour he must not take it off until God has decided between him and his enemy."

144 Muslim traditions refer to several dates for the battle, around the fifteenth of Shawwāl in the year A.H. 3. This was reportedly about thirteen months after Badr. See ʿUmarī, *Sīra*, 378.

145 See Ṭabarī, *History*, 7:118, where he states, "God sent down his victory and made good his promise to them. They cut down the enemy with their swords until they put them to flight. There was no doubt about the defeat the Muslims had inflicted on the Meccans." See Ṭabarī, *Ta'rīkh*, 1400; also Ibn Hishām, *Sīra*, 2:77; Ibn Hishām, *Life*, 379.

146 Petersen, *ʿAlī*, 17.

147 Wāqidī, *Maghāzī*, 224–225; Ibn Qutayba, *Maʿārif*, 159; Bayhaqī, *Dalā'il*, 3:220, 3:227; Dhahabī, *Ta'rīkh*, 2:167. According to al-Ṭabarī, "When the archers saw the Messenger of God and his companions in the heart of the polytheists' camp and plundering them, they hurried down to the booty." Ṭabarī, *History*, 7:115.

over us, do not come to our assistance."[148] Nonetheless, the archers reportedly disobeyed Muhammad's instructions. This careless action provided a huge opportunity for a Meccan counterattack against the Muslims, fulfilled largely by the clever warrior Khālid ibn al-Walīd.[149] The result of the counterattack was that many Muslims were slaughtered, and even Muhammad was severely injured.[150] The literary detail regarding the result of disobeying Muhammad's command is a creative design by the narrators. Not only does it emphasize that obeying Muhammad is as important as obeying Allah, but it also idealizes Muhammad by establishing a memory that includes severe repercussions due to violating his instruction.[151] Moreover, the defeat and killing of the Muslims as well as the injuring of Muhammad at Uḥud appear as a clear fulfillment of the dream Muhammad saw before the battle, in which he was forewarned not to leave Medina.[152] Still, there is an apparent silence among narrators concerning whether Muhammad violated a divine warning. After all, the idealized picture of Muhammad would require deafening silence when it is due; thus the religious authors appear to have ignored this turbulent detail. Overall, Muslim traditions largely attribute the Muslims' defeat to two major factors: (1) the hypocrisy of the Muslims who followed ᶜAbdullāh ibn Ubayy and withdrew before the battle, and (2) the disobedience of the Muslim archers to Muhammad's command.

In analyzing the narrative of Uḥud, I offer five critical observations. First, the narrative is better viewed as a religious lesson rather than a precise description of past events. Classical Muslim historians appear to have successfully formed a tale aimed at exhorting Muslims to fight in battles, warning them against disobeying Muhammad's commands, and discouraging them against retreating from battle by labeling such an action as religious hypocrisy.[153] This is what some Islamicists identify as "salvation

[148] See Ṭabarī, *History*, 7:113; Ṭabarī, *Ta'rīkh*, 1394. Wāqidī, *Maghāzī*, 224–225; Ibn Qutayba, *Maᶜārif*, 159; Bayhaqī, *Dalā'il*, 3:227.

[149] Ibn Saᶜd, *Ṭabaqāt*, 2:30; Ibn Hishām, *Sīra*, 2:78; Ṭabarī, *History*, 7:112–113; Ibn Ḥibbān, *Thiqāt*, 225; Kalāᶜī, *Iktifā'*, 1:373; Ibn ᶜAbd al-Barr, *Istīᶜāb*, 2:427ff.; Ibn al-Athīr, *Usd*, 2:140ff. For Khālid, see Dhahabī, *Ta'rīkh*, 3:230ff.; Dhahabī, *Siyar*, 1:366ff.; Ibn Saᶜd, *Ṭabaqāt*, 4:190ff.; Khalīfa, *Ṭabaqāt*, 51; Ibn Maᶜīn, *Ta'rīkh*, 3:20; Ibn Hajar, *Iṣāba*, 2:215ff.

[150] Wāqidī, *Maghāzī*, 237, 295; Ṭabarī, *Ta'rīkh*, 1408–1409; Ṭabarī, *History*, 7:123–125; Kharkūshī, *Sharaf*, 3:32; Bayhaqī, *Dalā'il*, 3:270; Suhaylī, *Rawḍ*, 6:58; Kalāᶜī, *Iktifā'*, 1:380; Ibn Kathīr, *Sīra*, 3:47; Ḥalabī, *Insān*, 2:310, 320.

[151] One may also argue that the literary feature is designed to explain and correspond to verses in the Qur'ān, including Q 3:165–166, where the verses refer to a disaster that struck the believers—by Allah's permission—when the two armies met.

[152] See Ṭabarī, *History*, 7:108, which claims that Muhammad interpreted the dream.

[153] See Rubin, *Eye*, 1–3, where he argues that the *Sīra* accounts reflect "the self-image of medieval Islamic society" (3). Like Rubin, I examine these texts "for the sake of the stories recorded in them, not for the sake of the events described in these stories" (1). This is often labeled a "literary"

history."[154] These traditions do not describe actual historical events. Consider how traditions insist on portraying an initial Muslim victory followed by a defeat only after Muhammad's commands were disobeyed. This portrayal has various gaps.[155] Where is the divine support for the believers? Unlike Badr, there were no angels or archangels at Uḥud.[156] Nor were there any miracles performed by Muhammad to blind and confuse the Meccans. The entire tradition seems tendentious.[157] Moreover, the initial victory is hard to believe.[158] We are told that the battle was almost over and that the Muslims won and began collecting the spoils. However, the same Muslim tradition indicates that Muslims were unsuccessful at seizing any spoils, even before the counterattack.[159] This reported initial victory invites us to believe that the Muslims were successful in reaching the Meccan locations and in beginning to plunder—a mere seven hundred Muslims overcame three thousand Meccans and were ready to declare victory. These details are unconvincing and, more importantly, do not sit well with the supposedly divine warning given to Muhammad, through a dream, instructing him not to leave Medina to march to Uḥud. Was the divine dream false? If the Muslims were to win, then the divine dream—revealing that Muhammad would be injured and the Muslims massacred if they were to leave Medina and march to Uḥud—was

approach. In agreement with Rubin, Hawting states, "It is difficult to see how anyone could expect to recover real facts about Muḥammad's life from the sort of traditions and reports examined here" (127). Hawting, "Review," 126–129.

[154] Rippin writes that from a "salvation history" standpoint, "The actual 'history' in the sense of 'what really happened' has become totally subsumed within later interpretation and is virtually, if not totally, inextricable from it," or, in other words, "The records we have are the existential records of the thought and faith of later generations." Rippin, "Literary," 156. Wansbrough, *Sectarian*, 45; Wansbrough, *Qur'ānic*, 121–148.

[155] See Watt, *Muḥammad*, 25. Although Watt often trusts the general outline in Muslim sources, he states, "We may admit, then, that the official Muslim account [of Uḥud] has to be modified along these lines."

[156] See the critical observations about Uḥud in Ibrahim, *Stated*, 81, where I write, "In this situation, there is no supernatural guidance, nor is there mention of Gabriel, who supported the Muslims at Badr." See also Watt, *Muḥammad*, 27, where he evaluates the Muslims' defeat at Uḥud, and states, "Muhammad's earlier claim that Badr was a sign of God's favour raised theological difficulties, which his opponents in Medina and elsewhere were not slow to press. Did Uḥud not show that God favoured the Meccans, and that Muhammad was no prophet?"

[157] For a Muslim thinker skeptical of the miracles mentioned in Muslim traditions, see Djait, *Waḥy*, 79–80. For a modern Shīʿite perspective on fabricating traditions by Muslim narrators, see Subḥānī, *Kulliyyāt*, 25–28.

[158] See Watt, *Muḥammad*, 24, where he is skeptical of the claims of the initial victory. For an exaggerated report of this initial victory, see Wāqidī, *Maghāzī*, 229; see also Wāqidī, *Life*, 113, where it reads, "God never granted such a victory on a field to his Prophet as He granted him and his companions on the day of Uḥud, until they disobeyed the Prophet and disputed his command."

[159] Wāqidī, *Maghāzī*, 231; Wāqidī, *Life*, 114. See also Watt, *Muḥammad*, 24, where he concludes that the "source material also admits that they did not in fact secure any booty."

disingenuous. It is plausible to deduce that the story of the divinely given dream is an interpolation by some storytellers to maintain that Allah was actively supporting the Muslims by forewarning Muhammad—but this interpolated detail creates more confusion than clarity, as it sheds doubt on Muhammad's assumed ability to heed Allah's warnings.

Second, Muslim traditions accuse ᶜAbdullāh ibn Ubayy of being a hypocrite when he decided not to march to Uḥud. However, the same traditions reveal that Muhammad initially agreed with ᶜAbdullāh and did not want to leave Medina.[160] Muslim historians appear confused as to how to depict ᶜAbdullāh.[161] How can he be a weak believer if Muhammad agreed with him? Muhammad was reportedly reluctant to march to Uḥud and was uncertain in making that decision—even those believers who exhorted him to march to war were not confident and eventually "regretted what they did."[162] In a sense, Muhammad changed his opinion and decided to march to Uḥud after initially agreeing with ᶜAbdullāh. These competing reports about Muhammad and ᶜAbdullāh are another indication of the confusion of the jumbled narrators who were unable to develop a coherent and unified story. The scene of the defeated Muslims, under Muhammad's leadership, posed a moral dilemma to religious narrators. These writers were accustomed to sorting through circulating traditions in search of acceptable details, and this process resulted in disoriented portrayals at various points. This is evident in how the same pool of traditions portray ᶜAbdullāh in a significantly positive light in a different setting. He is identified as a major Arab leader of Medina before the Muslims even came to it as well as a notable, honorable man, upon whose dignity everyone agreed.[163] He was reportedly a skillful warrior and a chief of the Medinan tribe of al-Khazraj.[164] In one Muslim memory, he appears to have been an astute tribal warrior who was familiar with Medina's surroundings. We are told that, immediately before the battle, ᶜAbdullāh

[160] Ibn Hishām, *Sīra*, 2:63; Ṭabarī, *Ta'rīkh*, 1387. Ibn Shabba, *Ta'rīkh al-Madīna*, 349ff. Al-Ṭabarī reports, "The opinion of ᶜAbd Allāh b. Ubayy b. Salūl was the same as the opinion of the Messenger of God on this matter, that he should not go out to meet the enemy." Ṭabarī, *History*, 7:108.

[161] See Watt, *Muḥammad*, 21, where he writes of the difficulty of reconstructing the course of the battle due to the source problems; however, he still approaches the sources with a hope that they have some truth in them: "if we accept the general soundness of the material, a rough outline does emerge."

[162] Wāqidī, *Maghāzī*, 214; Wāqidī, *Life*, 106.

[163] Nuwayrī, *Nihāyat*, 16:356.

[164] On ᶜAbdullāh, see the valuable discussion in ᶜAlī, *Mufaṣṣal*, 7:139, and 9:209–210. For primary sources, see Khalīfa, *Ta'rīkh*, 114; Ibn Qutayba, *Maᶜārif*, 1:159; Fasawī, *Maᶜrifa*, 2:428; Balādhurī, *Ansāb*, 1:274, where he identifies ᶜAbdullāh as the "head of the hypocrites." See also al-Masᶜūdī, *Tanbīh*, 1:211; Maqdisī, *Bad'*, 4:200.

pled with Muhammad: "Listen to me in this affair, for I know that I inherited this opinion from the elders of my people, and the decision makers among them, for they were the people of war and experience."[165] ʿAbdullāh knew that the battle was going to be dangerous. When Muhammad dismissed his opinion, ʿAbdullāh reportedly stated, "Muhammad disobeyed me and obeyed [the counsel of] *al-wildān* (immature men)."[166] Still, we should note that before ʿAbdullāh withdrew from marching to the battle, the Muslims were reportedly divided, as some desired war but others hated it.[167] Even some of those Muslims who initially desired war reportedly regretted their decision: "*istakrahnā* (we compelled) the Prophet and we should not have done so."[168] In fact, some traditions portray Muhammad as hesitant and indecisive, acting in haste and disobeying the intuition of some Muslims, especially after he saw the reported divine dream.[169] All of these literary pieces do not reflect factual encounters, but indicate a confusion in Muslim traditions as to how to portray a man negatively, only because he reportedly attempted to avoid an inevitable suicide at the hands of the Meccans at Uḥud. After all, based on the results of the Battle of Uḥud, ʿAbdullāh proved to be a competent military leader and wise in his counsel.[170] Additionally, one cannot ignore the likelihood that this negative depiction of ʿAbdullāh relates to the general disposition of the tradition to portray the *anṣār* less favorably than their Meccan counterparts, especially those from the Quraysh, as we explained earlier.[171]

Third, the majority of traditions unequivocally attribute the Muslims' defeat to the archers' disobedience to Muhammad's commands.[172] Many modern and contemporary Muslims follow the same logic.[173] However, this

[165] Wāqidī, *Maghāzī*, 210; Wāqidī, *Life*, 104.

[166] Suhaylī, *Rawḍ*, 5:302; Ṭabarī, *Ta'rīkh*, 1390; Wāqidī, *Maghāzī*, 216, 219. See the comments of Watt, *Muḥammad*, 21.

[167] Wāqidī, *Maghāzī*, 209. Ibn Hishām, *Sīra*, 2:62; Bayhaqī, *Dalā'il*, 3:163.

[168] Ibn Hishām, *Sīra*, 2:63; Ṭabarī, *Ta'rīkh*, 1390. Kharkūshī, *Sharaf*, 3:21; Ibn Ḥibbān, *Sīra*, 1:220; Suhaylī, *Rawḍ*, 5:302; Ibn Kathīr, *Sīra*, 3:26.

[169] Compare Yaʿqūbī, *Ta'rīkh*, 2:47, and Ṭabarī, *Ta'rīkh*, 1387; also Ibn Hishām, *Sīra*, 2:62 and 2:64. On Muhammad's hesitancy in this situation, see ʿAbd al-Raḥmān, *Judhūr*, 121.

[170] The wise counsel of ʿAbdullāh is reported by Wāqidī, *Maghāzī*, 210; Wāqidī, *Life*, 104, where it reads, "O Messenger of God, our city is a virgin and she will not be forced against us ever. We will never go out to an enemy unless the enemy takes us, and one did not enter upon us ever, except we captured him."

[171] See the discussion earlier in chapyrt 2. See also ʿAbd al-Karīm, *Quraysh*, 377–392; Qimanī, *Ḥizb*, 51ff. Cf. Ibn Hishām, *Sīra*, 2:406–407; Ibn Kathīr, *Sīra*, 3:676; Ḥalabī, *Insān*, 3:175.

[172] See Watt, *Muḥammad*, 23, where he states, "The unsatisfactory outcome of the battle is attributed to the disobedience of the majority of the archers."

[173] See Haykal, *Ḥayāt*, 308–310. Sharīf, *Makka*, 467. For a traditional apologetic argument for the Muslims' defeat, see Mubārakpūrī, *Rawḍat*, 112.

cannot be accurate—the portrayed battle itself was an inevitable suicide mission for the Muslims. The traditions include conflicting information and reflect a more complex portrayal that does not place blame on the archers: The Meccans had over four times as many soldiers as the Muslims. Muhammad knew he should not leave his protected location in Medina. He was in agreement with those Muslims who hated marching to war. He saw a dream or divine vision warning him of the slaughter of the Muslims. The attempt of Muslim narrators to attribute the defeat to the archers' mistake does not seem plausible.[174] Similarly, the traditions claiming an initial significant victory for the Muslims are unconvincing. After all, the same traditions reveal that the Meccans were equipped and ready for the fight, while the Muslims were in disharmony, exhibiting clear floundering and uncertainty.[175] A more persuasive argument for the defeat emerges if we only consider the reported balance of power in this battle: The Muslims were at a significant disadvantage from the beginning, which is evident in how Muhammad himself was injured and almost died.[176] Again, like the accounts of Badr, similar trends appear in the accounts of Uḥud, as Muslim historians appear to flounder in attempts to *author* history rather than *detail* what might have actually occurred. This is evident in a report by al-Wāqidī in which he seeks to justify the lack of angels appearing at Uḥud to aid the Muslims. He reports that Allah was about to send down three thousand angels to support the Muslims, but when he saw their distress, he raised the number to five thousand; however, the Muslims did not *ṣabarū* (wait and persevere patiently) to receive the support.[177]

Fourth, the traditional Muslim approach of portraying the *maghāzī* as self-defense campaigns for religious proclamation does not ring true in the case of Uḥud. This approach appears in the apologetic claims of Muslim scholar Ḥusayn Haykal (1888–1956) in his argument regarding what motivated

174 See Ibrahim, *Stated*, 83, where I write, "It appears that the classical narrators forged the report of the victory in order to ensure that the 'defeat' story made sense. Hypothetically, even if we accept the claim that the mistake of the archers affected the victory, this claim cannot be the sole reason for the defeat."

175 See Yaᶜqūbī, *Taʾrīkh*, 2:47; Ṭabarī, *Taʾrīkh*, 1383–1385. In explaining how the Meccans were well prepared for the battle, I highlight that they "collected money, prepared warriors, plotted tactics, and were determined to win." Ibrahim, *Stated*, 83.

176 Ṭabarī, *Taʾrīkh*, 1409.

177 Wāqidī, *Maghāzī*, 320. See similar arguments in ᶜAbd al-Jabbār, *Tathbīt*, 2:420. We can also consider one interesting literary feature in the account of Uḥud as compared to that of Badr. At Badr, we are told, Muslims killed seventy of the Meccans and took seventy captive. At Uḥud, the numbers are the same, only this time they are in reverse. For Badr, see Ṭabarī, *Taʾrīkh*, 1290, 1354; Ṭabarī, *History*, 7:34, 81. Ibn Hishām, *Sīra*, 1:714. Yaᶜqūbī, *Taʾrīkh*, 2:46. For Uḥud, see Ṭabarī, *History*, 7:81–82; Ṭabarī, *Taʾrīkh*, 1355.

Uḥud. Haykal insists that Muhammad and the believers were driven by a zeal to defend *al-ʿaqīda* (Islamic dogma), *al-īmān* (the faith), and *al-dīn* (the religion) of Allah as well as a desire to secure *al-waṭan* (the homeland) and its *maṣāliḥ* (interests).[178] Haykal's assessment appears unrealistic and seems not to engage the Muslim accounts but to interpret events apologetically.

I argue that this battle—as a religious narrative—is better viewed as the inevitable consequence of a desire for revenge—a tribal expedition prepared and executed by the Meccan Quraysh in retaliation against the Muslims after its defeat at Badr. Religious proclamation neither is reported nor should be expected. This is evident in a statement by classical Shīʿite historian al-Yaʿqūbī, where he writes that at Uḥud, "the Quraysh gathered and got prepared *li-ṭalab tha'ruhā* (to seek its revenge)."[179] It is plausible to deduce that Muslims at Uḥud were involved in one campaign in a series of Meccan-Medinan combats.[180] This is clear in a unique—and to some extent, interesting—account by the renowned Muslim historian al-Ṭabarī, in which he comments on the Muslims' defeat at Uḥud. He contrasts Uḥud with Badr and states that, "at Uḥud, [the Muslims] were punished for what they had done [to the Meccans at Badr]."[181] For al-Ṭabarī, the defeat of the Muslims was a punishment for what they had done to the Meccans one year earlier. Whether al-Ṭabarī's quote refers to Allah or the Meccans as the agent(s) who punished the Muslims is uncertain; however, this unique report is given in the context of how Muslims killed the Meccan prisoners after the Meccans surrendered and how the Muslims quarreled over the ransom money at Badr. Al-Ṭabarī's report presents a disruption in a seemingly unified claim concerning the reasons for the defeat at Uḥud. This particular report of al-Ṭabarī reflects an important phenomenon in Islamic historiography. On the one hand, the report is better viewed as a reflection of a circulated memory among some Muslims—up until the time of al-Ṭabarī—who viewed the actions of Muhammad and the Muslims at Badr—particularly the killing and imprisoning of their own relatives—as appalling and thus punishable by the deity. In this memory, the Muslim defeat at Uḥud was a divine

[178] Haykal, *Ḥayāt*, 305. For another apologetic Sunnī argument, see Ṣallābī, *Ghazawāt*, 92, where he claims that Uḥud was a battle to defend Islam against the Meccans who diligently spent money to prevent people from conversion.

[179] Yaʿqūbī, *Ta'rīkh*, 2:47.

[180] See Watt, *Muḥammad*, 21, where he explains this series of expeditions: "When Abū Sufyān raided Medina to show that Mecca was not 'down and out', Muḥammad gave a counter-display of his power by pursuing him with at least 200 men."

[181] Ṭabarī, *History*, 7:81–82; Ṭabarī, *Ta'rīkh*, 1355. The same account is found in Jawzī, *Muntaẓim*, 3:114; Ibn Kathīr, *Tafsīr*, 2:159, 4:19.

punishment against the Muslims who acted unjustly against their own families. Granted, this memory should not be viewed as a reflection of a factual history, but it reiterates the contention that Muslim narrators often manipulated traditions to convey their sectarian inclinations and advance their preferred sympathies. On the other hand, al-Ṭabarī's report indeed appears rare, but that is as of *now*—it most likely has not always been this way. From the earliest generations of Islam, one may deduce, this report—as a memory of the believers—emerged with other competing reports. As Muslims circulated their memories of the past, they created and shaped their tradition. As a pool of memories, this tradition included numerous reports. Some of these reports were elevated and emphasized by narrators, particularly scholars of traditions, while others were rendered into oblivion.[182] Some reports tendentiously gained momentum and thus formed the orthodox memory, while others were dismissed as less valuable and thus became unconventional—although they did not vanish from the memory of the community, as evidenced by this report by al-Ṭabarī.[183] This elevation and suppression of reports results in new ways of viewing the past, as the memory is developed and shaped.[184] Indeed, this report by al-Ṭabarī is an exception. It highlights the struggle between the Muslims and the Meccans as a series of continuous combats, and the Muslims were not always blameless. Still, the vast majority of traditions attribute the Muslims' defeat at Uḥud to the disobedience of the archers to Muhammad's commands, to the hypocrisy of ᶜAbdullāh when he withdrew from marching to the battle, or to Allah's desire to teach the Muslims a lesson.[185]

[182] Sarah Savant studies religious loyalty and belonging "from the twin angles of tradition and memory," as she traces *revisions* and *elisions* to the collective memory of the new Iranian Muslims. Savant, *New*, 1–30. Savant builds on various theories, including Jan Assmann's "mnemohistory" and Maurice Halbwachs's "collective memory." Assmann studies how Moses is remembered in European history in the seventeenth and eighteenth centuries, and argues that the "past is not simply 'received' by the present. The present is 'haunted' by the past and the past is modeled, invented, reinvented, and reconstructed by the present." Assmann, *Moses*, 9. See also Assmann, *Cultural*, 55, where he argues that memory (and thus forgetting) is socially and culturally shaped, emphasizing the existence of an "alliance between power and forgetting" of cultural memory. See Spiegel, "Memory," 149–162; Hutton, *History*, 1–22; Halbwachs, *On Collective*; Fentress and Wickham, *Social*; Innes, "Memory"; Steinbock, *Social Memory*.

[183] See Savant, *New*, 4, where she argues, "As a tradition accumulates weight and authority, it shapes collective agreements about the past, thereby creating memories."

[184] Sarah Savant, by focusing on the role of memory and its revision and erasure, argues, "Conversion to Islam led Iranians to recall their past in new ways and to accumulate new memories about their history." Savant, *New*, 3.

[185] See Ṭabarī, *History*, 7:113; Ṭabarī, *Taʾrīkh*, 1394. Wāqidī, *Maghāzī*, 224–225; Ibn Qutayba, *Maᶜārif*, 159; Bayhaqī, *Dalāʾil*, 3:227. For classical Muslims who claim that the defeat was a lesson from Allah to the Muslims, see the commentaries on Q 3:140 in Muqātil, *Tafsīr*, 1:193; Qurṭubī, *Tafsīr*, 4:218; Riḍā, *Manār*, 4:148.

In the same vein, al-Ṭabarī considers Muhammad's injury. In reporting its severity, he states that Muhammad's "lower lateral incisor was broken, his helmet was shattered on his head, and the blood flowed over his face; the Prophet's companions fled and took to the mountain."[186] This is expected in tribal battles, rather than assuming divine protection apart from the natural course of raids. However, the severe injury of Muhammad and his near death—as literary features—do not sit squarely with other reports that seek to assign him complete divine protection.[187] This undoubtedly perplexed the narrators, and they diligently attempted to tweak the narrative to state that Muhammad, one day following the defeat, was back on the battlefield, leading the Muslims in more military combats.[188] Was Muhammad divinely protected against harm? Some said his divine protection began only after Uḥud, while others claimed he was only protected against getting killed.[189]

Fifth, the matter of the spoils of war is worth noting. At Badr and Uḥud, many Muslim soldiers reportedly rushed to secure the spoils. At Badr, the warriors disputed the distribution of spoils, which led Muhammad to postpone dividing and distributing them.[190] The matter was unsatisfying and completely out of their control. At Uḥud, however, the soldiers—particularly the archers—appear to have desired to secure their own portions without waiting until after the battle.[191] Al-Wāqidī reports, "The Muslims were busy with the spoils and the plunder."[192] They were not ready to wait for Muhammad or anyone else to distribute spoils. They wanted the matter to be done by their own hands. "It seems safe to assume the archers wanted to secure the maximum portion of the spoils of war."[193] This expedition—as a

[186] Ṭabarī, *History*, 7:81–82; Ṭabarī, *Ta'rīkh*, 1355. Ibn Hishām, *Sīra*, 2:86; Ibn Hishām, *Life*, 383.

[187] See, for instance, the views of Muslim traditionists on the verse "And Allah will *yaᶜṣimuka* (shield, defend, or protect you) from people" (Q 5:67). See Muqātil, *Tafsīr*, 1:492; Ṭabarī, *Jāmiᶜ*, 10:469 (Muhammad used to be protected by people, until Allah revealed this verse), 10:471 (Muhammad used to fear the Quraysh, until Allah revealed this verse to assure him of protection); Zamakhsharī, *Kashshāf*, 2:688; Rāzī, *Mafātiḥ*, 12:399–401 (the protection was only against getting killed, the verse was revealed *after* Uḥud); Qurṭubī, *Jāmiᶜ*, 6:242–244; Riḍā, *Manār*, 6:391; Kharkūshī, *Sharaf*, 1:465; ᶜAbd al-Jabbār, *Tathbīt*, 1:7, 2:346.

[188] Wāqidī, *Life*, 163; Wāqidī, *Maghāzī*, 334. See Spiegel, "Revising," 1–19.

[189] See Rāzī, *Mafātiḥ*, 12:401.

[190] See Wāqidī, *Maghāzī*, 99–100; Wāqidī, *Life*, 50–51. Watt, *Muḥammad*, 12.

[191] For a secondary study on four expected material rewards for Muslim soldiers in battles, see Ibrahim, *Stated*, 72. For primary sources, see Yaḥyā ibn Ādam, *Kharāj*, 58–61, 82; Ibn Sallām, *Amwāl*, where he discusses *al-fay'* (87–96, 132–145, 301–311), distinguishes *al-fay'* from the *ghanīma* (342–349), and explains the *salb* (403–408). See Ibn Zanjawayh, *Amwāl*, 477ff.; Ibn Qudāma, *Mughnī*, 6:453ff. For a Muslim secondary study, see ᶜUmarī, *Sīra*, 511–512; cf. ᶜAbd al-Karīm, *Shadwu*, 1:75–77. For a non-Muslim view, see Kister, "Land," 273.

[192] Wāqidī, *Life*, 114; Wāqidī, *Maghāzī*, 230.

[193] Ibrahim, *Stated*, 83.

literary tale—does not seem to have been a battle for religious proclamation but a natural tribal raid driven by loot-lust.[194] The Muslim thinker Khalīl ᶜAbd al-Karīm, in his examination of Muslim raids, observes that many of Muhammad's *ṣaḥāba* (companions) were often concerned with *al-ghanīma* (the spoils of war).[195] The arguments of ᶜAbd al-Karīm are plausible and fit the natural course of tribal raids and expeditions among the Arabs, although they do not align with traditional claims suggesting the raids were for self-defense and religious proclamation.[196]

Without a doubt, the Muslims' defeat at Uḥud resulted in a challenge to the religious support they claimed one year earlier at Badr. After all, seventy Muslims were killed and seventy others taken captive.[197] In addition, there were many important companions and relatives of Muhammad among the dead. How could Allah leave his people to be defeated by pagan unbelievers? How could he leave his prophet to be injured and almost die? Where was the angelic support to save the Muslims from death and injury? Why were there no miraculous deeds to change the balance of power in the battle? These unanswered questions likely puzzled the narrators, but they resorted to their religious disposition and painted the defeat as a divinely given lesson for the Muslims to never disobey Muhammad.[198] However, as Watt observes, the defeat creates a significant challenge to the ideology repeatedly advanced in the traditions portraying the Muslim community with unequal superiority and unmatched divine support.[199]

The Battle of Uḥud was the first significant defeat of the Muslims in their fight with the Meccan Quraysh. It was a major setback. However, storytellers insist, Muslims soon reunited, learned a valuable lesson, and prepared to

[194] See Roohi, "Muḥammad's Disruptive," 40–80, especially 74, where he argues, "Had the early traditionists understood the attribution to the Prophet of caravan looting as a matter of discomfort, the number of caravan raids would most likely have undergone a decline in the period between Ibn Isḥāq and al-Wāqidī. In reality, however, the situation was vice versa."

[195] See ᶜAbd al-Karīm, *Shadwu*, 1:85ff., as he examines two battles. Compare with the traditional interpretation in Haykal, *Ḥayāt*, 281.

[196] For pre-Islamic tribal raids among the Arabs, see ᶜAlī, *Mufaṣṣal*, 10:5–140; 7:142–414.

[197] These numbers are curious and appear fabricated, as they reflect the same counts of Badr among the Meccans, only this time they are given about the Muslims. At badr, we are told, the Muslims "killed seventy of [the unbelievers of Mecca] and took seventy of them captive." See Ṭabarī, *History*, 7:34, 81; Ibn Hishām, *Sīra*, 1:714. Yaᶜqūbī, *Ta'rīkh*, 2:46.

[198] See, for example, al-Qurṭubī claiming that Muhammad's injury was an example of consolation and comfort to the Muslims. Qurṭubī, *Jāmiᶜ*, 14:155.

[199] Watt, *Muḥammad*, 26–27. Medieval Christians used the defeat at Uḥud to question the divine support assumed by Muslims. See the example of ᶜAbd al-Masīḥ al-Kindī in his *Risāla* as found in Newman, ed., *Early Christian-Muslim*, 430–432.

exact their own revenge. The Medina-Mecca combat appears as a long military conflict that lasted about eight years. During this combat, the Meccans grew weaker, while the Medinan Muslim community grew stronger. This is evident in many Muslim victories over the Meccans reportedly achieved in the following years. We now turn to these victories.

4
Muhammad's Triumph over the Meccans

> I have endeavoured in this book, I believe on sufficient grounds, to show that neither the wars of Mohammad were offensive, nor did he in any way use force or compulsion in the matter of belief.—Moulavi Chirágh Ali (1844–1895)[1]

According to Muslim traditions, many confrontations occurred between the Muslims and the Meccan tribe of the Quraysh during the final decade of Muhammad's life. While the previous chapter focused on the Battle of Badr and the Battle of Uḥud, in this chapter we cover three more encounters between the two camps: the Battle of the Trench, the Battle (and treaty) of Ḥudaybiyya, and the conquest of Mecca.[2] Muhammad was reportedly the commander of the Muslims in all three battles. The Battle of the Trench, also known as al-Khandaq (ditch) or al-Aḥzāb (the confederates), occurred two years after Uḥud; there, the Muslims successfully defeated the confederates (Meccans and the allies). The Battle of the Ḥudaybiyya took place one year after al-Khandaq and appears as a tactical treaty, although Muslim narrators insist it was a successful *ghazwa* (raid). This treaty provided Muhammad and his followers a time of relief, with less tension with the Quraysh—a time needed to focus on other enemies. Two years after the Ḥudaybiyya, Muhammad launched the conquest of Mecca. It is described as the greatest conquest of all, although it appears as a negotiated surrender that declared him the major king of West Arabia. As in the previous chapters, in the following discussion I examine the Medinan-Meccan confrontations with a

[1] Ali, *Critical*, i.

[2] Some of the other raids include the raid to al-Sawīq (2/624), al-Qarada (3/624), Ḥamrā' al-Asad (3/625), Badr al-Mawᶜid (4/625), and others. These were indeed important raids, but their significance is not by any means comparable to the major five discussed in this chapter. Some classical historians do not even mention these minor battles. For example, see the list of Muhammad's raids included by Ibn Ḥabīb, *Muḥabbar*; Khalīfa, *Ta'rīkh*; Yaᶜqūbī, *Ta'rīkh*. For the Mecca-Medina combat, see Sharīf, *Makka*, 433–495.

Muhammad's Military Expeditions. Ayman S. Ibrahim, Oxford University Press. © Oxford University Press 2024.
DOI: 10.1093/oso/9780197769171.003.0004

special emphasis on their stated motivations, goals, and results. In examining these *maghāzī* accounts, I view them as literary representations of what "the medieval historians, at best, believed to have taken place or, at worst, desired their audience to believe about the era they described."[3] We should view these accounts as largely the product of ᶜAbbāsid-era historians, who designed ideological stories to educate Muslims and fashioned figurative tales to relay to non-Muslims important matters regarding Islam and its prophet.

The Battle of the Trench (5/627)

This battle is known as al-Khandaq (the Trench) or al-Aḥzāb (the Confederates or the Allied Parties).[4] Muslim narrators depict it as a military siege of Medina led by about tne thousand Meccans and their allies—all forming the so-called *al-aḥzāb*, that is, the confederates.[5] The *aḥzāb*, we are told, consisted of the Meccan Quraysh, the tribe of Ghaṭafān, and some Jews from the tribes of Banū al-Naḍīr and Banū Qurayẓa.[6] The siege reportedly occurred in 5/627, only two years after the Muslims' defeat at Uḥud in 3/625.[7]

[3] Ibrahim, *Conversion*, 22. Our sources provide a "representation rather than record," as the historians were authors "who wrote well after the events they describe." Robinson, *Empire*, viii. See also Petersen, *ᶜAlī*, 11–20; Khalidi, *Images*, 151–280; Hibri, *Parable*, ch. 1; Hagen, "Imagined," 97–111; Wansbrough, *Sectarian*, ix, 118–119; Wansbrough, "Res," in *Method*, ed. Berg, 10–19; Rippin, "Literary," 155–156. Rubin, *Eye*, 1–3.

[4] For the account of the battle, see Wāqidī, *Maghāzī*, 440ff.; Ibn Hishām, *Sīra*, 2:214ff.; Ibn Hishām, *Life*, 668–713; Balādhurī, *Futūḥ*, 17ff.; Balādhurī, *Origins*, 34ff.; Yaᶜqūbī, *Ta'rīkh*, 2:50; Ṭabarī, *Ta'rīkh*, 1463–1485; Ibn Qutayba, *Maᶜārif*, 161–166; Ibn ᶜAbd al-Barr, *Durar*, 1:169ff.; Kalāᶜī, *Iktifā'*, 1:420ff. For Muslim secondary studies, see Sharīf, *Makka*, 364ff.; Abū Māyla, *Sarāyā*, 173–178; Abū Māyla, *Ghazwat*, 52ff.; Ṣaᶜīdī, *Tārīkh*, 107–113; Ṣaᶜīdī, *Dirāsāt*, 126–130. For a non-Muslim study, see Watt, *Muḥammad*, 35ff. For the confederates, see Ibn Hishām, *Sīra*, 2:215, where he states that Abū Sufyān was the leader of the *mushrikūn* (polytheists, associaters); Bayhaqī, *Dalā'il*, 3:394; Suhaylī, *Rawḍ*, 6:197.

[5] This number is unrealistic. See Shoemaker, *Creating*, 98, where he explains that Mecca, in the late ancient Near East, "was a very small village with only a few hundred inhabitants, perhaps around five hundred or so, with around 130 free adult men."

[6] See Ibn Hishām, *Sīra*, 1:561 and 2:214–215, where the author states that some Jews of Banū al-Naḍīr went all the way to Mecca to incite the Quraysh against Muhammad. Ibn Ḥibbān, *Sīra*, 1:254, indicates that the people of Banū al-Naḍīr were furious because Muhammad expelled them from Medina, so they traveled to Mecca to instigate the Meccans, calling them to fight Muhammad, promising that they would join the confederates, and aiming to *nasta'ṣilahu wa man maᶜahu* (completely destroy him and those with him). See the comments on this by Sharīf, *Makka*, 337; also Qimanī, *Ḥurūb*, 243ff. Rodinson, *Muhammad*, 210–211.

[7] Muslim historians make competing and contradicting claims about the dates of many battles; al-Khandaq is not an exception. See Bayhaqī, *Dalā'il*, 3:392ff. and 5:463, where he relies heavily on Mūsā ibn ᶜUqba's accounts, which place the battle a year earlier (in the year A.H. 4). Compare with Suhaylī, *Rawḍ*, 6:196 and 6:243, as he relies on Ibn Hishām's *Sīra* and places the battle in the year A.H. 5; see the similar dating in Wāqidī, *Maghāzī*, 440, and Ibn Kathīr, *Sīra*, 3:132ff. See also Yaᶜqūbī 2:50, where he states that it was in the year A.H. 6. For contradictions in the chronology of the *maghāzī*, see Jones, "Chronology," 245–280; Schacht, "On Mūsā," 288–300; Schoeler, "Mūsā," 67–97.

At al-Khandaq, after the confederates seized Medina for about three weeks or a month, their siege failed and they retreated.[8] The Muslims reportedly won greatly, although the confederates had given their very best effort.[9] The narrative is a medieval religious memory, projected back in history for religious and sociopolitical purposes. It provides a whole cluster of exhorting insights and spiritual prophecies—not historical details. The Muslims are portrayed as under siege by unbelieving pagans and Jews, yet they still won; one lesson advanced by the narrators, we may deduce, is a call for the Muslims to be patient under affliction, as Allah is with the believers (Q 2:153), and he will thwart the schemes of the unbelievers. The narrative paints the Jews in a dark light, portraying them as hypocrites and deceivers whose loyalty cannot be trusted. They are an unfaithful camp that is clearly on the decline. In contrast, the story idealizes Muhammad, elevating him as a growing star in Arabia, an unstoppable conquest initiator and commander whose strength and power constantly astonish the Bedouins.

More importantly, the storytellers do not relinquish the chance to advance sympathies appealing to the early ᶜAbbāsids, by introducing a unique Persian character and displaying him as the genius mind behind the victory.[10] The new convert to Islam Salmān the Persian reportedly advised Muhammad to dig a trench around Medina.[11] The Muslims' staying in

[8] The siege was reportedly "for over twenty nights—nearly a month—with no warfare between the troops." Ṭabarī, *History*, 8:17.

[9] See Djait, *Fitna*, 26–28, where he views al-Khandaq as the second most important Muslim victory. See also Djait, *Masīrat*, 127–131. In describing the efforts of the Meccans in this battle, Watt writes, "It was the supreme effort of the Meccans to break Muḥammad's power." Watt, *Muḥammad*, 36.

[10] Savant, *New*, 61–89. The Persians were known as crucial agents in the ᶜAbbāsid revolution and to the ᶜAbbāsid caliphs. For the Persian influence on the ᶜAbbāsids, see, for instance, the role of the Persian Abū Muslim al-Khurāsānī as described in Dīnawarī, *Akhbār*, 338ff.; Ibn al-Athīr, *Kāmil*, 4:358ff.; Dhahabī, *Ta'rīkh*, 8:25ff.; Dhahabī, *Siyar*, 6:48ff.; Ibn ᶜAsākir, *Ta'rīkh*, 35:408ff.; Ibn Khallikān, *Wafayāt*, 3:145–156; Ṣafadī, *Wāfī*, 18:161; Ziriklī, *Aᶜlām*, 3:337–338. For a broader discussion, see Kennedy, *Prophet*, 123ff., especially 132–140; Kennedy, *Caliphate*, ch. 3; Hibri, *Abbasid*, 55–56; Khuḍarī, *Dawla*, 19–40, especially 38–40, also 63–64 and 67; Ḍayf, *ᶜAṣr*, 9–12; Agha, *Revolution*, 53–86; Muṣṭafā, *Ta'rīkh*, 1:191; Sourdel, "al-Faḍl b. Yaḥyā al-Barmakī," *EI²*, 2:732; Sourdel, "al-Barāmika," *EI²*, 1:1033ff.; Bouvat, *Les Barmécides*, 25ff. For how caliphal influence shaped traditions, see Black, *History*, 27ff.; Lassner, *Shaping*, 24–30; Lassner, *Medieval*, 138; Lecker, "Notes," 233–254; Lecker, "Glimpses," in *Cambridge Companion*, ed. Brockopp, 62; Lecker, *Muslims*, 92 and Appendix B, 154–155; Robinson, *Historiography*, 40.

[11] The word "advised" is used by Ṭabarī, *History*, 8:8. On Salmān's advising Muhammad, see ᶜAbd al-Jabbār, *Tathbīt*, 2:450; also Suhaylī, *Rawḍ*, 6:195, where he claims that the trench was a Persian war tactic with which Arabs were not familiar—a claim explained by Sharīf, *Makka*, 328–329. For Salmān and his life, see Ibn Saᶜd, *Ṭabaqāt*, 4:56ff. (he was a convert to Christianity from Zoroastrianism but later converted to Islam after meeting Muhammad); Ibn Ḥibbān, *Thiqāt*, 141, 249–257, 266; Balādhurī, *Ansāb*, 1:485–489; Dāraquṭnī, *Mu'talif*, 2:785; Ibn Manda, *Maᶜrifat*, 726–727 (Salmān lived for 250 years!); Ibn ᶜAbd al-Barr, *Istīᶜāb*, 2:634–638; Ibn ᶜAsākir, *Ta'rīkh*, 21:373–459 (Salmān actually lived for 350 years, although some say only 250 [p. 459]); Ibn al-Athīr, *Usd*, 2:510; Dhahabī, *Siyar*, 1:505–557; Samᶜānī, *Ansāb*, 6:47–48. For a secondary study on Salmān, see Savant, *New*, 61–89.

Medina and not going out to meet the enemy—like they did at Uḥud—proved to be a successful military tactic. This trench, we are told, served as a barrier that allowed the Muslims to defeat the confederates and force them to retreat in humiliation.[12] Salmān the Persian's portrayal in the Trench's accounts aims to signify a national Persian pride, intending to exhort and appeal to the new Sassanid converts—after all, they largely supported the ᶜAbbāsids against the Umayyads.[13] Creatively developed by ᶜAbbāsid-era historians, the narrative is dispositioned to relay that one of the Persian Muslims is a cherished companion of Muhammad and is credited with a significant role in the triumph over the unbelievers. Salmān, as a literary depiction, appears standing with distinction next to Muhammad, proposing a uniquely innovative idea—digging a trench—that no Arab had seen before.[14] He is an example, the rationale goes, for Muslims—especially those of Persian origin—to emulate in their devotion to Muhammad. Salmān's portrayal is built on many other literary layers, scattered elsewhere in Muslim traditions. He reportedly wandered for years in Syria in search of Muhammad as the final prophet, until he met him and converted to Islam in Muhammad's presence.[15] The entire narrative is better viewed as a religious figurative tale. This is evidenced in how the narrators claim that, since the Muslims' victory was significant, some verses in the Qur'ān foretold and declared it.[16] After the victory, Muhammad announced that Allah beat the confederates.[17]

[12] One should not think of Medina as a city with walls. It is an oasis. On the geography of Medina, see Yaᶜqūbī, *Buldān*, 97–98; Ibn Khuradādhbih, *Masālik*, 128–132; Hamdānī, *Ṣifat*, 47–48; Iṣṭakhrī, *Masālik*, 18–19; Ibn al-Faqīh, *Mukhtaṣar*, 23–27. Concerning the location of the trench, see Wāqidī, *Maghāzī*, 450–452, which states that the trench was outside Medina between two mountains—one called Banū ᶜUbayd and the other Rātij—and that some Muslims actually claimed the trench had gates, but no one knew where they were. See also Kharkūshī, *Sharaf*, 3:47. Note that later Muslims tried to use the trench in other battles and it did not work. See Ibrahim, *Stated*, 115, where I write, "The trench was a sufficient barrier for the Meccan horses, but not an actually defensible location, as was proved about 150 years later when Muḥammad al-Nafs al-Zakiyya tried to use it against the ᶜAbbāsid army, and it did not succeed." See Ibn al-Athīr, *Kāmil*, 5:130.

[13] Hibri, *Parable*, 14–15.

[14] Suhaylī, *Rawḍ*, 6:195; Sharīf, *Makka*, 328–329.

[15] Ibn Saᶜd, *Ṭabaqāt*, 4:56ff.; Hibri, *Parable*, 14–15. His depiction at the Trench is a climax of his portrayal, although he will continue being active in the life of the Muslims for years after Muhammad's death. See his role at the conquest of Ctesiphon. Ṭabarī, *Ta'rīkh*, 2437.

[16] For its mention in the Qur'ān, see Ibn Hishām, *Sīra*, 2:245; Suhaylī, *Rawḍ*, 6:242. For exegetes describing the Qur'ānic statements on the battle, see Muqātil, *Tafsīr*, 3:455ff.; Ṭabarī, *Jāmiᶜ*, 14:469ff., 15:278ff.; Zamakhsharī, *Kashshāf*, 3:518ff.; Rāzī, *Mafātiḥ*, 25:153ff.; Qurṭubī, *Jāmiᶜ*, 14:113ff.; Bayḍāwī, *Anwār*, 4:224ff.

[17] Ibn Hishām, *Sīra*, 2:412; Bayhaqī, *Dalā'il*, 3:88; Kalāᶜī, *Iktifā'*, 1:509, 2:31. After the battle, Gabriel instructed Muhammad not to rest but to go immediately to fight Banū Qurayẓa. Bayhaqī, *Dalā'il*, 7:66. On killing men and taking women and children captive, see Suhaylī, *Rawḍ*, 6:248.

In this section, I discuss the battle of al-Khandaq; however, before doing so, we should note that in the two-year period between Uḥud and al-Khandaq, the fighting continued between the Muslims and the Meccans and resulted in several confrontations.[18] Looking at these minor confrontations briefly is important before we examine the major accounts of al-Khandaq. Based on many Muslim historical reports, it is plausible to deduce that after the defeat at Uḥud, the morale among Muslims was significantly low.[19] The defeat was not only a military blow but also a huge hit to the Muslim's presumed religious hegemony and supposed divine protection.[20] Muhammad had to act quickly. One day after Uḥud, while he was severely wounded, he reportedly sought to chase the Meccans before they reached Mecca. Portraying him as a fearless commander, the traditions reveal that Muhammad gathered the *wujūh* (notables) of the Arabs in Medina and exhorted the believers to fight.[21] With enthusiasm, the Muslims responded to Muhammad's command and declared their devotion to Allah, as they "jumped to their weapons and did not stop for their wounds."[22] They all marched to attack the Meccans. We are told that Muhammad "went out while he was wounded. On his face were the traces of two links, and a cut on his forehead at the root of his hair. His tooth had splintered, his upper lip cut from within, his right shoulder weakened by the blow from Ibn Qamī'a, and the two sides of his knees bruised."[23] The portrayal idealizes Muhammad and presents him as an unstoppable warrior. This combat became known in Muslim traditions as the raid of Ḥamrā' al-Asad, which is the name of the location—some eight miles from Medina.[24] While Muslim traditions portray the raid of Ḥamrā' al-Asad as one of the brave military decisions by the Muslims to avenge their defeat by the Meccans, we are also told that there was no fight. The literary details concerning the raid, its timing, and its precursors—from a military standpoint—are hardly plausible, especially if we consider Muhammad's severe injury and the overall morale of the Muslims.[25] However, these details are meaningful tools for the

[18] See al-Qimanī, *Ḥurūb*, 217–272; Djait, *Masīrat*, 121–127.

[19] See Ṭabarī, *Ta'rīkh*, 1403; Ṭabarī, *History*, 7:120, where he speaks of the Muslim retreat and calls it a catastrophe: "When this catastrophe befell the Muslims, they were afflicted in three ways; some were killed, some wounded, and some put to flight." The catastrophe was magnified by the "Mutilation of the Muslim Dead" at the hands of Meccan women. Ṭabarī, *Ta'rīkh*, 1415ff.

[20] Watt, *Muḥammad*, 29–30.

[21] Wāqidī, *Life*, 163; Wāqidī, *Maghāzī*, 334.

[22] Wāqidī, *Life*, 163; Wāqidī, *Maghāzī*, 335.

[23] Wāqidī, *Life*, 164.

[24] Ṭabarī, *Ta'rīkh*, 1427ff.; Ṭabarī, *History*, 7:138ff.

[25] Wāqidī, *Maghāzī*, 335–339; Watt explains, "Contact was not made with the enemy, though they were apparently still in the vicinity. To make his demonstration more impressive Muhammad had his men work hard collecting wood by day and lighting fires by night." Watt, *Muḥammad*, 29. See Ṭabarī,

storytellers in order to develop their religious instruction for their Muslim audience. Muslim historians, as religious instructors, needed a picture of fearless and unstoppable soldiers, strivers (*mujāhidūn*) in Allah's path, despite the defeat—and that is what they created. Still, as a literary tale, we may deduce that the raid served mainly as a declaration of power to save face. The narrators' aim was likely to highlight how Muhammad sought to attack the Meccans in order to demonstrate that the Muslims still possessed zeal and power to fight—or that he needed to prevent any further escalated attacks by the Meccans.[26] We are told that after no confrontation had transpired, the Muslims returned to Medina, while the Meccans went their way to Mecca. The raid of Ḥamrā' al-Asad appears as the first in a series of minor battles during the two-year period between Uḥud and al-Khandaq—a strategic period for the Muslims and the Meccans.[27]

The Muslim narrators placed considerable emphasis on the theme of the rising hegemony of the Muslims by detailing many raids with high frequency in a short time. This theme serves the religious philosophy of the narrators. After Uḥud and before al-Khandaq, Muhammad continued raiding the Meccan Quraysh and their allies. We read of raids targeting the Meccans, including the expedition of Badr al-Mawᶜid (one year after Uḥud) and al-Rajīᶜ (three years after the *hijra*),[28] and others against their allies—such as the tribes of Asad, Ghaṭafān, and Banū al-Muṣṭaliq—as in the expeditions of Bi'r Maᶜūna, Dhāt al-Riqāᶜ, Dūmat al-Jandal, and al-Muraysiᶜ.[29] These raids were

History, 7:129, where he describes the severity of the Muslim defeat and states that, after the battle, the wife of Abū Sufyān, Hind, "and the women who were with her stopped to mutilate the Messenger of God's dead companions, cutting off their ears and noses until Hind was able to make anklets and necklaces of them." See also Ṭabarī, *Ta'rīkh*, 1415.

[26] Al-Ṭabarī reports that Abū Sufyān and some of his army desired to return to attack Medina and said, "We killed a proportion of Muḥammad's companions, including leaders and nobles, and now we have turned back home before exterminating them. Let us return to Medina for the rest of them and finish them off." Ṭabarī, *History*, 7:140.

[27] See the analysis of the confrontations between the Muslims and the Meccans during this two-year period in Qimanī, *Ḥurūb*, 217–272.

[28] On al-Rajīᶜ, see Wāqidī, *Maghāzī*, 354, which states that Muhammad sent Muslims to spy on the Meccan Quraysh. See also Ṭabarī, *Ta'rīkh*, 1431–1432, where this raid is dated as the first in the year A.H. 4. See Ṭabarī, *History*, 7:143. The Muslims were unsuccessful in this raid, and many of them were killed. See Watt, *Muḥammad*, 34. To revenge the death of some Muslims at al-Rajīᶜ, Muhammad reportedly led a minor expedition against Banū Liḥyān a few months later. See Ṭabarī, *Ta'rīkh*, 1501–1502. Similarly, shortly before the treaty of Ḥudaybiyya, Muhammad reportedly led a raid—more like a skirmish or a chasing—to Dhū Qarad. Ṭabarī, *Ta'rīkh*, 1502–1510. According to al-Ṭabarī, Dhū Qarad was followed by Banū al-Muṣṭaliq—these were the last two raids before the treaty of Ḥudaybiyya.

[29] On Bi'r Maᶜūna, see Ṭabarī, *Ta'rīkh*, 1441, where he states that the expedition targeted Najd and was a "disaster" for the Muslims. See Ṭabarī, *History*, 7:151. See Watt, *Muḥammad*, 34, where he defines the Muslim defeat at Bi'r maᶜūna as a "misfortune." See Roohi, "Form-Critical," 267–338,

arguably limited in their goals, as compared to other major battles. They were part of the continued tribal conflict between the Muslims, on the one hand, and the Meccans and their allies, on the other. This is evident if we observe the precursors of Uḥud, when Muhammad reportedly targeted the tribe of Ghaṭafān—the allies of Mecca—a few months before Uḥud in the raid of Dhū Amarr (also known as the raid to Ghaṭafān).[30] Moreover, according to Muslim traditions, Muhammad deployed two strategic military tactics: he (1) diligently worked to suppress the power of the Medinan Jews and (2) skillfully planned the assassination of major individuals among his enemies. The former is evident in the expulsion of two major Jewish tribes from Medina—Banū Qaynuqāᶜ was expelled before Uḥud and Banū al-Naḍīr shortly after (we discuss these expeditions in the next chapter).[31] The latter is evident in that Muhammad instructed the assassination of Abū Sufyān from among the Meccans (an unsuccessful attempt) and several other Jewish leaders, such as the poet Abū ᶜAfak (an outspoken critic of Muhammad) and two chiefs of Banū al-Naḍīr, Abū Rafiᶜ ibn Abī al-Ḥuqayq and Kaᶜb ibn al-Ashraf.[32] These reported assassinations are better viewed as religious tales *by* and *for* later

where he studies the stories of al-Rajīᶜ and Bi'r Maᶜūna raids critically. For Dhāt al-Riqāᶜ, see Ṭabarī, *Ta'rīkh*, 1454–1460, where he states that the expedition occurred in the year A.H. 4 immediately after the expedition of Banū al-Naḍīr and targeted the Arab tribes of Anmār and Thaᶜlaba. See also Wāqidī, *Maghāzī*, 395. For Dūmat al-Jandal, see Ṭabarī, *Ta'rīkh*, 1463–1464, where he explains that the raid occurred shortly before al-Khandaq and targeted the tribe of Quḍāᶜa—allies of Ghaṭafān and almost five hundred miles from Medina—but there was "no clash with the enemy." See Ṭabarī, *History*, 8:4–5. See Watt's comments on the raid in *Muḥammad*, 35. The raid of al-Muraysiᶜ (a water well where the raid occurred) is also known as the expedition against the Banū al-Muṣṭaliq (the tribe attacked). Al-Wāqidī dates it a few months before al-Khandaq in the year A.H. 5, while al-Ṭabarī claims it occurred shortly after al-Khandaq in the year A.H. 6. See Wāqidī, *Maghāzī*, 404–414; Wāqidī, *Life*, 198–202; Ṭabarī, *Ta'rīkh*, 1511–1517; Ṭabarī, *History*, 8:51–57. Historians claim that the tribe of Banū al-Muṣṭaliq was planning to attack Medina, and Muhammad launched a preventive raid to confront them. Al-Wāqidī summarizes the raid and states that Muhammad "commanded his companions to attack. They attacked as a single man and not a man among [the enemies] escaped. Ten of them were killed and the rest of them were taken captive. The Messenger of God captured men women and children [*sic*]. Cattle and sheep were plundered. Only one man was killed from the Muslims." Wāqidī, *Life*, 199. Watt, *Muḥammad*, 35. The raid was infamous because immediately after it, Muhammad's wife ᶜĀ'isha was accused of adultery in an incident known as *al-ifk* (the lie), but Allah and Muhammad declared her innocence. See Ṭabarī, *Ta'rīkh*, 1518–1531. Ibrahim, *Muhammad*, 55–57.

30 For the raid of Dhū Amarr, see Wāqidī, *Maghāzī*, 193–196; Ibn Hishām, *Sīra*, 2:46–48. Dhū Amarr is a valley near Medina. Al-Ṭabarī dates the raid at the beginning of the year A.H. 3. See Ṭabarī, *History*, 7:93–95, where he writes that Muhammad stayed for a month in the valley "and then returned to Medina without any fighting."

31 See Qimanī, *Ḥurūb*, 229ff., where he analyzes Muhammad's treatment of the Jews of Banū al-Naḍīr after Uḥud. For the expulsion of Banū al-Naḍīr, see Ṭabarī, *Ta'rīkh*, 1448ff., where he places it in the year A.H. 4 before al-Khandaq. See also Ṭabarī, *History*, 7:156ff.

32 See Wāqidī, *Maghāzī*, 3, where he lists the sequence of the raids, placing Qaynuqāᶜ and Banū al-Naḍīr before al-Khandaq. For the incursion to murder Abū Sufyān, see Ṭabarī, *History*, 7:147–150.

Muslims—during and after the time of documentation—concerning ways to treat opponents and critics.[33] Overall, the narratives convey that, between Uḥud and al-Khandaq, Muhammad's side grew stronger, eliminated enemies, and created alliances.

As for the Meccan side, based on Muslim accounts, we can deduce that the Meccans seem to have lost a great opportunity after Uḥud, as they did not maximize their advantage by striking while they had a prime opportunity. They simply returned to Mecca and began celebrating.[34] This naïve retreat—as reported in Muslim traditions—might actually reinforce the tendentiousness of the accounts. The narrators design an unfavorable depiction of the Meccan pagans. From a tactical standpoint, the Meccan retreat granted the Muslims time and opportunity to reunite and rearrange their military ranks. With the exception of the unsuccessful raids of al-Rajīᶜ and Bi'r Maᶜūna, the Muslims are reported to have grown in power between Uḥud and al-Khandaq.[35] As for the Meccans, "The only possibility of raising a more powerful army was [for them] to attract the active support of some of the great nomadic tribes to the east and northeast of Medina, using propaganda about Muḥammad's weakness, memories of the prestige of Quraysh, promises of booty, and even straight bribes."[36] After all, at Uḥud, the Meccans

For the incursion of killing Abū ᶜAfak and how Muhammad commissioned the companion Sālim ibn ᶜUmayr to fulfill it, see Wāqidī, *Maghāzī*, 174ff.; also Ibn Hishām, *Sīra*, 2:635–636. As for the Jew Abū Rāfiᶜ, he was another critic of Muhammad and known as Sallām ibn Abī al-Ḥuqayq. He was one of the leaders of the confederates. He reportedly *ḥazzab al-aḥzāb* (created the alliances). See Kalāᶜī, *Iktifā'*, 1:444, which states that Abū Rāfiᶜ was a main conspirator against the Muslims. See Wāqidī, *Maghāzī*, 373–393, where it explains that Muhammad planned to assassinate Abū Rāfiᶜ and sent the companion Ibn ᶜAtīk to murder him. See also Ibn Hishām, *Sīra*, 2:273–274, where he claims that the al-Aws clan killed Kaᶜb ibn al-Ashraf for Muhammad before Uhud, while the Khazraj clan killed Abū Rāfiᶜ after Uḥud after they asked Muhammad's permission as they competed with the al-Aws. See also Bayhaqī, *Dalā'il*, 3:408, where he claims that the Jews of Banū Qurayẓa and Banū al-Nadir were the main agents who created the confederates against the Muslims. See similar accounts on the role of the Jews in creating the *aḥzāb* (confederates) in Ibn ᶜAbd al-Barr, *Durar*, 1:169; Suhaylī, *Rawḍ*, 6:196. For murdering Kaᶜb ibn al-Ashraf, see Wāqidī, *Maghāzī*, 184–192; Ibn Hishām, *Sīra*, 2:54–57. For secondary studies, see Sharīf, *Makka*, 364; Abū Māyla, *Sarāyā*, 173–178; Abū Māyla, *Ghazwat*, 52ff. and 1121. See Watt, *Muḥammad*, 31–32, where he discusses two assassinations instructed by Muhammad between Uḥud and al-Khandaq.

33 See Ibn Taymiyya, *Ṣārim*, 70–91. See the critical observations of Roohi, "Muḥammad's," 40–80.

34 Some Meccan soldiers acknowledged this tactical mistake. Ṭabarī, *Ta'rīkh*, 1429; Ṭabarī, *History*, 7:40.

35 See Roohi, "Form-Critical," 267–338, where he argues that the stories of al-Rajīᶜ and Bi'r Maᶜūna raids "reflect far more about the circumstances of their composition and redaction than about first/seventh-century Arabia." See Watt, *Muḥammad*, 34, where he writes, "The misfortunes at Bi'r Ma'unah and ar-Rajīᶜ (about July 625) may have caused temporary gloom in Medina, but for the rest of the period up to the siege the tide seemed to be turning in favour of the Muslims."

36 See Watt, *Muḥammad*, 30.

reportedly gathered their maximum power (three thousand soldiers).[37] After Uḥud, the Meccans needed more support. They worked diligently to create alliances with Arab nomads who neighbored Medina, including the tribes of Banū Sulaym, Banū Ghaṭafān, and Banū Ḍamrah.[38] This endeavor reportedly resulted in the formation of the confederates consisting of the Meccan Quraysh, Arab nomads, and some Medinan Jews. They marched to attack Muhammad and eliminate him completely.

Here we highlight major Muslim accounts on the Battle of the Trench; then we offer several critical comments. The battle is portrayed as a siege of Medina initiated by wicked non-Muslim schemers who wanted to get revenge against Muhammad. Some Muslim historians claim that the Jews initiated the scheme by contacting the Quraysh in Mecca, while others insist that the Meccans approached the Jews first.[39] The story suggests that some Jews, especially those of Banū al-Naḍīr, have attempted to exact their revenge against Muhammad for expelling them from their homes a few months earlier—they were eager to gain back their homes in Medina.[40] As news of the approaching confederates reached Muhammad, the Muslims were reportedly worried. Following the advice of Salmān the Persian, every capable Muslim in town, including Muhammad himself, began the fast task of digging a trench to protect Medina, accomplishing it in six days.[41] Some Muslim hypocrites, we are told, disobeyed Muhammad and did not participate in the digging.[42] This literary detail reflects a tool of the narrators, serving as a warning against

[37] Watt, *Muḥammad*, 19–21. The number is clearly hyperbolic and ideologically driven to amplify the Muslim victory. See Shoemaker, *Creating*, 98.

[38] For these tribes, see ᶜAlī, *Mufaṣṣal*, 7:257–259 (Banū Sulaym was a rich tribe and in strong alliance with the Jews of Medina and the Quraysh); 11:240 (Banū Sulaym and Banū Ghaṭafān worshipped the idol al-ᶜUzza); 7:246 (Banū Ghaṭafān accepted a tribal alliance with the Jews and the Meccans); 2:57 (Banū Ḍamrah were allies to Banū Ghaṭafān); 14:39–41 (early in his time in Medina, Muhammad made a treaty with Banū Ḍamrah). See also Fück, "Ghaṭafān," *EI*², 2:1023–1024. See Watt, *Muḥammad*, 30, where he comments that "The chief of B. Ḍamrah (a little north-west of Mecca) had been led to believe that Muḥammad was 'finished' after Uḥud, and was greatly surprised to see the strong Muslim force at [the second] Badr in April 626." See the claim of Banū Ḍamrah in Wāqidī, *Maghāzī*, 388; Wāqidī, *Life*, 190.

[39] See Yaᶜqūbī, *Ta'rīkh*, 2:50, where he claims that the Quraysh initiated the conversation with the Jews. Ibn Hishām and al-Ṭabarī state the opposite. Ibn Hishām, *Sīra*, 2:214; Ṭabarī, *Ta'rīkh*, 1457–1458. See also Dhahabī, *Ta'rīkh*, 2:283ff.

[40] Wāqidī claims that the Jews of Banū al-Naḍīr "promised [Ghaṭafān] dates of Khaybar for a year, if they would help them and march with the Quraysh to Muḥammad." Wāqidī, *Life*, 217. See also Watt, *Muḥammad*, 36–38, where he writes of this as "a bribe" given to Ghaṭafān to join the confederates, but Muhammad made them a better offer "of a presumably higher bribe if they would withdraw" (38).

[41] Ṭabarī, *Ta'rīkh*, 1465–1466. Ṭabarī, *History*, 8:8.

[42] See Ṭabarī, *Ta'rīkh*, 1465; Ṭabarī, *History*, 8:8–9, where it reads, "Certain men of the hypocrites hung back from the Messenger of God and from the Muslims in their work."

religious disobedience. Unlike these Muslim hypocrites, some Jews reportedly helped Muhammad dig the trench and provided him with tools. We are told that Muslims "borrowed many tools of iron, hoes and baskets from the [Jews of] Banū Qurayẓa. They dug the trench with [Muhammad], for they were at that time at peace with the Prophet."[43] With these Jews' help, the Muslims successfully dug the trench that secured the area north of Medina; the southern parts were guarded by mountains.[44]

When the battle started, the Muslims had only three thousand while the confederates totaled ten thousand.[45] Once more, we encounter a literary detail that exaggerates the power of the Muslims and the Meccan pagans. Muslim historians fashion this report to amplify the Muslims' future victory. We are told that the confederates marched with horses to attack Medina, but the trench served as a barrier.[46] Despite their number and all of their might, the confederates failed, scattered, and withdrew, granting the Muslims a huge victory. Muslim traditions provide reasons for the Muslim victory. While nothing could dissuade the Muslim historians from emphasizing Allah's role in bringing victory to Muhammad and the believers, the narratives point to an inevitable Muslim victory—there were *natural* factors contributing to the victory. According to the story, digging the trench and thus being protected inside Medina served as a strategic military decision that played a significant role in the victory. Two Muslims should be thanked for such a strategic decision: Salmān the Persian and ᶜAbdullāh ibn Ubayy ibn Salūl. The former suggested digging the trench, while the latter—being an experienced

[43] Wāqidī, *Life*, 218; Wāqidī, *Maghāzī*, 445. See also Ḥalabī, *Insān*, 2:628, where he states, "and [the Muslims] borrowed from Qurayẓa plenty of tools."

[44] Ṭabarī, *Ta'rīkh*, 1470; Ṭabarī, *History*, 8:13. Cf. Yāqūt, *Muᶜjam*, 4:182. See also Yaᶜqūbī, *Buldān*, 97–98; Hamdānī, *Ṣifat*, 47–48; Ibn al-Faqīh, *Mukhtaṣar*, 23–24.

[45] See Ibn Hishām, *Life*, 452–453; Ṭabarī, *Ta'rīkh*, 1470; Kalāᶜī, *Iktifā'*, 2:162–163; Ibn Ḥibbān, *Sīra*, 1:254ff. These numbers are likely exaggerated. See the Muslim scholar Djait, *Masīrat*, 129, where he rejects these exaggerated figures and asserts his belief that the actual amount may have been half or even one-fourth of these fanciful accounts. See also Ḥusayn, *Shaykhān*, 103, where he writes of exaggeration in traditions about numbers. Similarly, see ᶜAbd al-Hādī ᶜAbd al-Raḥmān, *al-Tārīkh wa-l-usṭūra*; al-Raḥmān, *Judhūr al-quwwa*, 7ff., where he labels accounts as illogical (11–12). Non-Muslim scholars share similar views. See Donner, *Conquest*, 126, where he highlights contradictions regarding the number of warriors. For the "erratic" and fanciful numbers of warriors in historiography, see Hoyland, *God's Path*, 42. Recent research highly questions these numbers. See Shoemaker, *Creating*, 111–112, where he studies Medina in the late ancient Near East and argues, "Like Mecca, Yathrib was not sizeable enough even to be called a town, let alone a 'city.' It was in fact not a single organized settlement but rather 'an oasis comprising a somewhat looser collection of disparate settlements' located around the region's various water sources." Shoemaker quotes Munt, *Holy*, 49–50. Watt argues that the three thousand Muslims were "practically all the inhabitants of Medina with the exception of the Jewish tribe of Qurayẓah." Watt, *Muḥammad*, 36. These exaggerations are found in Muslim sources and non-Muslim sources. Hoyland, *Seeing Islam*, 186.

[46] Ṭabarī, *Ta'rīkh*, 1475. Horses are not suitable for crossing deserts. See Crone, *Slaves*, 22–23, 220.

Medinan warrior—told Muhammad not to leave Medina, a piece of advice that was reportedly ignored two years earlier and caused the Muslims a huge defeat at Uḥud.[47] These two men thus played a significant role in bringing victory to the Muslims.

A third person crucial in achieving the victory was Nuᶜaym ibn Masᶜūd. He was from the tribe of Ghaṭafān, and everyone thought he was a part of the confederates.[48] However, he reportedly converted secretly to Islam shortly before the battle and played a vital role in dissolving the confederates.[49] To mislead the Meccans, Nuᶜaym spoke with them before his conversion, assuring them of his support, yet later he became loyal to Muhammad.[50] He spread dissonance among the confederates and secretly encouraged the Jews of Banū Qurayẓa to continue supporting Muhammad, and they did.[51] Nuᶜaym's tale functions—both stylistically and thematically—as a religious precedent and moral example of plotting and scheming in battles. The story of deceiving the enemy is built on a strong philosophy established by Muhammad in a reported saying during the battle of Uḥud that *al-ḥarb khidᶜa* (war is deceit).[52] Muhammad's statement, in historiographical accounts, received more fame and higher emphasis when he used it again in exhorting Nuᶜaym to deceive his unbelieving people of the Ghaṭafān tribe.[53]

A fourth person who reportedly played a significant role in the victory was Muhammad himself. As he deployed Nuᶜaym to mislead Ghaṭafān, Muhammad simultaneously, in a tactical move, met with leaders of the

[47] Yaᶜqūbī, *Ta'rīkh*, 2:50; Ṭabarī, *Ta'rīkh*, 1475; Kalāᶜī, *Iktifā'*, 2:166; see also Suhaylī, *Rawḍ*, 6:210. Compare with Ṭabarī, *Ta'rīkh*, 1387, concerning the defeat at Uḥud. Salmān the Persian was celebrated as the reason for the victory: "It is said that Salmān the Persian advised the apostle to make it. A traditionist told me that on this day the Muhājirs claimed that Salmān belonged to them, while the Anṣār said that he was their man; but the apostle said, 'Salman belongs to us, the people of the house.'" Ibn Hishām, *Life*, 764. On al-Khandaq as a Persian military tactic, see Watt, *Muḥammad*, 36–37.

[48] On Nuᶜaym ibn Masᶜūd, see Ibn Saᶜd, *Ṭabaqāt*, 2:53–56, 4:209–210; Ibn ᶜAbd al-Barr, *Istīᶜāb*, 4:1508; Ibn al-Athīr, *Usd*, 5:328; Dhahabī, *Siyar*, *sīra* 1:495–496; Ṣafadī, *Wāfī*, 27:97.

[49] Many accounts describe Nuᶜaym as the believer who *khadhal al-mushrikūn* (disappointed the polytheists). See Ibn ᶜAbd al-Barr, *Istīᶜāb*, 4:1508; Ibn al-Athīr, *Usd*, 5:328; Dhahabī, *Siyar*, *sīra* 1:495–496; Ṣafadī, *Wāfī*, 27:97.

[50] See the change in Nuᶜaym's loyalty in two reports by al-Ṭabarī, *Ta'rīkh*, 1459 and 1480; also Ṭabarī, *History*, 7:166 and 8:23. See Nuᶜaym's deception of the Meccans in Ṭabarī, *Ta'rīkh*, 1482; Ṭabarī, *History*, 8:24.

[51] Wāqidī, *Maghāzī*, 480–482; Ibn Hishām, *Sīra*, 2:229; Ibn Hishām, *Life*, 458; Ṭabarī, *Ta'rīkh*, 1480–1481; Ibn Ḥibbān, *Sīra*, 1:259; Kalāᶜī, *Iktifā'*, 2:172.

[52] Wāqidī, *Maghāzī*, 299; Bukhārī, *Ṣaḥīḥ*, 4:63–64; 4:200; Muslim, *Ṣaḥīḥ*, 2:746; 3:1361–1362.

[53] Wāqidī, *Maghāzī*, 487; Ibn Hishām, *Sīra*, 2:229; Ibn Ḥibbān, *Sīra*, 1:259; Kharkūshī, *Sharaf*, 4:255; Bayhaqī, *Dalā'il*, 3:405; 3:432; Suhaylī, *Rawḍ*, 6:219; Kalāᶜī, *Iktifā'*, 1:428; Fasawī, *Maᶜrifa*, 1:300; Maqdisī, *Bad'*, 4:219; Dhahabī, *Ta'rīkh*, 2:293; Ibn Ḥibbān, *Thiqāt*, 1:270; Abū Nuᶜaym, *Maᶜrifat*, 5:2668. Later Muslims used Muhammad's precedent in war. Ṭabarī, *Ta'rīkh*, 3086; Ṭabarī, *History*, 16:24; Ibn al-Athīr, *Kāmil*, 2:559.

tribe of Ghaṭafān and offered them a huge sum of money (one-third of the crop of Medina) so that they would abandon the confederates.[54] The tribe of Ghaṭafān proved to be less concerned with either party—the tribe was practical and reportedly ready to be bought by the one who paid the most. The story of Muhammad's tactical dealings with the tribe of Ghaṭafān appears to serve as a product of the medieval narrators who sought to construct a tradition with a discernible set of religious values and moral meanings.[55] To achieve victory, the rationale goes, one must use the tools one has, creating alliances or dissolving them, offering incentives or withholding them, and speaking openly or concealing the truth. While Muhammad does not appear as a divinely guided prophet in these tactical steps, the narrative marvels at his ability to win with different strategies.

In addition to the four men, the Muslim traditions highlight the role of the Jews of Banū Qurayẓa in the Muslims' victory, even though the Muslims treated them harshly—in an expedition—after the battle.[56] These Jews reportedly supported Muhammad not only in digging the trench but also in refusing to assist the confederates—a decision that helped the Muslims greatly.[57] When the confederates sought the support of Banū Qurayẓa, the chiefs of the Jews reportedly refused not only by demanding guarantees from the confederates but also by claiming they could not fight on a Saturday.[58] This reluctance of the Jews of Banū Qurayẓa played a significant role in improving the chances of a Muslim victory by discouraging the confederates. While we examine the relations between Muhammad and the Jews in the next chapter, this literary detail about the helpful Jews is important to note, as it reveals the existence of competing depictions of the Jews not only in the Trench narratives but in the Muslim pool of memory generally. The Trench narratives include two competing literary threads: on one hand, the Jews initiated the wicked scheme, contacted the Quraysh, and consolidated the confederates; on the other hand, the Jews opposed the confederates, provided Muhammad with tools and dug the trench with the Muslims, and refused to ally with the unbelievers against the believers. The existence of these two

[54] Ibn Hishām, *Sīra*, 2:223; Ibn Hishām, *Life*, 545; Kalāʿī, *Iktifā'*, 2:165; Suhaylī, *Rawḍ*, 6:208. The Ghaṭafān demanded half of the harvest, but Muhammad offered them "a third of the date harvest of Medina on condition that they and their followers go back." See Ṭabarī, *Ta'rīkh*, 1474; Ṭabarī, *History*, 8:17. On this negotiation, see the discussion in Watt, *Muḥammad*, 38.

[55] Hibri, *Reinterpreting*, 12–13; Hibri, *Parable*, 23.

[56] We discuss the raid to Banū Qurayẓa in the next chapter.

[57] Ṭabarī, *Ta'rīkh*, 1482; Ibn Ḥibbān, *Sīra*, 1:261.

[58] Ibn Hishām, *Sīra*, 2:230; Ibn Hishām, *Life*, 456; Ṭabarī, *Ta'rīkh*, 1482; Ṭabarī, *History*, 8:24.

competing threads can be evaluated in various ways. From a critical standpoint, the competing portrayals of the Jews may emphasize the contention we discussed earlier as to how a specific tradition may gain momentum and get elevated, while another gets suppressed into oblivion.[59] Two accounts, we may argue, circulated among the Muslim narrators—one portraying the Jews as helpful to Muhammad while the other depicted them as wicked hypocrites. With the passing of time, one narrative gained more recognition than the other, thus receiving a push and becoming the orthodox tale. In exploring many Muslim historical accounts on the Trench, it appears that the recognition of the helpful Banū Qurayẓa in the precursor of the battle is not widely asserted. Even when they are recognized, their positive portrayal is soon eclipsed into oblivion—in the same pool of traditions—when Muhammad launches an attack against them immediately after the Battle of the Trench is won. It appears that the narrators could not resist portraying the Jews unfavorably, even with the existence of a memory which depicted them favorably.

Additionally, the existence of competing reports about the Jews may well reflect different attitudes of the narrators about the Jewish community at the time of documentation. After all, as we have argued repeatedly, a historiographical account reflects the religious sympathies and sociopolitical inclinations of the traditionists. While the emergence of a tradition advances the time of documentation and the attitudes of the narrators, its survival depends on its circulation by Muslim storytellers, whether it is elevated or sent to oblivion. A narration is thus a devised message, conveyed to an audience at a certain time and in a specific context that defines and shapes the literary text. Moreover, as I argued in a previous publication, the Muslim narration serves to relay messages to Muslims and non-Muslims alike.[60] In this regard, we may deduce, the story of the Trench serves as a warning message to the Jews who resided in Muslim lands during the time of writing: their

[59] Patrick Geary, in studying European society in the tenth through the eleventh centuries, discusses the "creative forgetting" by both individuals and communities, to readjust their sense of connection to their past by creating new memories more suitable for their present, using a process of transmission, adaptation, and suppression. See his work *Phantoms of Remembrance* and his article "Oblivion between Orality and Textuality in the Tenth Century," in *Medieval Concepts*, ed. Althoff and Geary, 111–122, especially 111. See also Borrut, *Entre*, 80; Savant, *New*, 3. See Steinbock, *Social Memory*, where he analyzes the uses and meanings of the past in fourth-century Athens and argues that the communicated, idealized, and distorted memories of the past should be viewed not as an unreliable counterpart of history but as a valuable key to understanding a community's mentality and worldview. On memory and forgetting, see also Assmann, *Moses*, 9; Assmann, *Cultural*, 55; Spiegel, "Memory," 149–162.

[60] Ibrahim, *Conversion*, 3–7, 55–99, especially 97–99, also 231–245.

ancestors lost and were eclipsed by the growing Muslim power, as a reflection of the hegemony and truthfulness of Islam; they must heed the lesson, change course, forsake Judaism, and convert to Islam. Of course, one can also argue that the account is exegetical in nature—a story building on anti-Jewish material in the Qur'ān.[61]

As a literary tale, furthermore, the tradition insists on comparing the Jews to the Muslims. The Medinan Jews were in disarray after Muhammad eliminated many of them, forcing them to leave Medina. This is evident in how the Jews of Banū al-Naḍīr and those of Banū Qurayẓa reportedly played opposite roles in this battle. The role of Banū Qurayẓa—as a literary fiction—cannot be denied, especially as it appears that their support had strengthened the unity among the Muslims and magnified the disharmony among the confederates. The Jews of Banū Qurayẓa were in Medina and refused to support the cause of their fellow Jews of Banū al-Naḍīr who were a major part of the confederates. The ideological thrust of the tale is clear: The disarray of Jews is a stark contrast to the unity of the Muslims under Muhammad. Similarly, another comparison is advanced in relation to the confederates. While Muslims were secured and united behind a trench, the confederates were in chaos and disharmony: We read of the disagreement between the Meccan Abū Sufyān and the Jew Ḥuyayy ibn Akhṭab (of Banū al-Naḍīr)—two chiefs among the confederates.[62] Allah "caused them to abandon each other," the storytellers assure us.[63]

One final *natural* factor reportedly helped the Muslims greatly: severe weather conditions during the battle. While the Muslims were in Medina, sheltered and protected behind the mountains and the trench, the confederates were out in the open and thus vulnerable to the elements.[64] We read of "bitter cold winter nights" and "a wind that began overturning the [confederates'] cooking pots and blowing away their tents."[65] These reports are designed by believers to show nature taking the side of the Muslims. While some may

[61] See Mazuz, "Jewish-Muslim," 946–947; Stillman, *Jews*, 149–151; Sirry, *Scriptural*, 4, 32, 49–52. Cf. Cook, *Commanding*, 13–30. See Muqātil, *Tafsīr*, 1:490, 5:91; Ṭabarī, *Jāmiʿ*, 10:450–459; Thaʿlabī, *Kashf*, 4:87–88.

[62] See Wāqidī, *Maghāzī*, 484; Wāqidī, *Life*, 237. Al-Ṭabarī reports that Allah caused the disagreement to occur among the unbelievers. Ṭabarī, *Ta'rīkh*, 1483; Ṭabarī, *History*, 8:25. Watt observes that the Meccans "gathered a vast confederacy, including some of the nomadic tribes in no way subject to them." Watt, *Muḥammad*, 36.

[63] Ṭabarī, *History*, 8:25.

[64] See Ṭabarī, *Ta'rīkh*, 1483; Kalāʿī, *Iktifā'*, 2:174. For the mountains of Medina, see Yaʿqūbī, *Buldān*, 97–98.

[65] Ṭabarī, *History*, 8:25.

view the severe weather conditions as a natural factor that affected the balance of power, a believer may perceive them as divine elements through which Allah created confusion among the unbelievers. Overall, it is plausible to argue that—based on the literary evidence—several natural factors provided the Muslims a great victory.

But Muslim historians seem unsatisfied with portraying the victory as merely a natural success. They report the battle and the victory in religious manner, highlighting that the victory came from Allah, who supported his believers by granting Muhammad great miracles. Various Muslim historians devote a specific section of their accounts of the expedition to *muʿjizāt al-khandaq* (the miracles at the trench)—accounts that are better viewed as exegeting Qur'ānic passages claimed by Muslims to relate to the battle (e.g., Q 33:9–24).[66] We are told that Muhammad spat on rocks, making them as soft as sand in order to help Muslims dig the trench in tough soil.[67] To feed the Muslims as they worked hard at digging the trench, we are invited to believe, Muhammad multiplied a handful of dates and fed the thousands.[68] These miracles reportedly served as a sign for "God's justifying His apostle and confirming his prophetic office," especially because "Muslims saw [these miracles] with their eyes."[69] Needleless to say, some of the miracles appear similar to some biblical accounts—a fact that may indicate that Muslim historians were likely seeking to appeal to Christians and Jews at the time of writing.[70] Arguably, the entire tradition is designed to magnify and prove Muhammad's prophethood: While the Muslims were digging the trench, the story alleges, Muhammad prophesied of future victories over many unbelievers. He was using a pick on a large, hard rock: when the pick hit the rock, three flashes of lightning sparked. Muslims asked Muhammad about the meaning of the three flashes, and he declared, "The first means

[66] See Muqātil, *Tafsīr*, 3:455ff.; Ṭabarī, *Jāmiʿ*, 14:469ff., 15:278ff.; Zamakhsharī, *Kashshāf*, 3:518ff.; Rāzī, *Mafātiḥ*, 25:153ff.; Qurṭubī, *Jāmiʿ*, 14:113ff.; Bayḍāwī, *Anwār*, 4:224ff. Cf. with historical accounts in Ibn Hishām, *Sīra*, 2:245; Suhaylī, *Rawḍ*, 6:242.

[67] Ibn Hishām, *Sīra*, 2:218–219; Ibn Hishām, *Life*, 451, where he claims that Muhammad's miracle made a rock as if "it were soft sand."

[68] Ibn Hishām, *Sīra*, 2:219; also Ibn Hishām, *Life*, 452, where he states that a little ewe fed the Muslim workers at the trench.

[69] Ibn Hishām, *Life*, 451. For a critical assessment of these miracles, see Ibrahim, *Stated*, 90–91.

[70] For the tendentiousness of Muslim historical reports, see Ibrahim, *Conversion*, chs. 3–4. Crone, *Slaves*, 10; Crone, *Meccan*, 230; Crone, "How Did," 387–399; Robinson, *Historiography*, 38; Sellheim, "Prophet," 53–73 and 49–53; Wansbrough, *Qur'ānic*, 58. In examining the miracles at al-Khandaq, I indicate, "It seems reasonable to argue that these reports of miracles are later interpolations that seek to bolster the *umma*'s faith by portraying the Khandaq military victory as Allah's mighty work." Ibrahim, *Stated*, 91.

that God has opened up to me the Yaman; the second Syria and the west; and the third the east."[71] These literary features reflect one more indicator for the tendentiousness of the tradition: It is a medieval religious memory, designed after conquering many lands and projected back in history for ideological purposes. While religious enthusiasts appreciate a belief in these supernatural elements (e.g., miracles and prophecies), we should note that the tradition itself appears to advance that the Muslim victory was well expected due to natural factors. But, again, Muslim traditionists served as religious authors of history. Just as they did in reporting the Muslims' victory at Badr, these storytellers appear eager to interpolate supernatural literary elements in fashioning the Muslim's victory at al-Khandaq, although none of these elements appeared at the Muslims' defeat at Uḥud. Since the religious lesson desired from Uḥud is different from that of Badr and al-Khandaq, the narratives are adjusted accordingly. Still, while Muslim historians mention miracles during the battle, the Qur'ān does not explicitly mention any in its presumed verses on the incident (Q 33:9–24). In fact, the Qur'ān seems to emphatically deny, in many verses, that Muhammad performed miracles, highlighting that his only miracle was the Qur'ān itself.[72] Muslim historians seem to have needed literary embellishments to magnify the Muslim victory and provide proofs for Muhammad's prophethood and abilities.[73]

The Muslim victory at al-Khandaq was huge, placing the Meccans and their allies among the Arab Bedouins and the Jews in a severe failure. Muhammad beat them and dissolved their confederacy. Though the non-Muslims reportedly did their very best, they lost drastically. This victory marked a new era for Muhammad and the Muslims, as their growing power could have not been underestimated any further by their enemies. This is evidenced in how the Meccans were ready to make a deal with Muhammad. One year after al-Khandaq, the treaty of Ḥudaybiyya (6/628) was reportedly cut between Muhammad and the Meccans. While it was mainly a treaty and a peace pact, Muslim accounts portray it as a *ghazwa* (raid). Thus, in the next section, we turn to the raid of the Ḥudaybiyya.

[71] Ibn Hishām, *Sīra*, 2:219; Ibn Hishām, *Life*, 452; Ṭabarī, *Ta'rīkh*, 1468.

[72] See Q 6:37; 11:12; 13:7; 17:59; 28:48; 29:50–51. For a study on how the Qur'ān denies that Muhammad performed miracles, see Ibrahim, *Quran*, 119–122; also Ibrahim, *Stated*, 114. For Muslim views that are critical of the miracles in Muslim tradition, see the Moroccan historian Jābrī, *Mawāqif*, 49–50; also the Tunisian scholar Djait, *Masīrat*, 127–131. For an apologetic claim by a classical Muslim defending Muhammad's miracles, see ʿAbd al-Jabbār, *Tathbīt*, 1:58.

[73] I provide three possible reasons for why classical Muslim narrators resorted to interpolating supernatural components in their accounts. See Ibrahim, *Stated*, 91.

The Raid of the Ḥudaybiyya (6/628)

According to Muslim traditions, the incident of the Ḥudaybiyya occurred in A.H. 6, only one year after the Muslims' victory over the confederates at al-Khandaq.[74] The name "al-Ḥudaybiyya" refers to a water-well location—about fifteen miles north of Mecca—where the incident reportedly occurred.[75] It was about nine days' travel from Medina toward Mecca and only one day's travel from Mecca—it was thus very near to the Meccan territory.[76] This incident reportedly provided a huge step forward for Muhammad's power and dominion in Arabia to grow, largely unchallenged by the Meccans. The Muslim sources report it as both a strategic *ṣulḥ* (peace treaty) and successful *ghazwa* (raid), although it did not involve any fighting and was merely a truce agreement.[77] This reiterates a major contention of this study: classical narrators marvel at Muhammad's *maghāzī* and highlight their scope, motive, success, and frequency. The literary context here also implies that Muhammad is more and more on the offensive—he is moving farther south from Medina and approaching the Meccan territory from the north.

Classical historians report that Allah himself initiated the incident of the Ḥudaybiyya when he spoke to Muhammad in a dream.[78] In the dream, Muhammad entered *al-bayt* (the House, i.e., the Kaᶜba in Mecca) and began performing the rituals of the *ḥajj* (pilgrimage), including shaving his head and standing on Mount ᶜArafāt.[79] When he woke up, we are told, the meaning

[74] For accounts on the Ḥudaybiyya, see Maᶜmar, *Expeditions*, 21–33; Ibn Hibbān, *Sīra*, 1:280ff.; Khalīfa, *Ta'rīkh*, 1:81ff.; Ibn Ḥabīb, *Muḥabbar*, 1:115; Ibn Qutayba, *Maᶜārif*, 162; Fasawī, *Maᶜrifa*, 1:25; Balādhurī, *Futūḥ*, 35ff.; Masᶜūdī, *Tanbīh*, 1:221ff.; Kharkūshī, *Sharaf*, 3:55ff.; Bayhaqī, *Dalā'il*, 4:99ff.; Ibn ᶜAbd al-Barr, *Durar*, 1:191–196; Suhaylī, *Rawḍ*, 7:51ff.; Kalāᶜī, *Iktifā'*, 1:464ff.; Ibn Kathīr, *Sīra*, 3:293ff.; Ḥalabī, *Insān*, 3:12ff.; Maqdisī, *Bad'*, 4:224; Dhahabī, *Ta'rīkh*, 2:363ff. For Muslim perspectives, see the important recent secondary study by Ḥakamī, *Marwiyyāt*, which is a graduate research project (completed under the supervision of Professor Akram ᶜUmarī) focusing on the Raid of the Ḥudaybiyya (6/628); also Ṣallābī, *Sīra*, 657ff.; ᶜUmarī, *Sīra*, 434–453; Ṣaᶜīdī, *Tārīkh*, 113–119.

[75] A stage is a one-day desert journey. See Yaᶜqūbī, *Buldān*, 152. For the geographical location of the Ḥudaybiyya, see Bakrī, *Muᶜjam*, 2:430, 3:811 (a water well, seven stages from Medina and only one from Mecca); Hamadānī, *Amākin*, 1:713 (a small village); Yāqūt, *Muᶜjam*, 2:229 (small village, nine stages from Medina and only one from Mecca; should be rendered Ḥudaybiyya, not Ḥudaybiya); Samhūdī, *Wafā'*, 3:181 (a valley, a small village with a water well); Balādī, *Muᶜjam*, 94–95. On the name and its proper rendition, see Ḥakamī, *Marwiyyāt*, 17–18.

[76] See Watt, "al-Ḥudaybiya," *EI*², 3:539.

[77] For referring to Ḥudaybiyya as an expedition, see Wāqidī, *Maghāzī*, 571; Wāqidī, *Life*, 281; Ibn Hishām, *Sīra*, 2:608; Bayhaqī, *Dalā'il*, 3:398; Suhaylī, *Rawḍ*, 7:520; Kalāᶜī, *Iktifā'*, 1:464; Ibn Kathīr, *Sīra*, 2:355; Ḥalabī, *Insān*, 1:298; 3:12. For referring to it as a treaty, see Wāqidī, *Maghāzī*, 610, 623, 701; Ibn Hishām, *Sīra*, 2:322; Ṭabarī, *Ta'rīkh*, 1502; Bayhaqī, *Dalā'il*, 4:160, where he states that "the treaty of the Ḥudaybiyya was a great conquest"; Ibn ᶜAbd al-Barr, *Durar*, 1:330; Suhaylī, *Rawḍ*, 7:76; Kalāᶜī, *Iktifā'*, 1:472 (both conquest and treaty); Ibn Kathīr, *Sīra*, 3:324; Ḥalabī, *Insān*, 3:102.

[78] See Wāqidī, *Maghāzī*, 571, where it is called *ru'yā* (vision).

[79] Wāqidī, *Maghāzī*, 572; Wāqidī, *Life*, 281. On the Kaᶜba, see Ibrahim, *Islam*, 26–27.

of the dream was explained through a divine revelation of a verse from the Qur'ān (*sūrat al-Fatḥ* Q 48:24). The verse indicates that Allah restrained the unbelievers from the believers *bi-baṭni Makka* (in the valley of Mecca) and granted the believers a great victory over them.[80] Muhammad reportedly believed that Allah instructed him to march to Mecca, and then enter the city to perform the *ḥajj*. It is unclear, in Muslim traditions, whether Muhammad was planning to perform any *new* rituals specific to Islam or mainly aiming to follow pre-Islamic pagan rituals, especially as Mecca was reportedly full of idols and pagan worship at that time.[81] These reports may emphasize the tendentiousness of the narratives and how later historians projected the *ḥajj* rituals backward upon the accounts describing the time when the Kaᶜba was presumably the place of pagan worship—this is, of course, unless one accepts that Muhammad was seeking to perform pagan rituals in a house full of idols.[82] This account draws significant attention from many scholars, including some Muslims. The Tunisian Muslim scholar Hichem Djait argues that Muhammad practically and openly recognized *al-ḥajj al-wathanī* (the pagan pilgrimage), affirming most of its *shaᶜā'ir* (rituals).[83] For Djait, the Islamic *ḥajj* is directed to Allah alone, although "pagan elements always remain present."[84]

While the dream was reportedly divinely given to Muhammad alone, it appears that he realized that the step of marching to Mecca was understandably risky. After all, he was Mecca's biggest enemy at that time. Muhammad knew he could not go unsupported by himself to the Kaᶜba and anticipated that the Meccans would forbid him from entering the Sacred House or even Mecca entirely. Consequently, he reportedly summoned Muslims—both *muhājirūn* (Meccan emigrants) and *anṣār* (Medinan supporters)—in

[80] On this verse, see Muqātil, *Tafsīr*, 4:57, 4:75; Ṭabarī, *Jāmiᶜ*, 22:236–238; Zamakhsharī, *Kashshāf*, 4:341; Rāzī, *Mafātīḥ*, 28:81; Qurṭubī, *Jāmiᶜ*, 16:278–282. Most exegetes directly link the verse to the Ḥudaybiyya incident.

[81] On the *ḥajj* and its roots in pre-Islamic history, see Peters, *Muslim*, 3–41; Hawting, "Origins," 23–48; Hawting, ed., *Development*, especially ch. 14 by Snouck Hurgronje, "Meccan Feast," and ch. 15 by Lazarus-Yafeh, "Religious Dialectics"; also Gaudefroy-Demombynes, *Le pèlerinage*. On the circumambulation as a ritual found in other non-Muslim traditions before Islam, see Buhl, "Ṭawāf," *EI*², 10:376. See Djait, *Masīrat*, 154, where he argues that Muhammad adopted elements of the pilgrimage from pre-Islamic pagan rituals.

[82] On tendentious accounts, see Petersen, *ᶜAlī*, 18, where he observes that recording history "left a wide margin for tendentious presentation." See Crone, *Meccan*, 230.

[83] Djait, *Masīrat*, 154. He adds that Muhammad was going to his enemies to fulfill the known *ḥajj*, but with a "spiritual newness" (154).

[84] See Djait, *Masīrat*, 154–155, where he argues that these pagan elements include the sacredness of the Kaᶜba, circumambulation around it, sacrificing animals, shaving heads at the end of the rituals—all of these elements were pagan in their essence. Cf. Peters, *Muslim*, 3–41; Hawting, "Origins," 23–48.

addition to some non-Muslim Arab Bedouins and asked them to march with him to Mecca. We are told that many hastened to support him, although some Arab tribes—including Banū Bakr and Juhayna—were reluctant to do so.[85] These Arabs viewed Muhammad's march to Mecca as launching a war against the Quraysh; they wondered, "Does Muḥammad want to attack, with our help, a people well-prepared and equipped in spears and weapons?"[86] It appears plausible that non-Muslim Arabs believed that Muhammad was preparing for war against the Quraysh. Still, Muhammad was able to unite between fourteen hundred and sixteen hundred men to join him, although al-Ṭabarī puts the number as high as nineteen hundred.[87] With these men, Muhammad eventually began his travel toward Mecca with the goal of entering Mecca's most holy place to perform the *ḥajj*.

However, this narrative has gaps in it. There are two observations about its literary details—both related to the existence of competing accounts within the same Muslim tradition. First, the narrators state that Muhammad was willing to receive support from pagan Arab Bedouins—clearly non-Muslims—to march with him to Mecca, lest an attack occurred from the pagans of the Quraysh. While these details are not to be treated as factual, they conflict with other traditions that convey the opposite: Muhammad forbade the unbelievers from joining his troops, as "non-Muslims should not be recruited to fight for Muslim causes alongside Muslim combatants."[88] Here we encounter contradicting traditions—a feature that reiterates the contention we observed earlier: competing reports stem together—in response to various contexts and reflecting each narrator's sympathies—and circulate within the same pool of memory, yet only some of these get brought to general acceptance and thus orthodoxy, while others become marginal, rarely

[85] See Ṭabarī, *History*, 8:68, where he states that "Many of the Bedouins were slow in coming to him" to join in the march to Mecca. They *yatashāghalūn* (have pretended to be occupied) "with their possessions, children, and descendants." Wāqidī, *Maghāzī*, 574; Wāqidī, *Life*, 282. Ibn Hishām, *Sīra*, 2:308.

[86] Wāqidī, *Maghāzī*, 574; Wāqidī, *Life*, 282. These Arabs reportedly predicted, "Muḥammad and his companions will never return from this journey of theirs."

[87] Ṭabarī, *Ta'rīkh*, 1529; Ṭabarī, *History*, 8:69, where he reports, "The Messenger of God set out from al-Ḥudaybiyah with between thirteen and nineteen hundred of his companions." However, see Ṭabarī, *History*, 8:69, where he provides a different number: The Muslims "were fourteen hundred." For more competing reports on the number of the Muslims, see Wāqidī, *Maghāzī*, 574. See Ibn Hishām, *Sīra*, 2:309, where the number is fourteen hundred; also Ibn Ḥibbān, *al-Thiqāt*, 1:295, where the number is eighteen hundred. See Muslim perspectives on these numbers in ᶜUmarī, *Sīra*, 435; also Ḥakamī, *Marwiyyāt*, 39–53.

[88] See the quote in the valuable study of Yarbrough, "I'll Not Accept," in *Authority*, ed. Alain Delattre et al., 44–95. Some accounts indicate that *mushrikūn* (polytheists, associaters) joined Muhammad's camp to fight alongside him in the Battle of Ḥunayn. Ibn Saᶜd, *Ṭabaqāt*, 2:114–116. See Ibrahim, *Conversion*, 85.

recognized, or sent to forgetfulness. Second, in the same vein, the narrators observe that the Arab tribes, before the raid, still thought highly of the Quraysh and declared that the tribe was strong and prepared, although all along the Muslim narrators—arguably the *authors* of the accounts—have been describing the Quraysh as confused, floundering, and vulnerable. Here we notice two competing threads in the same tradition: in one, the Quraysh is weak, vulnerable, and declining in power and appeal among the Arabs; in the second, the Quraysh is well equipped with spears and weapons and should be avoided. The narrative even calls us to believe that, in two years, the Quraysh will totally collapse and surrender to Muhammad. When put together, the details of the traditions reflect a tendentious picture with many gaps in it. Still, there is one more observation to make on the literary detail that Muhammad sought the support of unbelievers against other unbelievers.[89] This does not sit well with Muslim claims that Muhammad's raids were for the purpose of religious proclamation. The story reflects a tribal combat, in which Muhammad was willing to ally with anyone—even unbelievers—to secure power, consolidate alliances, and ensure victory over the Quraysh.

The narrative of the Ḥudaybiyya includes more competing reports. While the report of a divine dream or vision may appeal to religious enthusiasts, other Muslim accounts seem to shed doubts on the divine initiation of the Ḥudaybiyya through a dream, portraying the incident as entirely Muhammad's plan to fight Mecca. Without any reference to a divine dream, al-Ṭabarī reports that Muhammad "set out to make the lesser pilgrimage" and "called on the Arabs and Bedouin desert dwellers who were around him to help by setting out with him, for he feared that Quraysh would oppose him with fighting or turn him away from the [Holy] House."[90] This might indicate that Muhammad was determined to march to Mecca at all costs, whether he received a dream from Allah about it or not.[91] He desired to perform the pilgrimage to make a point to the Quraysh, conveying that they could not ban him anymore. As for the divine dream, it might have been the case that later narrators added it as a literary embellishment to justify the initiation of the raid. All of these literary reports are better viewed as figurative stories: The historiographical accounts are representative of the inclinations

[89] Cf. Yarbrough, "I'll not Accept," 44–95.
[90] Ṭabarī, *Ta'rīkh*, 1529–1530.
[91] In explaining Muhammad's political aspirations, Watt observes that Muhammad's "primary intention was no doubt simply what he said, to perform the pilgrimage; but this had certain political implications, and it was probably in these that he was chiefly interested." Watt, *Muḥammad*, 47.

of the narrators rather than factual records of days past. Here, the narrators present two Muhammads—one driven by divine inspiration, the other determined to provoke his enemies in their heartland. Both are cherished by storytellers in different times and circumstances. These two Muhammads are shaped by different literary details and reflect the various preferences of the Muslim narrators from different times. At one time, the rationale goes, a determined Muhammad is needed in order to make a point about bravery and assertiveness. At other times, the need for a lesson on waiting for divine guidance necessitates a depiction of Muhammad following a dream given by Allah. The competing reports, we may argue, merge together within the memory of the believers, but they do not all receive the same recognition or wide circulation.

Even if we hypothetically accept the claim about a divine dream given to Muhammad, we should note that some reports emphasize that the Muslims were *certainly* determined to conquer Mecca: They "set out to Mecca, *lā yashukkūna fī al-fatḥ* (not doubting conquering it) because of the vision [Muhammad] saw."[92] This report suggests that there was certainty among Muslims that entering Mecca would be to conquer the Quraysh with Allah's support. This narrative highlights readiness to conquer Mecca, not perform a ritual, and reflects the tendency of the narrators to use literary details to communicate religious lessons for their audience: a divine dream guarantees supernatural support in battle. In fact, some modern Muslim scholars dismiss classical accounts claiming that the Muslims did not have weapons and argue that the believers were *actually* ready for war, not merely seeking pilgrimage.[93] Their argument may be supported by a tradition stating that the Muslims who marched to the Ḥudaybiyya had weapons with them and were ready for fighting.[94] Other Muslim scholars—by relying on opposing accounts—disagree and insist that Muslims neither carried weapons nor sought war.[95] Here, again, a modern historian stumbles in a tangled spider web of competing narrations, each reflecting different depictions yet all aiming to relay specific religious meanings to the recipient.

We are told that since the victory would be granted by Allah, "[the Muslims] set out without weapons except for the sword in its scabbard"

[92] Wāqidī, *Maghāzī*, 572; Wāqidī, *Life*, 281. Ibn Hishām, *Sīra*, 2:318. See also the Muslim view of ᶜUmarī, *Sīra*, 445.

[93] See ᶜUmarī, *Sīra*, 435, 445.

[94] Bukhārī, *Ṣaḥīḥ*, 4:103.

[95] See the traditional Muslim argument of Ṣallābī, *Sīra*, 662.

and that a "group of [Muhammad's] companions drove the sacrificial animals."[96] To reveal his intention, Muhammad reportedly said, "I do not like to carry weapons as a pilgrim."[97] These literary details are devices for religious insights: even if the Muslims had no weapons, the lesson goes, a victory over the enemy could be gained entirely by a divine intervention. This lesson can arguably be gleaned by Muslims who were the target audience of these stories; however, the narrators might have also aimed to draw parallels with biblical narratives, to convey a message to adherents of these religions who resided under Muslim rule at the time of writing. If the Jews, the rationale goes, experienced victory over the enemy when Moses raised his hand on the mountain, seeking divine support (Exodus 17), then later Jews should pay attention to the new and true Moses among them, that is, Muhammad, who appears in these stories as a divinely guided and supported commander, fearless to march to battle and mighty to succeed in wars. Some even perceive direct Jewish influences on the formation of the traditions—because Muslim narrators wrote their texts with Bible stories in mind. They narrated in response to and in dialogue with biblical accounts. Ultimately, the narratives as literary tools can take on different meanings when contrasted and compared with a broader pool of religious traditions.[98]

As expected, when the Meccan Quraysh heard of Muhammad's plan and his marching men, they thought it was an imminent attack.[99] In a tactical move, Muhammad reportedly chose a different route to travel in order to avoid any possible interception by the Quraysh.[100] The route was rocky with scarce water wells for travelers, and "there were complaints about the small quantity of water [from some Muslims]."[101] Consequently, Muhammad reportedly needed to perform a miracle in order to provide water to the Muslims, especially as "the polytheists had arrived earlier at Baldaḥ and taken its water."[102] This literary detail makes the miracle inevitable as a divine sign against schemes of wicked unbelievers. Muhammad "washed his mouth, then spat in the bucket," emptied the water in an old well, and stirred the water with an arrow—the well then "became agitated with fresh

96 Wāqidī, *Life*, 281. See ᶜUmarī, *Sīra*, 435, where he disputes al-Wāqidī's claim and asserts that Muslims actually were prepared with weapons because they did not trust the Meccans.
97 Wāqidī, *Maghāzī*, 572.
98 Hibri, *Parable*, 342 n. 58.
99 Wāqidī, *Maghāzī*, 579.
100 Ṭabarī, *Ta'rīkh*, 1534; Ṭabarī, *History*, 8:74. Ibn Hishām, *Sīra*, 2:309.
101 Ṭabarī, *Ta'rīkh*, 1535; Ṭabarī, *History*, 8:75.
102 Wāqidī, *Life*, 289. ᶜUmarī, *Sīra*, 438.

water."[103] The Muslims rejoiced, and the water well "leveled to its edge and then spilled over its sides until they drank to the last of them."[104] In another miraculous report, Allah sent down rain on Muhammad "several times and the water increased."[105] Whether it was rains or the restoration of an old well, the narrators insist that the miracles accompany Muhammad. The literary details of signs and wonders are crucial for an audience living well after the presumed time of Muhammad. These tales edify the believers and give them reason to claim that their prophet had also performed miracles like the biblical characters in days past. However, the reports of miracles are opposed by other traditions. In a report contradicting the claims of miracles, al-Wāqidī writes that Muhammad attempted several times to find water in various places, but all of his attempts went in vain, until he found some water in a place called al-Kharrār.[106] With these competing reports, we can still deduce that much in this representation is meant to magnify the prophethood of Muhammad, especially by drawing parallels with biblical characters.

Muhammad and the Muslims then proceeded to Mecca, and they all began preparing for the *ḥajj* rituals at the Ḥudaybiyya, as they expected to enter Mecca the following day.[107] Muhammad did not plan for war but was ready for it if necessary: "We only come to circumambulate this House," Muhammad said, "but we will fight whoever obstructs us from it."[108] Muhammad appears to have realized that "The Quraysh are a people injured and exhausted by the war."[109] He was determined to proceed. The narrators needed to depict a wounded and weakened Quraysh for the tale to continue to unfold, highlighting the growing power of Muhammad—although the remaining details of the Ḥudaybiyya encounter may suggest that the Quraysh was not that weak.[110]

At this point, the Muslims arrived at the little town, the Ḥudaybiyya. Muslim traditions are ambiguous about the sequence and details of events, advancing competing reports. By the time these men arrived at the

[103] Wāqidī, *Life*, 289; Wāqidī, *Maghāzī*, 588–589. For a Muslim discussion of the miracle, see Ḥakamī, *Marwiyyāt*, 98–100.

[104] Wāqidī, *Life*, 289.

[105] Wāqidī, *Maghāzī*, 589; Wāqidī, *Life*, 289.

[106] Wāqidī, *Maghāzī*, 578.

[107] Wāqidī, *Maghāzī*, 578.

[108] Wāqidī, *Maghāzī*, 593; Wāqidī, *Life*, 291. Ibn Hishām, *Sīra*, 2:308. Cf. ᶜUmarī, *Sīra*, 435.

[109] Wāqidī, *Maghāzī*, 593; Wāqidī, *Life*, 291. Ibn Hishām, *Sīra*, 2:309.

[110] In a competing account, we are told that the Quraysh was "a people well-prepared and equipped in spears and weapons." Wāqidī, *Life*, 282; Wāqidī, *Maghāzī*, 574. The non-Muslim Arabs predicted, "Muḥammad and his companions will never return from this journey of theirs."

Ḥudaybiyya, the Quraysh had to act quickly, as the Muslims were reportedly only one day's journey from Mecca.[111] The Meccans sent a small group of fifty or two hundred warriors, including the shrewd commanders Khālid ibn al-Walīd and ᶜIkrima ibn Abī Jahl, to investigate why over a thousand Muslims were approaching Mecca.[112] In one report, we read that this small group harassed the Muslims by throwing rocks and random arrows at them.[113] In another, Muhammad reportedly caught the Meccans then released them untouched and unhurt, assuring them that he did not come for war but only wanted to visit the House to perform a pilgrimage.[114] The literary details—Meccans throwing rocks and Muhammad catching and releasing them—seem to moralize and idealize the Muslims by amplifying their piety and magnifying the wickedness of the people of the Quraysh, thus granting the Muslims a religious justification and right to advance forward to Mecca. The entire narrative is tendentious, serving as a moralizing construction in the shape of a historical narrative.

But there is a unique literary detail worth noting. When Muhammad caught the Quraysh people, they reportedly rebuked him, saying, "We have not heard of a man who exterminates his roots," thereby indicating their disapproval of how Muhammad was fighting and killing his relatives.[115] This report might represent an early memory: Due to its negative portrayal of Muhammad, the report may have needed some embellishments in later generations—a recurrent case in Muslim historiography that often results in the existence of rare reports and, at times, contradicting versions. Still, the narrators in this report may have sought a lesson for the believers: the devotion of Muhammad to his new mission had surpassed and eclipsed his earlier loyalties and commitments. Some scholars argue that a negative charge about Muhammad indicates a factual account, but I do not think this is plausible.[116]

[111] See Dhahabī, *Ta'rīkh*, 2:363, where he states that the location was only nine miles from Mecca. See also Bakrī, *Muᶜjam*, 2:430; 3:811.

[112] For the number of Meccans coming to meet Muhammad, see Wāqidī, *Maghāzī*, 579; cf. 582. For secondary references on ᶜIkrima, see Lecker, *Jews*, 20; Hibri, *Parable*, 62; Haykal, *Life*, 272–279; Kennedy, *Prophet*, 36, 47–49.

[113] Ṭabarī, *Ta'rīkh*, 1542; Ṭabarī, *History*, 8:81. On Khālid, see Dhahabī, *Siyar*, 1:366ff. and 2:111ff.; Zubayrī, *Nasab*, 320. For a Shīᶜite perspective on Khālid, see Yaᶜqūbī, *Ta'rīkh*, 2:147; Ḥā'irī, *Dā'irat*, 9:40–41, where Khālid is called *sayyi' al-ᶜāqiba* (someone of a bad destiny [at Judgment Day]).

[114] Muhammad reportedly said, "I do not desire to carry weapons as a pilgrim." Wāqidī, *Life*, 281.

[115] Wāqidī, *Life*, 292; Wāqidī, *Maghāzī*, 595.

[116] See Hibri, *Parable*, 330 n. 6, where he rightly critiques the sanguine views of Schoeler, who argues, "Characteristics and anecdotes of this sort should be seen as being reliable, since they have resisted the tendency towards idealization." Schoeler, "Character," 362. Watt uses similar arguments when he treats the Satanic Verses incident and argues for its factual nature. See Watt, *Muḥammad*, 103; Watt, *Muḥammad: Prophet and Statesman*, 61.

The tradition presents a pool of memories of and by the faithful, tweaked over time, adjusted to convey competing leanings. The reports are rewritten, rearranged, abridged, and blended. It is impossible to discern what may have been a truthful record, if it ever existed.[117]

In response to the disapproving words of the Qurashites, Muhammad planned to send some of his companions to the Quraysh to negotiate and declare his intentions. He asked his major companion ᶜUmar ibn al-Khaṭṭāb to go to speak with the Meccans, but ᶜUmar declined and told Muhammad it was a huge risk and suggested sending ᶜUthmān instead.[118] Muhammad then commissioned ᶜUthmān, who accepted the mission. Muhammad instructed him to march to Mecca and meet "Abū Sufyān and the dignitaries of Quraysh, to inform them that [Muhammad] had come not for war but only to visit the House and venerate its sanctity."[119] This report is important to examine, as it compares two men who later became caliphs: ᶜUmar and ᶜUthmān. The literary comparison judges two Rāshidūn caliphs through the lens of ᶜAbbāsid-era historians: ᶜUmar appears hesitant, disobedient, and to some extent cowardly, declaring, "I fear the Quraysh"[120]—while ᶜUthmān appears brave, fearless, and obedient to Muhammad. While *most* traditions often idealize ᶜUmar and represent ᶜUthmān negatively, especially in the later part of his reign, here we encounter a tale that seems to make the opposite claim, by highlighting ᶜUthmān favorably and contrasting him with a less favorable ᶜUmar.[121] Contrary to the way ᶜUmar is often depicted as *zāhid* (an ascetic) who never compromises in applying Allah's laws strictly

[117] Ibrahim, *Conversion*, 20–24; Wellhausen, *Arab*, xii; Juynboll rightly states, "It is no longer possible to sift the genuine Zuhrī traditions from the fabricated ones, or as is my contention, even the genuine Ibn Shihāb al-Zuhrī traditions from the possible hundreds of pseudo-Zuhrī ones." Juynboll, *Muslim*, 158. In the same vein, see Ibn Maᶜīn, *Ta'rīkh*, 4:464, where it is reported, "They used to bring to al-Zuhrī writings which he never read or heard of, asking him whether they could narrate them on his authority, and he would agree." Cf. Schoeler, *Biography*, 23–26. See also Crone, *Slaves*, 10; Crone, *Meccan*, 230; Crone, "How Did," 387–399; Crone, "Pagan," 140–164. See also Hibri, *Parable*, 16–17, where he correctly observes, "The task of the historian of the Rāshidūn period, therefore, becomes more challenging and *without a recognizable frame* after the dissolution of the caliphate in Medina" (17, emphasis mine).

[118] Ṭabarī, *Ta'rīkh*, 1543. See also Wāqidī, *Life*, 295, which reports ᶜUmar as saying, "I fear the Quraysh are against me. They know of my hostility towards them." See Ibn Hishām, *Sīra*, 2:315.

[119] Ṭabarī, *Ta'rīkh*, 1542–1543. See Ibn Hishām, *Sīra*, 2:315, which states that ᶜUthmān was sent to Abū Sufyān and *ashrāf* (the notables) of the Quraysh.

[120] Ibn Hishām, *Sīra*, 2:315; Wāqidī, *Life*, 295; Ṭabarī, *History*, 8:82.

[121] For the evolving depiction of ᶜUthmān, see Keaney, "Remembering." See the valuable study on the Rāshidūn by Hibri, *Parable*, 77–153. In his examination of ᶜUthmān's portrayal, Hibri argues, "Thus, there seem to be some gaps of logic in [ᶜUthmān's] companionship career that entice the historian to presume that much of ᶜUthmān's prestige in appearing to accompany Abū Bakr and ᶜUmar during the days of the Sīra represents *a back-projection of Sunnī praise on account of his having become third caliph.*" See Hibri, *Parable*, 123 (emphasis mine).

and properly, here ᶜUthmān appears in a better light.[122] This is a narration with a moral, religious, and political sentiment. While ᶜUthmān as Muhammad's envoy to the Quraysh does actually make sense, because he was from the same Umayyad family as the notable Abū Sufyān (which might have granted ᶜUthmān a significant advantage), the report itself is designed to advance more positive depictions: If many consider ᶜUmar pious and just, we are invited to believe that ᶜUthmān, too, was pious, willing, and brave, despite other questionable reports about him. This positive report might reflect later Sunnite embellishments in favor of ᶜUthmān.[123] The reason is that ᶜUthmān was important to proto-Sunnī and Sunnī claims both against the ᶜAlids and about the so-called Rightly Guided Caliphs, but he was a controversial figure. His depiction required some embellishments: the ᶜAbbāsid-era historians were ready to redesign and rewrite aspects of his portrayal by fashioning idealistic accounts that contrasted him with ᶜUmar, a more positive figure. The logic is that through the creation and circulation of some positive depictions of ᶜUthmān, his admirers would successfully balance a hostile set of claims against him; consequently, negative narratives would become diluted and harsh memories would be eliminated. This outcome is evident in the way ᶜUthmān's positive depiction continues to develop in the Ḥudaybiyya narrative.

When ᶜUthmān met the Meccans and began negotiating the Muslims' desire to enter Mecca to visit the Kaᶜba, we are told, the Meccans did not listen to him and treated him poorly. Although he was of a prestigious status among the Quraysh, they reportedly imprisoned him.[124] ᶜUthmān appears as a pious Muslim who endured persecution willingly and bravely. False reports

[122] See Hibri, *Parable*, 15.

[123] See Hibri, *Parable*, 123. One of the earliest extant pro-ᶜUthmān accounts can be found in Sayf ibn ᶜUmar's *Kitāb al-Ridda*. This pro-ᶜUthmān disposition appears in the so-called ᶜUthmāniyya movement. For Sayf's *Kitāb al-Ridda* and the ᶜUthmāniyya, see Ibrahim, *Conversion*, 107–110, where I discuss various sources and resources on Sayf; also Petersen, *ᶜAlī*, 78–82; Zahniser, "ᶜUthmānīya," 161ff. Sayf was ᶜUthmānī, with clear pro-ᶜAbbāsid and anti-Shīᶜite tendencies. See Sayf, *Kitāb al-ridda*, 1:57–58; 1:139–140. See the evaluation of Sayf by Petersen, *ᶜAlī*, 78–83, where Sayf is responsible for the "fabrication" and "adaptational process" of traditions; also Crone, "Review," 237–240; Hawting, "Review of Sayf," 546–547. For a somewhat positive assessment of Sayf's work, see Landau-Tasseron, "Sayf," 1–26. For al-Ṭabarī's reliance on Sayf, see Thompson, "Re-reading," 71ff., et passim; Hinds, "Sayf," 3–16; also Shoshan, *Arabic*, 7–8. For the ᶜAbbāsid policy against Shīᶜites, see Ṣadūq, *ᶜUyūn*, 1:108–112; Isfahānī, *Maqātil*, 387ff. See also the studies by Dūrī, *ᶜAṣr*, 110ff.; Amīn, *Aᶜyān*, 1:24ff.; Abū Khalīl, *Hārūn*, 194ff.; Wurayyimī, *Fī al-I'tilāf*, 117ff., 146, 191ff.; Kennedy, *Prophet*, 141; Kennedy, *Caliphate*, 92–93.

[124] Ṭabarī, *Ta'rīkh*, 1543. Ibn Hishām, *Sīra*, 2:315.

traveled to the Muslims claiming that the Meccans killed ᶜUthmān.[125] As a result, Muhammad and the Muslims prepared for war, as Muhammad declared, "We will not leave until we fight it out with the enemy."[126] The Muslims declared they would support him, giving him the oath of allegiance in what was later identified as *bayᶜat al-Riḍwān* (the oath of allegiance in good pleasure).[127] This oath meant that the Muslims were ready to follow whatever Muhammad decided—"it was an agreement unto death."[128] The narrative drives a moral-religious lesson, inviting later Muslims to imitate the actions of their pious forefathers. It is plausible to view this oath as an exegetical report on some Qur'ānic passages, including Q 48:18, where the scripture emphasizes that Allah was pleased with the believers when they swore allegiance and loyalty, under the tree, to the leader. A tradition is designed to exegete the Qur'ān, especially as it refers to the sworn allegiance under the tree. Still, al-Ṭabarī complicates the seemingly unified picture, as he reports that these Muslims "swore" they would not retreat or flee, but they "did not swear allegiance to [Muhammad] to the death."[129] Competing accounts are evident, but the existence of a memory about a reluctant set of warriors may indicate that some of the Muslims by now were uncertain of the consequence of the clash against the Quraysh.[130] In fact, some refused to give the oath of allegiance to Muhammad, and shortly after, we are told, Muhammad received the news that ᶜUthmān was not killed.[131] The literary detail of reluctant soldiers in Muhammad's camp may highlight a precedent, designed by traditionists, for later Muslims to avoid. Nonetheless, with over a thousand battle-ready Muslims, Mecca had to count the cost. It was a time for negotiation. This led to the treaty of the Ḥudaybiyya.

[125] Ṭabarī, *History*, 8:82; Ṭabarī, *Ta'rīkh*, 1543. Other reports claimed that ᶜUthmān performed parts of the pilgrimage when he was at Mecca instead of waiting to be joined by the Muslims. Wāqidī, *Maghāzī*, 601–602. Ibn Hishām, *Sīra*, 2:315.

[126] Ṭabarī, *Ta'rīkh*, 1543.

[127] Fazārī, *Siyar*, 1:189; Wāqidī, *Maghāzī*, 603–604; Ibn Hishām, *Sīra*, 2:315. On *bayᶜat al-Riḍwān*, see Ḥakamī, *Marwiyyāt*, 133–157. On the oath of allegiance as *bayᶜa*, see Marsham, "Oath of Allegiance," in *Princeton Encyclopedia*, ed. Böwering et al., 401; see also his study on *bayᶜa* as particularly directed to Muhammad within the "Conquest Society": Marsham, *Rituals*, 40ff.

[128] See Watt, *Muḥammad*, 50. See Ibn Abī Khaythama, *al-Ta'rīkh al-kabīr (Part 2)*, 1:258, where Muhammad sought *al-qitāl* (fighting), and the Muslims gave him allegiance *ᶜalā al-mawt* (to death).

[129] See Ṭabarī, *History*, 8:83, where it reads, "We swore allegiance to the Messenger of God that we would not flee; we did not swear allegiance to him to the death." Cf. Wāqidī, *Maghāzī*, 603; Ibn Hishām, *Sīra*, 2:315. This is contradicted by Bukhārī, *Ṣaḥīḥ*, 9:78, which states that they gave the oath of allegiance "until death." See the Muslim perspectives concerning "allegiance to death" by ᶜUmarī, *Sīra*, 440, and also Ṣallābī, *Sīra*, 670.

[130] See Djait, *Masīrat*, 165, where he argues that Muslims were doubting Islam and becoming angry, and this was the reason why Muhammad needed a *bayᶜa* (oath of allegiance).

[131] Ibn Hishām, *Sīra*, 2:315–316.

The Quraysh reportedly sent to Muhammad a man named Suhayl, instructing him, "Go to Muḥammad and make peace with him. Let the only provision of the peace with him be that he shall go away from us this year; for, by God, the Arabs must never say that he entered our territory by force."[132] Thus, it appears that Mecca initiated the peace conversation with Muhammad to protect its prestigious status among the Arabs.[133] This literary detail may be viewed as describing the Quraysh as peaceful, but, considering the bias of our narrators, it can better be understood to suggest that Mecca is on the decline in its power and prestige because of the growing influence of the Muslims—all that drives the Quraysh is concerns of being ashamed among the Arabs. After all, it is reported that, immediately after the Battle of the Trench, Muhammad spoke of the Quraysh and swore, "Now we shall *naghzūhum* (invade, attack them) and they will not *yaghzūnanā* (invade, attack us)."[134] It appears that the narrators desired to show determination and insistence on the part of Muhammad, as this depiction reflects strength and hegemony. In fact, the Quraysh appear to have been willing to allow some Muslims to enter the sacred place, if they "desire to enter and circumambulate the house," but not to have all Muslims enter, lest their doing so would be viewed as conquering Mecca by assault.[135]

Eventually, when Muhammad met Suhayl, they reportedly spoke for a long time, then Muhammad declared, "The people [of Quraysh] intended peace when they sent this man." Al-Ṭabarī reports that the "two men negotiated with each other, and peace was made between them."[136] However, some Muslims were reportedly angry about the peace agreement, as they desired war, but Muhammad went ahead for the final terms of the treaty.[137] There is a clear tension in the narrative: some reports insist that the Muslims *only* wanted to perform the *ḥajj* rituals, while other traditions reveal they chiefly sought to conquer Mecca. These two threads are vivid in the narratives and

[132] Ṭabarī, *History*, 8:84; Ṭabarī, *Ta'rīkh*, 1545; Wāqidī, *Maghāzī*, 605–606; Ibn Hishām, *Sīra*, 2:316.

[133] See Wāqidī, *Maghāzī*, 579, which reports that they were alarmed and declared, "[Muhammad] desires to enter upon us with his forces as pilgrims of *ʿUmra*. The Bedouin have heard about it. He would enter upon us by force, and between us and him is that which is between us from the war." Wāqidī, *Life*, 284.

[134] Ṭabarī, *History*, 8:40; Ṭabarī, *Ta'rīkh*, 1499. Dhahabī, *Ta'rīkh*, 2:304.

[135] Wāqidī, *Life*, 297; Wāqidī, *Maghāzī*, 605. For the details of the agreement according to the Quraysh's desire, see Wāqidī, *Maghāzī*, 605–606, where the Meccans were mostly concerned with their prestigious status among the Arabs and did not want the Bedouins to say that Muhammad entered Mecca *ʿanwa* (by assault).

[136] Ṭabarī, *History*, 8:84; Ṭabarī, *Ta'rīkh*, 1545.

[137] ʿUmar reportedly approached Muhammad and said, "For what reason do we give a lower position in our religion?" Wāqidī, *Maghāzī*, 606.

deeply intertwined—one cannot untangle them. They represent variations in the memory of the episode among Muslims. Still, it appears that it was important for the narrators to emphasize this tension, as they advanced the religious crux of their narrative: Muslims have a right to enter Mecca to perform the rituals of the *ḥajj*, whether peacefully or by assault. The logic goes: If the Muslims were prevented from entering Mecca, then an attack on the Quraysh would be legitimate—even considered defensive. This rationale for initiating wars appears in the writings of classical, modern, and contemporary Muslim exegetes and scholars.[138]

The peace treaty between Muhammad and the Quraysh included various items.[139] Most importantly, it established that "warfare shall be laid aside by the people for ten years, during which the people shall be safe and refrain from [attacking] each other."[140] Nonetheless, in forming the treaty, it appears that Muhammad had to make three *religious* concessions: one related to Allah, another related to Muhammad's prophethood, and a third concerning Meccan converts to Islam.[141] These concessions are important to examine—not as factual occurrences, but as literary devices shaped by the narrators. When Muhammad demanded that the agreement begin with the Islamic introductory phrase "in the name of Allah," Suhayl opposed and said, "I do not know this one. Write rather, 'In your name, O god.' "[142] Muhammad

[138] For classical Muslims, see Muqātil, *Tafsīr*, 1:167; Zamakhsharī, *Kashshāf*, 1:235, 2:21; Qurṭubī, *Jāmiʿ*, 2:347–348; Bayḍāwī, *Anwār*, 1:128–129. For modern Muslims, see Riḍā, *Manār*, 2:168, where he interprets Q 2:290–292 and claims that the verses were revealed during the Ḥudaybiyya incident and aimed to exhort the Muslims who did not want *al-qitāl* (fighting) in the sacred mosque. For Riḍa, the verses allow them to fight, because the battle is in self-defense and in Allah's path since the Muslims were seeking to worship in *bayt Allāh* (Allah's house); preventing them was tantamount to declaration of war against them. A similar justification appears in Haykal, *Ḥayāt*, 256–258. For contemporary Muslim scholars, see ʿUmarī, *Sīra*, 434–437; Ṣallābī, *Sīra*, 657. See the discussion of various classical and modern interpretations of these verses in Ibrahim, *Stated*, 215–216.

[139] For a secondary study on the items of the treaty, see Ṣallābī, *Sīra*, 673–674; Ḥakamī, *Marwiyyāt*, 166.

[140] Ṭabarī, *History*, 8:86; Ṭabarī, *Taʾrīkh*, 1546. Ibn Hishām, *Sīra*, 2:317–318. There are scholarly doubts about the number "ten" for the designated years for peace in the treaty. If we consider that Abū Sufyān reportedly sought to "prolong" the treaty less than two years after its establishment when he traveled from Mecca to Medina to meet Muhammad, it does not seem plausible for a commander to seek to renew a treaty that was still valid. See Ṭabarī, *Taʾrīkh*, 1418. See the comments of Djait, *Masīrat*, 156 and 173, where he does not trust the reliability of the "ten years" claim and argues the period was likely only "two years." Djait's opinion goes against traditional Muslim claims, such as Ḥakamī, *Marwiyyāt*, 166; Ṣallābī, *Sīra*, 674; ʿUmarī, *Sīra*, 443.

[141] See the details in Wāqidī, *Maghāzī*, 610–612. For a Muslim perspective on these compromises, see ʿUmarī, *Sīra*, 441–442, where he dilutes them and argues that they were simple "disagreements," although he later asserts that Muslims were unhappy about these points (443). See also the Sunnī scholar Ṣallābī, *Sīra*, 673, where he argues that Muhammad's concessions were in his pursuit of the policy of "wisdom, flexibility, and patience." See similar arguments by Muslim scholar Ḥakamī, *Marwiyyāt*, 170, where he claims that some Muslims were "hurt" by the signing of the treaty.

[142] Ṭabarī, *History*, 8:85–86; Ṭabarī, *Taʾrīkh*, 1546.

reportedly conceded. He then wanted the agreement to acknowledge his prophethood as being Allah's apostle and demanded the writing of the statement, "This is that whereon Muḥammad the Messenger of God has made peace with Suhayl."[143] Suhayl again objected to the statement and said, "If I testified that you are the Messenger of God, I would not fight you. Write rather your name and the name of your father."[144] In concession, Muhammad agreed and said to the scribe, "Write: This is that whereon Muḥammad the son of ᶜAbdallāh has made peace with Suhayl."[145] It appears that Muhammad was willing to concede these two religious claims in order to accomplish the final goal of cutting the treaty with the Meccans. His aspiration for political achievement appears to have surpassed other priorities. Moreover, a third concession was on a major consequence for converts to or from Islam: If anyone from the Quraysh seeks to join Muhammad's camp (i.e., desires to convert to Islam), then this individual cannot do so without "the permission of his [Meccan] guardian."[146] If permission is not granted, then Muhammad, based on the Ḥudaybiyya agreement, must reject the individual, refuse the conversion, and send him back to the Quraysh. The opposite, however, is not acceptable: "whoever shall come to Quraysh from those who are with the Messenger of God, they shall not return him to [Muhammad]."[147] It is clear that this item in the treaty favored the Meccans over the Muslims and was advantageous for the pagans. The literary report of the three concessions reflects Muhammad as chiefly a tribal leader who mainly cared about tribal consolidation and resourceful advancement. As a literary tale, it might have been fashioned by the narrators to exhort the believers to follow Muhammad's footsteps and seek strategic political agreements above religious sentiments in times of war. Still, this account seems to sit poorly with apologetic claims that the raids were essentially sacred campaigns for religious reasons.

[143] Ṭabarī, *History*, 8:86; Ṭabarī, *Ta'rīkh*, 1546.

[144] Ṭabarī, *History*, 8:86; Ṭabarī, *Ta'rīkh*, 1546. Decades later, Muᶜāwiya referred to this dispute, as he was writing his agreement to cease war with Caliph ᶜAlī. Muᶜawiya refused to describe ᶜAlī as *Amīr al-mu'minīn* (the commander of the believers). Abū Ḥanīfa al-Dīnawarī, *Akhbār*, 206–207. Cf. Ibn ᶜAbd Rabbih, *ᶜIqd*, 2:233. Ibn ᶜAbd Rabbih (d. 328/940) is pro-Umayyad. See Ibn al-Faraḍī, *Ta'rīkh*, 1:49–50; Yāqūt, *Muᶜjam*, 1:463ff.; Dhahabī, *Ta'rīkh*, 24:221; Dhahabī, *Siyar*, 15:283ff. On the religio-political orientation of *Kitāb al-ᶜIqd al-farīd*, see Toral-Niehoff, "Writing," 80–95.

[145] Ṭabarī, *History*, 8:86; Ṭabarī, *Ta'rīkh*, 1546.

[146] Ṭabarī, *History*, 8:86; Ṭabarī, *Ta'rīkh*, 1546.

[147] Ṭabarī, *History*, 8:86; Ṭabarī, *Ta'rīkh*, 1546. This item appears to exclude women and children, according to a report by Wāqidī, *Maghāzī*, 631–632; Wāqidī, *Life*, 310–311. See Ibn Qudāma, *Mughnī*, 9:230, where he reports that it was Allah who instructed excluding women. On excluding women and children, see ᶜUmarī, *Sīra*, 452.

Some Muslim scholars view these as not compromises at all, and argue that Muhammad was strategic and prudent to reach his goals—he did not concede to that which opposed his religious convictions.[148] But these opinions are challenged by the Muslim traditions themselves. We are told that these three concessions made many Muslims angry. ᶜUmar—one of Muhammad's close companions—doubted Islam on that day and declared, "Why should we grant what is detrimental to our religion?"[149] He reported his experience thus: "Surely doubt entered me at that time. I disputed the Prophet returning answer for answer, and I have not disputed like that with him ever."[150] Of course, this depiction of ᶜUmar is better viewed as a designed portrayal by the medieval narrators that fits squarely in his overall image in the sources as a strict, sharp, and angry person—characteristics that elevated him to the role of a just caliph.[151] The picture revolves on his values of firmness and inflexibility in matters of faith.[152] In fact, we are told that Muhammad instructed the Muslims to "avoid (or be careful of) ᶜUmar's anger, as Allah becomes angry with ᶜUmar's anger."[153] The tendentiousness of the report is glaring.

But ᶜUmar was not the only one. We are told that many doubted Islam on that day, to such an extent that Muhammad had to openly exhort those who remained in their commitment to Islam—"Because they did not doubt."[154]

[148] Ṣallābī, *Sīra*, 673; ᶜUmarī, *Sīra*, 434–437.

[149] Ṭabarī, *History*, 8:86; Ṭabarī, *Ta'rīkh*, 1546. See also Wāqidī, *Maghāzī*, 606; Ibn Hishām, *Sīra*, 2:315–316. Avraham Hakim studies several early traditions that compare Muhammad's authority with that of ᶜUmar, and traces how competing traditions were at play to support the caliph's authority, but later Muslims "preferred to formulate [their] law based on the prophetical authority and not the caliphal one." See Hakim, "Muḥammad's Authority," 181–200. For Shīᶜite perspectives on ᶜUmar's disagreement with Muhammad, see Sulaym ibn Qays, *Kitāb Sulaym*, 418, 363; Naṣr ibn Muzāḥim, *Waqᶜat*, 215–216; Ibn Shādhān, *Īḍāḥ*, 1:229ff.; Masᶜūdī, *Ithbāt*, 145ff. See also Khalidi, *Arabic*, 48. For scholarly discussions of the works of Sulaym and Naṣr, see Ibrahim, *Conversion*, 35–41 and 118–121, respectively. On Sulaym's work, see Djebli, "Sulaym b. Kays," *EI²*, 9:818–819; Amir-Moezzi, *Silent*, 13–22; Modarressi, *Tradition*, 82–83; Crone, *Nativist*, 43; Donner, "Umayyad," 187. For a negative assessment of Naṣr's work, see al-Qazwīnī, *Irshād*, 2:572. Abū Jaᶜfar al-ᶜUqaylī (d. 323/934) places Naṣr among the weak narrators. ᶜUqaylī, *Ḍuᶜafā'*, 4:300. Ibn al-Nadīm places Naṣr in the same class as Abū Mikhnaf (d. 157/774). Ibn al-Nadīm, *Fihrist*, 93; Ṣafadī, *Wāfī*, 27:56. On Naṣr and his work, see Sezgin, *Ta'rīkh*, 1:2:137–138; Brockelmann, *History*, 1:211; Brockelmann, *Ta'rīkh*, 3:37; Muṣṭafā, *Ta'rīkh*, 1:67. Petersen, *ᶜAlī*, 24. On Abū Mikhnaf, see Sezgin, *Ta'rīkh*, 1:2:127–130; Brockelmann, *Ta'rīkh*, 3:36. See also Abū Mikhnaf, *Kitāb Maqtal al-Ḥusayn*.

[150] Wāqidī, *Life*, 298; Wāqidī, *Maghāzī*, 607. See the two secondary studies of Ouardi, *Les califes maudits* and *Les derniers jours*; also Hichem Djait, *Fitna*, 26ff.

[151] See Hibri, *Parable*, 80, where he compares the depiction of ᶜUmar in the *Sīra* with Paul in Christianity.

[152] On this image of ᶜUmar, see Ibn Saᶜd, *Ṭabaqāt*, 3:222, 3:265, where ᶜUmar is portrayed as the strictest among the *umma* of Muhammad.

[153] Khaṭīb, *Ta'rīkh*, 3:439; Ibn ᶜAsākir, *Ta'rīkh*, 44:72.

[154] Ṭabarī, *History*, 8:89; Ṭabarī, *Ta'rīkh*, 1550.

Not only did some Muslims doubt Islam, but some openly disobeyed Muhammad.[155] When Muhammad completed the signing of the document, he instructed the Muslims to stand up, sacrifice, and shave, "But not a man among them responded"—he "repeated his command thrice, yet not one among them obeyed."[156] This drove Muhammad to be "in great anger."[157] In reading these accounts within the frame of representations, one may view in them some raw, early memories of the faithful that required tweaking and adjustment by later traditionists. The accounts appear to reflect unembellished portrayals of the human side of Muhammad and his companions, depicting major companions doubting Islam and Muhammad himself getting angry when he is disobeyed.[158] Of course, one can identify a theological disposition designed in this account in the form of an exhortation to the believers to not question Muhammad, but instead to trust, obey, and follow his wisdom. In a sense, this may be practically done—in later generations—by submitting and applying Muhammad's reported *aḥādīth* (traditions, sayings), which were subsequently developed by Muslim traditionists.[159] But not every tale in Muslim historiography must have a theological point; sometimes the lesson is moral. Contrary to what Muslims often claim and argue about the earliest companions, they are not often portrayed in the most affirmative ways in historiographical sources.[160]

In contrast to Muhammad's three major concessions, the Meccan pagans seem to have made one major compromise. They demanded that the Muslims return to Medina and not enter Mecca this time; they promised Muhammad that in the next year, the Meccans "will go out, away from you, and you shall enter Mecca with your companions and stay there for three nights: you shall have with you the weapons of a rider, with the swords in scabbards; you shall

155 Ibn Hishām, *Sīra*, 2:319.

156 Wāqidī, *Life*, 302. Wāqidī, *Maghāzī*, 613. See the argument of ᶜUmarī, *Sīra*, 446, where he claims that Muslims were not disobedient but angry, as they tried to annul the treaty. See similar views in Ṣallābī, *Sīra*, 680.

157 Wāqidī, *Life*, 302.

158 On Muhammad's anger, see Ibn ᶜAsākir, *Ta'rīkh*, 4:63, 16:243.

159 See Goldziher, *Muslim*, 2:44, where he observes, "It is not surprising that, among the hotly debated controversial issues of Islam, whether political or doctrinal, there is not one in which the champions of the various views are unable to cite a number of traditions." He adds, "Anything which appears desirable to pious men was given by them a corroborating support reaching back to the Prophet. This could easily be done in a generation in which the Companions, who were represented as the intermediaries of the Prophet's words, were no longer alive" (2:42).

160 See Hibri, *Parable*, 343 n. 58, where he observes, "There are in fact a variety of instances where the Prophet had to manage a situation of uncooperative companions, and theology is not usually the foundation of much of this discourse as much as morality."

not enter with other weapons."[161] This concession settled the peace treaty, and both parties signed it.[162]

Classical Muslim historians portray the Ḥudaybiyya as one of the greatest victories of Islam, claiming that many joined Muhammad's camp—that is, "converted" to Islam—after it.[163] Even Allah, we are told, revealed to Muhammad verses from the Qur'ān, highlighting the incident as a great victory and conquest (Q 48:1).[164] Traditions claim that "No victory greater than this one had been won previously in Islam."[165] Before it, "There had been only fighting when the people met together," but "when the truce took place, and war laid down its burdens, and all the people felt safe with each other, they met with each other in conversation and debate, and no one possessing understanding was told about Islam but embraced it."[166] The literary detail of embracing Islam is important to highlight. In this context, it appears, embracing Islam reflects making an alliance with Muhammad and his community.[167] Conversion here is not about religious devotion to a set of theological claims. Practically, upon signing the treaty, Arabs reportedly began to choose sides, whether to ally themselves with Muhammad or the Quraysh. After all, the agreement established that "anyone who wishes to enter into treaty and pact with the Messenger of God may do so, and anyone who wishes to enter into treaty and pact with Quraysh may do so."[168] The prestigious Khuzāᶜa tribe hastened and said, "We have a treaty and pact with the Messenger of God," while the tribe of Banū Bakr, "jumped up and said, 'We have a treaty and compact with Quraysh.'"[169] These tribal alliances would prove essential a short while later, as this treaty did not last for

[161] Ṭabarī, *History*, 8:86; Ṭabarī, *Ta'rīkh*, 1547.

[162] Still, Suhayl and Muhammad disagreed and argued concerning who would keep the document—they ended up copying the agreement and each party took a copy. Wāqidī, *Maghāzī*, 612. Wāqidī, *Life*, 301. Reportedly, Muhammad's cousin, ᶜAlī, wrote the agreement. Ṭabarī, *Ta'rīkh*, 1546. Cf. Ibn ᶜAbd Rabbih, *ᶜIqd*, 4:245. See also Majlisī, *Biḥār*, 20:140.

[163] Wāqidī, *Maghāzī*, 624.

[164] See Wāqidī, *Maghāzī*, 618–624, where al-Wāqidī interprets the Qur'ānic passage against the background of the Ḥudaybiyya, emphasizing victory and conquests: "the *fatḥ* (conquering, or opening) of the Quraysh and their reconciliation." See also Wāqidī, *Life*, 304; Ibn Hishām, *Sīra*, 2:320.

[165] Ṭabarī, *History*, 8:90; Ṭabarī, *Ta'rīkh*, 1550; Wāqidī, *Life*, 300; Wāqidī, *Maghāzī*, 610.

[166] Ṭabarī, *History*, 8:90; Ṭabarī, *Ta'rīkh*, 1551; Wāqidī, *Maghāzī*, 624; Wāqidī, *Life*, 307.

[167] See Ibrahim, *Stated*, 97–98, 151, and 236, where I write, "Becoming a 'Muslim' probably meant declaring loyalty and adherence to ruling elites, mostly Meccan aristocrats." On this meaning of conversion, see also Ibrahim, *Conversion*, 30, 88, 162, 208, 210; Sharīf, *Makka*, 561, and 533, where he rightly observes that conversion to Islam was *maẓharan li-dukhūlihim fī al-niẓām al-jadīd wa-iqrārihim bi-l-wiḥda al-ᶜarabiyya* (a manifestation of people joining into the new system as well as their affirmation of the Arabian unity).

[168] Ṭabarī, *History*, 8:86; Ṭabarī, *Ta'rīkh*, 1546–1547.

[169] Ṭabarī, *History*, 8:86; Ṭabarī, *Ta'rīkh*, 1547; Wāqidī, *Maghāzī*, 612; Wāqidī, *Life*, 301. Ibn Hishām, *Sīra*, 2:318. See Watt, *Muḥammad*, 48–49.

long.[170] In less than two years, Muhammad and the Muslims announced that the treaty was broken because a tribe allied with the Meccans had supposedly attacked a tribe allied with the Muslims.[171] This led to the greatest conquest against the Quraysh.[172] Still, Muslim historians claim that "in those two years as many or more entered Islam as had been in it before."[173]

Before we critically analyze crucial literary details in the accounts of Ḥudaybiyya, we should observe that the story is designed to emphasize a huge triumph for the Muslims, highlighting that the treaty provided them at least three strategic results.[174] The first is the Meccans' recognition of Muhammad as an equal.[175] They could not deny any further the importance of their opponent whom they forced to emigrate from his hometown six years earlier. This is a significant success that Muhammad achieved in a relatively short period of time. It is plausible to deduce that the narrators were aiming to highlight the growing power of the Muslims to fit within the developing story that will reach its climax shortly with the conquest of Mecca. Another notable result is that after the treaty, major Meccan pagans reportedly shifted their loyalties by joining Muhammad's camp through their open declaration of conversion to Islam. These converts, the narrative suggests, must have realized that Muhammad was growing in power. Two men were significantly important in this regard: Khālid ibn al-Walīd and ᶜAmr ibn al-ᶜĀṣ.[176] These men were shrewd military commanders from

170 See Hamidullah, *Battlefields*, 81, where he argues, "It was these subsidiary parties who dragged the main groups into the war."

171 We are told, "Indeed there was peace for twenty-two months until they destroyed the contract." Wāqidī, *Life*, 307. Wāqidī, *Maghāzī*, 624. However, see ᶜUmarī, *Sīra*, 453, where he argues that the peace period was actually seventeen or eighteen months.

172 See Ṭabarī, *Ta'rīkh*, 1619ff., where it reports that supporters of the Quraysh (Banū Bakr) and allies of Muhammad (Banū Khuzāᶜa) clashed, which led to the breaking of the treaty in the precursors of the conquest of Mecca in the year A.H. 8. See also Wāqidī, *Maghāzī*, 612; Wāqidī, *Life*, 301.

173 Ṭabarī, *History*, 8:90; Ṭabarī, *Ta'rīkh*, 1550–1551.

174 For Muslim views on the results, see Ḥakamī, *Marwiyyāt*, 158–166; Ṣallābī, *Sīra*, 687–694; ᶜUmarī, *Sīra*, 443; also the nonconventional views of the Muslim scholar Djait, *Masīrat*, 156, where he argues that Muhammad was politically and diplomatically genius in this treaty, as he believed it would provide future unmatched opportunities. For non-Muslim arguments on the results of the treaty, see Watt, *Muḥammad*, 50–51.

175 See Watt, *Muḥammad*, 48–49, where he argues, "The clause suggests that the two sides are being treated equally, and in a sense it is a recognition by Quraysh of Muḥammad's equality with themselves." Unlike Watt, Djait, *Masīrat*, 156, argues that the treaty did not regard both parties equally, suggesting that the Muslims conceded more than the Meccans did.

176 For the conversion of the two men, see Ibrahim, *Conversion*, 166 n. 366, where I argue, "It appears that, for ᶜAmr and Khālid, conversion was a decision to join the victorious camp, especially when we consider that ᶜAmr converted after he spoke with al-Najāshī, who declared that Islam was going to surpass every other religion (Wāqidī, *Maghāzī*, 742–745). ᶜAmr then met Khālid, who stated, 'All people now entered Islam and if we wait our necks will be smitten.' Both ᶜAmr and Khālid then converted, in what appears an inauthentic conversion."

the Quraysh.[177] Khālid and ᶜAmr's joining Muhammad's camp reportedly caused a huge embarrassment and loss for the Quraysh and resulted in a momentous victory for the Muslims.[178] As a literary tale, the account of the "conversion" of Khālid and ᶜAmr is important to highlight. The men seem to have merely joined the victorious camp with no supernatural experience or spiritual change. Their conversion was not a transformation in religious loyalty, but merely a calculated political step. Still, the narrators—who served as religious storytellers—needed to fashion a picture that fit within their religious framework. They shaped the victory narrative as a declaration of the hegemony of Islam, which astonished the Arab warriors, persuading them to choose Islam. A third important result of the Ḥudaybiyya was that it ensured lessened tension between the Muslims and the Meccans and thus allowed the former, we are invited to believe, not only to grow in power but also to focus on other opponents, including the Jews of Medina and its surroundings (the topic of the next chapter).[179] Because of the assurance of the peace pact with the Meccans, Muhammad was able to launch several raids, establishing dominion over neighboring locations in Arabia. Al-Ṭabarī lists many of these raids, depicting them as an inevitable result of the Muslims securing the treaty with the Meccans. He reports that in one of these raids, Muhammad sent the Muslim companion ᶜUkkāsha with forty men to a nearby water well east of Medina called al-Ghamr, which belonged to the tribe of Banū Asad.[180] Securing water wells in Arabia is a major necessity. The example of al-Ghamr is one of many and reflects that the decreased tension with the Meccans allowed Muhammad to grow his strategic expansion in controlling Arabia. The story indicates that after the Ḥudaybiyya, the Muslims were able to launch more raids in order to expand their control over strategic lands near Medina. The frequency of the raids and the apparent repetition in the

[177] Wāqidī, *Maghāzī*, 624. See Wāqidī, *Life*, 307. ᶜAmr ibn al-ᶜĀṣ was initially reluctant to convert and said, "If all Quraysh converted, I will not." Wāqidī, *Maghāzī*, 742. Djait argues that Muhammad was a "great political commander" who knew how to "turn the page" by ignoring the past bad behaviors of Khālid in order to benefit from his skills in the fight against the Meccans. Djait, *Masīrat*, 169. See also ᶜUmarī, *Sīra*, 453, where he argues that there seems to have been a change in the agreement by allowing these two men to leave the Quraysh and join Muhammad, since there is no mention in the traditions that the Quraysh allowed them to join Muhammad.

[178] See Djait, *Masīrat*, 169, where he explains the significance of Khālid and ᶜAmr to the balance of power in the Medinan-Meccan combat.

[179] See Hamidullah, *Battlefields*, 110, where he argues, "The pact at Hudaibiyah with the Meccans left the Prophet with hands free to deal with the growing danger at Khaibar." See Khaṭṭāb, *Rasūl*, 287–289; also Watt, *Muḥammad*, 51, where he explains, "by ending the state of war with Mecca, [Muhammad] had gained a larger measure of freedom for the work of extending the influence of the religious and political organization he had formed."

[180] Ṭabarī, *Ta'rīkh*, 1554; Ṭabarī, *History*, 8:93. On al-Ghamr, see Yāqūt, *Muᶜjam*, 4:211.

accounts serve to emphasize the religiously driven theme of Islam's victory, advancement, and superiority.[181]

In analyzing the accounts of the Ḥudaybiyya, I offer four critical observations. First, the Ḥudaybiyya incident was a strategic truce agreement, even though many classical historians depict it as a raid. It did not involve any fighting. It was a successful political move with huge benefits and implications. The narrative seems to point to a major claim: The Ḥudaybiyya elevated Muhammad's status as a tribal leader and transformed the balance of power in Arabia. Muhammad had now become a recognized tribal leader in Arabia, and he was not to be underestimated either in his power or in his influence and reach.[182] This is echoed, in part, in the way the Tunisian Muslim historian Hichem Djait interprets the event of the Ḥudaybiyya. He views it as "a religious treaty and a political victorious conquest."[183] While one may indeed find evidence for a plausible reading of a political victory, it is not certain how the treaty could be viewed as a religious treaty, especially if one considers Muhammad's concessions to the Meccans.

Second, the Muslims reportedly initiated the incident of the Ḥudaybiyya. Whether it was Allah's divine dream or Muhammad's desire to return to his hometown is not significant in this regard.[184] The Meccans did not initiate the incident. One plausible reading suggests that Muhammad, in a bold move, gathered hundreds of Arabs and marched to Mecca supposedly to perform ritual worship. This move must have provoked the Meccans who had reportedly lost to the Muslims a year earlier in the Battle of the Trench. In reading the narratives as representations created by later generations, we should not attempt to place significant weight on the question of whether Muhammad had sought to attack the Quraysh or simply to perform the *ḥajj*. We cannot know, and, more importantly, these are representations designed by the storytellers, who aim to advance religious philosophy. The tension in the narratives seems to aim to conflate the two.[185] Some may argue that the

[181] Hibri, *Parable*, 18.

[182] See Watt, *Muḥammad*, 51, where he explains, "In making a treaty with the Meccans as an equal [Muhammad] had received public recognition of the position that was clearly his after the failure of the siege of Medina."

[183] Djait, *Masīrat*, 153.

[184] See Ṭabarī, *Taʾrīkh*, 1529–1530.

[185] For some traditions that suggest that Muhammad's primary goal was actually to conquer Mecca, see Ṭabarī, *Taʾrīkh*, 1529–1530. Additionally, we read of Muhammad's sworn declaration—sometime before he received the divine dream—about the Meccans, "Now we shall *naghzūhum* (invade, attack them) and they will not *yaghzūnanā* (invade, attack us)." Ṭabarī, *History*, 8:40. See also the argument of the Muslim scholar ʿUmarī, *Sīra*, 435, where he (1) rejects accounts stating that

month during which this incident occurred was a sacred month in which fighting was not allowed; however, Muhammad and the Muslims had already demonstrated that they did not necessarily care to follow these tribal customs any longer.[186]

Nevertheless, if one assumes that Muhammad's sole desire was to perform the pilgrimage, then one is faced with a dilemma. According to traditions, Mecca and the Kaᶜba were full of idols and pagan worshippers at the time. It is uncertain precisely what pure Islamic rituals were supposed to be performed by the Muslims in a completely pagan town. This is arguably a clear gap in the tradition. While classical historians seem to have worked diligently to fill the gaps in the overall picture, they left many questions unanswered. On the one hand, as observed earlier, one may conclude that the Islamic pilgrimage was not initially different from the pagan one.[187] On the other hand, some may argue—less compellingly—that Muhammad was trying to send a comforting message to the Meccans, conveying that his new religion was not a threat to their pagan worship or wealth.[188] Still, it appears that Muslim historians, in their formation of religious traditions, have projected their contemporary understanding of Mecca back onto history. After all, the Mecca of the time of the writing of historical traditions (at least two centuries after Muhammad) was different from the presumed Mecca of the pagan Quraysh. Moreover, even if we assume Muhammad's intention to be completely as stated—that is, he only wanted to perform pilgrimage and not enact war—we still have to deduce that the offensive move against the Meccans was a calculated political step and Muhammad was keen to accomplish it. As a tribal leader, Muhammad must have realized the significant implications of embarrassing the Quraysh and emphasizing himself as an equal leader.[189] At least the

Muslims did not seek war and did not have weapons, and (2) argues that they were actually ready to fight the Meccans.

[186] On the Muslim violation of the sacred months, see Ibn Hishām, *Sīra*, 2:308. See the discussion in Ibrahim, *Stated*, 72–73; also Watt, *Muḥammad*, 47, where he rightly observes that the month of the Ḥudaybiyya "was, of course, one of the sacred months in which there was supposed to be no bloodshed, but Muḥammad had not shown himself specially observant of sacred times, and was clearly relying, not solely on the sanctity of the season, but partly on the number of his followers." See also the arguments of the Muslim scholar Qimanī, who points out that Muhammad's followers did not keep the sacred months but violated them by shedding blood, stealing possessions, and taking people captive. Qimanī, *Ḥizb*, 153.

[187] See Peters, *Muslim*, 3–41; Hawting, "Origins," 23–48.

[188] According to Watt, "The performance of the pilgrimage would be a demonstration that Islam was not a foreign religion but essentially an Arabian one, and in particular that it had its centre and focus in Mecca." Watt, *Muḥammad*, 47. Watt's argument here echoes Djait's argument that Islamic rituals were not that different from pagan ones. Djait, *Masīrat*, 154.

[189] See Watt, *Muḥammad*, 47.

Muslim narrators portrayed him in such a way. In the same vein, some may argue that Muhammad was trying to be friendly to the Meccans,[190] but this does not seem to ring true. The narratives drive a clear point: Muhammad was ready to engage with the Meccans as an equal opponent. He did not need to appease or please them. He was now a true enemy who must be feared. The accounts portray him as a commander in chief leading hundreds of Muslims—who gave him their allegiance, promising no retreat until death—to enter the place from which he was forced out. These narratives do not sit well with traditional claims that all of Muhammad's raids were conducted in self-defense.[191]

Third, the accounts depict the Meccan Quraysh as the first to seek peace with Muhammad. This is a curious literary feature to highlight. While the peace treaty was not initiated by the Muslims, we should note that the Quraysh did not appear to seek peace because they were peacemakers. Rather, they reportedly feared the huge embarrassment they may receive—as a prestigious Arab tribe—if Arabs learned that Muhammad—with his fourteen hundred or nineteen hundred followers—was able to enter Mecca, especially after the Quraysh's humiliating defeat one year earlier. This literary detail—the Quraysh fearing shame and embarrassment—aims to defame the Meccans and convey their motives unfavorably. Importantly, the Ḥudaybiyya narratives demonstrate that the main goal of both parties was not *necessarily* peace but political gain and advancement.[192] Mecca wanted to protect its prestigious status in order to keep its trade growing and its significance rising among the Arabs, while Muhammad aimed to obtain a period of lessened tension at all costs so that he could focus on other political matters.[193] Both parties gained that which they sought; however, both likely realized that the "peace" was not going to last long. They just needed a temporary truce. This is

190 See the unconvincing argument of Watt, where he claims that "demonstration of such a kind at such a time would impress upon the Meccans that Islam was not a threat to the religious importance of Mecca. It would also suggest that Muhammad was prepared to be friendly on his own terms, of course." Watt, *Muḥammad*, 47. Contrary to Watt's assertions, see the arguments of Sunnī scholars Ḥakamī, *Marwiyyāt*, 158–166; Ṣallābī, *Sīra*, 687–694; ʿUmarī, *Sīra*, 443. For them, it was the time for jihad and fighting, not being friendly to the Meccans, who were the greatest enemy of the Muslims at the time.

191 See the apologetic work by Moulavi Chirágh Ali (1844–1895), *Critical Exposition*. See also the studies of Khalidi, "Muslim Debates," 305–323; Hardy, *Muslims*, 112–113. See also Ibrahim, *Stated*, 1–5.

192 See Watt, *Muḥammad*, 48, where he argues that the treaty "gives some satisfaction to both parties."

193 See Watt, *Muḥammad*, 49, where he explains, "Muḥammad had by implication given up the blockade of Mecca. Mecca could presumably now resume her trade with Syria, though her monopoly of this trade was gone."

reportedly evident in how Muhammad was willing to compromise on major ideological points—points presumably essential to his Islamic message.[194] The agreement did not affirm his religious status, nor did it adopt his claims about Allah, not to mention the clear disadvantage of making it difficult for pagan Meccans to convert to Islam. Muhammad, the story reveals, accepted these compromises likely because he aimed to attain more imminent political goals. He appears to have been willing to sit on the fence regarding essential religious terms in order to achieve strategic military results. This is evident in the reported reactions of many Muslims—some questioned Muhammad, and some actually doubted or abandoned Islam.[195] Ultimately, Muhammad's designed portrayal at the Ḥudaybiyya is unique: He appears as a skillful tribal leader who acted politically and strategically, even though his moves drove many to question him and his presumed message. He was determined to advance his tribal influence by luring the Meccans to make a deal at all costs. His example, in conceding and compromising on religious grounds, may reflect a lesson of a strategic political warrior, not a moral theological preacher. Contrary to traditional Muslim suggestions, it is better to view Muhammad here as a tribal commander, not an ascetic proselytizer.[196] The Muslim historian Djait argues, "When Muslims think within religious boundaries, Muhammad thinks according to political considerations (and restrictions), as if he—in this moment—distances himself from religious enthusiasm."[197]

Fourth, the Ḥudaybiyya account appears to have been designed to emphasize that Mecca—not only Muhammad and the Muslims—was required to offer some compromises in order to achieve the deal. While the Meccans initially forbade Muhammad from entering Mecca, they must have realized they could not do this anymore. To save face, they said they could allow Muslims in the city in the following year, at which time the Meccans would leave the Kaᶜba so that the Muslims could perform their pilgrimage unchallenged and

[194] See Djait, *Masīrat*, 156, where he calls the treaty an "unequal pact" and argues that the angry Muslims were right in their reaction against the treaty, because it was not treating the two parties equally. See also ᶜUmarī, *Sīra*, 446, where he states it was an unequal pact, although he still considers it a great victory.

[195] Wāqidī, *Maghāzī*, 608. Watt argues, "The treaty was thus favourable to Muhammad's long-term strategy, but for the moment left him to deal with the disappointment of his followers at the apparent failure of the expedition." Watt, *Muḥammad*, 49. See also Watt, "al-Ḥudaybiya," *EI*^{2}, 3:539, where he argues, "The expedition to Khaybar about six weeks later was in part to console [the Muslims] for this disappointment."

[196] This is evident in the way some modern Muslim historians attempt to distinguish Muhammad's roles. See Djait, *Masīrat*, 154, where he calls for a distinction between Muhammad *al-insān* (the man) and Muhammad *al-nabī* (the prophet).

[197] Djait, *Masīrat*, 156–157.

alone.[198] They also compromised by allowing Arabs to join either party. This compromise cost them greatly, both politically and strategically. They basically offered Muhammad the greatest opportunity of all, as they opened the gate wide for Arab tribes to choose Muhammad. Unlike Muhammad's compromises, this Meccan compromise was a fatal tactical error. Tribes could now—as the story reveals—hasten to abandon the Qurayshite alliance, to unite with the growing power of the Muslims under the leadership of the "King of the Hijaz (Western Arabia)," as some called Muhammad a few months later.[199] The Jewish community is a case in point: by signing the treaty, the Meccans lost any possible support they may have potentially received from the Jews; otherwise, they would have jeopardized their relationship with the Muslims.[200] The powerful tribe of Khuzāᶜa is another example. Even before the treaty, some of their men joined the fourteen hundred or nineteen hundred people who marched with Muhammad to Mecca.[201] This suggests that the tribe was already sensing that Muhammad's star was glowing and his political future was promising. Once the treaty was cut, the Khuzāᶜa tribe reportedly joined Muhammad and abandoned the Quraysh. Not only did Khuzāᶜa and other tribes make the switch from the Quraysh to Muhammad, but notable individuals did so as well.[202] Thus, while the Quraysh and the Muslims offered compromises, it appears that the Meccans' loss was severer. It marked their exponential decline in power and prestige, allowing Muhammad an unchallenged path to becoming the major leader of Arabia.

The medieval narrators offer us a literary story demonstrating that the raid and treaty of the Ḥudaybiyya served Muhammad and the Muslims greatly. While many Muslims were reportedly disappointed with Muhammad for his compromise on religious grounds, he proved tactically and politically shrewd more than they could have imagined. By initiating the march to Mecca, he was going on the offensive, declaring his readiness for escalation and confrontation, in order to convey that he was already an equal opponent. By granting

[198] Cf. Watt, *Muḥammad*, 48.

[199] Ṭabarī, *Ta'rīkh*, 1576, 1582; Yaᶜqūbī *Ta'rīkh*, 2:56; Ibn Hishām, *Sīra*, 2:336; Suhaylī, *Rawḍ*, 7:104; Ibn Kathīr, *Sīra*, 3:374; Bayhaqī, *Dalā'il*, 4:230–232, where the title is rendered "the king of Yathrib."

[200] See also Hamidullah, *Battlefields*, 81, where he argues, "The Meccans may or may not have known that in this way they were deserting the Jews of Khaibar, and consequently they were also losing Jewish help against the Muslims."

[201] See Ibn Hishām, *Sīra*, 2:311–312, which states that Khuzāᶜa joined Muhammad, as they used to spy for him, revealing to him all of what was happening in Mecca among the Quraysh.

[202] Watt observes, "Instead of vigorously prosecuting the struggle with Mecca, [Muhammad] was angling for the conversion of Quraysh to Islam." Watt, *Muḥammad*, 49.

the Meccans that which they demanded, he demonstrated that he was willing to compromise, politically and religiously. Muhammad's goals were far higher and aiming beyond the present moment. Arguably, Muhammad's reported adoption of violence in his *maghāzī* does not make him a precedent for generations seeking mutual coexistence and peacebuilding but offers an image for how political leaders operate and calculate their gains and losses. As an astute warrior, he knew that the time would soon come for his total and complete victory over the Meccans. It was not long before he found the opportunity to declare that Mecca had broken the treaty and thus must be fought. This led to the greatest victory of Muhammad over the Meccans, only two years later, in the conquest of Mecca.

The Conquest of Mecca (8/630)

Muslim traditions represent the conquest of Mecca (8/630) as *fatḥ*.[203] The Arabic term *fatḥ* literally means "opening" or "clearing up."[204] It does not connote "invading," "assailing," or "assaulting" other territories.[205] It can also mean "judgment."[206] The term appears in the Qur'ān several times (e.g., Q 4:141; 48:1; 57:10) and is explicitly linked to victory in battles (Q 61:13; 110:1). It denotes a unique *religious* description of a military expedition.[207]

203 Wāqidī, *Maghāzī*, 780ff.; Ibn Hishām, *Sīra*, 2:389ff.; Balādhurī, *Futūḥ*, 35ff.; Ṭabarī, *Ta'rīkh*, 1619ff.; Bayhaqī, *Dalā'il*, 5:5ff.; Suhaylī, *al-Rawḍ*, 7:191ff.; Kalāʿī, *Iktifā'*, 1:473.

204 See Rāzī, *Mukhtār*, 233; Fīrūzābādī, *Qāmūs*, 232.

205 For the ideological use of the term *fatḥ*, see Ibrahim, *Stated*, xiii, 14, 17–18; also Donner, "Arabic *Fatḥ*," 1–14, where he examines the rendering of the term as "conquest" and argues that it is more complex than this "rigid" translation.

206 See Rāzī, *Mukhtār*, 233, where he takes *iftaḥ* (open) as meaning *uḥkum* (judge). See also Fīrūzābādī, *Qāmūs*, 232, where he understands *fatḥ* as referring to *naṣr* (victory) and *iftitāḥ* (opening) non-Muslim lands in military activity. See also Ṭabarī, *Jāmiʿ*, 10:405–406, where he explains that the *fatḥ* of Mecca was *qaḍā'* (judgment) in order to distinguish *al-īmān* (faith and belief) from *al-kufr* (unbelief and infidelity). Cf. Baer, *Honored*, 13.

207 See Muqātil, *Tafsīr*, 2:380 (the *fatḥ* of Mecca was Allah's promise to Muhammad), 4:97 (it was to humiliate the polytheists), 4:905 (*Sūrat al-fatḥ*, Q 48, was revealed after the conquest of Mecca and al-Ṭā'if); Ṭabarī, *Jāmiʿ*, 10:405–406 (the *fatḥ* was *qaḍā'*, i.e., judgment), 16:456–459 (the *fatḥ* was Allah's promise), 22:201 (the raid of the Ḥudaybiyya and the conquest of Mecca were both *fatḥ*, and even the *bayʿat al-Riḍwān* was *fatḥ*), 22:217 (the raid to Khaybar was also *fatḥ*), 23:175 (Ḥudaybiyya and Mecca were both *fatḥ*), 24:667–668 (the major *fatḥ* only refers to the conquest of Mecca); al-Zamakhsharī, *Kashshāf*, 2:531 (Allah's promise), 4:331 (*Sūrat al-fatḥ*, Q 48, refers to the conquest of Mecca), 4:341 (Muhammad saw the *fatḥ* of Mecca in a dream, and the vision of a prophet is a divine revelation), 4:474 (the *fatḥ* of Mecca was for *ʿizz al-islām*, i.e., Islam's supremacy); Rāzī, *Mafātiḥ*, 19:43 (the *fatḥ* was Allah's promise), 28:65 (several meanings for the term *fatḥ* in Q 48), 28:66 (the *fatḥ* of Mecca was an act of cleansing the house of Allah from idols), 29:452 (the *fatḥ* refers mainly to the conquest of Mecca, and nothing else can compare to it); Qurṭubī, *Jāmiʿ*, 16:271, 278 (the raid to Khaybar was also a *fatḥ*, like that of Mecca), 16:279 (the *fatḥ* was Allah's promise to Muhammad that foretold of the conquering of Mecca); Bayḍāwī, *Anwār*, 5:186 (the *fatḥ* of Mecca was for *ʿizz al-islām*,

As a term, it is ideological, coined and designed in relation to the *maghāzī* in order to convey a Muslim view of the military activities as actions in Allah's path and for the cause of Islam. The term always connotes victory and hegemony.[208] For Muslim storytellers, the conquest of Mecca was not an invasion but an "opening" of Mecca to the light of Islam, as the Muslims' military activity aimed at "clearing up" the way for Muhammad and his message to prevail in Mecca against Meccan hostility and opposition. The conquest—as traditionists saw it—was a divine "judgment" between good and evil, declaring Islam victorious in the land. Early Muslims have cherished the term, as evidenced in how *fatḥ* (pl. *futūḥ*) was later adopted by Muslim historians to represent the Muslim conquests led by Muhammad's successors against the Byzantine and Persian Empires. Still, the conquest of Mecca is unmatched in Muslim historiography. Muslim historians go even further in marveling at and cherishing the event and describe it as *fatḥ al-futūḥ*, meaning the conquest of all conquests, or the greatest of all victories.[209]

This conquest reportedly occurred in 8/630—only two years after the Ḥudaybiyya (6/628) and two years before Muhammad's death (11/632).[210] The traditions of the conquest appear to represent a composition, shaped by medieval Muslim narrators, with a discernible set of religious meanings. While many describe it as a conquest, it appears in classical traditions "as a negotiated surrender, rather than a victory achieved after battle."[211] Just

i.e., Islam's supremacy); Riḍā, *Manār*, 2:22 (*Sūrat al-fatḥ*, Q 48, was revealed to describe the conquest of Mecca), 2:177 (the first *ḥajj* for the Muslims was one year after the *fatḥ* of Mecca and was led by Abū Bakr, not Muhammad), 4:8 (Mecca was conquered by the sword), 6:357 (the *fatḥ* of Mecca made Islam prevalent as it was Allah's promise), 10:176 (the goal of the *fatḥ* of Mecca was *hadm dawlat al-shirk*, i.e., the destruction of the state [or land] of polytheism). For *bayᶜat al-Riḍwān* as *fatḥ*, see Kalāᶜī, *Iktifā'*, 1:473.

208 See also Watt, *Muḥammad*, 66–67.

209 It may also be rendered the victory of victories. For the term *fatḥ al-futūḥ* as a reference to the conquest of Mecca, see Rāzī, *Mafātiḥ*, 32:337; Nīsābūrī, *Gharā'ib*, 6:585; Ḥaraḍī, *Bahjat*, 1:397; Abū Shuhba, *Sīra*, 2:12, 435; Qimanī, *Ḥurūb*, 2:329ff. We should note, however, that Muslim traditions use the same term with other conquests, including the conquest of Jalūlā' (A.H. 17) and the conquest of Nihāwand (A.H. 21). For the term's use with Jalūlā', see Khalīfa, *Ta'rīkh*, 1:137; Balādhurī, *Futūḥ*, 264; Kalāᶜī, *Iktifā'*, 2:494; Dhahabī, *Ta'rīkh*, 3:161; Ibn ᶜAbd al-Barr, *Istīᶜāb*, 4:1546; Ibn al-Athīr, *Usd*, 5:353; Ṣafadī, *Wāfī*, 27:129. For the term's use with Nihāwand, see Balādhurī, *Futūḥ*, 302; Ṭabarī, *Ta'rīkh*, 2629; Kalāᶜī, *Iktifā'*, 2:563; Maqdisī, *Bad'*, 5:180; Ibn al-Athīr, *Kāmil*, 2:399; Ibn Kathīr, *Bidāya*, 7:120; Ibn Ḥajar, *Iṣāba*, 4:383.

210 The conquest was in January 630. In this year, al-Ṭabarī reports four *maghāzī* occurred prior to the conquest of Mecca: the incursions against Banū al-Mulawwiḥ and Dhāt al-Salāsil, followed by the one of al-Khabaṭ (tree leaves), and finally the raid to Mu'ta. In these expeditions, Muhammad relied on various Muslim commanders to lead. See Ṭabarī, *History*, 8:139–159. We discuss Mu'ta in chapter 7.

211 Ibrahim, *Stated*, 96. Watt, *Muḥammad*, 65ff.; see also Djait, *Masīrat*, 173 and 176, where he rightly observes that there was only a little fight in the conquest of Mecca.

as the Ḥudaybiyya is considered a *ghazwa* (raid) even though it did not involve fighting, *fatḥ al-futūḥ* is described as a glorious Muslim triumph over the Meccans even though Muhammad did not need to fight and only a little bloodshed occurred.[212] The reason for the lack of fighting was simple: the Meccans surrendered and gave in completely after negotiating with Muhammad. This surrender—as a literary detail—was not tranquil and easy. It is worth studying, as it explains not only the growing power of Muhammad and his dominion over large parts of Arabia but also what conversion to Islam actually meant on the day of the conquest. More importantly, the study of the Meccan surrender sheds light on how Muslim historians used their historical narratives to advance their sectarian and political views.

The period between the treaty of the Ḥudaybiyya (6/628) and the conquest of Mecca (8/630) was significant in advancing Muhammad's power.[213] The narrators paint a picture that the treaty offered him and his Medinan community a great opportunity to focus on enemies beyond the Meccan Quraysh.[214] Within two years after the treaty, Muhammad was able to eliminate any significant threat from the nomadic tribes and the Jews neighboring Medina.[215] Concerning the Arab nomads, he was able to persuade a large number of them to join his expanding dominion in the regions of Western Arabia, the Hijaz.[216] Their joining of his camp—an act of surrender—is

212 For Muslim secondary studies on the conquest, see Ṣallābī, *Sīra*, 748ff.; ᶜUmarī, *Sīra*, 473ff.; Djait, *Masīrat*, 167–182; Ṣaᶜīdī, *Tārīkh*, 120–123; Ṣaᶜīdī, *Dirāsāt*, 111–116. Still, some Muslim sources claim that Mecca was conquered *ᶜanwa* (by assault), while others claim that it was conquered *ṣulḥan* (peacefully). See Ibn ᶜAbd al-Barr, *Durar*, 1:217–218, where he provides contradicting claims yet states that most scholars argue that Mecca was conquered *ᶜanwa* (by assault). See also Masᶜūdī, *Tanbīh*, 1:231–232; Suhaylī, *Rawḍ*, 7:225; and Ḥalabī, *Insān*, 3:117, where both views are given. For reports that Mecca was conquered *ᶜanwa*, see Ṭabarī, *History*, 8:182; Kharkūshī, *Sharaf*, 3:369; Ibn Kathīr, *Sīra*, 3:547, 3:577. See the important work of Shāfiᶜī, *Umm*, 7:382, where he insists that Mecca was conquered peacefully. For a Muslim secondary study on these conflicting views, see Abū Shuhba, *Sīra*, 2:459–462. For an important study on the difference between "by assault" and "peacefully" in relation to the Muslim conquests of Egypt and Iraq, see Noth, "The '*Ṣulḥ*'–'*ᶜAnwa*,'" in *Expansion*, ed. Donner, 177–187. For an interesting early report, see Khaṭīb, *Ta'rīkh*, 12:233, where he states that Muhammad confirmed that Mecca was conquered *ᶜanwa*, and when people questioned his statement later, Muhammad declared that he made that claim up to refute his adversary's opinions. We should note that al-Shāfiᶜī's interpretations influenced the adoption of the *ṣulḥ* argument in following generations. On al-Shāfiᶜī and his contribution to Muslim jurisprudence, see van Ess, *Theology*, 1:44, 2:89, 2:795, 2:816, 3:192–193; Abū Zayd, *Falsafat*, 12ff. For primary sources, see Ibn al-Nadīm, *Fihrist*, 209; Khaṭīb, *Sharaf aṣḥāb*, 1:46; Bayhaqī, *Manāqib*, 1:399–401. On his life, see Ali, *Imam Shafiᶜi*. On his work, methods, and influence, see Abū Khalīl, *Hārūn*, 194ff.; Wurayyimī, *Fī al-I'tilāf*, 117ff., 146, 191ff.; Chaumont, "al-Shāfiᶜī," *EI*², 9:181–185; el-Shamsy, *Canonization*, 147ff., especially 157ff.; Lowry, *Early*, 1–22; Lowry, "al-Shāfiᶜī," in *Islamic*, ed., Arabi et al., 43ff.; Robinson, "Ibn al-Azraq," 16.

213 For primary sources on this period, see Wāqidī, *Life*, 311–384; Ṭabarī, *History*, 8:71–159.

214 Ibrahim, *Stated*, 85–100.

215 On controlling the Jews and the Arab nomads, see the valuable observations of Djait, *Masīrat*, 167; also Watt, *Muḥammad*, 65.

216 Watt, *Muḥammad*, 65.

described in Muslim traditions as their embrace of Islam.[217] This literary representation is important: just as a military raid is described as *fatḥ* (opening), the surrender to Muhammad's political rule is explicitly advanced as religious conversion. The texts reflect the religious opinion and thought of later generations—not the time they describe. As for the Jews, Muhammad successfully eliminated any significant presence of them in Medina before the treaty of the Ḥudaybiyya. After it, he continued with the elimination of two major Jewish settlements near Medina, Khaybar and Fadak.[218] This way, he was able to establish dominion and control over the majority of Western Arabia. In fact, we are told that he attempted to attack the Christian Byzantine Empire and its subordinate Arab Christian neighboring villages in the Battle of Mu'ta, which appears to have been more of a failed skirmish with a great Muslim loss.[219] With all of these military campaigns, we are invited to believe, Muhammad consolidated power and accomplished great momentum as a commander. However, the logic goes, no success could be considered and no victory could be celebrated if Mecca remained unconquered.[220]

Mecca meant a great deal to Muhammad. It was his homeland, from which, according to traditions, he was unjustly forced to depart eight years earlier. When he left Mecca, he fled in secret.[221] He was vulnerable and without support, but now he was significantly different in terms of power and

[217] For accepting Islam as an act of surrender, see Sharīf, *Makka*, 533; Ibrahim, *Stated*, 154, 156; ᶜAqqād, *Mawsūᶜat*, 857; Ibrahim, *Conversion*, 80–89. For the meaning of *aslam* (converted to Islam) in this context, see Rāzī, *Mukhtār*, 153, where *aslam* is taken to mean *istaslam* (surrendered and submitted); see Ibn Manẓūr, *Lisān*, 12:293, where *aslam* is understood as connoting *istaslam wa inqād* (surrendered and yielded), *islām wa istislām* as referring to *inqiyād* (surrender and yielding), and *islām* as meaning *khuḍūᶜ wa iltizām* (subordination and commitment). See also Fīrūzābādī, *Qāmūs*, 1122, where *aslam* is taken to mean *inqād wa ṣār musliman* (yielded and became Muslim). See also ᶜAbd al-Karīm, *Quraysh*, 294.

[218] These are discussed in the next chapter. See Wāqidī, *Life*, 311ff. (Khaybar) and 347ff. (Fadak).

[219] We discuss Mu'ta in chapter 7. For the account of the raid, see Wāqidī, *Life*, 372ff.; also Ṭabarī, *History*, 8:152ff. Djait argues that Mu'ta was a certain defeat for the Muslims, although he doubts greatly the traditions about it. Djait, *Masīrat*, 170. See also the Muslim views of Hamidullah, *Battlefields*, 100, who argues, "There had been actual fighting at Mu'tah between the Muslim army and the Byzantine army, with great loss to the Muslims." For traditional Muslim interpretations arguing that the battle was actually a victory for the Muslims, see ᶜUmarī, *Sīra*, 467–470, where he considers the Muslim retreat *fatḥan ᶜaẓīman* (a great victory). Like ᶜUmarī's views, see Ṣallābī, *Sīra*, 732ff., especially 737, where he claims that the one hundred thousand Byzantines became discouraged and realized that the three thousand Muslims would never be beaten. See also Abū Māyla, *Ghazwat*, 342–353, especially 345, where he completely denies that the Muslims were defeated by the Byzantines.

[220] See the comments about the importance of Mecca to Muhammad in Djait, *Masīrat*, 171.

[221] Ibn Hishām, *Sīra*, 1:485; Ibn Ḥibbān, *Sīra*, 1:129; Kharkūshī, *Sharaf*, 2:341; ᶜAbd al-Jabbār, *Tathbīt*, 2:320, 2:365–366; Bayhaqī, *Dalā'il*, 2:471; Ibn ᶜAbd al-Barr, *Durar*, 1:80–81; Suhaylī, *Rawḍ*, 4:134.

preparation. He was the glowing star of Arabia.[222] The narratives of the conquest convey religious meaning in a form of literary composition: subduing all tribes and controlling all lands could not be compared to humiliating the pagan Quraysh. While this is the overall religious sentiment in the sources, a critical reading of the accounts may suggest that Muhammad and his companions were patiently waiting for the opportune time to launch the attack, especially as they almost entered the sacred city two years earlier, when the Quraysh forbade them, leading to the treaty of the Ḥudaybiyya.[223] The narrators successfully develop a tale with stimulating turns—beginning with precursors, moving to conflicts, and leading to the great victory. We are invited to believe that now the Muslims were much more capable militarily to conquer the Quraysh. However, they did not want to break the treaty needlessly. They only needed a justification for the conquest—an incident to break the peace agreement with the Quraysh and thus trigger the fight. For Muslims, if the Meccans would not initiate a fight, then the second-best option had to be in the hands of the allies who joined the Ḥudaybiyya treaty.[224] If an ally of Mecca attacked an ally of Muhammad, then the treaty would be considered violated.

The opportunity came on a silver platter—the story alleges—when news erupted that one of Mecca's allies attacked one of Muhammad's allies. We are told, in *most* traditions, that Banū Bakr (Quraysh's ally) attacked Banū Khuzāᶜa (Muhammad's ally), and the Quraysh *secretly* supported Banū Bakr.[225] Banū Bakr and Banū Khuzāᶜa had been in a tribal conflict for a long time, even before the emergence of Islam (with many incidents of mutual attacks between the two tribes).[226] However, the treaty of the Ḥudaybiyya

[222] Ṭabarī, *Ta'rīkh*, 1576, 1582; Yaᶜqūbī, *Ta'rīkh*, 2:56; Ibn Hishām, *Sīra*, 2:336; Suhaylī, *Rawḍ*, 7:104; Ibn Kathīr, *Sīra*, 3:374; Bayhaqī, *Dalā'il*, 4:230–232.

[223] In describing the situation from a nonreligious lens, Muslim historian Djait argues that after the Ḥudaybiyya, Muhammad needed to wait patiently and anticipate a political—instead of psychological—victory, as he needed to seek "power and influence" instead of a "religious miracle." Djait, *Masīrat*, 168–169. In another work, Djait studies Ibn Hishām's *Sīra* and argues that as early as the *hijra*, Muhammad was ready to declare outright war against Mecca—he was just waiting for the optimal timing. Djait, *al-Fitna*, 27.

[224] See Ibrahim, *Stated*, 96, where I argue, "It is unlikely that the Meccans wished to break the treaty, as they must have been aware of Muhammad's growing power."

[225] Wāqidī, *Maghāzī*, 780ff.; Wāqidī, *Life*, 384ff.; Ibn Hishām, *Sīra*, 2:322 (precursors), 2:389–390 (allies and breach of the treaty); Balādhurī, *Futūḥ*, 35ff.; Balādhurī, *Origins*, 60ff. For Djait, this reported violation of the treaty was *al-dharīᶜa al-muthlā* (the ideal excuse, or justification) for Muhammad to launch the conquest of Mecca. Djait, *Masīrat*, 174.

[226] For the reports that the conflict began in pre-Islamic times, see Wāqidī, *Maghāzī*, 781; Ibn Hishām, *Sīra*, 2:389; Ibn Ḥibbān, *Sīra*, 1:320–321; Ibn ᶜAbd al-Barr, *Durar*, 1:211; Suhaylī, *Rawḍ*, 7:191–192; Kalāᶜī, *Iktifā'*, 1:499; Ibn Kathīr, *Sīra*, 3:528–529; Ḥalabī, *Insān*, 3:102; Dhahabī, *Ta'rīkh*, 2:521–522; Ibn Kathīr, *Bidāya*, 4:318. For a secondary study on the conflict, see Djait, *Masīrat*, 173–174.

obviously created an additional dimension: any new attack between the two tribes would be a violation of the Ḥudaybiyya agreement since they both joined the treaty on opposing sides. Practically, whether the Quraysh actually supported Banū Bakr against Banū Khuzāʿa is unimportant, as the alleged attack itself was sufficient for the Muslims to consider the treaty violated. It was important for the narrators, it appears, in their designing the tale, to depict Muhammad as the defender of an ally, not as the breaker of a treaty. This depiction sets forth moral and ideological meanings. Still, similar to that which we encountered in other raids, conflicting accounts cast doubt on the seemingly clear Muslim portrayal. The matter of "who" first violated the treaty does not appear as a clear-cut report in historical accounts. Some Muslim accounts reveal an opposite scenario, highlighting that it was actually Muhammad's ally (Khuzāʿa)—not the Quraysh's ally—who started the attack. The renowned classical Muslim historian al-Balādhurī (d. ca. 279/892) reports that "One of the clan of Khuzāʿah [Muhammad's ally] hearing one of the clan of Kinānah [Quraysh's ally] sing a poem satirizing the Prophet, attacked him and crushed his head."[227] According to this account, a man from Khuzāʿa started the attack by killing another man from the Quraysh's allies, not the other way around—unless one considers the singing of a satirizing poem to equate to a tribal attack or a breach of a treaty. But al-Balādhurī's report is not an exception. Seemingly supporting the report, al-Ṭabarī (d. 310/923) provides a revealing account, indicating that Muhammad's allies might have been responsible for the initial attack: "a group of Banū Kaʿb [Muhammad's allies] fought with a group of Banū Bakr [Quraysh's allies])."[228] This report specifies Banū Kaʿb (not Banū Bakr) as the first in the fight, or at least indicates that the fight was mutually initiated. As literary representations, these conflicting historiographical reports should no longer surprise us. We have repeatedly encountered them in the tradition, and they appear to be literary devices the narrators deployed to elevate memories and suppress others at different times. It is tempting here to view evidence of a layering of historical accounts. In essence, we have two conflicting memories, existing simultaneously, within the same tradition of the conquest of Mecca: one making Muhammad a victim and the other making him a perpetrator. The former fits the orthodoxy established by medieval

[227] See Balādhurī, *Futūḥ*, 35; Balādhurī, *Origins*, 60.

[228] The Arabic account reads, *fa-iqtatalat ṭā'ifa min Banī Kaʿb wa ṭā'ifa min Banī Bakr*. Ṭabarī, *Ta'rīkh*, 1634; Ṭabarī, *History*, 8:175.

historians through their ample accounts, while the latter sits poorly with the overall narrative. One way to view the confused tradition is that most likely the story about Muhammad's ally violating the treaty had existed and circulated among the faithful for some time; however, this created a dilemma for medieval orthodoxy. The story needed to be adjusted by a new memory, established through the creation of a conflicting report suggesting the opposite. The circulating of the new memory, making it orthodoxy, would eventually send the other to oblivion. In all cases, knowing who started the tribal conflict is not essential in this regard, as the Muslims were reportedly eager to launch an attack to declare victory over the Quraysh once and for all.

Al-Ṭabarī writes that this reported violation of the treaty *ahāj* (stimulated or triggered) the conquest of Mecca.[229] We are told that a group of men from Banū Khuzāᶜa traveled from Mecca to Medina to meet Muhammad, their closest and strongest ally. They appealed to him for revenge because "Quraysh had backed the Banū Bakr against them."[230] Muhammad was reportedly ready to aid them, as he knew that the Quraysh could not be trusted. This literary detail strengthens the scheme of the story by portraying Muhammad as a trusted and committed ally. He prepared ten thousand soldiers from among his devoted Muslims and some Arab allies and planned to march to Mecca.[231] The Quraysh were terrified by news of the breach of the treaty and the imminent attack, as they *rahabū alladhī ṣanaᶜū* (had become fearful of what they had done).[232] Through these traditions, the narrators add layers of literary support to place the blame on the Meccans, thus legitimizing the conquest as an act of justice against treaty breakers. Consequently, the Meccans chose one of their most prestigious notables, Abū Sufyān, who was known as *sayyid* (the master of) Quraysh, and sent him to win Muhammad over.[233]

[229] For historical context, see Ṭabarī, *Taʾrīkh*, 1618–1621, and especially 1621 for the quote. See also Ibn Hishām, *Sīra*, 2:322ff.; Ibn Hishām, *Life*, 542; Dhahabī, *Taʾrīkh*, 2:521ff. We should note that the violation of the treaty does not seem to be the only reason for launching the conquest; as al-Ṭabarī explains, "This [violation] was one of the things that prompted the conquest of Mecca." Ṭabarī, *History*, 8:162.

[230] Ṭabarī, *Taʾrīkh*, 1622; Ṭabarī, *History*, 8:163.

[231] Ibn Hishām, *Sīra*, 2:322, 400, 421; Ṭabarī, *Taʾrīkh*, 1628, 1659; Ṭabarī, *History*, 8:168, 9:8; Wāqidī, *Maghāzī*, 801. Many scholars doubt these exaggerated numbers. See, for instance, Djait, *Masīrat*, 175. Djait argues that the Arabs who joined Muhammad were not necessarily Muslims but those who adopted a "superficial" conversion (*islāman saṭḥiyyan*) (177). The number of ten thousand soldiers is fanciful and a clear exaggeration. See Munt, *Holy*, 49–50; Shoemaker, *Creating*, 111–112.

[232] Ṭabarī, *Taʾrīkh*, 1622.

[233] Ibn Hishām, *Life*, 543; Ibn Hishām, *Sīra*, 2:395–396; Ṭabarī, *Taʾrīkh*, 3:1622. For Abū Sufyān's begging Muhammad, see the accounts in Bayhaqī, *Dalāʾil*, 5:7–10, where the author details that the Meccan leader asked Muhammad several times to extend the agreement. For primary sources on Abū Sufyān, see Khalīfa, *Taʾrīkh*, 1:166; Khalīfa, *Ṭabaqāt*, 39; Ibn Qutayba, *Maᶜārif*, 73–74, 136 (Muhammad married his daughter), 344–345; Fasawī, *Maᶜrifa*, 3:167; Dhahabī, *Taʾrīkh*, 3:368ff.;

The literary choice of Abū Sufyān is crucial, as, at this point in the tale, the narrators—serving the ᶜAbbāsids and their orthodoxy narrative—bring a major Umayyad figure to the scene and depict him unfavorably, specifically as a polytheist unbeliever. This portrayal of Abū Sufyān is contrasted—as we shall see—with Muhammad and his uncle al-ᶜAbbās, who are both depicted positively in support of ᶜAbbāsid claims for power. The Quraysh reportedly assigned specific goals for Abū Sufyān's visit to Muhammad: Abū Sufyān "had been sent by Quraysh to strengthen the agreement with the apostle and to ask for an extension, for they were afraid of the consequences of what they had done to Muḥammad."[234] Muhammad was capable of reading the political scene, especially after the Banū Khuzāᶜa sought his help. He even *prophesied*, we are told, that Mecca would send Abū Sufyān and revealed to his companions, "I think you will see Abū Sufyan come to strengthen the pact and extend the term."[235] Here the narrators, as religious instructors, seize the chance to prove Muhammad's prophethood by advancing a literary claim of a fulfilled prophecy. And, lest the reader imagine that the Quraysh sought peace and reconciliation, the same literary device insists the Quraysh were cowards and terrified of Muhammad, not seekers of peace.

Abū Sufyān's journey from Mecca to Medina was about a ten-day travel.[236] In his way, about two days after leaving Mecca, he met some of the men of Khuzāᶜa who were just with Muhammad in order to seek his aid in exacting their revenge upon the Quraysh.[237] Abū Sufyān guessed that they had met and spoken with Muhammad, which led him to realize that his task of winning Muhammad over had become even harder.[238] Once Abū Sufyān arrived in Medina, he sought to meet with some Muslim companions before he actually met with Muhammad. He reportedly wanted these companions to intercede for him with Muhammad. Muslim traditions depict a severely humiliating experience for Abū Sufyān in each of these meetings with

Dhahabī, *Siyar*, 2:105ff.; Ibn Abī Ḥātim, *Jarḥ*, 4:426; Ibn ᶜAbd al-Barr, *Istīᶜāb*, 2:714; Ibn ᶜAsākir, *Ta'rīkh*, 23:421ff.; Ibn al-Athīr, *Usd*, 3:9; Ibn Ḥajar, *Iṣāba*, 3:332. For secondary studies on Abū Sufyān, see Ibrahim, *Conversion*, 71ff.; ᶜAlī, *Mufaṣṣal*, 7:110ff.; Gabriel, *Muhammad*, 169–170; Watt, "Abū Sufyān," *EI*², 1:151.

234 Ibn Hishām, *Life*, 543; Ibn Hishām, *Sīra*, 2:395–396; Bayhaqī, *Dalā'il*, 5:7–8; Ibn ᶜAbd al-Barr, *Durar*, 1:212; Suhaylī, *Rawḍ*, 7:200; Kalāᶜī, *Iktifā'*, 1:500; Ibn Kathīr, *Sīra*, 3:529; Ḥalabī, *Insān*, 3:104.

235 Ṭabarī, *Ta'rīkh*, 1622; Ṭabarī, *History*, 8:163.

236 A stage is a one-day desert journey. See Yaᶜqūbī, *Buldān*, 152, where he states that the distance between Mecca and Medina is ten stages. The entire distance equals to 225 miles in the desert.

237 They reportedly met in ᶜUsfān, which is two day's travel from Mecca. See Yaᶜqūbī, *Buldān*, 2:63.

238 Ṭabarī, *Ta'rīkh*, 1623; Ṭabarī, *History*, 8:164.

Muhammad's companions.[239] This humiliating depiction of the Umayyad notable, we should note, is better viewed as deliberate ᶜAbbāsid propaganda against the Umayyads.[240] The vast majority of our Muslim sources reached us from ᶜAbbāsid-era historians, who attempted to depict the Umayyads—of whom Abū Sufyān was a major leader—negatively. In a previous publication, I analyzed pre-ᶜAbbāsid accounts—attributed to al-Zuhrī and Mūsā ibn ᶜUqba—on Abū Sufyān's encounters with Muhammad and other people of Banū Hāshim and demonstrated that Abū Sufyān's journey is depicted differently, precisely as a journey of soul searching to accept Islam instead of shame and degradation.[241]

The ᶜAbbāsid version of Abū Sufyān's encounters with Muslims begins with a meeting with his daughter Umm Ḥabība, who was, at the time, a convert to Islam and married to Muhammad.[242] Umm Ḥabība reportedly despised her own father and said to him, "You are an unclean polytheist."[243] She did not want to support Abū Sufyān with her husband. Here the narrators communicate a religious philosophy: Islam surpasses familial ties and tribal bonds. Abū Sufyān left her and went to speak with Muhammad, but Muhammad "gave him no reply."[244] The image of Muhammad refusing to speak with Abū Sufyān reflects how the Umayyad family displeased the most important human figure of Islam. In humiliation, Abū Sufyān sought to talk with two major companions of Muhammad, Abū Bakr and ᶜUmar. Here the literary tale enforces a contrast between the first two highly praised Rāshidūn caliphs and the notable Umayyad aristocrat. Both harshly refused Abū Sufyān's plea for help. Abū Bakr said, "I will not [speak to Muhammad for you]," while ᶜUmar declared, "I intercede for you with the Messenger of God! By God, if I found only ant grubs [to eat], I would fight you!"[245] This

[239] For these encounters, see Wāqidī, *Maghāzī*, 792ff.

[240] See Ibrahim, *Conversion*, 70–75, where the conversion of Abū Sufyān is analyzed against the backdrop of anti-Umayyad propaganda; see also 20–25, 223–227; Sellheim, "Prophet," 33–91; Ḍayf, *ᶜAṣr*, 9–33; Mu'nis, *Tanqiyat*, 53ff. See Petersen, *ᶜAlī*, 17, 19, 20, and 50, where he concludes, "The formation of the historical tradition consists above all in reflections of the political and religious conflicts of its own age" (50). See also Judd, *Religious*, 143ff., where he argues that al-Ṭabarī's *Ta'rīkh* distorted the image of the Umayyads and that many historians followed his footsteps in advancing anti-Umayyad rhetoric.

[241] Ibrahim, *Conversion*, 70–75.

[242] For her marriage to Muhammad, see Ṭabarī, *History*, 109–110. Al-Wāqidī provides a contradicting report and states that Abū Sufyān met Muhammad first, then Umm Ḥabība. Wāqidī, *Maghāzī*, 792. On Umm Ḥabība as a companion of Muhammad, see Ibn Manda, *Maᶜrifat*, 1:951–953; Ibn Abī Khaythama, *Ta'rīkh (Part 3)*, 2:18; also Abū Nuᶜaym, *Maᶜrifat*, 6:3479.

[243] Ṭabarī, *Ta'rīkh*, 1623; Ṭabarī, *History*, 8:164. See Wāqidī, *Life*, 390–391, where it states that she speaks to her father, "you are an unclean man and a polytheist."

[244] Ṭabarī, *Ta'rīkh*, 1623; Ṭabarī, *History*, 8:164.

[245] Ṭabarī, *Ta'rīkh*, 1623; Ṭabarī, *History*, 8:164.

harsh response reflects the religious sympathies and political preferences that directed the literary choices of the ᶜAbbāsid-era historians. It was crucial for the narrators who formed the historical orthodoxy to show Abū Bakr and ᶜUmar in the most positive way, and here Abū Sufyān is despised and rejected by the two highly respected pious caliphs. This detail serves ᶜAbbāsid orthodoxy, and specifically a Sunnī disposition.[246] Abū Sufyān then approached Muhammad's daughter Fāṭima and her husband, ᶜAlī: "Intercede for us with the Messenger of God," Abū Sufyān pled. ᶜAlī responded, "Woe to you, Abū Sufyān. By God, the Messenger of God has determined on a matter about which we cannot speak to him."[247] This detail seems to appeal to the pro-ᶜAlids and Shīᶜites, implying they both should reject the Umayyads who did not accept Islam from the start. In desperation, Abū Sufyān "stood up in the mosque and said [to the Muslims], 'People, I hereby make peace among the people.' Then he mounted his camel and departed [back to Mecca]."[248]

Arguably, the narrators established reasons for rejecting the Umayyad Abū Sufyān and his plea to maintain and prolong the treaty—by using images of esteemed personages highly important to the ᶜAbbāsid and ᶜAlid claims—in order to develop the next phase of the story. Muhammad began his preparation to march to Mecca: "He proceeded on [toward Mecca] and encamped at Marr al-Ẓahrān with 10,000 Muslims."[249] Marr al-Ẓahrān, we are told, was about five miles from Mecca.[250] Muhammad made these plans in secrecy: These "reports had been kept hidden from Quraysh; no news was reaching them about the Messenger of God, and they did not know what he would do."[251] It was clear that a Muslim attack was imminent. The reports are pointedly exaggerated to elevate the power of Muhammad and the hegemony of Muslims. The storytellers establish that the Medinan camp under

[246] See Hibri, *Parable*, 77–78.

[247] Ṭabarī, *Ta'rīkh*, 1624; Ṭabarī, *History*, 8:164.

[248] Ṭabarī, *Ta'rīkh*, 1624; Ṭabarī, *History*, 8:165. See Wāqidī, *Maghāzī*, 795, where he writes that the Quraysh became skeptical of Abū Sufyān's delay, "accused him when he delayed with severe accusations," and declared, "we think he has converted and follows Muḥammad secretly and hides his Islam." Wāqidī, *Life*, 391. On the importance of ᶜAlī to the ᶜAlids and Shīᶜites, see the valuable (yet controversial) Arabic study of Wardī, *Wuᶜᶜāẓ*, 182ff.; also Khuḍarī, *Dawla al-umawiyya*, 364–406.

[249] Ṭabarī, *Ta'rīkh*, 1628; Ṭabarī, *History*, 8:168. Wāqidī, *Maghāzī*, 802.

[250] Yaᶜqūbī, *Buldān*, 4:319 (one day's travel from Mecca); Bakrī, *Masālik*, 403 (five miles from Mecca); Hamadānī, *Amākin*, 827 (very near to Mecca); Hamdānī, *Ṣifat*, 185; Samhūdī, *Wafā'*, 4:143. See also the secondary study Balādī, *Muᶜjam*, 288.

[251] Ṭabarī, *Ta'rīkh*, 1628; Ṭabarī, *History*, 8:168. See Wāqidī, *Life*, 401, where he reports, "Not a word of the Prophet's march to [Mecca] had reached the Quraysh." See also Wāqidī, *Maghāzī*, 802, 814. Here, Muhammad prayed to Allah, "Keep spies and news from Quraysh until we take them by surprise in their territory." Ṭabarī, *History*, 8:166.

Muhammad's leadership had grown significantly in power, while the Meccan Quraysh had lost its strength and prestige. In about eight years, Muhammad had successfully crippled their might and esteem.

At Marr al-Ẓahrān, Muhammad and his ten thousand soldiers were ready to march against Mecca, fully armored and prepared for an attack. To intimidate the Quraysh and their spies, we are told, Muhammad "commanded his companions to light fires, and they lit ten thousand fires," in a demonstration of strength and might.[252] Abū Sufyān traveled again to meet Muhammad in order to prevent a war, and upon seeing the fires, he reportedly exclaimed, "I have never seen fires like those I see today!"[253] Before meeting Muhammad, Abū Sufyān met with Muhammad's uncle, al-ᶜAbbās ibn ᶜAbd al-Muṭṭalib.[254] This is a significant literary detail that deserves close scrutiny, as it seeks to contrast the ᶜAbbāsids with the Umayyads by forging a discourse between two notables from the two families. The narrative elevates al-ᶜAbbās as the central character at this conjuncture. Since he serves as the progenitor of the ᶜAbbāsids, his image is of significant importance for the ᶜAbbāsid claims of power.[255] He appears as a leading supporter of Muhammad and a principal chastiser of Abū Sufyān. We are told that al-ᶜAbbās heard Abū Sufyān's exclamation about the fires lit by the Muslims and said, "Here is the Messenger of God behind me. He has come against you with a force you cannot resist—10,000 Muslims." Terrified and desperate, Abū Sufyān begged al-ᶜAbbās for advice, to which al-ᶜAbbās responded, "Mount the rump of this mule, and I will ask the Messenger of God to grant you a promise of safety; for, by God, if he gets hold of you, he will cut off your head."[256] The narrators paint a picture—for the purpose of advancing political legitimacy and religious superiority—in which al-ᶜAbbās surpasses Abū Sufyān in power, wisdom, prestige, and more importantly, Muhammad's favor. The picture establishes the ᶜAbbāsids as legitimate supporters and successors of Muhammad, in contrast to the Umayyads who delayed supporting Muhammad and accepting his religious status. As al-ᶜAbbās went with Abū Sufyān to meet Muhammad, ᶜUmar wanted to "cut off his head," but al-ᶜAbbās declared, in

[252] Wāqidī, *Life*, 401.

[253] Ṭabarī, *Ta'rīkh*, 1631; Ṭabarī, *History*, 8:171.

[254] The entire conversation between al-ᶜAbbās and Abū Sufyān is better viewed as anti-Umayyad propaganda, designed and documented under ᶜAbbāsid patronage. See the detailed study in Ibrahim, *Conversion*, 71ff.; Sellheim, "Prophet," 33–91.

[255] See the examination of al-ᶜAbbās's developing portrayals in Muslim historiography at Ibrahim, *Conversion*, 218–223. See Brown, *Muhammad*, 87, where he explains how the *Sīra* depicts the enemies of al-ᶜAbbās unfavorably and al-ᶜAbbās in a good light. Watt, "al-ᶜAbbās," *EI*², 1:9.

[256] Ṭabarī, *Ta'rīkh*, 1631; Ṭabarī, *History*, 8:172. See also Wāqidī, *Maghāzī*, 815.

front of Muhammad, "I have granted him protection."[257] Muhammad accepted, offered Abū Sufyān protection, and said, "Bring him to me tomorrow morning."[258] The narrative here advances al-ᶜAbbās as a powerful, just, and persuasive intercessor in front of Muhammad. The point of the fiction is arguably obvious: the progenitor of the ᶜAbbāsid family is not only a devout Muslim who is the closest to Muhammad, but also the protector of the Umayyad elite Abū Sufyān. The impressive image enforces ᶜAbbāsid legitimacy by painting the dynasty as the closest to Muhammad and as the pious protectors of Islam.

The following morning, Muslims brought the Meccan leader to Muhammad. The Muslims sought to offer Abū Sufyān the chance to convert to Islam, which required him to declare the *shahāda* (profession of faith), which includes two parts—the first is testifying that there is no god but Allah, and the second is affirming that Muhammad is Allah's messenger. Muhammad asked Abū Sufyān, "Hasn't the time come for you to know that there is no god but God?"[259] In a positive affirmation, Abū Sufyān responded, "I think that if there were another god along with God, he would have availed me somewhat." Abū Sufyān thus needed one more step to convert to Islam. Muhammad reportedly asked him, "Hasn't the time come for you to know that I am the Messenger of God?" With hesitation and uncertainty, Abū Sufyān responded, "As to that I still have some doubt."[260] Here is another literary detail, devised by ᶜAbbāsid-era narrators, which aims to portray Abū Sufyān and his entire Umayyad family as weak Muslims who doubted Muhammad until the end. In response to this uncertain statement, al-ᶜAbbās shouted, "Woe to you! Recite the testimony of truth before, by God, your head is cut off!" This detail makes al-ᶜAbbās the sole convincer of the Umayyad chief to accept Islam. The picture shows the ᶜAbbāsids as politically and religiously superior to the Umayyads.

Abū Sufyān appears to have realized the severity of the situation. He thus submitted, surrendered, and accepted Islam by openly reciting the *shahāda*.[261] This became the orthodox ᶜAbbāsid tale of Abū Sufyān's conversion. The

[257] Ṭabarī, *Taʾrīkh*, 1632; Ṭabarī, *History*, 8:172.

[258] Ṭabarī, *Taʾrīkh*, 1632; Ṭabarī, *History*, 8:173.

[259] Ṭabarī, *Taʾrīkh*, 1632; Ṭabarī, *History*, 8:173.

[260] Ibn Hishām, *Life*, 547–548; Ibn Hishām, *Sīra*, 2:403. Al-Ṭabarī renders it, "As for this matter, there is something of it in my mind." Ṭabarī, *History*, 8:173. See Wāqidī, *Maghāzī*, 815, 818, where he renders it, "O Muḥammad, indeed within me about this thing is a slight gap, so I will postpone it." Wāqidī, *Life*, 401, 403.

[261] Ṭabarī, *Taʾrīkh*, 1632; Ṭabarī, *History*, 8:173; Wāqidī, *Maghāzī*, 816. See the accounts of Wāqidī, *Maghāzī*, 812ff., and Ibn Hishām, *Sīra*, 2:403ff., where Abū Sufyān's conversion is portrayed as a result of the effort and guidance of al-ᶜAbbās. I argue that the ᶜAbbāsid-era historians elevate their

ᶜAbbāsid-era historians successfully created an inauthentic Umayyad Abū Sufyān to paint a picture despising rivals and advancing religio-political legitimacy. This is evident in the ᶜAbbāsid-era account labeling Abū Sufyān as *mushrik najis* (an unclean associater).[262] However, as I observed earlier, in pre-ᶜAbbāsid accounts, Abū Sufyān's conversion to Islam appears as "a genuine process of questioning and contemplating Muhammad's prophethood and his message."[263]

Abū Sufyān's conversion to Islam was a significant turning point in the course of events. The Muslim troops were ready to march against Mecca—only this time the Muslims knew that the Meccans had no chance whatsoever, because their leader openly declared his *islām* (submission). Before the troops marched against Mecca, we are told that al-ᶜAbbās spoke with Muhammad again for the sake of Abū Sufyān's dignity and honor: "Abū Sufyān is a man who loves glory. Grant him something that shall be [a cause of glory for him] among his clansmen." Muhammad accepted and promised, "Yes; whoever enters the house of Abū Sufyān shall be safe."[264] This meant that Muhammad granted safety and amnesty to anyone who sought security under Abū Sufyān. This literary report credits al-ᶜAbbās once more with rehabilitating the image of the Umayyad notable, thus amplifying the role, status, and prestige of the progenitor of the ᶜAbbāsids. In his detention by the Muslims, we are told, Abū Sufyān saw Muhammad's tribes and troops lining up, ready for war, and his heart sank.[265] He then saw Muhammad leading a huge squadron of Muslims "in iron [armor], with only their eyes visible."[266] Abū Sufyān asked al-ᶜAbbās about this squadron. "This is the Messenger of God amid the Emigrants and Anṣār," al-ᶜAbbās responded. Here, there is an

progenitor, al-ᶜAbbās, and represent Abū Sufyān—the major Umayyad figure—unfavorably, portraying him as a weak Muslim who merely accepted Islam to save his life. On these historiographical portrayals and their political and religious biases, see Ibrahim, *Conversion*, 218–228. See also Ibn Ḥibbān, *Sīra*, 1:329; Kalāᶜī, *Iktifāʾ*, 1:504; Ibn Kathīr, *Sīra*, 3:549; Ḥalabī, *Insān*, 3:114.

262 Ibn Ḥibbān, *Sīra*, 1:322; Ibn Hishām, *Sīra*, 2:396; Ibn Hishām and Ibn Isḥāq, *Life*, 547–548; Ṭabarī, *Taʾrīkh*, 1623; Ṭabarī, *History*, 8:164; Bayhaqī, *Dalāʾil*, 5:8; Ibn ᶜAbd al-Barr, *Durar*, 1:213; Suhaylī, *Rawḍ*, 7:200; Ibn Kathīr, *Sīra*, 3:530; Ḥalabī, *Insān*, 3:105; Dhahabī, *Taʾrīkh*, 2:524.

263 Ibrahim, *Conversion*, 72. See also Zuhrī, *Maghāzī*, 87ff. Mūsā ibn ᶜUqba, *Maghāzī*, 272. We should note that al-Zuhrī and Mūsā indicate that Abū Sufyān traveled more than once between Mecca and Medina to dialogue with Muhammad about Islam. See ᶜAbd al-Karīm, *Quraysh*, 382–383, where he argues that Abū Sufyān was mainly concerned with economic interests and benefits over any religious aspects.

264 Ṭabarī, *Taʾrīkh*, 1633; Ṭabarī, *History*, 8:173. Cf. Ibn Hishām, *Life*, 547–548; Ibn Hishām, *Sīra*, 2:403.

265 Wāqidī, *Maghāzī*, 815. Moreover, when the Muslims woke up early to perform the ritual prayer, "Abū Sufyān *faziᶜa* (was terrified) of their call to prayer." Wāqidī, *Life*, 401.

266 Ṭabarī, *Taʾrīkh*, 1633; Ṭabarī, *History*, 8:174. See Ibn Hishām, *Life*, 548.

important literary detail to emphasize: The pro-ᶜAlid, pro-ᶜAbbāsid historian al-Wāqidī portrays a uniquely tendentious picture.[267] As he paints Abū Sufyān as reluctant and cowardly, he elevates two esteemed characters at the same incident. He portrays ᶜAlī ibn Abī Ṭālib as a hero leading a majestic procession of Muslim soldiers, and al-ᶜAbbās as a chastiser and instructor who threatens and curses Abū Sufyān several times.[268] The elevation of ᶜAlī and al-ᶜAbbās above Abū Sufyān not only serves ᶜAbbāsid orthodoxy and advances anti-Umayyad rhetoric, but also reveals the Shīᶜite inclination of al-Wāqidī.[269] This is evident if we compare his accounts to the *Sīra* of Ibn Hishām, for instance, who is known for his anti-ᶜAlid sympathies and thus does not refer to a majestic procession led by ᶜAlī in the precursors of the conquest.[270] In portraying ᶜAlī during Abū Sufyān's conversion, anti-ᶜAlid Ibn Hishām paints ᶜAlī as an aggressive man who reprimanded and refused to help Abū Sufyān—and also disobeyed Muhammad.[271]

In apparent awe and undeniable defeat, Abū Sufyān told al-ᶜAbbās, "Your nephew's kingdom has become great!"[272] At this point, the Muslims released Abū Sufyān and instructed him, "Go join your people now, and

[267] On al-Wāqidī's sectarian and political inclinations, see Ibrahim, *Conversion*, 110–116. See Petersen, *ᶜAlī*, 18, where he writes that recording history "left a wide margin for tendentious presentation" (18). Ibn al-Nadīm, *Fihrist*, 98; Ṭūsī, *Fihrist*, 3; Khalīfa, *Ṭabaqāt*, 1:472, 641; Ibn Qutayba al-Dīnawarī, *Maᶜārif*, 518. See also Brockelmann, *Ta'rīkh*, 3:16; Brockelmann, *History*, 1:123; Petersen, *ᶜAlī*, 83ff., where al-Wāqidī is one of the major historians responsible for creating the ᶜAbbāsid "orthodox" tradition. In studying al-Wāqidī's accounts, Petersen concludes, "Wāqidī did not prepare [his] material thoroughly until after his arrival at Baghdad, and . . . he worked under the influence of the views of his Iraqian [*sic*] environment" (86). See also Ziriklī, *Aᶜlām*, 6:311–312.

[268] Wāqidī, *Maghāzī*, 814–823. See the comments on these portrayals of ᶜAlī and al-ᶜAbbās in Ibrahim, *Conversion*, 157–158, where I argue, "Al-Wāqidī contrasts the Umayyad Abū Sufyān with ᶜAlī and al-ᶜAbbās and utilizes the theme of insincere conversion to portray the Umayyads negatively by describing their major historical figure as an inauthentic Muslim who chiefly sought gain, honor, and pride" (158).

[269] On the bias against the Umayyads, see Mu'nis, *Tanqiyat*, 53ff.; Borrut, *Entre*, 6, 8–9. On the anti-Umayyad "pious opposition," see Watt, *Muḥammad*, 73–75, 348–353.

[270] On Ibn Hishām's sectarian sympathies and political inclination, see Ibrahim, *Conversion*, 121–128. Rudolf Sellheim argues that the *Sīra* is not only anti-Umayyad and pro-ᶜAbbāsid but precisely anti-ᶜAlid. See Sellheim, "Prophet." Berg, "ᶜAbbāsid," 17ff.; Lassner, *Middle*, 314 n. 5; Lassner, *Medieval*, 138; Rubin, "Prophets," 41–65. On the ᶜAbbāsid "competing claims" against the ᶜAlids, see Hibri, "Redemption," 241–265, especially the conclusion, 263–265; Rubin, "Prophets," 41–65. Robinson states, "The rise of the historiographic tradition, whether or not it was triggered by caliphal patronage, was a deeply political process." Robinson, *Historiography*, 40; Lassner, *Shaping*, 24–30.

[271] See Ibn Hishām, *Sīra*, 2:396 (ᶜAlī's aggressiveness) and 2:397 (ᶜAlī's disobedience). Compare with the Shīᶜite-sympathetic Wāqidī, *Maghāzī*, 2:814–823. See Lecker, "Wāqidī's Account," 15–32; Lecker, "Notes," 233–254.

[272] Ṭabarī, *Ta'rīkh*, 1633; Ṭabarī, *History*, 8:174; Wāqidī, *Maghāzī*, 822. Al-ᶜAbbās responded to Abū Sufyān, "it was due to the prophethood." This entire dialogue appears tendentious. See Sellheim, "Prophet," 33–91. For a more favorable account of Abū Sufyān's conversion, see Mūsā ibn ᶜUqba, *Maghāzī*, 269–273. See Ibrahim, *Conversion*, 71ff., where I analyze various reports of Abū Sufyān's conversion, demonstrating the biases of the historians.

warn them!"[273] While we cannot trust the details of the story, we can deduce that, based on the ᶜAbbāsid narratives, Abū Sufyān was never convinced of Muhammad's prophethood, although he acknowledged Allah's deity. As portrayed in Muslim traditions, the "conversion of Abū Sufyān was a decision made under the threat of losing his head."[274] This picture is precisely what the ᶜAbbāsid-era historians sought to advance, although its degree of factual reality is questionable.

Abū Sufyān departed to Mecca in haste. When he reached the Kaᶜba, he shouted, "People of Quraysh, behold Muḥammad has come upon you with forces you cannot resist," and added, "Anyone who enters my house will be safe."[275] This was a warning for his Meccans, calling them to show total surrender. At the same time, Muhammad moved his troops even closer to Mecca and declared his aspiration, "I hope that my Lord will gather [the Meccans] to me, all of them through the conquest of Mecca, and strengthen Islam through them and defeat the [tribe of] Hawāzin. I wish that God would grant me plunder from their wealth and their children."[276] This aspiration reflects that, for Muhammad, conquering Mecca would lead to overcoming other major Bedouin tribes. The narrators found it appealing to portray Muhammad as praying to Allah to help him "plunder" wealth and children from other Arabs. This picture—a divinely supported commander who plunders others' possessions—appealed to medieval traditionists. Muhammad then divided his soldiers into four battalions and commissioned them to march and surround Mecca from all directions.[277] The four battalions did not seem to face any significant resistance, except just a little, as all of the Meccans appear to have accepted the new reality.[278] The death casualties were few—twenty-eight non-Muslims and only two Muslims who were killed by mistake.[279] "People began to rush to their houses and lock themselves in. They threw the

[273] Ṭabarī, *Ta'rīkh*, 1633; Ṭabarī, *History*, 8:174.

[274] Ibrahim, *Stated*, 97. See similar comments in Djait, *Masīrat*, 179, where he states that Abū Sufyān was a reasonable man, not vulgar, and sometimes naïve, with "no great religious convictions, even when he converted to Islam." Still, al-Wāqidī claims that "Allah cast Islam in [Abū Sufyān's] heart." Wāqidī, *Maghāzī*, 807.

[275] Ṭabarī, *Ta'rīkh*, 1633; Ṭabarī, *History*, 8:174. See Wāqidī, *Maghāzī*, 823, where he renders the statement "This is Muhammad with ten thousand [soldiers] wearing iron, *fa-aslimū* (so convert to Islam)." See also Wāqidī, *Life*, 405.

[276] Wāqidī, *Life*, 402; Wāqidī, *Maghāzī*, 816.

[277] Wāqidī, *Maghāzī*, 825; Wāqidī, *Life*, 406.

[278] Traditions claim that only one of the four battalions, led by Khālid ibn al-Walīd, fought the Meccans after being attacked. Wāqidī, *Maghāzī*, 826; Wāqidī, *Life*, 407. For secondary studies on the situation with Khālid, see Watt, *Muḥammad*, 66; Djait, *Masīrat*, 178.

[279] Wāqidī, *Maghāzī*, 828.

weapons in the streets so that the Muslims could take them."[280] The Meccans totally surrendered, and it was obvious that Muhammad accomplished a marvelous triumph and conquered Mecca, only eight years after the Quraysh forced him out of it.[281]

Once Muhammad entered Mecca victoriously, we are told, "The people stood before him to swear allegiance to him, and so the people of Mecca became Muslims."[282] As Abū Sufyān did earlier, they too declared their *islām* (submission). Here, conversion to Islam appears as political surrender, and unsurprisingly this image was greatly acceptable, even advanced, by medieval historians. The narratives do not indicate any religious proclamation regarding faith. Rather, we are told, people simply surrendered their weapons and gave an oath of allegiance to Muhammad, thus becoming Muslims. This does not reflect *īmān* (faith and devotion), but *istislām* (surrender).[283] Muslim traditions point out that Muhammad quickly completed several important tasks once he entered Mecca.

First, he cleansed the Kaᶜba from idolatry, by destroying all of its three hundred idols.[284] In what is reported as a miraculous deed, whenever Muhammad came close to any idol, "he pointed at it with the staff in his hand" and proclaimed a Qur'ānic verse, "The truth has come and the falsehood has vanished—indeed, falsehood will definitely vanish" (Q 17:81). Upon the declaration of the verse, *fayaqaᶜ al-ṣanam li-wajhihi* (the idol fell on its face).[285] The literary detail of cleansing the Kaᶜba serves as a religious

[280] Wāqidī, *Life*, 407; Wāqidī, *Maghāzī*, 826.

[281] Ibrahim, *Stated*, 4; Qimanī, *Ḥurūb*, 1:38–40; Qimanī, *Ḥizb*, 8; Djait, *Masīrat*, 167, 171. In praising Muhammad's skills, Watt writes, "Muḥammad's own tact, diplomacy, and administrative skill contributed greatly [to the victory]." See Watt, *Muḥammad*, 69, where he adds, "In all this one cannot but be impressed by Muḥammad's faith in his cause, his vision and his far-seeing wisdom" (70).

[282] Ṭabarī, *Ta'rīkh*, 1636; Ṭabarī, *History*, 8:176. While Djait advances often critical historical analyses of the Muslim sources, here he claims that the conquest of Mecca was "a divine *fatḥ* (conquest)." Djait, *Masīrat*, 180—although he acknowledges that the Arabs who embraced Islam on that day, and later, were "definitely" converting *bi-dāfiᶜ min ḥubb al-maghānim* (motivated by the love of the spoils of war).

[283] Many Shīᶜites distinguish *īmān* (the act of believing in the heart) from *islām* (converting to Islam). See Sulaym ibn Qays, *Kitāb Sulaym*, 288, 325, 337. Naṣr ibn Muzāḥim, *Waqᶜat*, 29–30. See the comments on this distinction in Ibrahim, *Conversion*, 81–83. For the meaning of *aslam* (converted), see Rāzī, *Mukhtār*, 153, where the word means *istaslam* (surrendered); see also Ibn Manẓūr, *Lisān*, 12:293, where *aslam* means *istaslam wa-inqād* (surrendered and submitted), and *islām wa-istislām* refers to *inqiyād* (surrender and yielding); also, *islām* means *khuḍūᶜ wa-iltizām* (obedience and adherence); also Fīrūzābādī, *Qāmūs*, 1122, where *aslam* means *inqād wa-ṣār musliman* (yielded and became Muslim).

[284] See the comments on destroying the idols in Watt, *Muḥammad*, 69, where he observes, "The Kaᶜbah and the private houses were cleansed of idols. Parties were sent to destroy [other idols outside Mecca]."

[285] Wāqidī, *Life*, 409; Wāqidī, *Maghāzī*, 832.

fable to instruct Muslims and non-Muslims alike. It can arguably appeal to Muslims by stressing the most important doctrine of Islam, *tawḥīd* (divine unicity, unitarianism), displaying Muhammad as its utmost implementer—the destroyer of statues and idols. Similarly, the narrators may have desired to present Islam to non-Muslims in the conquered lands. The act of Muhammad cleansing the Kaᶜba parallels Jesus cleansing the temple in Matthew 21:12–17 and John 2:11–12—a message that clearly appeals to many Christians and even to Jews familiar with the biblical text.[286] This way, Muhammad's image conveys that a new day of victory has come, as the cleansing of the holy house is now done by Muhammad—the final prophet who makes things right, pure, and complete. Likewise, the narrators emphasize Muhammad's commitment to *tawḥīd*, by highlighting him as sending his commanders to neighboring towns to destroy other idols that the Arabs used to worship.[287]

Second, Muhammad granted safety to all of the Meccans who entered either Abū Sufyān's house or the Kaᶜba as well as to all of those who surrendered, remained in their houses, and showed no resistance.[288] This meant that Muhammad reportedly pardoned his enemies, despite all of that which they had done against him and his family. In the Kaᶜba, as a victorious commander, he proclaimed to the "people of Quraysh and people of Mecca," "Go, for you are *al-ṭulaqā'* (the pardoned and set-free persons, sg. *ṭalīq*)."[289] The term *ṭulaqā'* is an important literary sobriquet that received significant attention in Muslim sources and became a historiographical theme with religious meaning.[290] These *ṭulaqā'* were Meccan pagans who presumably converted to Islam to save their lives "after their political defeat at the conquest of Mecca."[291] Overall, the term is viewed negatively in Muslim sources.[292]

[286] See Rosenthal, "Influence," 35–45.

[287] Al-Ṭabarī devotes an entire section, titled "The Destruction of Idolatrous Shrines." Ṭabarī, *Ta'rīkh*, 1648ff.; Ṭabarī, *History*, 8:187ff. See the early work of Hishām ibn al-Kalbī, *Aṣnām*, 25, 31–33, where the destruction of the idols is not represented as a miracle, but as an act of Muhammad piercing one idol after another, in their eyes and faces. Hishām ibn al-Kalbī (d. 204/819) was known as a devoted Shīᶜite. See Najāshī, *Rijāl*, 434 (#1166); Ḥillī, *Khulāṣat*, 437. See also Petersen, *ᶜAlī*, 76. On Hishām ibn al-Kalbī (d. 204/819) and his father, Muḥammad al-Kalbī (d. 146/763), see Ibrahim, *Conversion*, 116; Anbārī, Nuzhat, 75–76; Ibn Ḥibbān, *Majrūḥīn*, 3:91.

[288] Ṭabarī, *Ta'rīkh*, 1633; Ṭabarī, *History*, 8:174.

[289] See Ṭabarī, *History*, 8:182, where the term *ṭulaqā'* is rendered as, "those whose bonds have been loosed." Ṭabarī, *Ta'rīkh*, 1642.

[290] For the *ṭulaqā'* theme in historiography, see Ibrahim, *Conversion*, 79–89, 206–209.

[291] See Ibrahim, *Conversion*, 5, 82–83. See the usage of the term by Ibn Hishām, *Sīra*, 2:412; Ibn Ḥibbān, *Sīra*, 1:337, 2:536, where Muᶜāwiya (son of Abū Sufyān) is one of the *ṭulaqā'*. See also Kalāᶜī, *Iktifā'*, 1:510; Suhaylī, *Rawḍ*, 7:232. Cf. Naṣr ibn Muzāḥim, *Waqᶜat*, 29–30. On how the *ṭulaqā'* have later served alongside Muhammad at Ḥunayn, see Ibn Abī Khaythama, *Ta'rīkh (Part 2)*, 2:978.

[292] See Ibn al-Athīr, *Kāmil*, 5:115, where the opposite of the term is honor, notability, and dignity.

It often refers to sons of the curse.[293] According to al-Ṭabarī, the term *ṭulaqāʾ* had later become a common description of "the people of Mecca."[294] It is frequently used by pro-ᶜAlīd and ᶜAbbāsid writers to designate Umayyad figures.[295] In coining this term, ᶜAbbāsid-era writers created a religious stigma against their Umayyad rivals, painting them as disingenuous Muslims who only converted after their defeat in battle to save their own lives. The stigma sets them—in contrast to ᶜAbbāsids and ᶜAlids—as Muhammad's enemies whom he graciously pardoned, which was the only reason they survived and entered Islam.

Third, among the *ṭulaqāʾ*, there was a group of converts to Islam who have been identified as the *muʾallafa qulūbuhum*. This phrase refers to people "whose hearts were reconciled."[296] These, traditions reveal, were *min ashrāf al-nās* (of the Meccan notables) who received material gifts and special incentives from Muhammad in exchange for their acceptance of Islam.[297] Like the *ṭulaqāʾ*, the *muʾallafa qulūbuhum* appears as a historiographical theme, this one describing inauthentic converts. Here, once again, we encounter an emphasis on the contention that on the day of the conquest of Mecca conversion to Islam reflected a tribal surrender to a victorious leader, sometimes through material enticements.[298] The people of the *muʾallafa*

[293] Balādhurī, *Ansāb*, 2:74, 5:319. ᶜUmar reportedly prevented the *ṭulaqāʾ* and their decedents from joining the *shūrā* (consultation) council of the Muslims. Dhahabī, *Taʾrīkh*, 3:466; Balādhurī, *Ansāb*, 10:434–435.

[294] Ṭabarī, *Taʾrīkh*, 1633; Ṭabarī, *History*, 8:174. For studies on the *ṭulaqāʾ*, see Ibrahim, *Conversion*, 81–83, 207–208, and 223; Bosworth, "Ṭulakāʾ," *EI²*, 10:603; Crone, *Meccan*, 214; Hawting, *First*, 23; ᶜAlī, *Mufaṣṣal*, 14:153. See also Urban, "Identity," 125–126, where she compares *ṭulaqāʾ* and *mawālī* (non-Muslims who convert to become "clients" under Muslims).

[295] See Ibrahim, *Conversion*, 82–83.

[296] The term *muʾallafa qulūbuhum* appears in Qur'ān 9:60. For a thorough explanation, see the Muslim jurist Riḍā, *Manār*, 10:14, 10:229 (Muhammad gave them great incentives, and the *muʾallafa qulūbuhum* were from among the *ṭulaqāʾ*), 10:372, 408 (the *muʾallafa* were weak in their faith), 10:426 (they included two kinds: *kuffār wa muslimūn*, i.e., unbelievers and believers). See Thaᶜlabī, *Kashf*, 5:58–59; Qurṭubī, *Jāmiᶜ*, 8:180–181; Mujāhid, *Tafsīr*, 370; Muqātil, *Tafsīr*, 2:176–177; Ṭabarī, *Tafsīr*, 14:323, 18:7; Zamakhsharī, *Kashshāf*, 2:281–283; Ibn Abī Khaythama, *al-Taʾrīkh al-kabīr, Akhbār al-makkiyyīn*, 1:230, 1:235; Ibn Abī Khaythama, *Taʾrīkh (Part3)*, 1:185–187, 2:23–24. See also Ibn Ḥajar, *Fatḥ*, 1:80, where the *muʾallafa* is understood as linguistically meaning *taʾlīf wa tajmīᶜ* (i.e., harmonizing and bringing people together), and 6:252, where they are described as converting with an unfaithful conscience; Bayḍāwī, *Anwār*, 3:86; Shaᶜrāwī, *Khawāṭirī*, 6:3544, 11:6835. Ed., "al-Mu'allafa Ḳulūbuhum," *EI²*, 7:254. For the significance of rewards among Arab soldiers and how Muhammad used these incentives strategically to win them, ᶜAbd al-Karīm, *Shadwu*, 1:75ff.

[297] Ibn Hishām, *Sīra*, 2:492. For an example of how the incentives worked to win people over to Islam, see Wāqidī, *Maghāzī*, 854–855, where he details the matter of Ṣafwān's conversion to Islam after he saw the spoils of war. On Ṣafwān, see Ibrahim, *Conversion*, 85–86; also Djait, *Masīrat*, 180.

[298] The modern Muslim historian Aḥmad al-Sharīf explains that conversion to Islam was *maẓharan li-dukhūlihim fī al-niẓām al-jadīd wa-iqrārihim bi-l-wiḥda al-ᶜarabiyya* (a manifestation of their joining the new system and their affirmation of the Arabian unity). Sharīf, *Makka*, 533. Like Sharīf, the Moroccan historian ᶜĀbid al-Jābrī argues that "Islam" in that early stage was *islāman siyāsiyyan* (Islam of a political nature) and meant *iᶜtirāfan bi-zaᶜāmat dawlat al-rasūl* (a recognition

qulūbuhum were indeed of certain eminence to Muhammad. He reportedly granted them gifts in order to win their hearts over through that which they loved most—materialistic gains.[299] Some narrators reveal that the *mu'allafa* were Arab elites who received wealth from Muhammad after converting to Islam: When they loved the incentives, they declared, "this is a good religion," but when they did not like them, they mocked Muhammad and abandoned him.[300] The presence of this literary feature demonstrates that, for the medieval narrators, there was no concern whatsoever with depicting the acceptance of Islam for materialistic incentives. Still, we should also note that the list of the *mu'allafa qulūbuhum* is given by ᶜAbbāsid-era narrators, which explains why most of the people included in the list were Umayyad figures, portrayed as worldly people who converted without a sincere conviction about Islam.[301] This is evident in how the major Umayyad notables Abū Sufyān and his son Muᶜāwiya are identified as part of this group.[302]

Fourth, while Muhammad reportedly declared a general amnesty and pardoned his enemies on the day of the conquest, he "commanded that six men and four women should be killed."[303] The reasons for this instruction generally revolve around the people's reported apostasy after they accepted Islam or the accusation that some of them "used to molest" Muhammad.[304] At least one of the four women—Hind, who was Abū Sufyān's wife—saved her life when she came in disguise and sought Muhammad's forgiveness, declaring her submission as she "became a Muslim and swore allegiance."[305] These pardonings and executions should be interpreted as authored accounts with religious purposes. Here, the narrators appear occupied with forming a religious ultimatum: Although Muhammad granted amnesty to many and offered incentives to lure people's hearts to his leadership, some mistakes are

of the Messenger Muhammad's state). See Jābrī, *Naqd*, 3:165–166. In the same vein, Djait argues that the tribes who accepted Muhammad's leadership were *muta'aslimūn*, not Muslims. The term *muta'aslimūn* suggests that they were declaring submission, even pretending surrender, to a powerful leader, not to a religious prophet. Djait, *Masīrat*, 170 and 177.

299 Rosenthal calls the *mu'allafa qulūbuhum* the sympathizers of Muhammad. Rosenthal, *Man*, 404–405.

300 Thaᶜlabī, *Kashf*, 5:58–59.

301 See Ibn Hishām, *Sīra*, 2:492–493; Wāqidī, *Maghāzī*, 939. See Ibrahim, *Conversion*, 155–166, where the theme of sincere conversion is discussed.

302 See Qurṭubī, *Jāmiᶜ*, 8:180–181.

303 Ṭabarī, *Ta'rīkh*, 1642; Ṭabarī, *History*, 8:181. Wāqidī, *Maghāzī*, 825; Wāqidī, *Life*, 406. Watt writes, "There was also a small number of persons specified by name as excluded from the general amnesty." Watt, *Muḥammad*, 68.

304 Ṭabarī, *History*, 8:178–179.

305 Ṭabarī, *History*, 8:179; Wāqidī, *Maghāzī*, 850.

unforgivable, as he was still adamant about killing specific enemies. These enemies, the story suggests, abandoned Islam or showed hostility or outright rejection toward Muhammad—and these actions are never permissible. The narrators used their reports to create a disposition against insulting Muhammad or abandoning Islam—two matters that became highly important to later Muslim jurists and resulted in consequential religious rulings.[306]

The reported victory of the Muslims in the conquest of Mecca is marvelous in so many ways, not least among them that it was reportedly accomplished in only eight years after the Muslims were expelled from Mecca. In this relatively short period, Muhammad successfully became the major leader of the Hijaz, and his community grew in power, unity, and accumulated resources. Through treaties, alliances, and skillful tactics in his *maghāzī*, Muhammad consolidated his tribal dominion and advanced his influence among the Arabs. Those who harassed, persecuted, or despised him in the past had reportedly realized and acknowledged his victory. The Muslim traditions paint an impressive picture of a capable statesman with a religious mission. With his enemies, he deployed tactics and embraced patience, knowing when to withdraw from treaties and when to advance militarily. With his allies and companions, he defended them when they called for his support, exhorted them when they doubted, and encouraged them when they got discouraged. Muhammad reportedly believed in his goals and sincerely chased them. While the reported Muslim victory in the conquest of Mecca is great in and of itself, one can argue that it is even more spectacular. Just consider that within those same eight years, Muhammad was successful in overcoming not only the mighty Quraysh and the major Arab tribes but also the united, organized, and devoted Jewish community, both in Medina and in its neighboring lands. Muhammad's reported victory over the Jewish tribes is the topic of the following chapter.

306 See how some of the ten names are explicitly used by later jurists to justify similar treatment of Muslims insulting Muhammad or abandoning Islam in Ibn Taymiyya, *Ṣārim*, 1:109–110, 1:142; Ibn Qayyim, *Zād*, 3:362.

5
Muhammad's Confrontations with the Jews

You brethren of monkeys and pigs!—Prophet Muhammad crying out at the Jews of Banū Qurayẓa, according to Ibn Shihāb al-Zuhrī

The Jews and the Christians say, "We are Allah's sons and his beloved." Respond: "Why does he then chastise you for your transgressions? No. You are merely humans from among whom he created."—*Sūrat al-Mā'ida* (Qur'ān 5:18)

The last hour will not be established until you fight with the Jews—the stone behind which a Jew will be hiding will say, "O Muslim! There is a Jew hiding behind me, so kill him!"—A prophecy attributed to Muhammad, reported by Imām Bukhārī in his *bāb qitāl al-yahūd* (book of fighting against the Jews)

It seems safe to say that the conflict with the Jews of Medina was so deep that even when the Qur'ān deals with Jesus the Medinan revelations are governed by polemics against Jews.—Muslim scholar Munᶜim Sirry[1]

If the portrayal of Muhammad's victory over the Meccan pagans is a marvelous picture of hegemony in itself, it is significantly more so once we consider how the Muslim traditions describe his elimination of the Jews of Medina within the same time period. If idol worshippers are described as his main rivals in Mecca, the Jews are depicted as his major enemy in Medina.[2]

[1] Zuhrī, *Maghāzī*, 81; Bukhārī, *Ṣaḥīḥ*, 4:42; Sirry, *Scriptural Polemics*, 44.

[2] For the Jews of the Hijaz, their lives and history, see the valuable Arabic studies by Jamīl, *Nabī*, 32–53; Sayyid, *Yahūd*, 7–38; Kanᶜān, *Muḥammad*, 335–352; Ṣāliḥ, *Yahūd*. For non-Muslim studies, see Mazuz, *Religious*, 9–24; Wolfensohn, *Ta'rīkh*, 1–34 (the Jews in the Hijaz), 50–80 (the Jews in Medina); Wensinck, *Mohammed*; Newby, *History*; also Hoyland, "Jews," 91–116.

Muhammad's Military Expeditions. Ayman S. Ibrahim, Oxford University Press. © Oxford University Press 2024.
DOI: 10.1093/oso/9780197769171.003.0005

According to Muslim narratives, the powerful, organized, and well-established Jewish community of Medina, where it had reportedly existed for centuries,[3] was totally subdued or entirely expelled from Medina within seven years after the Muslims arrived in the city. While the tradition claims that one of the earliest actions Muhammad accomplished upon arriving at Medina was cutting a peace treaty with several Jewish clans,[4] this hoped-for peace did not yield fruit, because the Jews were soon accused of disloyalty and hypocrisy. At every turn, the traditions describe the Jews of Medina as ungrateful, insincere, deceitful, and disingenuous people who sought to harm the Muslims and refused to accept Muhammad's religious message.[5] The tradition emphasizes repeatedly that Muhammad could never trust

[3] See Stillman, "Yahūd," *EI*², 11:239, where he writes, "Jews had lived in various parts of the Arabian Peninsula since Antiquity, and the numbers of those living in northwestern Arabia must have been swelled by refugees from Judaea when the great rebellions against Rome were suppressed in A.D. 70 and 135." See also ᶜAlī, *Mufaṣṣal*, 12:98. For the Jews in the Qur'ān, see Rubin, "Jews and Judaism," *EQ*, 3:21–34, especially 3:23–25, where he studies "the qur'ānic attack on the Jews" and examines verses describing their insubordination and disbelief (e.g., Q 2:79–80; 2:94; 2:111; 3:23–24; 4:49; 5:18; 62:6), arguing that the "key term conveying the idea of God's anger with the Jews is *ghaḍab*, 'wrath'" (3:25). See also Margoliouth, *Mohammed*, 22. For verses on Allah's wrath against the Children of Israel and how he cursed those with whom he has been angry, which led to them turning into apes and pigs, see Q 2:65; 5:60; 7:166. On the matter of turning the evil Jews into apes and pigs, Muslim exegetes disagree on whether the transformation was an actual physical change in their appearance, or the statement referred to a mere symbolic change. See Muqātil, *Tafsīr*, 1:113, 1:125 (Allah transformed them physically into monkeys); Ṭabarī, *Jāmiᶜ*, 2:168–170 (physical transformation); Thaᶜlabī, *Kashf*, 1:212 (actual bodily transformation into apes); Zamakhsharī, *Kashshāf*, 1:653 (bodily transformation, in which the young people were transformed into apes, while the elderly into pigs); Rāzī, *Mafātiḥ*, 3:541 (the transformation can be physical or figurative in reference to their hearts); Qurṭubī, *Jāmiᶜ*, 1:439–440, 2:58 (similar to al-Rāzī's interpretation); Bayḍāwī, *Anwār*, 2:134 (figurative, not physical); Riḍā, *Manār*, 6:371 (transforming them was actually physical, although some believe it was spiritual); Quṭb, *Fī ẓilāl*, 1:77 (figurative); Shaᶜrāwī, *Khawāṭirī*, 6:3254 (not physical, as they were cursed into possessing the characteristics of monkeys). It appears that, roughly, classical exegetes argued for a physical transformation, while modern interpreters tweaked the interpretations to fit a modern understanding suitable for their day. Rubin argues, "Transformation into apes recurs elsewhere in the Qur'ān as a punishment inflicted on the Children of Israel for violating the Sabbath" (*EQ*, 3:25). In a tradition attributed to Muhammad, he was concerned that some Jews were transformed into lizards. He reportedly said, "Allah cursed or became angry against a tribe from the Sons of Israel *famasakhahum* (and transformed them) to animals that move on the earth. Thus, I do not know, perhaps this *ḍabb* (lizard) is one of them. So I do not eat it, nor do I prohibit the eating of it." Muslim, *Ṣaḥīḥ*, 3:1546.

[4] On the *Ṣaḥīfa* (the so-called Constitution of Medina), see Ibn Hishām, *Sīra*, 1:501–504; Ibn Hishām, *Life*, 231–233; Suhaylī, *Rawḍ*, 4:171–173; Kalāᶜī, *Iktifā'*, 1:296–298; Ibn Sayyid al-Nās, *ᶜUyūn*, 1:227–229; Ibn Kathīr, *Sīra*, 2:321; Ibn Kathīr, *Bidāya*, 3:273. For modern Muslim studies on the *Ṣaḥīfa*, see the important analysis of ᶜUmarī, *Sīra*, 272–298, where he is skeptical of its origins, although he still affirms its contents and attempts to trace its statements in authentic traditions. See also Mubārakpūrī, *Raḥīq*, 168–169; Sharīf, *Makka*, 316–322; Ṣallābī, *Sīra*, 323–354; Khaṭṭāb, *Rasūl*, 70–74. For a recent critical study, see Ibrahim, *Muhammad*, 71–77, where reasons for skepticism toward the authenticity of the *Ṣaḥīfa* are given. See also the important work by Lecker, "Constitution," 1–78, in which he provides a translation of the document and analyzes details about its documentation and content. Cf. Shoemaker, *Creating*, 26–29. Lecker and Shoemaker appear to accept that its validity as an early document traces back to Muhammad's time; however, we should note we only know about it from later traditions.

[5] For a modern Muslim polemic against the Jews, portraying them as ungrateful and hypocritical based on the Qur'ān and the *sunna*, see Ṣāliḥ, *Yahūd*, 11–27, 51–45, 91–98, 141–149. Within the

them; consequently, he commissioned calculated assassinations of notable Jews, led several *maghāzī* to subdue Jewish tribes within Medina, and raided two Jewish settlements in neighboring regions.

These stories of Jewish-Muslim tensions are just that. While many Muslims may believe these traditions as factual,[6] they are better viewed as a product of medieval historians who designed a particular depiction of the Jews. Through these tales, traditionists portrayed an image of a rival religious community that challenged the believers upon their arrival in Medina. The challenge was inherently religious, around theological claims, but was soon crystalized into a tribal military struggle.[7] If we consider the late date of documenting these traditions, they are arguably exegetical in nature.[8] Not only do they appear to explain verses in the Qur'ān that depict the Jews negatively (e.g., Q 2:61), but they also form a religious anti-Jewish disposition,

overall negative portrayal of the Jews in Muslim traditions, it is not surprising that historiographical accounts describe very few Jews as to have reportedly accepted Muhammad's message. These include two Jewish rabbis, ᶜAbdullāh ibn Salām and Mukhayriq. Both converted to Islam and fought for Muhammad. For a study on Jewish intellectuals who converted in classical Islam, see Stroumsa, "On Jewish," 179–197; cf. Leveen, "Mohammed," 399–406. For how the Jews are portrayed as teachers of Muhammad, see Anthony, *Muhammad*, 74–75, 167. For Mukhayriq, see Wāqidī, *Maghāzī*, 262–263; Ibn Hishām, *Sīra*, 1:514–519; Ibn Saᶜd, *Ṭabaqāt*, 1:388–389. As for Ibn Salām, see Wāqidī, *Maghāzī*, 329, 509; Ibn Hishām, *Sīra*, 1:516; Ibn Saᶜd, *Ṭabaqāt*, 2:268–269; ᶜAlī, *Mufaṣṣal*, 12:138, where he writes that traditions seem to exaggerate about Ibn Salām being a knowledgeable rabbi. It is noteworthy to mention that classical historians highlight the conversion of these Jewish rabbis as a testimony for Islam's truthfulness, contrasting them with Jews who refused Muhammad, portraying the latter as ungrateful and hypocritical. For hypocrite Jews who accepted Islam disingenuously, see Ibn Hishām, *Sīra*, 1:527; cf. the comments of the Muslim scholar Ḥanafī, *Min*, 3:271–272. For other Jews who converted to Islam while they were not rabbis, see, for instance, the account of Nuᶜaym ibn Masᶜūd in Wāqidī, *Maghāzī*, 480; Ibn Hishām, *Sīra*, 1:557. On conversion of Jews as a literary theme of Islam's supremacy, see Ibrahim, *Conversion*, ch. 1.

[6] For modern and contemporary Muslims who believe the traditions about Muhammad and the Jews to document actual historical episodes and to a large extent prescriptive on Muslim-Jewish relations, see Hamidullah, *Battlefields*, 103–117; Mubārakpūrī, *Raḥīq*, 214–219; Abū Māyla, *Sarāyā*, 20, 64, 127; ᶜUmarī, *Sīra*, 299–317; Ṣallābī, *Sīra*, 323–354, 454–467; Sharīf, *Makka*, 245–263. A "traditional" Muslim is defined in this study as a believer "adopting a traditional and mostly conservative approach toward Islamic origins. When used in relation to non-Muslim authors, it refers to scholars who are likely to view the sources' reliability positively." See Ibrahim, *Conversion*, xx.

[7] See Mazuz, "Jewish-Muslim," 946–973, where he argues that Muslim anti-Jewish polemics began early with the Qur'ānic assertions against the Jews and their beliefs, particularly their rejection of Muhammad's prophethood, but soon multiplied in *ḥadīth* and *sīra* literature. For polemics in religious discourse, see Beck, *Mature*, 21.

[8] For verses in the Qur'ān that portray the Jews negatively, see Q 2:61; 2:65; 5:60–64; 7:166. For more verses, see Mazuz, "Jewish-Muslim," 946–947; Stillman, *Jews*, 149–151. On these verses and the anti-Jew traditions advanced by Muslim exegetes, see classical works such as Muqātil, *Tafsīr*, 1:490, 5:91; Ṭabarī, *Jāmiᶜ*, 10:450–459; Thaᶜlabī, *Kashf*, 4:87–88, 5:66; Zamakhsharī, *Kashshāf*, 1:654–657; Rāzī, *Mafātiḥ*, 12:393–398; Qurṭubī, *Jāmiᶜ*, 6:237–239; Bayḍāwī, *Anwār*, 2:135. Modern exegetes generally follow the same line of thought. Riḍā, *Manār*, 6:374–376; Quṭb, *Fī ẓilāl*, 2:906–908; Shaᶜrāwī, *Khawāṭirī*, 6:3261–3264. See Margoliouth, *Mohammed*, 22–23, 32, 54, where he comments on anti-Jewish polemics in the Qur'ān; also Margoliouth, *Mohammedanism*, 130; Bar-Asher, *Jews*, 27–57.

likely suitable for later Muslim generations who sought to relay anti-Jewish polemics in dealing with Jews living in the conquered lands.[9]

In this chapter, the study focuses on five major *maghāzī* led by Muhammad against three Jewish tribes in Medina—Banū Qaynuqāᶜ, Banū al-Naḍīr, and Banū Qurayẓa—and two Jewish settlements—Khaybar and Fadak—in its neighboring lands.[10] I analyze that which the Muslim traditions reveal concerning the motivations and results of these military combats. I treat these traditions as ideological literary tales, designed by classical Muslim historians in their attempt to comment on certain political, religious, and sociocultural matters at the time of writing.[11] In the absence of eyewitnesses and actual documentation, the drawing of straightforward links between historiographical reports and events that may have happened centuries earlier is problematic.[12] While traditional Muslims have often viewed these stories as reliable, factual, and prescriptive, I view them as descriptive of later times and as homiletic in nature, aiming to communicate religious appeals to Muslims and non-Muslims in later generations. For Muslims, these

[9] On Muslim anti-Jewish polemics, their contexts and emergence, see Perlmann, "Study of Muslim Polemics," 4–59; Perlmann, "Muslim-Jewish Polemics," 11:396–402; Mazuz, *Religious*, 1–23, 69–80; Firestone, "Muhammad," 1–16; Stillman, *Jews*, 12–21, 149–151, 275–276; Adang, "Medieval Muslim Polemics," 143–159; Adang and Schmidtke, "Polemics," where they argue, "The Muslim polemic against Judaism and its adherents is a phenomenon as old as Islam, and the Qur'ān was its very first source." For Qur'ānic polemic against other religions, see Azaiez, *Le contre-discours*. See also Perlmann, "Medieval Polemics," 103–138; Bar-Asher, *Jews*, 27–57, 109–120; O'Sullivan, "Anti-Jewish Polemic," 49–68, where he argues that Muslim anti-Jewish polemics appear to have emerged within a larger context of Christian anti-Jewish polemics; Cf. Déroche, "Polémique," 141–161; Cameron, "Byzantines," 249–274; Gil, *Jews*, 73; Powers, *Muḥammad*, 272 n. 50; Reinink, "Beginnings," 165–187; also, to a lesser extent, see Haldon, *Byzantium*, 345–347. See Olster, *Roman*, 18–19, 29, and 116–178, where he examines Christian anti-Jewish polemics, and, in relation to Islam, he argues, "The Arab invasions inspired the Christians to write anti-Jewish texts; they inspired the Jews to write anti-Christian texts" (175); cf. 12–13, 90, 158, where Olster discusses the Muslim anti-Jewish writings. For a classical Muslim polemic against the Jews, see Ibn Ḥazm, *Faṣl*, 82–92, et passim; Maghribī, *Badhl*, 101–146. For a secondary study on these two works, see Perlmann, "Study," 36–59, 65–93, respectively. See also Nirenberg, *Anti-Judaism*, ch. 4, where he discusses "The Role of Jewish Enmity in the Construction of Muhammad's Biography." For a modern Muslim polemic against the Jews, see Ṣāliḥ, *Yahūd*, 11–27. On Muslim polemic against *ahl al-kitāb* in general, see the important volume by Waardenburg, ed., *Muslim Perceptions*. We should note a methodological problem in Mazuz's *Religious*. While he states that he understands the textual problems of the Muslim sources, he still treats them largely as true indications of Muhammad's encounters with the Medinan Jews. Mazuz's core conclusion is that Muhammad encountered "Talmudic-Rabbinic Jews in almost every respect" (99). There is no independent evidence to support that assertion.

[10] In a Shīᶜite report, Medina had three *buṭūn* (clans) of Jews: Qaynuqāᶜ, Naḍīr, and Qurayẓa. See Majlisī, *Biḥār*, 90:69, where the Jews envied Muhammad after the Arab tribes of al-Aws and al-Khazraj allied with him. For a summary on how Muhammad dealt with the Jews in the Hijaz in general, see Ibn Qayyim, *Aḥkām*, 1:167–168, 1:372, 1:392. For a study on the Jews, particularly of Yemen, under Muslim rule in early Islam, see Tobi, *Jews*, 34–46; see his examination of the Jewish-Muslim tribal relations on 142–155.

[11] See Roohi, "Muḥammad's Disruptive," 40–80; Hibri, *Parable*, xi. Hibri, *Reinterpreting*, 13.

[12] Ibrahim, *Conversion*, 1–2.

memorable stories of Muhammad attacking the Jews serve as a testimony of Islam's superiority and militaristic hegemony over a religious rival. For non-Muslims, especially Jews in conquered lands, these traditions become a warning, exhorting the Jews to heed the calling of Islam, lest they face similar reckonings as their forefathers experienced. As for Muslim-Jewish relations in our day, our world can benefit greatly from the critical approach of treating these traditions as figurative and hyperbolic, as the stakes are higher if one were to view them as factual and literal, let alone prescriptive.

The Raid against Banū Qaynuqāc (2/624)

The narrators designed a particular explanation for how the armed conflict between the Muslims and the Jews erupted. They emphasize two major literary claims: the military clash with the Jews began after Muhammad secured a momentous victory over the pagans of Mecca in the Battle of Badr, and the clash started because the Jews were jealous of the Muslims' victory and broke the peace agreement with Muhammad. To set the historical background for the initial military clash with the Jews, al-Ṭabarī reports that after Muhammad "killed many polytheists of Quraysh at Badr," the Jews "were envious and behaved badly towards him."[13] This report is also given by al-Wāqidī and paints a general image of the Jews as jealous of the Muslims and as covenant-breakers—a necessitated depiction to establish reasons not only for the first Muslim raid against the Jews but also for the deterioration of Muslim-Jewish relations presumably occurring in the following few years.[14] The image displays the Jews negatively, especially as Ibn Hishām describes it in religious terms: "When God smote Quraysh at Badr, the apostle assembled the Jews in the market of the Banū Qaynuqāc when he came to Medina and called on them to accept Islam before God should treat them as he had treated Quraysh."[15] This tradition describes the Jews as religiously misguided—unable to recognize the victory Allah granted to the Muslims and how this was a sign for Muhammad's prophethood. While, at this time, no fight erupted as a response to their religious unbelief, the

13 Ṭabarī, *History*, 7:85; Ṭabarī, *Ta'rīkh*, 1359–1360. For a comparison of the texts of Ibn Isḥāq's *Sīra* with Wāqidī's *Maghāzī* on the Medinan Jews, see Faizer, "Muhammad," 463–489.

14 Wāqidī, *Life*, 87. Wāqidī, *Maghāzī*, 175–176.

15 Ibn Hishām, *Life*, 260. See also Ibn Hishām, *Sīra*, 1:552. For the expulsion of Banū Qaynuqāc and their history in the Hijaz, see Wolfensohn, *Ta'rīkh*, 110–120.

Muslim tradition highlights the Jews as hypocrites, ungrateful, and envious of the Muslims, as they reportedly said, "Muḥammad has not met anyone who is good at fighting. Had he met us, he would have had a battle which would be unlike a battle with anyone else."[16] This literary account is shared by various classical Muslim historians and seems to depict the Jews as arrogant, boastful, and prideful. They also appear as imprudent people who lack wisdom and insight,[17] especially as they challenge Muhammad and threaten the Muslims.[18] It is plausible to deduce that this overall negative literary image is designed to correspond to verses in the Qur'ān that present the Jews as ungrateful transgressors who often fought and killed the prophets (Q 2:61).[19] Against this background and without particularities, we are told, the Jews "also infringed the contract in various ways."[20] By identifying the Jews as rivals who do not keep covenants, the storytellers designed a historical context for the Muslim-Jewish armed conflict and established the precursor for the first Muslim raid against the Jews.

One month after the Battle of Badr, Muhammad reportedly led his first *ghazwa* (raid) to target the Jewish tribe of Banū Qaynuqāᶜ.[21] The tribe was one of the three major Jewish tribes that resided for centuries in Medina.[22] The people of Banū Qaynuqāᶜ were reportedly known for their goldsmith trade (*ṣāgha*) and armorers, and they had their own trading market (*sūq*).[23]

16 Ṭabarī, *History*, 7:85; Ṭabarī, *Ta'rīkh*, 1359–1360. Ibn Hishām, *Sīra*, 1:552, 2:47. For a study on Muhammad's legendary encounters with the Jews and their rabbis, see Hirschfeld, "Historical," 100–116.

17 For a traditional Sunnī reading of the report, see Ṣallābī, *Sīra*, 454–455, where the author suggests that the Jewish response was disrespectful and demonstrated a lack of commitment to the peace treaty with Muhammad that led to the fight. Similarly, see ᶜUmarī, *Sīra*, 299–300, where he argues that Muhammad fought them because of their apparent willingness to violate the peace treaty, not because of their religious unbelief since, at this stage, says ᶜUmarī, Islam allowed the Jews to remain on their faith—a matter that changed later when the jihad was ordered against the unbelievers.

18 Ḥanafī, *Min*, 3:271–287. Djait, *Masīrat*, 113–116.

19 See Ibn Hishām, *Sīra*, 1:540, where he refers to Q 3:12–13 as a text revealed concerning boastful and ungrateful Jews in Medina, just before the fight with Banū Qaynuqāᶜ erupted.

20 See Ṭabarī, *History*, 7:85; Ṭabarī, *Ta'rīkh*, 1359–1360.

21 See a Shīᶜite account in Majlisī, *Biḥār*, 20:5ff. The date is about March 624.

22 These Medinan Jews are depicted in Muslim traditions as in disharmony and continuous tension, especially as Banū Qaynuqāᶜ allied themselves with al-Khazraj, while Banū al-Naḍīr and Banū Qurayẓa did so with al-Aws (al-Khazraj's rival). See Ibn Hishām, *Sīra*, 1:540; Ibn Hishām, *Life*, 253; Majlisī, *Biḥār*, 90:69; Ibn Qayyim, *Aḥkām*, 3:1404. On the disharmony between the Jewish tribes in Medina and their competing allies, see ᶜAlī, *Mufaṣṣal*, 12:109; Mubārakpūrī, *Raḥīq*, 163; Djait, *Masīrat*, 115.

23 Ṭabarī, *Ta'rīkh*, 1361; Ṭabarī, *History*, 7:87. Ibn ᶜAsākir, *Ta'rīkh*, 4:218, 13:190–193; Djait, *Masīrat*, 113–115; Gil, *Jews*, 639; ᶜAlī, *Mufaṣṣal*, 7:264, 12:112, 13:58, 13:309–310, 14:65, 14:250. According to ᶜAlī, *Mufaṣṣal*, 12:98, the Jews of Medina consisted of tribes, clans, and families. They were not Bedouins in the sense of traveling in different lands, but rather they dwelled in specific locations, grew their families, and relied on developing and advancing skillful professions including blacksmiths, goldsmiths, and in some cases agriculture and trading. Some *speculate* that the

The Muslim tradition highlights Banū Qaynuqā^{c} as the first violator of the peace agreement with the Muslims. While Muhammad had reportedly invited the Medinan Jews to Islam, there is a specific report dedicated to him inviting Banū Qaynuqā^{c} in particular. He summoned Banū Qaynuqā^{c} in their market and addressed them: "O Jews, beware lest God bring on you the like of the retribution which he brought on Quraysh. Accept Islam, for you know that I am a prophet sent by God."[24] Through this report, it appears, classical historians justify any retaliatory action against the Jews, since, the logic goes, they were warned and invited to convert to Islam. To present the people of Banū Qaynuqā^{c} as unbelievers, classical historians claim that Muhammad emphasized, "You will find this [i.e., I am a prophet sent by God] in your scriptures and in God's covenant with you."[25] This literary detail clearly links historiographical accounts with the Qur'ān and reflects the apparent exegetical nature of various historical traditions.[26]

Still, the religious ignorance of the Jews did not solely or immediately trigger the armed fight. Their refusal of conversion to Islam, according to traditions, was followed by a uniquely random incident: A few Jews of Banū Qaynuqā^{c} killed a Muslim man for murdering a Jew who offended an Arab woman by lifting up her dress at the market.[27] This incident, we are invited to believe, meant for the Muslims that the peace treaty with the Jews was violated—this ignited the fight. Despite the apparent literary detail that a Jew was the first murdered person in the incident, we are told, the Jews were first to break the peace agreement with the Muslims. Although the historicity of the entire story is questionable, the tradition of this unnamed Arab woman appears unstable and unconvincing.[28] In their attempt to create a justifying tale for the presumed attack of the Jews, medieval narrators seem to have done a poor job: The woman is not even identified as a Muslim, but simply

Jews came to the Hijaz sometime after the destruction of the Jewish temple in 70 C.E. See Watt, *Muḥammad*, 193–194, where he writes, "the Jews appear to have been pioneers in agricultural development" (193). See also Rodinson, *Muhammad*, 29, 61, 139; Margoliouth, *Mohammed*, 54–55.

[24] Wāqidī, *Maghāzī*, 176; Wāqidī, *Life*, 87; Ibn Hishām, *Life*, 363; Ibn Hishām, *Sīra*, 2:47; Ṭabarī, *History*, 7:85; Ṭabarī, *Ta'rīkh*, 1360.

[25] Ṭabarī, *History*, 7:85; Ṭabarī, *Ta'rīkh*, 1360; Wāqidī, *Maghāzī*, 176; Wāqidī, *Life*, 87; Ibn Hishām, *Life*, 363; Ibn Hishām, *Sīra*, 2:47.

[26] See Q 7:157, "Those who follow the messenger—the unlettered prophet—whom they find written in that which they have of the Torah and the Gospel . . ." See Cook, *Commanding*, 13–30.

[27] Wāqidī, *Maghāzī*, 177–178; Wāqidī, *Life*, 88. Ibn Hishām, *Life*, 363–364; Ibn Hishām, *Sīra*, 2:47–49.

[28] Watt considers the incident trivial and arbitrary. Watt, *Muḥammad*, 15. Rodinson, *Muhammad*, 172.

as an Arab: "and even if she were Muslim, there is no mention of her tribe, clan, family, or even her name. There is also no mention of the Muslim man who took revenge for her; he is unknown."[29] The story seems to have been forged by Muslim historians to justify a reported attack. More importantly, the same pool of memory includes competing reports that suggest other scenarios for the initiation of the attack. According to al-Ṭabarī, Gabriel came from heaven to Muhammad with a verse from the Qur'ān, "If you fear the betrayal of some people, then throw it back to them equally" (Q 8:58), to which Muhammad responded, "I fear the Banū Qaynuqāᶜ," and "It was on the basis of this verse that the Messenger of God advanced upon them."[30] It appears from this tradition that the revealed verse propelled Muhammad to raid the Jews as he was afraid of them. The point is not which tradition is more plausible or convincing, but rather to reiterate that the same pool of Muslim memory provides competing scenarios on what broke the treaty and initiated the raid.

Ultimately, according to traditions, the raid against the Jews was inevitable; consequently, Muhammad led a group of Muslims and forced a siege against the tribe for fifteen days, until they "surrendered unconditionally" and he expelled them from their homes.[31] We are told that Allah "gave their property as booty to his Messenger and the Muslims."[32] According to traditions, the Jews were over seven hundred men, not including women and children.[33] While this ending may possibly appear as a satisfying finale for the account of the raid against Banū Qaynuqāᶜ, it is not so for classical Muslim historians, as we repeatedly encountered how they design literary reports to derive religious instructions. In this tale, storytellers added two unique details—one about Muhammad's treatment of the surrendered Jews, and the

[29] See Ibrahim, *Stated*, 84, where I write, "This entire story appears to be random and tendentious; quite likely forged and deliberately documented to justify the actions against the Jews." See also the excellent comments of the Muslim scholar Qimanī, *Ḥurūb*, 1:120, where he dismisses the story completely and argues it was fabricated to justify the attack. Even some conservative Muslims argue that the story is unconvincing and that its *isnād* is weak. See ᶜUmarī, *Sīra*, 300, where he is skeptical of the narrative of the Arab woman, but nonetheless argues that, for him, as a historiographical report, the story *yusta'nas bi-hā* (is comforting or plausible).

[30] Ṭabarī, *Ta'rīkh*, 1360. See also Ṭabarī, *History*, 7:85, where he renders the verse, "And if thou fearest treachery from any folk, then throw back to them their treaty fairly."

[31] Ibn Hishām, *Life*, 363; Ibn Hishām, *Sīra*, 2:47. Ṭabarī, *History*, 7:85; Ṭabarī, *Ta'rīkh*, 1360. Some traditions indicate that these Jews were sent all the way to Greater Syria, particularly to a place called Adhriᶜāt. See Ibn al-Athīr, *Kāmil*, 2:30.

[32] Ṭabarī, *Ta'rīkh*, 1361. See also Ṭabarī, *History*, 7:87, where it reads, "The Banū Qaynuqāᶜ did not have any land, as they were goldsmiths. The Messenger of God took many weapons belonging to them and the tools of their trade."

[33] Ṭabarī, *Ta'rīkh*, 1361. See also Ṭabarī, *History*, 7:86. Ibn Hishām, *Sīra*, 2:48; Ibn Hishām, *Life*, 363.

other comparing two Muslims, particularly concerning their responses to Muhammad expelling the Jews from Medina.

Concerning Muhammad's treatment of the surrendered Jews, the narrators depict him as truly angry with the people of Banū Qaynuqāᶜ. After they gave in, "They were fettered and he wanted to kill them."[34] Of course, the veracity of this report is hard to establish, and—as we repeatedly voice skepticism toward the reliability of historiographical accounts—it is better viewed as a creation of Muslim historians for religious instructions. The report reflects a precedent they attributed to Muhammad in his treatment of surrendered Jews, and likely aimed to form and advance anti-Jewish sentiments in medieval times, particularly in the conquered lands where Muslims ruled over non-Muslims.[35] As it stands, the report matters significantly to Muslims who view Muhammad as the exemplary man for humankind. If he was angry with the Jews and wanted to fetter and kill them after they surrendered, the logic goes, he definitely had a reason and his example is to be imitated. From a critical standpoint, there is no way to establish the historicity of this report. It is better viewed as fashioned by classical narrators to communicate a warning message to their audience: to Muslims, warning them against trusting the Jews, and to non-Muslims, particularly Jews in conquered lands, threatening similar consequences should they follow in the footsteps of their forefathers.

In the same vein, storytellers also develop a literary comparison between two Medinan Muslims—ᶜAbdullāh ibn Ubayy ibn Salūl and ᶜUbāda ibn al-Ṣāmit—who reportedly responded differently to Muhammad expelling the Jews from their homes. Both men were from the Arab tribe of al-Khazraj, which was a major tribe among the Muslim *anṣār* (supporters of Muhammad).[36] Seizing the Jews of Banū Qaynuqāᶜ and expelling them from their homes created a tribal dilemma, because this Jewish tribe was

[34] Ṭabarī, *History*, 7:86; Ṭabarī, *Taʾrīkh*, 1360.

[35] See Mazuz, "Jewish-Muslim," 946–973; Perlmann, "Medieval," 103–138; Adang and Schmidtke, "Polemics." On fabricating accounts and attributing them to previous authorities, see Yāqūt, *Muᶜjam al-udabāʾ*, 3:1201–1204; Ibn al-Muᶜtazz, *Ṭabaqāt*, 69; Jumaḥī, *Ṭabaqāt*, 1:48.

[36] See the valuable explanation of ᶜAbdullāh's background in ᶜAlī, *Mufaṣṣal*, 9:209–210. For primary sources on ᶜAbdullāh as one of the major chiefs of al-Khazraj, see Khalīfa, *Taʾrīkh*, 114; Ibn Qutayba, *Maᶜārif*, 1:159; Fasawī, *Maᶜrifa*, 2:428; Balādhurī, *Ansāb*, 1:274; Masᶜūdī, *Tanbīh*, 1:211; Maqdisī, *Badʾ*, 4:200. For ᶜUbāda, see Ibn Saᶜd, *Ṭabaqāt*, 3:412; Khalīfa, *Taʾrīkh*, 66; Ibn Hishām, *Sīra*, 1:431; Ibn Qutayba, *Maᶜārif*, 1:255; Fasawī, *Maᶜrifa*, 1:316; Maqdisī, *Badʾ*, 4:166; Ibn al-Athīr, *Usd*, 3:158–159; Ibn al-Athīr, *Kāmil*, 2:30; Dhahabī, *Taʾrīkh*, 2:147; Dhahabī, *Siyar*, 2:5–10; Ibn ᶜAbd al-Barr, *Istīᶜāb*, 2:807–809; Ibn ᶜAsākir, *Taʾrīkh*, 26:175–207; Ṣafadī, *Wāfī*, 16:353; Ibn Ḥajar, *Iṣāba*, 3:505–506.

reportedly allied with al-Khazraj.[37] From the standpoint of a tribal alliance, ᶜAbdullāh and ᶜUbāda, as members of al-Khazraj, should have defended the Jews against mistreatment and expulsion; however, these two men were now Muslims, presumably adhering primarily to Islam and submitting to Muhammad's commands. The Muslim tradition highlights that ᶜAbdullāh opposed Muhammad and desired to treat the Jews kindly, while ᶜUbāda declared he was not bound anymore to any agreement with the Jews. When ᶜAbdullāh saw the misery of the Jews of Banū Qaynuqāᶜ after they surrendered, he reportedly spoke to Muhammad on their behalf: "Muhammad, deal kindly with my *mawālī* (clients), because they are the allies of al-Khazraj."[38] Knowing that ᶜAbdullāh was a major chief of al-Khazraj, this request was legitimate and reasonable from a tribal standpoint, but it reportedly made Muhammad furious.

According to Muslim accounts, Muhammad initially did not answer ᶜAbdullāh, putting him off for a while, until ᶜAbdullāh put his hand into Muhammad's collar and begged, "Treat my *mawālī* well," to which Muhammad "was so angry that his face became almost black."[39] "Damn you," Muhammad shouted, "let me go." "No, by God," ᶜAbdullāh responded, "I will not let you go until you treat my *mawālī* well."[40] These literary details reflect a designed image, created by classical historians to portray ᶜAbdullāh negatively, in opposition to Muhammad's desires and instructions. This is evidenced in how ᶜAbdullāh was repeatedly identified in the traditions as a *munāfiq* (hypocrite, or lukewarm believer), as we discussed in the accounts of the Battle of Uḥud in chapter 3. Still, there is a critical observation on ᶜAbdullāh's portrayal in the traditions: If we were to accept the general outline of the dispute between Muhammad and ᶜAbdullāh, it is plausible to deduce that Muhammad's new status—as the highest leader in Medina—threatened the status and the stature of ᶜAbdullāh, who resided there all his life and until less than two years earlier was known and acknowledged as a chief leader in Medina.[41] A few months earlier, the story suggests, ᶜAbdullāh's

[37] See Ibn Hishām, *Life*, 253, 363; Ibn Hishām, *Sīra*, 1:540. See also ᶜAlī, *Mufaṣṣal*, 12:109; Djait, *Masīrat*, 115. In a Shīᶜite report, from a tribal alliance perspective, the Medinan Jews were weakened after al-Aws and al-Khazraj entered Islam. See Majlisī, *Biḥār*, 20:167.

[38] Ibn Hishām, *Sīra*, 1:540; Ibn Hishām, *Life*, 363. Ṭabarī, *Ta'rīkh*, 1361; Ṭabarī, *History*, 7:86.

[39] Ibn Hishām, *Life*, 363. According to al-Ṭabarī, Muhammad "was so angry that they could see shadows in his face (that is, his face colored)." Ṭabarī, *History*, 7:86.

[40] The reasoning of ᶜAbdullāh reportedly appears in his statement to Muhammad: "Four hundred men without armour and three hundred with coats of mail, who defended me from the Arab and the non-Arab alike, and you would mow them down in a single morning?" Ṭabarī, *History*, 7:86.

[41] See the comments of Watt, *Muḥammad*, 15.

word was heeded and opinion respected. With Muhammad's arrival in Medina, we are invited to believe, all power and status were given to him, and men like ᶜAbdullāh were marginalized. While this line of thought may explain the reported enmity between Muhammad and ᶜAbdullāh, the fact is that, critically speaking, this line of thought is hard to believe and it exposes the exaggerated Muslim accounts. To believe these accounts, we must accept that a vulnerable Muhammad—who was severely persecuted for thirteen years in Mecca—had successfully emigrated from his hometown to Medina and, in less than two years, managed to control major Arab tribes, convince their chiefs to submit to his leadership, lead dozens of raids, suppress a well-established Jewish tribe that excelled in armorers, and assassinate those who insulted him, among other things. The hyperbolic nature of these traditions cannot be overstated.

In contrast to ᶜAbdullāh, the Muslim tradition brings another Muslim, ᶜUbāda, to the scene. Unlike ᶜAbdullāh, ᶜUbāda reportedly went to Muhammad and "renounced all responsibility for [the Jews]" for the sake of Allah and Muhammad, and said, "O Allah's apostle, I take Allah and his messenger and the believers as my allies, and I renounce my agreement and friendship with these *kuffār* (infidels)."[42] ᶜUbāda, thus, agreed with Muhammad's treatment of the Jews and revoked his earlier alliance with them. This literary comparison between ᶜAbdullāh and ᶜUbāda is better viewed as a parable—as compared to a record of actual events—designed by Muslim historians for religious and political purposes. One point of the comparison is clear: ᶜUbāda is a better Muslim than ᶜAbdullāh—the reader is invited to believe—because loyalty to Islam surpasses tribal loyalties, and commitment to Muhammad and Allah replaces previous commitments.[43] The ᶜAbdullāh-ᶜUbāda contrast is further emphasized, as the tradition highlights that Muhammad entrusted ᶜUbāda to take charge of expelling the Jews from Medina all the way to regions in Syria, where they soon perished.[44] If Muhammad entrusted ᶜUbāda, the logic of the fiction goes, he is an example of a praiseworthy Muslim after Muhammad's own heart.[45] Furthermore, the contrast is overamplified by claiming that Allah revealed verses of the Qur'ān to respond to ᶜAbdullāh and ᶜUbāda. We are told that Allah revealed, "O you who have believed, take

[42] Ibn Hishām, *Sīra*, 2:49. Ibn Hishām, *Life*, 363.

[43] After all, Muhammad is reported to have once declared that *maḥā al-islām al-ᶜuhūd* (Islam erased the [previous] treaties). See Ṭabarī, *Ta'rīkh*, 1450; Ṭabarī, *History*, 7:158, where it is rendered "Islam has wiped out the old covenants." See Ibrahim, *Stated*, 89.

[44] See Ṭabarī, *History*, 7:87. Cf. Ibn al-Athīr, *Kāmil*, 2:30.

[45] For a Sunnī praise of ᶜUbāda, see Ṣallābī, *Sīra*, 457–458.

not the Jews and the Christians as allies" (Q 5:51), to instruct the Muslims in this situation—clearly commending ᶜUbāda and chastising ᶜAbdullāh.[46] In fact, Ibn Hishām designates a specific section to detail verses revealed on that occasion.[47] Not only do these reported verses suggest that classical historians often formed historiographical reports as exegetical accounts; they also indicate how the religious instruction of the fiction receives more weight when accompanied by assumed divine approval.

But there is more to say concerning the literary comparison between ᶜAbdullāh and ᶜUbāda. The glaring contrast between the two Muslims seems to drive another theological instruction: Follow the example of ᶜUbāda, do not trust the Jews under your rule, and treat them harshly.[48] This theological message arguably suited medieval times when Muslims ruled over the Jews in conquered lands. By creating anti-Jewish traditions, centered on narratives of dedication and devotion to Muhammad, classical historians advanced polemical rhetoric against the conquered Jews. Moreover, these classical historians clearly did not find their portrayal of Muhammad offensive. They designed a specific image for Muhammad, suitable for their time, portraying him as strong, unyielding, superior, and, to some extent, harsh and unforgiving with his enemies—either the hypocrite Jews or lukewarm Muslims. This "Muhammad," as a literary image, appealed to religious and sociopolitical medieval contexts. Indeed, as I often argue, Muslim historiographical accounts are fashioned in a way to respond to the necessities of their time of documentation.[49]

In the same vein, classical historians, in their *representation* of the raid against Banū Qaynuqāᶜ, report other anti-Jewish tales surrounding this military activity. We are told that there were three calculated assassinations to eliminate specific Jews who are identified as enemies of Muhammad. These assassinations are portrayed as *sarāyā* (incursions)—military activities Muhammad commissioned: one to get rid of a woman named ᶜAṣmā' bint

[46] Dhahabī, *Ta'rīkh*, 2:147.

[47] Ibn Hishām, *Sīra*, 2:49–50. See also Ṭabarī, *Ta'rīkh*, 1360; Ṭabarī, *History*, 7:86, where he reports that *surāt al-Anfāl* (Q 8:58) was revealed to correspond to that situation. For a Sunnī study on the list of verses presumably revealed in this situation, see Ṣallābī, *Sīra*, 458–459.

[48] This seems to correspond with two verses in the Quran, "O Prophet, *jāhid* (wage jihad) against the unbelievers and the hypocrites and be harsh upon them. Their refuge is hellfire, and wretched is the destiny" (Q 9:73; 66:9).

[49] On inventing historiographical reports, see Robinson, *Historiography*, 12, where he writes, "The answers were given [by Muslim historians] because belief now required them." See also Kennedy, *Prophet*, 348, 355; Rosenthal, *Historiography*, 29, 84, 166; Abū Rayya, *Aḍwā'*, 85–92; ᶜAbd al-Raḥmān, *Judhūr*, 7–9; ᶜAlawī, *Maḥaṭṭāt*, 19–20.

Marwān, another to murder an older Jew named Abū ᶜAfak, and a third to eliminate a notable Jew named Kaᶜb ibn al-Ashraf.[50] In the traditions, there is no dispute about Abū ᶜAfak and Kaᶜb ibn al-Ashraf being Jews, but reports about ᶜAṣmā' are contradictory, although several accounts identify her as a Jewess.[51] ᶜAṣmā' bint Marwān and Abū ᶜAfak were reportedly killed before the raid against Banū Qaynuqāᶜ, and Kaᶜb ibn al-Ashraf after it. These three individuals are painted as having envied the victory of the Muslims at Badr and harshly insulted Muhammad, which led to their deaths. Their killing—as a literary theme—serves the same goals as the portrayal of the raid against Banū Qaynuqāᶜ.

Shortly after the Muslims' victory at Badr, ᶜAṣmā' reportedly "insulted the Prophet, vilified Islam and incited the people against the Prophet with poetry."[52] As for Abū ᶜAfak, "He was an old man who had reached one hundred and twenty years when the Prophet arrived in Medina. He provoked the enmity of the Prophet and did not enter Islam."[53] In response to ᶜAṣmā', Muhammad said to his companions, "Who will rid me of [her]?"[54] A Muslim named ᶜUmayr reportedly hastened and on that very night "went to her house and killed her."[55] ᶜUmayr "placed his sword upon her heart and pierced her until it came out from behind her. Then he returned to pray the dawn prayer with the Prophet in Medina."[56] In a literary detail to magnify his heroic deed, we are invited to believe that ᶜUmayr was blind.[57] When Muhammad heard the news of killing ᶜAṣmā', he praised ᶜUmayr and said,

50 See Wāqidī, *Maghāzī*, 172–193; Wāqidī, *Life*, 85–96. Other Jews were reportedly targeted by the Muslims, such as al-Yusayr ibn Rizām and Sallām ibn Abī al-Ḥuqayq, but they are not connected to the raid against Banū Qaynuqāᶜ. See Ibn Hishām, *Sīra*, 2:618 (for al-Yusayr) and 2:191 (on Sallām). Unlike al-Wāqidī, Ibn Hishām places the murder of Abū ᶜAfak before ᶜAṣmā'. See Ibn Hishām, *Sīra*, 2:636; Ibn Hishām, *Life*, 675. For a recent study on the assassinations of Muhammad's antagonists, see Roohi, "Between," 425–472, where he concludes, "Our accounts exhibit striking resemblances with one another in both form and content, a point seriously undermining the trustworthiness of the *sīra* as a straightforward source for reconstructing the Prophet's life."

51 For ᶜAṣmā' as a Jewess, see Ibn al-Athīr, *Usd*, 4:325; Ibn Ḥajar, *Iṣāba*, 5:264; Ḥalabī, *Insān*, 3:222; Taymiyya, *Ṣārim*, 1:97. It appears that medieval Muslim authors referred to her as Jewish whenever it suited their religio-political aims in writing. For the competing reports, see Abū Māyla, *Sarāyā*, 132–139. See the Muslim study of Jamīl, *Nabī*, 101–106, where she is considered a Jewess.

52 Wāqidī, *Life*, 85; Wāqidī, *Maghāzī*, 172.

53 Wāqidī, *Life*, 86; Wāqidī, *Maghāzī*, 174.

54 Ibn Hishām, *Life*, 676.

55 Ibn Hishām, *Life*, 676. On ᶜUmayr, see Ibn Saᶜd, *Ṭabaqāt*, 2:20–21; Ibn Ḥibbān, *Thiqāt*, 1:208; Abū Nuᶜaym, *Maᶜrifat*, 4:2096; Ibn ᶜAbd al-Barr, *Istīᶜāb*, 3:1217; Dhahabī, *Siyar*, *sīra* 1:370; Ṣafadī, *Wāfī*, 1:75; Ibn Ḥajar, *Iṣāba*, 4:398–399.

56 Wāqidī, *Life*, 86. The image painted by classical historians is even more graphic, as we are also told that when ᶜUmayr entered the home, ᶜAṣmā' had her children "sleeping around her, and one suckled at her breast" (86). The image is that ᶜUmayr never hesitated to get rid of her.

57 Ibn Saᶜd, *Ṭabaqāt*, 2:20; Abū Nuᶜaym, *Maᶜrifat*, 4:2096; Ibn Hajar, *Iṣāba*, 4:599.

"You have helped Allah and his apostle."[58] The fate of the Jew Abū ᶜAfak was similar to that of ᶜAṣmā'. Envious of Muhammad's victory at Badr, Abū ᶜAfak reportedly insulted him in a poem. In response, Muhammad asked the Muslims, "Who will deal with this *khabīth* (vicious, malevolent man) for me?"[59] In response, a Muslim named Sālim vowed to kill Abū ᶜAfak, "waited for a heedless moment," and killed him.[60]

Many religious enthusiasts treat the narratives of the killing of ᶜAṣmā' and Abū ᶜAfak as factual; consequently, the reports become theologically prescriptive and arguably drive negative anti-Jewish perspectives.[61] Contemporary Sunnī scholar Birayk Abū Māyla views the story of ᶜAṣmā' as a true record that shows love and dedication to Muhammad and that anyone who insults him must be killed.[62] Some medieval thinkers used these stories as a warning against offending Muhammad.[63] When taken literally, these narratives do not, at face value, advance positive notions about the Jews; moreover, if viewed as prescriptive, they could lead to religious intolerance.[64] From a critical standpoint, the storytellers seem to have designed the accounts of ᶜAṣmā' and Abū ᶜAfak as a theological exhortation to Muslims to emulate the examples of ᶜUmayr and Sālim. Undoubtedly, the narrators labeled these assassinations as *sarāyā* (incursions), to form a

[58] Ibn Hishām, *Life*, 676.

[59] Ibn Hishām, *Sīra*, 2:636. Ibn Hishām, *Life*, 675.

[60] Wāqidī, *Life*, 87; Wāqidī, *Maghāzī*, 175. Ibn Hishām, *Sīra*, 2:636. Ibn Hishām, *Life*, 675. On Sālim, see Ibn Saᶜd, *Ṭabaqāt*, 2:21; Ibn Ḥibbān, *Thiqāt*, 3:158; Ibn Manda, *Maᶜrifat*, 1:720; Abū Nuᶜaym, *Maᶜrifat*, 3:1366; Ibn ᶜAbd al-Barr, *Istīᶜāb*, 2:576; Ibn al-Athīr, *Usd*, 2:387; Dhahabī, *Siyar*, *sīra* 1:371; Ṣafadī, *Wāfī*, 1:75; Ibn Ḥajar, *Iṣāba*, 3:8–9. For a Muslim study on Abū ᶜAfak, see Jamīl, *Nabī*, 106–108.

[61] For some Muslim scholars who treat these tales as factual, see Ṣallābī, *Sīra*, 458–459; Abū Māyla, *Sarāyā*, 129–139; Mubārakpūrī, *Raḥīq*, 1:219–222. For Muslims who attempt to historicize the narratives, see Akyol, *Islam*, 58–59; Akyol, *Reopening*, 157–180, 231–234; Abou El Fadl, "Place of Tolerance," 3–26. See also Abou El Fadl's critique of what he identifies as the "unreasonable interpretations" in Abou El Fadl, *Speaking*, ch. 4. See the valuable conclusion of Shoemaker, *Apocalypse*, 182–183.

[62] Abū Māyla, *Sarāyā*, 137.

[63] See Ibn Taymiyya, *Ṣārim*, 1:95–97 (on ᶜAṣmā') and 1:104–105 (on Abū ᶜAfak), where he uses the narratives to argue for defending Muhammad by killing the insulters. Ibn Taymiyya insists that if a Muslim or non-Muslim insults Muhammad, the religious penalty for that individual is death without any possibility of repentance. Ibn Taymiyya, *Ṣārim*, 1:300. It appears that, for Ibn Taymiyya, insulting Allah followed by repentance can be forgiven, but insulting Muhammad earns the death penalty with no question. Cf. Ibn Taymiyya, *Ṣārim*, 1:546. See also Ibn Qayyim, *Aḥkām*, 3:1414–1445; Ibn Qayyim, *Zād*, 3:362; ᶜIyāḍ ibn Mūsā, *Shifā*, 2:215–216; Khaṭṭāb, *Rasūl*, 151. On the Muslim penalty for insulting Muhammad, Friedmann, *Tolerance*, 149–152.

[64] This is why modernist Muslim readings often aim to reinterpret these narratives, arguing they have no bearing on later times. See Akyol, *Islam*, 58–59; Akyol, *Reopening*, 157–180, 231–234; Fadel, "Is Historicism," 131–176.

religious disposition of Islam's preeminence in general and against insulting Muhammad in particular.

As with ᶜAṣmā' and Abū ᶜAfak, the tradition reports the assassination of the Jew Kaᶜb ibn al-Ashraf, albeit in more detail. Kaᶜb is depicted as one of the most jealous, resentful, and hostile Jews against Muhammad and Muslims.[65] He is a Jew, because his mother belonged to the Jewish tribe of Banū al-Naḍīr, although his father was an Arab from Banū Ṭayyi'.[66] Arguably, Kaᶜb ibn al-Ashraf, as a literary figure, serves as a link between the raid against Banū Qaynuqāᶜ and the following raid against the second major Medinan Jewish tribe, Banū al-Naḍīr. His assassination allegedly occurred between the two raids.[67] The tradition claims that Kaᶜb was a famous poet among the Arabs—a lax, indulgent, and wealthy man, who was famous for his *jamāl* (physical beauty) in Medina.[68]

The literary plot to assassinate Kaᶜb has various turns: He was reportedly envious of the Muslims' victory at Badr and, in particular, angry about the killing of the notables of the Quraysh.[69] He reportedly traveled all the way to Mecca to praise Muhammad's enemies, the Quraysh, and to incite them against the Muslims.[70] At Mecca, Kaᶜb began reciting poems, arousing the Quraysh's anger against the Muslims, fueling their hatred toward Muhammad, and stirring them to wage war against him. In response to his poems, some Muslims began reciting satirical poems, mocking him and his Meccan hosts, thus forcing him to return to Medina.[71] At Medina,

[65] Wāqidī, *Life*, 91–96; Wāqidī, *Maghāzī*, 184–193; Ibn Hishām, *Sīra*, 2:51–54; Ibn Hishām, *Life*, 364–369; Ṭabarī, *Ta'rīkh*, 1368–1373; Ṭabarī, *History*, 7:94–98; Bayhaqī, *Dalā'il*, 3:195; Dhahabī, *Ta'rīkh*, 2:157–161. For a Muslim study on Kaᶜb, see Jamīl, *Nabī*, 108–120.

[66] Ṭabarī, *Ta'rīkh*, 1368; Ṭabarī, *History*, 7:94. For a contemporary Sunnī study on Kaᶜb, see Abū Māyla, *Sarāyā*, 139–152.

[67] In a Shīᶜite tradition, Kaᶜb was alive and active in his treachery against Muhammad during the raid against Banū al-Naḍīr—Kaᶜb was only killed when Gabriel instructed Muhammad to kill him. See Majlisī, *Biḥār*, 20:158, 163, 173.

[68] See Ibn Ḥabīb, *Muḥabbar*, 117, 282, 390. Watt, *Muḥammad*, 210–211; Hamidullah, *Battlefields*, 205, 242; Mubārakpūrī, *Raḥīq*, 219–220. For contemporary studies of Kaᶜb, see Ṣallābī, *Sīra*, 459–467; ᶜUmarī, *Sīra*, 302–304. Most traditionists label the incident *sarriyat qatl* (the incursion of murdering) Kaᶜb. See Ibn Saᶜd, *Ṭabaqāt*, 2:24, 3:338; Ibn ᶜAsākir, *Ta'rīkh*, 55:261; Ibn Sayyid al-Nās, *ᶜUyūn*, 1:384. Some refer to it by its leader, Muḥammad ibn Salma. See Ḥalabī, *Insān*, 3:227, 3:522. A group of traditionists refers to this military mission as *sariyya ilā* (an incursion against or toward) Kaᶜb. See Ṭabarī, *Ta'rīkh*, 1368; Ṭabarī, *History*, 7:94; Masᶜūdī, *Tanbīh*, 1:209; Maqdisī, *Bad'*, 4:197; Jawzī, *Muntaẓim*, 3:158.

[69] The similarities between the traditions of ᶜAṣmā', Abū ᶜAfak, and Kaᶜb are glaring and suggest tendentiousness and that historians seem to have forged history rather than documenting it. Robinson, *Historiography*, 38. Crone, *Meccan*, 230.

[70] See Wāqidī, *Life*, 91, where he summarizes the situation: "Ibn al-Ashraf was a poet who had insulted the Prophet and his companions with his poetry, and incited the disbelieving Quraysh against them."

[71] Wāqidī, *Maghāzī*, 186; Wāqidī, *Life*, 92. Ibn Hishām, *Sīra*, 2:52.

Kaᶜb continued to mock Muhammad and the companions, to the extent that he "composed love poetry on some of the women of the Muslims, causing them offence."[72] His portrayal highlights a viciously anti-Muslim character. To stop Kaᶜb's offense, we are told, Muhammad asked the Muslims, "Who will rid me of Ibn al-Ashraf?"[73] In response, a group of five men plotted to kill Kaᶜb, by misleading him into leaving his house in the middle of the night. They succeeded in executing him brutally, by beheading him.[74] They reportedly "brought Ibn al-Ashraf's head to [Muhammad]."[75] The five men, we are told, were all from the Medinan tribe al-Aws—one of two major tribes of the *anṣār*.[76] To add literary embellishments of religious zeal and devotion to Muhammad, storytellers claim two of these five men were Kaᶜb's own milk-brothers.[77] This is one reason Kaᶜb believed them as they deceived him through sweet talk. While the killing report suggests treachery, betrayal, and deception, traditional Muslim interpretations emphasize Kaᶜb as an evil Jew, a violator of a treaty who deserved death.[78]

Like the accounts of ᶜAṣmā' and Abū ᶜAfak, Kaᶜb's tale is better treated as a theological homily, clearly serving as a warning for non-Muslims, especially Jews, against offending Islam's prophet.[79] This is evidenced in a report of how the Jews were intimidated after Kaᶜb's assassination: "The Jews became fearful. Not one of their leaders ventured out. They did not speak for they feared they would be sought out in their homes just as Ibn al-Ashraf

[72] Ṭabarī, *History*, 7:95. Ibn Hishām, *Life*, 367.

[73] Ṭabarī, *History*, 7:95. See also Bukhārī, *Ṣaḥīḥ*, 5:90–91; Muslim, *Ṣaḥīḥ*, 3:1425, where the tradition claims that Muhammad asked, "Who is ready to kill Kaᶜb ibn al-Ashraf who has *ādhā* (really harmed) Allah and his apostle?" Some traditions add that Muhammad said that Kaᶜb—through his poems—had strengthened the unbelievers over the believers. See Bayhaqī, *Dalā'il*, 3:195; Dhahabī, *Ta'rīkh*, 2:157–161.

[74] Muslim historians report that which Kaᶜb's wife told him in their private room, discouraging him from going to meet the Muslims: "Surely you are a fighting man and such a man does not go out at this hour?" Wāqidī, *Life*, 94; Ibn Hishām, *Sīra*, 2:56. The account is clearly fictional. On the date of the incursion, see Wāqidī, *Life*, 91, where he writes that Kaᶜb was killed in the twenty-fifth month after the *hijra*—only four or five months after the raid to Banū Qaynuqāᶜ, which reportedly occurred in the twentieth month after the *hijra* (cf. Wāqidī, *Life*, 87).

[75] Ṭabarī, *History*, 7:98. Ṭabarī, *Ta'rīkh*, 1373. Wāqidī, *Maghāzī*, 190; Wāqidī, *Life*, 94.

[76] Their leader was reportedly Muḥammad ibn Maslama, and thus the *sariyya* is named after him. See Ḥalabī, *Insān*, 3:227, 3:522.

[77] Ṭabarī, *Ta'rīkh*, 1368–1372. Watt, *Muḥammad*, 210. Rodinson, *Muhammad*, 176–177.

[78] Abū Māyla, *Sarāyā*, 147; ᶜUmarī, *Sīra*, 304; ᶜUmarī, *Mujtamaᶜ*, 142–143. Interestingly, a Sunnī tradition suggests that Muᶜāwiya viewed Kaᶜb's murder as *ghadran* (treachery). See Bayhaqī, *Dalā'il*, 3:193. For a classical claim justifying the act of deceiving Kaᶜb, see Ibn Qayyim, *Zād*, 3:171.

[79] For Muslim jurists who used Kaᶜb's story to derive juristic rulings, especially on non-Muslims insulting Muhammad, see Ibn Qayyim, *Aḥkām*, 3:1414–1445. See the recent study by Roohi, "Murder," 1–20, where he examines various accounts of assassinating Kaᶜb, and argues that the story presents "seriously distorted material with logical absurdities and discrepancies that cannot easily be reconciled."

was."[80] And to the Muslims, Kaᶜb's tale appears to drive an exhortation: Strive to the end in defending Muhammad and Islam. This exhortation is hard to miss, as it is evidenced in two important literary details. First, we are told, on the morning following Kaᶜb's assassination, Muhammad instructed the Muslims, "Whoever of the Jews falls into your hands, kill him"—in response, the Muslim Muḥayyiṣa killed the Jew Ibn Sunayna.[81] The literary statement aims to encourage Muslims to follow course, and weighs greatly for those who believe it as a prophetic factual statement.[82] Second, since the Muslim group that killed Kaᶜb were all from the tribe of al-Aws, we are invited to believe that their rivals, the tribe of al-Khazraj, were jealous and sought to show similar dedication to Muhammad by killing another Jew. The tribe reportedly succeeded and killed the Jew Sallām ibn Abī al-Ḥuqayq.[83] The targeting of the Jews—as these accounts suggest—becomes a testimony of religious zeal and devotion. The narrators seem to have shaped a particular religious disposition to their Muslim audience: all praiseworthy believers should strive to show devotion to Muhammad and defend him against wicked Jews.

But there is also the intertwining of the Qur'ān into the historiographical account of Kaᶜb's assassination. Muslim traditionists describe Allah as a major actor in the matter. We are told that, because of Kaᶜb's desire to support the pagans of Mecca and their false deities, Allah revealed *sūrat al-Nisā'* (Q 4:51), to point to Jews who—despite receiving the Scriptures—identified the *kuffār* (unbelieving infidels) as "better guided than the believers."[84] Here, once again, we encounter an example of how historiographers shape the historical narratives to exegete verses from the Qur'ān. The verse of the Qur'ān—which arguably does not directly reveal a context—becomes abundantly clear by a fashioned narrative, exegeting the verse's meaning and placing it in a sacred religious history. The literary detail of Allah revealing a verse to address Kaᶜb's situation places Kaᶜb in a dark light and, in turn, suggests that Jews are generally untrustworthy.[85]

[80] Wāqidī, *Life*, 95; Wāqidī, *Maghāzī*, 191.

[81] Ṭabarī, *History*, 7:97; Ṭabarī, *Ta'rīkh*, 1372. The tradition is repeated in many sources. See Ibn Hishām, *Life*, 369; Ibn Hishām, *Sīra*, 2:58; Wāqidī, *Maghāzī*, 191; Wāqidī, *Life*, 95; Bayhaqī, *Dalā'il*, 3:200; Suhaylī, *Rawḍ*, 5:292; Kalāᶜī, *Iktifā'*, 1:369; Ibn Sayyid al-Nās, *ᶜUyūn*, 1:353; Ibn Kathīr, *Sīra*, 3:15.

[82] Abū Māyla, *Sarāyā*, 150.

[83] For how al-Khazraj attempted to imitate al-Aws after the latter killed for Muhammad, see Ibn Ḥibbān, *Sīra*, 1:239–240; Ḥalabī, *Insān*, 3:227, 3:522. For Sallām's murder, see Wāqidī, *Maghāzī*, 392; Ibn Hishām, *Sīra*, 2:273–274; Bayhaqī, *Dalā'il*, 4:33–38; Suhaylī, *Rawḍ*, 5:290; Kalāᶜī, *Iktifā'*, 1:444–445; Ibn Sayyid al-Nās, *ᶜUyūn*, 2:114. See Watt, *Muḥammad*, 213.

[84] Ṭabarī, *Tafsīr*, 8:464–465.

[85] For Muslim exegetes using Kaᶜb's tradition in connection to Q 4:51, see Muqātil, *Tafsīr*, 1:397; Ṭabarī, *Jāmiᶜ*, 8:462–470; Thaᶜlabī, *Kashf*, 3:327–328; Zamakhsharī, *Kashshāf*, 1:521; Rāzī, *Mafātiḥ*,

Kaᶜb's narrative smoothly links two Medinan Jewish tribes and their fates at the hands of the Muslims. As a literary tale, Kaᶜb's assassination is designed to reflect an escalation against the Jews of Medina. After the Muslim raid against the Jews of Banū Qaynuqāᶜ, the elimination of Kaᶜb is reported and his background as being from the Jewish tribe of Banū al-Naḍīr is established as an important literary detail. Soon after his assassination, the Muslims reportedly launched a raid against his tribe, Banū al-Naḍīr, thus expelling them from Medina. We now turn to this raid.

The Raid against Banū al-Naḍīr (4/625)

After the reported murder of Kaᶜb, the Muslim tradition continues to represent the Jews as a threat—a consolidated religious group unable to accept Muhammad's prophethood. We are told that their presence at Medina with their holy book and their resistance to Islam create significant disharmony, where Muhammad is supposedly the sole leader.[86] As they remain in their unbelief, insult Muhammad, and criticize the Muslims, the traditions convey a growing enmity and hostility between the two religious groups.[87] A little over a year after the expulsion of the Jews of Banū Qaynuqāᶜ, *most* traditions emphasize, "The Prophet *ajlā* (expelled) the Banū al-Naḍīr from their homes."[88] According to this dating, expelling the tribe of Banū al-Naḍīr from Medina occurred in the fourth *hijrī* year (ca. May 625)—*after* the Muslim defeat at the Battle of Uḥud in A.H. 3 (ca. March 625). However, some earlier traditions provide a significantly contradictory dating, placing it over a year

10:101; Qurṭubī, *Jāmiᶜ*, 5:248; Riḍā, *Manār*, 5:126–128; Shaᶜrāwī, *Khawāṭirī*, 4:2314–2315. See Roohi, "Murder," 1–20, where he studies accounts of assassinating Kaᶜb and argues that "our reports have been doctored for political reasons."

86 According to Majlisī, *Biḥār*, 20:160, the reason for expelling Banū al-Naḍīr and other Jews from Medina is the Muslim ruling to have no religion other than Islam in the Arabian Peninsula. This echoes a tradition attributed to Muhammad, "I will surely expel the Jews and Christians from the Arabian Peninsula, until I will leave none but Muslim." Muslim, *Ṣaḥīḥ*, 3:1388; ᶜAbd al-Razzāq, *Muṣannaf*, 6:54, 10:358; Ibn Ḥanbal, *Musnad*, 1:329, 1:341–343; Ibn Zanjawayh, *Amwāl*, 1:275; Ḥākim, *Mustadrak*, 4:305. See Margoliouth, *Mohammedanism*, 56–57.

87 For religious roots of the enmity between Muhammad and the Jews, see the observations of two modern Muslim scholars: Qimanī, *Ḥurūb*, 2:243, and Djait, *Masīrat*, 113–116. Cf. Rodinson, *Muhammad*, 192–193.

88 Ṭabarī, *Ta'rīkh*, 1448. The entire account of Banū al-Naḍīr covers 1448–1453. Cf. Ṭabarī, *History*, 7:156. For the history of Banū al-Naḍīr and their expulsion, see Wolfensohn, *Ta'rīkh*, 110–132.

earlier, precisely after Badr and before Uḥud.[89] This contradiction is significant enough to examine.

There are two groups of historiographical traditions: a minority that dates the expulsion of Banū al-Naḍīr to the third year after the *hijra*, particularly six months after Badr but clearly before Uḥud, and a majority that claims it occurred over a year later, in the early months of the fourth year.[90] The two groups can roughly be identified as pre-ᶜAbbāsid and ᶜAbbāsid, respectively. The minority group relies on a presumably early report attributed to Umayyad-era (pre-ᶜAbbāsid) traditionist Ibn Shihāb al-Zuhrī (d. 124/742),[91] while the majority group largely adopts the dating claimed by ᶜAbbāsid-era historians, including al-Wāqidī (d. ca. 207/823) and Ibn Hishām (d. 218/833)—a dating that was eventually crystalized and circulated as historiographical orthodoxy after al-Ṭabarī (d. 310/923) adopted it.[92] This

[89] For a scholarly discussion on the contradictions concerning the date of the raid, see ᶜUmarī, *Sīra*, 304–306. An early tradition, attributed to al-Zuhrī and his teacher ᶜUrwa, alleges that the raid occurred only six months after Badr, clearly claiming it preceded Uḥud. See Zuhrī, *Maghāzī*, 71; Maᶜmar, *Expeditions*, 41. See also the same report in ᶜAbd al-Razzāq, *Tafsīr*, 3:296; Ibn Zanjawayh, *Amwāl*, 91–93. For a high view of al-Zuhrī and ᶜUrwa as traditionists, see Suyūṭī, *Ṭabaqāt*, 30, 49–50, 62, et passim. However, see Ibn Qayyim, *Zād*, 3:223, where he dismisses al-Zuhrī's early date of the raid, calling him "erroneous" or "delusional" (*wahmun minhu aw ghalaṭun ᶜalayhi*).

[90] See Ibn Qayyim, *Zād*, 3:223, where he argues that Muhammad had four major raids against the Jews: Qaynuqāᶜ after Badr, Naḍīr after Uḥud, Qurayẓa after al-Khandaq, and Khaybar after al-Ḥudaybiyya. See Bayhaqī, *Dalā'il*, 3:176–180, where he provides three possible dates. He seems to agree with al-Zuhrī on the early date, although he also asserts that Mūsā ibn ᶜUqba and Ibn Isḥāq date it after Uḥud. For Mūsā ibn ᶜUqba, his life, works, and their textual problems, see Ibrahim, *Conversion*, 49–55.

[91] See Zuhrī, *Maghāzī*, 71; Maᶜmar, *Expeditions*, 41; ᶜAbd al-Razzāq, *Muṣannaf*, 5:358; Mūsā, *Maghāzī*, 210–212. For a study on Zuhrī's *Maghazī* and its textual problems, see Ibrahim, *Conversion*, 41–49, where I explain how his *maghāzī* reports were reportedly documented by ᶜAbd al-Razzāq al-Ṣanᶜānī (d. 211/827) who heard them as a narration from his Baṣran teacher, Maᶜmar ibn Rāshid (d. 153/770), who was a dedicated student of al-Zuhrī. See also Schoeler, *Biography*, 25, where he argues that ᶜAbd al-Razzāq gained his *maghāzī* reports from his teacher Maᶜmar, who, in turn, had obtained "roughly half of his traditions from his teacher az-Zuhrī." On ᶜAbd al-Razzāq al-Ṣanᶜānī's *Muṣannaf*, see the important study of Motzki, "Muṣannaf," 1–21, where he views the value of this early source positively and writes, "We are now able to raise the question of the historical value of the *hadīth* texts anew" (21). On al-Zuhrī, see ᶜIjlī, *Ta'rīkh*, 412; Ibn Abī Ḥātim, *Jarḥ*, 8:71ff.; Fasawī, *Maᶜrifa*, 1:639; Harawī, *Dhamm*, 3:3; Abū Zurᶜa, *Ta'rīkh*, 411; Ibn ᶜAsākir, *Ta'rīkh*, 55:294–388; Ibn Ḥabīb, *Muḥabbar*, 476. Dhahabī, *Siyar*, 5:326–350; Dhahabī, *Tadhkirat*, 1:83–85; Yāqūt, *Muᶜjam*, 3:1201–1204; Ibn al-Muᶜtazz, *Ṭabaqāt*, 69; Jumaḥī, *Ṭabaqāt*, 1:48. See also Ziriklī, *Aᶜlām*, 7:97; Sezgin, *Ta'rīkh*, 1:2:74–79. On Maᶜmar, see Ibn Saᶜd, *Ṭabaqāt*, 5:546, 7:361; Khalīfa, *Ṭabaqāt*, 1:520; ᶜIjlī, *Ta'rīkh*, 1:435; Ibn Abī Ḥātim, *Jarḥ*, 8:255; Ibn Ḥibbān, *Thiqāt*, 7:484; Ibn ᶜAsākir, *Ta'rīkh*, 59:390–422; Ibn Khallikān, *Wafayāt*, 3:216; Dhahabī, *Siyar*, 7:5ff.; Ibn Ḥajar, *Tahdhīb*, 10:243–246; also Ziriklī, *Aᶜlām*, 7:272; Kaḥḥāla, *Muᶜjam*, 12:309. See also Ibrahim, *Conversion*, 46 n. 65, where I argue, "If Maᶜmar was a devoted student of al-Zuhrī, it should be noted that he lived under the ᶜAbbāsids." Petersen views Maᶜmar as pro-ᶜAbbāsid. Petersen, *ᶜAlī*, 85. See also Motzki, *Analysing*, 4–11; Motzki, *Origins*, 27; Motzki, "Dating," 240; Motzki, "Muṣannaf," 3. Cf. Shoemaker, "In Search," 257–344.

[92] Al-Wāqidī (d. ca. 207/823), Ibn Hishām (d. 218/833), and Ibn Saᶜd (d. 230/844) claim it occurred in Rabīᶜ al-Awwal of the Islamic fourth year, thirty-seven months after the *hijra*. See Wāqidī, *Maghāzī*, 363; Ibn Hishām, *Sīra*, 2:190: Ibn Saᶜd, *Ṭabaqāt*, 2:43. See Yaᶜqūbī, *Ta'rīkh*, 2:49, where he dates the

contradiction reinforces our skepticism of the reliability of the sources and strengthens our conviction that classical Muslim historians *authored* history rather than recorded it. The accounts appear in disunity, and the reconstruction of a clear and coherent overall account of Islam's origins—in this case, the sequence of Muhammad's *maghāzī*—is impossible if we rely on the Arabic Muslim sources.

But there is more to the contradicting reports about the expelling of Banū al-Naḍīr. The accounts are not only inconsistent about the date of the event, but, more importantly, concerning major details of the raid and what initiated it. There are two competing scenarios with starkly different literary contents. While the pre-ᶜAbbāsid account of al-Zuhrī provides a portrayal for what caused the expulsion of Banū al-Naḍīr, his report is largely rejected and transformed to a different narrative under the ᶜAbbāsids. In al-Zuhrī's account, we are told that, six months after Badr, Muhammad's Meccan tribe, the Quraysh, conspired with the Medinan Jews to attack the Muslims. Instead of keeping their peace treaty with Muhammad, we are told, Banū al-Naḍīr "chose treachery."[93] They told Muhammad, "Come out to meet us with thirty of your companions, and we will come forth with thirty rabbis." Intending to harm Muhammad, they deceptively said, "If the rabbis believe in the truth of what you say and believe in you, then we shall all believe." Al-Zuhrī reports that Muhammad agreed and went to meet them. When they saw him with thirty Muslims, they wanted to isolate him: "Come forward with only three of your companions." Muhammad reportedly accepted and came forward with three of his men, not knowing that the "Jews had brought daggers and concealed them, for they wanted to assassinate [him]." A *nāṣiḥa* (faithful and honest) Jewess from Banū al-Naḍīr, we are told, sent to her brother, who converted earlier to Islam, and informed him "about the plans of al-Naḍīr to betray the Messenger of God." Her brother disclosed the matter to Muhammad, who hurriedly turned back. The next morning, Muhammad came "with several arrays of armed men and besieged them." He offered them a peace treaty,

raid four months after Uḥud. Ṭabarī, *Ta'rīkh*, 1448. On al-Ṭabarī's influence on historiography, see Ibrahim, *Conversion*, 3–4; Borrut, *Entre*, 103–107. Chase Robinson calls al-Ṭabarī's *Ta'rīkh* "the definitive record of the first three centuries of Islam," "the *ne plus ultra* of Islamic historical writing," and concludes that "in several respects, al-Tabari can be said to mark the end of the beginning of Islamic historiography." Robinson, "Islamic," in *Oxford*, ed. Foot and Robinson, 239–240. See also Robinson, "Local," 521–536; Dūrī, *Baḥth*, 154; Dūrī, *Rise*, 159; Khalidi, *Arabic*, 73–74; Shoshan, *Poetics*, 109ff.

[93] See Zuhrī, *Maghāzī*, 71–74; ᶜAbd al-Razzāq, *Muṣannaf*, 5:357–538. All quotes in this paragraph are from Maᶜmar, *Expeditions*, 68–71.

but they refused, "so he and the Muslims fought against them that very day."[94] The next day, Muhammad reportedly headed back to Banū al-Naḍīr: He "fought them and eventually they surrendered, agreeing to be exiled." This pre-ᶜAbbāsid scenario concludes, "Their exile was the first time a people had been banished to Syria."

But there is a significantly different scenario for their eviction—a tale adopted and approved by ᶜAbbāsid-era historians.[95] We are told that in the early months of the fourth *hijrī* year (ca. May 625)—a few months after the Muslim defeat at Uḥud—a random killing occurred. The Muslim companion ᶜAmr ibn Umayya al-Ḍamrī killed two men of the tribe of Banū ᶜĀmir—a tribe that had *ᶜaqd al-jiwār* (a neighbor's covenant) with the Muslims.[96] Consequently, the Muslims had to pay Banū ᶜĀmir the *diyyat al-qatīl* (blood-money) in compensation for the killing.[97] To pay Banū ᶜĀmir, we are told, Muhammad sought some financial provision from the Jews. Joined by a group of his companions, Muhammad approached Banū al-Naḍīr and demanded that they contribute toward the blood-money.[98] The sources do not reveal the particular reason why Muhammad asked Banū al-Naḍīr to contribute to the blood-money, especially as they had no connection with the killing in the first place; however, al-Ṭabarī observes that Banū al-Naḍīr had *ḥilf wa-ᶜaqd* (a treaty and a covenant) with Banū ᶜĀmir.[99] If they had supported the Muslims, the logic goes, they would presumably violate their covenant with Banū ᶜĀmir. In what seems a generous gesture, Banū al-Naḍīr,

[94] Here al-Zuhrī adds a strange detail that, once Muhammad left Banū al-Naḍīr, he marched to another Jewish tribe, Banū Qurayẓa, and offered them a peace treaty, which they accepted. Maᶜmar, *Expeditions*, 70.

[95] For this scenario, albeit with some literary variations, see Wāqidī, *Maghāzī*, 363ff.; Ibn Hishām, *Sīra*, 2:190ff.: Ibn Saᶜd, *Ṭabaqāt*, 2:43ff.; Balādhurī, *Futūḥ*, 18–21; Balādhurī, *Origins*, 34–39; Balādhurī, *Ansāb*, 1:339; Ṭabarī, *Ta'rīkh*, 1448–1453; Ṭabarī, *History*, 7:156–161.

[96] See Ibn Hishām, *Sīra*, 2:186, where he also claims that ᶜAmr ibn Umayya was not aware of Muhammad's promise to Banū ᶜĀmir. Ṭabarī, *Ta'rīkh*, 1448.

[97] The chief of the tribe wrote to Muhammad, "You have killed two men whom you had given a promise of protection, so send their blood-money." Ṭabarī, *History*, 7:156. It is worth noting that, in a Shīᶜite report, Kaᶜb ibn al-Ashraf was still alive during the raid against Banū al-Naḍīr and Muhammad asked him to contribute to the blood-money. See Majlisī, *Biḥār*, 20:163.

[98] The group seemed like a battalion of Muslims (from Meccan *muhājirūn* and Medinan *anṣār*), including the major companions Abū Bakr, ᶜUmar, ᶜAlī, and others. Ṭabarī, *History*, 7:157. Ibn Hishām, *Sīra*, 2:190.

[99] Ṭabarī, *Ta'rīkh*, 1448; Ṭabarī, *History*, 7:159. See Ṣallābī, *Sīra*, 549, where he argues that the Jews were obliged to contribute to the blood-money because this was an item in their agreement with Muhammad. This seems inaccurate, especially as Ṣallābī affirms—in detailing of the items of the treaty with the Jews—that it reads, "incumbent upon the Jews their expenditure and upon the Muslims theirs." Cf. Lecker, "Constitution," 37; also Ṭabarī, *Ta'rīkh*, 1449; Ṭabarī, *History*, 7:157, where the Jews reportedly said to Muhammad, "We will give you the help which you want and which you have asked from us."

we are told, accepted Muhammad's request and affirmed they would contribute to the blood-money. Nonetheless, the narrative indicates that they lied and intended to assassinate Muhammad. While Muhammad and his companions were waiting to receive their money, he reportedly received *al-khabar min al-samā'* (news from heaven) that these Jews were planning to kill him by dropping a huge rock from the roof on his head.[100] He quickly returned home, told the Muslims of the treachery of the Jews, and instructed the companions "to get ready to fight them."[101] Consequently, Muhammad reportedly marched toward Banū al-Naḍīr and seized them "for fifteen days until he had reduced them to a state of utter exhaustion," before burning their palm trees to force them to surrender and evacuate.[102] Then, Banū al-Naḍīr surrendered and showed a desire for peace and Muhammad reportedly ordered them to get out *min bilādih* (of his lands), declaring that *maḥā al-islām al-ᶜuhūd* (Islam erased the treaties).[103] Ultimately, the Jews surrendered and left their homes, as well as "their gold, silver, and weapons."[104] Muhammad reportedly expelled them to Adhriᶜāt in Syria.[105] He then "seized the wealth

[100] See Ibn Hishām, *Sīra*, 2:190; Ṭabarī, *History*, 7:159; ᶜAbd al-Jabbār, *Tathbīt*, 2:489. In a Shīᶜite report, Kaᶜb was involved in the treachery and wanted to assassinate Muhammad, but Gabriel descended from heaven to warn Muhammad. See Majlisī, *Biḥār*, 20:163. Still, some historians do not mention the matter of the divine news. See Balādhurī, *Origins*, 34, "The Jews intended to drop a stone on him but the Prophet left them and sent them word ordering them to evacuate his city [Yathrib] because of their perfidy and violation of covenant. The Jews refused to comply, and announced hostility." See Rodinson, *Muhammad*, 139, where he argues for an Aramaic root for the name Yathrib.

[101] Ṭabarī, *Ta'rīkh*, 1449; Ibn Hishām, *Sīra*, 2:190; ᶜAbd al-Jabbār, *Tathbīt*, 2:489. See Djait, *Masīrat*, 116, where he estimates Muhammad's army, after Uḥud, to be approximately five hundred men. For Muhammad, we are told, the Jews had violated their agreement with him when they intended treachery. See Wāqidī, *Maghāzī*, 367; also Wāqidī, *Life*, 180, where Muhammad said, "You have broken the agreement which I have made for you with what treachery you planned against me." He then added, "Leave from my land. I have granted you a period of ten days. Whoever is seen after that, his head will be cut off!"

[102] Yaᶜqūbī, *Ta'rīkh*, 2:50; Wāqidī, *Maghāzī*, 372; Wāqidī, *Life*, 182–183, where in response to destroying the palm trees, "the [Jewish] women tore their dresses, struck their cheeks, crying out in affliction." See Majlisī, *Biḥār*, 20:165, where he asserts that their palm trees were particularly cherished among the tribe and the Muslim action hurt them greatly, as it meant a huge economic loss for the Jews. For distributing their lands and possessions, Ibn Shabba, *Ta'rīkh*, 488ff. See Djait, *Masīrat*, 116, where he explains the economic disaster of burning the palm trees for the Jews.

[103] Ṭabarī, *Ta'rīkh*, 1450. Still, some contradicting reports indicate that the Jews refused Muhammad's request to leave their homes: "We will not leave from our homes and our possessions. You can do whatever you want." This forced Muhammad to expel them by assault. See Wāqidī, *Life*, 181; Wāqidī, *Maghāzī*, 370. Eventually, he reportedly evicted them from "their homes," making them "Muhammad's home." Compare Ṭabarī, *Ta'rīkh*, 1448 and 1450, respectively.

[104] Yaᶜqūbī, *Ta'rīkh*, 2:50. For burning the palm trees and what it meant for the Jews, see Ṭabarī, *Ta'rīkh*, 1449. For distributing their lands and possessions, Ibn Shabba, *Ta'rīkh*, 488ff.

[105] Ṭabarī, *Ta'rīkh*, 1451; Ṭabarī, *History*, 7:159. In his *Tafsīr*, 23:262, al-Ṭabarī indicates that Muhammad expelled them to Syria and Khaybar—a detail that will be used in the raid against Khaybar.

and the weapons" for himself.[106] This concludes the ᶜAbbāsid-era scenario—a tale that became the official narrative for the eviction of Banū al-Naḍīr, thus sending al-Zuhrī's scenario largely into oblivion.

The comparison of the two scenarios reflects competing Muslim memories for expelling Banū al-Naḍīr. In the first, we have the Quraysh and Banū al-Naḍīr conspiring against the Muslims, after the victory at Badr and *before* Uḥud. The Jewish scheme to kill Muhammad was thwarted by the act of a faithful Jewish woman. This scenario elevates a Jewess for saving Muhammad's life and does not include reports about a Muslim killing two Arabs, blood-money, Muhammad demanding money from the Jews, or news from heaven warning Muhammad of a rock dropping from the roof. In the second scenario, the incident occurs months *after* Uḥud. Following a blood-money dispute and a reported Jewish treachery, Muhammad's life is spared by a revelation from heaven, propelling him to march against Banū al-Naḍīr, seizing them for two weeks before taking their possessions, and expelling them to Syria. Largely, the first scenario is pre-ᶜAbbāsid, while the second is ᶜAbbāsid.

Muslim scholars, past and present, acknowledge the contradictions between the two scenarios concerning the date of the raid and the content of the narratives.[107] In my estimation, the clear contradictions between the two accounts support our earlier contention that specific narratives were *selectively* and *tendentiously* elevated among Muslims and thus received recognition and formed orthodoxy, while others were marginalized and became unconventional or sent to oblivion—although, to be sure, they did not entirely disappear from the memory of the community.[108] I argue that the pre-ᶜAbbāsid

[106] Wāqidī, *Life*, 185. In response to Muhammad's seizing the wealth, a Muslim asked him about the portion designated to him and that to the Muslims; Muhammad reportedly said, "I will not apportion something God most high has given me to the exclusion of the believers" (185). See also Wāqidī, *Maghāzī*, 377; Bayhaqī, *Dalā'il*, 3:185. To affirm Muhammad's action regarding the spoils, we are told, Allah revealed Q 59:7, which refers to the gains granted by Allah to his messenger. Here, Muslim historiographical accounts serve as exegesis of the Qur'ān. Still, in a competing report, we are told that Muhammad gave the booty entirely to the Meccan *muhājirūn* (emigrants), after the Medinan *anṣār* (supporters) declared they needed no spoils. Wāqidī, *Maghāzī*, 379. On this contradiction, see Majlisī, *Biḥār*, 20:166, where he states that all spoils of Banū al-Naḍīr were given to Muhammad alone, although he gave some to the Meccan *muhājirūn*.

[107] For classical Muslims who acknowledge the contradictions between the two scenarios, see Bayhaqī, *Dalā'il*, 3:176–190; Ibn Kathīr, *Tafsīr*, 8:57–59; Ibn Qayyim, *Zād*, 3:223; Ibn Ḥajar, *Fatḥ*, 7:331–334. For contemporary Muslims who do the same, see ᶜUmarī, *Sīra*, 304–306; Ṣallābī, *Sīra*, 548–551. For a Shīᶜite study of the contradictory dates, see Majlisī, *Biḥār*, 20:160–165, especially 164. He attempts to harmonize the two scenarios by combining them in one narrative, leaving aside the discrepancy concerning the date of the raid.

[108] A few ᶜAbbāsid-era traditionists continue to refer to al-Zuhrī's account. Ibn Zanjawayh, *Amwāl*, 91–93; Ḥākim, *Mustadrak*, 2:525; Bayhaqī, *Dalā'il*, 3:179. Even later Muslims did the same. See Dhahabī, *Ta'rīkh*, 2:150–151; Dhahabī, *Siyar*, *sīra* 1:379–380; Ibn Ḥajar, *Fatḥ*, 7:331–334. On how

memory of evicting Banū al-Naḍīr—designed by Umayyad-era traditionists, such as ᶜUrwa and al-Zuhrī—was less desirable for the ᶜAbbāsid historians. They were addressing different sets of religious questions and responding to changing sociopolitical demands; consequently, the tale needed to be *rewritten.*[109] For instance, if pre-ᶜAbbāsid Umayyad-era traditionists adopted a memory of a Jewess saving Muhammad's life, ᶜAbbāsid historians were dealing with different religious and political contexts, which propelled them to tweak the memory to show Allah—not a Jewess—at work to save Muhammad. After all, these same historians invited us to believe that, a few years later, a Jewess poisoned Muhammad at Khaybar and was responsible for his death.[110] The Umayyad memory seems to have needed adjustments under their ᶜAbbāsid rivals.

But the religious memory of the faithful is not only tweaked and adjusted, it is also *selective.*[111] The Umayyad-era account of evicting Banū al-Naḍīr did not *entirely* vanish under the ᶜAbbāsids.[112] A unique case in point is the account of Shīᶜite historian Ibn Wāḍiḥ al-Yaᶜqūbī (d. 284/897 or 292/905),

the pre-ᶜAbbāsid stance eventually permeated ᶜAbbāsid historiography, see Hibri, "Redemption," 254; Hughes, *Muslim*, 115–116; Petersen, *ᶜAlī*, 133ff., 173; Ibrahim, *Conversion*, 171, 199–201, 217.

[109] For rewriting history, see Ibrahim, *Conversion*, 3–4, 23–24, 31–33; Wellhausen, *Arab*, xi–xii; Borrut, *Entre*, 37–40. Hoyland, "Arabic," 211–233; Robinson, *Historiography*, 38; Robinson, *Empire*, 1–31; Petersen, *ᶜAlī*, 17, 50; Anthony, *Muhammad*, 129ff. For how some Umayyad figures paid attention to history writing, see Ibrahim, *Conversion*, 31–32, where I argue, "Scholars now agree that Muslims paid attention to history writing during the Umayyad Caliphate, although most of this corpus has not survived." Antoine Borrut convincingly argues that most of our historiographical reports were filtered and redacted under the ᶜAbbāsids. See Borrut, *Entre*, 59–108, where he writes of "le prisme déformant des grands auteurs et compilateurs de l'âge Abbasside" (61).

[110] See Ṭabarī, *History*, 9:163ff.; Ibn Hishām, *Life*, 678ff.; Bukhārī, *Ṣaḥīḥ*, 3:163, 6:9; Dārimī, *Musnad*, 1:207–209; Muslim, *Ṣaḥīḥ*, 4:1721; Ibn Saᶜd, *Ṭabaqāt*, 2:82, 2:155; Masᶜūdī, *Tanbīh*, 1:223; Ibn al-Athīr, *Kāmil*, 2:100; Ibn Ḥibbān, *Thiqāt*, 2:16–17; Dhahabī, *Ta'rīkh*, 1:523, 2:437; Dhahabī, *Siyar*, *sīra* 2:88; Ibn Ḥajar, *Iṣāba*, 8:155. Ibn Qayyim al-Jawziyya, *Zād*, 3:297–300. For a study on the different Sunnī and Shīᶜite arguments regarding the incident of poisoning Muhammad, see Ibrahim, *Muhammad*, 98–103; Madelung, *Succession*, 356–359; Watt, *Muḥammad*, 54, 234; Rodinson, *Muhammad*, 254; Szilágyi, "After the Prophet's Death." Mubārakpūrī, *Raḥīq*, 344–345. See Spiegel, "Revising," 1–19, where she explores "the various forces that may help to explain the ongoing historiographical phenomenon of revision."

[111] On the religious memory, Sarah Savant focuses on the role of memory and its revision and erasure, and argues, "Conversion to Islam led Iranians to recall their past in new ways and to accumulate new memories about their history." Savant, *New*, 3. On the relationship between history and memory, see Spiegel, "Memory," 149–162; Borrut, *Entre*, ch. 1; Hutton, *History*, 1–22; Halbwachs, *On Collective*; Fentress and Wickham, *Social*; Innes, "Memory"; Clanchy, *From Memory*, ch. 9; Robinson, *Historiography*, 172–177; Geary, *Phantoms*, 111–122; Hirschler, *Written*. See also the recent study of Steinbock, *Social Memory*. Fred Donner rejects the term "collective memory" and suggests instead "collective images" or "collective visions" of the past, calling it history. Donner, *Narratives*, 139. On the interdependency between memory and written reports (literacy), see Carruthers, *Book of Memory*, where she examines the training, usage, and formation of memory in European cultures during the Middle Ages.

[112] See Ibn Zanjawayh, *Amwāl*, 91–93; Ḥākim, *Mustadrak*, 2:525; Bayhaqī, *Dalā'il*, 3:179.

who reportedly served under the ᶜAbbāsids.[113] He does not adhere *exactly* to the narrative adopted by his ᶜAbbāsid contemporaries. In his recounting of Banū al-Naḍīr's expulsion from Medina, al-Yaᶜqūbī adopts the date preferred by ᶜAbbāsid-era historians while utilizing pieces from the Umayyad-era substance of the story. For him, like his ᶜAbbāsid contemporaries, the raid occurred after Uḥud and after assassinating Kaᶜb ibn al-Ashraf, but, unlike them, the eviction was a result of Muhammad simply sending "them a message, saying: 'Leave your dwellings and your property.' "[114] For al-Yaᶜqūbī, Muhammad "marched against them after the mid-afternoon prayer, fought them, and killed a group of them.... When they saw that they had no strength to fight the Messenger of God, they sued for peace, and he granted it, provided that they left their lands."[115] Although al-Yaᶜqūbī dates the raid at four months after Uḥud, he does not follow the general contour of the ᶜAbbāsid-approved narrative: two men killed, blood-money sought, Jewish treachery followed, and the assassination of Muhammad divinely thwarted. Clearly, al-Yaᶜqūbī has a large pool of memory of the incident. From that pool, he selects pieces from the pre-ᶜAbbāsid content and the ᶜAbbāsid dating that form his designed account of the raid.

In my estimation, al-Yaᶜqūbī's account reflects a memory of the incident without ample ᶜAbbāsid-era embellishments.[116] His version should not be viewed as more historically reliable, but at least it does not exaggerate literary details. Unlike the pre-ᶜAbbāsid version, the ᶜAbbāsid account incorporates ample literary features which not only appear unrealistic in nature but also create various unanswered questions: Why did Muhammad initially march

[113] For primary sources and secondary studies on al-Yaᶜqūbī, see Ibrahim, *Conversion*, 197–199. Yāqūt, *Muᶜjam*, 2:557; Millward, "A Study"; Millward, "Adaptation," 329–344; Brockelmann, "Al-Yaᶜqūbī," *EI*², 11:257–258; Dūrī, *Rise*, 66; Petersen, *ᶜAlī*, 169; Donner, *Narratives*, 134; Khalidi, *Arabic*, 120ff., 131ff.; Robinson, *Historiography*, 36, 76, 98, 136–137; Muṣṭafā, *Ta'rīkh*, 1:250–253. We should note that his Shīᶜite sympathy is disputed and not conclusively solved among scholars. See Brockelmann, "Al-Yaᶜqūbī," *EI*², 11:257; Anthony, "Was Ibn Wāḍiḥ," 15–41; Daniel, "al-Yaᶜqūbī and Shiᶜism Reconsidered," in *ᶜAbbasid*, ed. Montgomery, 209ff.

[114] Yaᶜqūbī, *Works*, 3:648. Yaᶜqūbī, *Ta'rīkh*, 2:49–50. Cf. See Zuhrī, *Maghāzī*, 71; ᶜAbd al-Razzāq, *Muṣannaf*, 5:357–538; Maᶜmar, *Expeditions*, 41. Like al-Yaᶜqūbī, see Ṭabarī, *Tafsīr*, 23:262, and Thaᶜlabī, *Kashf*, 9:268, where both report the pre-ᶜAbbasid concise account, but place the raid after Uḥud. See also Ṭabarī, *Ṭa'rīkh*, 1451; Ṭabarī, *History*, 7:159, where he provides al-Zuhrī's account in his details of the fourth *hijrī* year.

[115] Yaᶜqūbī, *Works*, 3:648.

[116] On al-Yaᶜqūbī's tendency to resist adding embellishments, see Ibrahim, *Conversion*, 221, where I examine his portrayal of al-ᶜAbbās ibn ᶜAbd al-Muṭṭalib and argue, "Al-Yaᶜqūbī is clearly unwilling to follow the common trend of his contemporaries. He does not add embellishments in order to depict al-ᶜAbbās favorably." See also Berg, "ᶜAbbāsid," 13, where he argues, "Most [ᶜAbbāsid] historians, however, added embellishments in ways that reflected well on [al-ᶜAbbās] or, even more telling, suppressed some of the earlier, less flattering references."

with many Muslims to Banū al-Naḍīr, demanding their contribution to the blood-money?[117] We are told that Muhammad was escorted by *katā'ib* (battalions or armed troops).[118] This description sounds like the precursor of a battle, although the Jews were reportedly not involved in the killing. In one reading, this can be largely viewed as a provocative request to the Jews, perhaps to justify the expulsion. After all, their contribution would constitute a violation of their commitments to their tribal allies, the tribe of Banū ᶜĀmir. The ᶜAbbāsid version has more gaps. It invites us to believe that the Jews *openly* agreed to contribute to the blood-money, then conspired *secretly* to assassinate Muhammad. How could they kill Muhammad—with a rock from the roof—while he was surrounded by his skillful companions? Why did the heavenly warning come to Muhammad *after* he and his companions traveled all the way to the meeting? Is it not more plausible for the divine warning to have come beforehand? More importantly, why was the heavenly news needed when the tradition itself highlights that Muhammad overheard what the Jews secretly conspired?[119] Undoubtedly, these unanswered questions are avoided in al-Yaᶜqūbī's succinct account, which largely follows a concise pre-ᶜAbbāsid version of the tale.[120] Nonetheless, we should also note that al-Yaᶜqūbī's adopted version necessitated a tweak of the earlier report, presumably to fit his sectarian and sociopolitical context. He avoids the literary detail of a Jewish woman saving Muhammad's life—a report that was likely unsuitable for his ᶜAbbāsid-era demands.

There are three final observations on the narrative of the raid against Banū al-Naḍīr. First, as a literary fiction, the ᶜAbbāsid narrative is significantly longer than the pre-ᶜAbbasid report. It appears that a religious tradition collects additional layers by time, since it seeks to highlight a religious memory of the faithful in changing terms and contexts.[121] As a memory of the faithful, a tradition seems to develop, either by adding to or removing

[117] For some of the unanswered questions in the narrative, see Ibrahim, *Stated*, 87–90.

[118] Bayhaqī, *Dalā'il*, 3:179. See Wāqidī, *Maghāzī*, 364, where he reports that the Muslims with Muhammad were about ten men, including major companions.

[119] Wāqidī, *Maghāzī*, 364; see Wāqidī, *Life*, 178, where it reads, "While the Messenger of God was leaning against one of their houses, some of them withdrew and whispered to each other."

[120] Al-Zuhrī's narrative states, "The Messenger of God besieged them until they surrendered and entered exile, agreeing to take with them only what wealth and effects their camels could carry, minus any arms, meaning weaponry." Maᶜmar, *Expeditions*, 67.

[121] In a previous publication, I wrote, "Tracing the development in the supernatural tales of Islamic origins suggests that later authors provided a more fanciful and exaggerated picture." Ibrahim, *Stated*, 117.

from its core as its context dictates.[122] Thus, although the story of expelling Banū al-Naḍīr from Medina consisted of a few lines in an Umayyad version, it required pages in later times. Second, the narrative of the raid against Banū al-Naḍīr advances a strong Muslim polemic against the Jews, aiming to portray them as disloyal and treacherous people who cannot be trusted. Muslim historians—to amplify their unfavorable portrayal of the Jews—claim that verses of the Qur'ān have come down to judge the Jews of Banū al-Naḍīr.[123] Through this claim, the historical narrative gains higher weight and exegetes the Qur'ān.[124] Here, once again, we witness how historiographical reports are designed to serve as exegetical devices for Islam's Scripture. Indeed, this narrative is a product of the time of writing, with implications related to its immediate context. Third and finally, regarding the time of the raid, although we cannot determine it as a fact, from a literary standpoint, a date *after* the Muslim defeat at Uḥud appears more compelling. As a tale with turns, twists, and plots, a claim of a victory over the Jews after the Muslim defeat at Uḥud seems needed to balance the tradition. Perhaps a realization of that sort prompted the ᶜAbbāsid-era historians to adjust the received memory from earlier generations, thus moving the date of the raid to a year later. After all, the picture of the Muslim defeat at Uḥud was dark, especially as Muhammad was reportedly wounded severely and nearly died.[125] A portrayal of a victory seems needed. In the same vein, placing the expulsion of Banū al-Naḍīr both after Uḥud and also after the assassination of Kaᶜb ibn al-Ashraf—one of this Jewish tribe—appears plausible. From the perspective of the balance of power, the Muslims, as portrayed in the tradition, are presumably now stronger than the Jews after a series of successful attacks: Within the preceding year alone, we are invited to believe, the Muslims expelled the Jews of Banū Qaynuqāᶜ, seized their possessions, and assassinated two important

[122] Sarah Savant studies the role of memory and the way it is revised or erased, and writes, "As a tradition accumulates weight and authority, it shapes collective agreements about the past, thereby creating memories." Savant, *New*, 4.

[123] Wāqidī, *Maghāzī*, 380–383. See Ibn Hishām, *Sīra*, 2:192–193, where, we are told, that *sūrat al-Ḥashr* (Q 59) was entirely revealed to show how Allah wreaked his vengeance on the Jews of Banū al-Naḍīr and how he gave Muhammad power over them. See also Zuhrī, *Maghāzī*, 73–75.

[124] In one twist in the narrative, a Jew declares to another Jew, "By God you know and we know that he is the Messenger of God, and that we have his description with us. Indeed, we did not follow him, but envied him when prophecy left the Banū Hārūn." Wāqidī, *Life*, 180. This historiographical report supposedly refers to Q 7:157, where the verse states that the description of an *ummī* (unlettered) prophet, presumably Muhammad, is found in the Torah and the gospel. If a Jew admits and confesses to this claim, the logic goes, the Jews during the time of documenting these traditions should take notice and follow him.

[125] Wāqidī, *Maghāzī*, 237, 295; Ṭabarī, *Ta'rīkh*, 1408–1409; Kharkūshī, *Sharaf*, 3:32; Bayhaqī, *Dalā'il*, 3:270.

Jews, Abū Rāfiᶜ and Kaᶜb. Now, the tale continues, the second Jewish tribe is expelled. Thus, the momentum is now with the Muslims, and they should seize the opportunity to consolidate power and suppress any possible regrouping of the Jews. Here, the tradition zeroes in on the third Jewish tribe in Medina, the Banū Qurayẓa, portraying them as disloyal, ungrateful, and treacherous members of Medina.[126] They, too, must go.

The Raid against Banū Qurayẓa (5/627)

The general contour of the traditions depicts Muhammad as to have led four major raids against the Jews, each occurring as subsequent to another battle with the Meccan pagans: expelling Qaynuqāᶜ occurred after Badr, while al-Naḍīr after Uḥud, Qurayẓa after al-Khandaq, and Khaybar after al-Ḥudaybiyya.[127] According to al-Ṭabarī, al-Khandaq was soon followed by attacking Banū Qurayẓa—both are thematically connected and reportedly occurred in the last three months of the fifth *hijrī* year (ca. February–April 627).[128] The story of al-Khandaq, which we studied in the previous chapter, serves as a link between expelling Banū al-Naḍīr before it and attacking Banū Qurayẓa after it.[129] At al-Khandaq, Banū al-Naḍīr appears as a chief treacherous actor among the unbelievers, and Banū Qurayẓa allegedly assisted them.[130] If Banū Qurayẓa assisted the enemy, the logic goes, they should be fought.

[126] According to Shīᶜite traditions, Banū al-Naḍīr were wealthier than Banū Qurayẓa. See Majlisī, *Biḥār*, 20:166, where he also highlights that the former were about 1,000 men, while the latter totaled 700. However, his claim on Banū Qurayẓa is contradicted by other traditions. The raid against them resulted in the beheading of "600 or 700 in all, though some put the figure as high as 800 or 900." See Ibn Hishām, *Life*, 464; Ṭabarī, *Ta'rīkh*, 1493; Ibn Ḥibbān, *Sīra*, 1:266. See also Masᶜūdī, *Tanbīh*, 217, where the number is 750 men.

[127] Ibn Qayyim, *Zād*, 3:223; Ibn Qayyim, *Aḥkām*, 3:1453. Fadak was not a major raid. It was subsequent to Khaybar. See Ibrahim, *Stated*, 94–96.

[128] Ṭabarī, *Ta'rīkh*, 1463–1500; Ṭabarī, *History*, 8:5–41. See Zuhrī, *Maghāzī*, 79, and Maᶜmar, *Expeditions*, 82, where al-Khandaq and Qurayẓa are linked together in one section. Like the contradictions we discussed earlier concerning the date of the raid against Banū al-Naḍīr, there are some inconsistencies in the traditions about the date of Banū Qurayẓa, albeit to a lesser extent. A few traditionists claim the raid occurred a year earlier, i.e., in the fourth year, not the fifth. See Bayhaqī, *Dalā'il*, 3:393–394; Ibn Ḥazm, *Jamharat*, 1:343; Ibn Ḥazm, *Muḥallā*, 1:104–105, where he claims al-Khandaq was one year after Uḥud. See also Bukhārī, *Ṣaḥīḥ*, 3:177. For a Muslim attempt to harmonize the discrepancy, see ᶜUmarī, *Sīra*, 311–312.

[129] As explained in the previous chapter, the Battle of al-Khandaq (5/627), or the Trench, was reportedly a tribal siege of Medina led by *al-aḥzāb* (the confederates), which consisted of the Meccan Quraysh, the tribe of Ghaṭafān, and some Jews. See Ibn Hishām, *Sīra*, 1:561 and 2:214–215.

[130] Ṭabarī, *Ta'rīkh*, 1463; Ṭabarī, *History*, 8:6. Ibn Hishām, *Sīra*, 1:561; Ibn Ḥibbān, *Sīra*, 1:254; Ḥalabī, *Insān*, 2:423. Sharīf, *Makka*, 337; Qimanī, *Ḥurūb*, 243ff.

To depict the deceitfulness of Banū Qurayẓa, Muslim narrators provide details of a private dialogue that reportedly occurred in a closed room between the leader of Banū Qurayẓa (Kaᶜb ibn Asad) and one of the leaders of the confederates (Ḥuyayy ibn Akhṭab).[131] This dialogue, we are invited to believe, proves that the Jews of Banū Qurayẓa conspired against the Muslims.[132] Arguably, the details of the dialogue could never have been obtained unless the Muslim informants were present with the two leaders.[133] This dialogue is a literary construction that reflects the tendentious nature of the traditions. It reinforces, once more, our contention that Muslim narrators *authored* their reports.

However, despite the fanciful nature of this dialogue and its apparent bias, the account itself is contradicted by many other reports in the tradition. Some Muslim accounts actually defend Banū Qurayẓa and demonstrate them as supporting the Muslims in the battle. During the battle of al-Khandaq, Banū Qurayẓa reportedly refused to cooperate with the confederates.[134] The Jews told the Quraysh that it was a holy day and they could not work: "Today is the Sabbath, a day on which we do no labor. One of us violated it once, and you know what befell him."[135] They even reportedly provided Muhammad and the Muslims with tools to dig the trench.[136] These accounts contradict the picture of Banū Qurayẓa helping the confederates. Here, in the same Muslim tradition, we have roughly two competing sets of accounts—one claiming

[131] Wāqidī, *Maghāzī*, 455–458; Ibn Hishām, *Sīra*, 2:220–221; Ṭabarī, *Ta'rīkh*, 1482; Ibn Ḥibbān, *Sīra*, 1:261; Ibn Ḥabīb, *Muḥabbar*, 113; Kalāᶜī, *Iktifā'*, 2:173; ᶜAbd al-Jabbār, *Tathbīt*, 2:449; Bayhaqī, *Dalā'il*, 3:400–401; Ibn ᶜAbd al-Barr, *Durar*, 1:171–172; Suhaylī, *Rawḍ*, 6:204–205; Ibn Sayyid al-Nās, *ᶜUyūn*, 2:88–89; Ḥalabī, *Insān*, 2:423; Dhahabī, *Ta'rīkh*, 2:287–288. See also Mubārakpūrī, *Raḥīq*, 283; Sharīf, *Makka*, 391–392; ᶜAlī, *Mufaṣṣal*, 12:140. For a secondary study on the incident, see Peters, *Muhammad*, 222. See also Mazuz, *Religious*, 9–24, especially 12. Watt, *Muḥammad*, 265: "Thus as Muhammad became stronger, there was no longer any question of 'normal relations' of the old type between the *ummah* and non-Muslim tribes." See also Wolfensohn, *Ta'rīkh*, 133–156.

[132] Some historians did not care much about providing a reason to prove that Banū Qurayẓa violated the treaty with Muslims. See Yaᶜqūbī, *Ta'rīkh*, 2:53, where he simply asserts that Banū Qurayẓa broke their treaty with Muhammad. Cf. Ibn Hishām, *Sīra*, 1:561; Ḥalabī, *Insān*, 2:423.

[133] In a previous publication, I summarized and commented on the dialogue. See Ibrahim, *Stated*, 117, where I write, "Ḥuyayy desires to enter the house of Kaᶜb; the latter refuses, and the former insists. They keep talking, until Kaᶜb lets Ḥuyayy in. They converse and negotiate terms, and so forth. This looks like a drama. One wonders how the Muslim authors knew the details of this conversation. The story and the dialogue seem invented to place Banū Qurayẓa in a bad light, affirming they betrayed Muhammad, and thus deserve what happened to them."

[134] See Ṭabarī, *History*, 8:25, where the Jews told the Quraysh, "We will not fight on your side until you give us some of your men as hostages." See Watt, *Muḥammad*, 36, where he argues that Qurayẓa "seem to have tried to remain neutral." For a modern Muslim perspective on contradictory *sīra* accounts, see Ḥanafī, *Min*, 3:19–21.

[135] Ṭabarī, *Ta'rīkh*, 1482.

[136] Wāqidī, *Maghāzī*, 445; Ḥalabī, *Insān*, 2:628. On the Jews assisting the Muslims, see Qimanī, *Ḥurūb*, 2:247; Sharīf, *Makka*, 391; Watt, *Muḥammad*, 38, 214; Rodinson, *Muhammad*, 209.

that Banū Qurayẓa assisted the confederates and another demonstrating that they supported the Muslims. The point of the comparison is not that one set is more reliable or factual, but rather that we have competing claims coexisting in the same pool of memories. Depending on the narrator, some reports are adopted and elevated, while others are dismissed. Again, the entire tradition suffers from disunity and competing claims—it is impossible to reconstruct what actually occurred.

Ultimately, once the Muslims defeated the enemies at al-Khandaq, we are told, Allah did not allow Muhammad to rest and instructed him to march to attack Banū Qurayẓa. The attack is represented in the traditions as an extermination of the Jewish tribe, as their fate was—unlike the other two Jewish tribes—not eviction or enslavement.[137] When Muhammad reportedly returned home after the battle of al-Khandaq, Gabriel came to him "wearing a cloth-of-gold turban" and admonished him, "Have you laid down your arms?" When Muhammad responded affirmatively, Gabriel said, "The angels have not laid down their arms! I have just returned from pursuing the enemy." This reproach is followed by an instruction and a promise: "God commands you, Muḥammad, to march to the Banū Qurayẓah" and "I, too, will betake myself to the Banū Qurayẓah."[138] This literary construction sets the stage for the whole narrative of the raid against the Jews. As designed by Muslim storytellers, this tale invites the reader to trust that the marching of Muslims against Banū Qurayẓa is a religiously driven mission instead of a military assault—it is a task commissioned by Allah and supported by his angel who partakes in the mission himself. Muhammad, in the tale, was merely an executer of Allah's judgment against the Jews. Additionally, the literary report enforces a disposition of urgency for the believers to not cease until they have eliminated the evil in the land.[139] Critically, the story is formed to instruct an immediate audience of believers to follow the footsteps of forged literary characters.

Muhammad and the Muslims approached the fortresses of Banū Qurayẓa, and he reportedly shouted at the Jews, "You brothers of

[137] See the comments of Michael Fishbein in his foreword of Ṭabarī, *History*, 8:xiv–xv.

[138] Ṭabarī, *History*, 8:27. Ibn Hishām, *Sīra*, 2:233–234.

[139] We are told that Muhammad sent "a crier to announce to the people that whoever would heed and obey [the divine command] should not pray the afternoon prayer until they were in [the territory of] the Banū Qurayẓah." Ṭabarī, *History*, 8:28. Ibn Hishām, *Sīra*, 2:234. The report suggests that gathering all the believers to march to war and the travel to Banū Qurayẓa took less than four hours, since Muhammad had just finished the noon prayer. Wāqidī, *Maghāzī*, 497. See Majlisī, *Biḥār*, 20:210, 217, where he claims that the dwelling place of Banū Qurayẓa was two miles from Medina.

apes!"[140] Offended with his statement, the Jews responded, "You did not used to be so obscene, O Muhammad."[141] Muhammad's statement and the response of the Jews is a fashioned dialogue to advance an anti-Jewish stigma that fits medieval polemics against the Jews. It is plausible to deduce that Muslim traditionists interacted with many Jews in the conquered lands and used these literary tales to design an image of the Medinan Jews. Moreover, these historians shaped the tradition to serve as an exegetical tool, especially as the Qur'ān itself includes verses claiming that Allah punished some evil Jews by transforming them into apes (Q 2:65; 5:60; 7:166).[142] By identifying the Jews as apes, Muslim narrators attribute a phrase to Muhammad that emphasizes him as a divinely guided commander who echoes that which the Qur'ān already declares. Storytellers amplify the stigma against the Jews by developing a subsequent report that shows the Jews as intentionally wicked and deliberately evil people who knowingly disobey the divine: a Jew of Banū Qurayẓa—after hearing Muhammad calling them apes—told the other Jews, "it has become clear to you that he is indeed a prophet sent [from God] and that it is he whom you used to find [mentioned] in your book."[143] Thus, here is a literary portrayal of a Jew affirming in front of other Jews that they certainly know the truth—that Muhammad is a prophet and that he is mentioned in the Jewish Scripture—but decide to ignore it. Not only is a Jew chastising his fellow believers, but storytellers create an anti-Jewish report and place it in the mouths of the Jews themselves. We are told that, when the Jews heard Muhammad's statement calling them apes, they affirmed that their evil predecessors were truly transformed to apes as a divine punishment.[144] The tendentiousness of the traditions is glaring, and, based on these literary structures, the rationale goes, fighting Banū Qurayẓa was not only commanded but justified and even commended.

140 Ṭabarī, *History*, 8:28. The statement reads, "You brethren of monkeys and pigs!" in Zuhrī, *Maghāzī*, 81; Maᶜmar, *Expeditions*, 87. See Majlisī, *Biḥār*, 108:288. See also Wāqidī, *Maghāzī*, 499, where he observes that the Jews insulted Muhammad first. See the study of Firestone, "Apes," 26–48.

141 Zuhrī, *Maghāzī*, 81; Maᶜmar, *Expeditions*, 87.

142 See Muqātil, *Tafsīr*, 1:113, 1:125; Ṭabarī, *Jāmiᶜ*, 2:168–170; Thaᶜlabī, *Kashf*, 1:212; Zamakhsharī, *Kashshāf*, 1:653; Rāzī, *Mafātiḥ*, 3:541; Qurṭubī, *Jāmiᶜ*, 1:439–440, 2:58 (similar to al-Rāzī's interpretation); Bayḍāwī, *Anwār*, 2:134; Riḍā, *Manār*, 6:371; Quṭb, *Fī ẓilāl*, 1:77; Shaᶜrāwī, *Khawāṭirī*, 6:3254. On these verses, see Firestone, "Apes," 26–48. On the Qur'ānic anti-Jewish verses, see Mazuz, "Jewish-Muslim," 946–947; Bar-Asher, *Jews*, 27–57; Perlmann, "Medieval," 103–138; Adang and Schmidtke, "Polemics."

143 Ṭabarī, *History*, 8:30; Wāqidī, *Maghāzī*, 503; Ibn Hishām, *Sīra*, 2:235.

144 See Ṭabarī, *History*, 8:30, where some Jews said, "Profane our Sabbath and do on it what none of our predecessors has ever done, except those you know about and they were transformed in a way that you surely know?"

Muhammad and the Muslims besieged the tribe for twenty-five or thirty days, according to varying traditions, "until the siege exhausted them and God cast terror into their hearts."[145] The reference to the terror casted "into their hearts" connects the historiographical report to the Qur'ān, where it emphasizes Allah strengthening his believers and casting terror into the hearts of the unbelievers, thus allowing the believers to strike the necks and every fingertip of the unbelievers (Q 8:12). As we encountered repeatedly, Muslim historians serve as exegetes who design historical tales to unlock scriptural references. Whether it was the siege exhaustion or Allah's terror in their hearts, or both, the Jews of Banū Qurayẓa reportedly surrendered. Unlike his treatment of the earlier two tribes (Qaynuqāᶜ and al-Naḍīr), Muhammad did not expel them. He reportedly first "imprisoned them" in one house.[146] This appears as an exaggerated report, because it is soon followed by the claim that the Jewish men alone were between six hundred and nine hundred—one house can hardly receive an entire tribe.[147] However, as a hyperbolic literary description, the exaggeration seems to be fashioned to emphasize hatred, revenge, and rage. After he imprisoned them, the traditions reveal that "they were told to submit to the judgment of the Messenger of God," but a Muslim companion warned them by giving them "a sign that it would mean slaughter."[148] Muhammad then reportedly asked them whether they would accept the judgment of one they choose. The Jews said, "We will submit to the judgment of Saᶜd ibn Muᶜādh."[149] They reportedly chose Saᶜd because he was a chief of al-Aws tribe, which had a covenant with Banū Qurayẓa.[150] They thought he would keep the covenant and protect

[145] Ṭabarī, *History*, 8:30. Ibn Hishām, *Sīra*, 2:235. See a contradicting report in Wāqidī, *Maghāzī*, 496, where he states he seized them for only fifteen days, as Muhammad vowed, "O Allah's enemies, we will not leave your fortress until you starve to death. You—in your dwellings—are like foxes in their holes" (499).

[146] Ṭabarī, *History*, 8:35. According to al-Wāqidī, the Jews begged Muhammad to treat them as he did with Banū al-Naḍīr and expel them, but he refused, and said, "No. You will submit only to my judgment." Wāqidī, *Life*, 246; Wāqidī, *Maghāzī*, 501.

[147] Ṭabarī, *Ta'rīkh*, 1493; Ṭabarī, *History*, 8:35.

[148] Ṭabarī, *History*, 8:29.

[149] Ṭabarī, *History*, 8:29. Wāqidī, *Maghāzī*, 512.

[150] On Saᶜd, Wāqidī, *Ridda*, 1:44 (Allah's throne trembled for Saᶜd's death); Ibn Saᶜd, *Ṭabaqāt*, 3:320–332; Khalīfa, *Ṭabaqāt*, 139 (grandson of Imru' al-Qays and wounded at al-Khandaq); Balādhurī, *Ansāb*, 1:328, 1:346; Ibn Ḥabīb, *Muḥabbar*, 1:276; Ibn Ḥabīb, *Munammaq*, 1:408 (he was the first to ride a horse in Allah's cause); Fasawī, *Maᶜrifa*, 1:247 (Muhammad sat near Saᶜd's tomb and remembered him); Masᶜūdī, *Tanbīh*, 1:217 (he was *sayyid* al-Aws, i.e., their chief), 4:220, 5:114 (he was an early convert in Medina); Jawzī, *Muntaẓim*, 3:242–246; Dhahabī, *Ta'rīkh*, 2:309–330; Dhahabī, *Tadhkirat*, 3:224 (his death); Dhahabī, *Siyar*, 1:279–296; ᶜAlī, *Mufaṣṣal*, 7:137, 8:150 (called the chief of *al-anṣār*); Ibn Qāniᶜ, *Muᶜjam*, 1:251; Ibn Ḥibbān, *Thiqāt*, 1:96–97 (he accepted Islam in the First Aqaba Pledge); Dāraquṭnī, *Mu'talif*, 1:395; Ibn Manda, *Maᶜrifat*, 1:935; Abū Nuᶜaym, *Maᶜrifat*,

them as his tribal allies. Even the people of al-Aws reportedly pled with Saᶜd to have mercy on the Jews, as they were allies.[151] Nonetheless, Saᶜd was a convert to Islam, and his loyalty, we are invited to believe, was completely to Islam and Muhammad. Saᶜd stated his decree: "the men should be killed, the property divided, and the women and children taken as captives."[152]

Saᶜd and his decree against the Jews are better viewed as a medieval literary construction with religious meanings. Saᶜd is a fashioned depiction of a Muslim who shows a loyalty to Islam that surpasses any other tribal commitments. His character is designed in a way to reinforce a repeated theme in Islamic historiography: *maḥā al-islām al-ᶜuhūd* (Islam has wiped out the old covenants).[153] This is evident in how Saᶜd's depiction in the tradition includes various hyperbolic literary features to present him as an exemplarily hero for Islam. He is a wounded solider, we are told, at the battle of al-Khandaq, but his dedication to obey Muhammad's orders until the end is unmatched—this is what propels him to travel while wounded to speak judgment against the Jews. Saᶜd, we are told, was *jasīman jamīlan* (corpulent and beautiful), who heroically mounted a donkey to travel in obedience to Muhammad's call.[154] Even his severe judgment against the Jews, the tradition insists, was approved by Allah and praised by Muhammad.[155] We are invited to believe that Saᶜd, because of his judgment against Banū Qurayẓa, was rewarded by seventy thousand *malak* (archangels) welcoming him upon his death.[156] The exaggerating nature of the report is glaring, as it is much more than the number of angels who appeared at Badr. However, Muslim historians seem to have designed a character of a Muslim saint, so to speak, to exhort Muslims in a particular ideological path: Follow the footsteps of

3:1241–1243; Ibn ᶜAbd al-Barr, *Istīᶜāb*, 2:602–605; Ibn al-Athīr, *Usd*, 2:420; Ṣafadī, *Wāfī*, 1:55, 1:89, 9:154; Ibn Ḥajar, *Iṣāba*, 3:70–72.

[151] See Ibn Hishām, *Sīra*, 2:239; Ibn Hishām, *Life*, 464.

[152] Ibn Hishām, *Life*, 464; Ibn Hishām, *Sīra*, 2:240; Zuhrī, *Maghāzī*, 81; Maᶜmar, *Expeditions*, 87; Ibn Ḥibbān, *Sīra*, 1:265. Peters writes, "The penalty was a harsh one, and perhaps even somewhat surprising in the light of Muhammad's earlier treatment of the Jews of Medina, but the later Muslim jurists took their cue from Sura 8 of the Quran." Peters, *Muhammad*, 224.

[153] Ṭabarī, *Ta'rīkh*, 1450; Ṭabarī, *History*, 7:158. See Ibrahim, *Stated*, 89. See also Watt, *Muḥammad*, 215, where he argues, "The point at issue was whether allegiance to the Islamic community was to be set above and before all other alliances and attachments."

[154] Ibn Hishām, *Sīra*, 2:239; Ibn Hishām, *Life*, 463.

[155] See Ibn Hishām, *Life*, 464, where Muhammad tells Saᶜd, "You have given the judgement of Allah above the seven heavens."

[156] Bayhaqī, *Dalā'il*, 4:29–28. The word used is not *malāk* (angel), but rather *malak*, which refers to a high-level archangel. See Ibrahim, *Stated*, 117.

this brave solider who is devoted to Islam, dedicated to Muhammad, and does not trust evil Jews.

Nonetheless, these storytellers, in an attempt to magnify the image of Saᶜd, seem to create contradictory reports. While in some accounts Saᶜd is chosen by the Jews to state their judgment, other reports insist that Muhammad himself assigned the task to Saᶜd.[157] This apparent contradiction reflects, once again, a disunity in the overall tradition, but more importantly, a tweaked memory. The discrepancy points to how the memory of the believers adjusts itself over time to serve varying purposes. While the Jews choosing Saᶜd to judge them seems suitable for a particular context, it appears to credit the Jews with the high honor of assigning Saᶜd an esteemed status. This memory did not fit in other times, so it needed to be tweaked and its report was rewritten to credit Muhammad himself with designating Saᶜd as honorable. Saᶜd's severe judgment against the Jews—massacring the men, taking women and children captive, and dividing the possessions—should be viewed in the framework of descriptions aiming to drive anti-Jewish sentiments in medieval times. When Muslims, past and present, take these fictional tales as factual, religious coexistence crumbles, especially as some historiographical reports claim that their disastrous fate was the consequence of their refusal to accept Islam after Muhammad called them to embrace it.[158]

The story continues by presenting Muhammad as taking charge of applying Saᶜd's judgment against the Jews. Muhammad reportedly went to an open area—a market in Medina—and dug several trenches, and the Jewish men were brought to him in batches, and he *ḍarab aᶜnāqahum* (cut off their heads) in those trenches.[159] While this literary description shows Muhammad as slaughtering the men himself, other reports contradict this picture by claiming that, after he ordered the digging of the trenches, "he sat down, and ᶜAlī and al-Zubayr began cutting off their heads in his presence."[160] Each report, as I repeatedly argue, seems to advance a religious philosophy: One narrative highlights Muhammad as the agent of vengeance against the Jews, but another paints him as a commander who is served by virtuous Muslims accomplishing the task in his presence. Still, there is a third

[157] See Ibn Hishām, *Sīra*, 2:239, where Muhammad chose Saᶜd to yield to the request of the al-Aws tribe to have mercy on the Jews.

[158] Zuhrī, *Maghāzī*, 81; Maᶜmar, *Expeditions*, 87.

[159] Ṭabarī, *Ta'rīkh*, 1493; Ibn Hishām, *Sīra*, 2:240; Ibn Hishām, *Life*, 464; Ibn Ḥibbān, *Sīra*, 1:266.

[160] Ṭabarī, *History*, 8:40–41; Ṭabarī, *Ta'rīkh*, 1499–1500.

competing report, in which Muhammad assigns the killing of the Jews to Muslims from the tribe of al-Khazraj—a tribe that rivaled al-Aws (an ally to Banū Qurayẓa). The report reveals that the Muslims of al-Khazraj "began to cut off their heads with great satisfaction."[161] While the Muslims of al-Khazraj reportedly "showed their pleasure" in killing the Jews, the Muslims of al-Aws—the allies of Banū Qurayẓa—did not show satisfaction, which prompted Muhammad to hand them the last twelve Jews to kill.[162] The literary features of brutality, vengeance, and fury are clearly emphasized—and largely exaggerated—in this tradition. This third report uses Muhammad's esteemed status in Islam—as the exemplary Muslim—to exhort medieval believers to find pleasure in treating the unbelievers harshly.[163]

In the same vein, we are told, Muhammad himself killed only one Jewish woman in this incident, because she had murdered a Muslim earlier at al-Khandaq. Muhammad "called for her and beheaded her in retaliation."[164] The tradition on this woman is ambiguous, as she is unnamed in many accounts,[165] but it depicts Muhammad as revenging for the Muslims and as unforgiving to any person who attacks a Muslim. In these traditions, religious scholars create an overall feeling that the Jews cannot be tolerated, as evidenced in how Muhammad found it impossible to coexist with their ancestors in Medina. Storytellers justify revenge and unforgiving sentiments against Jews in later generations by forming a narrative and attributing it to Muhammad—the most important human figure for Muslims.

This anti-Jewish sentiment is further amplified with more literary constructions. We are told that Muhammad beheaded "600 or 700 in all, though some put the figure as high as 800 or 900."[166] The literary depiction of Muhammad's hatred and rage against the Jews continues as Muslim

[161] Ibn Hishām, *Sīra*, 2:59; Ibn Hishām, *Life*, 464.

[162] Ibn Hishām, *Sīra*, 2:59; Ibn Hishām, *Life*, 464. According to Wāqidī, *Maghāzī*, 515, al-Aws detested the killing of the Banū Qurayẓa "because of the significance of their confederacy." Wāqidī, *Life*, 253.

[163] The brutality of the historiographical details could be viewed as exegeting Islam's Scripture, when it presumably addresses Muhammad, "O Prophet! *jāhid* (strive against) the *kuffār* (infidels) and the *munāfiqūn* (hypocrites, or lukewarm believers) and be harsh with them. Their ultimate destination is hellfire—the most miserable ending" (Q 9:73). Muslim exegetes link this verse with the treatment of the Jews. See Muqātil, *Tafsīr*, 2:135.

[164] Ṭabarī, *History*, 8:41; Ṭabarī, *Ta'rīkh*, 1500.

[165] Ibn Hishām and al-Ṭabarī do not mention her name, although al-Ṭabarī claims she was a wife of a man from Banū Qurayẓa. Ṭabarī, *History*, 8:41.

[166] Ibn Hishām, *Life*, 464; Ṭabarī, *Ta'rīkh*, 1493; Ibn Ḥibbān, *Sīra*, 1:266. See also Masᶜūdī, *Tanbīh*, 1:217, where he claims the number is 750 men. When the Jewish women "learned of the killing of their men they screamed and ripped their clothes from the neckline, tore their hair, and slapped their cheeks for their men." Wāqidī, *Life*, 254.

historians claim that, after the killing of the men, Muhammad "divided the wealth, wives, and children of the Banū Qurayẓah among the Muslims."[167] The number of captive women and children was reportedly one thousand.[168] These literary claims can hardly be linked to actual events. Classical Muslim historians needed religious lessons, and these actions—killing, dividing property, and enslaving women and children—are attributed to Muhammad himself and are thus religiously sanctioned and legitimate. These literary tales become prescriptive for Muslims who choose to consider them factual and apply them literally, as evidenced in how renowned medieval jurists relied on the tale of Banū Qurayẓa to issue prescriptive rulings in life affairs.[169]

Muslim traditionists continue *authoring* their narratives of the raid of Banū Qaurayẓa, by describing how Muhammad dealt with the Jewish women and children after he enslaved them. Concerning the Jewish women, we are told that Muhammad sold all *al-sabāyā* (the captive women) and used the money to buy horses and *silāḥan* (weapons). This literary report is important to emphasize for at least two reasons. First, we are invited to believe that, for Muhammad and the Muslims, horses and weapons were of a higher value than the slaves of war—he sold the female war captives to strengthen his army. The spoils of war and the accumulated wealth were reportedly plentiful.[170] The narrators devised an image suitable for their time of empire expansion. They did not concern themselves with whether these women were treated fairly or justly, as these were not important matters during medieval times, but they emphasized the consolidation of power and accumulation of wealth. This is clearly a compelling narrative for the Muslim elites, the rulers in the Islamic caliphate. Second, the literary image suggests that Muhammad did not free the female slaves of war but sold them as captives to accumulate more wealth and power. Arguably, this religious disposition was important

[167] Ṭabarī, *Ta'rīkh*, 1497. See Yaᶜqūbī 2:53 and Mūsā ibn ᶜUqba, *Maghāzī*, 223.

[168] Waqidī, *Maghāzī*, 523.

[169] For instance, see Ibn Taymiyya, *Ṣārim*, 1:257–261; also Ibn Taymiyya, *Fatāwā*, 3:301, where he uses the tradition of Banū Qurayẓa literally and articulates a religious ruling based on Muhammad's treatment of them. See also Ibn Qayyim, *Zād*, 3:59, 3:106, 3:117, 3:120–130; ᶜIyāḍ ibn Mūsā, *Shifā*, 1:351–352. For some modern and contemporary Muslims who treat the story of Banū Qurayẓa as factual and prescriptive in religious relations, see Hamidullah, *Battlefields*, 105–106; Mubārakpūrī, *Raḥīq*, 288–292; ᶜUmarī, *Sīra*, 311–317; Ṣallābī, *Sīra*, 617–622; Sharīf, *Makka*, 391–393. Cf. Shoemaker, *Apocalypse*, 182–183.

[170] See Wāqidī, *Maghāzī*, 422–424, where he devotes a section to "the record of the portioning of the booty and its sale." See Wāqidī, *Life*, 256–258. The modern historian Meir Kister, in his analysis of this raid, rightly concludes, "The military strength of the Muslim community of Medina grew due to the weapons taken as booty; the sale of the captured women and children as slaves for horses and weapons enabled to enlarge the Muslim military force for further conquests." See Kister, "Massacre," 96.

to Muslim narrators. If Muhammad did not free his captives and instead sold them, the logic goes, Muslims can and should emulate him. The report uses Muhammad, the most important human figure for Muslims, to justify and legitimize selling and exchanging slaves of war—a claim advanced in many traditions.[171] Though this report is suitable for medieval Islam, it creates problems for modern religious discussions.[172] However, in Muhammad's treatment of the Jewish women, the narrators report an exception: he *iṣṭafā li-nafsihi min nisā'ihim* (selected for himself one of their women), Rayḥāna bint Zayd, as his wife, although she refused to convert to Islam.[173] According to al-Wāqidī, Muhammad "took her for himself as the leader's share. She was beautiful."[174]

Concerning Muhammad's treatment of the Jewish children, they were reportedly all taken captive—except *man kān muḥtaliman aw nabatat*

[171] The traditions insist that Muhammad owned, sold, and exchanged slaves. See Bukhārī, *Ṣaḥīḥ*, 9:89. Both Bukhārī and Muslim refer to Anjasha as Muhammad's Ethiopian black slave. Bukhārī, *Ṣaḥīḥ*, 8:35, 38, 47; Muslim, *Ṣaḥīḥ*, 3:115, 4:1811, 1812. We are also told of ᶜĀ'isha's slave girls. Bukhārī, *Ṣaḥīḥ*, 3:148; 5:168; Muslim, *Ṣaḥīḥ*, 4:1957; see Mālik ibn Anas, *Muwaṭṭa'*, 5:1385, where he names one of ᶜĀ'isha's slaves. Furthermore, we are told that Muhammad's daughter Fāṭima heard that Muhammad "obtained a few *raqīq* (slaves)." Bukhārī, *Ṣaḥīḥ*, 7:65. The Arabic sources use terms such as *ghulām*, *ama*, *sabiyya*, and *raqīq* to refer to slaves and war captives. For these terms, see Ibn Manẓūr, *Lisān*, 11:224 (a *ghulām* is a noun given to *al-ᶜabd* or *al-ama*, i.e., male or female slave); 4:489–490, 4:611, 4:617, 5:18, 6:179, 6:242 (*al-ama*, female slave, opposite to *al-ḥurra*, i.e., free woman); 5:383, 8:350, 14:367 (*sabiyya*, female slave, war captive); 2:143, 10:124 (*raqīq* refers to *ama*, a singular of *imā'*, and *ᶜabd* from *ᶜabīd*; *raqīq* means *mamlūk*, i.e., owned). For studies on slavery in Islam, see Ibrahim, *Muhammad*, 167–168; Levy, *Social*, 53–90; Clarence-Smith, *Islam*, 1–20, and 22–48; Mendelsohn, *Slavery*; Brockopp, *Early*, 115–160; also Brockopp, "Slavery"; Robinson, "Neck-Sealing," 401–441. See also the Muslim feminist Ali, *Marriage*, 187ff.; Saad, "Legal"; Myrne, *Female*, chs. 1–3; Myrne, "Slaves for Pleasure," 196–225. For women and slavery in Islamic history, see the volume Gordon and Hain, eds., *Concubines and Courtesans*. On slavery and slaves among Arabs in history until recently, see Lewis, *Race*; Brown, *Slavery*; Sowell, *Black*; Sowell, *Thomas*; also the edited volume Willis, ed., *Slaves and Slavery*.

[172] See the discussions in Ibrahim, *Muhammad*, 167–168; Clarence-Smith, *Islam*, 1–20; Brown, *Slavery*, chs. 1–3.

[173] Ṭabarī, *Ta'rīkh*, 1497–1498; Wāqidī, *Maghāzī*, 523; Yaᶜqūbī, *Ta'rīkh*, 2:53. On Rayḥāna, see Wāqidī, *Maghāzī*, 520, where she was reluctant to convert to Islam; Zubayr ibn Bakkār, *Muntakhab*, 47–48; Dhahabī, *Ta'rīkh*, 1:597–598; Ziriklī, *Aᶜlām*, 3:38. For secondary studies, see Ibrahim, *Conversion*, 136–137; Watt, *Muḥammad*, 397; ᶜAbd al-Raḥmān, *Nisā'*, 11–12, where she does not consider Rayḥāna one of the Mothers of the Believers; also Jamīlī, *Nisā'*, 115–116, who does not consider Rayḥāna at all. On how classical Muslims viewed Rayḥāna unfavorably, see Yitzhak, "Muhammad's Jewish Wives," 1–14. For Muhammad's wives in general, see Stowasser, "Wives of the Prophet," *EQ*, 4:506–521; Musᶜad, *Wives*; Lings, *Muhammad*, 233; Hyakal, *Ḥayāt*, 326–336, 350, 358. For a feminist treatment of Muhammad's wives, see Mernissi, *Women*, 115–140; Awde, *Women*, 10, where she is one of two concubines. See also Ruṣāfī, *Shakhṣiyya*, 416ff.; ᶜUmarī, *Risāla*, 95–110. For a conservative traditional Muslim study on Rayḥāna, see Ṣallābī, *Sīra*, 625, where he argues that Rayḥāna was reluctant to accept Islam but Allah opened her heart, at which time Muhammad gave her the choice to be freed or to become one of those whom Muhammad's right hand possesses (Q 4:25), and she chose the latter. Ṣallābī seems to rely on Ibn Hishām, *Sīra*, 2:245. On whether she was a wife or concubine, see Ibn Qayyim, *Zād*, 1:110; also Majlisī, *Biḥār*, 22:193.

[174] Wāqidī, *Life*, 255; Wāqidī, *Maghāzī*, 520.

ᶜānatah (those who attained nocturnal emission or puberty hair), who were murdered,[175] as Muhammad "commanded that all of them who had reached puberty should be killed."[176] This report advances an awkward literary image: the Muslims examined young boys to determine whether they attained puberty to execute them. This is an unmatched report in Muslim traditions and serves as another literary construction that advances sentiments of cruelty against the Jews—which is likely the religious message that medieval Muslim historians sought to convey in their immediate context: no mercy for the Jews, and do not spare any adult among them. Arguably, these accounts could have also aimed to terrorize the Jews who lived in the Islamic caliphate during the time of documentation.[177] It is plausible to deduce that these texts were shaped to humiliate the Jewish community in the conquered lands and to establish hegemony for Muslims as elites and religious notables.

Finally, there are some concluding observations on the Muslim accounts of the raid against Banū Qurayẓa. More than once, we encountered incoherence and disunity in the reports. The literary accounts include significant gaps, as the Muslim historians arguably attempted to *author* historiographical accounts rather than to document what actually happened. The image of a vengeful, unforgiving, and aggressive Muhammad—who slaughters people and takes women and children captive—likely appealed to medieval Muslims who had no concern about depicting their prophet in such a way, as they served the men in power—the ruling elites in the Muslim caliphate. These historians wrote to answer questions related to their time and to articulate depictions suitable for a period of empire expansion. They were unconcerned with modern questions surrounding peace building and religious coexistence. This is one reason why their portrayal of Muhammad created major challenges for modern and contemporary Muslims who sought to present Muhammad and Islam to non-Muslims in modern times.[178] The story of Muhammad's treatment of Banū Qurayẓa has been a sensitive narrative for obvious reasons, not least its uniquely violent literary account.

[175] Balādhurī, *Futūḥ*, 22; Balādhurī, *Origins*, 41. Ibn Saᶜd, *Ṭabaqāt*, 2:72.

[176] Ṭabarī, *History*, 8:38; Ṭabarī, *Ta'rīkh*, 1496. Dhahabī, *Ta'rīkh*, 2:314; Ibn Kathīr, *Bidāya*, 4:144.

[177] See Watt, *Muḥammad*, 217, where he argues that the brutal treatment of Banū Qurayẓa sent a clear warning to every Jew in Medina. While Watt largely treats the narratives as factual, his observation here points to how medieval Jews—who heard or read this Muslim tradition—might have felt as they resided in the Islamic caliphate.

[178] For an example of how Christians used these Muslim traditions in polemics against Muhammad and Islam, see Ibrahim and Hackenburg, *In Search*, 266, 310. See also Ibrahim, ed., *Medieval*, where over ten medieval Arabic-speaking Christians provide views on Muhammad and his message.

Overall, modern and contemporary Muslim thinkers treat the accounts of Banū Qurayẓa in at least three ways.

Some Muslims insist the story is factual—it is descriptive of the nature of the Jews and prescriptive for Muslims throughout all times.[179] These are the Muslim traditionalists who trust the tradition and defend its portrayal of early Islam. For them, the Jews have always been described in the Qur'ān as disloyal, and Muslim traditions simply follow course and present proof for the Jewish behavior.[180] For these Muslims, the Jews are the vilest of creatures (Q 98:6) who have violated their covenant with Muhammad and deserve destruction. This line of argument appears in the well-known study on Muhammad's life by Akram al-ᶜUmarī, who states, "We do not adjust Islam and its history to the taste of people and their intellectual ideologies in any given age."[181] In his examination of the raid of Banū Qurayẓa, al-ᶜUmarī criticizes some Muslim thinkers who deny that the raid occurred; he argues that the account is factual.[182]

Unlike al-ᶜUmarī's approach, other Muslims—although trusting the tradition's reliability and viewing the historiographical narratives as factual—acknowledge the moral problems of the story and call it annihilation, butchery, or massacre.[183] Some of these thinkers attempt to justify the incident. One justification claims that the murder of the Jewish men might appear aggressive in our day, but it was actually in harmony with Jewish Scriptures.[184] Still, this reasoning does not answer the aggressive portrayal

[179] See the Muslim studies of Mubārakpūrī, *Raḥīq*, 288–292; ᶜUmarī, *Sīra*, 311–315; Sharīf, *Makka*, 392–393 (the destruction of the Jews was a natural consequence of their treachery—all problems inside Medina were solved by destroying Banū Qurayẓa); Ṣallābī, *Sīra*, 610–611.

[180] See Riḍā, *Manār*, 3:192, 3:298, 11:110; Quṭb, *Fī ẓilāl*, 6:3952; Shaᶜrāwī, *Khawāṭirī*, 8:4666, 17:10417; Khaṭṭāb, *Rasūl*, 243–247.

[181] ᶜUmarī, *Mujtamaᶜ*, 23. Similarly, Khaṭṭāb, *Rasūl*, 246. In response, see Shoemaker, *Apocalypse*, 182–183, where he argues, "So long as we refuse to acknowledge and address these more 'illiberal' elements at the foundation of the Islamic tradition, they will continue to thrive in the minds of those fanatics who believe it is essential to follow the tradition exactly as Muhammad taught it and as his earliest followers observed it."

[182] ᶜUmarī, *Mujtamaᶜ*, 22–23; Mubārakpūrī, *Rawḍat*, 130–131; Mubārakpūrī, *Raḥīq*, 314.

[183] See Ramadan, *Understanding*, 78 (annihilation); Djait, *Fitna*, 28 (butchery); Qimanī, *Ḥurūb*, 2:262 (massacre). After calling it *majzara* (butchery), Tunisian Muslim scholar Hichem Djait states that the incident inaugurated "a truly violent *dawla* (state)" where violence became frequent as Arabs never saw it before—a frequently applied practice. He believes that the believers, under Muhammad, formed a *dawla* (state), *innamā buniyat ᶜalā al-ḥarb, ᶜala tashkīl quwwat tadakhkhul* (that was built on war, by establishing an aggressive intervention force). See Djait, *Fitna*, 26–27, 28. See Ibrahim, *Stated*, 92.

[184] See, for instance, Ramadan, *Understanding*, 78, where he claims that "the rule applied to Bani Qurayza is not Islamic, but an application of Deuteronomy, the enemy's book" (78), and affirms that this "annihilation" "represents an award rendered in arbitration," and that this "is in full agreement with the rules set forth in the Geneva Convention of 1949 with regard to prisoners of war and protected persons." For a traditional claim on Muhammad's kindness to the Jews, see Adil, *Muhammad*, 392. See the discussion of these studies in Ibrahim, *Stated*, 92.

of enslaving women and children.[185] Another justification relies on reading the narrative through historicism, arguing that the treatment of the Jews was suitable for the seventh-century context but is not prescriptive for all times and places.[186] A third group of Muslim studies represents the deniers of the incident who insist that it never happened.[187] Muslim apologist W. N. Arafat dismisses the incident entirely, claiming it is a myth, and argues that the Jews themselves created the story: "So then the real source of this unacceptable story of slaughter was the descendants of the Jews of Medina, from whom Ibn Isḥāq took these 'odd tales.'"[188] One problem with this line of thought is the pervasiveness of its occurrence in early Muslim sources—if one claims it never occurred, the reliability of the entire tradition is at stake, unless one picks and chooses from the accounts without any consistent methodology.

Unlike these Muslim arguments, non-Muslim thinkers *largely* do not exercise the same sensitivity toward the tradition—they refer to Banū Qurayẓa's incident as extermination, genocide, or butchery.[189] Still, some non-Muslims read the accounts as factual and provide reasons for the incident and its violent details.[190] A case in point is W. M. Watt, who defends

[185] In an interesting apologetic claim, Moulavi Chirágh Ali, *Critical Exposition*, 37–38, argues that Muhammad did not actually approve Saᶜd's judgment. Cf. ᶜAbd al-Raḥmān, *Judhūr*, 148ff., where he understands the story as a tactical move by Muhammad.

[186] Abou El Fadl, *Great*, 5–6, et passim; Abou El Fadl, *Speaking*, ch. 4; Akyol, *Islam*, 58–59; Akyol, *Reopening*, where he writes, "in the case of Banu Qurayza, even a massacre of all men [occurred], although there is some doubt about this grim story." Fadel, "Is Historicism," 131–176. For battles in Arabia, see ᶜAbd al-Karīm, *Mujtamaᶜ*, 21–27; ᶜAlī, *Mufaṣṣal*, 5:333ff. (reasons for raids), 5:399ff. (wars and conquests), 4:271ff. (the general rules of the Arabian society). See also Bodley, *Messenger*, 31–33; Grunebaum, *Classical*, 18. On manslaughter, vendetta, and raid customs in Arabia, see Rodinson, *Muhammad*, 14ff.

[187] See Ahmad, *Muhammad*, 9–10, where he claims that massacring men is never condoned by Islam and argues that the stories about murdering or expelling the Jews were forged by ᶜAbbāsid traditionists with anti-Jewish polemical motivations. See also Arafat, "New," 100–107; Ali, *Critical*, 37–38. See also the recent study by Akyol, *Islamic Moses*, which argues that the raid never happened.

[188] Arafat, "New," 106.

[189] See Anthony, *Muhammad*, 13 n. 45 (massacre); Rodinson, *Muhammad*, 213–214 (massacre); Stillman, *Jews*, 137; Bat Ye'or, *Islam*, 37. See also Michael Fishbein in his foreword of Ṭabarī, *History*, 8:xiv–xv. Gerhard Bowering writes, "In the aftermath of the 'Battle of the Trench,' Muhammad felt free to deal harshly with the Banu Qurayza, executing their men and selling their women and children into slavery." Bowering, "Muhammad," in *Princeton*, ed. Bowering, 375. Bernard Lewis writes that Muhammad gave the Jews of Banū Qurayẓa a choice between conversion and death. Lewis, *Jews*, 10, 83.

[190] See Watt, "Condemnation," in his *Early*, 1–11, previously published in 1952 as an article in *The Muslim World*; Watt, *Muḥammad*, 215, 328. See also Stillman, *Jews*, 16, where he argues that the execution was "not unusual according to the harsh rules of war during that period." Djait, in what appears to disagree with Stillman, argues that the punishment, particularly against women and children, was unusual among the Arabs. Djait, *Fitna*, 28. Tor Andræ views this incident in religious terms. He argues that Muhammad targeted Banū Qurayẓa because they "were the sworn enemies of Allah and His revelation." Andræ, *Mohammed*, 155. For some non-Muslim popular writers, see the arguments of contemporary British writer Karen Armstrong (1944–), *Muhammad*, 113–201.

Muhammad's actions against the Jews, writing, "The treatment of the Jewish clan of Qurayẓah by the Muslims was simply the regular Arab practice, but on a larger scale than usual, since the Muslims were stronger than even the average strong tribe."[191]

Unlike these approaches and interpretations, I believe that the accounts of the raid of Banū Qurayẓa are better viewed in the same way we treat Islamic historiography in general. They are the product of medieval historians who *authored* historiographical reports for sectarian, religious, and political goals. These historians did not necessarily aim to record past encounters. Rather, they shaped literary stories, communicating religious lessons, first, to exhort and educate Muslims on matters pertaining to faith and practice, and second, to communicate Islamic dispositions to non-Muslims in the conquered lands. With the accounts of Banū Qurayẓa, we are invited to believe that the Muslims had completely eradicated the Jews from Medina after they expelled the other two tribes earlier. They gained more power and accumulated more wealth. Nevertheless, the tradition reveals that there remained two Jewish settlements on the outskirts of Medina—Khaybar and Fadak. After the elimination of the Jews inside Medina, Muslim storytellers affirm that Muhammad and the Muslims were ready to march to these two settlements, to ensure the suppression of any possible Jewish threat.

The Raids to Khaybar and Fadak (7/628)

We are now in the early months of the seventh year after the *hijra*—almost two years after the elimination of Banū Qurayẓa (5/627) and only a few months after Muhammad's successful treaty of Ḥudaybiyya (6/628) with the Meccan Quraysh. Since Muhammad secured a phase of less tension with the Meccans and reportedly succeeded in getting rid of all the Jews within Medina, the logic goes, he is now ready to consolidate power, advance hegemony, and accumulate more resources, especially by eliminating any possible Jewish threat from outside Medina.[192] This frames the literary context of Muhammad's raid against Khaybar, which is a Jewish settlement in an oasis located about one hundred miles to the north of Medina.[193] Al-Balādhurī

[191] Watt, *Muḥammad*, 296; see also his broader defense of Muhammad's moral behavior in pp. 327–328.

[192] See Peters, *Muhammad*, 228.

[193] For the geography of Khaybar, see Ibn Khuradādhbih, *Masālik*, 248; Ibn al-Faqīh, *Buldān*, 83; Bakrī, *Muʿjam*, 2:521 (it is a three-day journey from Medina); Zamakhsharī, *Jibāl*, 126; Hamadānī,

states, "The Prophet *ghazā* (invaded) Khaybar in the year 7."[194] The use of the verb *ghazā* highlights initiation, determination, and assertiveness.[195] The Muslim tradition reveals that, after Muhammad's several attacks against the Medinan Jews, many of them fled Medina to Khaybar; consequently, the logic goes, it was important for the Muslims to secure Medina's northern region, since the southern region was relatively safe after the Treaty of Ḥudaybiyya.[196]

The Muslim narrators—as religious authors of historical accounts—design the initial marching steps toward Khaybar in theological terms. Muhammad's companions declared, "We will go out with you to Khaybar. Surely it is the countryside of the Ḥijāz with rich food and property."[197] Since this report shows Muslims seeking wealth and worldly gain, we are told, Muhammad deviated their attention from seeking the spoils and affirmed, "You will not go out with me unless you desire *jihād*. As for plunder, there will be none."[198] The narrative portrays Muhammad's companions as driven by worldly lusts, and this communicates a theological meaning to later Muslims: As you march into battle, seek jihad for Allah's cause, not for wealth. The narrators describe the raid not as a tribal attack but as a religious mission. This theological disposition is echoed in another account claiming that Allah protected the Muslims by dissuading the Arabs of Ghaṭafān from supporting the Jews of Khaybar.[199] To show the raid as a divinely commissioned activity, we are told that Kināna ibn Abī al-Ḥuqayq, who was the chief of Khaybar, had a situation at home: His beautiful wife Ṣafiyya bint Ḥuyayy reportedly wished for a different husband, specifically *malik al-ḥijāz Muḥammadan* (the king of the Hijaz, Muhammad).[200] The storytellers invite us to believe that Ṣafiyya

Amākin, 453 (it has fortresses, plants, and plenty of palm trees); Yāqūt, *Muʿjam*, 2:409 (it contains seven fortresses and ample palm trees); Samhūdī, *Wafā'*, 4:74; Balādī, *Muʿjam*, 118. See Vaglieri, "Khaybar," *EI²*, 4:1137–1138. Wolfensohn, *Ta'rīkh*, 157–174.

194 Balādhurī, *Futūḥ*, 23; Balādhurī, *Origins*, 42. See also Ibn Hishām, *Life*, 510–523; Ṭabarī, *Ta'rīkh*, 1575; Yaʿqūbī, *Ta'rīkh*, 2:56; Bayhaqī, *Dalā'il*, 4:194; Mūsā ibn ʿUqba, *Maghāzī*, 247.

195 On the verb *ghazā*, see Ibn Manẓūr, *Lisān*, 3:384, 8:237, 15:123–125. For a secondary study on Khaybar, see Mubārakpūrī, *Raḥīq*, 338–342.

196 See Ṭabarī, *Tafsīr*, 23:262, where he observes that Muhammad expelled Banū al-Naḍīr to Syria and Khaybar. *Ta'rīkh*, 1451; Ṭabarī, *History*, 7:159. Sharīf, *Makka*, 393; Watt, *Muḥammad*, 31, 212.

197 Wāqidī, *Life*, 312; Wāqidī, *Maghāzī*, 634.

198 Wāqidī, *Life*, 312; Wāqidī, *Maghāzī*, 634. See Watt, *Muḥammad*, 51.

199 Ṭabarī, *Ta'rīkh*, 1576. Ibn Hishām, *Sīra*, 2:328. See Wāqidī, *Maghāzī*, 642, where half of the date harvest of Khaybar was promised to Ghaṭafān if they helped the Jews. See Watt, *Muḥammad*, 36, 93.

200 Ṭabarī, *Ta'rīkh*, 1576, 1582; also Ibn Hishām, *Sīra*, 2:336; Yaʿqūbī, *Ta'rīkh*, 2:56; Zuhrī, *Maghāzī*, 161–162. In al-Bayhaqī, it is rendered "the king of Yathrib" (*Dalā'il*, 4:230–232). The Hijaz is the region where Mecca and Medina are located in western Arabia. On Safiyya, see Khalīfa, *Ta'rīkh*, 1:82, 86; Khalīfa, *Ṭabaqāt*, 1:640; Ibn Saʿd, *Ṭabaqāt*, 2:82, 8:95ff.; Ibn Ḥabīb, *Muḥabbar*, 1:90 (the dream or vision she saw); Fasawī, *Maʿrifa*, 1:508; Balādhurī, *Ansāb*, 1:442–443; Dhahabī, *Ta'rīkh*, 2:421ff.; Dhahabī, *Siyar*, 2:231–235; Ibn al-Athīr, *Usd*, 7:168; Ibn Ḥajar, *Iṣāba*, 8:210. For secondary studies on

even had a dream that her husband interpreted for her: "This simply means that you covet the king of the Hijaz, Muhammad."[201] The report is hard to believe if we consider that, according to traditions, Muhammad killed Ṣafiyya's father two years earlier at the Banū Qurayẓa affair.[202] However, the Muslim narrators fashion the report to elevate Muhammad as the growing star of Arabia who was desired even by his supposed enemies. As Muhammad marched to Khaybar, he reportedly declared, "Allāhu Akbar, Khaybar is destroyed."[203] While the traditionists can hardly relinquish their commitment to painting a raid in religious colors, they also need to portray the Jews of Khaybar negatively—particularly as violators of trust who deserve death. Thus, an incident must be designed to demonstrate the Jewish betrayal.

Muhammad reportedly arrived at Khaybar and demanded the *kanz* (treasure) of Banū al-Naḍīr from the Jewish chief Kināna.[204] Shocked at the request, Kināna reportedly said he was unaware of any treasure, but a Jew from Khaybar informed Muhammad of a possible location.[205] When the Muslims searched for the treasure, they reportedly found it—which confirmed Kināna was a liar and the Jews were treasonous. Muhammad sentenced Kināna to death and instructed the Muslim companion al-Zubayr, "Torture him until you root out what he has."[206] The Muslim tradition presents a picture of a painful and humiliating murder: "So [al-Zubayr] kindled a fire with flint and steel on [Kināna's] chest until he was nearly dead. Then the apostle delivered him to Muhammad b. Maslama and he struck off his head."[207] As with other literary pictures we have encountered, this one aims to convey how severe the Jews' punishment should be due to their treachery and betrayal. This account serves as a clear warning to the Jews in the Muslim Empire. After Kināna's death, his wife Ṣafiyya was reportedly given to Muhammad as a

Ṣafiyya, see Watt, *Muḥammad*, 396–397; Awde, *Women*, 10, 58–59, 85–90; Firestone, "Prophet," 33; Ruṣāfī, *Shakhṣiyya*, 416ff.; ᶜUmarī, *Risāla*, 95–110.

201 Ibn Hishām, *Life*, 515. Her story will conclude after the raid, as Muhammad will select her as a wife for himself.

202 Wāqidī, *Maghāzī*, 513, 516. Ibn Hishām, *Sīra*, 2:241. Ṣafiyya was likely seventeen years old at Khaybar. See Balādhurī, *Ansāb*, 1:422–444; also Watt, *Muḥammad*, 396–397.

203 Ibn Hishām, *Life*, 511.

204 On Kināna, see Ibn Saᶜd, *Ṭabaqāt*, 8:95–97, 8:175 (Kināna was from Banū al-Naḍīr, and married Ṣafiyya after she was married to Salām ibn Mishkam from Banū Qurayẓa); Ibn Manda, *Maᶜrifat*, 965; Ibn ᶜAbd al-Barr, *Istīᶜāb*, 4:1871 (he was a poet); Ibn al-Athīr, *Usd*, 7:168 (poet); Dhahabī, *Siyar*, 2:231 (Jewish poet); Ṣafadī, *Wāfī*, 16:188 (poet). See also ᶜAlī, *Mufaṣṣal*, 18:338, 348.

205 Ibn Hishām, *Sīra*, 2:336. Ṭabarī, *Ta'rīkh*, 1582.

206 Ṭabarī, *History*, 8:122–123; Ṭabarī, *Ta'rīkh*, 1582.

207 Ibn Hishām, *Life*, 515. Ṭabarī, *Ta'rīkh*, 1582; Ṭabarī, *History*, 8:123.

wife.[208] The picture of a prophet marrying a beautiful woman soon after he killed her husband and family is designed by the Muslim narrators to advance the rights, privileges, and advantages of Muhammad among the Muslims.[209] This is evidenced in a claim that Ṣafiyya was initially among the portion of the captives given to Diḥya al-Kalbī, one of Muhammad's companions, but she was then taken and solely designated to Muhammad himself because she was *sayyidat* (the notable lady of) Qurayẓa and al-Naḍīr.[210]

With the victory of Muslims over the Jews of Khaybar, we are told, "The women of Khaybar were distributed among the Muslims."[211] This literary picture, it appears, is designed by Muslim narrators to entice Muslim warriors due to the materialistic benefits soldiers could obtain in battle. Still, traditionists report that some Muslims did not act honorably with the Jewish women. These Muslims reportedly raped pregnant Jewish women, which propelled Muhammad to declare such acts as forbidden.[212] This report contrasts the Muslim warriors' worldly behavior with the religious notion that these soldiers were *zuhhād* (ascetics) marching in battle to proclaim Islam.[213] Ultimately, after the killing of the chief of Khaybar, Muhammad reportedly "seized the property piece by piece and conquered the forts one by one as he came to them."[214] Some claim that Muhammad "besieged the inhabitants between thirteen and nineteen nights."[215] He even "took the children captive."[216] Eventually, as he besieged the Jews of Khaybar, "they were certain that they would perish," so "they asked him to banish them and spare

208 Ṭabarī, *Ta'rīkh*, 1576. See also Ibn Hishām, *Sīra*, 2:331; Ibn Hishām, *Life*, 511; Ibn Ḥabīb, *Muḥabbar*, 90.

209 See the claims of Ibn Qayyim, *Zād*, 3:130.

210 Ibn al-Athīr, *Usd*, 7:168 (poet); Dhahabī, *Siyar*, 2:231. We are told that Diḥya asked Muhammad for Ṣafiyya, but Muhammad chose her for himself and gave Diḥya her two cousins. Ibn Hishām, *Life*, 511.

211 Ibn Hishām, *Life*, 511.

212 Ibn Hishām, *Sīra*, 2:330; Suhaylī, *Rawḍ*, 7:96. Additionally, we are told, "The Muslims ate the meat of the domestic donkeys and the apostle got up and forbade the people to do a number of things which he enumerated." Ibn Hishām, *Life*, 511. See the juristic application by Shāfiᶜī, *Musnad*, 3:53.

213 See the discussion in Ibrahim, *Stated*, 163, 237. See the tendentious report in Bukhārī, *Ṣaḥīḥ*, 5:8; Muslim, *Ṣaḥīḥ*, 4:1967, where it claims that Muhammad stated, "Do not insult my companions, do not insult my companions." Similarly, see Bukhārī, *Ṣaḥīḥ*, 3:171; Muslim, *Ṣaḥīḥ*, 4:1963, where Muhammad reportedly prophesied, "The best of people is *qarnī* (my generation, century), then those following them."

214 Ibn Hishām, *Life*, 511. Ibn Hishām, *Sīra*, 2:328.

215 Ṭabarī, *History*, 8:117; Ṭabarī, *Ta'rīkh*, 1577.

216 Yaᶜqūbī, *Ta'rīkh*, 2:56. In a Shīᶜite report, al-Yaᶜqūbī writes, "[Muhammad] divided their women, their men, and the loads of dates, wheat, and barley among the Banū Hāshim; then he made division among the people as a whole." Yaᶜqūbī, *Works*, 3:656. The Shīᶜite sympathy is clear in the report. This report is echoed in Wāqidī, *Maghāzī*, 660, and Ibn Zanjawayh, *Amwāl*, 188, 194, but they do not mention Banū Hāshim in particular, only his relatives generally. Watt writes on the apparent partiality of Muhammad in this incident and justifies the action by claiming, "It must be

their lives, which he did."[217] Like earlier discussions on literary depictions of the raids against the Jews, it is important to reiterate that these reports are better viewed as not necessarily factual but instead as devising a religious message for later Muslim and non-Muslim generations in the Islamic caliphate.

As for the wealth and spoils gained from Khaybar, Muhammad reportedly *ḥāz al-amwāl kullahā* (had taken possession of all their property).[218] He took one-fifth of the spoils for himself and distributed the rest to the Muslims.[219] The tradition provides ample reports on the abundance of wealth that Muslims gained from Khaybar. When Muhammad seized a particular fortress, we are told, Allah "opened it" for the Muslims to conquer: "There was no fortress in Khaybar more abounding in food and fat meat than it."[220] Some Muslims exclaimed, "We have never been full [of food] except after we conquered Khaybar."[221] Even Muhammad's wife ʿĀ'isha reportedly said after conquering Khaybar, "Now we will always be over satisfied from dates."[222] For the narrators, it appears, the abundance of spoils reflects a sign of divine support for the Muslims. As a literary construction, wealth and spoils undoubtedly serve as a compelling motivation for Muslim soldiers during a time of empire expansion: Imitate Muhammad's companions, strive in jihad for Allah, and gain his divine favor by fighting the enemy and accumulating wealth. This religious lesson appears at the core of the narrative of Khaybar.

Finally, after their defeat and surrender, the Jews begged Muhammad "to employ them on the property with half share in the produce, saying, 'We know more about it than you and we are better farmers.'"[223] Muhammad agreed to this arrangement, but declared, "O community of Jews, by God, to

remembered, however, that Muhammad stood in a special relation to the clans of Hāshim and al-Muṭṭalib; he was their leader among the Muslims." Watt, *Muḥammad*, 260.

[217] Ṭabarī, *History*, 8:123; Ṭabarī, *Ta'rīkh*, 1582.

[218] Ibn Hishām, *Sīra*, 2:337; Ibn Hishām, *Life*, 515. Fazārī, *Siyar*, 239. There are contradicting accounts. Some claim that Muhammad took only a portion of the spoils for himself, while others imply he seized all of them. Watt rightly observes, "Some sources imply that at Khaybar and Fadak also the lands fell entirely to Muḥammad." Watt, *Muḥammad*, 256.

[219] Ṭabarī, *Ta'rīkh*, 1590; Ṭabarī, *History*, 8:130; Wāqidī, *Maghāzī*, 660; Ibn Sallām, *Amwāl*, 70–71; Ibn Zanjawayh, *Amwāl*, 94; Abū Yūsuf, *Kharāj*, 62, 103. There are contradicting reports about the distribution of the spoils. See Ṭabarī, *History*, 8:128 n. 528; Vaglieri, "Khaybar," *EI*², 4:1137–1138.

[220] Ṭabarī, *History*, 8:117; Ṭabarī, *Ta'rīkh*, 1577.

[221] Bukhārī, *Ṣaḥīḥ*, 5:140.

[222] Bukhārī, *Ṣaḥīḥ*, 5:140. For a study on ʿĀ'isha, see Spellberg, *Politics*, 27–99.

[223] Ibn Hishām, *Life*, 515. Wāqidī, *Maghāzī*, 690. Abū Yūsuf, *Kharāj*, 62, 103. See Watt, *Muḥammad*, 256–257, where he explains how this rule was later used by Muhammad's successors.

me you are the most loathsome creation of God,"[224] and, "if we wish to expel you we will expel you."[225] This is a multilayer report with a clear anti-Jewish disposition. The literary image of the Jews begging Muhammad to work in their former lands seems to create a parable of Islam's hegemony over the Jews. The additional literary layer of Muhammad loathing the Jews seems to fit the religious tension of the medieval time of documentation. Once more, we encounter a designed narrative that serves as a warning for the Jews in conquered lands. Overall, the reports convey that divine support is with the Muslims, as evidenced in how they are victorious and their enemies are now working for them.

With the Muslim victory in seizing Khaybar, the tradition reveals, there is only one major nearby Jewish settlement, Fadak, left to be subdued.[226] However, the battle against Fadak was arguably over before it started, because its people were reportedly terrified when they heard of what the Muslims did at Khaybar. The people of Fadak sent to Muhammad, "asking him to banish them and spare their lives, and they would leave him their property; and he did so."[227] They surrendered and gave all their lands to Muhammad and the Muslims. Since the Muslims won over Fadak without any attack, its spoils were reportedly treated differently than those of Khaybar. While Muhammad reportedly divided portions of the spoils of Khaybar among the Muslims, "Fadak belonged exclusively to [him]."[228] The tradition highlights that the subjugation of Khaybar and Fadak meant the end of the Jewish presence within and outside Medina; however, Muhammad knew that some Jews

224 Wāqidī, *Life*, 340; Wāqidī, *Maghāzī*, 691.

225 Ibn Hishām, *Life*, 515. See also Ṭabarī, *Ta'rīkh*, 1590; Ṭabarī, *History*, 8:130.

226 For Fadak, see Bakrī, *Muʿjam*, 3:1015–1016 (an agricultural village, located about two days' journey from Khaybar, which has plentiful fruits and water wells); Zamakhsharī, *Jibāl*, 1:255 (a village with palm trees and plentiful agriculture); Yāqūt, *Muʿjam*, 4:238–240 (located two or three days' travel from Medina, i.e., about ninety-five miles, and has a sparkling water well and plenty of palm trees); Samhūdī, *Wafā'*, 4:126; Balādī, *Muʿjam*, 235. See also Adam, "Fadak," *EI*², 2:725–727.

227 Ṭabarī, *History*, 8:123; Ṭabarī, *Ta'rīkh*, 1583. Ibn Hishām, *Life*, 515.

228 Ṭabarī, *History*, 8:123; Ṭabarī, *Ta'rīkh*, 1583. See Ibn Sallām, *Amwāl*, 70–71; Ibn Zanjawayh, *Amwāl*, 94; Abū Yūsuf al-Anṣārī, *Kharāj*, 62, 103. Many Shīʿite traditions claim that Muhammad designated Fadak to his daughter Fāṭima. See Majlisī, *Biḥār*, 29:111, 205. On the matter and the dispute between Abū Bakr and Fāṭima over Muhammad's inheritance, particularly Fadak, see Yāqūt, *Muʿjam*, 4:238–240; Vaglieri, "Fāṭima," *EI*², 2:244–245; Adam, "Fadak," *EI*², 2:725; Bājī, *Taʿdīl*, 3:1295. Khaybar became the *fay'* of the Muslims. Ṭabarī, *History*, 8:123; Ṭabarī, *Ta'rīkh*, 1583. For the terms *ghanīma* and *fay'*, as descriptions of spoils, see Yaḥyā ibn Ādam, *Kharāj*, 58–61, 82; Ibn Sallām, *Amwāl*, 87–96, 132–145, 301–311 (*al-fay'*); 342–349 (distinguishing *ghanīma* and *fay'*); 403–408 (*salb* and *fay'*). An English translation of *Kitāb al-amwāl* is now available as *The Book of Revenue*. See the *fay'* on 17–24 and 211–239 and the *salb* on 295–304. See also Ibn Qudāma, *Mughnī*, 6:453ff. See Kister, "Land," 273; Løkkegaard, "Fay'," *EI*², 2:869–870; Løkkegaard, "Ghanīma," *EI*², 2:1005–1006; Ibrahim, *Stated*, 72; ʿAbd al-Karīm, *Shadwu*, 1:75–77. For a Shīʿite view on *fay'* and *ghnīma*, see Khū'ī, *Prolegomena*, 247, where they are both the same.

resided in a nearby location named Wādī al-Qurā. This was not a Jewish settlement, but a small land where Arab Bedouins and some Jews lived. Consequently, Muhammad marched to Wādī al-Qurā with a small army "seeking those Jews who lived there."[229] The Jews, we are told, began to attack the Muslims with spears, so Muhammad "charged his companions to fight."[230] The Muslims fought the Jews until they surrendered. We are told that Muhammad "conquered them by force."[231] This is why Muhammad reportedly treated the matter of the spoils as he did in Khaybar. He "apportioned what he took among his companions," but "left the dates and land in the hands of the Jews and employed them on it."[232] As we encountered in many incidents, the Muslim narrators design the raid in a religious manner and claim that Allah "plundered their property and [the Muslims] took furniture and goods in plenty."[233] As compared to Khaybar, the incident of Wādī al-Qurā appears in the tradition as a minor *ghazwa* (raid).[234] However, as a literary construct, it seeks to describe the total elimination of the Jews in the Hijaz. It invites the reader to see an image of no Jewish influence in the land of Muhammad. Watt observes, "The fall of Khaybar and surrender of the other Jewish colonies may be said to mark the end of the Jewish question during Muhammad's lifetime."[235]

Muhammad is now portrayed as the king of the Hijaz. However, the glowing picture is distorted. After his victory over Khaybar, we are told, a tragedy occurred: When he sat down to rest, a wicked Jewess named Zaynab bint al-Ḥārith reportedly offered to cook him a meal, and he accepted—but she poisoned it.[236] The reports are contradictory on the incident, particularly

229 Wāqidī, *Life*, 349; Wāqidī, *Maghāzī*, 709.

230 Wāqidī, *Life*, 349.

231 Wāqidī, *Life*, 349.

232 Wāqidī, *Life*, 350.

233 Wāqidī, *Life*, 350.

234 Ibn Hishām, *Sīra*, 2:338–339; Wāqidī, *Life*, 349–350. Similarly, there were some Jews in Taymā' and when they heard about Muhammad's "conquest of Khaybar, Fadak and Wādī al-Qurā," they "made peace with the Messenger of God on the *Jizya*." Wāqidī, *Life*, 350. See Watt, *Muḥammad*, 218. On the issue of non-Muslims surrendering to Muslims after defeat in battles, see Milka Levy-Rubin, *Non-Muslims*, 32–56.

235 Watt, *Muḥammad*, 219; Margoliouth, *Mohammed*, 22. Wolfensohn, *Ta'rīkh*, 175–186.

236 Ibn Hishām, *Sīra*, 2:338; Ibn Saᶜd, *Ṭabaqāt*, 1:343, 2:82, 2:154; Ṭabarī, *History*, 8:123–124; Ṭabarī, *Ta'rīkh*, 1583–1584; Bukhārī, *Ṣaḥīḥ*, 4:99; 5:141; 7:193; Kharkūshī, *Sharaf*, 4:292, 4:539; Masᶜūdī, *Tanbīh*, 1:223; Bayhaqī, *Dalā'il*, 4:256–263; Suhaylī, *Rawḍ*, 7:110; Ibn Kathīr, *Sīra*, 3:395–400; Ibn Kathīr, *Bidāya*, 4:237–240; Jawzī, *Muntaẓim*, 3:297; Ibn al-Athīr, *Kāmil*, 2:100; Dhahabī, *Ta'rīkh*, 1:523, 2:435–437. After she poisoned Muhammad, Zaynab reportedly told him, "You know what you have done to my people. I said to myself, 'If he is a king I shall ease myself of him and if he is a prophet he will be informed (of what I have done).'" Ibn Hishām, *Life*, 516. See also Ibn Taymiyya, *Fatāwā*, 1:164; Ibn Taymiyya, *Majmūᶜ*, 35:217.

on whether he swallowed the food; however, on his deathbed, he declared, "I feel my aorta being severed because of the food I ate."[237] This is why, al-Ṭabarī reports, "The Muslims believed that in addition to the honor of prophethood that God had granted him the Messenger of God died a martyr."[238] The contradictions in the reports, I argue, are better viewed as reflecting a tweaked tradition. Later generations of traditionists have likely found the story of a Jewess poisoning Muhammad unacceptable, especially as it questions the divine protection and abilities of a prophet; thus, revisions of the memory and adjustments were necessary.[239] Still, this report displays an image of a horrific attack against Muhammad—it is plausible to view it as a Muslim literary device aiming to paint the Jews as the most vicious enemy of Islam, since, the logic goes, they hurt the most important human figure in the faith.

Arguably, the poison narrative remains a major source of anti-Jewish detestation in Muslim circles, despite its implausibility. Not only does it depict Muhammad as naïve, coveting a cooked meal by a Jewess after he reportedly killed members of her family (father, uncle, and husband) and took others captive, but it also invites us to believe that the effect of the poison remained in Muhammad's blood for over four years (Khaybar was in March–April 628, and he reportedly died in June 632).[240] Despite this reported poison and its continued effects, the tradition insists that Muhammad remained an

[237] Ṭabarī, *History*, 8:124. Ibn Hishām, *Life*, 210, 516. See a classical Sunnī explanation on the contradictions in the tradition in Ibn Qayyim, *Zād*, 3:398. For studies on the incident of poisoning Muhammad, see Ibrahim, *Muhammad*, 98–103; Margoliouth, *Mohammed*, 361; Watt, *Muḥammad*, 54, 234; Rodinson, *Muhammad*, 254; Pierce, "Remembering," 220ff. For a thorough overview of the literature on Muhammad's death and how the account was later used in anti-Muslim polemic, see Szilágyi, "After the Prophet's Death." See also feminist Muslim scholar Kecia Ali, *Lives*, 22, where she unconvincingly dismisses the poisoning narrative and calls those accounts relying on it "hostile accounts," because the "poisoning by a Jewish woman allows critics to view Muhammad as bereft of God's protection and therefore clearly not what he claimed to be."

[238] Ṭabarī, *History*, 8:124. See Faizer, "Ibn Isḥāq," where the author concludes, "[Muhammad] dies a martyr from that very poison, which was surely a fine note on which to conclude the life of this 'most heroic of Prophets'" (126). For a Shīʿite view on the poisoning of Muhammad, see Qummī, *Tafsīr*, 2:376; Majlisī, *Biḥār*, 22:516; 31:641; Ḥabīb, *Fāḥisha*, 455ff.

[239] See the valuable study of Ahmed, *Before*, 268–269, where he analyzes numerous accounts of the Satanic Verses tradition and argues, "Given the centrality of the *authoritative* persona of the Prophet to the logic of the Ḥadīth movement, it is obvious that the idea of an *infallible* or *impeccable* Prophet whose words and deeds might reliably be taken to establish a model for detailed pious mimesis must have possessed a particular appeal for the [traditionists]."

[240] See Rodinson, *Muhammad*, 254. The death of Muhammad, according to major Muslim traditions, was in 632; however, there are doubts concerning this date, especially as numerous sources—Jewish, Christian, Samaritan, and even Islamic—suggest that he was alive for two to three years after that and led the conquest of Palestine in 634–635. See Shoemaker, *Death*, 1–16.

unstoppable commander in chief, leading the conquest of Mecca a year after Khaybar. In fact, in the four years between Khaybar and his death, he reportedly led and commissioned major military activities to subdue strong Arab tribes and even targeted the Christian Byzantines. We look at these raids next.

6

The King of Arabia

Raiding the Bedouins

> Inform him that if he becomes a Muslim I will return his family and property to him and give him a hundred camels.—Muhammad reportedly incentivizing a tribal leader to surrender

> You have become the most wealthy among the Quraysh! Give me from this wealth.—Umayyad leader Abū Sufyān, speaking to Muhammad after the spoils were seized at the Battle of Ḥunayn[1]

With the elimination of the Jews from Medina and its surroundings, as well as the victory over the Quraysh in the conquest of Mecca, Muhammad is depicted in Muslim traditions as to have overcome his *major* enemies, but not all. While he is indeed identified as the king of Arabia, there were still strategic *maghāzī* that he needed to launch in order to suppress all his enemies.[2] Soon after the conquest of Mecca, we are told, he sent tactical military campaigns against specific Arab Bedouins. In particular, the tradition highlights three major expeditions: one against the Banū Jadhīma under the command of Muhammad's companion Khālid ibn al-Walīd, another against the strong tribe of Hawāzin in the Battle of Ḥunayn, and finally its subsequent siege of al-Ṭā'if to subdue the Thaqīf tribe. The first two military campaigns resulted in Muslim victories, while the siege did not yield military success. All these reportedly occurred in the eighth *hijrī* year. In the following year, many of the Arab tribes will reportedly come to Muhammad and offer him their *islām* (submission). The year is known in the tradition as *ᶜām al-wufūd* (the year of delegations), describing Arab tribes surrendering to Muhammad's leadership and converting to Islam.[3] Once Muhammad is able

[1] Wāqidī, *Life*, 467, 463.
[2] For a Muslim study on Muhammad's military skills, see ᶜAqqād, *ᶜAbqariyyat Muḥammad*, 28–56.
[3] See Ibn Saᶜd, *Ṭabaqāt*, 1:222ff.

Muhammad's Military Expeditions. Ayman S. Ibrahim, Oxford University Press. © Oxford University Press 2024.
DOI: 10.1093/oso/9780197769171.003.0006

to control all these Arab tribes under his leadership, the logic goes, he is able to attack the superpower of his day: the Byzantine Empire. In this chapter, we examine the traditions of the incursion to Banū Jadhīma, the Battle of Ḥunayn, and the raid to al-Ṭā'if, leaving the military campaigns targeting the Christian Byzantines to chapter 7.

The Incursion to Banū Jadhīma (8/630)

The tradition describes the raid to Banū Jadhīma as a consequence of the conquest of Mecca, when Muhammad "commanded [his companions] to attack those who were not following Islam."[4] He reportedly dispatched many companions—in *sarāyā* (incursions)—to various locations in Arabia and instructed them to destroy the idols wherever they found them.[5] Notably, Muhammad instructed the shrewd and skillful new convert Khālid ibn al-Walīd to march to Nakhla to destroy their major idol al-ᶜUzzā; consequently, Khālid "set out with thirty riders from his companions to al-ᶜUzzā and brought it down."[6] After Khālid successfully accomplished this task, Muhammad reportedly entrusted him to lead 350 Muslims to march "to the Banū Jadhīma, not on a mission of war, but, with an invitation to Islam."[7] Banū Jadhīma was a small Arab tribe south of Mecca, but this report is odd. It describes an army of Muslims heading to a nearby location with a missionary goal. If we accept this report, then other raids did not have such religious objectives. This, from a critical standpoint, questions the traditional Muslim claim that all the *maghāzī* aimed to proclaim Islam.[8] Ironically, while the report emphasizes a religious mission, it questions the religious nature and motivations of other

[4] Wāqidī, *Life*, 429. Al-Ṭabarī calls it *sariyya* (incursion) and *ghazwa* (raid), although Muhammad did not participate in it. Ṭabarī, *Ta'rīkh*, 1649.

[5] Ṭabarī, *Ta'rīkh*, 1649.

[6] Wāqidī, *Life*, 429. Muhammad also reportedly instructed ᶜAmr ibn al-ᶜĀṣ to destroy Hudhayl, and Saᶜd to bring down the idol Manāt. See ᶜUmarī, *Sīra*, 484. On Khālid, see Zubayrī, *Nasab*, 1:320–321; Ibn Saᶜd, *Ṭabaqāt*, 4:190–191; Khalīfa, *Ṭabaqāt*, 51; Ibn al-Athīr, *Usd*, 2:140; Balādhurī, *Ansāb*, 10:207–209; Dhahabī, *Siyar*, *sīra* 2:189–190, 1:366–383; Ṣafadī, *Wāfī*, 13:160–162; Ibn Ḥajar, *Iṣāba*, 2:215–218; Ibn Ḥazm, *Jamharat*, 1:147; Ziriklī, *Aᶜlām*, 2:300. See the Muslim study of ᶜAqqād, *ᶜAbqariyyat Khālid*, 11–60.

[7] Wāqidī, *Life*, 430. Here the tradition seems to highlight a change in the aim of warfare, as evidenced in the report stating, "There is no *hijra* (emigration) after *al-fatḥ* (the conquest of Mecca) but only *jihād* (striving and fighting) and good intention remain." Bukhārī, *Ṣaḥīḥ*, 3:14. Ṣallābī, *Ghazawāt*, 275.

[8] See Ibrahim, *Stated*, 1–9.

expeditions. Additionally, as a literary narrative, it contains more problematic features than expected.

When Khālid arrived at the location for his presumed religious proclamation, we are told, he "mistreated the Banū Jadhīma and killed some of them."[9] Muslim narrators describe a reason for this mistreatment: Decades earlier, before the advent of Islam, men from Banū Jadhīma reportedly killed Khālid's paternal uncle.[10] This is why, when Khālid arrived at Banū Jadhīma and they saw him, they were alarmed and "took up their weapons," but he assured them, "Put down your weapons, for the people have become Muslims."[11] He told them not to worry as he had already converted to Islam. They reportedly affirmed, "We are a Muslim community; we bless and trust Muḥammad. We built the mosque and call to prayer in it."[12] Still, one of the men of Banū Jadhīma did not trust Khālid and told his people, "It is Khālid. By God, after you lay down your weapons, it will be nothing but leather manacles, and after leather manacles it will be nothing but the smiting of necks. By God, I will never lay down my weapon!"[13] His people did not heed his advice and assured him, "The people have become Muslims."[14] Nonetheless, once Banū Jadhīma "laid down their weapons because of what Khālid had said," he "ordered that their hands should be tied behind their backs, then he put them to the sword, killing some of them."[15]

The account describes Khālid's treachery and deceit against fellow Muslims. The tradition points to him as a Muslim who "acted in the time of Islam according to the ways of *jāhiliyya* (the pre-Islamic time of ignorance)."[16] Angry about what Khālid did, one of Muhammad's companions rebuked Khālid, "You only took vengeance for your paternal uncle."[17] The rebuke indicates that some Muslims believed that Khālid purposefully planned on murdering people of Banū Jadhīma, although he was supposedly

[9] Ṭabarī, *Ta'rīkh*, 1649; Ṭabarī, *History*, 8:189. For a Sunnī study on the account, see ᶜUmarī, *Sīra*, 492–493, where he describes the incursion as a precursor of attacking Hawāzin, because Banū Jadhīma was south of Mecca on the road to Ṭā'if.

[10] Ṭabarī, *Ta'rīkh*, 1650; Ṭabarī, *History*, 8:189. Ibn Hishām, *Life*, 562.

[11] Ṭabarī, *History*, 8:189; Ṭabarī, *Ta'rīkh*, 1650.

[12] Wāqidī, *Life*, 430.

[13] Ṭabarī, *History*, 8:189; Ṭabarī, *Ta'rīkh*, 1650.

[14] Ṭabarī, *History*, 8:190.

[15] Ṭabarī, *History*, 8:190; Ṭabarī, *Ta'rīkh*, 1650.

[16] Ṭabarī, *Ta'rīkh*, 1651. See Watt, *Muḥammad*, 70, where he argues, "The standard account of this expedition, however, is hardly more than a circumstantial denigration of Khālid, and yields little solid historical fact." Watt, here, does not seem to consider the overall portrayal of Khālid in major Muslim histories, especially among Sunnīs.

[17] Ṭabarī, *History*, 8:190.

on a mission to proclaim Islam. We are told that, once Muhammad heard of what Khālid did, "he raised his hands to heaven and said, 'O God, I declare to Thee that I am innocent of what Khālid has done.' "[18] Muhammad reportedly disapproved of Khālid's actions, although he did not dismiss him and actually relied on him shortly afterward in major military expeditions.[19]

Overall, these reports represent a negative portrayal of Khālid, highlighting him as acting in ways unfitting of Islam.[20] While this portrayal is arguably the shortest literary description of the incident, which might reflect its succinct memory, Khālid's negative image did not seem to appeal to medieval traditionists, since he was reportedly one of Muhammad's major companions. His negative depiction required adjustment through literary embellishments, not only because of Khālid's importance for later *maghāzī* traditions, but, more importantly, because Khālid's negative portrayal might also place Muhammad in a dark light and question his wisdom. Muhammad had designated Khālid to lead this "missionary" raid, although the grudge of Khālid against Banū Jadhīma was reportedly known among the companions.[21] There seems to be a literary gap here, especially if one questions why a missionary envoy of 350 Muslims needed to march to Banū Jadhīma if the people had already accepted Islam. For these reasons, the logic goes, a tweak in the literary portrayal of Khālid seemed necessary. Muslim narrators, as we have often encountered in Arabic traditions, tweak narratives by creating opposing memories. This is one reason why competing reports justify Khālid's behavior and offer reasons for his killing of fellow Muslims.

In one report, we are told that, after killing the people, Khālid declared, "I did not fight until ᶜAbdallah b. Ḥudhāfah al-Sahmī commanded me to do so."[22] Here, the narrators defend Khālid by blaming another Muslim companion. In another report, Khālid insisted he was told that Muhammad himself "commanded [him] to kill them because of their resistance to Islam."[23] The report vindicates Khālid by establishing a competing memory highlighting

[18] Ṭabarī, *Ta'rīkh*, 1650. Ṭabarī, *History*, 8:190.

[19] See reports of Muhammad relying on Khālid in various expeditions after this incident. Wāqidī, *Maghāzī*, 897 (Ḥunayn); Ṭabarī, *History*, 9:58 (to Ukaydir at Dūmat al-Jandal), 9:82 (Banū al-Ḥārith), 9:90 (Yemen). Dūmat al-Jandal, where Ukaydir reportedly lived, was of economic and strategic importance; see Kennedy, *Prophet*, 35, 52; Muir, *Life*, 225; Eph'al, *Ancient*, 121.

[20] Khālid accepted Islam in Ṣafar in year A.H. 8, and the conquest of Mecca was seven months later, in Ramaḍān of the same year. Cf. Ṭabarī, *History*, 8:143 and 8:160. Still, a contradicting report—to embellish Khālid's image—suggests he was a secret Muslim since year A.H. 6. Ṭabarī, *History*, 8:71.

[21] Ṭabarī, *History*, 8:190.

[22] Ṭabarī, *History*, 8:190.

[23] Ṭabarī, *History*, 8:190.

him fulfilling prophetic instructions. It appears that the narrators worked diligently to provide excuses for Khālid, as evidenced in how they explicitly reported on what "some who would excuse Khālid said."[24] In a third report, we are invited to believe that Khālid killed the Muslims because it was not *absolutely* clear whether they converted to Islam—they did not give him the right answer: When they saw him, they declared *ṣabaʾnā, ṣabaʾnā* (we converted, we converted).[25] For Khālid, they did not clearly declare *aslamnā* (converted to Islam), and thus they deserved to be slain.[26] In this report, the narrators justify Khālid by claiming the massacre was a result of a mere misunderstanding. While this report might excuse Khālid, other accounts reveal that some major companions who were with him—including ᶜUmar's son—openly opposed and disobeyed his specific orders to kill fellow Muslims.[27] Ultimately, we have two sets of competing memories that disperse any particularities about Khālid's actions.

Still, more importantly, the narrators seemingly needed to distance Muhammad from receiving any blame for Khālid's actions; consequently, they shaped a report that Muhammad *openly* chastised Khālid in front of other companions: "Gently, Khālid, leave my companions alone, for by God if you had a mountain of gold and spent it for God's sake you would not approach the merit of my companions."[28] This report—though somewhat ambiguous—may convey that, for Muhammad, Khālid was not considered among the companions—a notion particularly stressed by Shīᶜite Muslims.[29] Muhammad's statement might even suggest that he excommunicated Khālid from among the companions; however, this appears doubtful, as ample traditions reveal that, soon after this incident, Muhammad commissioned Khālid to lead various expeditions, including the following Battle of

[24] Ibn Hishām, *Life*, 562; Ṭabarī, *History*, 8:190.

[25] Ibn Hishām, *Sīra*, 2:431; Bayhaqī, *Dalāʾil*, 5:114; Suhaylī, *Rawḍ*, 7:266. The narrators distinguish the term *ṣabaʾ* from *aslam*, although Muhammad was often identified as al-Ṣābiʾ since he abandoned the religion of Quraysh for Islam. See Ibn Manẓūr, *Lisān*, 1:107–108; Qurṭubī, *Jāmiᶜ*, 11:163; Riḍā, *Manār*, 7:311; Rāzī, *Mafātiḥ*, 17:308. However, the word *ṣābiʾ* appears to be a general reference to someone who abandons a religion for another, i.e., a mere convert. See Qurṭubī, *Jāmiᶜ*, 1:434.

[26] See the explanation of Ibn Ḥajar, *Fatḥ*, 8:57–58; Ibn Kathīr, *Sīra*, 3:592–594; Ibn Kathīr, *Bidāya*, 4:358–360; Ḥalabī, *Insān*, 3:277–278; Dhahabī, *Taʾrīkh*, 2:567; Ibn Qayyim, *Zād*, 3:365. For secondary Muslim studies that excuse Khālid's action and argue that *ṣabaʾnā* is different from *aslamnā*, see ᶜUmarī, *Sīra*, 492–494; Mubārakpūrī, *Raḥīq*, 377; Qarībī, *Marwiyyāt*, 77–79; Abū Māyla, *Sarāyā*, 247–249, 252–253.

[27] Bayhaqī, *Dalāʾil*, 5:114; Ibn Kathīr, *Sīra*, 3:593; Dhahabī, *Taʾrīkh*, 2:567.

[28] Ibn Hishām, *Life*, 562.

[29] See Sulaym ibn Qays, *Kitāb Sulaym*, 227, 387, 390–394; Naṣr ibn Muzāḥim, *Waqᶜat*, 195, 206; Ṣadūq, *Man lā*, 4:121, 4:503; Isfahānī, *Maqātil*, 23; Yaᶜqūbī, *Taʾrīkh*, 2:62–63; Majlisī, *Biḥār*, 98:43.

Ḥunayn.[30] After all, a year earlier, Muhammad named Khālid "the sword of Allah," and the title remained after the Banū Jadhīma's incident.[31]

Evidently, the traditionists were keen to polish Khālid's reputation. Their embellishments of his portrayal—in ample Muslim traditions—are glaring and inescapable. One proto-Sunnī historian insists that Muhammad instructed *lā tasibbū Khālidan, innahu sayfu-Allāhi* (do not insult Khālid, for he is the sword of Allah).[32] Another traditionist invites us to believe that Khālid performed miracles: When he saw a container of wine, he prayed to Allah to turn it into honey, and he did.[33] We are also told that a man presented Khālid with poison—the unfearful Khālid drank it and was not affected.[34] Some traditionists even designate sections in their works to detail the virtues of Khālid.[35] Arguably, Khālid's portrayal is important to the overall Sunnī perspective, and some Sunnīs insist he was one of the greatest companions who served Islam.[36] The matter is clearly opposite among the

[30] Soon after Banū Jadhīma, Muhammad reportedly relied on Khālid at Ḥunayn. Wāqidī, *Maghāzī*, 897; Wāqidī, *Life*, 440. See also Ibn Hishām, *Life*, 565, where he states that, after Banū Jadhīma, Muhammad sent Khālid to Nakhla to destroy al-ᶜUzzā. See also various reports in Ṭabarī, *History*, 9:58, 82, 90.

[31] Ṭabarī, *History*, 8:71; 8:158. On Khālid as *sayfu-Allāhi* (Allah's sword), see Zubayrī, *Nasab*, 320; Fasawī, *Maᶜrifa*, 1:312. Muhammad reportedly continued to identify Khālid as "Allah's Sword" after the massacre of Banū Jadhīma. See Wāqidī, *Maghāzī*, 1030; Ibn Saᶜd, *Ṭabaqāt*, 1:220; Suhaylī, *Rawḍ*, 7:397; Ḥalabī, *Insān*, 3:290; Ibn ᶜAsākir, *Ta'rīkh*, 68:234; Ibn Ḥajar, *Iṣāba*, 1:381.

[32] Balādhurī, *Ansāb*, 10:208; also Ibn Ḥajar, *Maṭālib*, 16:309, where he provides two versions of the same *ḥadīth*; one states, "Do not insult," and the other, "Do not hurt." The tendentiousness of these statements is glaring. On al-Balādhurī's background, works, and religio-political sympathies, see Ibrahim, *Conversion*, 192–194. For primary sources, see Ibn al-Nadīm, *Fihrist*, 113; Yāqūt, *Muᶜjam*, 2:530–535; Dhahabī, *Siyar*, 13:162–163; Ibn Taghrībirdī, *Nujūm*, 3:83. See also Robinson, *Historiography*, 39–40; Becker and Rosenthal, "Al-Balādhurī," *EI*², 1:971–972; Petersen, *ᶜAlī*, 109–112; Dūrī, *Rise*, 61–64; Ziriklī, *Aᶜlām*, 1:267; Kaḥḥāla, *Muᶜjam*, 2:201–202. See also the introduction of the editor S. D. Goitein in *Ansāb al-ashrāf*, 9–16. See also the pro-Umayyad praise of Khālid in Zuhrī's account of how Muhammad cared for Khālid at Ḥunayn: "There Khālid stood leaning against the rear of his mount, and the Messenger of God went to him and tended to his wound." Maᶜmar, *Expeditions*, 107; Zuhrī, *Maghāzī*, 93.

[33] Ibn Ḥajar, *Iṣāba*, 2:218.

[34] Ibn Ḥanbal, *Faḍā'il*, 2:816. On Ibn Ḥanbal and his life and thought, see Hurvitz, "Aḥmad"; Hurvitz, *Formation*; Spectorsky, "Aḥmad," in *Islamic*, ed. Arabi et al., 85–106; Melchert, "Aḥmad Ibn Ḥanbal," 22–34; Melchert, *Aḥmad*; Melchert, *Formation*, ch. 7; Patton, *Aḥmed*, 2–20, 126–127; Roberts, "Early," 55; Zaman, *Religion*, 71ff.; Hoyland, "Arabic," 211–233.

[35] See Bukhārī, *Ṣaḥīḥ*, 5:27ff., where he devotes a section to *manāqib* (the virtues of) Khālid; see also 5:144, where a *ḥadīth* is narrated on Khālid's authority. Like al-Bukhārī, Ibn Ḥanbal, *Faḍā'il*, 2:813–817, designates an entire section for "The Virtues of Khālid," which includes a miracle performed by Khālid and statements of Muhammad praising him. On *manāqib* in general, see Pellat, "Manāḳib," *EI*², 6:349ff.; Bosworth, "Manāqib," in *Encyclopedia*, ed. Meisami and Starkey, 2:504–505.

[36] For primary sources reflecting Khālid's importance for the proto-Sunnī and Sunnī claims, see Balādhurī, *Ansāb*, 10:207–209; Ibn Abī Ḥātim, *Jarḥ*, 3:351; Ibn Ḥibbān, *Thiqāt*, 2:60–62; Ibn Manjawayh, *Rijāl*, 1:182, 186; Iṣfahānī, *Maᶜrifat*, 2:925–930; Ibn ᶜAbd al-Barr, *Istīᶜāb*, 2:427–430; Ibn ᶜAsākir, *Ta'rīkh*, 16:216–281 (Khālid was a *ḥadīth* narrator, with various examples); Dhahabī, *Siyar*, 1:366–383; Ṣafadī, *Wāfī*, 13:160–162; Ibn Ḥajar, *Iṣāba*, 2:215–218; Ibn Ḥajar, *Tahdhīb*, 3:120, 3:124; Ibn Ḥazm, *Jamharat*, 1:147. See also the Sunnī studies of Abū Māyla, *Sarāyā*, 247–255; Ṣallābī, *Sīra*, 766–767; Mubārakpūrī, *Raḥīq*, 358–359.

Shīᶜites.[37] The narrative of the incursion against Banū Jadhīma highlights a religious missionary activity that turned into a military massacre. Despite his reported mistreatment of fellow Muslims, the narrators seem to take pride in Khālid's commandership and skill.[38] Throughout the Arabic sources, he continues to be praised as the "Sword of Allah," and most narrators advance depictions that adjust his memory to fit the overall narrative of companions marching in battles for Allah's sake.

Like the classical narrators, many Muslim thinkers, past and present, follow similar patterns and attempt to polish Khālid's image.[39] For some Muslims, Khālid *ijtihad fa'khṭa'* (strived to do right, but got it wrong) and the proof of his innocence is that Muhammad did not punish him.[40] It appears that the literary portrayal of Khālid represents an evolving memory of some Arabs who might have joined Islam only to align themselves with the winning camp. Arabic sources claim that Khālid was one of the Meccan aristocrats and fought viciously against Muhammad in several major battles, including Badr, Uḥud, and al-Khandaq. He waited until the balance of power was clearly leaning toward Muhammad to "accept" Islam. Accepting Islam in his portrayal, it appears, was a mere act of tribal submission to the winning leader.[41] This is evidenced in how Khālid, a few years later, reportedly behaved

[37] For negative Shīᶜite views on Khālid and his sons, see Sulaym ibn Qays, *Kitāb Sulaym*, 227 (Khālid leads a conspiracy to murder ᶜAlī), 387 (Khālid attempts to hit Fāṭima), 390–394 (Khālid attempts to kill ᶜAlī). Naṣr ibn Muzāḥim, *Waqᶜat*, 195, 206; Kulaynī, *Kāfī*, 8:112; Ṣadūq, *Man lā*, 4:121, 4:503; Isfahānī, *Maqātil*, 23; Yaᶜqūbī, *Ta'rīkh*, 2:62–63; Majlisī, *Biḥār*, 98:43 (ᶜUmar plans to kill ᶜAlī with the help of Khālid).

[38] See Kennedy, *Great*, 75, where he writes, "It was Khālid who united the different Muslim armies on his arrival, it was Khālid who began the conquest of Damascus by opening the East Gate, and it was Khālid who devised the tactics that won the battle of Yarmūk."

[39] See, for example, the Muslim study of ᶜAqqād, *ᶜAbqariyyat Khālid*, 45–50, especially 47, where the author defends Khālid and insists that he never acted intentionally to murder Muslims. See similar Muslim defense for Khālid in ᶜUmarī, *Sīra*, 492–494; Qarībī, *Marwiyyāt*, 80–83, where he lists several excuses for Khālid's actions. See also Haykal, *Ḥayāt*, 430; Mubārakpūrī, *Raḥīq*, 377; Abū Māyla, *Sarāyā*, 247–249, 252–253. See also classical works in defense of Khālid, including Ibn Ḥajar, *Fatḥ*, 8:57–58; Ibn Kathīr, *Sīra*, 3:592–594; Ibn Qayyim, *Zād*, 3:365.

[40] See ᶜUmarī, *Sīra*, 494. Ṣallābī, *Ghazawāt*, 276.

[41] Khālid only converted after realizing with ᶜAmr ibn al-ᶜĀṣ that "all people now entered Islam and if we wait our necks will be smitten." Wāqidī, *Maghāzī*, 744; Wāqidī, *Life*, 366. See Ibrahim, *Conversion*, 166. For primary sources indicating conversion as a tribal submission, see Ibn Ḥabīb, *Munammaq*, 1:203, 1:250; Ibn Qutayba, *Maᶜārif*, 1:70, 1:332, 1:608; Balādhurī, *Ansāb*, 1:55, 1:198, 1:378, 1:384, 1:366; Abū Zurᶜa, *Ta'rīkh*, 1:169; Yaᶜqūbī, *Ta'rīkh*, 2:27–31, 2:38, 2:54, 2:59–61, 2:65, 2:85–86 (many delegations); Ibn Abī Khaythama, *Ta'rīkh (Part 2)*, 1:156, 1:198; Ibn Abī Khaythama, *Ta'rīkh (Part 3)*, 2:371; Zubayrī, *Nasab*, 1:254; Ibn Shabba, *Ta'rīkh*, 48, 365, 499. For more references, see Ibrahim, *Conversion*, 162, 210. Muslim historian Aḥmad al-Sharīf explains that accepting Islam during that time was *maẓharan li-dukhūlihim fī al-niẓām al-jadīd wa-iqrārihim bi-l-wiḥda al-ᶜarabiyya* (a manifestation of their joining into the new system, and their affirmation of the Arabian unity). Sharīf, *Makka*, 533. For the lexical meaning of *aslam*—i.e., converting to Islam—see Rāzī, *Mukhtār*, 153, where *aslam* relates to Islam and means *istaslam* (surrendered, submitted); see Ibn Manẓūr, *Lisān*, 12:293, where *aslam* means *istaslam wa-inqād* (surrendered and yielded), and *islām*

similarly: During the so-called *ḥurūb al-ridda* (the Apostasy Wars), Khālid humiliated a fellow Muslim named Mālik, killed him, and then fornicated with his wife.[42] Khālid's portrayal in the sources is clearly mixed, probably because the narrators appear to have valued his military accomplishments and diligently attempted to tweak his memory. When a memory of Khālid circulates suggesting that his sword was the ultimate say, classical narrators seem willing and ready to present a competing report, thus dispersing any negativity.

The incursion to Banū Jadhīma appears in the sources as a link between the conquest of Mecca and the Battle of Ḥunayn. The sources paint a picture of Muhammad's rapid tribal advancement and his steady consolidation of power over the surrounding lands of Mecca and Medina. This is why, the logic goes, after overcoming Mecca, Muhammad wanted to ensure the surrender of its neighboring lands, such as that of Banū Jadhīma. However, the sources are clear: Once Quraysh submitted to Muhammad in Mecca, there was no other tribe stronger than Hawāzin. This will lead us to the Battle of Ḥunayn, where we turn next.

The Battle of Ḥunayn (8/630)

The tradition describes Hawāzin as a strong and influential Arabian tribe.[43] It includes various clans, most notably the Thaqīf, who resided largely in

wa-istislām refers to *inqiyād* (surrender and yielding); also, *islām* means *khuḍūᶜ wa-iltizām* (subordination and commitment); also Fīrūzābādī, *Qāmūs*, 1122, where *aslam* means *inqād wa-ṣār musliman* (yielded and became Muslim).

[42] On the incident of murdering Mālik ibn Nuwayra, see Ibrahim, *Stated*, 137–138. For primary sources, see Ṭabarī, *Taʾrīkh*, 1880, 1924–1926; Dhahabī, *Taʾrīkh*, 3:32ff. Khālid reportedly considered Mālik an apostate, which resulted in ordering his killing. However, Mālik and his people reportedly *adhdhanū wa aqāmū al-ṣalāt* (performed the call to prayer and the prayer as well). Ṭabarī, *Taʾrīkh*, 1925. In what seems to be a literary embellishment, we are told that Khālid instructed the Muslim guards *adfiʾū asrākum* (make your prisoners warm), which some of them interpreted to mean "kill your prisoners." Ṭabarī, *Taʾrīkh*, 4:1925. Muslim narrators describe a horrific scene: "Khālid required that Mālik's head should be cooked in a pot, from which Khālid ate, as he intended to scare the apostates in Arabia with this act." Ibrahim, *Stated*, 138. On the same day, Khālid took Mālik's wife, Layla bint al-Minhāl, and fornicated with her. Ibn al-Athīr, *Kāmil*, 287. Khālid's actions were reportedly despised by major companions. ᶜUmar demanded Khālid's dismissal, while ᶜAlī sought to apply the *ḥadd* (punishment) on Khālid. Dhahabī, *Siyar*, 1:376. See Madelung, *Succession*, 50. Muslim authorities include Mālik among Muhammad's *ṣaḥāba* (companions) and reveal that Mālik *lam yartadd* (did not apostatize). Ibn Ḥajar, *Iṣāba*, 10:8; Ibn al-Athīr, *Usd*, 5:49. See also the Shīᶜite accounts of Yaᶜqūbī, *Taʾrīkh*, 2:131; Ibn Aᶜtham, *Futūḥ*, 1:19–20. On Ibn Aᶜtham and his work, see the comments of Noth/Conrad, *Early*, 29.

[43] On Hawāzin, see Watt, "Hawāzin," *EI*[2], 3:285–286. Watt, *Muḥammad*, 70–75, 95–105. See also ᶜAlī, *Mufaṣṣal*, 2:56–57 (the families and clans of Hawāzin, and its link to Thaqīf), 7:334 (one of the

al-Ṭā'if, southeast of Mecca.[44] In Muhammad's time, Hawāzin was reportedly as powerful as the Quraysh of Mecca, and the two tribes had a history of rivalry.[45] As the tradition invites us to believe, once Muhammad overcame Quraysh at the conquest of Mecca, the time had come to ensure Hawāzin's submission, which is described as its conversion to Islam.[46] The narrative of Hawāzin's conversion revolves around the significant events of the Battle of Ḥunayn, often known in the tradition as the Day of Ḥunayn, which was less than a month after the conquest of Mecca.[47] According to traditions, Ḥunayn was the most important military encounter between Muhammad and the Bedouins of Arabia.[48]

The overall narrative of Ḥunayn begins with Hawāzin being alarmed because of Muhammad's victory over the mighty people of Mecca; consequently, the people of Hawāzin and Thaqīf and their Bedouin allies, we are told, began preparing to attack the Muslims.[49] Their leader was Mālik

strongest Arabian tribes), and 10:30–36 (enmity between Hawāzin and Ghaṭafān). For its importance and connection to Muhammad, see Ibn Saᶜd, *Ṭabaqāt*, 1:50 (Ḥalīma, Muhammad's nursing mother, descended from Hawāzin), 8:217 (Umm al-Faḍl, first female convert after Khadīja and wife of al-ᶜAbbās, was from Hawāzin); Khalīfa, *Ṭabaqāt*, 1:29; Ibn ᶜAsākir, *Ta'rīkh*, 3:97 (Ḥalīma), 9:255 (Umayya ibn Abī al-Ṣalṭ was from Thaqīf of Hawāzin). For its significant places, see Yaqūt, *Muᶜjam*, 3:1290; Ibn al-Athīr, *Usd*, 7:69; Ṣafadī, *Wāfī*, 13:83; Ibn Hajar, *Iṣāba*, 8:87; Bakrī, *Masālik*, 1:343 (the Kurds are from Kurd ibn Mard from Hawāzin); Bakrī, *Muᶜjam*, 3:961–962; Zamakhsharī, *Jibāl*, 1:180, 333; Hamadānī, *Amākin*, 1:84, 100, 448, 611, 887; Samhūdī, *Wafā'*, 4:54; Balādī, *Muᶜjam*, 71.

44 The ancestor Hawāzin had only one son named Bakr, from whom different branches of the Hawāzin tribe emerged following his four sons: Muᶜāwiya, Saᶜd, Munabbih, and Zayd. The sons of Munabbih included Thaqīf. Ibn Qutayba, *Maᶜārif*, 1:86, 91; Masᶜūdī, *Tanbīh*, 1:179; ᶜAlī, *Mufaṣṣal*, 2:57. See Lecker, "Thaḳīf," *EI*², 10:432; Lecker, "al-Ṭā'if," *EI*², 10:115–116. On the relationship between Hawāzin and Thaqīf, see ᶜUmarī, *Sīra*, 489–490; Ṣallābī, *Sīra*, 780; Ṣallābī, *Ghazawāt*, 287; Shams al-Dīn, *Majmūᶜ*, 202–205.

45 See ᶜAlī, *Mufaṣṣal*, 7:83–85; Watt, "Hawāzin," *EI*², 3:285. Watt, *Muḥammad*, 71.

46 See Ṭabarī, *History*, 8:170, where he states that, when Muhammad marched to Mecca, "some said his destination was Quraysh, some said it was Hawāzin, and some said it was Thaqīf." See also Ṭabarī, *History*, 8:175. On this confusion regarding the destination, see ᶜUmarī, *Sīra*, 491. Djait argues that Muhammad only targeted big towns in his raids, and when he attacked small villages, it was only to seize spoils without real fighting. Djait, *Masīrat*, 183.

47 See Wāqidī, *Maghāzī*, 889 and 892. The conquest of Mecca was reportedly on the thirteenth of Ramaḍān, and Ḥunayn was on the tenth of the following month, Shawwāl. Cf. Ṭabarī, *Ta'rīkh*, 1636, 1654. Cf. Balādhurī, *Ansāb*, 1:364, where he claims that Muhammad stayed in Mecca for twelve days before heading to Ḥunayn. Watt states that the battle took place on January 31, 630. Watt, *Muḥammad*, 72; ᶜUmarī, *Sīra*, 495. For details on the Battle of Ḥunayn, see the thorough study of Muslim scholar Ibrāhīm Qarībī, *Marwiyyāt*, 1–840, where he examines numerous primary sources on the account (for the date of the battle, see 99–105). While he discusses the incident from a rather conservative Sunnī perspective, his collection of sources is helpful. See also Haykal, *Ḥayāt*, 432–443; Djait, *Masīrat*, 183–194. For a non-Muslim study, see Watt, *Muḥammad*, 70–73.

48 Watt observes, "Ḥunayn was the major encounter during Muhammad's lifetime between the Muslims and the nomadic tribes." Watt, *Muḥammad*, 72.

49 Wāqidī, *Maghāzī*, 885; Wāqidī, *Life*, 435; Ibn Hishām, *Sīra*, 2:437; Ibn Hishām, *Life*, 566–587; Ṭabarī, *Ta'rīkh*, 1654–1655; Yaᶜqūbī, *Ta'rīkh*, 2:63–64.

ibn ᶜAwf al-Naṣrī, who was thirty years old at the time and ordered them to bring "with them their wealth and their women and the children."[50] Mālik reportedly "wanted to place behind every man his family, his property, his children and his wives so that he will fight for them."[51] The image is that Hawāzin brought all its might and resources, and "help came to them from every direction."[52] They were twenty-four thousand soldiers, and the Muslims were only twelve thousand (ten thousand from Medina and two thousand from Mecca).[53] Muhammad was reportedly willing to receive aid from notable Arab polytheists: He "was told that Ṣafwān b. Umayyah had armor and weapons. Therefore, he sent to him, although he was at that time a polytheist."[54]

At night before the battle started, the narrators point to horror occurring in the Hawāzin camp. When Mālik sent spies to Muhammad's camp, they returned to him with "their limbs dislocated" from fear, and reported, "We saw white men on piebald horses.... Surely, we do not fight people of the earth but rather people from the heavens."[55] The tendentiousness of this report is

[50] Wāqidī, *Life*, 436. Ṭabarī, *Taʾrīkh*, 1654; Ibn Hishām, *Sīra*, 2:437. Mālik eventually converted to Islam after Ḥunayn and became one of the *muʾallafa qulūbuhum* (converts through financial incentives). Ibn Qutayba, *Maᶜārif*, 1:315, 1:324.

[51] Wāqidī, *Life*, 436.

[52] Wāqidī, *Life*, 436.

[53] See Majlisī, *Biḥār*, 44:66, 38:220, who states the number of the unbelievers was twenty-four thousand; however, many traditionists avoid specifying an exact number, so the exact figure is ambiguous, unlike the number of the Muslims. Ibn Ḥajar agrees with this number and states it might have been even higher. Ibn Ḥajar, *Fatḥ*, 8:29. Still, Wāqidī, *Maghāzī*, 893, puts the number at twenty thousand. Ṭabarī, *History*, 9:8. Watt, *Muḥammad*, 72. On the number of the soldiers in both armies as found in Muslim traditions, see the study Qarībī, *Marwiyyāt*, 110–116. We should note that this might be one of the largest numbers given in the tradition for a Muslim army during Muhammad's lifetime. See ᶜUmarī, *Sīra*, 496. We should note that the two thousand soldiers from Mecca were presumably from those who accepted Islam on the day of the conquest of Mecca, known as the *ṭulaqāʾ*, i.e., the pardoned and set-free Meccans who embraced Islam to save their lives and spare their families. ᶜUmarī, *Sīra*, 496; Ṣallābī, *Sīra*, 780. For a study on the *ṭulaqāʾ*, with examples of primary sources and secondary studies, see Ibrahim, *Conversion*, 79–81. Of course, as we explained earlier, these numbers appear tendentious and exaggerated. See Munt, *Holy*, 49–50; Shoemaker, *Creating*, 98, 111–112.

[54] Ṭabarī, *History*, 9:7. See Wāqidī, *Life*, 437, where Muhammad relied on *mushrikūn* (polytheists) in his army. See Yaᶜqūbī, *Taʾrīkh*, 2:64, where he states that Muhammad took to the battle Muslims who converted "voluntarily and involuntarily." See Ibrahim, *Conversion*, 85–86; Crone, *Meccan*, 87, 89–91, 129–131; Sara Nur Yıldız, "Battling *Kufr*," in *Islam*, ed. de Nicola et al., 339; Watt, *Muḥammad*, 19; Ridgeon, *Jawanmardi*, 117, 152; Haykal, *Life*, 269–270, 272, 295, 436–441. Cf. Yarbrough, "I'll Not Accept," 44–95. Some of the soldiers among the Muslims reportedly wanted to worship a tree, and Muhammad rebuked them. Wāqidī, *Maghāzī*, 891; Ibn Hishām, *Sīra*, 2:442. When a polytheist spoke *shirk* (infidelity), Muhammad reportedly "said nothing to the disbeliever, nor did he punish him." The narrative suggests that Muhammad sought to secure soldiers at all costs. See ᶜUmarī, *Sīra*, 497, where he argues that the new converts had negative effects on the Muslim army due to a clear remnant of unbelief that was apparent in their deeds. Ṣallābī, *Sīra*, 787. For Muslim studies on the participation of the polytheists in this battle, see Qarībī, *Marwiyyāt*, 605–609; Shams al-Dīn, *Majmūᶜ*, 203–204.

[55] Wāqidī, *Life*, 438. Ṭabarī, *Taʾrīkh*, 1658.

blatant, as it estimates a dialogue presumably occurring in the enemy's camp, but it might also demonstrate how Muslim narrators relied on earlier literary compositions, such as biblical accounts highlighting terrified spies who have seen the strength of their enemies.[56] Eventually, in the morning the two camps met at the valley of Ḥunayn.[57] Muhammad reportedly appointed the shrewd warrior Khālid ibn al-Walīd—despite his questionable behavior a few days earlier at the incursion of Banū Jadhīma—to lead "the vanguard of the cavalry."[58]

As the Muslims marched to Ḥunayn, some warriors were reportedly prideful and boastful because of their number: "If we meet the [enemy] we will not care. One will not defeat us today for our small numbers."[59] The statement describes an arrogant and prideful stance among Muslims *iᶜjāban bi-kathratihim* (due to their large number).[60] This is why, we are told, Allah revealed a verse in the Qur'ān that rebuked them and asserted that he supported them "in many fields, and on the Day of Ḥunayn" (Q 9:25).[61] Narrators, as we repeatedly encounter, frame the historiographical narrative to exegete the Qur'ān, precisely establishing an interpretation and scriptural context linked to Muhammad's *Sīra*.[62] However, there is a problem with this

[56] See the account of Moses sending twelve spies to the promised land (Numbers 13). Similarly, we are told, Muhammad sent one of his companions to spy on Hawāzin. The companion reached all the way to their leader Mālik, then reported back to Muhammad an account of how Hawāzin underestimated the Muslims. Wāqidī, *Maghāzī*, 893–894.

[57] See Wāqidī, *Life*, 440, where he refers to the valley as an "empty hollow, possessing narrow gorges." The valley is located on the road between Mecca and Ṭā'if. Djait, *Masīrat*, 185. See Mattson, "Ḥunayn," *EQ*, 2:465–466, where the author states that Ḥunayn is "a deep, irregular valley, one day's journey from Mecca on the road to al-Ṭā'if." For the interconnected relations between Mecca and Ṭā'if, see ᶜUmarī, *Sīra*, 489, where he claims that Ṭā'if was the paradise land for the Meccan Quraysh, as people used to spend the summertime in Ṭā'if. Ibn Ḥajar asserts that Ḥunayn is fourteen miles from Mecca. Ibn Ḥajar, *Fatḥ*, 8:27. Mu'nis, *Ta'rīkh*, 547–548, 570–580.

[58] Wāqidī, *Life*, 440.

[59] Wāqidī, *Maghāzī*, 889. On this matter, see Shīᶜite traditions in Majlisī, *Biḥār*, 21:147. Watt argues that the Muslims were "over-confident." Watt, *Muḥammad*, 72. For a Sunnī perspective on reasons for the defeat, including the prideful attitude of the Muslims, see Qarībī, *Marwiyyāt*, 135, 141. See ᶜUmarī, *Sīra*, 496, and Ṣallābī, *Sīra*, 780, where they both identify the boastful Muslims as to have been from the *ṭulaqā'*, the new believers from Mecca, presumably weak Muslims who accepted Islam on the day of the conquest of Mecca. See Ibrahim, *Conversion*, 79–81. See also Riḍā, *Manār*, 10:220, where he states that four of the twelve thousand Muslims in the battle were *kuffār* (unbelievers).

[60] Bayḍāwī, *Anwār*, 3:76.

[61] See Mattson, "Ḥunayn," *EQ*, 2:465, where the author argues that Ḥunayn "is presented in Q 9:25–7 as a reminder that victory can only come from God, for despite their large number, the Muslims were quickly routed by the enemy, until their panicked retreat was transformed into a successful rally by divine intervention."

[62] See Reynolds, *Subtext*, 1–2, as he argues "the connection made by medieval Muslim exegetes between the biography of Muḥammad and the Qur'ān should not form the basis of critical scholarship" (2). For a Muslim study on the verses revealed during Ḥunayn and their interpretations, see Ṣallābī, *Ghazawāt*, 303.

tradition. In a competing account, we are told, the boastful statement is actually attributed not to prideful and boastful Muslims, but to Muhammad himself: When he saw the great number of soldiers accompanying him, he exclaimed, "We shall not be defeated today from a few."[63] While the two competing reports exist in the same pool of traditions, it appears that an earlier memory of Muhammad's voicing the statement did not appeal to traditionists; consequently, they tweaked it by creating a rival account to avoid placing Muhammad in a dark light, since the Qur'ān presumably questions the boastful believers. This is evident in the fact that a third competing report emerged claiming that the statement came from Abū Bakr.[64] Thus, we are invited to believe that the boastful statement was said, but no one knows *precisely* by whom.[65]

When the fight started, Hawāzin reportedly won and the Muslims retreated. One Muslim described the people of Hawāzin: "I had never, in that time, seen anything like such a dark multitude."[66] However, we are told, this initial victory of the unbelievers was soon reversed under Muhammad's bravery and leadership. He cried out, "O helpers of God and helpers of His messenger! I am the servant of God and his patient messenger!"[67] In a literary image that reflects bravery and devotion, we are told that, among the Muslim fighters, there was a pregnant woman who came to the battlefield with her husband and "had a dagger in her hand."[68] The report, it appears, is designed to exhort Muslims to follow course and show dedication. Eventually, the Muslims regrouped and displayed patience, as Muhammad reportedly "came forward with his spear, in front of the people," to the extent that Muslims were not harmed after that: "not a sword struck us nor a spear pierced us until God defeated them."[69] The narrative indicates that, due to Muhammad's leadership and courage, "The Hawāzin began to flee and those Muslims who had fled came back."[70] While the picture painted here seems to emphasize

[63] For reports affirming that Muhammad said the statement, see Ibn Hishām, *Sīra*, 2:444; Suhaylī, *Rawḍ*, 7:286; Kalāʿī, *Iktifāʾ*, 1:520; Maqdisī, *Badʾ*, 4:236; Ibn al-Athīr, *Kāmil*, 2:134. For traditions claiming it was an unidentified Muslim, see Ṭabarī, *Jāmiʿ*, 14:181; Zamakhsharī, *Kashshāf*, 2:259; Riḍā, *Manār*, 10:84, 10:220; Jawzī, *Muntaẓim*, 3:332.

[64] Wāqidī, *Maghāzī*, 890; Ibn Saʿd, *Ṭabaqāt*, 2:114; Ibn Kathīr, *Bidāya*, 4:369; Ibn Kathīr, *Sīra*, 3:610; Ḥalabī, *Insān*, 3:158; Dhahabī, *Taʾrīkh*, 2:574.

[65] This is Qarībī's conclusion after examining the contradicting traditions. Qarībī, *Marwiyyāt*, 135–139. See also Bayḍāwī, *Anwār*, 3:76, where he states that the statement was said by Muhammad, Abū Bakr, or someone else.

[66] Wāqidī, *Life*, 440.

[67] Wāqidī, *Life*, 441.

[68] Ṭabarī, *History*, 9:13. Ibn Hishām, *Sīra*, 2:446.

[69] Wāqidī, *Life*, 441.

[70] Wāqidī, *Life*, 441.

a religious exhortation, other reports indicate that Muhammad encouraged his soldiers to remain in the battle by incentivizing them that if a Muslim kills an unbeliever, "his booty belongs to him."[71] Nothing would mean more to a nomad warrior than seizing spoils.[72]

Still, the Muslim storytellers, as religious scholars, insist that the Muslim victory occurred after Muhammad performed a miracle: He threw pebbles at the unbelievers, saying, "Defeat them by the Lord of the Kaᶜba."[73] This hurt the eyes of the unbelievers, but, moreover, we are told that a divine intervention came in the form of "squadron upon squadron" of angels, shining like "white men on piebald horses" and "wearing red turbans that fell down between their shoulders, between the heaven and the earth."[74] These angels were distinguished from those who appeared at Badr—at that time they were wearing white turbans.[75] Still, some traditionists assure us that these angels, unlike the case at Badr, were not sent to fight but mainly to exhort the believers.[76] The religious disposition of the accounts is glaring: The Muslim narrators congest the accounts with metaphysical features to emphasize Allah's role in the Muslim victory. This is not a record of a certain past, but a homily of exhortation for the faithful. For Muslims, the miracle of Muhammad and the angelic support are signs of prophethood.[77] Muslim traditions report the result of the Battle of Ḥunayn in religious terms, as Hawāzin rapidly weakened, "until Allah defeated them."[78] Some unbelievers, we are told, fled to al-Ṭā'if, while others encamped in Awṭās and Nakhla—a literary detail to connect Ḥunayn with the following battle.[79] Ultimately, the narrative concludes, "By

[71] Wāqidī, *Life*, 445–446; Ibn Hishām, *Sīra*, 2:448. Of course, we are invited to believe, each warrior had to find a witness to testify to the killing in order to obtain the spoils later from Muhammad—which created quarrels among the Muslims after the battle. Wāqidī, *Maghāzī*, 907–908.

[72] See ᶜUmarī, *Sīra*, 497 and 515, where he states that most of the new converts and the Bedouins who joined Muhammad's army were after spoils and did not have sincere desire for jihad or religious zeal.

[73] Wāqidī, *Life*, 441; Maᶜmar, *Expeditions*, 104. See Muslim, *Ṣaḥīḥ*, 3:1398, where it reads, "by the Lord of Muhammad." For a modern Muslim perspective that questions some *sīra* traditions, see Ḥanafī, *Min*, 3:625–645, where he questions reports on Muhammad's miracles; also 3:19–21, where he argues that Muslim traditions include both truths and myths. It is clear that his assertions are brave, especially as they come from a Muslim scholar residing in the Arab World.

[74] Wāqidī, *Maghāzī*, 906; Wāqidī, *Life*, 445. The same description of the angels as "white men on piebald horses" is found elsewhere: Ibn Hishām, *Sīra*, 1:76; Wāqidī, *Maghāzī*, 409, 892; Ṭabarī, *Ta'rīkh*, 1663.

[75] Suyūṭī, *Durr*, 2:309. For angels with turbans, see Ibn Hishām, *Sīra*, 1:633, which states that at Badr the turbans of the angles were white, while at the battle of Ḥunayn they were red. See also Ṭabarī, *Ta'rīkh*, 1328; Suhaylī, *Rawḍ*, 5:86; Bayhaqī, *Dalā'il*, 3:61, 78. See Ibn Saᶜd, *Ṭabaqāt*, 1:338, and 2:11, which states that angels rode horses. ᶜAbd al-Jabbār, *Tathbīt*, 2:403ff.

[76] Majlisī, *Biḥār*, 21:147.

[77] Ṣallābī, *Sīra*, 784.

[78] Wāqidī, *Maghāzī*, 899.

[79] Ṭabarī, *Ta'rīkh*, 1665. ᶜUmarī, *Sīra*, 505.

God, I have not seen a defeat that was like it. The enemy fled in every direction."[80] As the unbelievers fled the scene of the battle, we are told, *al-riᶜda* (the trembling) wore them down and the *ruᶜb* (terror) filled their souls, so "Allah cast Islam in their hearts."[81] This concluding report suggests that, for the Muslim narrators, terror and trembling in the camp of unbelievers are signs of Islam's hegemony and superiority, as well as a testimony of divine intervention. Notably, conversion to Islam in this incident is not primarily a result of religious conviction or the spiritual experience of a faith capturing one's heart. Rather, the Muslim storytellers depict conversion as a result of terror overcoming the hearts of unbelievers after military defeat.

As with other *maghāzī* narratives, the account is better viewed as a religious parable. The narrators designed a message to the faithful, indicating that Allah's victory was bestowed upon the Muslims when they practiced patience against affliction and trial. Still, there are many literary features that require attention. Since traditionists never relinquish their commitment to their sectarian or political views, the ᶜAbbāsid-era historians seem to insist on inserting literary elements to magnify the role of al-ᶜAbbās ibn ᶜAbd al-Muṭṭalib—the ancestor of the ᶜAbbāsid Dynasty—in the victory.[82] When Muhammad wanted to cause confusion and disarray among the unbelievers, we are told, he asked al-ᶜAbbās, "Get me some pebbles!" Al-ᶜAbbās "brought pebbles from the ground," then Muhammad "threw them at the faces of the polytheists," saying, "Disgrace them! Be defeated by the Lord of the Kaᶜba."[83] The report invites us to consider that Muhammad did not pick the pebbles himself, but relied on al-ᶜAbbās who is portrayed as a devotee to Muhammad—a contributor to the miracle and to the victory. This is clearly a pro-ᶜAbbāsid account, especially if we compare it with the pre-ᶜAbbāsid account attributed to al-Zuhrī, in which Muhammad did not rely on al-ᶜAbbās but simply "grabbed a handful of small stones and cast them into the faces of infidels."[84] The pro-Umayyad al-Zuhrī did not seem to find it necessary to include al-ᶜAbbās in the miracle preceding the victory. It appears that ᶜAbbāsid-era historians seize any opportunity to design reports that esteem their progenitor al-ᶜAbbās and emphasize him as a strong

[80] Wāqidī, *Life*, 443; Wāqidī, *Maghāzī*, 903.
[81] Wāqidī, *Life*, 445; Wāqidī, *Maghāzī*, 907.
[82] See Djait, *Masīrat*, 185. Petersen, *ᶜAlī*, 17. Ibrahim, *Conversion*, 218–223; Berg, "ᶜAbbāsid," 13–38.
[83] Wāqidī, *Life*, 442.
[84] Zuhrī, *Maghāzī*, 93; Maᶜmar, *Expeditions*, 105.

supporter of Muhammad.[85] In the same vein, these historians aim to degrade key Umayyad figures and depict them as weak and untrue Muslims. In one report, we are told that the major Umayyad notable, Abū Sufyān—who presumably converted to Islam weeks earlier—gloated over the initial defeat of the Muslims and declared "that their defeat would continue to the seas."[86] This report portrays Abū Sufyān's conversion as disingenuous.[87] The depiction is clearly anti-Umayyad, serving ᶜAbbāsid propaganda against their rivals.

Similarly, the logic goes, pro-ᶜAlid and Shīᶜite historians seize the chance to emphasize the role of their major Imam, ᶜAlī ibn Abī Ṭālib, and elevate his Hāshimite household in the portrayal of the victory. Shīᶜite historian Ibn Wāḍiḥ al-Yaᶜqūbī writes that, under the heavy battle, "The Muslims were driven away from the Messenger of God, until he remained amid ten of the Banū Hāshim."[88] This report elevates Banū Hāshim as the only devoted Muslims who remained faithful and patient around Muhammad in the heat of battle.[89] Unsurprisingly, among those ten, al-Yaᶜqūbī observes, ᶜAlī and al-ᶜAbbās were the first two on the list.[90] Because al-Yaᶜqūbī was a Shīᶜite historian with clear pro-ᶜAlid and pro-ᶜAbbāsid sympathies, the placement of these two Muslims first on the list seems ideologically expected.[91] In the same vein, al-Yaᶜqūbī provides a unique report to conclude the narrative of the battle: After the victory occurred, ᶜAlī "advanced on the standard-bearer of the Hawāzin and killed him."[92] Here Shīᶜite traditions portray ᶜAlī in a

[85] See a similar account in Shīᶜite traditions by Majlisī, *Biḥār*, 21:181, where Muhammad clearly relies on al-ᶜAbbās in exhorting the soldiers. See also Ṭabarī, *History*, 9:11, where al-ᶜAbbās reportedly says, "I was with the Messenger of God, holding the bit of his white mule which I myself had inserted into the mule's mouth." Thus, we are told, al-ᶜAbbās was the closest to Muhammad and the holder of the bit of the mule. The image is pro-ᶜAbbāsid, showing their ancestor as a good Muslim supporting Muhammad in battles. Ibn Hishām, *Life*, 569.

[86] Wāqidī, *Life*, 446; Ibn Hishām, *Sīra*, 2:443; Ṭabarī, *Ta'rīkh*, 1660.

[87] For a detailed study on Abū Sufyān's conversion depiction between pre-ᶜAbbāsid and ᶜAbbāsid accounts, see Ibrahim, *Conversion*, 71–75, 157–158, 206–207. See also chapter 2 earlier, and Mu'nis, *Ta'rīkh*, 344–347.

[88] Yaᶜqūbī, *Works*, 3:664; Yaᶜqūbī, *Ta'rīkh*, 2:64.

[89] In other reports, the number of those who patiently stood firm was one hundred. Wāqidī, *Maghāzī*, 900. See Qarībī, *Marwiyyāt*, 169.

[90] See Ibn Qutayba, *Maᶜārif*, 1:164; Majlisī, *Biḥār*, 21:147, 21:166.

[91] On Ibn Wāḍiḥ al-Yaᶜqūbī, his works and religio-political leaning, see Ibrahim, *Conversion*, 197–199; Millward, "A Study of Al-Yaᶜqūbī." Yāqūt, *Muᶜjam*, 2:557; Millward, "Adaptation," 329–44; Brockelmann, "Al-Yaᶜqūbī," *EI*², 11:257–258; Dūrī, *Rise*, 66; Petersen, *ᶜAlī*, 169; Donner, *Narratives*, 134; Khalidi, *Arabic*, 120ff., 131ff.; Robinson, *Historiography*, 36 (al-Yaᶜqūbī's Shīᶜite views), 76 (his historiographic style), 98 (eschewing *isnād*, and how later mainstream historians followed his work in style), 136–137 (the uniqueness of al-Yaᶜqūbī's *Ta'rīkh*, especially as a Shīᶜite writing a universal history and relying on Christian and Jewish sources); Anthony, "Was Ibn Wāḍiḥ," 15–41; Daniel, "al-Yaᶜqūbī," in *ᶜAbbasid*, ed. Montgomery, 209ff.

[92] Yaᶜqūbī, *Works*, 3:665.

way that fits their sectarian disposition: He is a courageous commander for Islam, unstoppable in the midst of affliction. This is echoed in other Shīᶜite traditions designed to place ᶜAlī at the center of the Muslim troops, unyielding and undefeated.[93]

While one can recognize the tendency of Muslim historians to add literary embellishments to magnify religious and political figures important to their views, some literary constructions are illogical and unpersuasive. In one report, Muhammad stands with major companions after the victory and asks one among them named Ḥāritha about the number of Muslims who stood firm in the battle. "They were a hundred," Ḥāritha reported to Muhammad. Later in the day, Ḥāritha passed by Muhammad "while he was confiding in the angel Gabriel at the door of the mosque," at which time Gabriel asked Muhammad about Ḥāritha: "Who is this, O Muhammad?" When Muhammad said to Gabriel that the name of the soldier was Ḥāritha, Gabriel said, "This was one of the patient hundred on the day of Ḥunayn." Gabriel added, "If [Ḥāritha] greeted me, I would have greeted him back."[94] The report invites us to believe that the angel—the supposed agent of revelation—was unaware of the name of the Muslim soldier, despite recognizing his heroic participation in the battle. In the same vein, the literary exaggerations of the number of soldiers and the initial Muslim defeat are hard to reconcile.[95] We are invited to believe that twelve thousand Muslims—who were initially defeated by twenty-four thousand unbelievers—turned the defeat into victory in one day and with only four Muslims "martyred."[96] While the Muslim narratives initially describe Hawāzin and Thaqīf as mighty people of war, these same reports invite us later to view them as a group of amateurs, fleeing the battleground in a satirical way.[97] The apparent exaggeration in these tales reflects, once more, how the accounts are authored.

93 Majlisī, *Biḥār*, 44:66, 38:220.

94 Wāqidī, *Maghāzī*, 900.

95 See Djait, *Masīrat*, 185, where he argues that the Bedouins were destined to lose to city-dwellers like Meccans and Medinans, even with their large numbers. For a Muslim discussion on reasons for the initial defeat, see Ṣallābī, *Sīra*, 795; Ṣallābī, *Ghazawāt*, 303–305.

96 Wāqidī, *Maghāzī*, 922; Ibn Hishām, *Sīra*, 2:459. Watt, *Muḥammad*, 72. See also Qarībī, *Marwiyyāt*, 242, where only four Muslims were killed; also ᶜUmarī, *Sīra*, 504, where hundreds of the unbelievers were killed and only four of the Muslims. On the mythical and exaggerated elements in Islamic accounts, see ᶜAbd al-Raḥmān, *Judhūr*, 7–9; ᶜAbd al-Raḥmān, *Tārīkh*; also ᶜAlawī, *Maḥaṭṭāt*, 19–20. See also Munt, *Holy*, 49–50; Shoemaker, *Creating*, 98, 111–112; Ibrahim, *Stated*, 117; Hoyland, *God's Path*, 42; Cf. Hoyland, *Seeing*, 186, where similar exaggerated numbers of soldiers are found in non-Muslim sources.

97 On how Hawāzin was reportedly mighty in war (even more than Quraysh), see ᶜAlī, *Mufaṣṣal*, 7:85. This is echoed in Watt's observations, "It does not appear, however, to have been a stubbornly fought battle," and "This suggests that there was little hand-to-hand fighting." Watt, *Muḥammad*, 72.

The matter of the spoils and their distribution among the soldiers is noteworthy,[98] as the Muslim traditionists use the historiographical account to derive clear juristic rules and ideological instructions.[99] The reports on the ample spoils and their distribution should not be taken as factual, but instead as a demonstration of how Arab soldiers loved looting and sought spoils.[100] This is evident in a report that, during Muhammad's distribution of the spoils of Ḥunayn among the Muslims, they sought to snatch all they could get, to the extent that they tore Muhammad's mantle.[101] The report reflects a Muslim memory and reveals what the Arab soldiers cared about the most. Their pre-Islamic habits and customs continued well after their presumed conversion to Islam—only now the spoils and their pursuit were reportedly sought *fī sabīl Allāh* (for Allah's cause).[102] We are told that the captives were numerous and the spoils were plentiful, as Muhammad "held six thousand captives from the children and women, and innumerable camels and sheep."[103] Muhammad reportedly "ordered that the plunder be collected" and warned the Muslims, "Those who believe in God and the Last day will not be deceitful," which propelled the soldiers "to put away their plunder."[104] To ensure all spoils were

[98] For the juristic principles on distributing the spoils, see ᶜUmarī, *Sīra*, 511–512, where he states that one-fifth of the spoils should be given to Muhammad to use as he pleases, while the remaining portion should be distributed equally among the warriors who participated in the battle. For a study on the different kinds of plunders (*ghanīma fay'*, *nafl*, and *salb*), see Ibrahim, *Stated*, 72–73, where I write, "(1) *al-ghanīma* (booty or spoils of war), which is taken from unbelievers through fighting and killing; (2) *al-fay'*, which refers to money gained without the use of fighting, as it is given to the Muslim warriors through peace treaties or any sort of compromise with the enemies; (3) *al-nafl*, which is a part of *al-ghanīma* after dividing it; 4) *al-salb*, which refers to that which is seized or obtained by the *qātil* (killer) from the person killed." See also ᶜAbd al-Karīm, *Shadwu*, 1:75–77.

[99] For a detailed Muslim study on the juristic rules derived from the accounts of Ḥunayn, see Qarībī, *Marwiyyāt*, 511–743, also 840–843, where he lists numerous jurisprudence topics that, he believes, can be gleaned from the historical narratives of Ḥunayn and al-Ṭā'if. See also Ṣallābī, *Sīra*, 796–799; Ṣallābī, *Ghazawāt*, 305–307; ᶜUmarī, *Sīra*, 520–522.

[100] See ᶜUmarī, *Sīra*, 515, where he argues that most of the Muslims were primarily after spoils and wealth without a sincere devotion to Islam.

[101] See Ibn Hishām, *Life*, 594, where it states that they kept seeking the spoils, "until they forced him back against a tree and his mantle was torn from him and he cried, 'Give me back my mantle.'" See also Ibn Hishām, *Sīra*, 2:492; Ṭabarī, *Ta'rīkh*, 1679.

[102] See Donner, *Early*, 3–5; Ibrahim, *Stated*, 41–43, where I discuss motivations for the raids and conquests in secondary studies. Muir argues, "Arabian people, both town and Bedouin, were riveted to Islam by a common bond—the love of rapine and the lust of spoil." Muir and Weir, *Caliphate*, 43. See also Donner, "Introduction," in *Expansion*, ed. Donner, xx; Donner, *Early*, 251–71. Donner argues that the religious motivation among the Muslims was created by three major components: *umma*, *sharīᶜa*, and *tawḥīd* (the Muslim community, its law, and its strict monotheism). Donner, *Early*, 55–62.

[103] Ṭabarī, *History*, 9:26. Wāqidī, *Maghāzī*, 943. See Ibn Hishām, *Life*, 592, where the captive women included some of Muhammad's aunts—all were put in enclosures. See Ṭabarī, *Ta'rīkh*, 1675, where the detainees included paternal and maternal aunts of Muhammad. Majlisī, *Biḥār*, 21:181. See Djait, *Masīrat*, 187, where he rightly observes the exaggerated numbers provided by the narrators regarding the spoils.

[104] Wāqidī, *Life*, 450.

collected and brought to him, Muhammad reiterated, "Whoever takes something from the plunder, return it,"[105] before he commanded that all captives and spoils be taken to a different location named al-Jiᶜirāna, for him to divide them.[106]

The narrators seem to highlight the importance of giving all the spoils to Muhammad—it appears as a crucial religious lesson they want to advance for the faithful. They design additional traditions to make their point. We are told that a Muslim received a needle as plunder and gave it to his wife to sew her garments with; however, in obedience to Muhammad's instructions, this Muslim returned the needle.[107] Even a needle, we are invited to believe, had to be given to Muhammad. The narrators fashion the hyperbolic tradition to emphasize the importance of giving all spoils to the leader. In the same vein, we are told that another Muslim found a rope as plunder and asked Muhammad about how it would be divided among the believers. Muhammad responded, "My share of it is for you. What will you do with the shares of the Muslims?"[108] The point of the report is clear: all spoils must be given to Muhammad, who can divide them equally according to his wisdom. These tales became foundational for later Muslim jurists when devising their rules on plunder and the role of the *ḥākim* (ruler) in dividing and distributing it.[109]

Once Muhammad had all the spoils, we are told, "he waited for the delegation [of Hawāzin] to come to him," as he was probably hoping to negotiate with them over the spoils.[110] When they did not come, Muhammad "began with the wealth and apportioned it," and gave the first portion to a group of Muslims often labeled in the tradition as *al-muʾallafa qulūbuhum*, which identifies those who accepted Islam after their hearts were reconciled through materialistic incentives.[111] The tradition reveals that these were "certain men of eminence," and Muhammad gave them gifts "in order to

[105] Wāqidī, *Life*, 450.

[106] Wāqidī, *Maghāzī*, 923. Ibn Hishām, *Sīra*, 2:459. Ṭabarī, *Taʾrīkh*, 1669. The name is rendered al-Jiᶜrrāna and al-Jiᶜrāna. See Bakrī, *Muᶜjam*, 2:348; Bakrī, *Masālik*, 1:406; Zamakhsharī, *jibāl*, 1:95; Yāqūt, *Muᶜjam*, 2:142, 2:229 (he prefers al-Jiᶜrāna). See Mu'nis, *Taʾrīkh*, 575–576.

[107] Wāqidī, *Maghāzī*, 918.

[108] Wāqidī, *Life*, 450.

[109] See Ibn Qayyim, *Zād*, 3:425.

[110] Wāqidī, *Life*, 462–463.

[111] Ibn Qutayba, *Maᶜārif*, 1:324. Wāqidī, *Life*, 463. On this group of Muslims, see chapter 4 on the conquest of Mecca. See Ed., "al-Mu'allafa," *EI*², 7:254; Watt, *Muḥammad*, 73–75, 348–353; Ibrahim, *Conversion*, 157–158. See also Ibn Ḥajar, *Fatḥ*, 8:48. See Djait, *Masīrat*, 188, where he argues that these incentives for the *muʾallafa* were reasonable to win them over. For a detailed list of the gifts given to the *muʾallafa*, see Ṭabarī, *Taʾrīkh*, 1679–1680. Ibn Hishām, *Sīra*, 2:493–494.

conciliate them and to win over their hearts."[112] He reportedly won them over to Islam by bestowing on them what they loved the most: plunder and loot.[113] Thus, the gifts reportedly won people over to Muhammad and Islam. Expectedly, some Muslims complained as Muhammad reportedly did not distribute the incentives equally: it appears some men were more notable for him than others.[114] This propelled a Muslim to complain, "I don't think you have been fair."[115] While modern religious discussions might view this tradition as odd, medieval Muslims seem to have fashioned the narrative and found it plausible. For them, accepting Islam, at least in one of its aspects, was a tribal surrender to the victorious leader, and material enticements were a tool to motivate the elites to join the community of Muhammad. Still, it appears that Muhammad reportedly favored some of his Meccan relatives in the portions, as he "divided the spoils among those of Quraysh who had [recently] embraced Islam."[116] His decision propelled some Muslims of the Medinan *anṣār* to complain among themselves that Muhammad bestowed ample camels upon people of the Quraysh and ignored them although they fought too.[117] While this report appears to portray Muhammad negatively, it could be read as another testimony of how, as we discussed earlier,

[112] Ṭabarī, *History*, 9:31–32; Ibn Hishām, *Sīra*, 2:492; Wāqidī, *Maghāzī*, 854–855. Cf. Ibrahim, *Conversion*, 85–86; Djait, *Masīrat*, 180. For Sunnī discussions on the *mu'allafa* during Ḥunayn, see Qarībī, *Marwiyyāt*, 403–412, 696–707; Ṣallābī, *Sīra*, 787–788. For a religious justification for incentivizing people through gifts to embrace Islam, see Ṣallābī, *Sīra*, 788–791.

[113] One of those who received gifts testified, "By Allah, the messenger of Allah gave me what he gave me; he used to be the most detested person to me; however, he kept giving me until he is now the dearest of people to me." Muslim, *Ṣaḥīḥ*, 4:1806.

[114] Ṭabarī, *Ta'rīkh*, 1681–1682; Ṭabarī, *History*, 9:31–32. See Watt, *Muḥammad*, 73–74, where he creates a list of those who received incentives and writes, "The list is interesting as showing the importance of the various men." See also Haykal, *Ḥayāt*, 435–436. See ᶜUmarī, *Sīra*, 511–512, where he claims that many Muslims did not understand Muhammad's wisdom behind the distribution of the spoils, but it led many to be satisfied and embrace Islam. See similar arguments in Ṣallābī, *Sīra*, 788–791.

[115] See Ṭabarī, *History*, 9:34–35, where, in response to this Muslim, Muhammad "became angry and said, 'Woe to you! If justice is not to be found with me, then with whom is it to be found?'" For a Muslim defense of Muhammad's unequal distribution of the plunders, see Qarībī, *Marwiyyāt*, 390–400; ᶜUmarī, *Sīra*, 514.

[116] Ṭabarī, *History*, 9:3; Ṭabarī, *Ta'rīkh*, 1655. For a traditional Muslim interpretation of this action, see Haykal, *Ḥayāt*, 442.

[117] Wāqidī, *Maghāzī*, 926; Ibn Hishām, *Sīra*, 2:498. Their complaint is as follows: "The Messenger of God has found his community. When there is battle, we are his companions; as for when he apportions, it is his community and his tribe." Wāqidī, *Life*, 468. Ṭabarī, *Ta'rīkh*, 1655, 1683; Bayhaqī, *Dalā'il*, 5:176; Dhahabī, *Ta'rīkh*, 2:601; Bukhārī, *Ṣaḥīḥ*, 5:185; Muslim, *Ṣaḥīḥ*, 2:733. Qarībī, *Marwiyyāt*, 403, 418. Cf. Ibn Ḥanbal, *Musnad*, 18:255, where he reports a negative tradition about the *anṣār*, suggesting they should have not complained and preferred gaining Muhammad and his approval over worldly matters. See also Ibn Ḥajar, *Fatḥ*, 8:48–55, 10:512. See Djait, *Masīrat*, 188, where he argues that the Medinan *anṣār* were right to sense injustice and partiality. See ᶜUmarī, *Sīra*, 514, where he justifies Muhammad's actions towards the *anṣār* and argues that Muhammad convinced them later to accept receiving less than others.

there seems to be a tendency among traditionists to design narratives with a religio-political disposition to praise Muhammad's family (Hāshim) and tribe (Quraysh), often at the expense of the Medinan Muslims.[118] As an example of this tendency as it relates to the narrative of Ḥunayn, we are told that a polytheist man named ᶜUthmān was killed in the battle. When Muhammad heard of his death, he reportedly said, "May God deprive him of His mercy! He used to hate the Quraysh."[119] The narrators create a literary construction and attribute it to Muhammad in order to demonstrate a clear praise of his tribe, the Quraysh.[120]

But, as designed by the traditionists, Muhammad's portrayal at Ḥunayn includes exceptional features and virtuous actions. In what appears as a sign of humility and austerity, Muhammad is depicted as leading the battle riding "his white mule."[121] We are even told the name of this mule, Duldul.[122] While warriors seek to fight riding strong horses, we are invited to believe, Muhammad—the central hero of the battle—was showing humility, selflessness, and strictness, a clear example of a *zāhid* (ascetic), which is a beautiful description in Islam.[123] In one report, a woman among the slave captives

[118] See the earlier discussion in Chapter 2. See also Ibn Qutayba, *Maᶜārif*, 1:241; Fasawī, *Maᶜrif*, 1:279. See the studies of Qimanī, *Ḥizb*, 51ff.; ᶜAbd al-Karīm, *Quraysh*, 377–392; Wensinck, "al-ᶜAshara," *EI*², 1:693. Watt implies that Muhammad wanted to please the Meccans since they were the enemies of Hawāzin and had to adjust their feelings: "The Muslims, especially the Emigrants, had to adjust their feelings to the sudden change whereby their bitterest enemies had become allies." Watt, *Muḥammad*, 70.

[119] Ṭabarī, *History*, 9:14.

[120] See Mu'nis, *Ta'rīkh*, 597–602, where he argues that, according to historical reports, the Quraysh took clear steps to remove the Medinan *anṣār* from leadership roles.

[121] Ṭabarī, *History*, 9:11. A desert battle can hardly be fought by horses, let alone mules. See Crone, *Slaves*, 22–23, 220.

[122] Ṭabarī, *History*, 9:14. Cf. Tirmidhī, *Shamā'il*, 227. For a Muslim praise of Muhammad using a mule, see ᶜUmarī, *Sīra*, 501.

[123] For the term *zuhd* (renunciation, asceticism) and *zāhid* (ascetic) linguistically, see Rāzī, *Mukhtār*, 138, where *zuhd* is against *al-raghba* (desire or lust), *tazhhud* is *taᶜabbud* (adoration, worship), *tazhīd* is opposite of delighting in materialistic things, and *muzhid* is the *qalīl al-māl* (a person with scarcity of money). See Ibn Manẓūr, *Lisān*, 3:196–197, where *zuhd* is opposite of *al-raghba wa-l-ḥirṣ ᶜalā al-dunyā* (desire or lust, and being too attached to worldly matters); also Fīrūzābādī, *Qāmūs*, 1:286. For primary sources on *zuhd*, describing the term in relation to life and practice, see Ibn al-Mubārak, *Zuhd*, 69, where he explains—through a tradition—that whoever loves Allah, Allah loves him, and whoever knows *al-duniyā* (the world) *zahada fīhā* (does not seek much from it); Jāḥiẓ, *Bayān*, 3:85–138, where he dedicates a section on *zuhd* and explains what *al-nussāk* (ascetics) said about it; Ibn Qutayba, *ᶜUyūn*, 2:384–385, where he lists the characteristics of *al-zuhhād* (those who practice *al-zuhd*, ascetics); also Muslim, *Ṣaḥīḥ*, 4:2272ff., where he has a section on traditions on *zuhd*. See also Ibn Ḥanbal, *Zuhd*, where he lists the *zuhd* of various prophets, including Moses (63–66), Abraham (68), Jesus (76–89), and others. Ibn Ḥanbal also writes of the *zuhd* of Muhammad's companions, including Abū Bakr (89–94) and ᶜUmar (94–104). Similarly, see Abū Sufyān Wakīᶜ, *Zuhd*, 350, where he speaks of humility as a sign of *zuhd*, and 677, where *zuhd* is *ḥayā'* (modesty, decent courtesy, or the honorable quality of shyness); Ibn ᶜAbd Rabbih, *ᶜIqd*, 2:212–225, 3:119, 3:126; Ibn Taymiyya, *Zuhd*, 9–118, et passim; Ibn Taymiyya, *Jawāb*, 6:43. For the eternal rewards of *zuhd*, see Ibn Mūsā, *Zuhd*, 55–75. For an excellent study on *zuhd*, see Melchert, *Before*, 10–12, 130,

was treated harshly by the Muslims, so she revealed to them that she was Muhammad's foster-sister and named al-Shaymā'—but they did not believe her.[124] When Muhammad learned of the situation, he asked her for proof, so she showed him "a bite mark" and said, "You bit me there while I was carrying you." Once he "knew the mark," Muhammad reportedly protected her and rebuked the Muslims. He then wept with her and preached Islam to her. When she converted, we are told, he gave her four slaves and sent her back to her family.[125] This tale aims to praise Muhammad's character, portraying him as caring toward women and especially his family. While, to a contemporary mind, the tale might appear exaggerated—especially considering the bite mark and how unaware Muhammad was of al-Shaymā' for over fifty years—the story undoubtedly resonated with medieval Muslims and provided them an image of their prophet to emulate. In another report, we are told that the Muslims "hastened in killing children of the enemy," because "they are the children of polytheists." When Muhammad heard, he rebuked the Muslims and repeated three times, "Children should never be killed!"[126] Here, the traditionists design an image of Muhammad as full of mercy and compassion, especially caring toward all human life. The historical narrative not only magnifies Muhammad's character, but also exhorts Muslims to emulate him in his desire to protect children in war. His compassion toward children is amplified in another report that portrays him as seeking to protect defenseless women in times of war. We are told that he "passed a dead woman," and when he asked about her, they said she was a "woman whom Khālid killed." Muhammad, we are told, instantaneously sent an envoy to Khālid, forbidding him from killing "women and old men."[127] The point of the account is not to document a precise historical past, but to educate and edify Muslims through the creation of a meaningful tale.

Similarly, the narrators use Muhammad's example to provide juristic answers to Muslims on treating female war captives. In one report, Muhammad speaks to his soldiers about their female captives: "Pregnant women among the prisoners may not be 'trampled' until they are

165–166, et passim; also Netton, *Islam*, 91, where *zuhd* is described as asceticism, renunciation, and abstinence, making the deity the only goal.

[124] Ṭabarī, *Ta'rīkh*, 1668.
[125] Wāqidī, *Maghāzī*, 913. Cf. Ṭabarī, *Ta'rīkh*, 1668, where he does not mention her conversion and only refers to two slaves.
[126] Wāqidī, *Life*, 444.
[127] Wāqidī, *Life*, 448. For a juristic treatment of the issue, see Qarībī, *Marwiyyāt*, 548–557.

delivered."[128] Here the narrators establish a juristic ruling by relating it to a statement attributed to Muhammad at Ḥunayn. In another account, Muslim storytellers—again, relying on Muhammad's example—provide an answer on how to deal with a female captive who is not pregnant. We are told that Muhammad instructed the soldier who wants to have intercourse with a female prisoner to "wait until she menstruates."[129] Here the historical narrative serves as a religious homily, instructing the faithful on practical matters. This is further evidenced in how the narrative of Ḥunayn states that Muslims had asked Muhammad about *al-ᶜazl* (birth control), and he replied, "Pregnancy does not require all the 'water,' and when God desires it, nothing will prevent it."[130] Whatever this answer actually means is not the issue. The point is how narrators frame historiographical accounts to address important questions for Muslims. When Muhammad provides an answer, the logic goes, it is legitimate, authoritative, and prescriptive.[131] In the same vein, we are told, some Muslim soldiers seized female captives and wanted to *yaqaᶜū ᶜalayhunna* (have intercourse with them); however, the men detested the fact that these women were married. When the men asked Muhammad, he reportedly received a divine answer, as Allah revealed a verse from the Qur'ān, conveying that married women are forbidden for the believers, *illā mā malakat aymānukum* (except those whom your right hands possess) (Q 4:24).[132] In this report, the historiographical account is fashioned not only to provide a juristic ruling but also as an exegetical device of *asbāb al-nuzūl* (the occasions of revelation) of Islam's Scripture.[133] One historical narrative, designed by traditionists, serves later Muslims as both a connection between

[128] Wāqidī, *Life*, 451. See Qarībī, *Marwiyyāt*, 513–527.

[129] Wāqidī, *Life*, 451.

[130] Wāqidī, *Life*, 451. Ḥalabī, *Insān*, 3:180. For a Muslim study on the matter, see Qarībī, *Marwiyyāt*, 532–535.

[131] Goldziher observes, "Anything which appears desirable to pious men was given by them a corroborating support reaching back to the Prophet. This could easily be done in a generation in which the Companions, who were represented as the intermediaries of the Prophet's words, were no longer alive." Goldziher, *Muslim*, 2:42.

[132] Wāqidī, *Life*, 451. See Shāfiᶜī, *Tafsīr*, 2:574–581, where he lists several interpretations of the verse, relying on the reported incident at Ḥunayn. The verse seems to forbid Muslim soldiers from having sex with married female captives, except with captives labeled *illā mā malakat aymānukum*. The phrase perplexes Muslim exegetes, who offer various interpretations. Some argue that *mā malakat* may still refer to a married woman whom a solider owns through purchase or *nikāḥ* (marriage) after separating her from her husband. See Ṭabarī, *Jāmiᶜ*, 8:140–158 (female captives—if separated from their men—can be given to Muslims), also 6:561–574; Thaᶜlabī, *Kashf*, 3:280–285; Zamakhsharī, *Kashshāf*, 1:497 (married women captured in battles are allowed for soldiers); Rāzī, *Mafātiḥ*, 10:31–35; Qurṭubī, *Jāmiᶜ*, 5:120–123 (married women could be used either through purchase or marriage after separation from husbands); Riḍā, *Manār*, 5:3–17.

[133] See Wāḥidī, *Asbāb*, 152–153, where he relates the verse to the incident at Ḥunayn.

the Qur'ān and its presumed historical context, as well as a religious homily on treating women captives during and after the time of documentation.

The historiographical accounts of Ḥunayn take us immediately to the siege of al-Ṭā'if, which is reported in various traditions as a *ghazwa* (raid) led by Muhammad. We are told that Muhammad and the Muslims could not rest after the Battle of Ḥunayn, as the unbelievers fled to various locations, including al-Ṭā'if, Awṭās, and Nakhla. Additionally, the people of Hawāzin—we are invited to believe—have not yet come with their notables to declare submission to Muhammad by accepting Islam. The situation is not yet cleared up. Muhammad, the logic goes, must strike while the iron is still hot—he must march and subdue the stronghold of the defeated people of Hawāzin and Thaqīf who shielded themselves behind the high mountains of al-Ṭā'if. As he places the siege against al-Ṭā'if, the story goes, he was surprised by the results. The siege eventually failed and the Muslims retreated.

The Raid to al-Ṭā'if (8/630)

According to traditions, "When he had finished at Ḥunayn," Muhammad and his companions "went directly to al-Ṭā'if and encamped there for a fortnight, waging war against Thaqīf."[134] This detail presents the raid of al-Ṭā'if as closely related to Ḥunayn, to the extent that the distribution of the spoils of Ḥunayn was reportedly postponed by marching to al-Ṭā'if. The dividing and distribution of the loot will reportedly wait until the raid to al-Ṭā'if concludes.[135] The narrators depict this attack against al-Ṭā'if as a strategic necessity. Apparently, Muhammad wanted to send a clear message to the Bedouins—especially those of Hawāzin and Thaqīf—that the Muslims were serious and the war would not end before the unbelievers chose to submit and accept his prophethood. Notably, the battles of Ḥunayn and al-Ṭā'if are reportedly Muhammad's last military incursions against the polytheists of Arabia.[136]

Geographically, al-Ṭā'if is strategically located. It is about seventy-five miles southeast of Mecca and is well known as the summertime destination for the wealthy people of the Hijaz—it is a mountaintop location with

[134] Ṭabarī, *History*, 9:20. For a traditional Muslim study on the incident, see Ṣallābī, *Ghazawāt*, 287–311.

[135] Cf. Ṭabarī, *History*, 9:20 and 9:26. See the Muslim study Shams al-Dīn, *Majmūʿ*, 202–208.

[136] Ṣallābī, *Sīra*, 802.

beautiful weather, plentiful water and trees, and protection in fortified highlands with walls surrounded by valleys.[137] Religiously, al-Ṭā'if was reportedly a central location of the worship of the goddess al-Lāt, and it was known as the dwelling place of the Thaqīf clan.[138] This is why, the Muslim rationale goes, Thaqīf must be fought and the statue of pagan infidelity destroyed; however, the high and fortified location of al-Ṭā'if served as a natural protection for its people.[139]

Before leaving Ḥunayn, Muhammad "dispatched Khālid ibn al-Walīd from Ḥunayn to lead the attack."[140] Khālid's portrayal as a reliable commander continues in the tradition, despite his reported mistreatment of people. Behind the fortress walls of al-Ṭā'if, we are told, the people of Thaqīf and all those who fled after Ḥunayn sought protection as the Muslims approached them. It appears that it was a matter of life or death for the people of Thaqīf, as they planned a fierce resistance against the imminent Muslim attack—to the extent that they reportedly accumulated food provisions that would last them for a year.[141] As the Muslims marched to al-Ṭā'if, Muhammad received military tools in the form of *dabbāba wa-manjanīq* (war machines and mangonels) in addition to four hundred soldiers from the Arabian tribe of Banū Azad.[142] However, Thaqīf was ready, as they "repaired their fortress" and "locked themselves in."[143] The literary detail that they repaired their fortress appears hyperbolic, since the time between the battles of Ḥunayn and al-Ṭā'if was very short. The addition of this literary exaggeration seems to reflect the narrators' attempt to magnify the claims

137 See the excellent description of al-Ṭā'if in ᶜAlī, *Mufaṣṣal*, 7:142–156, where he writes it is located on Jabal Ghazwān, the coldest in Hijaz, and it has plenty of fruit trees, and its people work in agriculture. See also ᶜUmarī, *Sīra*, 489. For primary sources on al-Ṭā'if, see Ibn Khuradādhbih, *Masālik*, 134, 187; Hamdānī, *Ṣifat*, 1:120–121; Ibn al-Faqīh, *Mukhtaṣar*, 31–32; Balkhī, *Masālik*, 19–21 (the coldest place in the Hijaz); Bakrī, *Masālik*, 1:403; Bakrī, *Muᶜjam*, 1:65, 67, 78; Zamakhsharī, *Jibāl*, 1:216; Hamadānī, *Amākin*, 1:910; Yāqūt, *Muᶜjam*, 4:8–12.

138 See ᶜAlī, *Mufaṣṣal*, 7:145, where he writes that the statue of al-Lāt was in the form of a cubic rock, and it was destroyed when the people of Thaqīf in al-Ṭā'if accepted Islam.

139 ᶜAlī, *Mufaṣṣal*, 7:146–147. For the tactics of the people of Thaqīf in fighting the Muslims from the top of the mountain, see ᶜAlī, *Mufaṣṣal*, 7:151–152.

140 Wāqidī, *Maghāzī*, 923. For Muhammad's journey from Ḥunayn to al-Ṭā'if, see ᶜUmarī, *Sīra*, 508.

141 Ibn Saᶜd, *Ṭabaqāt*, 2:120. Wāqidī, *Maghāzī*, 924. ᶜUmarī, *Sīra*, 507.

142 Wāqidī, *Life*, 453. See Ibn Hishām, *Sīra*, 2:483, where it states that Muhammad was the first to use a *manjanīq* (mangonel) in Islam. For Muslim studies on Muhammad's use of these new war tools, see Ṣallābī, *Sīra*, 785; ᶜUmarī, *Sīra*, 508–509. In competing reports, we are told that Salmān the Persian advised Muhammad to use mangonels: "I think that you should establish a mangonel against their fortress." Wāqidī, *Life*, 454. As we encountered at al-Khandaq, literary embellishments about Salmān may reflect Persian influences under the ᶜAbbāsids. See chapter 4 earlier; also Savant, *New*, 61–89; Hibri, *Parable*, 14–15.

143 Wāqidī, *Life*, 453.

of the groundwork of the enemy to fit the scenario of the Muslim retreat. In a similar manner, the narrators, as religious authors, interrupt the narrative of the siege to inform the reader that, on his way from Ḥunayn to al-Ṭā'if, Muhammad stopped on the road, built a mosque, and prayed in it.[144] This describes a Muslim commander who is concerned with the religious health of his soldiers. Nonetheless, the same picture combines a literary claim that Muhammad saw a palace owned by Mālik, the leader of Hawāzin, and ordered the Muslims to set it ablaze.[145] We are invited to view Muhammad as both a divinely guided prophet and an assertive military commander.

When Muhammad besieged al-Ṭā'if, we are told, "Thaqīf fought the Muslims from behind the fort and none came out in the open."[146] The upper hand reportedly went to Thaqīf, as they threw ample arrows at the Muslims and wounded many.[147] The Muslims reportedly saw one of the unbelievers of Thaqīf "aim from above the fortress with about ten of his arrow heads as though they were spears, and not an arrow of his fell short of its mark."[148] The attack against the Muslims was described as severe, and the unbelievers were protected in "an inaccessible fortress."[149] This report might bring to question the exaggerated accounts of Ḥunayn when the Muslims—aided by angelic power—won a huge battle and only four Muslims died, since the report here describes a severe attack and no escape. Because Muhammad had to act quickly, he reportedly sought help from one of the Muslims, Ḥubāb, to find a better location. We previously encountered Ḥubāb at the Battle of Badr, where he advised Muhammad of a better location for the Muslims to camp that would strengthen them against the Meccans.[150] In obedience to Muhammad, Ḥubab "set out until he reached the place of the Mosque of al-Ṭā'if, outside the village and he came to the Prophet and informed him," as this new location was at a higher elevation and at the rear of the people of Thaqīf.[151] Muhammad reportedly ordered all the Muslims to move to the new location. This literary detail provides one more example of a Muslim memory that describes Muhammad's human limitations. While many may seek to view and present Muhammad as matchless in his abilities due to his

144 Wāqidī, *Maghāzī*, 924–925.
145 Wāqidī, *Maghāzī*, 925. Bayhaqī, *Dalā'il*, 5:157.
146 Ṭabarī, *History*, 9:20.
147 Wāqidī, *Maghāzī*, 925. Ibn Hishām, *Sīra*, 2:482–483.
148 Wāqidī, *Life*, 454.
149 Wāqidī, *Life*, 458.
150 Ṭabarī, *Ta'rīkh*, 1309; Wāqidī, *Maghāzī*, 53. Ṣallābī, *Sīra*, 397.
151 Wāqidī, *Maghāzī*, 926. For a Muslim discussion on Muhammad receiving the consultation of a companion, see Ṣallābī, *Sīra*, 786.

prophethood, the historiographical narratives offer a more complex picture, weaving competing memories together.[152] Still, we have a competing memory suggesting that Muhammad did not need this advice regarding location: "When his comrades were killed by arrows, the Prophet moved to higher ground and pitched his camp."[153] This report depicts Muhammad as knowledgeable and in control, having no need for advice about the best location. The existence of the two competing reports reflects, once more, a reoccurring pattern in Muslim historiography: when one narrative requires adjustment, the traditionists create another. With competing reports, particularities are dispersed, resulting in some accounts being elevated and others forgotten.

The siege tale continues, as we are told that the Muslims "entered under the war machine," then "crawled with it to the wall of the fortress to breach it, but the Thaqīf sent scraps of iron heated with fire against them and burned the war machine; so the Muslims came out from under it, and among them were those who were wounded."[154] Under the heavy attack, the Muslims reportedly had to seek negotiations with Thaqīf.[155] However, all attempts failed.[156] When weapons and armor did not work, Muhammad reportedly wanted to hurt the livelihood of Thaqīf by instructing the Muslims "to cut the grape vines and burn them," and exhorting them, "Who cuts a rope of grapes, for him is a rope in Paradise."[157] While this literary report may appear as a trivial detail, it reflects how traditionists shape their historical narratives in a form of religious homily—by legitimizing it through a tradition attributed to Muhammad—to incentivize Muslims to fight for Allah's cause. In Islamic historiography, the incentivizing of Muslim soldiers is a common theme, often advanced in the form of promising rewards in the hereafter for martyrs, accompanied by tangible material gains in this world upon victory. This is evident in a designed conversation between two Muslim companions during the siege. "If we conquer al-Ṭā'if," one disclosed to the other, "you should have women of the Banū Qārib, because they are the most beautiful you may ever

[152] Similarly, in another report, after fifteen days of the siege, Muhammad consulted a Muslim, asking "his opinion about continuing [the siege]." Ṭabarī, *History*, 9:24.

[153] Ṭabarī, *History*, 9:22; also Ibn Hishām, *Sīra*, 2:482.

[154] Wāqidī, *Life*, 455.

[155] Wāqidī, *Maghāzī*, 926; Ibn Hishām, *Sīra*, 2:483.

[156] See Wāqidī, *Life*, 454. After promising a Muslim the safety and protection to negotiate, we are told, the people of Thaqīf killed him; consequently, the Muslims ambushed a man from Thaqīf outside the fortress gate and brought him to Muhammad, and they "cut off his head."

[157] Wāqidī, *Life*, 455. Ṭabarī, *History*, 9:23.

catch; moreover, when ransomed, they will bring a larger ransom."[158] This narrative is clearly designed to entice men, as they were needed as warriors during times of expansion.[159]

Ultimately, the Muslims besieged al-Ṭā'if for fourteen, fifteen, eighteen, or nineteen days, depending on varying reports—but at the end there seemed to be no progress.[160] Twelve Muslims were killed, and they are described in the tradition as martyrs.[161] Consequently, Muhammad "left and halted at al-Jiʿrānah where the captives of Ḥunayn were held with their women and children."[162] While this appears as a failed siege, the narrators conclude by depicting Muhammad as a patient religious leader who remained faithful throughout the siege's duration and always prayed in the two tents he built for his two wives who joined him.[163] Still, al-Ṭā'if was not defeated and Thaqīf did not accept Islam. The traditions reveal that Thaqīf would resist submission to Muhammad for almost a year, until the following Ramaḍān, when they came as a delegation to accept Islam.[164]

In Muslim historiography, military victories and defeats are better treated as tales designed by the narrators to communicate Islamic meanings. This is why the story of the failure of the siege of al-Ṭā'if is filled with literary components, framing the defeat around religious lessons to the faithful in at least three ways.[165] First, we are invited to believe, the raid to al-Ṭā'if did not result in victory because Allah did not predestine it.[166] This is indicated in a dialogue between two major companions of Muhammad: ʿUmar and Abū Bakr. When ʿUmar was striving to overcome the fortress of al-Ṭā'if after days of the siege, Abū Bakr discouraged him from trying and said, "Allah

[158] Wāqidī, *Maghāzī*, 930. For women between Islam and *jāhiliyya* (pre-Islam), see Shepard, "Age of Ignorance," *EI*², 1:37ff., especially 38. For women and the "virtual" caste system, see Donner, *Early*, 11–50, especially 32; also Hoyland, *Arabia*, 132. On women in pre-Islamic Arabia, see El Cheikh, *Women*, 6ff.; Ahmed, *Women*, 41ff. (ch. 3, "Women and the Rise of Islam"); Stowasser, *Women*, 120; Abbott, "Women," 259–284; also Sayeed, *Women*.

[159] See more reported sensual accounts about women in al-Ṭā'if in Wāqidī, *Maghāzī*, 933.

[160] For the discrepancy regarding the duration of the siege, see Wāqidī, *Maghāzī*, 927. Cf. Ṭabarī, *Ta'rīkh*, 1670. Some even claim the siege was more than twenty, twenty-five, thirty, or even furty days. Ṭabarī, *History*, 9:22; Ibn Hishām, *Sīra*, 2:482; Bayhaqī, *Dalā'il*, 5:158; Muslim, *Ṣaḥīḥ*, 2:736. For a Muslim discussion on the discrepancies of the siege duration, see ʿUmarī, *Sīra*, 507–508.

[161] Ṭabarī, *Ta'rīkh*, 1674. Ibn Hishām, *Sīra*, 2:486–487.

[162] Ṭabarī, *History*, 9:21.

[163] Wāqidī, *Maghāzī*, 927. For a modern Muslim defense of Muhammad's wisdom in abandoning the siege, see Ṣallābī, *Sīra*, 787.

[164] Ṭabarī, *Ta'rīkh*, 1705; Ṭabarī, *History*, 9:62. Ibn al-Athīr, *Kāmil*, 2:150; Ibn ʿAbd al-Barr, *Durar*, 1:247; Suhaylī, *Rawḍ*, 7:413. See ʿUmarī, *Sīra*, 517; also Djait, *Masīrat*, 186–187.

[165] On the failure of this raid, see the discussion of Djait, *Masīrat*, 186–187. For Muslims who do not view it as a failure, see ʿUmarī, *Sīra*, 510.

[166] Wāqidī, *Maghāzī*, 935.

is not permitted the conquest."[167] Here, the narrators fashion a religious declaration for their audience: Muslims should yield to Allah's decree. The siege, the logic goes, was not a defeat after all, since Allah prevented the victory for a reason. Even if there is no explicit reason given, the believers are called to submit to Allah's predestination. One may wonder why Allah would allow the Muslims to march all the way to al-Ṭā'if and establish a siege for days, permitting deaths among Muslims, before conveying his decree to Muhammad? Moreover, if the divine decree was initially prescribed, why would Muhammad—after *fifteen days* of the siege—need to consult a Muslim companion concerning "his opinion about continuing [the siege]"?[168] There are gaps in the tradition. However, the religious sentiment of the tale seems to limit its scope and discourage skepticism. Because the defeat at al-Ṭā'if does not align with traditional arguments on Islam's hegemony, the failure of the siege has to be reframed. This is evidenced in how some traditional Muslim thinkers claim that Muhammad did not actually "intend" to conquer al-Ṭā'if per se. Rather, he was aiming to show the people of Thaqīf that he could get to them when he wanted.[169] Additionally, from a literary standpoint, the narrators appear to use the dialogue of Abū Bakr and ᶜUmar to elevate the religious status of the two companions, since both are important for Sunnī orthodoxy. In particular, Abū Bakr appears here as the closest friend of Muhammad, who conveyed to him Allah's decree and then later relayed it to ᶜUmar.[170] The image may even reflect a back-projection of Sunnī claims on the sequence of the two as the first two successors of Muhammad.

[167] Wāqidī, *Life*, 458.

[168] Ṭabarī, *Ta'rīkh*, 1673.

[169] See the unconvincing argument of ᶜUmarī, *Sīra*, 510, where he claims that Muhammad "did not intend with al-Ṭā'if's siege to conquer it." ᶜUmarī relies on a loose reading of *aḥādīth* in Bukhārī, *Ṣaḥīḥ*, 5:156, 9:140, and claims they are sound, arguing that Muhammad was only eager for them to accept Islam.

[170] Hibri, *Parable*, 77–78, 123. Another literary device seems to elevate Abū Bakr: Muhammad concluded the matter with the delegation of Hawāzin and returned to Medina, placing Abū Bakr in charge of Mecca and instructing him to lead the Muslims in performing the hajj and to teach them Islam. Ṭabarī, *Ta'rīkh*, 1658. This report is also mentioned in the pro-Umayyad account in Zuhrī, *Maghāzī*, 93; also Maᶜmar, *Expeditions*, 108–109. The literary portrayal elevates Abū Bakr as a trusted companion to lead. For al-Zuhrī's sectarian and political sympathies, see Ibrahim, *Conversion*, 41–49. However, this report about Abū Bakr is contradicted by other accounts claiming Muhammad appointed another Muslim, ᶜAttāb, over Mecca. See Wāqidī, *Maghāzī*, 889, 959; Khalīfa, *Ta'rīkh*, 1:87; Ibn Hishām, *Sīra*, 2:500; Ibn Ḥabīb, *Muḥabbar*, 1:11; Ibn Saᶜd, *Ṭabaqāt*, 2:110; Ibn Ḥibbān, *Sīra*, 1:359; Kharkūshī, *Sharaf*, 3:86; ᶜAbd al-Jabbār, *Tathbīt*, 2:559; Bayhaqī, *Dalā'il*, 5:121, 5:203; Ibn ᶜAbd al-Barr, *Durar*, 1:237; Suhaylī, *Rawḍ*, 7:367; Kalāᶜī, *Iktifā'*, 1:520. Even al-Ṭabarī himself contradicts his own account later. Ṭabarī, *Ta'rīkh*, 1685. For a classical Muslim praise of Abū Bakr, see Ibn Qutayba al-Dīnawarī, *Imāma*, 26–27; for Muslim secondary studies, see Najjār, *Khulafā'*, 37–117; Haykal, *Ṣiddīq*, 11:23; Ḥusayn, *Shaykhān*, 26–121. On Abū Bakr's changing image in various traditions, see Akpinar, "Narrative," 93ff. For secondary studies on ᶜUmar, see Najjār, *Khulafā'*, 117–257; Haykal, *Fārūq*, 74–90; Haykal, *Life*, 127ff. (his conversion added to Islam and reduced the

Second, the retreat of the Muslims—without overcoming their enemies—appears in the accounts as nonetheless a religious victory. Although the narrative insists that Muhammad departed without any success in overcoming the fortresses of al-Ṭā'if, we are told that he still had the upper hand in the entire situation: In the midst of the attack, Muhammad was still exercising dominance and even invited the people of Thaqīf to forsake their fortress, promising them, "Any slave who comes down from the fortress and comes out to us, is free! So some ten men set out from the fortress."[171] So the narrators emphasize that the raid was not a failure after all. They assert that some of the unbelievers heeded Muhammad's invitation, escaped their stronghold, declared conversion to Islam, and submitted to Muhammad. This is, we are invited to believe, a religious victory. In fact, we are told, Muhammad entrusted these new converts in the hands of Muslim men "to protect and host" them and to teach them the Qur'ān and the *sunan* (religious laws, prescriptions).[172] Thus, the siege, the logic goes, was not a failure.

Third, the narrative details the bravery of Muslim soldiers by advancing images of wounded and dying soldiers, thus creating exemplary tableaux for the faithful to emulate.[173] This is evidenced in literary images of heroism, as Muslims fight in Allah's path and refuse calls to retreat: "We will not turn back without conquering al-Ṭā'if! We will not leave until God conquers for us."[174] While this report indicates a failure of the siege was evident and soldiers were retreating, the narrators frame the story to highlight Muslims' religious zeal and devotion to Islam.[175] This religious disposition is strengthened by emphasizing Muhammad's superior ability to know the unknown. We are told that a Muslim warrior named ᶜUyayna went to speak with the unbelievers of al-Ṭā'if in their fortress and revealed to them that he was truly amazed with their success against the Muslims: "By God, surely

power of the Quraysh), 254 (his justice), 540ff. (his shock after Muhammad's death); ᶜUmarī, *Sīra*, 177–180; ᶜUmarī, *ᶜAṣr*, 75ff.; Ṣallābī, *Sīrat*, 17–25, et passim; Numani, *Umar*, 3–73; Crone, *Nativist*, 10 (his reported character, soft heart), 43–44 (Shīᶜite perspective on him); Crone, *Meccan*, 93ff., 96–98; Kennedy, *Armies*, 60–64 (his reign model), 71–75; Kennedy, *Great*, 51–54, 75–76, 91–93; Kennedy, *Prophet*, 41–44, 49ff. (his role and achievement in the conquests), and 86 (his caliphate); Ḥusayn, *Shaykhān*, 124ff.

171 Wāqidī, *Life*, 456. Ibn Hishām, *Sīra*, 2:478–479.
172 Wāqidī, *Life*, 456.
173 Wāqidī, *Maghāzī*, 931–932.
174 Wāqidī, *Life*, 458.
175 We are also told that some Muslims—in disobedience to Allah's decree—decided to remain and fight: "they fought and the Muslims were wounded." Wāqidī, *Life*, 459. The point is that Allah did not permit victory.

what I see among you gladdens me."[176] This is a negative portrayal of a lukewarm Muslim. When Muhammad asked him later about his encounter with the unbelievers, ᶜUyayna lied and said, "I invited them to accept Islam," but Muhammad knew ᶜUyayna was lying and confronted him. This report aims to demonstrate Muhammad's presumed prophetic abilities.[177] Of course, from a critical perspective, the account may be contrasted with earlier reports—in the same narrative of the siege—which display Muhammad's limited ability to know the unknown. However, as we often encounter in Muslim historiography, competing threads exist simultaneously, and—depending on preferences of the narrators—some reports are elevated while others are sent to oblivion. Still, in this report, Muhammad's religious example is further magnified, as he reportedly opposed Muslims who wanted to kill ᶜUyayna—after identifying him as a traitor—and instead let him go and declared, "The people will say that I kill my companions."[178]

The narrative of the raid or siege of al-Ṭā'if concludes with two brief claims: the fortress of al-Ṭā'if was not penetrated, and Muhammad instructed the Muslims to depart to al-Jaᶜrāna for him to manage the spoils and captives obtained from Ḥunayn.[179] Muhammad thus marched to al-Jaᶜrāna, which is ten miles from Mecca. Once he arrived in al-Jaᶜrāna, we are told, as he waited for the people of Hawāzin to come to declare their submission to him, he began to divide and distribute the spoils. Muhammad "had plundered much silver; four thousand measures," and the plunder was gathered in front of him. When Abū Sufyān saw that amount of silver, he declared, "You have become the most wealthy among the Quraysh!" In response, Muhammad smiled, which propelled Abū Sufyān to ask, "Give me from this wealth," and Muhammad gave him only four measures.[180] This report appears as another testimony of ᶜAbbāsid-era propaganda against Umayyad figures, depicting them as mainly seeking wealth and worldly gain, as we explained in the discussion of the conquest of Mecca. This is evidenced as the account indicates that Abū Sufyān asked Muhammad to also give to his two sons, Yazīd and Muᶜāwiya, and Muhammad accepted.[181]

176 Wāqidī, *Life*, 457. Ibn Hishām, *Sīra*, 2:485.
177 Wāqidī, *Maghāzī*, 932.
178 Wāqidī, *Life*, 457.
179 See Wāqidī, *Life*, 462, where it states, "The prisoners numbered six thousand and the camels numbered twenty four thousand. The amount of the plunder was not known. They had said more or less forty thousand."
180 Wāqidī, *Life*, 463.
181 Wāqidī, *Maghāzī*, 945. See ᶜAṭiyya, *Dimā'*, ch. 1, where Muᶜāwiya is identified as seeking *al-mulk* (dominion and power), not *al-khilāfa* (the rightful legitimate succession).

The ᶜAbbāsid-era historiographical orthodoxy, in many instances, displays the Umayyads unfavorably.

Ultimately, the people of Hawāzin came to Muhammad, who told them, "I waited for you until I thought you would not come."[182] We are told that they came as a high-status *wafd* (delegation or deputation) of fourteen notables representing various clans and families of the tribe, with the important exception of the people of Thaqīf.[183] The delegation declared its submission to Muhammad's leadership, and the tribe converted to Islam as a group.[184] This literary detail is important as it emphasizes the historiographical theme of collective conversion, where a group of people embraces Islam at once.[185] This reflects adopting Islam not as a set of beliefs or convictions, but rather as a declaration of tribal surrender. In a previous publication, I labeled this historiographical theme under conversion topoi of compromise, as it reflects "disingenuous conversions, where converts merely seek materialistic gain apart from genuine conviction or avoid murder by accepting Islam."[186] While the people of Hawāzin presumably declared their conversion, the narrative highlights them as primarily concerned with making a deal with a victorious leader in order to restore their properties and people. The delegation officially demanded the return of their captives and war spoils, but Muhammad relayed that he had already divided and distributed the spoils among the Muslims.[187] He presented them with a choice between wealth and their captives: "Are your sons and wives dearer to you or your possessions?"[188] They chose their captives. Thus, Hawāzin embraced Islam to save their families, but their action is depicted as religious conversion.

Similarly, we are told, Muhammad asked the people of Hawāzin about their leader, Mālik, who led them at the Battle of Ḥunayn. They said Mālik was among those shielded with Thaqīf at the fortress of al-Ṭā'if. Muhammad told the people, "Inform him that if he becomes a Muslim I will return his family and property to him and give him a hundred camels."[189] Muhammad's

[182] Wāqidī, *Life*, 465.

[183] See ᶜUmarī, *Sīra*, 517; also Djait, *Masīrat*, 186–187. Lecker argues that Thaqīf's reluctance to convert to Islam was due to economic rather than religious concerns. Lecker, "Idol," 331–346. For their reluctance, see Balādhurī, *Ansāb*, 1:367ff.; Ibn Ḥazm, *Jamharat*, 1:266–269; Samᶜānī, *Ansāb*, 3:139–141.

[184] Ṭabarī, *Ta'rīkh*, 1670.

[185] See Ibrahim, *Conversion*, 68, 79, 82–83.

[186] See Ibrahim, *Conversion*, 6, also 79–89, 130–143, 206–213.

[187] See Ṭabarī, *History*, 9:21, where it reads, "he set all their women and children free."

[188] Ṭabarī, *History*, 9:28; Wāqidī, *Maghāzī*, 951; Maᶜmar, *Expeditions*, 107.

[189] Wāqidī, *Life*, 467. Ṭabarī, *Ta'rīkh*, 1678.

offer appears strategic, as the conversion of Mālik, the logic goes, would lead to the conversion of his entire family and relatives. To place pressure on Mālik to yield and submit, Muhammad reportedly instructed the Muslims "to imprison his family," and declared, "I want the best for them," which presumably meant their conversion.[190] When Mālik heard Muhammad's offer, we are told, he fled the fortress of al-Ṭā'if in secret, as he feared the retaliation of the people of Thaqīf. Mālik reportedly joined Muhammad, who "returned his family and his property and gave him a hundred camels."[191] This tale highlights Mālik's deal with Muhammad and does not convey that Mālik received religious instruction of any sort. This is a case of *khuḍūᶜ wa-stislām* (submission and surrender), not a heartfelt conviction or change. Just as the case with the *mu'allafa qulūbuhum* who accepted Islam after receiving incentives at the conquest of Mecca, and the collective conversion of the entire Hawāzin tribe, Mālik's case highlights a calculated submission that is then shaped by the narrators as a case of religious conversion. Mālik reportedly converted to Islam and *ḥasuna islāmuh* (demonstrated a praiseworthy conversion).[192]

In the narrative of the aftermath of the Battle of Ḥunayn, we encounter the theme of collective conversion, as emphasized in how the *wafd* (delegation) of Hawāzin, as a tribe, accepted Islam. This literary detail reflects an important theme in Muslim historiography and serves as a literary thread between the Battle of Ḥunayn, the Hawāzin delegation, and the crucial following year, which is labeled in the tradition as *ᶜām al-wufūd* (the year of the delegations). The year is the ninth after the *hijra*, and the tradition alleges that many *wufūd* (delegations, deputations, or groups) came to declare allegiance, loyalty, and submission to Muhammad—a notion conveyed in the tradition as religious conversion.[193] Within one year, we are told, Muhammad received over sixty delegations from among the Arab tribes, as he extended his sway over the Arabian Peninsula.[194] The narrative of *ᶜām al-wufūd* is fashioned by the traditionists to exegete the Qur'ān, particularly its unique assertion on people entering Allah's religion *afwājan* (in multitudes, groups, or crowds) (Q 110:1–3). Eventually, with the submission of these tribes and clans, after

[190] Wāqidī, *Maghāzī*, 955.
[191] Wāqidī, *Life*, 467. Ibn Hishām, *Sīra*, 2:491.
[192] Wāqidī, *Maghāzī*, 955.
[193] See Ibn Hishām, *Sīra*, 2:559ff. As an example of the *wufūd*, see Landau-Tasseron, "Processes," 253–270, where she studies Banū Tamīm, their collective conversion, and the textual problems of their portrayals. For a list of the *wufūd*, see Ibn Saᶜd, *Ṭabaqāt*, 1:222ff.
[194] Watt, *Muḥammad*, 78.

the suppression of Quraysh, Hawāzin, and Thaqīf, Arabia has largely fallen under Muhammad's leadership. He has become, we are invited to believe, the major leader over the Bedouins.[195] This makes the ninth *hijrī* year, *ᶜām al-wufūd*, a remarkable representation of Muhammad's victory over Arabia. Moreover, his victory was even greater, as the traditions allege that, during the same year, he was not only satisfied with ruling over Arab delegations from all over Arabia that flocked to him from every direction, but he also aimed even higher. He sought to challenge the superpower of his day, the Christian Byzantine Empire. This crystalized in the battle of Tabūk, which was one of three reported major military campaigns led or commissioned by Muhammad to reach the Byzantines. Next we look at these campaigns.

[195] Watt, *Muḥammad*, 78.

7
Muhammad's Expeditions to Byzantine Frontiers

Invade by Allah's name and in his path. Fight those who believe not in Allah.—Muhammad instructs his Muslim soldiers before they march to Mu'ta, as reported by al-Wāqidī

O you who believed, fight the infidels who are adjacent to you and let them find in you *ghilẓa* (harshness). Know that Allah is with those who fear him.— *Sūrat al-Tawba* (Q 9:123), reportedly triggering the march to Tabūk

At the ninth hour, there was a battle between the Romans and the Arabs of Muḥammad. . . . The Romans fled, leaving behind the patrician *bryrdn*, whom the Arabs killed. Some 4000 poor villagers of Palestine were killed there, Christians, Jews and Samaritans. The Arabs ravaged the whole region.—Thomas the Presbyter, in his account dated Friday, February 7, 634, which describes the Battle of Dathin[1]

The Muslim tradition points to three major groups as targets of Muhammad's *maghāzī*: the pagans of the Arabian Peninsula, the Jews of Medina and its surroundings, and the Christians of the Byzantine Empire and its allies from the Arab Christian tribes who resided in its frontiers with Arabia. In previous chapters, we covered the confrontations between Muhammad and the first two groups. In this chapter, we focus on three specific military campaigns that Muhammad allegedly led or commissioned against the Byzantine

[1] Wāqidī, *Maghāzī*, 757–758; Ibn Kathīr, *Bidāya*, 5:5–6; Hoyland, *Seeing*, 120. Hoyland describes this report as "the first explicit reference to Muḥammad in a non-Muslim source, and its very precise dating inspires confidence that it ultimately derives from firsthand knowledge."

Muhammad's Military Expeditions. Ayman S. Ibrahim, Oxford University Press. © Oxford University Press 2024.
DOI: 10.1093/oso/9780197769171.003.0007

Empire and its Arab Christian allies: the battle of Mu'ta, the battle of Tabūk, and Usāma's expedition. Mu'ta reportedly occurred in the eighth year after the *hijra*, shortly before the conquest of Mecca—it is considered the first major military encounter between Muslims and Christians, marking the beginning of the Muslim pursuit to conquer Christian lands. Tabūk was reportedly in the ninth year, a little after Ḥunayn and during the year of delegations. Usāma's expedition was commissioned by Muhammad shortly before his sudden death, which essentially halted it soon after it began.

As we explained in previous chapters, the details of these military encounters are better viewed as *representations* of what the classical Muslim narrators sought to convey to their audience, rather than as factual records of past events. This chapter's study of the traditions of these three raids will reemphasize this point, especially considering their exaggerated and fanciful literary features. In a sense, if we consider how Muslim traditionists authored these traditions, it is plausible to deduce that they sought to design a picture in which Muhammad—as a mighty warrior and inspired prophet—successfully defeated all his enemies from among the pagans, Jews, and Christians. If Islam's most sacred text, the Qur'ān, interacts with Arabs, Jews, and Christians, the logic goes, Muhammad—as a designed portrayal in the traditions—won over them all. His literary image, as shaped by Muslim narrators, exegetes the Qur'ān and conveys a complex picture of a marauding commander and inspired prophet. His success in battle is framed as proof of his religious mission's origin.

The Raid to Mu'ta (8/629)

The raid to Mu'ta reportedly occurred in the eighth year of the *hijra*—two months after Khaybar and only four months before the conquest of Mecca.[2] Mu'ta is a *ḍayʿa* (village) in the region of Balqā' in Bilād al-Shām (Greater Syria).[3] Among traditionists, the expedition is called *ghazwa* (raid) and

[2] This was reportedly in August–September 629, parallel to the fifth *hijrī* month of Jumādā al-awwal in A.H. 8. See Ṭabarī, *History*, 8:152. Watt, *Muḥammad*, 53. Zayd led five other *sarāyā*. See Wāqidī, *Maghāzī*, 553, 555, 564; Ibn Kathīr, *Bidāya*, 4:203–204; Ibn Hishām, *Sīra*, 2:50, 2:635; Kharkūshī, *Sharaf*, 3:51, 3:391, 3:392, 3:533; Bayhaqī, *Dalā'il*, 4:84; Suhaylī, *Rawḍ*, 5:279, 7:547; Kalāʿī, *Iktifā'*, 1:366; Masʿūdī, *Tanbīh*, 1:219–220; Jawzī, *Muntaẓim*, 3:256–258. On these *sarāyā*, see Powers, *Muḥammad*, 75, 144. Some claim it was in the seventh *hijrī* year. See Khalīfa, *Ṭabaqāt*, 30, 32, 163. Note that Khalīfa contradicts himself in his *Ta'rīkh*, 86, and states it was in the eighth year. See Powers, *Zayd*, 49–50. For a thorough Muslim study on Mu'ta and its traditions, see Abū Māyla, *Ghazwat Mu'ta*, 235. For Shīʿite traditions on the raid, see Majlisī, *Biḥār*, 21:50ff.

[3] See Bakrī, *Masālik*, 1:414; Bakrī, *Muʿjam*, 4:1172; Zamakhsharī, *jibāl*, 1:299; Yāqūt, *Muʿjam*, 5:219–220. The location refers today to a small town in the center "of a fertile plain in the land

sariyya (incursion), often identifying it as the *ghazwa* (raid or battle) of Mu'ta or the *sariyya* (incursion) of Zayd ibn Ḥāritha, because he was reportedly the main commander whom Muhammad entrusted to lead, along with two others.[4] Zayd is known in the tradition as a slave, a *mawlā* of Muhammad,[5] and also as Muhammad's adopted son.[6] In a rare report, we are even told that

east of Jordan, east of the southern end of the Dead Sea, about two hours' journey south of Karak." F. Buhl, "Mu'ta," *EI*², 7:756–757. Today, the location is about 150 miles from Amman and 700 miles from Medina. See Abū Māyla, *Ghazwat Mu'ta*, 240. Majlisī, *Biḥār*, 21:57. Regarding al-Shām, this is not today's Syria. The term *Bilād al-Shām* in Muslim sources often refers to Greater Syria, which encompasses areas of today's Lebanon, Syria, Palestine, Egypt, and even sometimes Greece. See Ibn al-Faqīh, *Mukhtaṣar*, 91–93, in which he includes Gaza, Damascus, Jordan, Palestine, and other regions in al-Shām; Yaᶜqūbī, *Buldān*, 160ff.; Iṣṭakhrī, *Masālik*, 55ff.; Yaqūt, *Muᶜjam*, 3:311–315. See the recent study of Webb, "Pre-Islamic al-Shām," 135–164. Philip Hitti writes, "Syria, using the term in its old, geographical sense, occupies a unique place in the annals of the world. Especially because of the inclusion of Palestine and Phoenicia within its ancient boundaries." Hitti, *History of Syria*, 3; and Hitti, *Syria*, 1. See also Miller and Hayes, *History*, 36, 39, 317, 315, 325, et passim, where al-Shām encompasses the broader region of Syria-Palestine. See Ibrahim, *Stated*, 179.

4 See Khalīfa, *Ta'rīkh*, 86 (it is *waqᶜat*, i.e., the incident of Mu'ta); Fasawī, *Maᶜārif*, 144 and 205 (*yawm*, i.e., the day of Mu'ta), 163 (*baᶜtha*, i.e., military mission to Mu'ta); Ṭabarī, *Ta'rīkh*, 1614 (*ghazwa*); Masᶜūdī, *Tanbīh*, 1:230 (aimed to *ghazw* al-Rūm); Maqdisī, *Bad'*, 4:230 (*ghazwa*); Isfahānī, *Maqātil*, 1:31 (*ghazwa*); Jawzī, *Muntaẓim*, 3:318 (*sariyya*); Ibn al-Athīr, *Kāmil*, 2:115 (*ghazwa*); Dhahabī, *Ta'rīkh*, 2:479 (*ghazwa*); Ibn Kathīr, *Bidāya*, 4:284 (*ghazwa*); Ibn al-ᶜImād, *Shadharāt*, 1:126 (*ghazwa*). We should note that identifying it as a *ghazwa* might suggest that the narrators viewed it as one of the expeditions Muhammad led in person. See Abū Māyla, *Ghazwat Mu'ta*, 235–236.

5 For the term *mawlā* (pl. *mawālī*), see Urban, "Early," where she studies the creation and disappearance of the *mawālī* (non-Arab Muslims), and argues that the term almost disappeared when Islam became the faith of the majority in conquered lands. On the social status of the *mawālī* during the early ᶜAbbāsid era, see Dūrī, *ᶜAṣr*, 10ff.; Zaydān, *Ta'rīkh*, 4:340ff., where he explains how Arabs felt superior to non-Arab Muslims. For the role of the *mawālī* in the transmission of historical works, see Crone, "Mawālī," 184ff., where she studies their role in the transmission of one of the earliest Shīᶜite historical works, *Kitāb Sulaym*. On the issue of how the *mawālī*, including Ibn Isḥāq, al-Wāqidī, al-Balādhurī, al-Yaᶜqūbī, and others, were key figures in historical writing among Muslims, see Muṣṭafā, *Ta'rīkh*, 87; Gibb, *Studies*, 112; Hoyland, "Arabic," 233, where he explains the concerns of the Arab historians about the role of the non-Arab *mawālī*, who "held all the important positions in the land." For the tensions between the Arab Muslims and the *mawālī*, see the valuable study of Amīn, *Ḍuḥā*, 1:35–66, and his discussion on the *shuᶜūbiyya* (1:67ff.). On the *shuᶜūbiyya*, see Dūrī, *Judhūr*, 13ff.; Webb, *Imagining*, 246–249, 298–299, 312–313. The term *shuᶜūbiyya* refers to the anti-Arab disposition advanced by the *mawālī* in early Islam. See Enderwitz, "Shuᶜūbiyya," *EI*², 9:513ff., where *al-shuᶜūbiyya* is described as an anti-Quraysh movement, aiming to deny the matchless superior status of Muhammad's tribe; Bosworth, "Shuᶜūbiyya," in *Encyclopedia of Arabic Literature*, ed. Meisami and Starkey, 2:717. See also Dionisius Agius, "Shuᶜūbiyya Movement," 76–88; Gibb, *Studies*, 62–73; Zaydān, *Ta'rīkh*, 4:424ff. For early primary sources aiming at resisting *al-shuᶜūbiyya* and stressing the excellence of the Arabs, see Jāḥiẓ, *Bayān*, 2:5ff., where he devotes an entire section to respond critically to the *shuᶜūbiyya*; Ibn Qutayba, *Faḍl*, 56ff. The editors of Ibn Qutayba's work, Peter Webb and James Montgomery, describe the work as "The spirited defense of the Arabs," which "addresses us from an intellectually fertile but politically and socially precarious moment of early Islam" (x), serving "as a circling of the wagons to defend the social prestige of Arabness in the waning political system of the centralized Abbasid caliphate" (xiv).

6 Zayd was a slave purchased by Muhammad's wife, Khadīja, who then became Muhammad's adopted son. M. Lecker, "Zayd b. Ḥāritha," *EI*², 11:475. Zayd is mentioned in the Qur'ān, *sūrat al-Aḥzāb* (Q 33:37). On Zayd, see Ibn Saᶜd, *Ṭabaqāt*, 1:386 (Zayd was *mawlā*, i.e., a client of Khadīja); Ibn ᶜAsākir, *Ta'rīkh*, 3:147–169, 4:278; Ibn Ḥibbān, *Thiqāt*, 3:134 (Zayd is called "the son of Muhammad" until the revelation of the verse *udᶜūhum li-abā'ihim* (call them after their [biological] fathers)

Zayd had the unmatched honor of being the first male to convert to Islam.[7] Overall, the raid is heavily emphasized in the tradition. Due to its size and target, the narrators highlight it as one step farther for Muhammad's advancement northward, to bring more Arabs under his rule and even challenge the Christian Byzantine Empire.[8] After all, his stated intentions were reportedly declared three years earlier, when he "desired to approach the place closest to al-Shām," which initiated his raid to Dūmat al-Jandal, because he knew that "if he drew near to it, this would terrify Caesar."[9] Muhammad

(Q 33:5); Ibn Manda, *Maᶜrifat*, 1:960, 1:980, concerning the affair of Zaynab, Zayd, and Muhammad; Ibn al-Athīr, *Usd*, 2:350, where Zayd is identified as Muhammad's son; Dhahabī, *Ta'rīkh*, 1:330–333; Dhahabī, *Siyar*, *sīra* 1:111 and 1:220ff., where Zayd is the first male convert after ᶜAlī; also *sīra* 2:131ff. and 1:144, where Zayd converted after Khadīja, ᶜAlī, and Abū Bakr, and is followed by ᶜUthmān. For Muslim studies, see Haykal, *Life*, 78; ᶜAqqād, *ᶜAbqariyyat al-ṣiddīq*, 73. For a recent non-Muslim study on Zayd, see Powers, *Zayd*, 16–26, et passim; Powers, *Muhammad*, 72–92; also Ibrahim, *Conversion*, 60.

7 Zuhrī, *Maghāzī*, 46. Maᶜmar, *Expeditions*, 18–19. For the competition between Zayd, Abū Bakr, and ᶜAlī on the earliest to convert, see Ibrahim, *Conversion*, ch. 2. For Shīᶜite views, see Yaᶜqūbī, *Ta'rīkh*, 2:22; Raḍī, *Nahj*, 81, 100; Ṭabarsī, *Iḥtijāj*, 1:37, 1:271; Ṭabarsī, *Iᶜlām*, 1:102–103; Ṭabarī, *Dhakhā'ir*, 58–59; Majlisī, *Biḥār*, 38:272, 40:42, et passim; also Amīnī, *Ghadīr*, 3:219ff., where he lists one hundred traditions establishing that ᶜAlī was the earliest and first to convert to Islam; Amīnī, *Naẓra*, 149. The Sunnī jurist Yaḥyā ibn Maᶜīn, a friend of Ibn Ḥanbal, insists that Abū Bakr was the first to convert. Yaḥyā ibn Maᶜīn, *Maᶜrifat*, 1:151.

8 For the earliest Muslim-Byzantine encounters, see Kaegi, "Initial," 139–149; Kaegi, *Muslim*, 16–90; Kennedy, *Byzantine*, 141–183; Eger, *Islamic-Byzantine*. See also Cheikh and Bosworth, "Rūm," *EI²*, 8:601ff., where the term Rūm "occurs in Arabic literature with reference to the Romans, the Byzantines and the Christian Melkites interchangeably" (601). For a general introduction on Byzantium, see Cameron, *Byzantines*, 1–196; also her edited volume Cameron, ed., *Byzantine*; Haldon, *Byzantium*, 41–90 (politics of survival against the Muslim conquests), 143–170 (economic effects of the conquests); Mango, *Byzantium*. See also the edited volume by Bonner, ed., *Arab-Byzantine Relations*. For a study on reasons for the Byzantine failure in responding to the Arab conquests, see Kaegi, *Byzantium*, 26–180; Bonner, "Some Observations," 5–31. For a study on theological controversies in Byzantium, see Parry, *Depicting*, 67–199; Brubaker and Haldon, *Byzantium*, 286–294; El Cheikh, *Byzantium*, 39–54. See also the recent edited volume by Mike Humphreys, ed., *Companion*. For the Muslim-Byzantine encounter with particular emphasis on al-Shām, see Tannous, *Making*, 225–429; Khalek, *Damascus*; Khalek, "From Byzantium"; also the edited volume by Garsoïan, et al., eds., *East of Byzantium*. For the Umayyad-Byzantine religious rivalry, see Walker, *Catalogue*; Hoyland, *Seeing*, 552–553; also Mikhail, *From Byzantine*, 64–65, albeit with an emphasis on Egypt. For Syriac images of Muslim-Byzantine encounters, see Brock, "Syriac," 9–21.

9 Wāqidī, *Life*, 197. On Dūmat al-Jandal's location, see Ibn Khuradādhbih, *Masālik*, 129; Ibn al-Faqīh, *Buldān*, 437; Iṣṭakhrī, *Masālik*, 23; Zamakhsharī, *Jibāl*, 1:132; Hamadānī, *Amākin*, 1:438 (it is in Greater Syria, five days' journey from Damascus and fifteen from Medina); Yāqūt, *Muᶜjam*, 2:487–488 (seven stages from Damascus). See Watt, *Muḥammad*, 35, where he states that, "As Dūmah was some 500 miles from Medina there can have been no immediate threat to Muhammad," but he reportedly desired to march to it. See also Sharīf, *Makka*, 363 and 401, where he states that Dūmah is an oasis, about one hundred miles from Damascus on the frontier between the Hijaz and al-Shām. See ᶜAlī, *Mufaṣṣal*, 7:233–240. For reasons to initiate the raid to Dūmat al-Jandal, see Ṣallābī, *Sīra*, 732, where he claims that Arab Christian tribes in al-Shām created tension and enmity between the Muslims and Byzantines, which prompted several incursions, including Ḥismā and Wādī al-Qurā—both led by Zayd. On Ḥismā and Wādī al-Qurā, see Wāqidī, *Maghāzī*, 555, 617, and Ibn Hishām, *Sīra*, 2:612, 2:617, respectively. Dūmat al-Jandal was of economic and strategic importance; see Kennedy, *Prophet*, 35, 52; Muir, *Life*, 225; Eph'al, *Ancient*, 121.

reportedly "set out with a thousand Muslims" to attack a location almost five hundred miles north of Medina.[10] While this was presumably a minor raid, as Muhammad did not fight in it and his people fled, it showed his desire to subdue tribes in the northern parts of Arabia. Now, the logic goes, in his raid of Mu'ta, that Muhammad would proceed to accomplish his reported desire. However, in his summary of this raid, al-Ṭabarī reports an undesired result: Muhammad "sent out his expedition to Syria whose members met with disaster at Mu'tah."[11]

The details of the raid are as follows: It was launched as a Muslim response to an assault made by some Arab Christians against an envoy whom Muhammad sent to Buṣrā (Bostra, southern Syria).[12] We are told that Muhammad sent a Muslim named al-Ḥārith with a letter to the king of Buṣrā in al-Shām, although the sources do not indicate the purpose or contents of the letter.[13] When al-Ḥārith arrived in Mu'ta, he was intercepted by Shuraḥbīl ibn ᶜAmr al-Ghassānī, a Christian from the Ghassānid tribe—an ally of the Byzantines.[14] Shuraḥbīl was reportedly the governor of al-Balqā'

[10] Wāqidī, *Life*, 197. The raid did not have big goals, nor did it accomplish much: Muhammad "marched until he attacked their cattle and their shepherd," then "alighted in their yard, but he did not find anyone there." Muhammad reportedly did not fight. Wāqidī, *Life*, 197–198. However, he was reportedly keen to keep attacking, as he shortly sent a *sariyya* (incursion) to it in A.H. 6; also in A.H. 9 after Tabūk, he sent Khālid to it. See Wāqidī, *Maghāzī*, 560, 1025.

[11] Ṭabarī, *History*, 8:152. For secondary Muslim studies on Mu'ta, see the thorough work by Birayk Abū Māyla, *Ghazwat Mu'ta*, 231ff.; also Ṣallābī, *Sīra*, 732ff.; Ṣallābī, *Ghazawāt*, 244–254; ᶜUmarī, *Sīra*, 467ff. For recent non-Muslim studies, see Powers, *Zayd*, 49–67; Powers, *Muḥammad*, 72–119.

[12] The following summary of the raid relies on Wāqidī, *Maghāzī*, 755ff.; Wāqidī, *Life*, 372ff.; Ṭabarī, *Ta'rīkh*, 1610ff.; Ṭabarī, *History*, 8:152–161; Ibn Hishām, *Sīra*, 2:373ff.; Ibn Hishām, *Life*, 531–540. For a possible parallel in a Byzantine account, see Buhl, "Mu'ta," *EI*², 7:756, where he refers to an account by Theophanes, who claims that Muhammad sent four commanders "to the land east of Jordan against the Christian Arabs there." See Theophanes, *Chronicle*, 36. On Theophanes and his take on Mu'ta, see Conrad, "Theophanes"; also Powers, *Muḥammad*, 82–83. Kaegi, *Byzantium*, 71–74. On Buṣrā, see Ibn Khuradādhbih, *Masālik*, 77,97; Ibn al-Faqīh, *Buldān*, 202, 210; Iṣṭakhrī, *Masālik*, 65; Bakrī, *Masālik*, 1:464; Bakrī, *Muᶜjam*, 1:253; Zamakhsharī, *Jibāl*, 1:52; Yāqūt, *Muᶜjam*, 2:500; Maqrīzī, *Mawāᶜiẓ*, 4:101, 4:393.

[13] See the comments of Fishbein in Ṭabarī, *History*, 8:xviii, where he states, "the motive for this mission to Buṣrā remains a mystery."

[14] The Ghassānids (Banū Ghassān) refer to a Christian Arab dynasty in al-Shām (Greater Syria), with a Yamanī origin. They followed the Monophysite Christian tradition and were allied with the Byzantine Empire, especially in defending the frontiers against the Persians. Shahid, "Ghassān," *EI*², 2:1020–1021. On the Ghassānids, see the excellent study of Cheikho, *Naṣrāniyya*, 30–39, 136–137; also ᶜAlī, *Mufaṣṣal*, 6:77–136, where he explains that it is an Arab Christian tribe and kingdom; their name is derived from Ghassān, a water well where they resided (5:150, 6:77); the Ghassānids in Syria were rivals of the Manādhira in Iraq (5:245); the Ghassānid kingdom ruled the Christian Arabs of Bilād al-Shām under the patronage of the Byzantines (6:77) and had good trading relationships with Arabia, especially Mecca (6:81). See also Shahid, *Byzantium*, 3ff.; Avner, Nehmé, and Robin, "A Rock Inscription," 237–256; also see the articles in the edited volume by Genequand and Robin, *Les Jafnides*; Tannous, "Arabic," in *Medieval*, ed. Ibrahim, 7–14. On the "political" alliance between Christian Arab tribes in Northern Hijaz and the Byzantine Empire, see the traditional Islamic view in ᶜUmarī, *Sīra*, 467–468.

in al-Shām, appointed by Heraclius, the Byzantine emperor.[15] Shuraḥbīl, we are told, knew that al-Ḥārith was one of Muhammad's messengers and deliberately killed him.[16]

When Muhammad learned of the killing of al-Ḥārith, we are told, the news affected him greatly. He prepared an army with three thousand Muslim soldiers—the largest force until this point—to avenge his envoy's death.[17] To ensure the endurance and sustainability of the army, Muhammad reportedly appointed three commanders to lead in consecutive order—if one dies, the other succeeds him. Muhammad assigned Zayd ibn Ḥāritha as the initial holder of the banner of the army. If he died, we are told, Jaᶜfar ibn Abī Ṭālib would become the commander; if Jaᶜfar died, ᶜAbdullāh ibn Rawāḥa would take his place.[18] Zayd and Jaᶜfar were from the Quraysh and Banū Hāshim, while ᶜAbdullāh was from the Medinan *anṣār*.[19] For Muhammad to appoint three commanders, it appears, he was aware that the task was

[15] For the portrayal of Heraclius in Muslim sources, see Conrad, "Heraclius," 113–156. See Buhl, "Mu'ta," *EI*², 7:756. Ṣallābī, *Sīra*, 733. Mu'ta is south of al-Balqā', and al-Balqā' is south of Damascus. See Ibn Saᶜd, *Ṭabaqāt*, 2:97; Kharkūshī, *Sharaf*, 3:68; Jawzī, *Muntaẓim*, 3:318. On al-Balqā', see Hamdānī, *Ṣifat*, 170; Ibn Khuradādhbih, *Masālik*, 64–66; Ibn al-Faqīh, *Buldān*, 1:156; Bakrī, *Masālik*, 1:154 (northern frontier of the Arabian Peninsula), 1:168 (*al-ᶜamālīq*, i.e., the giants, resided there); Bakrī, *Muᶜjam*, 1:275, 4:1172 (Mu'ta is a village in al-Balqā'), 4:1280 (al-Balqā' is part of the greater area of Damascus); Zamakhsharī, *jibāl*, 1:53 (located in al-Shām), 1:299 (Mu'ta is a village in al-Balqā'); Hamadānī, *Amākin*, 1:137, 1:866; Yāqūt, *Muᶜjam*, 1:129–130, 214, 329, and especially 1:489 (al-Balqā' is a location in Damascus, between al-Shām and Wādī al-Qurā; full of villages and farming fields; well known for its wheat; its name is a reference to Bāliq from Lot; the Giants [*jābbarūn*, the mighty ones] resided there; some say that its name is derived from *balq*, meaning white and black mixed together). For secondary studies on Heraclius, see Drijvers, "Heraclius," 175–190; Whitby, "George," 157–173; Conrad, "Heraclius," 113–156; Kaegi, *Heraclius*, 19–121; Treadgold, *History*, 287–322.

[16] See Wāqidī, *Life*, 372, where the tradition claims, "Only he was killed for the Messenger of God." See Ṣallābī, *Sīra*, 732, where he blames the Arab Christians in al-Shām for creating tension between the Muslims and the Byzantines.

[17] In a contradicting tradition, the number of Muslims was six thousand. Ibn ᶜAsākir, *Ta'rīkh*, 2:9.

[18] On Jaᶜfar ibn Abī Ṭālib, see Ibn Abī Ḥātim, *Jarḥ*, 2:474, 482 (Jaᶜfar is called "with the two wings," *dhū al-janāḥayn*); Ibn Ḥibbān, *Thiqāt*, 3:49; Iṣfahānī, *Maᶜrifat*, 2:511 (named *al-ṭayyār*, i.e., the flying person, as Muhammad saw him with two wings in Paradise; Jaᶜfar was ten years older than ᶜAlī; Jaᶜfar received over seventy wounds at Mu'ta); Ibn ᶜAbd al-Barr, *Istīᶜāb*, 1:242–244; Ibn ᶜAsākir, *Ta'rīkh*, 27:250–298; Ibn al-Athīr, *Usd*, 1:541–542 (cousin of Muhammad, brother of ᶜAlī, known as Jaᶜfar *al-ṭayyār*, i.e., the flying, converted shortly after ᶜAlī); Dhahabī, *Siyar*, 1:206–217; Ṣafadī, *Wāfī*, 11:70–71; Ibn Ḥajar, *Iṣāba*, 1:592–593; Ibn Ḥajar, *Tahdhīb*, 2:98. See also Bukhārī, *Ṣaḥīḥ*, 5:19ff., where he designates a section of traditions on the virtues of Jaᶜfar. On ᶜAbdullāh ibn Rawāḥa, see Ibn Saᶜd, *Ṭabaqāt*, 3:398–400 (he was a believer from the *anṣār*, of al-Kazraj tribe, participated in Badr, Uḥud, al-Khandaq, and Khaybar, among others; he led a *sariyya* to kill a Jew at Khaybar, and he was martyred at Mu'ta). See also Jumaḥī, *Ṭabaqāt fuḥūl*, 1:215; Khalīfa, *Ṭabaqāt*, 162; Iṣfahānī, *Maᶜrifat*, 3:1638–1640; Ibn ᶜAbd al-Barr, *Istīᶜāb*, 3:898–900; Ibn ᶜAsākir, *Ta'rīkh*, 28:80–127; Ibn al-Athīr, *Usd*, 3:253; Dhahabī, *Siyar*, 1:230–239; Ibn Ḥajar, *Iṣāba*, 4:72–74. See the study by Schaade, "ᶜAbd Allāh b. Rawāḥa," *EI*², 1:50–51.

[19] Ibn Hishām, *Sīra*, 2:388. Ṣallābī, *Sīra*, 816.

dangerous and, to a large extent, a suicide mission.[20] In addition to the three commanders, Muhammad reportedly sent Khālid ibn al-Walīd—who accepted Islam less than three months earlier—to join the army. The narrators report that Muhammad accompanied the army, not to the battlefield, but to bid them farewell—a detail emphasized by various traditionists to reflect Muhammad's genuine concern and commitment to the cause of the military mission.[21] He instructed them to "fight those who disbelieve in God," but commanded them, "Do not betray or be extreme or kill children."[22] He also told the Muslims that Christians would have three options: converting to Islam, paying the *jizya* (poll tax, tribute), or fighting—a command that Muslim leaders also adopted in future battles.[23]

The Muslims marched from Medina to Syria to confront the Christians in Mu'ta. After they reportedly arrived in Maᶜān in al-Shām, they learned of the great Byzantine army led by Heraclius, the emperor himself, which had moved farther south to al-Balqā'.[24] The Muslims were shocked by the massive enemy forces awaiting them, as the traditions claim the unbelievers were one hundred thousand Byzantine soldiers and one hundred thousand Arab Christian auxiliaries, allies of the Romans.[25] These numbers, although

[20] See Buhl, "Mu'ta," *EI*², 7:756, where he states that Muhammad "must have fully recognised the hazardous nature of the enterprise." Sunnī scholar ᶜUmarī, *Sīra*, 467, affirms that Muhammad knew it was dangerous. However, ᶜUmarī unconvincingly argues that it was dangerous as the destination was far from Medina. Tunisian Muslim scholar Hichem Djait is skeptical of the account of Mu'ta. He questions its portrayal of Muhammad's wisdom and refers to him as having been *bilā ḥadhar* (not careful). Djait, *Masīrat*, 170.

[21] ᶜAbd al-Razzāq, *Muṣannaf*, 3:390.

[22] Wāqidī, *Life*, 372. In his directives, Muhammad reportedly spoke about offering Islam to Christians and imposing the *jizya* on those who refuse to convert to Islam—details that formed juristic legal rules for Muslims in generations to come. For detailed analyses of Muhammad's instructions and their juristic rules, see Abū Māyla, *Ghazwat*, 269; Ṣallābī, *Sīra*, 733.

[23] Wāqidī, *Maghāzī*, 757–758. Ṣallābī, *Sīra*, 733. On the three options given to Christians, see Ṭabarī, *Ta'rīkh*, 2109; Ibn Ḥibbān, *Sīra*, 2:446, 250; ᶜAbd al-Jabbār, *Tathbīt*, 1:236; Bayhaqī, *Dalā'il*, 5:247; Ibn ᶜAbd al-Barr, *Durar*, 1:242; Ibn Kathīr, *Sīra*, 4:3. See the studies by Ibrahim, *Stated*, 131, 155–156; Arnold, *Preaching*, 44–46; Muir and Weir, *Caliphate*, 111. On the roots and authenticity of the issue of non-Muslims surrendering to Muslims after defeats in battle, see Milka Levy-Rubin, *Non-Muslims*, 32–56.

[24] Wāqidī, *Maghāzī*, 760; Ibn Hishām, *Sīra*, 2:373. Maᶜān is in today's Jordan. Ṣallābī, *Sīra*, 734. See Buhl, "Mu'ta," *EI*², 7:756, where he is skeptical of the Muslim report that it was "the emperor Heraclius himself who assembled this great army." Similarly, see Djait, *Masīrat*, 170–171, where he is skeptical of the Muslim accounts and argues that Heraclius had already left Palestine before 630 C.E. In a curious Muslim tradition, a few months before Mu'ta, Heraclius received a letter (other reports refer to two letters) from Muhammad inviting him to accept Islam. While he valued Muhammad's invitation, Heraclius reportedly refused to follow Islam, although he believed in Muhammad's message, as he wanted to keep his worldly status. See Bukhārī, *Ṣaḥīḥ*, 6:35; also Yaᶜqūbī, *Ta'rīkh*, 2:83–84, although he places this after Tabūk. There are contradictions in the tradition regarding who led the Byzantines. See Abū Māyla, *Ghazwat*, 283–286.

[25] Cf. Ṭabarī, *Ta'rīkh*, 1611, and Ibn Hishām, *Sīra*, 2:373 (put the number as 200,000), while Wāqidī, *Maghāzī*, 760 (100,000). See also Ibn Ḥibbān, *Sīra*, 1:317 (100,000); Bayhaqī, *Dalā'il*, 4:360 (200,000); ᶜAbd al-Barr, *Durar*, 1:209 (200,000); Suhaylī, *Rawḍ*, 7:180 (250,000, including 50,000 Arabs); Ibn

upheld by Muslim narrators, are clearly exaggerated, probably to magnify the Muslim bravery and justify the eventual retreat and defeat.[26] Some Muslims, out of obvious fear, sought to retreat and return to Medina, as they reportedly desired *al-ᶜāfiya* (safety and protection).[27] Nonetheless, the tale claims that the Muslims became concerned and hesitated to engage in the battle. They decided to ask Muhammad's counsel as to whether they should wait for reinforcements or return to Medina. One of the three major commanders, ᶜAbdullāh ibn Rawāḥa, reportedly gave a stunning speech, exhorting the Muslims not to wait but to move forward and seek martyrdom: "Men, by God, what you loathe is the very thing you came out to seek—martyrdom. We do not fight the enemy by number, strength, or multitude; we fight them only by this religion with which God has honored us. Go forward, for it is one of two good things: victory or martyrdom."[28] With this stirring speech, the Muslims decided not to consult Muhammad, but to proceed to face the enemy. While some may view this literary report as merely an image of religious zeal and valor, it inspires Muslims to elevate jihad in Allah's path above any other considerations.[29]

After the Muslims decided to confront the Byzantines, we are told, the two armies met at Mu'ta with a vast difference in numbers—both in soldiers and equipment. An eyewitness of the battle, we are told, reported, "When we saw the polytheists we saw what was beyond us in numbers, and weapons and quivers."[30] In fact, we are invited to believe, "the commanders were at that time fighting on their feet," as a sign of bravery, devotion, and valor.[31] Importantly, while the Muslims were fighting in the battlefield at Mu'ta, we are told, Muhammad was at the mosque in Medina seeing a detailed vision of the front line and reporting it to his people. Thus, he is portrayed as a witness

Kathīr, *Sīra*, 3:458 (200,000, but some say 250,000, and the least number given is 150,000); Ḥalabī, *Insān*, 3:96 (200,000, or 250,000). See Abū Māyla, *Ghazwat*, 251, where he argues that the Arab Christians who allied themselves with the Byzantines deserved to be fought as a juristic command. Some Muslim scholars concede that the number of the Byzantines is exaggerated. See Sharīf, *Makka*, 534, where he argues that the Byzantines did not use this huge army even with the Persians. See also Abū Māyla, *Ghazwat*, 280–282, where he admits the number is exaggerated but provides several reasons for the possible exaggeration.

[26] See Buhl, "Mu'ta," *EI*^{2}, 7:756, where he observes, "the tendency of the stories to describe the dangers of the expedition and the overwhelming nature of the opposing force as very great in order to put the unfortunate result of the battle in a better light is quite evident."

[27] Ibn ᶜAsākir, *Ta'rīkh*, 2:15. Ṣallābī, *Sīra*, 735.

[28] Ṭabarī, *History*, 8:154; Ibn Hishām, *Sīra*, 2:373. Wāqidī, *Maghāzī*, 760.

[29] ᶜUmarī, *Sīra*, 468.

[30] Wāqidī, *Life*, 374.

[31] Wāqidī, *Life*, 374.

of the battle—through a divine vision—and its reporter. We are told, based on Muhammad's vision, that the first Muslim commander, Zayd, initiated the fight against the enemy, but he was soon killed.[32] Then Jaᶜfar took the commandership and fought fiercely. His right hand was severed, so he reportedly led the army and fought only with his left hand, until it was severed as well. He was eventually killed. Then ᶜAbdullāh led the army, until he was killed as well.[33]

After the deaths of the three commanders, the banner of the Muslims ended in the hands of the shrewd warrior Khālid ibn al-Walīd, who engaged the Byzantines in intense fighting, attempting to save the Muslim army from this disastrous situation. Some reports claim that he seized the commandership banner, while others assert that an older soldier gave it to him. More importantly, we are invited to believe that Khālid strategically took consecutive steps to safeguard the Muslim army and withdraw from the battlefield, although some accounts insist he led a Muslim victory.[34] It is impossible to determine what he did, but we are told that he *deceived* the Byzantines by altering the location of Muslim warriors between the right and the left of the battlefield—an act that confused the Byzantines into thinking the Muslims received huge enforcements.[35] Khālid thus intimidated them and tactically spared the Muslims. He is depicted as a hero, to the extent that Muhammad identified him as *Sayf Allāh* (Allah's sword). Ultimately, the Mu'ta account is treated in the tradition not as a defeat but as a tactical Muslim victory. We are invited to believe that Muslims harmed the Byzantines greatly and killed many of the unbelievers.[36] This concludes the overall narrative of the raid to Mu'ta.

Muslims past and present cherish the memory of the raid to Mu'ta, mostly highlighting it as a great strategic expedition.[37] However, as a literary

[32] He was fifty or fifty-five years of age at the time of his death. Lecker, "Zayd b. Ḥāritha," *EI*², 11:475. See Ibn Saᶜd, *Ṭabaqāt*, 3:34, where he states Zayd was fifty-five years old when he died.

[33] Ibn Hishām, *Sīra*, 2:378.

[34] Ṭabarī, *Ta'rīkh*, 1616–1617. See the discussion on Khālid in Anthony, *Muhammad*, 121–124.

[35] See Buhl, "Mu'ta," *EI*², 7:756, where he questions the Muslim claims on how the Muslims ended the battle and writes that the report about Khālid's plot to deceive the Byzantines "is not to be taken seriously."

[36] Abū Māyla, *Ghazwat*, 340–341. ᶜUmarī, *Sīra*, 468–469.

[37] The sources and studies that highly view Mu'ta are numerous. For classical sources, see, for instance, ᶜAbd al-Razzāq, *Muṣannaf*, 3:390; Khalīfa, *Ta'rīkh*, 86; Kharkūshī, *Sharaf*, 3:68; Fasawī, *Maᶜārif*, 144, 205, 163; Fasawī, *Maᶜrifa*, 3:258; Ṭabarī, *Ta'rīkh*, 1614; Masᶜūdī, *Tanbīh*, 1:230; Bukhārī, *Ṣaḥīḥ*, 5:143–144; Muslim, *Ṣaḥīḥ*, 3:1374; Ibn Ḥajar, *Fatḥ*, 7:498; ᶜAbd al-Jabbār, *Tathbīt*, 2:511; Maqdisī, *Bad'*, 4:230; Isfahānī, *Maqātil*, 1:31; Bayhaqī, *Dalā'il*, 4:361; Ibn ᶜAbd al-Barr, *Durar*, 1:209; Jawzī, *Muntaẓim*, 3:318; Suhaylī, *Rawḍ*, 7:172; Kalāᶜī, *Iktifā'*, 1:492; Ibn al-Athīr, *Kāmil*, 2:115; Dhahabī, *Ta'rīkh*, 2:479; Ibn Kathīr, *Bidāya*, 4:284; Ibn al-ᶜImād, *Shadharāt*, 1:126. For modern and contemporary Muslim studies, see Mubārakpūrī, *Raḥīq*, 355 (Mu'ta was the greatest war in

creation, the raid reflects a suicide mission that was later tweaked to resemble a victory.[38] This is one reason why the narrative includes unconvincing components and exaggerated features.[39] The hyperbolic nature of the accounts of Mu'ta reiterates our contention that the narrators appear to have *authored* history rather than recording or reporting it.[40] The tale, as we have it, is designed to advance religious claims and juristic rules, framed in historiographical reports.[41] There are five critical observations to make on the accounts and their exaggerated nature.

First, the Muslim tradition portrays the battle of Mu'ta as another attempt by the Muslims to advance northward into various Christian lands.[42] While the historiographical accounts claim the expedition was driven by revenge for the killing of Muhammad's envoy, it is plausible to view it, from a literary standpoint, as a natural consequence of the course of events. Three years earlier, Muhammad reportedly declared his desire to conquer Arab tribes in northern Hijaz and, we are told, he explicitly stated that he wanted to terrify the Byzantines.[43] It is conceivable to assume that the timing was right for him: On one hand, he had less tension with his major enemies, the Meccans, after cutting the peace treaty of Ḥudaybiyya.[44] On the other hand, he successfully suppressed the Jews after expelling them from Medina and its neighboring settlements. Now, the logic goes, he was ready to advance northward

Muhammad's lifetime); Sharīf, *Makka*, 403; Birayk Abū Māyla, *Ghazwat*, 231; Ṣallābī, *Sīra*, 732; ᶜUmarī, *Sīra*, 467.

[38] See the study of Sunnī scholar Abū Māyla, *Ghazwat*, 293–294, where he admits that, if we only take practical measures in mind, Mu'ta was a huge military mistake and a disaster; however, the battle was religious, says Abū Māyla, and it was jihad in Allah's path to protect *al-ᶜaqīda* (the Islamic dogma) and ensure its freedom to spread. See the comments of Tunisian Muslim scholar Djait, *Masīrat*, 170–171, where he is skeptical of the details of the raid and argues it was a complete defeat and a total disaster for Muslims.

[39] See Watt, *Muḥammad*, 53, where he argues, "The great expedition to Mu'tah is not merely part of the mysterious 'northern' policy [of Muhammad], but is in itself mysterious."

[40] Petersen, *ᶜAlī*, 11–20; Robinson, *Empire*, viii; Rubin, *Eye*, 1–3; Robinson rightly argues that Muslim historians—of al-Balādhurī's time—were authors rather than compilers of reports—they "impressed their vision upon the material" by "breaking them up, by rephrasing, supplementing and composing anew." See Robinson, *Historiography*, 35–36, 38. See Djait, *Masīrat*, 170–171, where he calls the Mu'ta narrative curious and unreasonable.

[41] The accounts address jihad, martyrdom, offering Islam to non-Muslims, treating conquered people, imposing the *jizya* (poll tax) on Christian subjects, and many other topics. Tunisian Muslim scholar Hichem Djait defines *jizya* as *gharāma* (a fine, financial penalty). Djait, *Masīrat*, 191; Cf. Cl. Cahen, "D̲jizya." *EI*[2], 2:559–567.

[42] See the earlier comments about Muhammad's raid and his commissioned incursion to Dūmat al-Jandal. Watt, *Muḥammad*, 105.

[43] Wāqidī, *Maghāzī*, 560, 1025. Muhammad would reportedly later send Khālid to Dūmat al-Jandal (*Maghāzī*, 1025).

[44] See Abū Māyla, *Ghazwat*, 259.

to subdue more Arab tribes. While these appear as possible logical reasons based on the overall literary story of the *maghāzī*, the tradition—as a religiously driven composition—provides one more appealing factor: Since al-Shām is adjacent to the Arabian Peninsula to the north and northwest, Muhammad sought to spread Islam in that region, beginning with the Arab tribes and hoping to eventually proceed to the heart of Byzantium. Here the historiographical narrative serves theological purposes. The way to advance Islam, as the tradition conveys, was to prepare to march to invade *fī sabīl Allāh* (for Allah's cause) and to offer Islam to the inhabitants of these lands—this claim is central to the narrative of Mu'ta.[45] Once the Muslim troops gathered near Medina to march to Mu'ta, Muhammad reportedly exhorted them, *ighzū b-ism Allāh* (invade in Allah's name), "fight Allah's enemy and your enemy in al-Shām."[46] Muhammad's exhortation is better viewed as a creation by the narrators to frame a military raid in a religious light. They also needed a reason for the story to start, so they forged an account of Muhammad's letter to the king of Buṣrā. It is curious how the tradition remains ambiguous about this letter and does not convey its message. While some scholars *hypothetically* assume it was similar to other letters that Muhammad allegedly sent to invite kings and rulers to Islam around the same time, the tradition does not state so.[47] The argument of these scholars is rather unconvincing, especially if we consider how Muslim narrators did not find it difficult to disclose the content of other letters.[48] The silence of the narrators regarding the content of this particular letter, it appears, amplifies the mysterious and mythical nature of the narrative.[49] One may argue that the massacre of Muhammad's envoy by a Christian ruler was a literary device to frame the raid not as an offensive Muslim attack but as a response to

[45] See Wāqidī, *Life*, 372, where Muhammad instructs the believers, "Raid, in the name of God and in the path of God, and fight those who disbelieve in God. Do not betray or be extreme or kill children. If you meet your enemy from the polytheists . . . invite them to enter Islam." See Abū Māyla, *Ghazwat*, 251, as he states that the chief reason for the raid was to fulfill Allah's command to fight the Christians (Q 9:29). See also Ṣallābī, *Sīra*, 733, where he claims the raid was mandatory to protect the Muslims in Arabia and to punish the Christians in the north who had often provoked the Muslims.

[46] Wāqidī, *Maghāzī*, 757–758. Muhammad's exhortation is mentioned twice. The Muslims gathered at al-Jurf, about three miles north of Medina. Powers, *Muḥammad*, 75. See Sunnī scholar ᶜUmarī, *Sīra*, 467, where he argues that there is no benefit from knowing the specific reason that triggered Mu'ta, as jihad has been already prescribed and it entailed the subjugation of the Arab Christian tribes in al-Shām and the expansion of the Islamic State. Abū Māyla, *Ghazwat*, 249.

[47] See Powers, *Zayd*, 50; Powers, *Muhammad*, 75.

[48] Ibn Hishām, *Sīra*, 2:607; Ibn ᶜAbd al-Ḥakam, *Futūḥ*, 67; Kalāᶜī, *Iktifā'*, 2:10–14; Ibn Sayyid al-Nās, *ᶜUyūn*, 2:326–328. Bukhārī, *Ṣaḥīḥ*, 1:8, 4:45, 6:36; Muslim, *Ṣaḥīḥ*, 3:1393–1397.

[49] On the mysterious nature of the military mission, see Watt, *Muḥammad*, 53; also the comments of Fishbein in Ṭabarī, *History*, 8:xviii.

assault. The tendentiousness of the report may also be gleaned from the insistence of the narrative that the envoy was killed *precisely* due to his known association with Muhammad. This, as a literary fiction, established a reason for marching to Mu'ta and fighting the avengers.

Second, the narrative is replete with metaphysical, mystical, and mythical elements. These reinforce our skepticism of its contents as a record of the past and reiterate our contention that the narrative should be valued more for its theological disposition and religious meaning, fashioned by traditionists, for later generations. In the Mu'ta story, we are invited to believe an image of the Byzantine Empire moving two hundred thousand or more of its warriors and allies to face an army of three thousand Bedouins marching to avenge the death of a Muslim.[50] At the same time, the narrative insists that these Muslims did fairly well in fighting and only had thirteen soldiers martyred, including the three commanders.[51] The exaggeration is glaring, but it serves the religious goals of the narrators.[52] The traditionists author religious reports and do not primarily seek to record a distant past. This is evident in how the sequence of the battle and the details of the wounds of the commanders are given to us—in details, including their number and locations—through a divine vision seen and authenticated by Muhammad himself.[53] In this vision, as Muhammad reportedly sat in his mosque in Medina, he saw his paternal cousin Jaᶜfar, the second commander, flying with the angels in paradise after he was martyred. This is why Jaᶜfar was called *al-ṭayyār* (the flying one) and *dhū al-janāḥayn* (the man with the two wings).[54] Not only does this report serve to direct the Muslims to the rewards of martyrdom, but it highlights Muhammad as deeply involved in the battle. In this portrayal, Muhammad is an eyewitness of the battle and, it could be argued, a participator in it—one more reason for some traditionists to insist on labeling it *ghazwa* (raid or battle) and not only *sariyya* (an incursion).[55]

[50] See the study of Tunisian scholar Djait, *Masīrat*, 170, as he argues that the account of Mu'ta is perplexing, as he cannot deny it occurred, nor can he deny it was a severe defeat for Muslims; however, says Djait, the account in the Muslim sources is unconvincing.

[51] ᶜUmarī, *Sīra*, 468. Wāqidī, *Maghāzī*, 769; Ibn Hishām, *Sīra*, 2:388. See Djait, *Masīrat*, 170, where he puts the number of the martyrs at eight and argues that the entire account is exaggerated.

[52] For a Muslim study on the exaggeration of these numbers at Mu'ta, see Djait, *Masīrat*, 170–171, where he questions Muhammad's wisdom in sending a mission to the north with apparent lack of planning and preparation.

[53] Wāqidī, *Maghāzī*, 761–762. See also Bukhārī, *Ṣaḥīḥ*, 5:143, where he provides two traditions—one claiming Jaᶜfar had fifty wounds and the other raising the number to over ninety.

[54] See Wāqidī, *Maghāzī*, 767; Bayhaqī, *Dalā'il*, 4:365; Ibn Abī Ḥātim, *Jarḥ*, 2:474, 2:482; Ibn Ḥibbān, *Thiqāt*, 3:49; Iṣfahānī, *Maᶜrifat*, 2:511; Ibn ᶜAbd al-Barr, *Istīᶜāb*, 1:242–244.

[55] The term *ghazwa* is often used with *maghāzī* led by Muhammad himself. See Abū Māyla, *Ghazwat*, 236, where he argues that Mu'ta is bigger than a *sariyya* because of the number of the

Not only was Muhammad involved in the battle, albeit through a vision, but Satan also was reportedly present. The tale invites us to believe that Zayd—as a commander of the army—insisted on seeking martyrdom in a conversation with Satan during the battle. In an attempt to dissuade Zayd from martyrdom, Satan came to him, we are told, "and made life attractive and death detestable to him." Zayd, as Muhammad's vision of the battlefield reveals, mocked Satan and said, "Now, when faith is deeply rooted in the hearts of the believers you will make the world attractive to me!"[56] This statement portrays a Muslim warrior gladly forsaking worldly pleasures and desiring martyrdom. The report serves as a parabolic homily for Muslims to imitate Zayd by striving for martyrdom in Allah's path, and it receives its authority from Muhammad's own mouth. The report fits medieval Islam and serves goals of caliphal expansion. This is not a suicide on a battlefield, according to one religious logic. Rather, it is spiritual heroism and is amplified further by the earlier speech of ᶜAbdullāh ibn Rawāḥa: He deterred the warriors—when they saw the enemy's numbers—from sending word to ask Muhammad how to proceed, and instead encouraged them to seek one of "two good results," victory or martyrdom.[57] The entire account is not designed to reveal what actually happened at Mu'ta, but to convey the thoughts and beliefs of religious storytellers. This is evident, once more, in how the traditionists invite us to imagine an unbelieving Jew—Nuᶜmān ibn Funḥuṣ—present among the Muslim soldiers while Muhammad instructed them about the sequence of the three commanders in the battle. When Nuᶜmān heard Muhammad's order of command, he reportedly told him, "If you are a prophet and you name whom you name, a few or many, they will be wounded all of them."[58] The storytellers design this portrayal to communicate a theological point, especially since we now know the result of the battle: even a Jew testified to Muhammad's prophethood. Indeed, it is difficult to imagine a Jew—after all that the Jews incurred in previous Muslim raids—somehow finding his way into the midst of the Muslim soldiers, listening to a military strategic plan,

soldiers, and it cannot be labeled a *ghazwa* since Muhammad did not participate in it. Nonetheless, Abū Māyla acknowledges that many traditionists call it a *ghazwa* due to its impact.

[56] Wāqidī, *Life*, 375.

[57] See Wāqidī, *Life*, 374, where ᶜAbdullāh exhorts the Muslims, "By God, we have never fought the people with great numbers or with many weapons, or with many horses, but only with this religion that God has blessed us."

[58] Wāqidī, *Life*, 372. The report also alleges that Nuᶜmān spoke with Zayd: "Make your testimony, for you will not return to Muḥammad ever, if he is a prophet." Since Zayd did not return, the logic of the story goes, then this is proof of Muhammad's prophethood. See Stroumsa, "Signs," 101–114.

and speaking with Muhammad himself about the plan; however, this appears to be the precise point derived by Muslim traditionists as they designed their story.

Third, the result of the raid—whether one calls it defeat, retreat, or victory—is worth examining. If we consider the vast difference in number and military power between the two armies and the swift deaths of the three commanders appointed by Muhammad, then this raid was a complete disaster and a humiliating experience for the Muslims. However, Muslim storytellers chose not to depart from their religious preferences. This is why there is significant confusion among the narrators as to whether this raid was a Muslim victory or defeat. The confusion, as we repeatedly encountered, reflects how storytellers *author* their accounts. In concluding his account on the raid to Mu'ta, al-Wāqidī reports the disastrous fate of the Byzantines: "And they were frightened, and withdrew, defeated. They were killed as never before."[59] Similarly, in his work on the proofs of Muhammad's prophethood, al-Bayhaqī summarizes the battle: *fa-hazama Allāhu al-ᶜaduwa wa-aẓhara al-muslimīna* (Allah defeated the enemy and made the Muslims victorious).[60] A defeat, it appears, is unfathomable in the framework of the theological understanding of divine support for Muhammad and the believers. Another traditionist describes the Byzantines and emphasizes that *fa-qutilū maqtalatan lam yuqtalhā qawmun* (they were definitely killed as no one else ever did).[61] This is why we are assured by storytellers that Muslims incurred minimal losses compared to the Christian Byzantines. If we take these reports at face value, which goes against plain reason, then the three thousand Muslims destroyed two hundred thousand Byzantines in an unprecedented, epic battle. This is difficult to believe, especially since the same tradition includes other reports that portray the exact opposite picture of a clear Muslim defeat. According to al-Wāqidī, who reported the Muslim victory earlier, the matter was complicated, and some Muslims affirmed that *Khālid inhazama bi-l-nās* (Khālid was defeated with the people).[62] One Muslim, presumably an eyewitness, reportedly declared, "The Muslims were defeated and it was the worst defeat I ever saw anywhere."[63] Another stated,

[59] Wāqidī, *Life*, 376.

[60] Bayhaqī, *Dalā'il*, 4:365. A similar account is advanced by Ibn Kathīr, *Bidāya*, 4:281. Cf. Stroumsa, "Signs," 101–114.

[61] Ibn Kathīr, *Bidāya*, 4:281. A similar account appears in Wāqidī, *Maghāzī*, 764.

[62] Wāqidī, *Maghāzī*, 764. While al-Wāqidī provides contradicting reports on the defeat and victory, he comments on this report of the defeat and states that it "is confirmed with us: that Khālid was defeated with the people."

[63] Wāqidī, *Life*, 375.

"The blood [of the Muslims] reached the horses on the spot near the hoof."[64] Similarly, Ibn Saᶜd, in reporting the conclusion of the raid for the Muslims, writes, *fa-kānat al-hazīma* (and there was the defeat).[65] Thus, the same tradition includes competing memories of the raid, particularly its conclusion. In fact, many narrators highlight a curious image: When the Muslims in Medina learned that the Muslim army was arriving back, they went out to meet them "and began to scatter dust in their faces, saying, '*yā furrār* (O deserters, fleers), did you flee from the path of God?' "[66] This report is curiously repeated by some narrators who claimed that the Muslims defeated the Byzantines.[67] However, this image—throwing dust at the Muslims upon their return from the battle and calling them *furrār*—cannot reflect a victory over the Byzantines.[68] Once more, we encounter a tweaked image. It appears that an earlier memory of a Muslim defeat at Mu'ta did not fit the narrative of Islam's hegemony, so the narrators adjusted it by adding embellishments. The memory that began as a Muslim defeat was then manipulated into a strategic withdrawal and finally ended as a declaration of Muslim victory and Byzantine humiliation.

Fourth, the floundering among the narrators in describing the events at Mu'ta reflects their attempts to not only forge a tale of victory but also to embellish Khālid's portrayal.[69] As we explained in the analysis of Khālid's incursion to Banū Jadhīma in the previous chapter, his portrayal is important to ᶜAbbāsid-era orthodoxy and the proto-Sunnī claims. Just as we find competing reports about the defeat at Mu'ta, we also encounter contradicting portrayals of Khālid. In one report, some Muslims declared after Mu'ta, "Surely Khālid fled from the polytheists."[70] This suggests he was a defeated coward. We are also told that, after the three commanders died, Khālid seized the commandership of the army forcibly, although "he was not one of

[64] Wāqidī, *Life*, 376.

[65] Ibn Saᶜd, *Ṭabaqāt*, 2:98.

[66] Wāqidī, *Life*, 376; Ibn Hishām, *Sīra*, 2:382–283; Ibn Saᶜd, *Ṭabaqāt*, 2:98; Ṭabarī, *History*, 8:159: "[The Muslims] began to throw dust at the army, saying, 'Fleers in the way of God!' "; Bayhaqī, *Dalā'il*, 4:374–375; Suhaylī, *Rawḍ*, 7:178–179; Kalāᶜī, *Iktifā'*, 1:496; Ibn Kathīr, *Sīra*, 3:469; Maqdisī, *Bad'*, 4:232; Jawzī, *Muntaẓim*, 3:319; Ibn al-Athīr, *Kāmil*, 2:114; Ibn al-Athīr, *Usd*, 7:414; Dhahabī, *Ta'rīkh*, 2:491; Ibn Kathīr, *Bidāya*, 4:283–284; Ibn Ḥajar, *Iṣāba*, 3:131.

[67] See, for instance, Wāqidī, *Maghāzī*, 465; Bayhaqī, *Dalā'il*, 4:375; Ibn Kathīr, *Bidāya*, 4:284.

[68] The narrators attempt to smooth the report on the "deserters" by claiming that Muhammad calmed the Muslims and said, "They are not deserters, but rather those who will return [to the battlefield], God willing!" Wāqidī, *Life*, 376. This report conveys that Muhammad reportedly acknowledged the defeat.

[69] Watt, *Muḥammad*, 54; Powers, *Muḥammad*, 79.

[70] Wāqidī, *Maghāzī*, 763.

the commanders."[71] This memory shows him as an unjustified leader who, through his aggressiveness, pushes himself to the top command. It is understandable that the traditionists needed to tweak this description, especially with the reported defeat of the Muslims, particularly for what he represents for the Sunnī claims. Consequently, the storytellers fashioned other opposing images of Khālid at Mu'ta. In response to those who claim that Khālid fled from the battlefield, the narrators assure us that an eyewitness swore, "No, by Allah, this never occurred."[72] By forging a statement from an eyewitness, the narrators cleared Khālid's image. As for those who claim that Khālid seized the commandership of the army, we are given a conflicting story: After the deaths of the three commanders, the commandership went to a Muslim man named Thābit, who delegated the commandership to Khālid. While initially Khālid *adamantly* refused to lead, at the insistence of Thābit and the Muslims Khālid finally yielded and "the people agreed upon Khālid."[73] This story is designed to justify Khālid and dispel accusations against him as an unjust commander who seized power. There are clear attempts to adjust Khālid's image in the tradition. Even the memory of Khālid's humiliating defeat has a solution in the hands of Muslim traditionists. They alternatively depict him as a hero who turned defeat into victory and deceived the Byzantines. We are invited to believe that once Khālid assumed commandership he tactically "made the rear guard his front and his front his rear guard. And his right became his left, and his left, his right."[74] By switching soldiers around, we are assured, Khālid confused the Byzantines, who declared, "Help has come to them," and "they were frightened, and withdrew, defeated."[75] Thus, a mysterious plot by Khālid reportedly confused hundreds of thousands of Byzantines and propelled them to run for their lives.[76] While Khālid's plot might seem curious to some, we are invited to view it as leading to an epic victory. While some religious enthusiasts may view these reports as factual, it is plausible to assume that the entire report about Khālid's plot aims

[71] Ṭabarī, *History*, 8:158. Ibn Kathīr, *Sīra*, 3:466; Ibn Kathīr, *Bidāya*, 4:281.

[72] Wāqidī, *Maghāzī*, 763.

[73] Wāqidī, *Life*, 376. In contradicting reports, Thābit refused to lead, which propelled the Muslims to choose Khālid. Ibn Hishām, *Sīra*, 2:379–380. Ṭabarī, *History*, 8:157.

[74] Wāqidī, *Life*, 376.

[75] Wāqidī, *Life*, 376.

[76] For a Muslim explanation of Khālid's plot, see Abū Māyla, *Ghazwat*, 326–330, where he claims a Muslim victory and that the army returned to Medina peacefully. Abū Māyla further argues that the tactical withdrawal led by Khālid was one of the most remarkable operations in military history (346). A similar claim on the tactical withdrawal is adopted by Ṣallābī, *Sīra*, 736–737, where he argues that this withdrawal should be viewed as *qimmat al-naṣr* (top triumph).

to embellish his portrayal as a commander who saved the army and spared many Muslims from massacre.[77]

Scholars have rightly recognized the hyperbolic nature of the Mu'ta narrative and argued for various possibilities for such exaggerated depictions, especially those of the three commanders and particularly that of Khālid.[78] From a critical standpoint, it is understandable that the Muslim storytellers would want to find a compelling historical context to elevate Khālid's portrayal. Due to Khālid's reported role in future raids, particularly in the so-called Apostasy Wars, the narrators needed to introduce Khālid in a glowing picture of heroism and valor, precisely as a Muslim warrior. Up to this point, Khālid's portrayal has largely focused on his association and participation with the polytheists of Mecca. The literary composition of Mu'ta allowed the possible inclusion and introduction of Khālid as a new convert who has now become a devoted Muslim warrior. This is evidenced in how the narrators elevate Khālid by designing a report of Muhammad specifically calling him *Sayf Allāh* (Allah's Sword) in recognition of his role at Mu'ta.[79] This alleged report, in no surprise, coincides with Khālid assuming commandership at Mu'ta after the murder of the three commanders.[80] Thus, the narrators present Khālid at Mu'ta as a skillful commander who led the Muslims to victory and was affirmed by Muhammad, who gave him the honorific title "Allah's Sword."[81]

[77] On the claims that Khālid's withdrawal was a great victory, see ᶜUmarī, *Sīra*, 468–469, where he argues that Khālid successfully led *insiḥāb munaẓẓam* (organized, gradual withdrawal), and claims that this withdrawal was *fatḥan ᶜaẓīman* (a great conquest). See also Ṣallābī, *Sīra*, 736, where he claims that Khālid's goal was to withdraw with the least amount of loss. Abū Māyla, *Ghazwat*, 324–325. In a more reasonable assessment, see Djait, *Masīrat*, 170–171, where he argues that Mu'ta was a Muslim defeat but Khālid's tactical withdrawal saved many Muslim lives.

[78] See Djait, *Masīrat*, 170–171. Additionally, Watt argues that the account of appointing Jaᶜfar and ᶜAbdullāh to succeed Zayd if he fell "is probably an invention to support the accusation that Khālid unjustifiably assumed supreme command." Watt, *Muḥammad*, 54. Powers views the narrative of Mu'ta in relation to how the Muslim memory disassociated Zayd from being Muhammad's beloved son and thus found the incident of Mu'ta as a suitable historical context for Zayd's death, to ensure he did not outlive Muhammad. Powers, *Muḥammad*, 73–80.

[79] Ṭabarī, *Ta'rīkh*, 1616–1617; Ṭabarī, *History*, 8:158. See Ibn Kathīr, *Sīra*, 3:466. In a later incident, Muhammad warns Muslims, "Do not curse Khālid ibn al-Walīd for surely he is one of the swords of God who drew his sword against the polytheists!" Wāqidī, *Life*, 434. Balādhurī, *Ansāb*, 10:208. Khālid appears to have cherished this title and used it in later correspondence with Caliph Abū Bakr. Kalāᶜī, *Iktifā'*, 2:204. Muhammad reportedly referred to Khālid with this title in correspondence with Ukaydir. Ibn Saᶜd, *Ṭabaqāt*, 1:220.

[80] Ṭabarī, *History*, 8:158. This is precisely the point where al-Ṭabarī alleges that Muhammad identified Khālid as "Allah's Sword."

[81] In the same vein, the narrators magnify his picture as a victorious commander at Mu'ta, by claiming that he used—and broke—nine swords in this battle alone. Bukhārī, *Ṣaḥīḥ*, 5:144; Ibn Ḥajar, *Fatḥ*, 7:516.

However, this scenario has problems. As we often encounter in Muslim historiographical reports, this narrative about Muhammad designating Khālid as Allah's Sword at Mu'ta is contradicted by other accounts which claim that the title was given later—specifically after Khālid's incursion to Banū Jadhīma, despite his problematic behavior.[82] Therefore, competing reports exist. Did Khālid become Allah's Sword at Mu'ta or later at the incursion of Banū Jadhīma? It appears that the traditionists needed to adjust this memory in light of not only the defeat at Mu'ta but also the questionable behavior of Khālid with Banū Jadhīma, as we explained in the previous chapter. If Muhammad named Khālid "Allah's Sword" at the incursion of Banū Jadhīma, the logic goes, the timing does not appear plausible, especially as Muhammad reportedly rebuked Khālid's vengeance against the men of Banū Jadhīma. It seems better, the same logic goes, to adjust the timing earlier—specifically at Mu'ta to improve Khālid's portrayal in light of the reported defeat and his role in it. Therefore, the storytellers design a new memory by moving Muhammad's designation of Khālid as Allah's Sword almost a year earlier. Still, this whole paradigm is rejected by many Shīᶜite scholars. For them, Muhammad's designation of Khālid is a Sunnī invention and implausible due to Khālid's behavior and manners, which are supported by sources deemed authoritative by Sunnīs themselves—if it were ever given to Khālid, it was not by Muhammad but instead by Abū Bakr.[83] Additionally, many Shīᶜites claim that the true "Sword of Allah" was no one but ᶜAlī, their first Imam.[84]

Fifth and finally, there appears to be an important non-Muslim textual testimony of Mu'ta. Scholars have rightly pointed to a brief account of the Battle of Mothous in *The Chronicle of Theophanes*, a Christian historical work that is attributed to a monk and covers roughly the period between 284 and 812 C.E.[85] Indeed, we should not elevate the importance of non-Muslim sources over Muslim ones, because both interacted with one another.[86]

[82] Balādhurī, *Ansāb*, 1:381–382.

[83] See Majlisī, *Biḥār*, 30:471, 30:486, 30:492, where he reports a Shīᶜite tradition that claims that Abū Bakr called Khālid "Allah's Sword" in response to ᶜUmar's furious criticism of Khālid after the killing of Mālik, and that the account attributed to Muhammad was invented by the liar Abū Hurayra; also 29:52, where it is clearly reported that Abū Bakr was the one who called Khālid "Allah's Sword," not Muhammad.

[84] Majlisī, *Biḥār*, 22:197, 40:33, where the tradition reads, "ᶜAlī is Allah's Sword against the infidels and hypocrites." See also more traditions in Majlisī, *Biḥār*, 38:90, 38:271, 63:146, 99:202, et passim.

[85] Buhl, "Mu'ta," *EI*², 7:756; Conrad, "Theophanes," 1–44; Powers, *Muḥammad*, 72–93, especially 82–83.

[86] I agree with Hoyland that we should not "champion non-Muslim sources over Muslim sources." See Hoyland, "Reflections," 113–140. Hoyland rightly observes that "Muslims and non-Muslims inhabited the same world, interacted with one another and even read one another's writings."

However, the Christian reference in Theophanes' *Chronicle* is a rare non-Muslim parallel to what Muslim accounts claim about military activities in Arabia. The Christian account includes similarities and dissimilarities when compared to the Muslim version of Mu'ta.[87] A stark difference relates to dating the battle to the reign of Abū Bakr, after Muhammad's death, although Theophanes describes Muhammad appointing four commanders in the army. Still, both versions describe a humiliating Muslim defeat and how the Byzantines killed their three commanders, with only the fourth—named Chaled in the Christian version—escaping.[88] The similarities between the two accounts propelled Conrad to argue convincingly that Theophanes must have had access to Arabic Muslim sources of the battle. This, in turn, results in Theophanes' work ceasing to be an independent witness of the raid.[89] Nonetheless, the rough outline of Theophanes suggests that a small Arab army attempted to reach Mu'ta and was destroyed by the Byzantines.

Whether Theophanes' account is *precisely* what the Muslim version of Mu'ta describes is unclear; however, Byzantine history describes a tribal skirmish—not a magnificent war, as alleged by the Muslim sources.[90] It is plausible to argue that the Muslim traditionists had no choice but to shape the narrative of Mu'ta as a huge success. They cannot relinquish their religious disposition. Their accounts of Mu'ta demonstrate how Muslim storytellers presented world events—in this case, a battle—as divinely directed proceedings that exemplified Allah's workings for Muhammad and his community.[91] Since this incident was reportedly the first occasion for Khālid's military prowess and shrewdness to manifest itself among the Muslims, embellishments and adjustments were necessary. Thus we ended

Hoyland, *God's Path*, 2–3; also, Borrut, *Entre*, 137ff. For scholarly discussions on Muslim and non-Muslim sources and their problems, see Donner, "Introduction," in *Expansion*, ed. Donner, xxvii–xxxi; Donner, *Narratives*, 1–5; Kaegi, *Byzantium*, 2–5, 8–14; Kaegi, *Muslim*, 1–10; Hoyland, *God's Path*, 231ff.; Dūrī, *Rise*, 3–11, and the excellent introduction of the book by Donner at vii–xvii. Cf. Conrad, "The Arabs," 173–195.

[87] See the detailed analyses of Powers, *Muḥammad*, 82–87, where he compares the Muslim version to the Christian one.

[88] Theophanes, *Chronicle*, 36.

[89] See the critical observations of Powers, *Muḥammad*, 85–86, as he challenges Conrad's position.

[90] See Powers, *Muḥammad*, 90, where he concludes, "It is certainly possible that a battle took place at Mu'ta, although it is likely that the dimensions of this military encounter were closer to those of a skirmish or raid than to that of a large battle."

[91] Scholars label this as "salvation history." See Wansbrough, *Quranic*, 43; Wansbrough, *Sectarian*, 20, 49; Wansbrough, "Res Ipsa Loquitur," in *Method*, ed. Berg, 7; Rippin, "Literary," 154. On Wansbrough's arguments, see Reynolds, "Introduction," in *Qur'ān*, ed. Reynolds, 12; Donner, *Narratives*, 35ff.; Motzki, "Alternative," in *Companion*, ed. McAuliffe, 60.

up with a manipulated story of a fanciful encounter between the Muslims and the Christian Byzantines.

The raid to Mu'ta appears in the tradition as one of the earliest *major* military encounters between Arab Muslims and Christians in al-Shām.[92] Still, the Muslims who were reaching out north to the Byzantine Empire, says the story, would not cease their efforts. In the following year, we are invited to believe, they organized a mightier army than the one marched to Mu'ta and sought to conquer the Christians at Tabūk. This would be the last *ghazwa* in Muhammad's lifetime.

The Raid to Tabūk (9/631)

A few days after the Muslims returned from Mu'ta, Muhammad entrusted another shrewd military commander, ᶜAmr ibn al-ᶜĀṣ, to lead an incursion to Dhāt al-Salāsil to punish the tribe of Quḍāᶜa, which reportedly cooperated with the Christians at Mu'ta.[93] ᶜAmr was a new convert like Khālid, and while his incursion was not large in its scope or results and eventually ended without a real fight, it showed Muhammad's reported determination to control regions in the northern parts of the peninsula.[94] About three months later, Muhammad reportedly led the greatest conquests of all: the conquest of Mecca, which opened the Hijaz for his leadership. About a year later, Muhammad reportedly led the battle of Tabūk.[95]

The raid to Tabūk was reportedly the final expedition that Muhammad led, and it occurred in the month of Rajab in the ninth *hijrī* year (ca. October 631), almost six months after the siege of al-Ṭā'if.[96] The Tabūk accounts are

[92] See Ṣallābī, *Sīra*, 737, where he claims that Mu'ta was the first major practical Muslim attack to "destroy the tyrannical Byzantine Empire in al-Shām."

[93] ᶜUmarī, *Sīra*, 471–472; also Ṣallābī, *Sīra*, 732, 744–747. See Djait, *Masīrat*, 170, where he seems to link Mu'ta and Dhāt al-Salāsil and argues that Muhammad desired to punish Quḍāᶜa, which was known for its military valor and strength.

[94] Following ᶜAmr's incursion, Muhammad reportedly commissioned two other minor incursions, one to al-Khabṭ led by ᶜUbayda and another to Khaḍira led by Abū Qatāda. See Wāqidī, *Maghāzī*, 774–780.

[95] Zuhrī, *Maghāzī*, 106; Maᶜmar, *Expeditions*, 130. See also Ibn Qutayba, *Maᶜārif*, 1:165, where he states that it was not only the last but also the farthest northward Muhammad went. Dīnawarī, *Akhbār*, 150.

[96] For primary sources on Tabūk, see Maᶜmar, *Expeditions*, 130–143; Wāqidī, *Maghāzī*, 989ff.; Wāqidī, *Life*, 485ff.; Ibn Hishām, *Sīra*, 2:515ff.; Ibn Hishām, *Life*, 602–610; Ibn Ḥibbān, *Sīra*, 366–372; Yaᶜqūbī, *Ta'rīkh*, 2:69–70; Ṭabarī, *Ta'rīkh*, 1692ff.; Ṭabarī, *History*, 9:47–62; Khalīfa, *Ta'rīkh*, 92–93; Ibn Ḥabīb, *Muḥabbar*, 1:116, 1:281–284; Ibn ᶜAbd al-Ḥakam, *Futūḥ*, 214; Ibn Qutayba, *Maᶜārif*, 1:165; Balādhurī, *Futūḥ*, 59–60; Balādhurī, *Origins*, 92–93; Dīnawarī, *Akhbār*, 150; Kharkūshī,

hardly records of a past event. Rather, they embody a fashioned narrative for religious representation and theological meaning—a Muslim homily on persevering under tough circumstances for the sake of defending the faith, marching in jihad against non-Muslim enemies, spending money to support military expeditions, and distinguishing between honest and disingenuous Muslims. The accounts are also designed to exegete specific verses in the Qur'ān, particularly in *sūrat al-Tawba* (Q 9), detailing juristic rules on *jizya* (poll tax) and *qitāl* (fighting), as well as providing explanations on Allah's forgiveness of believers who do not march in battles among others. As we encountered in the accounts of Mu'ta, those of Tabūk are replete with hyperbolic features and literary embellishments. Here, we describe what Muslim storytellers reveal about the raid and then analyze it critically.

Tabūk is a town located in northwestern Arabia (today's Saudi Arabia) and separated from the Red Sea by the Ḥismā mountains.[97] The Muslim narrative highlights at least four possible reasons for launching the raid to Tabūk. First, we are told that Muhammad initiated it, as he desired to march to fight the Byzantines: "He instructed [the Muslims] to get ready and told them *annahu yurīdu al-Rūm* (that he wanted to reach the Byzantines)."[98] According to this report, he "gave orders to prepare to raid the Byzantines" without any particular motive.[99] Second, other accounts describe the Byzantines and their Arab allies in al-Shām preparing to invade Medina, which prompted Muhammad to mobilize the Muslims to confront the enemy.[100] Third, the raid was

Sharaf, 3:87–88; Masᶜūdī, *Tanbīh*, 1:235; Maqdisī, *Bad'*, 4:239–240; Jawzī, *Muntaẓim*, 3:362–363; Bayhaqī, *Dalā'il*, 5:212–236; Ibn ᶜAbd al-Barr, *Durar*, 1:238–247; Suhaylī, *Rawḍ*, 7:383–413; Ḥalabī, *Insān*, 3:183–212; Ibn al-Athīr, *Kāmil*, 2:145–146; Dhahabī, *Ta'rīkh*, 2:627–642; Ibn Kathīr, *Bidāya*, 5:5–23. A rare report claims it was in the tenth year. See Abū Zurᶜa, *Ta'rīkh*, 165. For Shīᶜite traditions on the raid, see Majlisī, *Biḥār*, 21:252ff. For secondary Muslim studies on Tabūk, see ᶜUmarī, *Sīra*, 522–538; Ṣallābī, *Sīra*, 807–829; Ṣallābī, *Ghazawāt*, 312–356; Mubārakpūrī, *Raḥīq*, 398–403; Djait, *Masīrat*, 191–194; Shams al-Dīn, *Majmūᶜ*, 208–212.

97 Tabūk is a well-known location halfway between Medina and Damascus. See M.A. al-Bakhit, "Tabūk," *EI*², 10:50, where he states, "It seems to be the Thapaua of Ptolemy, and formed part of the Roman *Provincia Arabia* set up in A.D. 106. It was in the tribal area of the Banū Kalb, and later had a Byzantine military post." See Masᶜūdī, *Tanbīh*, 1:235, where he states that Tabūk is a twelve-night journey from Medina. See Ṣallābī, *Sīra*, 809, where he states that Tabūk was from the lands of Banū Quḍāᶜa, under the control of the Byzantines.

98 Ibn Hishām, *Sīra*, 2:516. See ᶜUmarī, *Sīra*, 522, where he states that Mu'ta and Tabūk has a specific target: the Byzantines and their Christian Arab allies.

99 Ibn Hishām, *Life*, 602. Ṭabarī, *Ta'rīkh*, 1693; Ibn Ḥibbān, *Sīra*, 366–367; Bayhaqī, *Dalā'il*, 5:213. See Ibn Ḥajar, *Fatḥ*, 8:112; also the arguments of Sunnī Muslim scholar ᶜUmarī, *Sīra*, 522, where he argues that one should not expect reasons for these *maghāzī*, as Allah prescribed jihad and Muslims must fulfill it—the raid to Tabūk was "a natural response to the *farīḍa* (religious duty) of jihad."

100 Wāqidī, *Maghāzī*, 990. This report is unique to al-Wāqidī, and many reiterated it based on his authority. However, in the final reports of Tabūk, al-Wāqidī negates this account and states, "News that had reached the Prophet, about Heraclius sending his companions and getting close to the South

initiated as a response to a divine command that instructed the Muslims to "fight those adjacent" to them from among the *kuffār* (unbelievers) "and let them find in you *ghilẓa* (harshness)" (Q 9:123). Since al-Shām is adjacent to Arabia and it contained unbelievers, the logic goes, launching the raid to Tabūk was in fulfillment of the divine command in the Qur'ān.[101] Fourth, Shīᶜite historian al-Yaᶜqūbī, in a unique report, emphasizes that Muhammad initiated the raid to avenge the death of his cousin Jaᶜfar ibn Abī Ṭālib at Mu'ta. This report is uniquely pro-Shīᶜite, as it advances sympathies to ᶜAlī's brother and indicates Muhammad's strong affection toward Banū Hāshim. Ultimately, whether it was the theological reason of the divine command, or the tribal motive of avenging the death of Jaᶜfar, or for the alleged purpose of confronting the Byzantine military machine advancing to Medina, the Muslim narrative reveals that Muhammad successfully gathered thirty thousand Muslims and ten thousand horses to march to Tabūk—the highest number of soldiers ever gathered by Muhammad in his lifetime.[102]

But the timing was difficult for the Muslims, who complained that Muhammad "ordered his companions to prepare to raid the Byzantines at a time when men were hard pressed; the heat was oppressive and there was a drought; fruit was ripe and the men wanted to stay in the shade with their fruit and disliked travelling at that season."[103] Muhammad directed them to

of al-Shām, was false." Wāqidī, *Life*, 499. Cf. Ibn al-Athīr, *Kāmil*, 2:145; Sharīf, *Makka*, 423; Djait, *Masīrat*, 190. In a comparable report, a Shīᶜite tradition indicates that Ukaydir, the Christian ruler of Dūmat al-Jandal in the north, prepared a strong army with mighty weapons to march against the Muslims in Medina. Majlisī, *Biḥār*, 21:258. For secondary references on Ukaydir, see Schick, *Christian*, 55.

[101] Ibn Kathīr, *Bidāya*, 5:5–6. We are also told that the raid was in fulfillment of another divine command for the Muslims to fight those who do not believe in Allah among those who were given the Scripture (Q 9:29). See ᶜUmarī, *Sīra*, 522–523, where he argues that, after the Muslims suppressed polytheists and Jews, now the time came for the Christians who had lost the true core of their religion.

[102] Zuhrī, *Maghāzī*, 107; Maᶜmar, *Expeditions*, 130. Wāqidī, *Maghāzī*, 996, 1003. We are told that Muhammad chose to march *ghāziyan* (raiding) with the Muslims on a Thursday, because he "liked going out on Thursdays." However, see Ibn Ḥabīb, *Muḥabbar*, 1:116, where he states that Muhammad left Medina on Monday, the first day of Rajab. See Masᶜūdī, *Tanbīh*, 1:235, where he adds twelve thousand camels to the army. See Djait, *Masīrat*, 191, where he is skeptical of the number of the Muslims and argues it might have been only somewhere between five thousand and ten thousand—it was a show of strength for the Arabs, especially the tribe of Quḍāᶜa, the allies of the Byzantines. For contradicting traditions on the number of Muslims, see Ibn Ḥajar, *Fatḥ*, 8:117–118, where he points to various traditions with varying numbers, including a little over ten thousand, thirty thousand, or even more than forty thousand. See ᶜUmarī, *Sīra*, 531. Note that, unlike camels, horses are not fit for crossing deserts. See Crone, *Slaves*, 22–23, where she writes, "Ecologically, the deprivation of the desert is extreme: sheep and goats can be reared only along the edges, but in the interior only camels can subsist." She also states, "Horses in the desert are as great a luxury as tomatoes in the Negev" (220).

[103] Ibn Hishām, *Life*, 602. See Wāqidī, *Life*, 486: "The people were in great need, and when the fruit had ripened, and shade was desired, the people wanted to stay, and hated going out in the conditions of that time." Zuhrī, *Maghāzī*, 106; Maᶜmar, *Expeditions*, 130. See Watt, *Muḥammad*, 189, where he

the right disposition and *ḥaḍḍahum ᶜalā al-qitāl wa-l-jihād* (exhorted them on fighting and jihad), thus stirring their hearts to join the army.[104] Preparing them to follow the path of jihad against *naṣārā al-Rūm* (the Byzantine Christians), Muhammad disclosed his goals for the raid to his soldiers—although he reportedly rarely did so—and exhorted them to preserve the faith and persevere for Allah, as the distance was long, the heat intense, and the enemy massive.[105] This is one reason the raid to Tabūk is known in the tradition as *ghazwat al-ᶜusra* (the raid of hardship).[106]

At every turn in the narrative of Tabūk, the Muslim narrators are sure to link each point in the course of events to the revelation of specific verses from the Qur'ān, particularly from *sūrat al-Tawba* (Q 9).[107] We are told that Muhammad's success in gathering this multitude of soldiers was due to following Allah's revelation, exhorting the Muslims to march forth—whether they were light or heavy in equipment and weaponry—to strive with their monies and lives for Allah's cause (Q 9:41). Many from the *muhājirūn* (Meccan Muslims), *anṣār* (Medinan Muslims), and other Arab tribes—who submitted and converted to Islam recently—joined the army. These are identified as faithful Muslims, but the tradition highlights some who lagged behind. We are told that some Muslims gave excuses for not going, but Allah did not accept their excuses, and others "were slow to make up their minds so that they lagged behind without any doubt or misgivings."[108] The narrative is shaped to provide a religious catalogue on discerning various kinds of Muslims based on their responses to marching for fighting and jihad.[109]

largely trusts the Muslim narrative as factual, and argues, "Muḥammad's grasp of events was so much wider than that of the majority of his followers that it must often have been difficult to bring them to accept his policies when these involved hardship" (189).

[104] Wāqidī, *Maghāzī*, 990–991. See Djait, *Masīrat*, 191–192, where he argues that Muhammad's goal was to prepare the faithful to always be ready for jihad, not necessarily to advance northward against the Byzantines—ultimately, the rule of Allah and his apostle must advance, so that everyone may accept it.

[105] Zuhrī, *Maghāzī*, 106; Maᶜmar, *Expeditions*, 130. Wāqidī, *Maghāzī*, 990; Ibn Hishām, *Sīra*, 2:516. Hamidullah, *Battlefields*, 93, 131, 136.

[106] ᶜAbd al-Razzāq, *Muṣannaf*, 9:354; Wāqidī, *Maghāzī*, 1023, 1055, 1062, 1074; Ibn Hishām, *Sīra*, 2:518. Ṣallābī, *Sīra*, 808.

[107] See Wāqidī, *Maghāzī*, 1022–1025, where he lists and explains the Qur'ānic verses revealed during the raid of Tabūk. For Shīᶜite traditions on the revelation of *Sūrat al-Tawba* (Q 9) during Tabūk, see Majlisī, *Biḥār*, 21:264ff.

[108] Ibn Hishām, *Life*, 603. See Wāqidī, *Life*, 487, where it reads, "People from the Hypocrites came to the Messenger of God and asked permission to be absent without cause, and he permitted them. There were roughly eighty Hypocrites who asked permission." Zuhrī, *Maghāzī*, 107; Maᶜmar, *Expeditions*, 130; Ṭabarī, *Ta'rīkh*, 1695.

[109] This is clear in a report of a conversation between Muslims, where one asks, "Do the men know the hypocrites among them?" to which a Muslim responded, "A man would know that hypocrisy

One Muslim named Jadd, we are told, gave an excuse to Muhammad: "Will you allow me to stay behind and not tempt me, for everyone knows that I am strongly addicted to women and I am afraid that if I see the Byzantine women I shall not be able to control myself."[110] Muhammad allowed him to stay behind, but Allah disapproved and revealed a verse chastising Jadd, declaring that some Muslims stay behind by claiming, "Do not tempt me," although they have surely fallen already into temptation (Q 9:49).[111] The tradition reveals some "powerful and healthy" people excused themselves from marching to Tabūk, and Muhammad "accepted their excuses and granted them permission," which did not please Allah; he rebuked them and admonished Muhammad in a Qur'ānic revelation (Q 9:43).[112]

In addition to Muslims who gave excuses to stay behind, the tradition refers to many *munāfiqūn* (lukewarm Muslims, or hypocrites) who did not want to join the army and discouraged Muslims from joining it: "Do not go forth in the heat."[113] On this occasion, Allah reportedly revealed verses in the Qur'ān to distinguish the faithful from the hypocrite among the believers, emphasizing that afflictions and hardships often reveal a person's true nature. In one verse, Allah warned these hypocrites that they should understand that the hellfire is hotter (Q 9:81). In the same vein, the narrators fashion reports to discourage Muslims from following the examples of the hypocrites. In a description of repentance in relation to those who did not accompany the army, an early account reveals a tale about a Muslim named Abū Lubāba. After he failed to accompany Muhammad, Abū Lubāba regretted his actions greatly. He tied himself to a pillar of the mosque and swore, "By God, I won't untie myself or taste food or drink until either I die or God accepts my repentance."[114] After seven days with no food or drink, "he collapsed to the ground unconscious," and that was when Allah "accepted his repentance." The story aims to rebuke those who did not join the army,

existed in his brother." Ibn Hishām, *Life*, 605; Wāqidī, *Maghāzī*, 1009; Ṭabarī, *Ta'rīkh*, 1698. See Mubārakpūrī, *Raḥīq*, 403; Ṣallābī, *Sīra*, 815.

110 Ibn Hishām, *Life*, 602. Wāqidī, *Maghāzī*, 992. It appears that Jadd's excuse was disingenuous, as he reportedly told his son, "O my little son, why should I go out in the wind and heat and difficulties to the Byzantines? By God, I am not secure from fear of the Byzantines in my own house in Khurbā, so how will I go out to them and raid them?" Wāqidī, *Life*, 486.

111 Ṭabarī, *Ta'rīkh*, 1693.

112 Wāqidī, *Life*, 501. See ᶜUmarī, *Sīra*, 526; Ṣallābī, *Sīra*, 815. This literary detail reflects one example of when Muhammad's deeds were not in agreement with Allah's will.

113 Ibn Hishām, *Life*, 603. ᶜUmarī, *Sīra*, 526.

114 Maᶜmar, *Expeditions*, 141; Zuhrī, *Maghāzī*, 112; ᶜAbd al-Razzāq, *Muṣannaf*, 5:405–406.

and it drives a theological parable on the utmost importance of never delaying to march for jihad.[115] The example of Abū Lubāba is not alone. Among the hypocrites, once again, we encounter the Medinan Muslim ᶜAbdullāh ibn Ubayy—who was a major figure at Uḥud and al-Khandaq, often identified as *ra's al-munāfiqūn* (the head of the hypocrites)—who did not march with Muhammad and "separated from him and stayed behind with the hypocrites and doubters."[116] It appears that ᶜAbdullāh's story always proves convenient when the narrators need a character to highlight examples of hypocrites and lukewarm believers, despite the literary fact that he was never dismissed from among the believers.

In contrast to these Muslim hypocrites, the tradition preserves a list of companions who gave significant portions of their wealth to prepare the soldiers for war: "The wealthy men provided mounts and stored up a reward with God."[117] This was reportedly in response to Muhammad's broad call for the Muslims to give for the army's preparation.[118] Major companions—including Abū Bakr, ᶜUmar, and ᶜUthmān—gave abundantly to prepare the army.[119] While Abū Bakr reportedly gave all his money and ᶜUmar gave half of his, ᶜUthmān's gift in particular was significant: He supplied the needs of one third of the army, as he gave "a larger sum than any had ever done."[120] "He spent the most, until that army had sufficient supplies, and it was said that every need was met. He even provided the ropes for their water containers."[121] This reportedly propelled Muhammad to praise ᶜUthmān's generosity and to state, "After this, nothing will harm ᶜUthmān whatever he does!"[122] While the choice of Abū Bakr, ᶜUmar, and ᶜUthmān—as literary

115 A similar story is reported about a Muslim man named Abū Khaythama, who did not initially join the army. Ten days after Muhammad departed with the army, Abū Khaythama came to his home on a hot day and found his two wives waiting for him: "Each one of them had sprayed her hut and cooled it with water for him, and prepared food for him in it." Instead of enjoying their company, Abū Khaythama reportedly felt remorse and regret that he was not with the army. He left quickly and joined the army near Tabūk. Wāqidī, *Life*, 488. See ᶜUmarī, *Sīra*, 529; Ṣallābī, *Sīra*, 820.

116 Ibn Hishām, *Life*, 603. ᶜAbdullāh appears to have believed that Muhammad's decision was not wise and said, "Muḥammad raids the Byzantines despite the strain of the situation and the heat and the distance of the land when he has no power over them! Does Muḥammad consider fighting the Byzantines a game? Those who pretend with him are of a similar opinion." Wāqidī, *Life*, 488.

117 Ibn Hishām, *Life*, 603. ᶜUmarī, *Sīra*, 524–525.

118 In one tradition, Muhammad reportedly promised, "Whoever equips the army of *al-ᶜusra* (the raid of hardship, i.e., Tabūk) will be granted paradise." Bukhārī, *Ṣaḥīḥ*, 4:13, 5:13. Bukhārī has an entire section on Tabūk (6:2–7).

119 Wāqidī, *Maghāzī*, 991. For depictions of ᶜUthmān in historical accounts, see Keaney, "Remembering."

120 Ibn Hishām, *Life*, 603. Ṭabarī, *Ta'rīkh*, 1694.

121 Wāqidī, *Life*, 486. Ibn Ḥibbān, *Sīra*, 366–367. See Sharīf, *Makka*, 297, 303; Ṣallābī, *Sīra*, 810.

122 Wāqidī, *Life*, 486.

portrayals—may reflect a later ᶜAbbāsid paradigm aiming to elevate a Sunnī preference, the account itself aims to drive the theological point that donating money to prepare soldiers is a virtuous act.[123] In the same vein, we are told that even poor Muslims gave for the cause of marching to Tabūk; additionally, women gathered "bracelets, bangles, anklets, earrings, rings and thongs" and sent them to Muhammad to offer to the Muslims in their preparations.[124] However, the hypocritical Muslims reportedly judged the rich who gave abundantly and mocked the poor who gave little—they accused the former of seeking haughty reputation and esteem, and mocked the latter by claiming that Allah does not need their small offerings as he is self-sufficient. This is why, we are told, Allah revealed a verse to Muhammad—again, from *sūrat al-Tawba* (Q 9)—rebuking the lukewarm believers who defame the sincere ones, and promising he will throw back their mockery on them and that their eternal destination will be a painful torment (Q 9:79). Thus, the historiographical narrative of Tabūk appears to be designed to exegete the Qur'ān and display a severe rebuke against the hypocrites who were reluctant to go forth in jihad and attempted to discourage the true believers from responding to Allah's call.

Unsurprisingly, in one report, these hypocritical Muslims used the house of Suwaylim the Jew for their meetings—a literary detail that further places them as lukewarm believers who made the wrong choice of befriending a Jew and staying behind.[125] Muhammad sent one of the Muslims to burn down Suwaylim's house to thwart the efforts of the hypocrites. We are told that the Muslim army included hypocrites and that they had a particular purpose for joining Muhammad: "Many people from the Hypocrites went out with him, and they did not go out except hoping for plunder."[126] Therefore, the accounts contrast charitable giving with insincere belief and highlight the evil-doing of hypocritical Muslims. Still, there was a category of believers, we are told, which included vulnerable and poor Muslims who could not join the army due to illness, old age, or poverty. Some of these were identified as the weepers. When they could not afford to march with the army, they reportedly stayed back, "their eyes flowing with tears for grief that they had not the

[123] Similarly, we can identify the report on al-ᶜAbbās sponsoring two men to join the army. Wāqidī, *Maghāzī*, 994.
[124] Wāqidī, *Life*, 486.
[125] Ibn Hishām, *Sīra*, 2:517. Ṣallābī, *Sīra*, 813.
[126] Wāqidī, *Life*, 490. There is a similar account in Wāqidī, *Maghāzī*, 1003, where a group of hypocrites were walking with Muhammad in Tabūk. ᶜUmarī, *Sīra*, 527.

wherewithal to meet the expense of the raid."[127] While they were discouraged and embarrassed to stay behind, Allah revealed a verse declaring these people were not to be blamed (Q 9:91–92).

Then Muhammad and the Muslims set out to march from Medina to Tabūk to confront al-Rūm (the Byzantines). He appointed Muḥammad ibn Maslama—or Sibāᶜ ibn ᶜUrfuṭa—to govern Medina while the army marched to Tabūk.[128] Some early accounts and Shīᶜite sources claim he appointed ᶜAlī.[129] The appointment of ᶜAlī seems to reflect an early memory that was later adjusted by ᶜAbbāsid-era historians to advance anti-ᶜAlid sympathies.[130] These historians emphasized that Muhammad simply instructed ᶜAlī to stay behind to look after his family—a decision that, we are told, propelled the hypocrites to speak negatively against ᶜAlī as being a burden on Muhammad. However, Muhammad reportedly encouraged ᶜAlī, "Are you not content, ᶜAlī, to stand to me as Aaron stood to Moses, except that there will be no prophet after me?"[131] This response presumably rebuked the hypocrites and honored ᶜAlī. As the army marched to Tabūk, we are told, some Muslims left the army and returned home—an action that propelled Muhammad to say to the Muslims, "Leave them, if there is good in them, Allah will bring them back to you; and if not, then Allah had relieved you of them."[132] Muhammad's statement, as articulated by the storytellers, drives a theological lesson on trusting Allah's will to guide people to the right path or lead them astray (Q 2:26; 4:88; 74:31).[133] In the same vein,

[127] Ibn Hishām, *Life*, 603. Wāqidī, *Maghāzī*, 993–994; Ibn Ḥabīb, *Muḥabbar*, 1:281; Ṭabarī, *Ta'rīkh*, 1694. These weepers asked Muhammad to help them, and he could not provide any means to help them join the army; consequently, we are told, a divine revelation described the incident, in which believers did not find what they needed to march for the battle, so they returned discouraged and "their eyes overflowing with tears" (Q 9:92). See Wāqidī, *Maghāzī*, 993. ᶜUmarī, *Sīra*, 529–530; Ṣallābī, *Sīra*, 812–813.

[128] Khalīfa, *Ta'rīkh*, 97; Wāqidī, *Maghāzī*, 995. Ṭabarī, *Ta'rīkh*, 1696. Masᶜūdī, *Tanbīh*, 1:235.

[129] Zuhrī, *Maghāzī*, 111; Maᶜmar, *Expeditions*, 140–141; ᶜAbd al-Razzāq, *Muṣannaf*, 5:405. This is echoed in an early Shīᶜite account indicating that Muhammad assigned "ᶜAlī as his deputy in charge of Medina." Yaᶜqūbī, *Works*, 3:671; Yaᶜqūbī, *Ta'rīkh*, 2:70; Majlisī, *Biḥār*, 21:260. See also the Sunnī tradition in Ibn Ḥajar, *Fatḥ*, 8:113.

[130] For ᶜAbbāsid-era historians, their religious inclinations and political sympathies, see Ibrahim, *Conversion*, 107–130, 180–199.

[131] Ibn Hishām, *Life*, 604. Ibn Ḥabīb, *Muḥabbar*, 1:126. In a Shīᶜite tradition, Allah gave Muhammad the choice to either lead the Tabūk army himself or let ᶜAlī lead it; however, Muhammad decided to march with the army and appointed ᶜAlī as his vicegerent on Medina. Majlisī, *Biḥār*, 21:260.

[132] Wāqidī, *Maghāzī*, 1000; Ṭabarī, *Ta'rīkh*, 1700. Many Muslims, we are told, hated to leave Medina at that time as they knew what the fight would entail, knowing "the Byzantines and their fighting ability." Ṭabarī, *History*, 9:48. Watt, *Muḥammad*, 189.

[133] For views of various exegetes on Allah leading people astray, see Ṭabarī, *Jāmiᶜ*, 1:408, 24:31; Thaᶜlabī, *Kashf*, 10:75; Zamakhsharī, *Kashshāf*, 4:650–652; Rāzī, *Mafātiḥ*, 2:368, 30:709–712; Qurṭubī, *Jāmiᶜ*, 19:78–79; Bayḍāwī, *Anwār*, 5:262; Ibn Kathīr, *Tafsīr*, 8:270; Quṭb, *Fī ẓilāl*,

Muhammad's example is highlighted in the narrative as a prophet enabled with divine abilities. We are told that, when he and the Muslims faced severe hunger and intense thirst, as the distance was long and the travel intense, Allah empowered Muhammad with divine miracles: In response to Muhammad's supplications, heavenly provisions of food came down and adequate rain supplied them with water.[134] When the water came down miraculously and "quenched the thirst of the last of them," we are told that Muhammad declared, "I witness that I am Allah's messenger."[135] It appears that the report is designed to serve as proof of Muhammad's prophethood, especially as each of these supernatural deeds, the narrators assure us, came accompanied with divine revelations of verses in the Qur'ān.[136] Similarly, many other signs and wonders were performed by Muhammad in the course of the battle. Upon arriving at Tabūk, Muhammad prophesied to the soldiers that a severe wind was coming and warned them about it—which protected the Muslims.[137] The storytellers emphasize him as knowing the unknown. In one report, Muhammad knew when a man questioned his prophethood in secret.[138] In another, he foretold that the soldier Abū Dharr was coming soon.[139] In a third, Muhammad sent Khālid to Dūmat al-Jandal to subdue it and foretold that he would find a Christian ruler named Ukaydir "hunting

6:3759. For studies, see Reynolds, *Allah*, 49; Ibrahim, *Muhammad*, 122. For a Shīʿite view of how Sunnīs differ in their perception of predestination, see Khū'ī, *Prolegomena*, 72–74. Cf. Ibrahim, *Islam*, 47–48.

[134] Ibn Hishām, *Sīra*, 2:522; Wāqidī, *Maghāzī*, 1008; Ṭabarī, *Ta'rīkh*, 1698. A presumably Muslim eyewitness declared, "I did not see a cloud in the sky," but Muhammad "did not stop praying until I saw clouds assemble from every direction. He did not leave his place until the heavens came down upon us with fresh water." Wāqidī, *Life*, 494; Ibn Ḥibbān, *Sīra*, 368. Ṣallābī, *Sīra*, 827; Ṣaʿīdī, *Dirāsāt*, 106–110.

[135] Wāqidī, *Maghāzī*, 1009. See the Sunnī study of Ṣallābī, *Sīra*, 825–826, concerning the miracles at Tabūk. For a Shīʿite view on Muhammad's miracles, see Khū'ī, *Prolegomena*, 39–41 (proof of prophethood), also 82–87.

[136] In a tendentious Shīʿite tradition, Muhammad prophesied before marching from Medina to Tabūk that he would return in eighty days, with ample plunder and without any fighting against the enemy. Majlisī, *Biḥār*, 21:259.

[137] Wāqidī, *Maghāzī*, 1006.

[138] Ibn Hishām, *Life*, 605; Ṭabarī, *Ta'rīkh*, 1699. See also Wāqidī, *Maghāzī*, 1010, where an anti-Jewish report alleges that there was a Jew who converted disingenuously and had "the deceit of the Jews and their bad faith." When he questioned Muhammad's prophethood, Muhammad reportedly knew and revealed to his companions what the Jew had in his heart. Wāqidī, *Life*, 494; Ibn Ḥibbān, *Sīra*, 368.

[139] Wāqidī, *Maghāzī*, 1000, 1004. See Ṭabarī, *Ta'rīkh*, 1700, a uniquely ʿAbbāsid-era report highly praising Abū Dharr as *ṣāḥib rasūl Allāh* (a companion of Allah's messenger). Abū Dharr appears in the tradition as an example of serious devotion to Islam. See Anthony, *Caliph*, 52. He converted to Islam after hearing Islam's message from relatives. See Ibn Saʿd, *Ṭabaqāt*, 4:169ff. (Abū Dharr and his family). For a Shīʿite view on Abū Dharr, see Khū'ī, *Prolegomena*, 156, 242.

wild cows," exactly as Khālid later found him.[140] These reports are designed as proofs of Muhammad's prophethood—a literary testimony of Allah's support for his prophet.

After traveling for about a month, the Muslims finally camped at Tabūk to confront the Byzantines.[141] The thirty thousand Muslims waited for the Byzantines to show up; however, no one came for ten nights, although other reports claim the Muslims remained there for twenty days.[142] No encounter and no fight occurred.[143] The traditionists claim that the Christians were terrified to face the Muslims, so they preferred safety and security and fled back to their lands. Despite their military might and numerous troops, they remained in al-Shām and preferred to avoid the Muslims.[144] Some of the Christian Arab tribes, who were allies of the Byzantines, accepted peace deals with the Muslims and paid the *jizya* (poll-tax) in return.[145] Through these treaties, we are told that Muhammad secured the northern frontier of the Hijaz.[146] The Muslims, we are told, finally left Tabūk victoriously after

[140] Ibn Hishām, *Life*, 607. Wāqidī, *Maghāzī*, 1025–1026; Ṭabarī, *Ta'rīkh*, 1702. Ṣallābī, *Sīra*, 819. In this incursion to Dūmat al-Jandal, Khālid had 420 soldiers with him, and they seized ample spoils.

[141] According to Yaᶜqūbī, *Ta'rīkh*, 2:70, the Muslims arrived in Tabūk in the following month of Shaᶜbān.

[142] See Ibn Hishām, *Sīra*, 2:527, and Wāqidī, *Maghāzī*, 1015, respectively. See Wāqidī, *Life*, 501. See also Ṭabarī, *Life*, 9:59–60, where he reports that Muhammad "stayed in Tabūk no more than ten nights and departed, returning to Medina." See Ibn Kathīr, *Bidāya*, 5:23, where he puts the number at ten nights.

[143] Balādhurī, *Futūḥ*, 59–60; Balādhurī, *Origins*, 92–93.

[144] See Wāqidī, *Maghāzī*, 1015, where it alleges that Heraclius stayed at Ḥimṣ in al-Shām to avoid confronting the Muslims at Tabūk. See Ṣallābī, *Sīra*, 822; also ᶜUmarī, *Sīra*, 535, where he questions traditions that Heraclius corresponded with Muhammad while the Muslims were at Tabūk. See ᶜAlī, *Mufaṣṣal*, 7:251, where he states that Muhammad came to Tabūk and found the Byzantines far from him, so he returned to Medina.

[145] See Yaᶜqūbī, *Works*, 3:671, where "Yuḥanna b. Ru'ba, the bishop of Ayla, came to him, made a treaty with him, and paid the poll-tax." Ayla is modern-day Eilat. See also Khalīfa, *Ta'rīkh*, 92; Ibn Hishām, *Sīra*, 2:525; Ṭabarī, *Ta'rīkh*, 1702; Balādhurī, *Futūḥ*, 59–60; Balādhurī, *Origins*, 92–93. On the *jizya*, see Cl. Cahen, "D̲j̲izya," *EI*², 2:559–567, where it is defined as "the poll-tax which, in traditional Muslim law, is levied on non-Muslims in Muslim states" (2:559). Like Yuḥanna, the Christian ruler of Dūmat al-Jandal, Ukaydir, made a deal with Muhammad: "Then Khālid brought Ukaydir to the apostle who spared his life and made peace with him on condition that he paid the poll tax." Ibn Hishām, *Life*, 608; Ibn Qutayba, *Maᶜārif*, 1:165; Ṭabarī, *Ta'rīkh*, 1702. We are also told, "The people of Jarbā' and Adhruḥ also offered him the poll tax." Ṭabarī, *History*, 9:58. See Yāqūt, *Muᶜjam*, 1:129–130, 2:118, 4:151, where Adhruḥ and Jarbā' are about one mile apart—both near al-Balqā', on the frontier of the Hijaz and al-Shām. ᶜAlī, *Mufaṣṣal*, 7:249. For Shīᶜite traditions on these locations and more, and the institution of the rule of peace in return for *jizya*, see Majlisī, *Biḥār*, 21:268–269. Djait defines *jizya* as *gharāma* (a fine, financial penalty). Djait, *Masīrat*, 191. See Hoyland, *Seeing*, 578, where he lists three non-Muslim sources that agree on the payment of the *jizya* to the Muslims between ca. 636 and 637. For a Shīᶜite view on the *jizya* verse, see Khū'ī, *Prolegomena*, 193.

[146] See Ṣallābī, *Sīra*, 822, where he claims that Muhammad, through these treaties with Arab Christian tribes, secured the north and *qaṣṣa ajniḥat al-Rūm* (severed the wings of the Byzantines, meaning destroyed their might).

seizing ample spoils of war.[147] On their way back to Medina, a group of Muslim hypocrites reportedly attempted to assassinate Muhammad; however, Allah protected him, spoiled their plot, and revealed a verse to rebuke their evildoing.[148] Ultimately, the Muslims returned from Tabūk to Medina in Ramaḍān, at which time the delegation of Thaqīf finally came to declare their submission and acceptance of Islam.[149] This concludes the overall narrative of the raid to Tabūk.

To analyze the accounts of the raid to Tabūk, there are four critical points to make. First, the Tabūk narrative is largely a religious sermon with only one final statement on the result of the battle. The entire account alleges to detail the initiation of the battle, the preparation of the army, the exhortation on jihad and fighting, the distinction between the various kinds of Muslims, the hardships of marching to war, the miraculous deeds of Muhammad in affirmation of his prophethood, and finally the arrival at the battle location. This long tale—with all its turns and details—is followed by no fight: the Muslim army just returned home. It is rather obvious that the narrative is not designed to detail an actual occurrence, but to present a religious discourse with theological objectives for later generations.[150] Still, there is a literary problem: The tale of Tabūk may shed doubts on Muhammad's wisdom in marching with thousands of soldiers in the heat of summer to no avail. However, some traditionists offer a curious explanation: Muhammad foreknew the result of the battle and foretold that the Muslims would return in precisely 80 days, with no fighting having occurred and no Muslim harmed.[151] While this may raise more questions, especially pertaining to the timing of marching hundreds of miles in the summer heat, it is clear that the reports of the conclusion of the raid are tendentiously short.[152] This reinforces our skepticism of the sources as a record of the past. The tradition

[147] The plunder was mostly seized by Khālid. See Ibn Kathīr, *Bidāya*, 5:23; Bayhaqī, *Dalāʾil*, 5:252; Dhahabī, *Taʾrīkh*, 2:647.

[148] See Ibn Qutayba, *Maᶜārif*, 1:343, where he lists the names of those who wanted to assassinate Muhammad—all of whom are identified as hypocrites and include ᶜAbdullāh ibn Ubayy and Saᶜd ibn Abī Sarḥ. See ᶜUmarī, *Sīra*, 536. For Shīᶜite traditions, see Majlisī, *Biḥār*, 21:97–98.

[149] Ṭabarī, *Taʾrīkh*, 1705; Ṭabarī, *History*, 9:62. Ibn al-Athīr, *Kāmil*, 2:150; Ibn ᶜAbd al-Barr, *Durar*, 1:247; Suhaylī, *Rawḍ*, 7:413.

[150] Hibri, *Parable*, 237; Donner, "Review," 570; Crone, *Meccan*, 224; Noth/Conrad, *Early*, 72.

[151] Majlisī, *Biḥār*, 21:259.

[152] While some may wonder whether Muhammad made a mistake by burdening thousands of Muslims to march all the way from Medina to Tabūk and back, Sunnī Muslim scholar Ṣallābī argues that the Byzantine crowds were not waiting at Tabūk, as they were concerned about fighting with the Muslims—even the Arab Christian tribes, says Ṣallābī, preferred to avoid the Muslims and pay the *jizya* instead. Ṣallābī, *Sīra*, 822; see also ᶜUmarī, *Sīra*, 535.

of Tabūk is symbolic with ideological significance, rather than a detailed record of a past battle. This is clear when one considers that the conclusion of the supposed battle occupies only one line in the tradition, while a sermon allegedly preached by Muhammad at Tabūk covers pages and details practical and juristic Islamic rulings on various topics. The narrative emphasizes the beliefs of the Muslims who fashioned the traditions.

Second, the storytellers—*aṣḥāb al-ḥadīth*, the lovers of the traditions—do not seem to relinquish their fondness for adding literary exaggerations.[153] We are invited to believe that Muhammad—only six months after his failed siege of al-Ṭā'if, when he had twelve thousand Muslims—now successfully gathered thirty thousand soldiers ready to confront the superpower of his day. Despite the fact that the number was already high at al-Ṭā'if, it grew even higher in a short period of time. The traditionists, it appears, keep generating generous estimates: at Mu'ta, we are told, the Muslims numbered three thousand, but four months later at the conquest of Mecca, they increased to ten thousand, and then, less than a year later at Tabūk, there were somehow thirty

[153] On *aṣḥāb al-ḥadīth*, see Ibrahim, *Conversion*, 28, 174. Crone, *Medieval*, 125ff. Crone calls proto-Sunnī scholars *ahl al-ḥadīth* or *aṣḥāb al-ḥadīth* (the Hadīth party or adherents of traditions, i.e., traditionists) (125). For a recent study on the influence of *aṣḥāb al-ḥadīth* on historical traditions, see Ahmed, *Before*, chs. 2–3, especially 35–37 and 45–47; Ḥammāmī, *Islām*, 55ff.; Abū Zayd, *Imām*, 37ff.; Abū Zayd, *Naṣṣ*, 13–65; Abū Zayd, *Naqd*, 117ff. For a classical praise of the traditionists, see Khaṭīb, *Sharaf*, 22ff. and 55ff., where he praises *aṣḥāb al-ḥadīth* and reports how Muhammad commanded honoring them; also Kabīr, *Shiʿār aṣḥāb*. For a classical Shīʿite view on *aṣḥāb al-ḥadīth*, see Ibn Shādhān, *Īḍāḥ*, 7–44. Concerning the time when Sunnism became an official sect, see Amīn, *Ẓuhr*, 789ff. For a modern Muslim discussion on the Ashʿarites and Muʿtazilites as the right and left in Islamic thought, respectively, see Ḥanafī, *Yamīn*, 5–41, where he praises the left as a better way forward for the world in which we live. On how Muʿtazilism challenged traditionists, see van Ess, *Theology*, 4:203, where he states, "The *miḥna* awakened theology even in circles close to the *aṣḥāb al-ḥadīth*." See 1:71, 2:390. For the *miḥna*, see Ibrahim, *Islam*, 37–40. On Muʿtazilism and its arguments, see the important masterpiece *Faḍl al-iʿtizāl wa-ṭabaqāt al-muʿtazila*, which contains texts written (or dictated) by three of its major thinkers, Abū al-Qāsim al-Balkhī (d. 319/931), ʿAbd al-Jabbār (d. 415/1024), and al-Ḥākim al-Jushamī (d. 494/1100): On the basic theology of Muʿtazilism, see 3–67; for its earliest advocates, see 180ff. See the study of Bennett, "Muʿtazilite," 142–158; el-Omari, "Muʿtazilite," 130–141. Theologically, Muʿtazilism was characterized by advocating for rationalism and opposing traditionists. See van Ess, *Theology*, 2:286ff., 3:483ff.; van Ess, *Flowering*, 9ff. (ch. 1) and 79ff. (ch. 3); van Ess, *Zwischen Hadit*, 61ff.; Martin et al., *Defenders*, 10–18 (for rationalism, reason, and doctrines), 26ff. (for its early stages of theological development). For their severe tension with Ibn Ḥanbal, see Ibn al-Jawzī, *Virtues*, 101–105, 135–163, 239–243, et passim. For the persecution of the Muʿtazila after the *miḥna*, see Tanūkhī, *Faraj*, 2:32ff. On the origins and arguments of Muʿtazilism, see Shahrastānī, *Milal*, 46ff.; Ibn al-Murtaḍā, *Ṭabaqāt*, 3ff. For secondary studies, see Yāsīn, *Sulṭa*, 106–125; Amīn, *Ḍuḥā*, 3:21ff.; Wurayyimī, *Fī al-I'tilāf*, 192; Corbin, *History*, 105–111; Gaudefroy-Demombynes, *Muslim*, 29ff.; Nawas, *Ma'mūn*, 14–16, 31ff.; Stroumsa, "Beginning," 265–293. For Muʿtazila as heretics (*zanādiqa*), see ʿAṭwān, *Zandaqa*, 11–26; Badawī, *Min*, 25–40; Ḥamad, *Zandaqa*, 21ff.; Shukr, *Zandaqa*, 121–124; Chokr, *Zandaqa*, section two. For modern Sunnī views opposing the Muʿtazila, see Tunisian scholar Ḥusayn, *Mawqif*, 113–168; Ḥusayn, *Sunna*, 17–21; also Muʿattiq, *Muʿtazila*, 283ff. For a brief comparison of Muʿtazilism and Shīʿism, see Amīn, *Ẓuhr*, 745ff., 809ff.; also Ansari and Schmidtke, "Shīʿī," 196–214.

thousand.[154] While Muslim enthusiasts often believe these numbers as accurate and view them as a reflection of Islam's hegemony in Arabia, scholars acknowledge them as exaggerations.[155] In the same vein, an additional element of exaggeration appears in the tradition's claim that Muhammad sought to challenge the Byzantine Empire, particularly in 630 C.E. In a convincing argument, Tunisian Muslim scholar Hichem Djait claims that the Byzantine superpower was far from the nascent Muslim community and probably did not even recognize the humble power of Muhammad in the Hijaz. Djait, questioning various elements of the Tabūk narrative as *ghayr maᶜqūla* (illogical), further highlights the hyperbolic nature of the tradition, because Heraclius, around that time, returned in a majestic way from Palestine to Byzantium[156] after reportedly restoring the Holy Cross to Jerusalem.[157] The apparent exaggerations of the storytellers are better viewed within the framework of their religious quest to fashion a compelling ideological tale; however, they often end up devising a floundering legend in the form of a historical report.

Third, medieval traditionists designed the narrative to respond to their political, sectarian, and social contexts. In this regard, Muhammad's statements—including his lengthy *khuṭba* (sermon, speech)—during the course of Tabūk serve the goals of later generations of Muslims. The Tabūk

[154] See Watt, *Muḥammad*, 257, where he examines the reported numbers of horses that the Muslims used in major expeditions of Muhammad, to highlight Muhammad's growing power. We should note that Watt appears, to a large extent, to treat these numbers as factual. See Hoyland, *Seeing*, 186, where similar tendencies of exaggerated numbers of soldiers can be traced in non-Muslim sources.

[155] See the Sunnī Muslim scholar Ṣallābī, *Sīra*, 818, where he views the number as a sign of Islam's success. Compare with Djait, *Masīrat*, 191, as he views these numbers as hyperbolic.

[156] Djait, *Masīrat*, 190–192. Djait blames the storytellers for these exaggerated reports and argues that a battle like Tabūk was not concerned at all with the Christians in the north, nor did it have anything to do with an alleged Muslim expansion in the north. Muhammad, says Djait, was satisfied with his Hijaz, and this battle was a strategic show of power to Arabian tribes such as Quḍāᶜa. Still, we should note that Djait treats the raid to Tabūk as to have actually occurred, even though he dismisses elements of it as exaggerations. Still, the Muslim tradition claims that Heraclius sent an envoy to Muhammad while in Tabūk to get answers about prophethood. Wāqidī, *Maghāzī*, 1018–1019. Even traditionalist Muslim scholar ᶜUmarī does not believe this narration about Heraclius' envoy to Muhammad. ᶜUmarī, *Sīra*, 535.

[157] For Heraclius' journeys around this time, particularly to restore the Holy Cross in March 630, see Drijvers, "Heraclius," 177–178, where the author writes, "In a nutshell, the most likely sequence of events is that after the successful conclusion of his Persian campaign in 628, Heraclius concluded a peace treaty with the Persians in the summer of 629. Included in this treaty was the deliverance of the relics of the Cross. The relics were handed over to Heraclius in Hierapolis. From there he journeyed, possibly with a detour through Armenia, to Palestine to restore the Cross in great ceremony to the Church of the Holy Sepulchre in Jerusalem on March 21, 630." See also Whitby, "George," 158–159; Conrad, "Heraclius," 151–152; Kaegi, *Heraclius*, 205–207, 256; Treadgold, *History*, 287–322, especially 299; Olster, *Roman*, 62.

narrative is shaped around these statements, aiming to provide *aḥkām* (rulings) on worship and practice by attributing them to the highest human authority in Islam.[158] For instance, in their attempt to stir medieval Muslims toward political expansion, the narrative begins with statements attributed to Muhammad on the rewards of *ghazw* (raiding) and *qitāl* (fighting) within the framework of jihad *fī sabīl Allāh* (in Allah's path). Once the army arrived at Tabūk, we are told, on the first morning Muhammad spoke at length and in depth with the Muslims about various religious matters including *ribā* (usury), lying, patience, eating *ḥarām* (unlawful) meat, insulting or killing a Muslim, forgiving one another, and controlling anger, among others.[159] Curiously, in his sermon, Muhammad highlighted the Qur'ān as the most worthy of books and its stories as the best of all. However, this appears to contradict the overall accepted tradition that the Qur'ān was not fully revealed nor completely compiled yet—the claim fits medieval Islam, not Muhammad's presumed time. In the same sermon, Muhammad reportedly praised his own *sunna* (laws, customs, and sayings) and affirmed that his *sunna* is the best of all. The claim seems more appropriate for later generations, when conversations about Muhammad's *sunna* and adhering to it were debated among Muslims. There can be little doubt that these statements were designed during later generations and projected back in time, thus receiving legitimacy through attribution to Muhammad. Additionally, these reported statements of Muhammad are not random pieces of the narrative, but the essential core of it. They are *significantly* strengthened through association with Qur'ānic revelations related to moments, individuals, and situations during the course of the raid. It is plausible to argue that the narrative—as formed by storytellers—not only provides rulings for later Muslims on worship and practice, but also unlocks and interprets mysterious passages of the Qur'ān. The narrative is chiefly concerned with ideological significance, not documentation of past events.

Fourth, the reported attempt to assassinate Muhammad on his way back from Tabūk to Medina, on al-ᶜAqaba road, is curious and worth examining. Both Sunnī and Shīᶜite traditions reveal that on his way back from Tabūk, a group of Muhammad's companions—labeled as hypocrites—attempted to assassinate him by hiding behind a rock to push him off a cliff.[160] We are

158 ᶜUmarī, *Sīra*, 537. Wāqidī, *Maghāzī*, 1016.

159 Wāqidī, *Maghāzī*, 1016.

160 Wāqidī, *Maghāzī*, 1045; Yaᶜqūbī, *Ta'rīkh*, 2:70; Ibn Ḥazm, *Muḥallā*, 12:156–161. Kharkūshī, *Sharaf*, 4:8 (only twelve people; Ḥudhayfa shouted at them and they ran; they were companions identified as *munāfiqūn*, i.e., hypocrites); Bayhaqī, *Dalā'il*, 5:260–261 (twelve masked men,

even told that Allah revealed a verse about these companions (Q 9:74), and many Qur'ān exegetes mention this assassination attempt.[161] The number of alleged hypocrites was between twelve and fifteen, although most accounts put it at fourteen. The reports of this incident are decidedly ambiguous and tendentiously short, particularly in Sunnī-approved narratives. However, in many Shīᶜite accounts, the incident receives significant attention and is reported to have included nine companions from the Quraysh, including Abū Bakr, ᶜUmar, ᶜUthmān, Muᶜāwiya, and ᶜAmr ibn al-ᶜĀṣ.[162] These companions are all anti-ᶜAlid and anti-Shīᶜite; including them thus fits the Shīᶜite sectarian and political perspectives. According to the Shīᶜite version, these hypocrites were not genuine Muslims, and they sought to seize power and kill Muhammad, particularly after he disclosed to them that he approved and assigned ᶜAlī's succession to him.[163] Conversely, the Sunnī narrative is curiously vague. It is not only short, but clearly lacks significant details; very few traditionists even disclosed the names of the hypocrites, with the exception of—unsurprisingly—ᶜAbdullāh ibn Ubayy, who is often depicted in the Sunnī-approved narrative as the head of the hypocrites. There are two critical observations on this reported incident.

First, I argue that it reflects an early memory of the faithful that was initially circulated among the believers. In later generations, particularly under the growing influence of *aṣḥāb al-ḥadīth* (traditionists),[164] the memory was

Muhammad was on his camel and ᶜAmmār was riding it, and the hypocrites wanted to push Muhammad, throwing him down the hill. Later, Muhammad did not want to tell the clans of the hypocritical companions, lest people say that Muhammad fought against his people), 5:262 (they were fourteen or fifteen masked men); Ḥalabī, *Insān*, 3:201–202; Dhahabī, *Ta'rīkh*, 2:648 (twelve masked men); Ibn Kathīr, *Bidāya*, 5:26 (twelve men, and Muhammad prophesied they would never enter Paradise). See also Muslim, *Ṣaḥīḥ*, 4:2144; Ibn Ḥanbal, *Musnad*, 38:347, 39:210–211; Ibn Qayyim, *Zād*, 3:477–478. For secondary Muslim studies, see Mubārakpūrī, *Raḥīq*, 400; Ṣallābī, *Sīra*, 829; ᶜUmarī, *Sīra*, 536.

[161] Wāḥidī, *Asbāb*, 256; Muqātil, *Tafsīr*, 2:183–184 (the hypocrites were fifteen, named twelve of them, and they included ᶜAbdullāh ibn Ubayy ibn Abī Salūl); Ṭabarī, *Jāmiᶜ*, 14:364 (included ᶜAbdullāh ibn Ubayy); Zamakhsharī, *Kashshāf*, 2:290–291 (the hypocrites were fifteen and wanted to kill Muhammad); Rāzī, *Mafātiḥ*, 16:103 (they were fifteen); Bayḍāwī, *Anwār*, 3:89; Ibn Kathīr, *Tafsīr*, 4:181; Riḍā, *Manār*, 10:476; Quṭb, *Fī ẓilāl*, 3:1677–1678; Shaᶜrāwī, *Khawāṭirī*, 9:5341.

[162] See Sulaym ibn Qays, *Kitāb Sulaym*, 154–155 (fourteen men, conspired with Abū Bakr and wrote an agreement in his home—the incident occurred at al-ᶜAqaba, but after Muhammad's farewell hajj); Majlisī, *Biḥār*, 21:230–231, and 28:100, where a Shīᶜite tradition indicates that these companions were fourteen, including nine from the Quraysh, among whom was Abū Bakr, ᶜUmar, ᶜUthmān, Ṭalḥa, Muᶜāwiya, and ᶜAmr. For Shīᶜite negative views on Abū Bakr, ᶜUmar, Muᶜāwiya, see Masᶜūdī, *Ithbāt*, 145ff.

[163] Sulaym ibn Qays, *Kitāb Sulaym*, 154–155. ᶜAskarī, *Tafsīr*, 387.

[164] Later Muslim traditionists began to censor accounts that depicted Muhammad as having limitations or weaknesses. See Ahmed, *Before Orthodoxy*.

no longer acceptable, because it appears unsuitable for some Sunnī claims. As it stands, the narrative shows Muhammad as limited and the companions as unfaithful—which does not fit the overall Sunnī paradigm on the *ᶜadālat al-ṣaḥāba* (the righteousness, integrity, and justice of the companions) and on Muhammad's *ᶜiṣma* (infallibility), especially as it pertains to claims of prophetic abilities, guidance, and protection.[165] Therefore, logically, the memory required adjustments. Consequently, attempts at abridging the report and suppressing its details were made, which resulted in significant ambiguity. It is curious that the Sunnī Muslim authority Ibn Ḥazm (d. 456/1064) not only describes the incident, but also acknowledges a disturbing report that identifies major companions—including Abū Bakr, ᶜUmar, ᶜUthmān, Ṭalḥa, and others—as part of the conspiracy to kill Muhammad, before denying the report completely.[166] Ibn Ḥazm's acknowledgment of the disturbing report does not appear in other Sunnī accounts. It seems that, while many Sunnī traditionists worked diligently to send this disturbing report into oblivion, Ibn Ḥazm—in an attempt to reject and deny the report—highlighted it. Ultimately, these attempts to suppress the report served proto-Sunnī and Sunnī points of view. As for the Shīᶜites, they do not endorse claims of the *ᶜadālat al-ṣaḥāba*, so they designed the narratives to display the

[165] For a Sunnī definition of *ṣaḥāba* and their status, see Ibn Hajar, *Iṣāba*, 1:8, where a companion is anyone who met Muhammad and remained a Muslim until death; in 1:131, he claims that all companions are *ᶜudūl* (just and of integrity) and whoever states the opposite is a heretic; and in 1:163, he claims that all of Muhammad's companions will be in Paradise. See Nawawī, *Taqrīb*, 92, where he states that all companions are *ᶜudūl* and lists some of them. See Ibn ᶜAbd al-Barr, *Istīᶜāb*, where the entire work details matters related to the companions; also Ibn Taymiyya, *Minhāj*, 3:371, where he criticizes the Shīᶜites on their views on *ᶜiṣma*; and in 8:474–475, he claims that all Meccan Muslims who emigrated with Muhammad were faithful and none of them was a hypocrite. On *ᶜadālat al-ṣaḥāba*, see Ibn Ḥibbān, *Ṣaḥīḥ*, 1:162; Ibn Ḥazm, *Ḥajjat*, 438; Dhahabī, *Siyar*, 2:601, 608. See also the secondary studies by Ḥammāmī, *Ṣūrat*, 318–320; Hibri, *Parable*, 8, 221–222, where he writes of how this doctrine "emerged that downplayed negative evaluations of the companions and shielded them from blame for the conflicts that occurred" (8). On how Sunnīs and Shīᶜites differ in viewing the *ṣaḥāba* (companions), see Juynboll, *Muslim*, 200–203. For the doctrine of *ᶜiṣma*, see Ibrahim, *Muhammad*, 61–62, 186–187; Reynolds, *Emergence*, 87–88, 139, 141, 171, 206; also Madelung and Tyan, "ᶜIṣma," *EI²*, 4:182; Paul E. Walker, "Impeccability," *EQ*, 2:505–507. Haykal, *Life*, 115–126; Pierce, "Remembering the Infallible Imams." The Shīᶜites reject the Sunnī claims on *ᶜadālat al-ṣaḥāba* and adopt a theological term and practice—the so-called *tabarrī* or *barāʾa*—in which they dissociate themselves from the evil companions by openly cursing them. See Sulaym, *Kitāb Sulaym*, 74–75, 166, 279, et passim. Dakake, "Loyalty," 347. For a contemporary Shīᶜite study, see the lengthy work of the Kuwaiti cleric Yāsir al-Ḥabīb, *Fāḥisha*, 103ff., et passim, where he counts the ungodly deeds of Muhammad's wife ᶜĀ'isha and the first three caliphs. See also Moroccan scholar Idrīs al-Ḥusaynī, *Khilāfa*, 69–112; and Lebanese scholar Kūrānī, *Ajwibat*, 5–8, 33–35, 78–85. On the Shīᶜite practice of cursing the early caliphs, see Kohlberg, "Barā'a," 139–175; Kohlberg, "The Term 'Rāfiḍa,'" 1–9. For primary sources on the *tabarrī*, see Kulaynī, *Kāfī*, 1:404, 2:244–245, and 8:246, where Abū Bakr and ᶜUmar were infidels who never repented. See also Ṭūsī, *Ikhtiyār*, 6–11. For a modern Shīᶜite view on jihad against the kuffār, see Khū'ī, *Prolegomena*, 233–238.

[166] Ibn Ḥazm, *Muḥallā*, 12:160.

major anti-ᶜAlid companions unfavorably. Still, the Shīᶜites needed to ensure that the doctrine of Muhammad's *ᶜiṣma* remained intact. Therefore, we are assured in Shīᶜite traditions that the Angel Gabriel himself forewarned Muhammad of the assassination plot.[167] This detail is eclipsed in the Sunnī version, where the warning came from one or two of the Muslims who were riding with Muhammad.[168] Once again, we encounter competing historiographical reports, shaped to fit the sectarian and political sympathies of the traditionists.

Second, while we cannot be certain of the details of the reported assassination attempt, the memory itself—as reflected in a circulated tradition—demonstrates disunity and the struggle for power among the believers during Muhammad's last days.[169] It is clear that early Muslim generations talked about these companions and their failed attempt. While the Shīᶜite accounts tend to focus on the evildoing of Abū Bakr, ᶜUmar, and ᶜUthmān (alongside Ṭalḥa, ᶜAmr, and ᶜĀ'isha)—portraying them as all conspiring to deny ᶜAlī the right to succeed Muhammad—the Sunnī traditions also convey a struggle for power in the last days of Muhammad. These Sunnī-approved traditions include at least three curious memories. In one instance, ᶜUmar reportedly denied Muhammad the chance to write his will on his deathbed. When Muhammad reportedly said, "Let me write for you *kitāb* (an account or a statement) after which you will not *taḍillū* (go astray)," ᶜUmar refused and told the Muslims that Muhammad "*ghalabahu al-wajaᶜ* (is overtaken by pain) and you have the Qur'ān—Allah's book is enough for us."[170] At face value, this tradition indicates that a Sunnī memory presents ᶜUmar in disharmony with Muhammad, to the extent that ᶜUmar reportedly silenced Muhammad from disclosing important matters pertinent to their future.[171] The point is not that this report on ᶜUmar is factual, but that it reflects how Muslims remembered the last days of Muhammad. These last days were arguably far from harmonious. In the same vein, this disunity appears in another tradition, in which Muhammad, again in his last days, was reportedly

[167] See Majlisī, *Biḥār*, 31:638 and 37:135, where Gabriel warned Muhammad and revealed the names of the hypocrites.

[168] See, for instance, Kharkūshī, *Sharaf*, 4:8; Bayhaqī, *Dalā'il*, 5:260–261; Ibn Qayyim, *Zād*, 3:477–478.

[169] See the recent works of Tunisian scholar Hela Ouardi, *Les derniers jours de Muhammad*; also her *Les califes maudits*. Ouardi criticizes the three caliphs and rejects their label, "califes bien guidés." For her, they sought power and dominion and betrayed Muhammad at his deathbed.

[170] Bukhārī, *Ṣaḥīḥ*, 7:120, 9:111.

[171] For a Shīᶜite criticism of ᶜUmar's actions, see Majlisī, *Biḥār*, 22:474, 30:533–535; Sulaym, *Kitāb*, 248, 249, 347–348.

furious that some companions—particularly his wife ᶜĀ'isha—poured "medicine" into his mouth against his will and his explicit instruction; subsequently, he required everyone in the room to drink from the same medicine after he was forced to take it.[172] In a third tradition, highlighted in Sunnī and Shīᶜite accounts, when Muhammad died, and before they even prepared him for burial, the Meccan Muslims were disputing with the Medinan Muslims in a meeting at the *saqīfa* regarding who would succeed Muhammad. Mysteriously, the man recommended by the Medinan Muslims was found dead, and Abū Bakr was declared a caliph—all this reportedly occurred on the same day that Muhammad died.[173] It is plausible to deduce that the *portrayal* of the Muslim community during Muhammad's last days was less positive than often assumed.

Finally, the traditionists designed the Tabūk narrative to reinforce the belief that Muhammad's *maghāzī* continued to target the Byzantine Christians, one of the major groups that Muhammad sought to suppress. The tradition paints an image of an unstoppable, unyielding, and unceasing commander who marches in battle against non-Muslims, particularly Christian Arab tribes. If they submit and accept Islam, they are spared. If they remain Christians or Jews, they must pay the *jizya* in return for peace. In all, the literary tale suggests that Islam is proceeding, advancing, and overcoming, as it is aided by Allah. This is one reason that Muhammad sought to challenge the Byzantines once more. He commissioned an incursion to al-Shām (Greater Syria) and appointed Usāma, the son of Zayd—who used to be Muhammad's adopted son, before the adoption was annulled—to lead it. While Tabūk was the last raid Muhammad led, Usāma's incursion was the last Muhammad commissioned, but he died before he dispatched the army.

Usāma's Incursion to Syria (11/632)

We are now in the last year of Muhammad's life, but he reportedly continued to commission his companions to lead religious and military missions.[174]

[172] Bukhārī, *Ṣaḥīḥ*, 6:14, 7:127. See Ibrahim, *Muhammad*, 100–101.

[173] On the *saqīfa*, see Ibrahim, *Stated*, 127–130; Ibrahim, *Muhammad*, 104–108; Madelung, *Succession*, 27–67. Cf. Veccia Vaglieri, "Ghadīr Khumm," in *EI*², 2:992–993; Mahmud Shahabi, "The Roots of Shiᶜism in Early Islamic History," in *Shiᶜism*, ed. Seyed Vali Reza Nasr et al., 15–16.

[174] Muhammad reportedly entrusted Abū Bakr to supervise the hajj in A.H. 9 and commissioned ᶜAlī to lead an incursion against Yemen in A.H. 10. Wāqidī, *Maghāzī*, 1077 (Abū Bakr leading three hundred Muslims to hajj); 1079 (ᶜAlī march to Yemen).

After his last hajj, known in the tradition as *ḥajjat al-wadāᶜ* (farewell pilgrimage),[175] Muhammad reportedly dispatched Usāma, the son of Zayd, to Mu'ta. This is another incursion to the northern village of Mu'ta, which we studied earlier in this chapter. The tradition highlights a major reason for this incursion: revenge for the death of Zayd and the other martyred commanders at Mu'ta.

A few days before the month of Ṣafar in the eleventh *hijrī* year (April–May 632), Muhammad reportedly continued to mention to the Muslims the martyrdom of Zayd and the other two commanders at Mu'ta. He "was extremely agitated over them," so he "commanded the people to prepare to raid the Byzantines, and he ordered them to hasten in raiding them."[176] In his honoring of Zayd's memory, Muhammad reportedly instructed Zayd's son, Usāma, to lead the army: "O Usāma, march in Allah's name and with his blessing, until you reach the location of your father's death: Step on them with the horses, because I have appointed you over this army."[177] Muhammad continued, "Shorten your stay with them. Take a guide with you. Send the spies and the foot soldiers to arrive ahead of you."[178] One day after this instruction, Muhammad reportedly "began a headache and a fever," but continued to direct Usāma: "Attack in Allah's name and in his path: Fight those who do not believe in Allah."[179] The army's preparation was underway, and it included major companions from the early Meccan *muhājirūn* (emigrants). However, since Usāma was reportedly eighteen years old, many older companions complained against Muhammad's choice: "Is this youth appointed over the first Muhājirūn? Many words were said about that."[180] In response to these complaints, Muhammad was furious and declared to the Muslims, "By Allah, if you *ṭaᶜantum* (question) my appointment of Usāma, then you have surely doubted my appointment of his father earlier."[181] He commanded, "Take care

[175] Called *ḥijjat al-islām*, Wāqidī, *Maghāzī*, 1089.
[176] Wāqidī, *Life*, 546. Wāqidī, *Maghāzī*, 1117.
[177] Wāqidī, *Maghāzī*, 1077. On Usāma ibn Zayd, see Ibn Saᶜd, *Ṭabaqāt*, 2:145–146, 4:45–53 (he was called Usāma *al-ḥubb*, the beloved, by Muhammad); Khalīfa, *Ṭabaqāt*, 32; ᶜIjlī, *Thiqāt*, 59; Ibn Ḥibbān, *Thiqāt*, 3:2; Ibn al-Athīr, *Usd*, 1:194–195 (Usāma was eighteen years old); Ibn Ḥajar, *Iṣāba*, 1:202–203 (Usāma was eighteen or twenty years old). Ibn ᶜAbd al-Barr, *Istīᶜāb*, 1:75–77 (he was eighteen, nineteen, or twenty). For a Shīᶜite perspective, see Majlisī, *Biḥār*, 28:306ff.; Ḥā'irī, *Dā'irat*, 3:304–305.
[178] Wāqidī, *Life*, 546.
[179] Wāqidī, *Maghāzī*, 1117. He continued, "Know that Paradise is under the flashing gleam." Wāqidī, *Life*, 546.
[180] Wāqidī, *Life*, 547. Ṭabarī, *Ta'rīkh*, 1794, 1849, where the Medinan *anṣār* were reportedly reluctant to yield to Usāma's leadership.
[181] Wāqidī, *Maghāzī*, 1119.

of him, for indeed he is one of your best."[182] While later traditionists portray the companions as righteous and shield them against negative depictions in order to match doctrinal claims on *ᶜadālat al-ṣaḥāba*, as we explained in the previous section, reports like these remain in the tradition and provide a less utopian image.

We are told that Muhammad continued to feel ill, but he insisted on dispatching Usāma's army, despite the pleading of many Muslims to postpone the mission: "Carry out the mission of Usāma." The Muslim soldiers came to bid farewell to Muhammad, as they prepared to march on the following day. When Usāma entered the room of Muhammad, he found him "slow and overwhelmed," because that was the day when the people gave Muhammad the medication. Usāma bowed his head and kissed Muhammad, and although Muhammad did not speak, he "began to raise his hand to the heavens, and then placed it on Usāma."[183] In a pro-ᶜAbbāsid literary detail, we are told, Muhammad was surrounded by his wives and al-ᶜAbbās.[184] Thus, the progenitor of the ᶜAbbāsids, we are told, was one of the nearest to Muhammad in his last days. Similarly, in a detail important to ᶜAbbāsid orthodoxy and particularly Sunnī-approved traditions, ᶜUmar was a member of Usāma's army, and Abū Bakr received permission from Muhammad to be absent because his marriage day to a new wife was imminent.[185] On the following morning, Usāma visited Muhammad, who was at the time awake and feeling much better, and Muhammad instructed Usāma, "With Allah's blessing, leave in the early morning." A day later, as Usāma's army marched from Medina to Syria, an envoy rushed to catch the Muslims only a few miles from Medina. The news was that Muhammad was dying. Usāma returned quickly to Medina with the army. On that day, Monday, 12 Rabīᶜ al-Awwal (June 8, 632), Muhammad "died when the sun declined from the meridian."[186] While this delayed Usāma's mission, we are told, Abū Bakr's first decision as Muhammad's caliph—on the following day—was to dispatch

[182] Wāqidī, *Life*, 547.
[183] Wāqidī, *Life*, 547.
[184] Wāqidī, *Maghāzī*, 1119.
[185] Wāqidī, *Maghāzī*, 1120. Abū Bakr reportedly was going to marry Ḥabība bint Khārija. On Ḥabība, see Ibn Saᶜd, *Ṭabaqāt*, 3:126; Ibn Ḥibbān, *Thiqāt*, 3:100; Ibn ᶜAbd al-Barr, *Istīᶜāb*, 4:1807; Ibn al-Athīr, *Usd*, 3:324; Ṣafadī, *Wāfī*, 11:231. To ensure that Abū Bakr's image as supportive of the raid is intact, the tradition alleges a heroic gesture from Abū Bakr to support Usāma's leadership: Usāma rode his horse, marching to Syria, while Abū Bakr reportedly walked next to him. Ṭabarī, *Ta'rīkh*, 1850. See Ibrahim, *Stated*, 139–141. We should note that in a Shīᶜite tradition, ᶜUmar did not join Usāma's army after all. Yaᶜqūbī, *Ta'rīkh*, 2:142.
[186] Wāqidī, *Life*, 547.

Usāma's army in fulfillment of Muhammad's wish.[187] In the immediate literary context, we are also told, once the news of Muhammad's death reached the Bedouins, many abandoned Islam and apostatized. This propelled Abū Bakr to instruct Usāma to fulfill Muhammad's command and complete the mission; additionally, the situation of all those who abandoned Islam triggered the so-called *ḥurūb al-ridda* (Apostasy Wars).[188]

While the narrative of Usāma's incursion to Syria is relatively short, there are two major critical observations. First, the account is crafted by storytellers to emphasize Muhammad as the commander in chief of the Muslims until his last breath. This image is how medieval traditionists sought to depict him, probably to instill in Muslims similar sentiments during an era of political expansion. The focus of the narrative is not *primarily* Usāma's army, but instead Muhammad, his illness, and his death. Usāma's tale is shaped to magnify Muhammad's portrayal and amplify his virtuous traits, his noble values, and his commendable words. The tradition insists that Muhammad's dedication to Islam is the source of his agitation regarding the murder of his former adopted son Zayd and the other commanders. We are invited to believe that Muhammad never forgets the slaughter of the Muslims and never forgives the wicked non-Muslims. He is portrayed as a war leader who does not yield until he avenges the deaths of his soldiers, but these elements are framed in the religious light of marching against non-Muslims in Allah's name, with his blessing, and in his path.[189] This paradigm, as we often encounter in Muslim historiography, is a source of pride to medieval storytellers who craft religious tales in the form of historical accounts. This is the "Muhammad" they cherish and the only "Muhammad" they want to advance. The narrative of Usāmā's raid is designed to serve Muhammad's image. The inclusion of various literary details about Muhammad's sickness and imminent death adds to the desired image by presenting the personal side of a dying soldier—a champion who never ceased to fight under affliction.

[187] Ṭabarī, *Ta'rīkh*, 1848. On Abū Bakr's portrayal as having been quick to fulfill Muhammad's wish, see Ḥusayn, *Shaykhān*, 16–18. See Ibn al-Athīr, *Usd*, 1:196, where he points out that Usāma was in harmony with Abū Bakr against ᶜAlī. For a study on Usāma's incursion, see Ibrahim, *Stated*, 139–141. The raid is depicted as a great success. Usāma raided various lands where the people *kharajū hurūban* (left and fled), and Usāma returned to Medina *sāliman ghāniman* (safely with plenty of spoils). Ṭabarī, *Ta'rīkh*, 1872–1873. Yaᶜqūbī, *Ta'rīkh*, 2:142.

[188] See Hibri, *Parable*, 296; Watt, *Muḥammad*, 79, "As his health continued to deteriorate (though he was still able to attend to business), disaffection grew. His death on 8 June 632 (13/ iii/ 11) led to the outbreak of a series of rebellions in various quarters of Arabia."

[189] See Shoemaker, *Apocalypse*, 183, where he rightly concludes, "The image of Muhammad as an often brutal warlord is ensconced in his traditional biographies—there is simply no avoiding this fact."

Second, the narrative of Muhammad's death requires attention. The story is full of gaps.[190] In one Sunnī-endorsed tradition, Muhammad—while on his deathbed—describes his pain to his beloved wife ᶜĀ'isha: "This is the time in which I feel a deadly pain from what I ate . . . at Khaybar."[191] The Khaybar incident was reportedly in A.H. 7, while Muhammad's death occurred in A.H. 11. However, the tradition insists that a Muslim man named Bishr ate of this very meal and died in the same day.[192] How did Muhammad survive for four years with poison in his blood? This is a gap in the tradition. There are competing reports and the confusion arguably stems from the attempts by medieval storytellers to *author* their accounts. While one report indicates that Muhammad *did* eat from the meal prepared by the Jewess Zaynab, other accounts—with different goals—emphasize that he chewed a piece but did not swallow it.[193] These conflicting reports serve different ends and varying times. Still, was he poisoned by the Jewess or not? The tradition is ambiguous; however, the storytellers likely sought to present Muhammad as a martyr—a dying solider—and therefore blamed the Jews.[194] This is why, on his deathbed, he reportedly said to Bishr's sister, "This is the time in which I feel *inqiṭāᶜ abharī* (my aorta is severed) from that which I ate with your brother at Khaybar."[195] Similarly, Muhammad is reportedly conveying to his wife ᶜĀ'isha "the pain caused by the food [he] ate at Khaybar" and affirming, "I feel as if *abharī* (my aorta, life artery) is being cut from that poison."[196] However, while the traditionists seek to present an image of a dying martyr, they create more problems: Where is Allah's protection? Why does he not shield Muhammad from being poisoned by a wicked Jewess? Indeed, the story of poisoning Muhammad creates problems when compared to verses in the Qur'ān. In one verse, there is the promise that "Allah will surely

[190] For a detailed discussion of primary sources and secondary studies on the incident, see Ibrahim, *Muhammad*, 98–103. For non-Muslim studies, see Watt, *Muḥammad*, 54, 234; Rodinson, *Muhammad*, 254; and Szilágyi, "After the Prophet's Death." See also Faizer, "Ibn Isḥāq," 126, where the author concludes, "Three years later, however, [Muhammad] dies a martyr from that very poison, which was surely a fine note on which to conclude the life of this 'most heroic of Prophets.'"

[191] Ibn Hishām, *Life*, 516.

[192] Ibn Hishām, *Life*, 516.

[193] Some reports claim that Muhammad "took hold of the shoulder and chewed a morsel of it, but he did not swallow it," as he declared, "This bone tells me that it is poisoned." Ibn Hishām, *Life*, 516.

[194] In connection to the poison incident, al-Ṭabarī reports, "The Muslims believed that in addition to the honor of prophethood that God had granted him the Messenger of God died a martyr." Ṭabarī, *History*, 8:124. Cf. Qummī, *Tafsīr*, 2:376; Majlisī, *Biḥār*, 22:516, 31:641; also Ḥabīb, *Fāḥisha*, 455ff.

[195] Ibn Hishām, *Sīra*, 2:338. See also Ibn Hishām, *Life*, 516, "I feel a deadly pain from what I ate with your brother at Khaybar."

[196] Bukhārī, *Ṣaḥīḥ*, 6:9. Ibn Hishām, *Sīra*, 2:338.

yaᶜṣimuka (shelter you) from the people" (Q 5:67).[197] This statement is arguably disrupted by the poison narrative, where no protection came. In another verse, Allah speaks about his apostle and warns, "If [Muhammad] were to forge concerning Us any sayings, We would have certainly seized him by the right hand and cut off his *watīn* (aorta, life artery)" (Q 69:44–46).[198] The verse is curiously alarming, as it states precisely that which the tradition—in later generations—claims about the way Muhammad died: "My aorta is being cut." The comparison between what the tradition claims and what the Qur'ān states creates a theological dilemma: did Muhammad disobey Allah and invent sayings that resulted in a divine death sentence? While the designed story seeks to establish a coherent picture, it ends up creating more problems due to the presence of competing memories. Unsurprisingly, the Shīᶜite version of the poison narrative not only opposes the Sunnī-approved story, but it also advances sectarian preferences and political sympathies unique to Shīᶜism.[199] Ultimately, the attempts by the storytellers to suppress the narrative of a Jewess poisoning Muhammad do not seem to have succeeded, as evidenced by their existence in the same pool of memory alongside contradicting accounts in an apparent dissonance with Qur'ānic statements.

197 Wāḥidī, *Asbāb*, 204–205; Muqātil, *Tafsīr*, 1:492 (the verse means that Allah will protect Muhammad from the Jews, shielding him against being killed); Ṭabarī, *Jāmiᶜ*, 10:472 (Allah will protect Muhammad against all harm from people); Zamakhsharī, *Kashshāf*, 2:218 (the word *yaᶜṣimuka* means *yaḥfaẓuka wa-yajᶜalu ᶜalyka wiqāya*, i.e., Allah protects you and places a shield upon you); Rāzī, *Mafātiḥ*, 12:401; Qurṭubī, *Jāmiᶜ*, 6:243–244 (the verse refers to a *ᶜiṣma*, i.e., protection, for Muhammad, so he could never leave out anything Allah said—it also refers to *ḥirāsa*, overarching shielding, against evildoers); Bayḍāwī, *Anwār*, 2:136 (guarantee from Allah for a *ᶜiṣma*, protection, for Muhammad against his enemies, so they cannot do anything to harm him); Ibn Kathīr, *Tafsīr*, 3:151 (the verse means that Allah shielded, supported, and made Muhammad victorious against his enemies, guaranteeing no one will harm him; Riḍā, *Manār*, 6:391 (instead of people protecting Muhammad, Allah promised in this verse to shield and protect him); Quṭb, *Fī ẓilāl*, 3:1138; Shaᶜrāwī, *Khawāṭirī*, 6:3289 (the verse means that no one can end Muhammad's life). For Shīᶜite traditions on this verse, see Majlisī, *Biḥār*, 89:164 (the verse means no one can kill Muhammad), also 60:38. It is obvious that the exegetes take this verse to describe a shield over Muhammad, protecting him from evil and evildoers, while the tradition reflects an opposite picture in various cases. Cf. Ṭabarī, *Ta'rīkh*, 1409, and Wāqidī, *Life*, 164, where Muhammad himself was injured and almost died at Uḥud, in addition to a story of death by poison.

198 Muqātil, *Tafsīr*, 2:231, 4:425 (*al-watīn* is the life artery, connected to the heart—if it is cut, a human dies); Ṭabarī, *Jāmiᶜ*, 23:593; Zamakhsharī, *Kashshāf*, 4:607; Rāzī, *Mafātiḥ*, 30:635 (a life artery connects the heart with the brain—if cut, a man dies); Qurṭubī, *Jāmiᶜ*, 18:276; Bayḍāwī, *Anwār*, 5:243.

199 Some Shīᶜites believe that Muhammad was poisoned by two of his wives, ᶜĀ'isha and Ḥafṣa. Qummī, *Tafsīr*, 2:376; ᶜAyyāshī, *Tafsīr*, 1:200; Majlisī, *Biḥār*, 22:516; 31:641. For the importance of the "poisoning" account in Shīᶜism as it reflects grief, martyrdom, and hope, see Pierce, "Remembering," 220ff. See more details in Ibrahim, *Muhammad*, 99–100. For a contemporary Shīᶜite study, see Ḥabīb, *Fāḥisha*, 455ff.

With Muhammad's death, his military career ended. According to al-Wāqidī, Muhammad launched and commissioned a total of seventy-four *maghāzī*.[200] His memory is cherished by many Muslims as a military warrior—a shrewd and skillful commander in chief who successfully suppressed all his enemies from among the pagans, Jews, and Christians. Still, one should consider: which Muhammad is cherished here? This is the "Muhammad" of Muslim tradition. As I explained in Chapter 1, we need to distinguish the Muhammad of history from the Muhammad of tradition—very little is known about the former, but the latter is portrayed by Muslim storytellers in numerous details depending on their social, sectarian, and political contexts.[201] Undoubtedly, some characteristics of the Muhammad of tradition may overlap with the Muhammad of history, but due to the textual problems of the Arabic Muslim sources, there is no feasible way to identify the historical Muhammad in the tendentious tradition. Finally, while the tradition pines to portray Muhammad as the sole ruler of Arabia at the time of his death, his reported dominion does not seem to have reached that far. The Muslim sources highlight him as having mainly controlled the western parts of Arabia, known as the Hijaz, all the way to the frontiers of Byzantium in the north and Yemen in the south.[202] Additionally, on his death day, the Muslims did not seem united or unified.[203] We are also told, "The Arabs had apostatized, either generally or as particular individuals in every tribe. Hypocrisy appeared, and the Jews and Christians began to exalt themselves, and the Muslims were like sheep on a cold and rainy night because of the loss of their Prophet and because of their fewness and the multitude of their enemy."[204] With this report, the tradition prepares the scene for Muhammad's successors. They will reportedly follow his footsteps in subduing tribes and nations, by launching the Arab Muslim conquests—a series of military activities described in the tradition as jihad *fī sabīl Allāh*.

[200] The list is found in Wāqidī's *Maghāzī* and observed by Watt, *Muḥammad*, 2, where he states, "Of the seventy-four expeditions listed by al-Wāqidī seven are assigned to the first eighteen months after the Hijrah."

[201] For a modern Muslim perspective which questions contradicting *sīra* accounts, see Ḥanafī, *Min*, 3:19–21, where he argues that Muslim traditions include both truths and myths. Cf. Anthony, *Muhammad*, 7–17.

[202] Djait, *Masīrat*, 197–199.

[203] This is clearly reflected in the incident of the *saqīfa*, when Abū Bakr became caliph on the very day of Muhammad's death. See Ibrahim, *Stated*, 127–130.

[204] Ṭabarī, *Ta'rīkh*, 1848, 1871; Ibn al-Athīr, *Kāmil*, 2:195.

Concluding Remarks

Which Muhammad? Whose *Maghāzī*?

> Therefore, when you encounter those who disbelieved, smite their necks until you have thoroughly slaughtered them. Then, tie them tightly. After that, until the war lays down its burdens, set them free either by generosity or ransom.—*Sūrat Muḥammad* (Q 47:4)

This book has aimed to examine the Muslim historiographical traditions of Muhammad's *maghāzī*. The focus was on the literary portrayals advanced by medieval Muslim narrators to describe the final ten years of Muhammad's life, particularly his military expeditions against the pagans, the Jews, and the Christians. I treated these traditions as *representations* of later Muslim generations, not as factual documentations of past events. The study thus focused on the Muhammad of tradition; it did not seek to reconstruct veracities of the Muhammad of history. The main objective of the book was to detail and analyze that which medieval Muslim traditionists reported in their historiographical works about the military career of their prophet. They fashioned an image of a divinely guided commander-in-chief who succeeded in subduing all his enemies. The book explored dozens of Muhammad's *maghāzī*, with a special emphasis on the major military expeditions that he led or commissioned—especially those that were reportedly consequential in his career. The Muslim storytellers presented his victories as proof of divine support, while his defeats were often relayed as divinely allowed setbacks for theological reasons and with religious meanings. These military activities, we are assured, were not the work of man, but rather a testimony of Allah's mechanics in supporting Muhammad and his believing community. We encountered the image of an unafraid, unstoppable, and unyielding warrior who chiefly sought Islam's hegemony. Muhammad was capable of creating alliances and dissolving treaties when necessary. His strength, wisdom, and

Muhammad's Military Expeditions. Ayman S. Ibrahim, Oxford University Press. © Oxford University Press 2024.
DOI: 10.1093/oso/9780197769171.003.0008

skill are repeatedly portrayed as astonishing to non-Muslims, who appear in the tradition as imprudent and deceived because they rejected his prophethood and religious mission. The result of these battles, the tradition alleges, was the ultimate elevation of Muhammad as the sole ruler in West Arabia—especially after numerous Arab tribes came collectively in delegations to give him their oath of allegiance, which is described in the tradition as their conversion to Islam.

The book has comprised eight chapters. In Chapter 1, I demonstrated how Muslims, from the earliest generations of Islam, have cherished and circulated numerous traditions about *maghāzī rasūl Allāh* (the expeditions of Allah's messenger). I began by exploring many examples of classical traditionists, to demonstrate the various ways they emphasized how the *maghāzī* demonstrated Allah's support for Muhammad and the believers. I then provided many examples of modern and contemporary Muslims who treated and interpreted the accounts of the *maghāzī*. Some of these Muslims consider the *maghāzī* narratives to be factual and prescriptive, while others contextualize and historicize the reports. By highlighting classical sources and modern studies on the *maghāzī*, I sought to establish the centrality and importance of the *maghāzī* among Muslims past and present. I proposed that a unique contribution of this current study is to bring together ample Arabic Muslim sources and numerous Muslim secondary studies to detail, study, and analyze the multifaceted accounts of Muhammad's military expeditions. The English-speaking world can hardly access a detailed account of Muhammad's *maghāzī*, let alone a critical examination of the topic. In addition to the Arabic Muslim sources and studies, this book builds on the valuable contributions of non-Muslim scholarship. This is why, in a lengthy section, I surveyed the non-Muslim claims, views, and arguments on Muhammad and his warring and plundering. I began with non-Muslim claims from the earliest period of Islam before focusing on the arguments of key Western scholars from the nineteenth century until our present day. With access to ample Arabic Muslim sources, integration of numerous Arabic Muslim studies, and the added benefit of many non-Muslim studies, this book hopes to contribute to the rich and vivid scholarship on this topic. After presenting Muslim claims and non-Muslim arguments, I defined my approach to Islamic historiography, highlighting the source problems and how they should give pause to any historian due to their internal literary inconsistencies and external textual challenges. I explained that I view the *maghāzī* accounts as products of the medieval storytellers, a testimony of their sociopolitical, sectarian, and religious contexts, rather than a record of a seventh-century Arabian past. Historiographical accounts are better viewed not as precise descriptions of that which actually happened but that which Muslim traditionists, at best, believed to have occurred or, at worst, sought to convey to their audience about past generations. Muhammad's *maghāzī*, as a literary genre, are fashioned tales by storytellers to convey theological meanings and establish religious claims suitable for the time of documentation.

I focused in chapter 2 on the initial military expeditions commissioned or led by Muhammad against the Meccan pagans of his Quraysh tribe. All occurred during the first two years after Muhammad's *hijra* (emigration) from Mecca to Medina and preceded the great battle of Badr. In this initial stage, Muhammad reportedly commissioned four *sarāyā* (incursions) and led four *maghāzī* (expeditions). In my analyses of the accounts of these military campaigns, I demonstrated how the narratives reflect the religious and sociopolitical agendas of the traditionists, who use literary features to advance their opinions. The sectarian sympathies and political dispositions of each historian influence the historiographical tales. Still, the narrators largely shape the accounts to portray the raids as fighting *fī sabīl Allāh* (in Allah's path)—a reoccurring theme that transforms a pre-Islamic understanding of tribal raiding into an ideological disposition of marching into battle for religious purposes. I highlighted clear discrepancies between various *maghāzī* narratives and argued that classical storytellers adjusted their reports to address the varying requirements of their times. This is evident in how ᶜAbbāsid-era historians tend to depict Umayyad figures—such as the Umayyad notable Abū Sufyān—unfavorably. Similarly, I demonstrated that these historians appear to have designed their accounts to magnify the status of the Meccan Muslims (*muhājirūn*) and amplify the role of Muhammad's Hāshimite family, by marginalizing the achievement and contribution of the Medinan Muslims (*anṣār*). More than once, I showed how the *maghāzī* accounts appear in disarray and disunity and deduced that the reconstruction of a precise, detailed, and coherent overall account is impossible if we rely on the Arabic Muslim sources. The arguments that I posed in this chapter are not unique to these initial *maghāzī* accounts, but will be demonstrated repeatedly in the analyses of other *maghāzī* in following chapters.

In chapters 3 and 4 I continued focusing on Muhammad's major confrontations with the Meccan pagans of his Quraysh tribe. Chapter 3 examined the Muslim victory at Badr (2/624) and their defeat at Uḥud (3/625), while chapter 4 discussed the accounts of the Battle of the Trench

(5/627), the raid of the Ḥudaybiyya (6/628), and the ultimate Muslim victory over the Meccans at the conquest of Mecca (8/630)—a victory that reportedly declared Muhammad the sole leader of the Meccan and Medinan Muslims. In analyzing the narratives, I treated them as literary stories, fashioned and created by traditionists to communicate meaningful religious dispositions. More than once, I demonstrated how ᶜAbbāsid-era historians seem to have worked diligently to elevate the status of figures crucial to ᶜAbbāsid legitimacy (e.g., al-ᶜAbbās ibn ᶜAbd al-Muṭṭalib) and how they also designed narratives to present Umayyad notables (e.g., Abū Sufyān and Muᶜāwiya) as weak Muslims who desired worldly gains and remained unbelievers until they were forced to submit to Muhammad at the conquest of Mecca. Muslim historians were unable to relinquish their religious sympathies or political inclinations in forming their narratives. They not only report stories—they author them.

The study of these accounts produced a curious observation: The literary shift in Muhammad's depiction between Mecca and Medina is unconvincing. At Mecca, he was persecuted and vulnerable, clearly uninterested in worldly matters, and acting as a humble ascetic and intimidated preacher for thirteen years. Once he moved to Medina, we are invited to believe, he suddenly assumed a tribal hegemony over various clans who had lived and flourished in the city for generations. Not only did he successfully convince them to accept his unquestioned leadership, but he reportedly persuaded them to fight for him. This sudden change in Muhammad's portrayal in the tradition, I argued, seems tendentious and reinforces the contention that traditionists authored their accounts. This also strengthens the contention that the biography of Muhammad is shaped to correspond to the Qur'ān and exegete it. We repeatedly encountered historiographical stories—such as at Badr and al-Khandaq—precisely fashioned to exegete specific verses from the Qur'ān.

The depiction of Muslims killing their enemies and plundering their possessions appeared in many of these *maghāzī* accounts. I explained that medieval Muslim traditionists seem to have found no concern with portraying Muhammad and the Muslims as seeking not only dominion by attacking the enemies but also wealth through plundering their possessions. Traditionists cherished and advanced a memory of Muhammad as a war initiator and a caravan interceptor. Seizing and distributing the spoils after battles is a repeated theme in the tradition. I explained that, while this portrayal may not fit today's religious discourses, it seems to have appealed to medieval generations and likely served as a religious exhortation in times of conquest. Indeed, a major argument of this study is that the *maghāzī* narratives—like the Muslim historiography as a whole—reflect not the time of Muhammad but that of their documentation, with its social, cultural, political, and religious concerns. Repeatedly I demonstrate that the storytellers clearly served as religious scholars, creating traditions with specific theological agendas. I traced the hyperbolic nature of many of their *maghāzī* accounts, as exemplified in exaggerated numbers of soldiers, and, more importantly, the tendentiousness of miraculous stories associated with some *maghāzī*. Some raids involved supernatural miracles to show Allah interceding for the believers, while others, we are told, lacked signs and wonders to teach the believers theological lessons. While the Qur'ān seems to insist that Muhammad's only miracle was the revealed message itself, later Muslim traditionists seem to have been unsatisfied with that and needed to devise stories of metaphysical and wondrous deeds to communicate the message of Islam in a religious milieu where stories of prophets performing miracles were the default. Another hyperbolic feature in the tradition appears in the speed and high frequency of reported expeditions: Muhammad is depicted as completely dedicated to raiding without ceasing. We are told that he almost died at Uḥud, then led a raid the following day. When he overcame the confederates at al-Khandaq, Allah sent him Gabriel to instruct him to march immediately to attack Banū Qurayẓa. This reflects a religious philosophy advanced by the storytellers, clearly highlighting their cherished memory of a divinely guided prophet who was victorious in battle. Again, the observations we highlighted in these two chapters are not exclusively related to the *maghāzī* discussed therein, but they also guide the study of other *maghāzī* traditions and historiographical accounts in general.

In chapter 5 I concentrated on Muhammad's confrontations with the Jews of Medina and its neighboring settlements. Through traditions, Muslim narrators designed an image of a rival religious community to the Muslims upon their arrival in Medina. The Jews are displayed as ungrateful and disingenuous, as they rejected Muhammad, his message, and his prophethood. The Muslim-Jewish tension appears as inherently religious, around theological claims, but it was soon crystalized into a tribal military combat. I examined the narratives of the Muslim raids against three major tribes in Medina—Banū Qaynuqāᶜ, Banū al-Naḍīr, and Banū Qurayẓa—before I analyzed the raids to the Jewish settlements of Khaybar and Fadak. The Muslim treatment of these Jews, as described in the tradition, varied between expulsion and annihilation. In the critical examination of these raids, I also studied what the tradition represents as *sarāyā* (incursions) in the form of strategic assassinations of notable Jews who openly showed enmity to Muhammad. I argued that these stories of raids and assassinations against the Jews are a product of medieval traditionists who likely sought to encourage an anti-Jewish disposition that is arguably more suitable for later generations living in the conquered lands. I highlighted several primary references and secondary studies on the Muslim anti-Jewish polemics before arguing that some of these stories seem to have been fashioned to exegete verses in the Qur'ān that depict the Jews negatively. Through various examples I demonstrated how historiographical reports appear to be shaped by the narrators to interpret Islam's Scripture, particularly advancing anti-Jewish sentiments. Still, in analyzing these anti-Jewish historiographical accounts, I highlighted stark contradictions in various narratives. The contradictions, I argued, appear to reflect competing memories within the same pool of traditions. I contended that, in changing times and circumstances, some accounts were *selectively* elevated and thus received recognition and formed orthodoxy, while others were sidelined and became unconventional or sent to oblivion—although, to be sure, they did not entirely vanish from the memory of the faithful. Historical narratives are not only written, but rewritten, tweaked, and adjusted to correspond to changing religious, social, and political necessities.

I devoted attention in Chapter 6 to Muhammad's final *maghāzī* against the Bedouins, which reportedly resulted in their total surrender to his leadership. The tradition describes that, after subduing the Jews of Medina and the pagans of Mecca, Muhammad needed to ensure the submission of various strong tribes in the Hijaz. While I highlighted various expeditions against the Bedouins, I focused on three in particular: the incursion against the Banū Jadhīma under the command of Muhammad's companion Khālid ibn al-Walīd, the raid against the strong tribe of Hawāzin in the Battle of Ḥunayn, and the siege of al-Ṭā'if. The first two resulted in Muslim victories, while the siege did not. Still, these raids are designed to highlight Muhammad as having become the major leader in Arabia. They reportedly occurred in the eighth *hijrī* year and were the precursor of the important ninth year in Islam, often known as *ʿām al-wufūd* (the year of delegations), when many *wufūd* (delegations, deputations, or groups) came to declare allegiance, loyalty, and submission to Muhammad—a notion conveyed in the tradition as religious conversion. In examining these narratives, I highlighted discrepancies in the reports and apparent attempts by the narrators to adjust the portrayals of individuals and the course of events. Not only did I explain that Khālid's early negative portrayal required adjustments by later Muslim generations due to his importance to the overall Sunnī tradition, but I also pointed to the literary embellishments applied to the siege of al-Ṭā'if to reframe it from a total defeat to a theological victory. I argued that Muslim traditionists appear to have designed military victories and defeats to communicate theological meanings, as evidenced in how the failure of the siege of al-Ṭā'if is framed around religious lessons to the faithful in several ways. Similarly, in the analysis of the historiographical narratives on the division and distribution of spoils among Muslims, I observed not only how the Muslim memory reveals what the Arab soldiers—even after their reported conversion to Islam—cared about the most, but also how the storytellers shape the accounts to derive juristic rules and religious lessons. Here I provided various examples of classical, modern, and contemporary Muslims who rely on these narratives to establish religious rulings on jihad, *qitāl*, *ghanīma*, *fay'*, and others. A historiographical Muslim narrative does not necessarily aim to be factual or to record a distant past, but more importantly to exegete Islam's Scripture and communicate theological meanings to the faithful.

In chapter 7 I studied the traditions of Muhammad's expeditions to the Christian Byzantine frontiers. While I highlighted his several reported attempts to raid Christian tribes in northern Hijaz and even attaining the Byzantine Empire superpower, I focused in particular on three important encounters: the raid to Mu'ta, the raid to Tabūk, and Usāma's incursion to Greater Syria. In studying Mu'ta, I highlighted the scholarly observation of its possible parallels to the battle of Mothous as reported in the Christian historical work *The Chronicle of Theophanes*. I compared the Muslim account to the Christian one and agreed with the scholarly contention that the Christian account appears to have been built largely on the Muslim version. In the analysis of Tabūk, I observed how the narrative is replete with hyperbolic and fanciful features, which reinforced my contention that traditionists authored accounts for religious and political reasons. The Tabūk account is fashioned as a theological homily that exegetes the Qur'ān and derives juristic rules for Muslims. It links the battle's events to *sūrat al-Tawba* (Q 9) and shapes historical anecdotes to establish various theological lessons: discerning religious hypocrisy, commending devotion to Muhammad, exerting patience under affliction, extolling the virtues of jihad in battle, and giving financially to prepare warriors for *qitāl* (fighting). The entire notion of attacking Christians in al-Shām, we are told, is built on a scriptural command, spurring the Muslims to fight those *adjacent* to them from among the unbelievers (Q 9:123)—if al-Shām contains non-Muslims and is adjacent to the Hijaz to the north, it should thus be fought. Additionally, if the Qur'ān interacts with pagans, Jews, and Christians, the logic goes, Muhammad's stories—which include raids against pagans and Jews—need to incorporate confrontations with Christians. Similarly, the narrators seem to have deployed their narratives to derive juristic decrees related to treating Christians under Islamic rule: When you, O Muslims, meet Christians in battles, give them a choice between converting to Islam, paying the *jizya* (poll tax, tribute), or yielding to the sword and fighting.

When I analyzed the historiographical accounts of these expeditions, I demonstrated how the sectarian inclinations and political leanings of Muslim historians are clearly evident in the way they design their narratives. A pro-Shīᶜite historian insists on portraying ᶜAlī and Banū Hāshim as the most crucial warriors for Muhammad, while ᶜAbbāsid historians do not hesitate to magnify the image of al-ᶜAbbās as the major aid of Muhammad, both on the battlefield and in performing miracles leading to the victory. This strengthens one of the overall arguments of this study: Muslim traditionists never relinquish their sectarian commitment or political sympathies when they design their narratives. Finally, in analyzing the accounts of Usāma's incursion to al-Shām, I explained how they seem to emphasize Muhammad as the military commander of the Muslims until his last breath, and that they are *primarily* concerned with magnifying and praising Muhammad, not the eighteen-year-old warrior Usāma. I interacted with the traditions of Muhammad's death that reportedly interrupted Usāma's military expedition. I discussed the ideological and textual problems of the poisoning episode of Muhammad, and I highlighted contradictory accounts concerning who poisoned him by contrasting Sunnī and Shīᶜite views on the incident. I argued that the poisoning traditions are full of gaps and unconvincing details, and I demonstrated, once more, that the narrators use the accounts to advance their sectarian and political agendas. On the one hand, by ascribing Muhammad's poisoning to a Jewess, storytellers advance the anti-Jewish disposition, portraying the Jews as the most vicious enemy of Islam who hurt the most important human figure in the faith. On the other hand, some Shīᶜite traditions seize the chance and credit Muhammad's poisoning to individuals loathed among the Shīᶜites, such as Abū Bakr, ᶜUmar, ᶜĀ'isha, and Ḥafṣa. Again, the argument holds true: Religious sympathies, sectarian inclinations, and political preferences influence historical representations.

In this concluding chapter I endeavored to summarize the main points of the book's chapters and their major observations and arguments. This book has been a journey into medieval Muslim thought on Muhammad and his role as a marauding military champion. The classical narrators designed his memory as a raid initiator, caravan interceptor, and plunder seeker—a memory that has been cherished by Muslims past and present. The depiction largely centers on a divinely guided messenger, with the Qur'ān in one hand and the sword in another. His commitment to Islam is uncompromised, and his devotion to Allah is unmatched. His success on the battlefield is both a sign of his divine mission and a testimony of divine support. He is wise and patient with his companions, unyielding and unstoppable with his enemies, and persistent and unrelenting with all unbelievers. At times, he is intolerant, strict, and unforgiving to those who insult him or hurt the Muslims, while at other times he extends forgiveness to vulnerable believers who fall into temptation. Due to competing traditions, Muhammad's portrayal is often unclear and contradictory. While very little is known about the Muhammad of history from contemporary and near-contemporary sources, details about the Muhammad of the tradition are ample in number, stunning in detail, and complex in composition. These stories are documented centuries after his death by religious zealots who served as authors of history. They tweaked, adjusted, and rewrote their narratives in response to their sociopolitical and sectarian contexts. When asked what is fiction and what actually occurred, one can only yield, *Allāhu aᶜlam* (Allah knows best).

About the Author

Ayman S. Ibrahim was born and raised in Egypt. He has taught in various countries within the Muslim world, and in the West at undergraduate and graduate levels. He completed his second PhD in 2018 at the Department of Middle Eastern History at the University of Haifa, Mount Carmel. He currently serves as Bill and Connie Jenkins Professor of Islamic Studies at Southern Seminary and the director of the Jenkins Center for the Christian Understanding of Islam. His publications include *The Stated Motivations for the Early Islamic Expansion* (Peter Lang, 2018), *Conversion to Islam* (Oxford University Press, 2021), *Basics of Arabic* (Zondervan, 2021), and *Medieval Encounters: Arabic-Speaking Christians and Islam* (Gorgias, 2022).

Book Synopsis

What is so fascinating about Muhammad's last ten years of life? In what ways did the earliest Muslims remember him and those years? In particular, what does the Muslim tradition reveal about Muhammad's military expeditions and their targets during these years? Did he really launch over seventy military campaigns? Why did he lead and commission these military activities? Were they for the purpose of proclaiming Islam to non-Muslims? Or were they conducted mainly to accumulate resources and advance tribal dominion? Did Muhammad really raid the Christian Byzantine Empire and expel the Jews from Medina? More importantly, can we be certain that these military activities actually occurred? Or did medieval Muslims invent these tales? These fundamental questions drive this study.

By relying on numerous Arabic Muslim sources, this study seeks to examine how medieval Muslims cherished and portrayed Muhammad's military career. They not only marveled at his battles—they also listed them, specified their targets, described the details from the battleground, and emphasized their tremendous successes. This study leads readers through a complex body of literature; provides insights regarding social, religious, and historical contexts; and creates a vivid picture of Muhammad's military expeditions according to the early Muslim historians. Readers join an intellectual journey, exploring numerous Muslim narratives and wrestling with their reliability. They will question whether Islam actually spread by the sword and deduce unconventional conclusions regarding Muhammad's military career as they unearth the link between historical narratives and historians' religious sympathies and political agendas. This book integrates and interacts with ample Arabic Muslim scholarly studies on the topic and analyzes their findings and arguments with the hope of making these valuable studies accessible to the English-speaking world.

Works Cited

ABBREVIATIONS

CMR Thomas, David, et al., eds. *History of Christian-Muslim Relations*. Leiden: Brill, 2009–.

EI2 Bearman, P., C. E. Bosworth, et al., eds. *Encyclopædia of Islam*, 2nd edition. Leiden: Brill, 1960–2002.

EI3 Krämer, Gudrun, Denis Matringe, John Nawas, et al., eds. *Encyclopædia of Islam*, 3rd edition. Leiden: Brill, 2007–.

EIR *Encyclopaedia Iranica Online*, edited by Ehsan Yarshater et al.

EQ Jane Dammen McAuliffe, ed. *Encyclopaedia of the Qur'ān*. Leiden: Brill, 2001–2006.

GAS Sezgin, Fuat. *Geschichte des arabischen Schrifttums*. 9 vols. Leiden: Brill, 1967–1984.

PRIMARY SOURCES

ᶜAbd al-Jabbār al-Hamadhānī. *Tathbīt dalā'il al-nubuwwa*. 2 vols. Cairo: Dār al-Muṣṭafā, n.d.

ᶜAbd al-Razzāq al-Ṣanᶜānī. *Muṣannaf*. 11 vols. Edited by Ḥabīb al-Raḥmān al-Aᶜẓamī. India: al-majlis al-ᶜilmī, 1403/1983.

ᶜAbd al-Razzāq al-Ṣanᶜānī. *Tafsīr*. 3 vols. Edited by Maḥmūd Muḥammad ᶜAbduh. Beirut: Dār al-kutub al-ᶜilmiyya, 1419/1998.

Abū Mikhnaf. *Kitāb Maqtal al-Ḥusayn*. Edited by Mushtaq Kurji and translated by Hamid Mavani. London: Shia Ithnasheri Community of Middlesex, 2002.

Abū Yūsuf al-Anṣārī. *Al-Kharāj*. Edited by Ṭāhā ᶜAbd al-Ra'ūf Saᶜd and Saᶜd Maḥmūd. Cairo: al-Maktaba al-Azhariyya li-l-turāth, n.d.

Abū Zurᶜa al-Dimashqī. *Ta'rīkh Abī Zurᶜa*. Edited by Shukr Allāh al-Qujānī. Damascus: Mujammaᶜ al-lugha al-ᶜArabiyya, 1980.

Anbārī, Kamāl al-Dīn al-. *Nuzhat al-albā' fī ṭabaqāt al-udabā'*. Edited by Ibrāhīm al-Sāmirrā'ī. Jordan: Maktabat al-manār, 1405/1985.

Andalusī, Ibn Saᶜīd al-. *Nashwat al-ṭarab fī tarīkh jāhiliyyat al-ᶜArab*. Edited by Naṣrat ᶜAbd al-Raḥmān. Amman: Maktabat al-Aqṣā, n.d.

Anonymous. *Akhbār al-dawla al-ᶜabbāsiyya*. Edited by ᶜAbd al-ᶜAzīz al-Dūrī and ᶜAbd al-Jabbār al-Muṭṭalibī. Beirut: Dār al-ṭalīᶜa, 1971.

ᶜAqīlī, Abū Jaᶜfar al-. *Al-Ḍuᶜafā' al-kabīr*. 4 vols. Edited by ᶜAbd al-Muᶜṭī Qalᶜajī. Beirut: Dār al-kutub al-ᶜilmiyya, 1404/1984.

Aṣbahānī, Abū al-Shaykh al-. *Akhlāq al-nabī*. 4 vols. Edited by Ṣāliḥ ibn Muḥammad al-Wanyān. Riyadh: Dār al-Muslim li-l-nashr wa-l-tawzīᶜ, 1998.

ᶜAskarī. *Tafsīr*. Edited by Madrasat al-Imām al-Mahdī. Qum: Maṭbaᶜat Mahr, 1409/1988.

ᶜAyyāshī, Muḥammad ibn Masᶜūd al-. *Tafsīr*. 2 vols. Tehran: al-Maṭbaᶜa al-ᶜilmiyya, 1380/2001.

Bājī, Abū al-Walīd al-. *Al-Taᶜdīl wa-l-tajrīḥ*. 3 vols. Edited by Abū Libāba Ḥusayn. Riyadh: Dār al-Liwā', 1406/1986.

Bakrī, Abū ᶜUbayd ᶜAbdullāh al-. *Al-Masālik wa-l-mamālik*. 2 vols. Beirut: Dār al-gharb al-Islāmī, 1992.

Bakrī, Abū ᶜUbayd ᶜAbdullāh al-. *Muᶜjam mā istaᶜjam min asmā' al-bilād wa-l-mawaḍiᶜ*. 4 vols. Beirut: ᶜĀlam al-kutub, 1403/1983.

Balādhurī, Aḥmad ibn Yaḥyā al-. *Ansāb al-ashrāf*, vol. V. Edited by S. D. Goitein. Jerusalem: Hebrew University Press, 1938.

Balādhurī, Aḥmad ibn Yaḥyā al-. *Ansāb al-ashrāf*. 13 vols. Edited by Suhayl Zakkār and Riyāḍ al-Ziriklī. Beirut: Dār al-fikr, 1417/1996.

Balādhurī, Aḥmad ibn Yaḥyā al-. *Kitāb futūḥ al-buldān*. Edited by Michael Jan de Goeje. Leiden: Brill, 1865–1866.

Balādhurī, Aḥmad ibn Yaḥyā al-. *The Origins of the Islamic State*. Translated by Francis Murgotten and Philip Khuri Hitti. New York: AMS Press, 1968.

Balkhī, Abū al-Qāsim al-, ᶜAbd al-Jabbār, and al-Ḥākim al-Jushamī. *Faḍl al-iᶜtizāl wa-ṭabaqāt al-muᶜtazila*. Edited by Fu'ād Sayyid. Beirut: Dār al-Fārābī, 1439/2017.

Barqī, ᶜAbd al-Raḥmān al-. *Rijāl al-Barqī: Ṭabaqāt*. Tehran: Manshūrāt Jāmiᶜat Ṭihrān, 1383/1963.

Bayḍāwī, ᶜAbdullāh al-. *Anwār al-tanzīl*. 5 vols. Edited by Muḥammad ᶜAbd al-Raḥmān. Beirut: Dār iḥyā' al-turāth al-ᶜArabī, 1418/1998.

Bayhaqī, Aḥmad ibn Ḥusayn al-. *Dalā'il al-nubuwwa*. 7 vols. Edited by ᶜAbd al-Muᶜṭī Qalᶜajī. Beirut: Dār al-kutub al-ᶜilmiyya, 1405/1984.

Bayhaqī, Aḥmad ibn Ḥusayn al-. *Manāqib al-Shāfiᶜī*. 2 vols. Edited by al-Sayyid Aḥmad Ṣaqr. Cairo: Dār al-turāth, 1390/1970.

Bukhārī, Muḥammad ibn Ismāᶜīl al-. *Ṣaḥīḥ*. 9 vols. Edited by Muḥammad Zuhayr al-Nāṣir. Beirut: Dār ṭawq al-najāh, 1422/2002.

Dāraquṭnī, Abū al-Ḥasan. *Al-Ḍuᶜafā' wa-l-matrukūn*. 3 vols. Edited by ᶜAbd al-Raḥīm Muḥammad al-Qashqarī. Medina: Majallat al-jāmiᶜa al-Islāmiyya, 1403/1983.

Dāraquṭnī, Abū al-Ḥasan. *Al-Mu'talif wa-l-mukhtalif*. 5 vols. Edited by Muwaffaq ᶜAbd al-Qādir. Beirut: Dār al-gharb al-Islāmī, 1406/1986.

Dārimī, ᶜAbd al-Raḥmān al-. *Musnad al-Dārimī*. 4 vols. Edited by Ḥusayn Salīm al-Dārānī. Saudi Arabia: Dār al-mughnī, 1412/2000.

Dāwūdī, Muḥammad Shams al-Dīn al-. *Tabaqāt al-mufassirīn*. 2 vols. Beirut: Dār al-kutub al-ᶜilmiyya, n.d.

Dhahabī, Shams al-Dīn al-. *Mīzān al-iᶜtidāl fī naqd al-rijāl*. 4 vols. Edited by ᶜAlī Muḥammad al-Bijāwī. Beirut: Dār al-maᶜrifa, 1382/1963.

Dhahabī, Shams al-Dīn al-. *Siyar aᶜlām al-nubalā'*. 25 vols. Edited by Shuᶜayb al-Arnā'ūṭ, et al. Beirut: Mu'assasat al-risāla, 1405/1985.

Dhahabī, Shams al-Dīn al-. *Tadhkirat al-ḥuffāẓ*. 4 vols. Beirut: Dār al-kutub al-ᶜilmiyya, 1419/1998.

Dhahabī, Shams al-Dīn al-. *Ta'rīkh al-Islām*. 52 vols. Edited by ᶜUmar ᶜAbd al-Salām Tadmurī. Beirut: Dār al-kitāb al-ᶜArabī, 1413/1993.

Dīnawarī, Abū Ḥanīfa al-. *Kitāb al-akhbār al-ṭiwāl*. Edited by Vladimir Jirjas. Leiden: Brill, 1888.

Fasawī, Yaᶜqūb ibn Sufyān al-. *Al-Maᶜrifa wa-l-tārīkh*. 3 vols. Edited by Akram Ḍiyā' al-ᶜUmarī. Beirut: Mu'assasat al-risāla, 1401/1981.

Fazārī, Abū Isḥāq al-. *Kitāb al-siyar*. Edited by Fārūq Ḥamāda. Beirut: Mu'assasat al-risāla, 1408/1987.

Fīrūzābādī, Majd al-Dīn al-. *Al-Qāmūs al-Muḥīṭ*. Edited by Muḥammad Nuᶜaym. Beirut: Mu'assasat al-risāla, 1426/2005.

Ghazālī, Abū Ḥāmid al-. *Iḥyā' ᶜulūm al-dīn*. 4 vols. Beirut: Dār al-maᶜrifa, n.d.

Ḥākim al-Kabīr al-. *Shiᶜār aṣḥāb al-ḥadīth*. Edited by Ṣubḥī al-Sāmirrā'ī. Kuwait: Dār al-khulafā', n.d.

Ḥalabī, ᶜAlī ibn Burhān al-Dīn al-. *Insān al-ᶜuyūn fī sīrat al-Amīn wa-l-Ma'mūn*. 3 vols. Beirut: Dār al-kutub al-ᶜilmiyya, 1427/2006.

Hamadānī, Abū Bakr al-. *Al-Amākin*. Edited by Ḥamad al-Jāsir. Riyadh: Dār al-Yamāma, 1415/1994.

Hamdānī, al-Ḥasan ibn Aḥmad al-. *Kitāb Ṣifat Jazīrat al-ᶜArab*. Edited by David Heinrich Müller. Leiden: Brill, 1884.

Ḥaraḍī, Yaḥyā al-. *Bahjat al-maḥāfil wa-baghyat al-amāthil*. 2 vols. Beirut: Dār ṣādir, 1417/1997.

Harawī, Abū Ismāᶜīl al-. *Dhamm al-kalām wa-ahli-h*. 5 vols. Edited by ᶜAbd al-Raḥmān al-Shibl. Medina: Maktabat al-ᶜulūm wa-l-ḥikam, 1418/1998.

Ibn ᶜAbd al-Barr, Yūsuf ibn ᶜAbdullāh. *Al-Durar fī ikhtiṣār al-maghāzī wa-l-siyar*. Edited by Shawqī Ḍayf. Cairo: Dār al-maᶜārif, 1991.

Ibn ᶜAbd al-Barr, Yūsuf ibn ᶜAbdullāh. *Al-Istīᶜāb fī maᶜrifat al-aṣḥāb*. Edited by Ṣubḥī al-Sāmirrā'ī. Kuwait: al-Dār al-salafiyya, 1404/1984.

Ibn ᶜAbd al-Ḥakam, ᶜAbdullāh. *Futūḥ Miṣr wa-akhbāruhā*. Edited by Charles Cutler Torrey. New Haven, CT: Yale University Press, 1922.

Ibn ᶜAbd al-Ḥakam al-Miṣrī. *Sīrat ᶜUmar ibn ᶜAbd al-ᶜAzīz*. Edited by Aḥmad ᶜUbayd. Beirut: ᶜĀlam al-kitāb, 1404/1984.

Ibn ᶜAbd Rabbih. *Al-ᶜIqd al-farīd*. 9 vols. Edited by Mufīd Qamīḥa. Beirut: Dār al-kutub al-ᶜilmiyya, 1404/1983.

Ibn Abī Ḥātim al-Rāzī. *Al-Jarḥ wa-l-taᶜdīl*. 9 vols. Hyderabad: Majlis dā'irat al-maᶜārif; Beirut: Dār Iḥyā' al-turāth, 1271/1952.

Ibn Abī Khaythama. *Al-Ta'rīkh al-kabīr, Akhbār al-makkiyyīn*. Edited by Ismāᶜīl Ḥusayn. Riyadh: Dār al-waṭan, 1997.

Ibn Abī Khaythama. *Al-Ta'rīkh al-kabīr* (Part 2). 2 vols. Edited by Ṣalāḥ Hilāl. Cairo: al-Fārūq li-l-nashr, 1427/2006.

Ibn Abī Khaythama. *Al-Ta'rīkh al-kabīr* (Part 3). 4 vols. Edited by Ṣalāḥ Hilāl. Cairo: al-Fārūq li-l-nashr, 1427/2006.

Ibn Abī Yaᶜlā. *Ṭabaqāt al-ḥanābila*. 2 vols. Edited by Muḥammad al-Fiqī. Beirut: Dār al-maᶜrifa, n.d.

Ibn ᶜAsākir. *Ta'rīkh Dimashq*. 80 vols. Edited by ᶜAmr ibn Gharāma al-ᶜUmrawī et al. Beirut: Dār al-fikr, 1415/1995.

Ibn Aᶜtham. *Futūḥ*. 8 vols. Edited by ᶜAlī Shīrī. Beirut: Dār al-Aḍwā' li-l-Ṭibāᶜa wa-l-nashr, 1411/1991.

Ibn al-Athīr, Abū al-Ḥasan ᶜAlī ibn Muḥammad. *Al-Kāmil fī al-tārīkh*. 10 vols. Edited by ᶜUmar ᶜAbd al-Salām Tadmurī. Beirut: Dār al-kitāb al-ᶜArabī, 1417/1997.

Ibn al-Athīr, Abū al-Ḥasan ᶜAlī ibn Muḥammad. *Usd al-ghāba fī maᶜrifat al-ṣaḥāba*. 8 vols. Edited by ᶜAlī Muᶜawwaḍ and ᶜĀdil ᶜAbd al-Mawjūd. 8 vols. Beirut: Dār al-kutub al-ᶜilmiyya, 1415/1994.

Ibn al-Faqīh, Muḥammad al-Hamadhānī. *Al-Buldān*. Edited by Yūsuf al-Hādī. Beirut: ᶜĀlam al-kitāb, 1416/1996.

Ibn al-Faqīh, Muḥammad al-Hamadhānī. *Mukhtaṣar kitāb al-buldān*. Edited by Michael Jan de Goeje. Leiden: Brill, 1885.

Ibn al-Faraḍī. *Ta'rīkh ᶜulamā' al-Andalus*. 2 vols. Edited by al-Sayyid al-Ḥusaynī. Cairo: Maktabat al-khānjī, 1408/1988.

Ibn al-Ghaḍā'irī, Aḥmad ibn Ḥusayn. *Rijāl*. Edited by Muḥammad Riḍā al-Jalālī. Qum: Dār al-ḥadīth, 1422/2002.

Ibn Ḥabīb, Muḥammad. *Al-Muḥabbar*. Edited by Ilse Lichtenstädter. Hyderabad, 1361/1942. Reprint, Beirut: Dār al-āfāq al-jadīda, n.d.

Ibn Ḥabīb, Muḥammad. *Al-Munammaq*. Edited by Khurshid Aḥmad Farūq. Beirut: ᶜĀlam al-kitāb, 1405/1985.

Ibn Ḥajar al-ᶜAsqalānī. *Al-Iṣāba fī tamyīz al-ṣaḥāba*. 8 vols. Edited by ᶜĀdil Aḥmad ᶜAbd al-Mawjūd and ᶜAlī Muḥammad Muᶜawwaḍ. Beirut: Dār al-kutub al-ᶜilmiyya, 1415/1995.

Ibn Ḥajar al-ᶜAsqalānī. *Fatḥ al-bārī fī sharḥ Ṣaḥīḥ al-Bukhārī*. 15 vols. Edited by Muḥib al-Dīn al-Khaṭīb. Beirut: Dār al-maᶜrifa, 1379/1960.

Ibn Ḥajar al-ᶜAsqalānī. *Lisān al-mīzān*. 7 vols. Beirut: Mu'assasat al-aᶜlamī, 1390/1971.

Ibn Ḥajar al-ᶜAsqalānī. *Tahdhīb al-tahdhīb*. 12 vols. Hyderabad: Dā'irat al-maᶜārif al-niẓāmiyya, 1326/1908.

Ibn Ḥajar al-ᶜAsqalānī. *Taqrīb al-tahdhīb*. Edited by Muḥammad ᶜAwwāma. Damascus: Dār al-rashīd, 1406/1986.

Ibn Ḥajar. *Al-Maṭālib al-ᶜāliya*. 19 vols. Edited by Saᶜd ibn Nāṣir al-Shathrī. Riyadh: Dār al-ghayth, 1419/1998.

Ibn Ḥanbal. *Al-Zuhd*. Edited by Muḥammad ᶜAbd al-Salām Shāhīn. Beirut: Dār al-kutub al-ᶜilmiyya, 1420/1999.

Ibn Ḥanbal. *Faḍā'il al-ṣaḥāba*. 2 vols. Edited by Waṣyullāh ᶜAbbās. Beirut: Mu'assasat al-risāla, 1403/1983.

Ibn Ḥanbal, Aḥmad. *Musnad*. 45 vols. Edited by Shuᶜayb al-Arnā'ūṭ et al. Beirut: Mu'assasat al-risāla, 1421/2001.

Ibn Ḥazm. *Al-Faṣl fī al-milal wa-l-ahwā' wa-l-niḥal*. 3 vols. Cairo: Maktabat al-khānjī, n.d.

Ibn Ḥazm. *Al-Muḥallā*. 12 vols. Beirut: Dār al-fikr, n.d.

Ibn Ḥazm. *Ḥajjat al-wadāᶜ*. Edited by Abū Ṣuhayb al-Karmī. Riyadh: Bayt al-afkār, 1988.

Ibn Ḥazm. *Jamharat ansāb al-ᶜArab*. Beirut: Dār al-kutub al-ᶜilmiyya, 1403/1983.

Ibn Ḥibbān. *Al-Majrūḥīn min al-muḥaddithīn wa-l-ḍuᶜafā' wa-l-matrukīn*. 3 vols. Edited by Maḥmūd Ibrāhīm Zāyid. Aleppo: Dār al-waᶜy, 1396/1976.

Ibn Ḥibbān. *Al-Sīra al-nabawiyya wa-akhbār al-khulafā'*. 2 vols. Edited by al-Sayyid ᶜAzīz et al. Beirut: al-kutub al-thaqāfiyya, 1417/1997.

Ibn Ḥibbān. *Al-Thiqāt*. 9 vols. Edited by Muḥammad ᶜAbd al-Muᶜīd Khān. Hyderabad: Dā'irat al-maᶜārif al-ᶜUthmāniyya, 1393/1973.

Ibn Ḥibbān. *Mashāhīr ᶜulamā' al-amṣār*. 9 vols. Edited by Marzūq ᶜAlī Ibrāhīm. Manṣūra, Egypt: Dār al-wafā', 1411/1991.

Ibn Ḥibbān. *Ṣaḥīḥ: al-Iḥsān fī taqrīb ṣaḥīḥ Ibn Ḥibbān*. 18 vols. Arranged by ᶜAlā' al-Dīn al-Fārisī. Edited by Shuᶜayb al-Arnā'ūṭ. Beirut: Mu'assasat al-risāla, 1408/1988.

Ibn Hishām, Abū Muḥammad ᶜAbd al-Malik. *Al-Sīra al-nabawiyya*. 2 vols. Edited by Muṣṭafā al-Saqqā et al. Cairo: Maktabat Muṣṭafā al-Ḥalabī, 1375/1955.

Ibn Hishām, ᶜAbd al-Malik, and Muḥammad Ibn Isḥaq. *The Life of Muhammad*. Translated by Alfred Guillaume. Oxford: Oxford University Press, 1967; 13th reprint, 1999.

Ibn al-ᶜImād. *Shadharāt al-dhahab fī akhbār man dhahab*. 11 vols. Edited by Maḥmūd al-Arnā'ūṭ and ᶜAbd al-Qādir al-Arnā'ūṭ. Damascus: Dār Ibn Kathīr, 1406/1986.

Ibn al-Jawzī. *Virtues of the Imām Aḥmad ibn Ḥanbal*. Volume 2. Edited and Translated by Michael Cooperson. New York: New York University Press, 2015.
Ibn al-Kalbī, Hishām. *Nasab Maᶜadd wa-l-Yaman al-kabīr*. 2 vols. Edited by Najī Ḥasan. Beirut: ᶜĀlam al-kutub, 1408/1988.
Ibn Kathīr, Abū al-Fidā' Ismāᶜīl. *Al-Bidāya wa-l-nihāya*. 15 vols. Edited by Ḥanān ᶜAbd al-Mannān. Beirut: Bayt al-afkār, 2004.
Ibn Kathīr, Abū al-Fidā' Ismāᶜīl. *Al-Sīra al-nabawiyya*. 4 vols. Edited by Muṣṭafā ᶜAbd al-Wāḥid. Beirut: Dār al-maᶜrifa, 1395/1976.
Ibn Kathīr, Abū al-Fidā' Ismāᶜīl. *Tafsīr*. 8 vols. Edited by Sāmī Muḥammad Salāma. Beirut: Dār Ṭība, 1420/1999.
Ibn Khaldūn. *Muqaddima*. 8 vols. Edited by Suhayl Zakkār and Khalīl Shiḥāda. Beirut: Dār al-fikr, 1421/2001.
Ibn Khaldūn. *The Muqaddimah: An Introduction to History*. Translated by Franz Rosenthal. Abridged and edited by N. J. Dawood. Princeton, NJ: Princeton University Press, 1989.
Ibn Khaldūn. *Prolégomènes, Texte arabe publié, d'après les manuscrits de la Bibliothèque impériale*. 3 vols. Translated by M. Quatremère. Paris: Benjamin Duprat, 1858.
Ibn Khallikān. *Wafayāt al-aᶜyān*. 7 vols. Edited by Iḥsān ᶜAbbās. Beirut: Dār ṣādir, 1900–1994.
Ibn Khayr al-Ishbīlī. *Fahrasat*. Edited by Muḥammad Fu'ād Manṣūr. Beirut: Dār al-kutub al-ᶜilmiyya, 1419/1998.
Ibn Khuradādhbih. *Al-Masālik wa-l-mamālik*. Edited by Michael Jan de Goeje. Leiden: Brill, 1889.
Ibn Manda. *Maᶜrifat al-ṣaḥāba*. Edited by ᶜĀmir Ṣabrī. UAE: UAE University, 1426/2005.
Ibn Manjawayh, Aḥmad ibn Ibrāhīm. *Rijāl Ṣaḥīḥ Muslim*. 2 vols. Edited by ᶜAbdullāh al-Laythī. Beirut: Dār al-maᶜrifa, 1407/1987.
Ibn Manẓūr, Jamāl al-Dīn Muḥammad. *Lisān al-ᶜArab*. 15 vols. Beirut: Dār ṣādir, 1955-1956.
Ibn al-Mubārak, ᶜAbdullāh. *Al-Zuhd wa-l-raqā'iq*. Edited by Ḥabīb al-Raḥmān al-Aᶜẓamī. Beirut: Dār al-kutub al-ᶜilmiyya, n.d.
Ibn Mūsā, Asad. *Al-Zuhd*. Edited by Abū Isḥāq al-Ḥuwaynī. Medina: Maktabat al-waᶜy al-Islāmī, 1413/1993.
Ibn Mūsā, ᶜIyāḍ. *Al-Shifā bi-taᶜrīf ḥuqūq al-Muṣṭafā*. 2 vols. Edited with notes by Aḥmad al-Shimnī. Dār al-fikr, 1409/1988.
Ibn al-Muṭahhar al-Ḥillī, al-Ḥasan ibn Yūsuf. *Khulāṣat al-aqwāl fī maᶜrifat ᶜilm al-rijāl*. Edited by qism al-ḥadīth fī mujammaᶜ al-buḥūth al-Islāmiyya. Mashhad, Iran: mujammaᶜ al-buḥūth al-Islāmiyya, 1981.
Ibn al-Muᶜtazz, ᶜAbdullāh. *Ṭabaqāt al-shuᶜarā'*. Edited by ᶜAbd al-Sattār Faraj. Cairo: Dār al-maᶜārif, n.d.
Ibn al-Nadīm, Muḥammad ibn Isḥāq. *Kitāb al-Fihrist*. Edited by Gustav Flügel. Leipzig: F. C. W. Vogel, 1872.
Ibn Qāniᶜ. *Muᶜjam al-ṣaḥāba*. 3 vols. Edited by Ṣalāḥ ibn Sālim al-Misrātī. Medina: Maktabat al-ghurabā', 1418/1997.
Ibn Qayyim al-Jawziyya. *Aḥkām ahl al-dhimma*. 3 vols. Edited by Yūsuf al-Bakrī and Shākir al-ᶜĀrūrī. Dammam: Ramādī li-l-nashr, 1418/1997.
Ibn Qayyim al-Jawziyya. *Zād al-maᶜād*. 5 vols. Beirut: Mu'assasat al-risāla, 1415/1994.
Ibn Qudāma al-Maqdisī. *Al-Mughnī*. 10 vols. Cairo: Maktabat al-Qāhira, 1388/1968.
Ibn Qutayba al-Dīnawarī. *Al-Imāma wa-l-siyāsa*. 2 vols. Edited by ᶜAlī Shīrī. Beirut: Dār al-aḍwā' li-l-ṭibāᶜa wa-l-nashr, 1411/1991.

Ibn Qutayba al-Dīnawarī. *Al-Maᶜārif.* Edited by Tharwat ᶜUkāsha. Cairo: Dār al-maᶜārif, 1981.

Ibn Qutayba al-Dīnawarī. *Faḍl al-ᶜArab wa-l-tanbīh ᶜalā ᶜulūmihā.* Edited by James Montgomery and Peter Webb. Translated by Sarah Savant and Peter Webb. New York: New York University Press, 2017.

Ibn Qutayba al-Dīnawarī. *ᶜUyūn al-akhbār.* 4 vols. Beirut: Dār al-kutub al-ᶜilmiyya, 1418/1997.

Ibn Saᶜd, Muḥammad. *Kitāb al-ṭabaqāt al-kabīr.* 8 vols. Edited by Muḥammad ᶜAbd al-Qādir ᶜAṭā. Beirut: Dār al-kutub al-ᶜilmiyya, 1410/1990.

Ibn al-Ṣalāḥ, ᶜUthmān. *Maᶜrifat anwāᶜ ᶜulūm al-ḥadīth.* Edited by ᶜAbd al-Laṭīf al-Hamīm and Māhir al-Faḥl. Beirut: Dār al-kutub al-ᶜilmiyya, 1423/2002.

Ibn Sallām al-Khuzāᶜī, Abū ᶜUbayd al-Qāsim. *Kitāb al-amwāl.* Edited by Muḥammad ᶜUmāra. Cairo: Dār al-shurūq, 1409/1989.

Ibn Sayyid al-Nās. *ᶜUyūn al-athar.* 2 vols. Edited by Ibrāhīm Ramaḍān. Beirut: Dār al-qalam, 1414/1993.

Ibn Shabba, ᶜUmar. *Ta'rīkh al-Madīna al-munawwara.* Edited by Fahīm Muḥammad Shaltūt. Jeddah, 1399/1979.

Ibn Shādhān, al-Faḍl. *Al-Īḍāḥ.* Edited by al-Sayyid Jalāl al-Dīn al-Ḥusaynī. Tehran: University of Tehran, 1363/1944.

Ibn Shāhīn. *Ta'rīkh asmā' al-thiqāt.* Edited by Ṣubḥī al-Sāmirrā'ī. Kuwait: al-Dār al-salafiyya, 1404/1984.

Ibn Taghrībirdī, Yūsuf. *Al-Nujūm al-zāhira fī mulūk Miṣr wa-l-Qāhira.* 16 vols. Cairo: Dār al-kutub, 1348/1929.

Ibn Taymiyya, Taqī al-Dīn. *Al-Fatāwā al-kubrā.* 8 vols. Beirut: Dār al-kutub al-ᶜilmiyya, 1408/1987.

Ibn Taymiyya, Taqī al-Dīn. *Al-Ṣārim al-maslūl ᶜalā shātim al-Rasūl.* Edited by Muḥammad ᶜAbd al-Ḥamīd. Saudi Arabia: Al-Ḥaras al-Waṭanī al-Saᶜūdī, n.d.

Ibn Taymiyya, Taqī al-Dīn. *Al-Zuhd wa-l-waraᶜ wa-l-ᶜibāda.* Edited by Ḥammād Salāma and Muḥammad ᶜUwayḍa. Amman: Maktabat al-manār, 1407/1986.

Ibn Taymiyya, Taqī al-Dīn. *Minhāj al-sunna al-nabawiyya.* 9 vols. Muḥammad Rashād Sālim. Riyadh: Jāmiᶜat al-imām Muḥammad ibn Saᶜūd, 1406/1986.

Ibn Zanjawayh, Ḥamīd ibn Mukhlid. *Kitāb al-amwāl.* Edited by Shākir Dhīb Fayyāḍ. Riyadh: Markaz al-malik Fayṣal, 1406/1986.

ᶜIjlī, Abū al-Ḥasan al-. *Ta'rīkh al-thiqāt.* Mecca: Dār al-Bāz, 1405/1984.

Iṣfahānī, Abū al-Faraj al-. *Maqātil al-Ṭalibiyyīn.* Edited by Kāẓim al-Muẓaffar. Najaf: Manshūrāt al-maktaba al-ḥaydariyya, 1385/1965.

Iṣfahānī, Abū Nuᶜaym al-. *Ḥilyat al-awliyā' wa-ṭabaqāt al-aṣfiyā'.* 10 vols. Beirut: Dār al-kutub al-ᶜilmiyya, n.d.

Iṣfahānī, Abū Nuᶜaym al-. *Maᶜrifat al-ṣaḥāba.* 7 vols. Edited by ᶜĀdil ibn Yūsuf al-ᶜAzāzī. Riyadh: Dār al-waṭan, 1419/1998.

Iṣṭakhrī, Abū Isḥāq al-Balkhī al-. *Kitāb al-masālik wa-l-mamālik.* Edited by Michael Jan de Goeje. Leiden: Brill, 1870.

Jāḥiẓ, Abū ᶜUthmān al-. *Al-Bayān wa-l-tabiyyīn.* 3 vols. Beirut: Dār al-hilāl, 1423/2002.

Jāḥiẓ, Abū ᶜUthmān al-. *Rasā'il.* 4 vols. ed. ᶜAbd al-Salām Hārūn. Cairo: Maktabat al-khānjī, 1384/1964.

Jawzī, Jamāl al-Dīn al-. *Al-Muntaẓim fī tarīkh al-mulūk wa-l-umam.* 17 vols. Edited by Muḥammad ᶜAbd al-Qādir ᶜAṭā and Muṣṭafā ᶜAbd al-Qādir ᶜAṭā. Beirut: Dār al-kutub al-ᶜilmiyya, 1412/1992.

Jumaḥī, Muḥammad ibn Sallām al-. *Ṭabaqāt fuḥūl al-shuᶜarā'*. 2 vols. Edited by Maḥmūd Shākir. Jeddah: Dār al-madanī, n.d.

Jurjānī, Ibn ᶜAdī al-. *Al-Kāmil fī ḍuᶜafā' al-rijāl*. 8 vols. Edited by ᶜĀdil ᶜAbd al-Mawjūd and ᶜAlī Muᶜawwaḍ. Beirut: Dār al-kutub al-ᶜilmiyya, 1418/1997.

Jūzjānī, Abū Isḥāq al-. *Aḥwāl al-rijāl*. Edited by ᶜAbd al-ᶜAlīm al-Bastawī. Faisalabad, Pakistan: Hadith Academy, n.d.

Kalāᶜī, Abū al-Rabīᶜ ibn Mūsā al-. *Al-Iktifā' fī maghāzī rasūl Allāh*. 2 vols. Beirut: Dār al-kutub al-ᶜilmiyya, 1420/1999.

Khalīfa ibn Khayyāṭ. *History on the Umayyad Dynasty 660–750*. Translated by Carl Wurtzel. Edited by Robert G. Hoyland. Liverpool: Liverpool University Press, 2016.

Khalīfa ibn Khayyāṭ. *Ta'rīkh*. 2 vols. Edited by Akram Ḍiyā' al-ᶜUmarī. Riyadh: Dār Ṭība li-l-nashr wa-l-tawzīᶜ, 1405/1985.

Khalīfa ibn Khayyāṭ. *Ṭabaqāt*. Edited by Suhayl Zakkār. Damascus: Dār al-fikr, 1414/1993.

Kharkūshī, Abū Saᶜd al-. *Sharaf al-muṣṭafā*. 6 vols. Mecca: Dār al-bashā'ir al-Islāmiyya, 1424/2003.

Khaṭīb al-Baghdādī, al-. *Sharaf aṣḥāb al-ḥadīth*. Edited by Muḥammad Saᶜīd Ughlī. Ankara: Dār iḥyā' al-sunna al-nabawiyya, 1972.

Khaṭīb al-Baghdādī, al-. *Ta'rīkh Baghdād*. 16 vols. Edited by Bashshār Maᶜrūf. Beirut: Dār al-gharb al-Islāmī, 1422/2002.

Kulaynī, al-Shaykh al-. *Al-Kāfī*. 8 vols. Edited by ᶜAlī Akbar al-Ghaffārī. Tehran: Dār al-kutub al-Islāmiyya, 1363/1944.

Mālik ibn Anas. *Muwaṭṭa'*. 8 vols. Edited by Muḥammad Muṣṭafā al-Aᶜẓamī. Abu Dhabi: Mu'assasat Zayd, 1425/2004.

Maᶜmar ibn Rāshid, and ᶜAbd al-Razzāq al-Ṣanᶜānī. *The Expeditions: An Early Biography of Muhammad*. Edited and Translated by Sean W. Anthony. New York: New York University Press, 2014.

Maqdisī, al-Muṭahhar ibn Ṭāhir al-. *Al-Bad' wa-l-ta'rīkh*. 6 vols. Port Said, Egypt: Maktabat al-thaqafa aldiiniyya, n.d.

Maqrīzī, Taqī al-Dīn al-. *Al-Mawāᶜiẓ wa-l-iᶜtibār fī dhikr al-khiṭaṭ wa-l-athār*. 4 vols. Beirut: Dar al-kutub al-ᶜilmiyya, 1418/1997.

Maqrīzī, Taqī al-Dīn al-. *Al-Nizāᶜ wa-l-takhāṣum fīmā bayna Banī Umayya wa-Banī Ḥāshim*. Edited by Ḥusayn Mu'nis. Cairo: Dār al-maᶜārif, 1984.

Masᶜūdī, Abū al-Ḥasan al-. *Ithbāt al-waṣiyya*. Qum: Mu'assasat Anṣāriyān, 2006 [1996].

Masᶜūdī, Abū al-Ḥasan al-. *Kitāb al-Tanbīh wa-l-ishrāf*. Edited by ᶜAbdullāh al-Ṣāwī. Cairo: Dār al-Ṣāwī, n.d.

Masᶜūdī, Abū al-Ḥasan al-. *Murūj al-dhahab*. 4 vols. Edited by Kamāl Ḥasan Marᶜī. Beirut: Al-maktaba al-ᶜaṣriyya, 2005.

Māwardī, Abū al-Ḥasan al-. *Al-Aḥkām al-sulṭāniyya*. Cairo: Dār al-ḥadīth, n.d.

Mizzī, Yūsuf ibn ᶜAbd al-Raḥmān al-. *Tahdhīb al-kamāl fī asmā' al-rijāl*. 35 vols. Edited by Bashshār ᶜAwwād Maᶜrūf. Beirut: Mu'assasat al-risāla, 1400/1980.

Mufīd, al-Shaykh al-. *Taṣḥīḥ iᶜtiqādāt al-imāmiyya*. Edited by Ḥusayn Dargāhī. Qum: al-mu'tamar al-ᶜālamī, 1413/1993.

Mujāhid ibn Jabr. *Tafsīr*. Edited by Muḥammad ᶜAbd al-Salām Abū al-Nīl. Cairo: Dār al-fikr al-Islāmī al-ḥadītha, 1410/1989.

Muqātil ibn Sulaymān. *Tafsīr Muqātil*. 5 vols. Edited by ᶜAbdullāh Maḥmūd Shiḥāta. Beirut: Dār iḥiyā' al-turāth, 1423/2002.

Murtaḍā, Aḥmad ibn Yaḥyā Ibn al-. *Kitāb ṭabaqāt al-muʿtazila*. Edited by Susanna Diwald-Wilzer. Beirut: Franz Steiner Verlag, 1380/1961.

Mūsā ibn ʿUqba. *Aḥādīth muntakhaba min maghāzī Mūsā ibn ʿUqba*. Abridged by Yūsuf ibn ʿUmar ibn Qāḍī Shuhba. Edited by Mashhūr Salmān. Beirut: Mu'assasat al-rayyān, 1991.

Mūsā ibn ʿUqba. *Al-Maghāzī*. Edited by Muḥammad Bāqshīsh Abū Mālik. Akadīr, Morocco: Jāmiʿat ibn Zahr, 1994.

Najāshī, Abū al-ʿAbbās al-. *Rijāl al-Najāshī*. Edited by Mūsā al-Zinjānī. Qum, Iran: Mu'assasat al-nashr al-Islāmī, 1418/1997.

Naṣr ibn Muzāḥim. *Waqʿat Ṣiffīn*. Edited by ʿAbd al-Salām Muḥammad Hārūn. Beirut: Dār al-Jīl, 1410/1990 [1382/1962].

Nawawī, Abū Zakariyya al-. *Al-Taqrīb wa-l-taysīr*. Edited by Muḥammad ʿUthmān. Beirut: Dār al-kitāb al-ʿArabī, 1405/1985.

Nawawī, Abū Zakariyyā al-. *Tahdhīb al-asmā' wa-l-lughāt*. 4 vols. Beirut: Dār al-kutub al-ʿilmiyya, n.d.

Nīsābūrī, Niẓām al-Dīn al-. *Gharā'ib al-Qur'ān wa-raghā'ib al-furqān*. 7 vols. Edited by Zakariyyā ʿUmayrāt. Beirut: Dār al-kutub al-ʿilmiyya, 1416/1996.

Nuwayrī, Aḥmad Ibn ʿAbd al-Wahhāb al-. *Nihāyat al-arab fī funūn al-adab*. 33 vols. Cairo: Dār al-kutub, 1423/2003.

Qazwīnī, Abū Yaʿlā al-Khalīlī al-. *Al-Irshād fī maʿrifat ʿulamā' al-ḥadīth*. 3 vols. Riyadh: Dār al-rushd, 1409/1989.

Qummī, ʿAlī ibn Ibrāhīm al-. *Tafsīr*. 2 vols. Edited by al-Sayyid al-Mūsawī al-Jazā'irī. Qum: Mu'assasat dār al-kitāb, 1387/1967.

Qurṭubī, Abū ʿAbdullāh al-Anṣārī al-. *Al-Jāmiʿ li-aḥkām al-Qur'ān*. 20 vols. Edited by Hishām Samīr al-Bukhārī. Riyadh: Dār ʿālam al-kutub, 2003.

Raḍī, al-Sharīf al-. *Nahj al-balāgha*. Edited by Ṣubḥī al-Ṣāliḥ. Beirut: Dār al-kitāb al-lubnānī, 1402/1982.

Rāzī, Abū Bakr al-. *Mukhtār al-Ṣiḥāḥ*. Edited by Yūsuf Muḥammad. Beirut: al-Maktaba al-ʿaṣriyya, 1420/1999.

Rāzī, Fakhr al-Dīn al-. *Mafātiḥ al-ghayb*. 32 vols. Beirut: Dār iḥyā' al-turāth al-ʿArabī, 1420/2000.

Ṣadūq, al-Shaykh al-. *Kitāb man lā yaḥḍuruh al-faqīh*. 4 vols. Edited by ʿAlī Akbar al-Ghaffārī. Qum: Mu'assasat al-nashr al-Islāmī, 1429/2008.

Ṣadūq, al-Shaykh al-. *ʿUyūn akhbār al-Riḍā*. 2 vols. Tehran: Manshūrāt Jahān, n.d.

Ṣafadī, Ṣalāḥ al-Dīn al-. *Al-Wāfī bi-l-wafayāt*. 29 vols. Edited by Aḥmad al-Arnā'ūṭ and Turkī Muṣṭafā. Beirut: Dār iḥyā' al-turāth, 1420/2000.

Samaw'al, Ibn ʿAbbās al-Maghribī al-. *Badhl al-majhūd fī ifḥām al-Yahūd*. Edited by ʿAbd al-Wahhāb Ṭawīla. Damascus: Dār al-qalam, 1410/1989.

Samʿānī, ʿAbd al-Karīm al-. *Ansāb*. Edited by ʿAbd al-Raḥmān al-Yamānī et al. Hyderabad: Dā'irat al-maʿārif al-ʿUthmāniyya, 1382/1962.

Samhūdī, Nūr al-Dīn al-. *Wafā' al-wafā' bi-akhbār dār al-Muṣṭafā*. 4 vols. Edited by Khālid ʿAbd al-Ghanī Maḥfūẓ. Beirut: Dār al-kutub al-ʿilmiyya, 1419/1998.

Sayf ibn ʿUmar. *Kitāb al-ridda wa-l-futūḥ wa-kitāb al-jamal wa-masīr ʿĀ'isha wa-ʿAlī*. A Critical Edition of the Fragments Preserved in the University Library of Imām Muḥammad ibn Saʿūd Islamic University in Riyadh, Saudi Arabia. 2 vols. Edited by Qāsim al-Sammarrā'ī. Leiden: Brill, 1995.

Shāfiʿī, ibn Idrīs al-. *Al-Umm*. 8 vols. Beirut: Dār al-maʿrifa, 1410/1990.

Shāfiʿī, ibn Idrīs al-. *Musnad*. 4 vols. Edited by Māhir al-Faḥl. Kewiut: Ghrās li-l-nashr, 1425/2004.

Shāfiᶜī, ibn Idrīs al-. *Tafsīr*. 3 vols. Edited by Aḥmad al-Farrān. Saudi Arabia: Dār al-tadmuriyya, 1427/2006.

Shahrastānī, Abū al-Fatḥ al-. *Kitāb al-milal wa-l-niḥal*. 3 vols. Syria: Mu'assasat al-ḥalabī, n.d.

Shīrāzī, Abū Isḥāq al-. *Ṭabaqāt al-fuqahā'*. Edited by Iḥsān ᶜAbbās. Beirut: Dār al-Rā'id al-ᶜArabī, 1970.

Suhaylī, Abū al-Qāsim al-. *Al-Rawḍ al-unuf fī sharḥ al-sīra al-nabawiyya li-Ibn Hishām*. 7 vols. Edited by ᶜUmar ᶜAbd al-Salām al-Salāmī. Beirut: Dār iḥyā' al-turāth al-ᶜArabī, 1421/2000.

Sulaym ibn Qays. *Kitāb Sulaym ibn Qays al-Hilālī: Asrār āl Muḥammad*. Edited by Muḥammad Bāqir al-Anṣārī. Qum: Dār al-hādī, 1420/2000.

Suyūṭī, Jalāl al-Dīn al-. *Al-Itqān fī ᶜulūm al-Qur'ān*. 4 vols. Edited by Muḥammad Abū al-Faḍl Ibrāhīm. Cairo: al-Hay'a al-Miṣriyya al-ᶜāmma li-l-kitāb, 1394/1974.

Suyūṭī, Jalāl al-Dīn al-. *Ṭabaqāt al-ḥuffāẓ*. Beirut: Dār al-kutub al-ᶜilmiyya, 1403/1983.

Suyūṭī, Jalāl al-Dīn al-. *Ta'rīkh al-khulafā'*. Edited by Ḥamdī al-Dimirdāsh. Mecca: Maktabat Nizār Muṣṭafā al-Bāz, 1425/2004.

Ṭabarī, Abū Jaᶜfar Muḥammad ibn Jarīr al-. *The History of al-Ṭabarī*. 40 vols. Edited by C. E. Bosworth, Jacob Lassner, et al. New York: State University of New York Press, 1980ff.

Ṭabarī, Abū Jaᶜfar Muḥammad ibn Jarīr al-. *Jāmiᶜ al-bayān fī ta'wīl al-Qur'ān*. 24 vols. Edited by Aḥmad Muḥammad Shākir. Beirut: Mu'assasat al-risāla, 1420/2000.

Ṭabarī, Abū Jaᶜfar Muḥammad ibn Jarīr al-. *Ta'rīkh al-rusul wa-l-mulūk*. 16 vols. Edited by Michael Jan de Goeje et al. Piscataway, NJ: Gorgias Press, 2005. Reprint.

Ṭabarī, Muḥib al-Dīn al-. *Dhakhā'ir al-ᶜuqbā*. Cairo: Dār al-kutub a-miṣriyya, 1356/1923.

Ṭabarsī, Abū ᶜAlī ibn Ḥasan al-. *Al-Iḥtijāj*. 2 vols. Edited by al-Sayyid Muḥammad Bāqir al-Kharasān. Najaf, Iraq: Dār al-nuᶜmān li-l-ṭibāᶜa wa-l-nashr, 1386/1966.

Ṭabarsī, Abū ᶜAlī ibn Ḥasan al-. *Iᶜlām al-warā bi-aᶜlām al-hudā*. 2 vols. Qum: Mu'assasat āl al-bayt li-iḥyā' al-turāth, 1417/1996.

Tanūkhī, al-Muḥsin al-. *Al-Faraj baᶜd al-shidda*. 5 vols. Edited by ᶜAbbūd al-Shāljī. Beirut: Dār ṣādir, 1398/1978.

Thaᶜlabī, Abū Isḥāq al. *Al-Kashf wa-l-bayān*. 10 vols. Edited by Abū Muḥammad ᶜĀashūr and Naẓīr Sāᶜidī. Beirut: Iḥyā' al-turāth, 1422/2002.

Thaqafī, Ibn Hilāl al-. *Kitāb al-ghārāt*. Edited by al-Sayyid al-Khaṭīb. Beirut: Dār al-aḍwā', 1407/1987.

Theophanes. *The Chronicle: An English Translation of Anni Mundi 6095–6305 (A.D. 602–813)*. Translated by Harry Turtledove. Philadelphia: University of Pennsylvania Press, 1982.

Tirmidhī, Abū ᶜĪsā al-. *Al-Shamā'il al-Muḥammadiyya*. Beirut: Dār iḥyā' al-trāth, n.d.

Ṭūsī, Abū Jaᶜfar ibn al-Ḥasan al-. *Al-Fihrist*. Qum: Manshūrāt al-Riḍā, n.d.

Ṭūsī, Abū Jaᶜfar ibn al-Ḥasan al-. *Ikhtiyār maᶜrifat al-rijāl* (abridgement of *Rijāl al-Kashshī*). Edited by Jawwād al-Iṣfahānī. Qum, Iran: Mu'assasat al-nashr al-Islāmī, 1427/2006.

Ṭūsī, Abū Jaᶜfar ibn al-Ḥasan al-. *Rijāl al-Ṭūsī*. Edited by Jawwād al-Iṣfahānī. Qum, Iran: Mu'assasat al-nashr al-Islāmī, n.d.

ᶜUqaylī, Abū Jaᶜfar al-. *Al-Ḍuᶜafā' al-kabīr*. 4 vols. Edited by ᶜAbd al-Muᶜṭī Qalᶜajī. Beirut: Dār al-kutub al-ᶜilmiyya, 1404/1984.

Wāḥidī, Abū al-Ḥasan ᶜAlī al-. *Asbāb nuzūl al-Qur'ān*. Edited by Kamāl Basyūnī Zaghlūl. Beirut: Dār al-kutub al-ᶜilmiyya, 1411/1991.

Wakīᶜ. *Akhbār al-quḍāt*. Edited by ᶜAbd al-ᶜAzīz al-Marāghī. 3 vols. Cairo: al-Maktaba al-tujāriyya, 1366/1947.

Wakīᶜ, Abū Sufyān. *Al-Zuhd*. Edited by ᶜAbd al-Raḥmān ᶜAbd al-Jabbār. Medina: Maktabat al-dār, 1404/1984.

Wāqidī, Abū ᶜAbdullāh ibn ᶜUmar al-. *Al-Maghāzī*, 3rd edition. 3 vols. Edited by Marsden Jones. Oxford: Oxford University Press, 1984.

Wāqidī, Abū ᶜAbdullāh ibn ᶜUmar al-. *Kitāb al-ridda wa-futūḥ al-ᶜIrāq*. Edited by Yaḥyā Wahīb al-Jabbūrī. Beirut: Dār al-gharb al-Islāmī, 1410/1990.

Wāqidī, Abū ᶜAbdullāh ibn ᶜUmar al-. *The Life of Muḥammad: Al-Wāqidī's Kitāb al-Maghāzī*. Edited by Rizwi Faizer and translated by Rizwi Fazier, Amal Ismail, and AbdulKader Tayob. London: Routledge, 2011.

Yaḥyā ibn Ādam. *Kitāb al-kharāj*. Edited by Ḥussayn Mu'nis. Cairo: Dār al-shurūq, 1987.

Yaḥyā ibn Maᶜīn. *Maᶜrifat al-rijāl* (narrated by Ibn Miḥriz). 2 vols. Edited by Muḥammad Kāmil al-Qaṣṣār. Damascus: Majmaᶜ al-lugha al-ᶜArabiyya, 1405/1985.

Yaḥyā ibn Maᶜīn. *Ta'rīkh* (narrated by al-Dūrī). 4 vols. Edited by Aḥmad Muḥammad Sayf. Mecca: Markaz al-baḥth al-ᶜilmī, 1399/1997.

Yaᶜqūbī, Aḥmad ibn Wāḍiḥ al-. *Kitāb al-buldān*. Edited by Theodor W. Juynboll. Leiden: Brill, 1860.

Yaᶜqūbī, Aḥmad ibn Wāḍiḥ al-. *Ta'rīkh*. 2 vols. Edited by M. Th. Houtsma. Leiden: Brill, 1883.

Yaᶜqūbī, Aḥmad ibn Wāḍiḥ al-. *The Works of Ibn Wāḍiḥ al-Yaᶜqūbī: An English Translation*. 3 vols. Edited by Matthew S. Gordon et al. Leiden: Brill, 2018.

Yāqūt al-Ḥamawī. *Kitāb muᶜjam al-buldān*. 5 vols. Beirut: Dār ṣādir 1397/1977.

Yāqūt al-Ḥamawī. *Muᶜjam al-udabā'*. 7 vols. Edited by Iḥsān ᶜAbbās. Beirut: Dār al-gharb al-Islāmī, 1414/1993.

Zamakhsharī. *Al-jibāl wa-l-amkina wa-l-miyāh*. Edited by Aḥmad ᶜAbd al-Tawwāb. Cairo: Dār al-fadīla, 1319/1999.

Zamakhsharī, Abū al-Qāsim al-. *Al-Kashshāf*. 4 vols. Beirut: Dār al-kitāb al-ᶜArabī, 1407/1986.

Zubayr ibn Bakkār. *Al-Muntakhab min azwāj al-nabī*. Edited by Sakīna al-Shihābī. Beirut: Mu'assasat al-risāla, 1403/1983.

Zuhrī, Muḥammad ibn Shihāb al-. *Al-Maghāzī al-nabawiyya*. Edited by Suhayl Zakkār. Damascus: Dār al-fikr, 1981.

Zuhrī, Muḥammad ibn Shihāb al-. *Marwiyyāt al-imām al-Zuhrī fī al-maghāzī*. 2 vols. Edited by Muḥammad al-ᶜAwājī. Medina: al-Jāmiᶜa al-Islāmiyya, 1425/2004.

SECONDARY STUDIES

Abbott, H. Porter. *The Cambridge Introduction to Narrative*. New York: Cambridge University Press, 2008.

Abbott, Nabia. "Women and the State on the Eve of Islam." *American Journal of Semitic Languages and Literatures* 58 (1941): 259–284.

ᶜAbd al-Karīm, Khalīl. *Mujtamaᶜ Yathrib*. Cairo: Dār sīnā li-l-nashr; Beirut: Mu'assasat al-intishār al-ᶜArabī, 1997.

ᶜAbd al-Karīm, Khalīl. *al-Qur'ān: al-Naṣṣ al-mu'assis wa-mujtamaᶜih*. 2 vols. Cairo: Dār Miṣr al-maḥrūsa, 2002.

ᶜAbd al-Karīm, Khalīl. *Quraysh: min al-qabīla ilā al-dawla al-markaziyya*, 2nd edition, Cairo: Dār sīnā li-l-nashr; Beirut: Mu'assasat al-intishār al-ᶜArabī, 1997.

ᶜAbd al-Karīm, Khalīl. *Shadwu al-rabāba bi-aḥwāl mujtamaᶜ al-ṣaḥāba*, 2nd edition. 3 vols. Cairo: Dār sīnā li-l-nashr; Beirut: Mu'assasat al-intishār al-ᶜArabī, 1998.

ᶜAbd al-Wahhāb, Muḥammad ibn. *Mukhtaṣar sīrat al-Rasūl*. Riyadh: Idārat al-thaqāfa wa-l-nashr fī kulliyyat al-sharīᶜa, 1419/2002.

Abou El Fadl, Khaled. "The Place of Tolerance in Islam." In *The Place of Tolerance in Islam*. Edited by Joshua Cohen et al., 3–26. Boston: Beacon Press, 2002.

Abou El Fadl, Khaled. *Rebellion and Violence in Islamic Law*. Cambridge: Cambridge University Press, 2006 [2001].

Abou El Fadl, Khaled. *Speaking in God's Name: Islamic Law, Authority and Women*. London: Oneworld Publications, 2014 [2001].

Abū Khalīl, Shawqī. *Hārūn al-Rashīd: Amīr al-khulafā' wa-ajall mulūk al-dunyā*. Damascus: Maktabat al-asad, 1996.

Abū Māyla, Birayk. *Al-Sarāyā wa-l-buᶜūth al-nabawiyya ḥawla al-Madīnā wa-Makka*. Edited by Akram Ḍiyā' al-ᶜUmarī. Dammam, Saudi Arabia: Dār ibn al-Jawzī, 1417/1997.

Abū Māyla, Birayk. *Ghazwat Mu'ta wa-l-sarāyā wa-l-buᶜūth al-nabawiyya al-shamāliyya*. Medina: al-Jāmiᶜa al-Islāmiyya, 1424/2004.

Abū Rayya, Maḥmūd. *Aḍwā' ᶜalā al-sunna al-Muḥammadiyya*, 6th edition. Cairo: Dār al-maᶜārif, 1994.

Abū Shuhba, Muḥammad ibn Sūwaylim. *Al-Sīra al-nabawiyya ᶜalā ḍū' al-Qur'ān wa-l-sunna*. 2 vols. Beirut: Dār al-qalam, 1427/2006.

Abū Zayd, Naṣr Ḥāmid. *Al-Imām al-Shāfiᶜī wa-ta'sīs al-wasaṭiyya*. Cairo: Sīna li-l-nashr, 1992.

Abū Zayd, Naṣr Ḥāmid. *Al-Naṣṣ, al-sulṭa, al-ḥaqīqa*. Beirut: al-Markaz al-thaqāfī al-ᶜArabī, 1995.

Abū Zayd, Naṣr Ḥāmid. *Falsafat al-ta'wīl*. Beirut: Dār al-tanwīr, 1983.

Abū Zayd, Naṣr Ḥāmid. *Naqd al-khiṭāb al-dīnī*. Cairo: Sīna li-l-nashr, 1994.

Adang, Camilla. "Medieval Muslim Polemics against the Jewish Scriptures." In *Muslim Perceptions of Other Religions*. Edited by Jacques Waardenburgh, 143–159. Oxford: Oxford University Press, 1999.

Adang, Camilla, and Sabine Schmidtke. "Polemics (Muslim-Jewish)." In *Encyclopedia of Jews in the Islamic World*. Executive editor Norman A. Stillman. https://www.google.com/books/edition/Encyclopedia_of_Jews_in_the_Islamic_Worl/vfiGtQEACAAJ?hl=en

Adil, Hajjah Amina. *Muhammad, the Messenger of Islam: His Life and Prophecy*. Washington, DC: Islamic Supreme Council of America, 2002.

Agha, Salih Said. *The Revolution Which Toppled the Umayyads: Neither Arab nor ᶜAbbāsid*. Leiden: Brill, 2003.

Agius, Dionisius A. "The *Shuᶜūbiyya* Movement and Its Literary Manifestation." *Islamic Quarterly* 24 (1980): 76–88.

Ahmad, Barakat. *Muhammad and the Jews*. New Delhi: Vikas Publishing House, 1979.

Ahmad, Bilal. "Leone Caetani's *Annali dell'Islām* on *Sīrah* of the Prophet Muḥammad." *Islamic Studies* 54, no. 3–4 (2015): 203–216.

Ahmed, Asad Q. *The Religious Elite of the Early Islamic Ḥijāz: Five Prosopographical Case Studies*. Oxford: Occasional Publications UPR, 2011.

Ahmed, Leila. *Women and Gender in Islam: Historical Roots of a Modern Debate*. New Haven, CT: Yale University Press, 1992.

Ahmed, Shahab. *Before Orthodoxy: The Satanic Verses in Early Islam*. Cambridge, MA: Harvard University Press, 2017.

Akpinar, Mehmetcan. "Representations of Abū Bakr (d. 13/634) in the Second/Eighth Century." PhD dissertation, University of Chicago, 2016.

Akyol, Mustafa. *Islam without Extremes: A Muslim Case for Liberty*. London: W. W. Norton, 2011.

Akyol, Mustafa. *Reopening Muslim Minds: A Return to Reason, Freedom, and Tolerance*. New York: St. Martin's Publishing Group, 2021.

Akyol, Mustafa. *The Islamic Moses: How the Prophet Inspired Jews and Muslims to Flourish Together and Change the World*. New York: St. Martin's Press, 2024.

ᶜAlawī, Hādī al-. *Maḥaṭṭāt fī al-tārīkh wa-l-turāth*. Damascus: Dār al-Ṭalīᶜa al-jadīda, 1997.

ᶜAlī, Jawwād. *Al-Mufaṣṣal fī tārīkh al-ᶜArab qabl al-Islām*. 11 vols. Baghdad: Jāmiᶜat Baghdād, 1431/1993.

Ali, Kecia. *Imam Shafiᶜi: Scholar and Saint*. Oxford: Oneworld Publications, 2011.

Ali, Kecia. *Marriage and Slavery in Early Islam*. Cambridge, MA: Harvard University Press, 2010.

Ali, Moulavi Chirágh. *A Critical Exposition of the Popular "Jihad": Showing That All the Wars of Mohammad Were Defensive; and That Aggressive War, or Compulsory Conversion, Is Not Allowed in the Koran*. Calcutta: Tracker, Spink and Co., 1885.

Althoff, Gerd, Johannes Fried, and Patrick J. Geary, eds. *Medieval Concepts of the Past: Ritual, Memory, Historiography*. Cambridge: Cambridge University Press; Washington, DC: German Historical Institute, 2002.

Amīn, Aḥmad. *Ḍuḥā al-Islām*. 3 vols. Cairo: al-Hay'a al-Miṣriyya al-ᶜāmma li-l-kitāb, 1997–1999 [1933].

Amīn, Aḥmad. *Ẓuhr al-Islām*. Cairo: Mu'assasat Hindāwī li-l-taᶜlīm wa-l-thaqāfa, 2013 [1945].

Amīn, al-Sayyid Muḥsin al-. *Kitāb aᶜyān al-shīᶜa*. 12 vols. Edited by Ḥasan al-Amīn. Beirut: Dār al-taᶜāruf li-l-maṭbūᶜāt, 1403/1983.

Amīnī, ᶜAbd al-Ḥusayn. *Kitāb al-ghadīr*. 11 vols. Beirut: Mu'assasat al-aᶜlamī, 1414/1994.

Amīnī, ᶜAbd al-Ḥusayn. *Naẓra fī minhāj al-sunna al-nabawiyya*. Edited by Aḥmad al-Kanānī. Beirut: Dār al-fikr, 1417/1996.

Amir-Moezzi, Mohammad Ali. *The Silent Qur'ān and the Speaking Qur'ān: Scriptural Sources of Islam between History and Fervor*. Translated by Eric Ormsby. New York: Columbia University Press, 2016.

Andersson, Tobias. *Early Sunnī Historiography: A Study of the* Tārīkh *of Khalīfa B. Khayyāṭ*. Leiden: Brill, 2018.

Andræ, Tor. *Die Person Muhammads in Lehre und Glauben seiner Gemeinde*. Stockholm: Norstedt & Soner, 1917.

Andrae, Tor. *Mohammed: The Man and His Faith*. London: Taylor & Francis, 2013.

Ansari, Hassan, and Sabine Schmidtke. "The Shīᶜī Reception of Muᶜtazilism (II): Twelver Shīᶜīs." In *The Oxford Handbook of Islamic Theology*. Edited by Sabine Schmidtke, 196–214. Oxford: Oxford University Press, 2016.

Anthony, Sean W. *The Caliph and the Heretic: Ibn Saba' and the Origins of Shī'ism*. Leiden: Brill, 2012.

Anthony, Sean W. *Muhammad and the Empires of Faith: The Making of the Prophet of Islam*. Berkeley: University of California Press, 2020.

Anthony, Sean. "Was Ibn Wāḍiḥ al-Yaᶜqūbī a Shiᶜite Historian? The State of the Question." *Al-ᶜUṣūr al-Wusṭā* 24 (2016): 15–41.

ᶜAqqād, ᶜAbbās Maḥmūd al-.*ᶜAbqariyyat al-ṣiddīq*. Beirut: Manshūrāt al-maktaba al-ᶜaṣriyya, n.d.

ᶜAqqād, ᶜAbbās Maḥmūd al-. *ᶜAbqariyyat Khālid*. Cairo: Dār nahḍat Miṣr, 2005.

ᶜAqqād, ᶜAbbās Maḥmūd al-. *ᶜAbqariyyat Muḥammad*. Fajjāla: Dār nahḍat Miṣr, 1999 [1977].

ᶜAqqād, ᶜAbbās Maḥmūd al-. *Mā yuqāl ᶜan al-Islām*. Cairo: Maktabat dār al-ᶜurūba, n.d.

ᶜAqqād, ᶜAbbās Maḥmūd al-. *Muᶜāwiya ibn Abī Sufyān*. Cairo: Hindāwī, Reprint 2013.

Arabi, Oussama, David Powers, and Susan Spectorsky, eds. *Islamic Legal Thought: A Compendium of Muslim Jurists*. Leiden: Brill, 2013.

Arnold, Thomas Walker. *The Preaching of Islam: A History of the Propagation of the Muslim Faith*. London: Constable, 1913.

Asadulla, Abubakr. *Islam vs. West: Fact or Fiction?* iUniverse, 2009.

Assmann, Jan. *Cultural Memory and Early Civilization: Writing, Remembrance, and Political Imagination*. New York: Cambridge University Press, 2011.

Assmann, Jan. *Moses the Egyptian: The Memory of Egypt in Western Monotheism*. Cambridge, MA: Harvard University Press, 1997.

ᶜAṭiyya, Rajā'ī. *Dimā' ᶜalā jidār al-sulṭa*. Cairo: Dār al-shurūq, 2017.

ᶜAṭwān, Ḥusayn. *Al-Zandaqa wa-l-shuᶜūbiyya fī al-ᶜaṣr al-ᶜabbāsī al-awwal*. Beirut: Dār al-jīl, 1984.

Avner, Uzi, Laïla Nehmé, and Christian Robin. "A Rock Inscription Mentioning Thaᶜlaba, an Arab King from Ghassān." *Arabian Archaeology and Epigraphy* 24 (2013): 237–256.

Awde, Nicholas. *Women in Islam: An Anthology from the Qur'ān and Ḥadīths*. New York: Routledge, 1999.

Aylāl, Rashīd. *Ṣaḥīḥ al-Bukhārī: Nihāyat usṭūra*. Morocco: Dār al-waṭan, 2017.

Azaiez, Mehdi. *Le contre-discours coranique*. Berlin: Walter de Gruyter, 2015.

ᶜAẓmah, ᶜAzīz al-. *Al-Masᶜūdī*. Beirut: Riad el-Rayyes Books, 2001.

ᶜAẓmah, ᶜAzīz al-. *Al-Turāth bayn al-sulṭān wa-l-tārīkh*. Casablanca: Dār Qurṭuba, 1987.

ᶜAẓmah, ᶜAzīz al-. *Ibn Khaldūn wa-tārīkhiyyatuh*. Beirut: Dār al-ṭalīᶜa li-l-nashr, 1987.

Badawī, ᶜAbd al-Raḥmān. *Mawsūᶜat al-mustashriqīn*. Beirut: Dār al-ᶜilm lil-malāyīn, 1993.

Badawī, ᶜAbd al-Raḥmān. *Min tārīkh al-ilḥād fī al-Islām*. Beirut: al-Mu'assasa al-ᶜArabiyya li-l-nashr, 1980.

Baer, Marc David. *Honored by the Glory of Islam: Conversion and Conquest in Ottoman Europe*. New York: Oxford University Press, 2008.

Baḥr al-ᶜUlūm, Muḥammad Mahdī. *Al-Fawā'id al-rijāliyya*. 4 vols. Najaf: Manshūrāt maktabat al-Ṣādiq, 1405/1984.

Bakhos, Carol, and Michael Cook, eds. *Islam and Its Past: Jahiliyya, Late Antiquity, and the Qur'an*. Oxford: Oxford University Press, 2017.

Balādī, ᶜĀtiq ibn Ghayth al-. *Muᶜjam al-maᶜālim al-jughrāfiyya fī al-sīra al-nabawiyya*. Mecca: Dār Makka li-l-nashr wa-l-tawzīᶜ, 1402/1982.

Bar-Asher, Meir M. *Jews and the Qur'an*. Translated by Ethan Rundell. Princeton, NJ: Princeton University Press, 2022.

Barth, Fredrik, ed. *Ethnic Groups and Boundaries: The Social Organisation of Culture Difference*. Boston: Little, Brown and Company, 1969.

Bearman, P., C. E. Bosworth, et al., eds. *Encyclopædia of Islam*, 2nd edition. Leiden: Brill, 1960–2002.

Bearman, Peri J., and Rudolph Peters, et al., eds. *The Islamic School of Law: Evolution, Devolution, and Progress*. Islamic Legal Studies Program, Harvard Law School, 2005.

Beaumont, Mark, ed. *Arab Christians and the Quran from the Origins of Islam to the Medieval Period*. Leiden: Brill, 2018.

Beck, Daniel. *Evolution of the Early Qur'ān: From Anonymous Apocalypse to Charismatic Prophet*. New York: Peter Lang, 2018.

Beck, Norman A. *Mature Christianity: The Recognition and Repudiation of the Anti-Jewish Polemic of the New Testament*. New Jersey: Associated University Press, 1985.

Becker, C. H. "The Expansion of the Saracens—the East." In *Cambridge Medieval History*. Edited by H. M. Gwatkin et al., 329–364. Cambridge: Cambridge University Press, 1913.

Becker, Carl Heinrich. "Julius Wellhausen." *Der Islam* 9 (1919): 95–99.

Begum, Rahmani Hassaan. "The Educational Movement of Sir Syed Ahmed Khan, 1858–1898." PhD dissertation, University of London, School of Oriental and African Studies, 1959.

Behzadi, Lale, and Jaakko Hämeen-Anttila, eds. *Concepts of Authorship in Pre-Modern Arabic Texts*. Bamberger Orientstudien 7. Bamberg: University of Bamberg Press, 2016.

Bennett, Clinton. "The Legacy of Karl Gottlieb Pfander." *International Bulletin of Missionary Research* 20, no. 2 (1996): 76–81.

Bennett, David. "The Muᶜtazilite Movement (II): The Early Muᶜtazilites." In *The Oxford Handbook of Islamic Theology*. Edited by Sabine Schmidtke, 142–158. Oxford: Oxford University Press, 2016.

Berg, Herbert. "ᶜAbbāsid Historians' Portrayals of al-ᶜAbbās b. ᶜAbd al-Muṭṭalib." In *ᶜAbbāsid Studies II: Occasional Papers of the School of ᶜAbbāsid Studies, Leuven, 28 June–1 July 2004*. Edited by John Nawas, 13–38. Leuven: Peeters Publishers, 2010.

Berg, Herbert. *The Development of Exegesis in Early Islam: The Authenticity of Muslim Literature from the Formative Period*. Richmond: Curzon, 2000.

Berg, Herbert. "The Implications of, and Opposition to, the Methods and Theories of John Wansbrough." *Method and Theory in the Study of Religion* 9, no. 1 (1997): 3–22.

Berg, Herbert, ed. *Method and Theory in the Study of Islamic Origins*. Leiden: Brill, 2003.

Berger, Peter L. *The Sacred Canopy; Elements of a Sociological Theory of Religion*. Garden City, NY: Doubleday, 1967.

Bernards, Monique, and John Abdallah Nawas, eds. *Patronate and Patronage in Early and Classical Islam*. Leiden: Brill, 2005.

Bernheimer, Teresa. *The ᶜAlids: The First Family of Islam, 750–1200*. Edinburgh: Edinburgh University Press, 2013.

Black, Antony. *History of Islamic Political Thought: From the Prophet to the Present*, 2nd edition. Edinburgh: Edinburgh University Press, 2011.

Bonner, Michael, ed. *Arab-Byzantine Relations in Early Islamic Times*. London: Taylor & Francis, 2017 [2004].

Bonner, Michael. "Some Observations concerning the Early Development of Jihad on the Arab-Byzantine Frontier." *Studia Islamica* no. 75 (1992): 5–31.

Borrut, Antoine. *Entre mémoire et pouvoir: L'espace Syrien sous les derniers Ommeyades et les premiers Abbassides (V. 72–193/692–809)*. Leiden: Brill, 2011.

Borrut, Antoine. "Vanishing Syria: Periodization and Power in Early Islam." *Der Islam* 91, no. 1 (2014): 37–68.

Borrut, Antoine, and Paul M. Cobb, eds. *Umayyad Legacies*. Leiden: Brill, 2010.

Borrut, Antoine, and Fred McGraw Donner, eds. *Christians and Others in the Umayyad State*. Chicago: Oriental Institute of the University of Chicago, 2016.

Bouvat, Lucien. *Les Barmécides d'après les historiens arabes et persans*. Paris: Ernest Leroux, 1912.

Böwering, Gerhard, et al., eds. *The Princeton Encyclopedia of Islamic Political Thought*. Princeton, NJ: Princeton University Press, 2013.

Breisach, Ernst, ed. *Classical Rhetoric and Medieval Historiography*. Kalamazoo: Medieval Institute Publications, Western Michigan University, 1985.

Brock, Sebastian P. "Syriac Views of Emergent Islam." In *Studies in the First Century of Islamic Society*. Edited by Gautier H. A. Juynboll, 9–21. Carbondale: Southern Illinois University Press Carbondale and Edwardsville, 1982.

Brockelmann, Carl. *History of the Arabic Written Tradition*. 2 vols. with 2 supplements. Translated by Joep Lameer. Leiden: Brill, 2017–2018.

Brockelmann, Carl. *Ta'rīkh al-adab al-ᶜArabī*. 6 vols. Edited by ᶜAbd al-Ḥalīm al-Najjār and Ramaḍān ᶜAbd al-Tawwāb. Cairo: Dār al-maᶜārif, 1977.

Brockopp, Jonathan E., ed. *The Cambridge Companion to Muḥammad*. Cambridge: Cambridge University Press, 2010.

Brockopp, Jonathan E. *Early Mālikī Law: Ibn ᶜAbd Al-Ḥakam and His Major Compendium of Jurisprudence*. Leiden: Brill, 2000.

Brockopp, Jonathan E. "Slavery in Islamic Law: An Examination of Early Mālikī Jurisprudence." PhD dissertation, Yale University, 1995.

Brown, Jonathan. "Did the Prophet Say It or Not? The Literal, Historical, and Effective Truth of Ḥadīths in Early Sunnism." *Journal of the American Oriental Society* 129, no. 2 (2009): 259–285.

Brown, Jonathan. *Misquoting Muhammad: The Challenge and Choices of Interpreting the Prophet's Legacy*. London: Oneworld, 2014.

Brown, Jonathan A. C. *Muhammad: A Very Short Introduction*. Oxford: Oxford University Press, 2011.

Brown, Jonathan A. C. *Slavery and Islam*. Oxford: Oneworld Publications, 2020.

Buaben, Jabal Muhammad. *Image of the Prophet Muhammad in the West: A Study of Muir, Margoliouth and Watt*. Leicester: Islamic Foundation, 1996.

Caetani, Leone. *Annali dell'Islam*. 10 vols. Milan: U. Hoepli, 1905–1926.

Cameron, Averil, ed. *The Byzantine and Early Islamic Near East III: States, Resources and Armies*. Princeton, NJ: Princeton University Press, 1995.

Cameron, Averil. *The Byzantines*. Malden, MA: Wiley-Blackwell, 2009.

Cameron, Averil. "Byzantines and Jews: Some Recent Work on Early Byzantium." *Byzantine and Modern Greek Studies* 20 (1996): 249–274.

Carlyle, Thomas. *On Heroes, Hero-Worship, and the Heroic in History*. London: James Fraser, 1841.

Carruthers, Mary J. *The Book of Memory: A Study of Memory in Medieval Culture*. Cambridge: Cambridge University Press, 2008.

Carvalho, Christina. "Christiaan Snouck Hurgronje: Biography and Perception." MA thesis, Universiteit van Amsterdam, 2010.

Cheikh, Nadia el-. *Byzantium Viewed by the Arabs*. Cambridge, MA: Harvard University Press, 2004.

Cheikho, Louis. *Al-Naṣrāniyya wa-ādābuhā bayna ᶜArab al-Jāhiliyya*. 2 volumes in 1. Beirut: Maṭbaᶜat al-Ābā' al-Mursalīn al-Yasūᶜiyyīn, 1912–1923.

Chokr, Melhem. *Zandaqa et zindīqs en islam au second siècle de l'hégire*. Paris: Presses de l'Ifpo, 2014.

Clanchy, M. T. *From Memory to Written Record: England, 1066–1307*. Cambridge, MA: Harvard University Press, 1979.

Clarence-Smith, William G. *Islam and the Abolition of Slavery*. Oxford: Oxford University Press, 2006.

Cole, Juan. *Muhammad: Prophet of Peace amid the Clash of Empires*. New York: Nation Books, 2018.

Conrad, Lawrence I. "The Arabs to the Time of the Prophet." In *The Cambridge History of the Byzantine Empire c. 500–1492*. Edited by Jonathan Shepard, 173–195. Cambridge: Cambridge University Press, 2019.

Conrad, Lawrence I. "Heraclius in Early Islamic Kerygma." In *The Reign of Heraclius (610–641): Crisis and Confrontation*. Edited by Gerrit J. Reinink and Bernard H. Stolte, 113–156. Leuven: Peeters, 2002.

Conrad, Lawrence I. "Recovering Lost Texts: Some Methodological Issues." *Journal of the American Oriental Society* 113, no. 2 (1993): 258–263.

Conrad, Lawrence I. "Theophanes and the Arabic Historical Tradition: Some Indications of Intercultural Transmission." *Byzantinische Forschungen: Internationale Zeitschrift für Byzantinistik* 15 (1990): 1–44.

Cook, David. *Martyrdom in Islam*. Cambridge: Cambridge University Press, 2007.

Cook, David. *Understanding Jihad*. Berkeley: University of California Press, 2005.

Cook, Michael. *Commanding Right and Forbidding Wrong in Islamic Thought*. Cambridge: Cambridge University Press, 2001.

Cook, Michael. *Muhammad*. Oxford: Oxford University Press, 1983.

Corbin, Henry. *History of Islamic Philosophy*. Translated by Liadain Sherrard and Philip Sherrard. London: Islamic Publications for the Institute of Ismaili Studies, 1993.

Crone, Patricia. "How Did the Qur'ānic Pagans Make a Living?" *Bulletin of the School of Oriental and African Studies* (University of London) 68, no. 3 (2005): 387–399.

Crone, Patricia. "*Mawālī* and the Prophet's Family: An Early Shīᶜite View." In M. Bernards and J. Nawas, eds., *Patronate and Patronage in Early and Classical Islam*, 167–194. Leiden; Boston: Brill, 2005.

Crone, Patricia. *Meccan Trade and the Rise of Islam*. Princeton, NJ: Princeton University Press, 1987.

Crone, Patricia. *Medieval Islamic Political Thought*. Edinburgh: Edinburgh University Press, 2014 [2004].

Crone, Patricia. *The Nativist Prophets of Early Islamic Iran: Rural Revolt and Local Zoroastrianism*. Cambridge: Cambridge University Press, 2012.

Crone, Patricia. "Pagan Arabs as God-Fearers." In *Islam and Its Past: Jahiliyya, Late Antiquity, and the Qur'an*. Edited by Carol Bakhos and Michael Cook, 140–164. Oxford: Oxford University Press, 2017.

Crone, Patricia. "Review of Sayf ibn ᶜUmar's *Kitāb al-Ridda wa'l-Futūḥ* and *Kitāb al-Jamal wa-masīr ᶜĀ'isha wa-ᶜAlī*." *JRAS Journal of the Royal Asiatic Society* 6, no. 02 (1996): 237–240.

Crone, Patricia. *Slaves on Horses: The Evolution of the Islamic Polity*. Cambridge: Cambridge University Press, 1980.

Crone, Patricia, and Michael A. Cook. *Hagarism: The Making of the Islamic World*. Cambridge: Cambridge University Press, 1977.

Crone, Patricia, and Martin Hinds. *God's Caliph: Religious Authority in the First Centuries of Islam*. Cambridge: Cambridge University Press, 1986.

Dabashi, Hamid. *Shiᶜism: A Religion of Protest*. Cambridge, MA: Harvard University Press, 2011.

Dakake, Maria Massi. "Loyalty, Love and Faith: Defining the Boundaries of the Early Shiᶜite Community." PhD dissertation, Princeton University, 2000.
Dakake, Maria Massi. "Writing and Resistance: The Transmission of Religious Knowledge in Early Shiᶜism." In *The Study of Shiᶜi Islam: History, Theology and Law*. Edited by Gurdofarid Miskinzoda and Farhad Daftary, 181–201. London: I. B.Tauris, 2014.
Dangar, Suleman Essop. *The Career of Abū Sufyān before and after His Conversion to Islam*. South Africa: University of Durban-Westville, 1987.
Daniel, Norman. *Islam and the West: The Making of an Image*. Edinburgh: Edinburgh University Press, 1960.
Danto, Elizabeth Ann. *Historical Research*. Oxford: Oxford University Press, 2008.
Dashti, Ali. *Twenty-Three Years: A Study of the Prophetic Career of Mohammad*. London: Routledge, 2013.
Ḍayf, Shawqī. *Al-ᶜAṣr al-ᶜAbbāsī al-awwal*. Cairo: Dār al-maᶜārif, 1966.
Décobert, Christian. *Le Mendiant et le combatant: L'institution de l'islam*. Paris: Ed. du Seuil, 1991.
Delattre, Alain, Marie Legendre, and Petra Sijpesteijn, eds. *Authority and Control in the Countryside: From Antiquity to Islam in the Mediterranean and Near East (6th–10th Century)*. Leiden: Brill, 2018.
de Nicola, Bruno, Sara Nur Yıldız, and A.C.S. Peacock, eds. *Islam and Christianity in Medieval Anatolia*. Aldershot, UK: Ashgate Publishing, 2015.
Déroche, Vincent. "Polémique anti-judaïque et émergence de l'islam." *Revue des Études Byzantines* 57 (1997): 141–161.
Djait, Hichem. *Al-Fitna*. Translated by Khalīl Aḥmad Khalīl. 4th reprint. Beirut: Dār al-Ṭalīᶜa, 2000 [1991].
Djait, Hichem. *Al-Waḥy wa-l-Qur'ān wa-l-nubuwwa*. Beirut: Dār al-Ṭalīᶜa, 1999.
Djait, Hichem. *Masīrat Muḥammad fī al-Madīna wa-intiṣār al-Islām*. Beirut: Dār al-Ṭalīᶜa, 2019.
Djait, Hichem. *Tārīkhiyyat al-daᶜwa al-Muḥammadiyya fī Makka*. Beirut: Dār al-Ṭalīᶜa, 2007.
Donner, Fred McGraw. "From Believers to Muslims: Confessional Self-Identity in the Early Islamic Community." *Al-Abḥāth* 50–51 (2002–2003): 9–53.
Donner, Fred McGraw, ed. *The Expansion of the Early Islamic State*, Formation of the Classical Islamic World 5. Aldershot: Ashgate, 2008.
Donner, Fred McGraw. *Muhammad and the Believers: At the Origins of Islam*. Cambridge, MA: The Belknap Press of Harvard University Press, 2010.
Donner, Fred McGraw. *Narratives of Islamic Origins: The Beginnings of Islamic Historical Writing*. Princeton, NJ: Darwin Press, 1998.
Donner, Fred McGraw. "Periodization as a Tool of the Historian with Special Reference to Islamic History." *Der Islam* 91, no. 1 (2014): 20–36.
Donner, Fred McGraw. "Review of *Parable and Politics in Early Islamic History: The Rāshidūn Caliphs* by Tayeb el-Hibri." *International Journal of Middle East Studies* 43, no. 3 (August 2011): 570–571.
Donner, Fred M. "Review of Robert Hoyland's In God's Path: The Arab Conquests and the Creation of an Islamic Empire." *Al-ᶜUṣūr al-Wusṭā* 23 (2015): 134–140.
Donner, Fred McGraw. "Talking about Islam's Origins." *Bulletin of SOAS* 81, no. 1 (2018): 1–23.
Donner, Fred McGraw. "Umayyad Efforts at Legitimation: The Umayyads' Silent Heritage." In *Umayyad Legacies*. Edited by Antoine Borrut and Paul M. Cobb, 187–211. Leiden: Brill, 2010.

Drijvers, Jan Willem. "Heraclius and the Restitutio Crucis: Notes on Symbolism and Ideology." In *The Reign of Heraclius (610–641): Crisis and Confrontation*. Edited by Gerrit J. Reinink and Bernard H. Stolte, 175–190. Leuven: Peeters, 2002.

Dunlop, Douglas Morton. "Some Remarks on Weil's History of the Caliphs." In *Historians of the Middle East*. Edited by Bernard Lewis and P. M. Holt, 326–327. London: Oxford University Press, 1962.

Dūrī, ᶜAbd al-ᶜAzīz al-. *Al-Judhūr al-tārīkhiyya li-l-shuᶜūbiyya*. Beirut: Dār al-ṭalīᶜa li-l-ṭibāᶜa wa-l-nashr, 1983 [1962].

Dūrī, ᶜAbd al-ᶜAzīz al-. *Al-ᶜAṣr al-ᶜAbbāsī al-awwal: Dirāsa fī al-tārīkh al-siyāsī wa-l-idārī wa-l-mālī*. Beirut: Dār al-ṭalīᶜa li-l-ṭibāᶜa wa-l-nashr, 1997 [1945].

Dūrī, ᶜAbd al-ᶜAzīz al-. *Baḥth fī nash'at ᶜilm al-ta'rīkh ᶜind al-ᶜArab*. Beirut: al-Maṭbaᶜa al-kāthūlīkiyya, 1960.

Dūrī, ᶜAbd al-ᶜAzīz al-. *The Rise of Historical Writing among the Arabs*. Translated by Lawrence I. Conrad. Princeton, NJ: Princeton University Press, 1983.

Eger, A. Asa. *The Islamic-Byzantine Frontier: Interaction and Exchange among Muslim and Christian Communities*. London; New York: I.B. Tauris, 2015.

El Cheikh, Nadia Maria. *Women, Islam, and Abbasid Identity*. Cambridge, MA: Harvard University Press, 2015.

Enayat, Hamid. *Modern Islamic Political Thought*. London: I. B. Tauris, 2005 [1982].

Engberts, Christiaan. "Orientalists at War: Personae and Partiality at the Outbreak of the First World War." In *Scholarly Personae in the History of Orientalism*. Edited by Christiaan Engberts and Herman Paul, 172–192. Leiden: Brill, 2019.

Engberts, Christiaan. *Scholarly Virtues in Nineteenth-Century Sciences and Humanities: Loyalty and Independence Entangled*. London: Palgrave Macmillan, 2021.

Eph'al, Israel. *The Ancient Arabs: Nomads on the Borders of the Fertile Crescent, 9th–5th Centuries B.C.* Leiden: Brill, 1982.

Esack, Farid. "In Search of Progressive Islam beyond 9/11." In *Progressive Muslims: On Justice, Gender and Pluralism*. Edited by Omid Safi, 78–97. Oxford: Oneworld Publications, 2003.

Fadel, Mohammad. "Is Historicism a Viable Strategy for Islamic Law Reform? The Case of 'Never Shall a Folk Prosper Who Have Appointed a Woman to Rule Them.'" *Islamic Law and Society* 18 (2011): 131–76.

Faizer, Rizwi Shuhadha. "Ibn Isḥāq and al-Wāqidī Revisited: A Case Study of Muḥammad and the Jews in Biographical Literature." PhD dissertation, McGill University, 1995.

Faizer, Rizwi Shuhadha. "Muhammad and the Medinan Jews: A Comparison of the Texts of Ibn Isḥāq's *Kitāb Sīrat Rasūl Allāh* with al-Wāqidī's *Kitāb al-Maghāzī*." *International Journal of Middle East Studies* 28, no. 4 (1996): 463–489.

Fentress, James, and Chris Wickham. *Social Memory: New Perspectives on the Past*. Cambridge: Blackwell, 1992.

Firestone, Reuven. "Apes and the Sabbath Problem." In *The Festschrift Darkhei Noam: The Jews of Arab Lands*. Edited by Carsten Schapkow, Shmuel Shepkaru and Alan T. Levenson, 26–48. Leiden: Brill, 2015.

Firestone, Reuven. "Muhammad, the Jews, and the Composition of the Qur'an: Sacred History and Counter-History." *Religions* 10, no. 63 (2019): 1–16.

Firestone, Reuven. "The Prophet Muhammad in Pre-modern Jewish Literatures." In *The Image of the Prophet between Ideal and Ideology*. Edited by Christiane J. Gruber and Avinoam Shalem, 27–44. Berlin: De Gruyter, 2013.

Foot, Sarah, and Chase F. Robinson, eds. *The Oxford History of Historical Writing*, Vol. 2. Oxford: Oxford University Press, 2012.

Friedmann, Yohanan. *Tolerance and Coercion in Islam: Interfaith Relations in the Muslim Tradition*. Cambridge: Cambridge University Press, 2003.
Fück, Johann. *Die arabische Studien in Europa bis in den Anfang des 20. Jahrhunderts*. Leipzig: Otto Harrassowitz, 1955.
Gabriel, Richard A. *Muhammad: Islam's First Great General*. Norman: University of Oklahoma Press, 2014.
Garsoïan, Nina G., Thomas F. Matthews, and Robert W. Thomson, eds. *East of Byzantium: Syria and Armenia in the Formative Period*. Washington, DC: Dumbarton Oaks, 1982.
Gaudefroy-Demombynes, M. *Le pèlerinage à la Mekke: Étude d'histoire religieuse*. Paris: n.p., 1923.
Gaudefroy-Demombynes, Maurice. *Muslim Institutions*. Translated by John P. Macgregor. London: George Allen & Unwin, 1955.
Geary, Patrick J. *Phantoms of Remembrance: Memory and Oblivion at the End of the First Millennium*. Princeton, NJ: Princeton University Press, 1994.
Geiger, Abraham. *Judaism and Islam*. Translated by F. M. Young. Edinburgh: Williams and Norgate, 1896.
Genequand, Denis, and Christian Julien Robin, eds. *Les Jafnides: des rois arabes au service de Byzance: VIe siècle de l'ère chrétienne: actes du colloque de Paris, 24–25 novembre 2008*. Paris: De Boccard, 2015.
Genette, Gérard. *Narrative Discourse: An Essay in Method*. Translated by Jane E. Lewin. Ithaca, NY: Cornell University Press, 1980.
Gibb, H. A. R. *Modern Trends in Islam*. Chicago: University of Chicago Press, 1947.
Gibb, H. A. R. *Mohammedanism: An Historical Survey*. New York: Oxford University Press, 1962 [1949].
Gibb, Hamilton A. R. *Studies on the Civilization of Islam*. Edited by Stanford J. Shaw and William R. Polk. Princeton, NJ: Princeton University Press, 1982 [1962].
Gilliot, Claude. *Exégèse, langue et théologie en Islam: L'exégèse coranique de Tabari (M. 311/923)*. Paris: Vrin, 1990.
Gilliot, Claude. "Récit, mythe et histoire chez Ṭabarī. Une vision mythique de l'histoire universelle." *MIDEO*, no. 21 (1993): 277–289.
Goitein, Shelomo Dov. "A Plea for the Periodization of Islamic History." *Journal of the American Oriental Society* 88, no. 2 (1968): 224–228.
Goitein, Shelomo Dov. *Studies in Islamic History and Institutions*. Leiden: Brill, 2010.
Goldziher, Ignác. *Muslim Studies*. 2 vols. Edited and translated by S. M. Stern. London: George Allen and Unwin, 1967–1971.
Gordon, Matthew S., and Kathryn A. Hain, eds. *Concubines and Courtesans: Women and Slavery in Islamic History*. Oxford: Oxford University Press, 2017.
Görke, Andreas. "Between History and Exegesis: The Origins and Transformation of the Story of Muḥammad and Zaynab bt Ǧaḥš." *Arabica* 65, no. 1–2 (2018): 31–63.
Görke, Andreas. "The Relationship between *Maghāzī* and *Ḥadīth* in Early Islamic Scholarship." *Bulletin of the School of Oriental and African Studies* 74, no. 2 (2011): 171–185.
Görke, Andreas, and Gregor Schoeler. "Reconstructing the Earliest *Sīra* Texts: The *Higra* in the Corpus of ᶜUrwa b. al-Zubayr." *Der Islam* 82 (2005): 209–220.
Görke, Andreas, Harald Motzki, Gregor Schoeler, and Bertram Thompson. "First-Century Sources for the Life of Muhammad: A Debate." *Der Islam* 89, no. 1 (2012): 2–59.
Griffith, Sidney H. "The Qur'an in Arab Christian Texts: The Development of an Apologetical Argument: Abū Qurrah in the Maǧlis of al-Ma'mūn." *Parole de l'Orient* 24 (1999): 203–233.
Gruber, Christiane J., and Avinoam Shalem, eds. *The Image of the Prophet between Ideal and Ideology*. Berlin: De Gruyter, 2013.

Guillaume, Alfred. "A Note on the Sīra of Ibn Isḥāq." *Bulletin of the School of Oriental and African Studies* 18, no. 1 (1956): 1–4.

Ḥā'irī, Muḥammad Ḥusayn al-Aᶜlamī, al-. *Dā'irat al-maᶜārif al-shīᶜīyya al-ᶜāmma*. 18 vols. Beirut: Mu'assasat al-aᶜlamī li-l-maṭbūᶜāt, 1413/1993.

Ḥabīb, Yāsir al-. *Al-Fāḥisha: al-wajh al-ākhar li-ᶜĀ'isha*. London: Khuddam al-Mahdi Organisation, 2010.

Hagen, Gottfried. "The Imagined and the Historical Muhammad." *Journal of the American Oriental Society* 129, no. 1 (January–March 2009): 97–111.

Ḥakamī, Ḥāfiẓ ibn Muḥammad ibn ᶜAbdullāh al-. *Marwiyyāt ghazwat al-Ḥudaybiyya: Jamᶜ wa-takhrīj wa-dirāsa*. Medina: Maṭābiᶜ al-jāmiᶜa al-Islāmiyya, 1406/1986.

Ḥākim al-Nīsābūrī al-. *Al-Mustadrak ᶜalā al-Ṣaḥīḥayn*. 4 vols. Edited by Muṣṭafā ᶜAbd al-Qādir ᶜAṭā. Beirut: Dār al-kutub al-ᶜilmiyya, 1411/1990.

Hakim, Avraham. "Muḥammad's Authority and Leadership Reestablished: The Prophet and ᶜUmar ibn al-Khaṭṭāb." *Revue de l'histoire des religions* 226, no. 2 (2009): 181–200.

Halbwachs, Maurice. *On Collective Memory*. Translated by Lewis A. Coser. Chicago: University of Chicago Press, 1992.

Haldon, John F. *Byzantium in the Seventh Century: The Transformation of a Culture*. Cambridge: Cambridge University Press, 1997 [1990].

Halm, Heinz. *Shiᶜism*. Translated by Janet Watson and Marian Hill. New York: Columbia University Press, 2004.

Ḥamad, Muḥammad ᶜAbd al-Ḥamīd al-. *Al-Zandaqa wa-l-zanādiqa: ta'rīkh wa-fikr*. Damascus: Dār al-ṭalīᶜa al-jadīda, 1999.

Hamidullah, Muhammad. *The Battlefields of the Prophet Muhammad with Maps, Illustrations and Sketches: A Contribution to Muslim Military History*. New Delhi: Nusrat Ali Nasri for Kitab Bhavan, 1992 [1983].

Ḥammāmī, Nādir. *Islām al-fuqahā'*. Beirut: Dār al-ṭalīᶜa li-l-nashr, 2006.

Ḥammāmī, Nādir. *Ṣūrat al-ṣaḥābī fī kutub al-ḥadīth*. Casablanca: al-Markaz al-thaqāfī al-ᶜArabī, 2014.

Ḥanafī, Ḥasan. *Al-Turāth wa-l-tajdīd: Mawqifunā min al-turāth al-qadīm*. 4th edition. Cairo: al-Mu'assassa al-jāmiᶜiyya, 1412/1992.

Ḥanafī, Ḥasan. *Al-Yamīn wa-l-yasār fī al-fikr al-dīnī*. Damascus: Dār ᶜAlā' al-Dīn, 1996.

Ḥanafī, Ḥasan. *Min al-naql ilā al-ᶜaql*. 3 vols. Cairo: al-Hay'a al-Miṣriyya al-ᶜāmma li-lkitāb, 2013.

Hardy, Peter. *The Muslims of British India*. Cambridge: Cambridge University Press, 1972.

Harris, Jonathan. *The Lost World of Byzantium*. New Haven, CT: Yale University Press, 2015.

Hartung, Jan-Peter. *A System of Life: Mawdūdī and the Ideologisation of Islam*. Oxford: Oxford University Press, 2014.

Hashmi, Sohail H., ed. *Just Wars, Holy Wars, and Jihads: Christian, Jewish, and Muslim Encounters and Exchanges*. Oxford: Oxford University Press, 2012.

Hawting, Gerald R., ed. *The Development of Islamic Ritual*. London: Routledge, 2017.

Hawting, G. R. *The First Dynasty of Islam: The Umayyad Caliphate AD 661–750*. New York: Routledge, 2002.

Hawting, Gerald R. "The Origins of the Muslim Sanctuary at Mecca." In *Studies on the First Century of Islamic Society*. Edited by G. H. A. Juynboll, 23–48. Carbondale: Southern Illinois University Press, 1982.

Hawting, G. R. "Review of *The Eye of the Beholder: The Life of Muḥammad as Viewed by the Early Muslims: A Textual Analysis* by Uri Rubin." *Journal of the Royal Asiatic Society*, 3rd series, 7, no. 1 (April 1997): 126–129.

Hawting, G. R. "Review of Sayf ibn ᶜUmar's *Kitāb al-Ridda wa'l-Futūḥ and Kitāb al-Jamal wa-masīr ᶜĀ'isha wa-ᶜAlī*. A Facsimile Edition of the Fragments Preserved in the University Library of Imam Muhammad Ibn Saᶜūd Islamic University in Riyadh, Saudi Arabia." *Bulletin of the School of Oriental and African Studies* (University of London) 60, no. 3 (1997): 546–547.

Haykal, Muḥammad Ḥusayn. *Al-Fārūq ᶜUmar*. Cairo: Maktabat al-nahḍa, 1963.

Haykal, Muḥammad Ḥusayn. *Al-Ṣiddīq Abū Bakr*. Cairo: al-Jihāz al-markazī li-l-kutub al-jāmiᶜiyya, 1402/1982. Reprint.

Haykal, Muḥammad Ḥusayn. *Fī manzil al-waḥy*. Cairo: Dār al-maᶜārif, 1986. Reprint.

Haykal, Muḥammad Ḥusayn. *Ḥayāt Muḥammad*. Cairo: Dār al-maᶜārif, 1977. Reprint.

Haykal, Muḥammad Ḥusayn. *The Life of Muhammad*. Oak Brook: American Trust Publications, 1976.

Hibri, Tayeb el-. *Parable and Politics in Early Islamic History: The Rashidun Caliphs*. New York: Columbia University Press, 2010.

Hibri, Tayeb el-. "The Redemption of Umayyad Memory by the ᶜAbbāsids." *Journal of Near Eastern Studies* 61, no. 4 (2002): 241–265.

Hibri, Tayeb el-. *Reinterpreting Islamic Historiography: Hārūn al-Rashīd and the Narrative of the ᶜAbbāsid Caliphate*. Cambridge: Cambridge University Press, 1999.

Hillenbrand, Carole. "William Montgomery Watt: The Man and the Scholar." In *Life and Work of W. Montgomery Watt*. Edited by Carole Hillenbrand, 3–14. Edinburgh: Edinburgh University Press, 2018.

Hinds, Martin. "Sayf ibn ᶜUmar's Sources on Arabia." In *Sources for the History of Arabia: Proceedings of the First International Symposium on Studies in the History of Arabia*. Volume 2. Edited by A. M. Abdalla et al., 3–16. Riyadh: University of Riyadh Press, 1979.

Hinds, Martin. *Studies in Early Islamic History*. Edited by Jere L. Bacharach, Lawrence I. Conrad, and Patricia Crone. Princeton, NJ: Darwin Press, 1996.

Hirschfeld, Hartwig. "Historical and Legendary Controversies between Mohammed and the Rabbis." *Jewish Quarterly Review* 10, no. 1 (1897): 100–116.

Hirschler, Konrad. *The Written Word in the Medieval Arabic Lands: A Social and Cultural History of Reading Practices*. Edinburgh: Edinburgh University Press, 2013.

Hitti, Philip K. *History of Syria: Including Lebanon and Palestine*. Piscataway, NJ: Gorgias Press, 2004.

Hitti, Philip K. *Syria, a Short History; Being a Condensation of the Author's "History of Syria, Including Lebanon and Palestine."* New York: Macmillan, 1959.

Hodgson, Marshall G. S. "How Did the Early Shīᶜa become Sectarian?" *Journal of the American Oriental Society* 75, no. 1 (1955): 1–13.

Hodgson, Marshall G. S. *The Venture of Islam: Conscience and History in a World Civilization*. 3 vols. Chicago: University of Chicago Press, 1975.

Horovitz, Josef. *The Earliest Biographies of the Prophet and Their Authors*. Edited by Lawrence I. Conrad. Princeton, NJ: Darwin Press, 2002.

Howard-Johnston, James. *Witnesses to a World Crisis: Historians and Histories of the Middle East in the Seventh Century*. Oxford: Oxford University Press, 2011.

Hoyland, Robert G. *Arabia and the Arabs: From the Bronze Age to the Coming of Islam*. London: Routledge, 2001.

Hoyland, Robert G. "Arabic, Syriac and Greek Historiography in the First ᶜAbbāsid Century: An Inquiry into Inter-cultural Traffic." *ARAM* 3, no. 1–2 (1991): 211–233.

Hoyland, Robert. "The Earliest Christian Writings on Muḥammad: An Appraisal." In *The Biography of Muḥammad*. Edited by Harald Motzki, 276–295. Leiden: Brill, 2000.

Hoyland, Robert G. *In God's Path: The Arab Conquests and the Creation of an Islamic Empire*. Ancient Warfare and Civilization. Oxford: Oxford University Press, 2015.

Hoyland, Robert G. "History, Fiction and Authorship in the First Centuries of Islam." In *Writing and Representation in Medieval Islam: Muslim Horizons*. Routledge Studies in Middle Eastern Literatures. Edited by Julia Bray, 16–46. New York: Routledge, 2006.

Hoyland, Robert. "The Jews of the Hijaz and Their Inscriptions." In *New Perspectives on the Qur'ān: The Qur'ān in Its Historical Context 2*. Edited by Gabriel S. Reynolds, 91–116. London: Routledge, 2011.

Hoyland, Robert G. "Reflections on the Identity of the Arabian Conquerors of the Seventh-Century Middle East." *Al-ᶜUṣūr al-Wusṭā* 25 (2017): 113–140.

Hoyland, Robert G. "Review of Fred Donner's *Muhammad and the Believers*." *International Journal of Middle East Studies* 44, no. 3 (2012): 573–576.

Hoyland, Robert G. *Seeing Islam as Others Saw It: A Survey and Evaluation of Christian, Jewish, and Zoroastrian Writings on Early Islam*. Studies in Late Antiquity and Early Islam 13. Princeton, NJ: Darwin Press, 1997.

Huart, Clement. *A History of Arabic Literature*. New York: D. Appleton and Company, 1903.

Hughes, Aaron W. *Muslim Identities: An Introduction to Islam*. New York: Columbia University Press, 2013.

Humphreys, R. Stephen. *Islamic History: A Framework for Inquiry*. Princeton, NJ: Princeton University Press, 1991.

Humphreys, R. Stephen. *Muᶜawiya ibn Abi Sufyan: The Savior of the Caliphate*. Oxford: Oneworld Publications, 2012.

Hurgronje, Christiaan Snouck. *Mekka*. La Haye: Martinus Nijhoff, 1888.

Hurgronje, Christiaan Snouck. *Mohammedanism: Lectures on Its Origin, Its Religious and Political Growth, and Its Present State. American Lectures on the History of Religions*. New York: Putnam's Sons, 1916.

Hurvitz, Nimrod. "Aḥmad ibn Ḥanbal and the Formation of Islamic Orthodoxy." PhD dissertation, Princeton University, 1994.

Hurvitz, Nimrod. *The Formation of Ḥanbalism*. Culture and Civilisation in the Middle East. London: Routledge Curzon, 2002.

Ḥusayn, Abū Lubāba. *Al-Sunna al-nabawiyya waḥy*. Medina: Dār al-malik Fahd, n.d.

Ḥusayn, Abū Lubāba. *Mawqif al-muᶜtazila min al-sunna al-nabawiyya*. Riyadh: Dār al-liwā' li-l-nashr wa-l-tawzīᶜ, 1407/1987.

Ḥusayn, Ṭāhā. *ᶜAlā hāmish al-sīra*. 2 vols. Cairo: Dār al-maᶜārif, n.d. Reprint.

Ḥusayn, Ṭāhā. *Al-Shaykhān*, 3rd edition. Cairo: Dār al-maᶜārif, 1966.

Ḥusaynī, Idrīs al-. *Al-Khilāfa al-mughtaṣaba*. Casablanca: Dār al-khalīj li-l-ṭibāᶜa wa-l-nashr, 1416/1996.

Hutton, Patrick H. *History as an Art of Memory*. Hanover, NH: University Press of New England, 1993.

Ibn Warraq, ed. *The Quest for the Historical Muhammad*. Amherst, NY: Prometheus Books, 2000.

Ibrahim, Ayman S. *A Concise Guide to Islam: Defining Key Concepts and Terms*. Grand Rapids: Baker Academic, 2023.

Ibrahim, Ayman S. *A Concise Guide to the Life of Muhammad: Answering Thirty Key Questions*. Grand Rapids: Baker Academic, 2022.

Ibrahim, Ayman S. *A Concise Guide to the Quran: Answering Thirty Critical Questions*. Grand Rapids: Baker Academic, 2020.

Ibrahim, Ayman S. *Conversion to Islam: Competing Themes in Early Islamic Historiography*. New York: Oxford University Press, 2021.

Ibrahim, Ayman S., ed. *Medieval Encounters: Arabic-Speaking Christians and Islam*. Piscataway, NJ: Gorgias, 2022.

Ibrahim, Ayman S. "Review of Juan Cole's *Muhammad: Prophet of Peace Amid the Clash of Empires*." *Review of Qur'ānic Research* 5, no. 2 (2019): 1–18.

Ibrahim, Ayman S. *The Stated Motivations for the Early Islamic Expansion (622–641): A Critical Revision of Muslims' Traditional Portrayal of the Arab Raids and Conquests*. Crosscurrents: New Studies on the Middle East. Series editors, J. Kevin Lacey and Sari Nusseibeh. New York: Peter Lang, 2018.

Ibrahim, Ayman S., and Clint Hackenburg. *In Search of the True Religion: Monk Jurjī and Muslim Jurists Debating Faith and Practice*. Piscataway, NJ: Gorgias, 2022.

Innes, Matthew. "Memory, Orality and Literacy in an Early Medieval Society." *Past & Present*, no. 158 (1998): 3–36.

Jābrī, Muḥammad ᶜĀbid al-. *Fikr Ibn Khaldūn: al-ᶜAṣabiyya wa-l-dawla*. Beirut: Markaz dirāsāt al-wiḥda al-ᶜArabiyya, 1994 [1971].

Jābrī, Muḥammad ᶜĀbid al-. *Mawāqif*. Morocco: Published Interview, 2003.

Jābrī, Muḥammad ᶜĀbid al-. *Naḥn wa-l-turāth*. Beirut: al-Markaz al-thaqāfī al-ᶜArabī, 1993 [1980].

Jackson, Roy. *Mawlana Mawdudi and Political Islam: Authority and the Islamic State*. New York: Taylor & Francis, 2010.

Jamīl, Muḥammad ibn Fāris al-. *Al-Nabī wa-yahūd al-madīna*. Riyadh: Markaz al-malik Fayṣal, 1422/2002.

Jamīlī, al-Sayyid al-. *Ghazawāt al-Nabī*. Beirut: Dār al-hilāl, 1416/1996.

Jamīlī, al-Sayyid al-. *Nisā' al-nabī*. Beirut: Dār al-hilāl, 1416/1996.

Jarrar, Maher. "Exegetical Designs of the Sīra: Tafsīr and Sīra." In *The Oxford Handbook of Qur'anic Studies*. Edited by M. A. S. Abdel Haleem and Mustafa Shah, 620–633. Oxford: Oxford University Press, 2020.

Johnston-Bloom, Ruchama. "Gustav Weil's Koranforschung and the Transnational Circulation of Ideas: The Shaping of Muhammad as Reformer." In *Modern Jewish Scholarship on Islam in Context: Rationality, European Borders, and the Search for Belonging*. Edited by Ottfried Fraisse, 95–120. Berlin: De Gruyter, 2018.

Johnston-Bloom, Ruchama. "Jews, Muslims, and Bildung: The German-Jewish Orientalist Gustav Weil in Egypt." *Religion Compass* 8 (2014): 49–59.

Johnston-Bloom, Ruchama. "Oriental Studies and Jewish Questions: German-Jewish Encounters with Muhammad, the Qur'an, and Islamic Modernities." PhD dissertation, University of Chicago, 2013.

Judd, Steven. *Religious Scholars and the Umayyads: Piety-Minded Supporters of the Marwānid Caliphate*. New York: Routledge, 2013.

Juynboll, G. H. A. *Muslim Tradition: Studies in Chronology, Provenance and Authorship of Early Ḥadīth*. Cambridge: Cambridge University Press, 1985.

Kaegi, Walter Emil. *Byzantium and the Early Islamic Conquests*. Cambridge: Cambridge University Press, 1992.

Kaegi, Walter E. *Heraclius, Emperor of Byzantium*. Cambridge: Cambridge University Press, 2003.
Kaegi, Walter Emil. "Initial Byzantine Reactions to the Arab Conquest." *Church History* 38, no. 2 (1969): 139–149.
Kaegi, Walter Emil. *Muslim Expansion and Byzantine Collapse in North Africa*. Cambridge: Cambridge University Press, 2010.
Kaḥḥāla, ᶜUmar Riḍā. *Muᶜjam al-mu'alifīn*. 13 vols. Beirut: Dār iḥyā' al-turāth al-ᶜArabī, n.d.
Kaḥḥāla, ᶜUmar Riḍā. *Muᶜjam qabā'il al-ᶜArab*. 5 vols. Beirut: Mu'assasat al-risāla, 1414/1994.
Kanᶜān, Jurjī. *Muḥammad wa-l-yahūdiyya*. Beirut: Baysān li-l-nashr, 1999.
Keaney, Heather. "Confronting the Caliph: ᶜUthmān b. ᶜAffān in Three ᶜAbbāsid Chronicles." *Studia Islamica*, new series, no. 1 (2011): 37–65.
Keaney, Heather. "Remembering Rebellion: ᶜUthmān b. ᶜAffān in Medieval Islamic Historiography." PhD dissertation, University of California, 2003.
Kennedy, Hugh. *The Armies of the Caliphs: Military and Society in the Early Islamic State*. New York: Routledge, 2013.
Kennedy, Hugh N. *The Byzantine and Early Islamic Near East*. Aldershot, UK: Ashgate, 2006.
Kennedy, Hugh. *Caliphate: The History of an Idea*. New York: New Books, 2016.
Kennedy, Hugh. *The Great Arab Conquests: How the Spread of Islam Changed the World We Live In*. Philadelphia: Da Capo, 2007.
Kennedy, Hugh. *The Prophet and the Age of the Caliphates: The Islamic Near East from the Sixth to the Eleventh Century*. Harlow: Longman, 1986. Reprint, 2004.
Kerr, David A. "Muir, William." In *Biographical Dictionary of Christian Missions*. Edited by Gerald H. Anderson, 478–479. New York: Macmillan Reference USA, 1998.
Keshk, Khaled. "The Depiction of Muᶜāwiya in the Early Islamic Sources." PhD dissertation, University of Chicago, 2002.
Keshk, Khaled. *The Historian's Muᶜāwiya: The Depiction of Muᶜāwiya in the Early Islamic Sources*. Germany: VDM Verlag Dr. Müller, 2008.
Keshk, Khaled. "When Did Muᶜāwiya Become Caliph?" *Journal of Near Eastern Studies* 69, no. 1 (April 2010): 31–42.
Khalek, Nancy. "From Byzantium to Early Islam. Studies on Damascus in the Umayyad Era." PhD dissertation, Princeton University, 2006.
Khalek, Nancy. *Damascus after the Muslim Conquest: Text and Image in Early Islam*. Oxford: Oxford University Press, 2011.
Khalidi, Omar. "Muslim Debates on Jihad in British India: The Writings of Chiragh ᶜAli and Abu al-Aᶜla Mawdudi." In *Just Wars, Holy Wars, and Jihads: Christian, Jewish, and Muslim Encounters and Exchanges*. Edited by Sohail Hashmi, 305–323. New York: Oxford University Press, 2012.
Khalidi, Tarif. *Arabic Historical Thought in the Classical Period*. Cambridge: Cambridge University Press, 1994.
Khalidi, Tarif. *Images of Muhammad: Narratives of the Prophet in Islam across the Centuries*. New York: Crown Publishing Group, 2009.
Khalidi, Tarif. *Islamic Historiography: The Histories of Masᶜūdī*. New York: SUNY Press, 1975.
Khaṭṭāb, Maḥmūd Shīt. *Al-Rasūl al-qā'id*. Beirut: Dar al-fikr, 1422/2002.
Khuḍarī, Muḥammad al-. *Al-Dawla al-ᶜAbbāsiyya*. Edited by Muḥammad al-ᶜUthmānī. Beirut: Dār al-qalam, 1406/1986 [1938].

Khuḍarī, Muḥammad al-. *Al-Dawla al-umawiyya*. Edited by Muḥammad al-ᶜUthmānī. Beirut: Dār al-qalam, 1406/1986 [1938].

Khū'ī, al-Sayyid Abū al-Qāsim al-Mūsawī al-. *The Prolegomena to the Qur'an*. Translated with an introduction by Abdulaziz A. Sachedina. New York: Oxford University Press, 1998.

Kindt, Tom, and Hans-Harald Müller, eds. *What Is Narratology?: Questions and Answers regarding the Status of a Theory*. Berlin: Walter de Gruyter, 2003.

Kister, M. J. "Land Property and Jihād: A Discussion of Some Early Traditions." *Journal of the Economic and Social History of the Orient* 34, no. 3 (1991): 270–311.

Kister, M. J. "The Massacre of the Banū Qurayẓa: A Re-examination of a Tradition." *Jerusalem Studies in Arabic and Islam* 8 (1986): 61–96.

Kister, M. J. "Mecca and Tamīm (Aspects of their Relations)." *Journal of the Economic and Social History of the Orient* 8 (1965): 113–163.

Kohlberg, Etan. "*Barā'a* in Shīᶜī Doctrine." *Jerusalem Studies in Arabic and Islam* 7 (1986): 139–175.

Kohlberg, Etan. *In Praise of the Few: Studies in Shiᶜi Thought and History*. Leiden: Brill, 2020.

Kohlberg, Etan. "The Term '*Rāfiḍa*' in Imami Shīᶜī Usage." *Journal of the American Oriental Society* 99 (1979): 1–9.

Krämer, Gudrun, Denis Matringe, John Nawas, et al., eds. *Encyclopædia of Islam*, 3rd edition. Leiden: Brill, 2007–.

Kūrānī al-ᶜĀmilī, ᶜAlī al-. *Ajwibat masā'il jaysh al-ṣaḥāba*. Beirut: Dār al-sīra, 1423/2002.

Lambton, A. K. S. "Obituary: Sir Hamilton Alexander Roskeen Gibb." *Bulletin of the School of Oriental and African Studies* (University of London) 35, no. 2 (1972): 338–345.

Lammens, Henri. "The Age of Muhammad and the Chronology of the Sira." In *The Quest for the Historical Muḥammad*. Edited by Ibn Warraq, 188–217. Amherst, NY: Prometheus Books, 2000.

Lammens, Henri. *Islam: Beliefs and Institutions*. Translated by Sir E. Denison Ross. London: Taylor & Francis, 2013 [1926].

Lammens, Henri. "L'Age de Mahomet et la chronologie de la sīra." *Journal Asiatique* 17 (1911): 209–250.

Lammens, Henri. *Le berceau de l'Islam: l'Arabie occidentale à la veille de l'Hégire*. Rome: Sumptibus Pontificii Instituti Biblici, 1914.

Lammens, Henri. "Qoran et tradition: Comment fut composé la vie de Mahomet." *Recherches de Science Religieuse* 1 (1910): 25–51.

Landau-Tasseron, Ella. "Processes of Redaction: The Case of the Tamīmite Delegation to the Prophet Muḥammad." *Bulletin of the School of Oriental and African Studies* 49, no. 2 (1986): 253–270.

Landau-Tasseron, Ella. "On the Reconstruction of Lost Sources." *Al-Qanṭara* 25 (2004): 45–91.

Landau-Tasseron, Ella. "Sayf Ibn ᶜUmar in Medieval and Modern Scholarship." *Der Islam* 67, no. 1 (1990): 1–26.

Lane, Edward William. *An Arabic-English Lexicon: Derived from the Best and the Most Copious Eastern Sources*. 8 vols. London: Williams and Norgate, 1863–1893.

Lang, Katherine H. "*Awā'il* in Early Arabic Historiography: Beginnings and Identity in the Middle ᶜAbbāsid Empire." PhD dissertation, University of Chicago, 1997.

Lapidus, Ira M. *A History of Islamic Societies*. Cambridge: Cambridge University Press, 2014.

Lassner, Jacob. *Islamic Revolution and Historical Memory: An Inquiry into the Art of ᶜAbbāsid Apologetics*. Ann Arbor: American Oriental Society, 1986.
Lassner, Jacob. *Medieval Jerusalem: Forging an Islamic City in Spaces Sacred to Christians and Jews*. Ann Arbor: University of Michigan Press, 2017.
Lassner, Jacob. *The Middle East Remembered: Forged Identities, Competing Narratives, Contested Spaces*. Ann Arbor: University of Michigan Press, 2000.
Lassner, Jacob. *The Shaping of ᶜAbbāsid Rule*. Princeton, NJ: Princeton University Press, 2017.
Lecker, Michael. *Dustūr al-Madīnah*. Princeton, NJ: Darwin Press, 2004.
Lecker, Michael. "Idol Worship in Pre-Islamic Medina (Yathrib)." *Le Museon* 106 (1993): 331–346.
Lecker, Michael. *Jews and Arabs in Pre- and Early Islamic Arabia*. Aldershot, UK: Ashgate, 1998.
Lecker, Michael. *Muslims, Jews and Pagans: Studies on Early Islamic Medina*. Leiden: Brill, 1995.
Lecker, Michael. "Notes about Censorship and Self-Censorship in the Biography of the Prophet Muḥammad." *Al-Qanṭara* 35, no. 1 (2014): 233–254.
Lecker, Michael. "A Review of *The Expeditions: An Early Biography of Muḥammad* by Maᶜmar Ibn Rāshid, edited and translated by Sean W. Anthony." *Journal of the American Oriental Society* 135, no. 4 (2015): 854–857.
Lecker, Michael. "Wāqidī's Account on the Status of the Jews of Medina: A Study of a Combined Report." *Journal of Near Eastern Studies* 54, no. 1 (1995): 15–32.
Leveen, Jacob. "Mohammed and His Jewish Companions." *Jewish Quarterly Review* 16, no. 4 (1926): 399–406.
Levy, Reuben. *The Social Structure of Islam*. New York: Cambridge University Press, 1971.
Levy-Rubin, Milka. *Non-Muslims in the Early Islamic Empire: From Surrender to Coexistence*. Cambridge: Cambridge University Press, 2011.
Lewis, Bernard. *The Jews of Islam*. London: Routledge, 2010.
Lewis, Bernard. *Race and Color in Islam*. New York: Harper & Row, 1971.
Lewis, Bernard. *Race and Slavery in the Middle East: An Historical Enquiry*. Oxford: Oxford University Press, 1990.
Lindstedt, Ilkka. "Al-Madā'inī and the Narratives of the ᶜAbbāsid Dawla." *Studia Orientalia Electronica* 5 (2017): 65–150.
Lings, Martin. *Muhammad: His Life Based on the Earliest Sources*. Rochester, NY: Inner Traditions City, 1987.
Lowry, Joseph Edmund. *Early Islamic Legal Theory: The* Risāla *of Muḥammad Ibn Idrīs Al-Shāfiᶜī*. Leiden: Brill, 2007.
Lucas, Scott C. *Constructive Critics,* Ḥadīth *Literature, and the Articulation of Sunnī Islam: The Legacy of the Generation of Ibn Saᶜd, Ibn Maᶜīn, and Ibn Ḥanbal*. Leiden: Brill, 2004.
Lyall, C. J. "Sir William Muir." *The Journal of the Royal Asiatic Society of Great Britain and Ireland* 37 (October 1905): 875–879.
Madelung, Wilferd. *The Succession to Muhammad: A Study of the Early Caliphate*. Cambridge: Cambridge University Press, 1997.
Majlisī, Muḥammad Bāqir al-. *Biḥār al-anwār*. 110 vols. Edited by ᶜAbd al-Raḥīm al-Shīrāzī et al. Beirut: Dār iḥiyā' al-turāth, 1983.
Makdisi, George, ed. *Arabic and Islamic Studies in Honor of Hamilton A. R. Gibb*. Leiden: Brill, 1965.
Mango, Cyril. *Byzantium: The Empire of New Rome*. New York: Charles Scribner's Sons, 1980.

Margoliouth, David Samuel. *The Early Development of Mohammedanism*. London: C. Scribner's Sons, 1914.

Margoliouth, David Samuel. *Mohammed. What Did They Teach?* London: Blackie & Son, Limited, 1939.

Margoliouth, David Samuel. *Mohammedanism*. London, 1911.

Margoliouth, David Samuel. *Mohammed and the Rise of Islam*. New York: G. P. Putnam, 1905.

Margoliouth, David Samuel. "Muhammad." In *Encyclopedia of Religion and Ethics*. Edited by John A. Selbie, James Hastings, and Louis H. Gray, 8:871–880. New York: Charles Scribner's Sons, 1925.

Marsham, Andrew. *Rituals of Islamic Monarchy: Accession and Succession in the First Muslim Empire*. Edinburgh: Edinburgh University Press, 2009.

Martin, Richard C. "The Religious Foundations of War, Peace and Statecraft in Islam." In *Just War and Jihad: Historical and Theoretical Perspectives on War and Peace in Western and Islamic Traditions*. Edited by John Kelsay and James Turner Johnson, 91–119. New York: Greenwood Press, 1991.

Martin, Richard C., Mark R. Woodward, and Dwi S. Atmaja. *Defenders of Reason in Islam: Muʿtazilism from Medieval School to Modern Symbol*. Oxford: Oneworld Publications, 1997.

Martinez-Gros, Gabriel. *L'idéologie Omeyyade: La construction de la légitimité du califat de Cordoue (Xe–Xie Siècles)*. Madrid: Casa de Velázquez, 1992.

Mazuz, Haggai. "Jewish-Muslim Polemics." In *The Cambridge History of Judaism: Jews in the Medieval Islamic World*. Volume 5. Edited by Phillip I. Lieberman, 946–973. Cambridge: Cambridge University Press, 2021.

Mazuz, Haggai. *The Religious and Spiritual Life of the Jews of Medina*. Leiden: Brill, 2014.

McAuliffe, Jane Dammen, ed. *The Cambridge Companion to the Qur'ān*. Cambridge: Cambridge University Press, 2006.

McAuliffe, Jane Dammen, ed. *Encyclopaedia of the Qur'ān*. 6 vols. Leiden: Brill, 2001–2006.

McDowell, Bill. *Historical Research: A Guide for Writers of Dissertations, Theses, Articles and Books*. London: Routledge, 2013.

Meisami, Julie Scott, and Paul Starkey, eds. *Encyclopedia of Arabic Literature*. Volume 2. London: Routledge, 1998.

Melchert, Christopher. "Aḥmad Ibn Ḥanbal and the Qur'ān." *Journal of Qur'ānic Studies* 6, no. 2 (2004): 22–34.

Melchert, Christopher. *Aḥmad ibn Ḥanbal*. Makers of the Muslim World. Oxford: Oneworld Publications, 2006.

Melchert, Christopher. *The Formation of the Sunnī Schools of Law*. Studies in Islamic Law and Society 4. Leiden: Brill, 1997.

Melchert, Christopher. *Before Sufism: Early Islamic Renunciant Piety*. Berlin: De Gruyter, 2020.

Mendelsohn, Isaac. *Slavery in the Ancient Near East*. New York: Oxford University Press, 1949.

Mernissi, Fatima. *Women and Islam: An Historical and Theological Enquiry*. Translated by Mary Jo Lakeland. Oxford: Basil Blackwell, 1991.

Mikhail, Maged S. A. *From Byzantine to Islamic Egypt: Religion, Identity and Politics after the Arab Conquest*. London: I. B. Tauris, 2014.

Miller, J. Maxwell, and John H. Hayes. *A History of Ancient Israel and Judah*. Philadelphia: Westminster Press, 1986.

Millward, William G. "The Adaptation of Men to Their Time: An Historical Essay by al-Yaᶜqūbī." *Journal of the American Oriental Society* 84, no. 4 (1964): 329–344.
Millward, William Guy. "A Study of al-Yaᶜqubī with Special Reference to His Alleged Shīᶜa Bias." PhD dissertation, Princeton University, 1962.
Modarressi, Hossein. *Tradition and Survival: A Bibliographical Survey of Early Shīᶜite Literature*. Oxford: Oneworld Publications, 2003.
Montgomery, James Edward, ed. *ᶜAbbasid Studies: Occasional Papers of the School of ᶜAbbasid Studies, Cambridge, 6–10 July 2002*. Leuven: Peeters, 2004.
Motzki, Harald. *Analysing Muslim Traditions: Studies in Legal, Exegetical and Maghāzī Ḥadīth*. Leiden: Brill, 2010.
Motzki, Harald. "Dating Muslim Traditions: A Survey." *Arabica* 52, no. 2 (2005): 204–253.
Motzki, Harald. "Der *Fiqh* des Zuhrī: Die Quellenprobiematik." *Der Islam* 68 (1991): 1–44.
Motzki, Harald. "The *Muṣannaf* of ᶜAbd al-Razzāq al-Ṣanᶜānī as a Source of Authentic *Aḥādīth* of First Century A.H." *Journal of Near Eastern Studies* 50, no. 1 (1991): 1–21.
Motzki, Harald. *The Origins of Islamic Jurisprudence*. Translated by Marion Holmes Katz. Leiden: Brill, 2002.
Mourad, Suleiman A. "On Early Islamic Historiography: Abū Ismāᶜīl al-Azdī and His *Futūḥ al-Shām*." *Journal of the American Oriental Society* 120, no. 4 (2000): 577–593.
Muᶜattiq, ᶜAwwād ibn ᶜAbdullāh al-. *Al-Muᶜtazila wa-uṣūluhum al-khamsa wa-mawqif ahl al-sunna minhā*. Riyadh: Dār al-rushd, 1416/1995.
Muir, William. *The Life of Mahomet*. London: Smith, Elder and Company, 1861.
Muir, William, and Thomas Hunter Weir. *The Caliphate, Its Rise, Decline, and Fall: From Original Sources*. Edinburgh: J. Grant, 1924.
Mu'nis, Ḥusayn. *Tanqiyat uṣūl al-tārīkh al-Islāmī*. Cairo: Dār al-rashād, 1997.
Mu'nis, Ḥusayn. *Ta'rīkh Quraysh*. Jeddah: al-Dār al-saᶜūdiyya li-l-nashr wa-l-tawzīᶜ, 1408/1988.
Munt, Harry. *The Holy City of Medina: Sacred Space in Early Islamic Arabia*. Cambridge: Cambridge University Press, 2014.
Musᶜad, Muḥammad Fatḥī. *The Wives of the Prophet Muhammad: Their Strives and Their Lives*. Cairo: Dār al-tawzīᶜ wa-l-nashr al-Islāmiyya, 2001.
Muṣṭafā, Shākir. *Al-Ta'rīkh al-ᶜArabī wa-l-mu'arrikhūn: dirāsa fī taṭawwur ᶜilm al-ta'rīkh wa-maᶜrifat rijālih fī al-Islām*, 3rd edition. 3 vols. Beirut: Dār al-ᶜilm lil-malāyīn, 1983.
Myrne, Pernilla. *Female Sexuality in the Early Medieval Islamic World: Gender and Sex in Arabic Literature*. London: I. B. Tauris, 2019.
Myrne, Pernilla. "Slaves for Pleasure in Arabic Sex and Slave Purchase Manuals from the Tenth to the Twelfth Centuries." *Journal of Global Slavery* 4, no. 2 (2019): 196–225.
Nagel, Tilman. *Allahs Liebling: Ursprung und Erscheinungsformen des Mohammedglaubens*. Munich: Oldenbourg Wissenschaftsverlag, 2008.
Nagel, Tilman. *Mohammed: Leben und Legende*. Munich: Oldenbourg Wissenschaftsverlag, 2008.
Najjār, ᶜAbd al-Wahhāb al-. *Al-Khulafā' al-Rāshidūn*. Edited by Khalīl al-Mays. Beirut: Dār al-qalam, 1414/1993.
Nasr, Seyyed Vali Reza. *Mawdudi and the Making of Islamic Revivalism*. New York: Oxford University Press, 1996.
Nasr, Seyyed Vali Reza. *Shiᶜism: Doctrines, Thought, and Spirituality*. New York: State University of New York Press, 1988.
Nef, John Ulric. *Towards World Community*. The Hague: W. Junk N.V., 1968.

Netton, Ian Richard. *Islam, Christianity and the Mystic Journey: A Comparative Exploration*. Edinburgh: Edinburgh University Press, 2011.

Neuwirth, Angelika, and Michael Sells, eds. *Qur'ānic Studies Today*. New York: Routledge, 2016.

Newby, Gordon Darnell. *A History of the Jews of Arabia: From Ancient Times to Their Eclipse under Islam*. Columbia: University of South Carolina, 1988.

Newman, N. A., ed. *The Early Christian-Muslim Dialogue; A Collection of Documents from the First Three Islamic Centuries (632–900 A.D.); Translations with Commentary*. Hatfield, PA: Interdisciplinary Biblical Research Institute, 1993.

Nickel, Gordon. "Scholarship and Islamic Sourcebooks: Telling the Truth about Islam." *Direction* 36, no. 2 (Fall 2007): 219–231.

Nirenberg, David. *Anti-Judaism: The Western Tradition*. London: W. W. Norton, 2013.

Noth, Albrecht, and Lawrence I. Conrad. *The Early Arabic Historical Tradition: A Source-Critical Study*. Princeton, NJ: Darwin Press, 1994.

Numani, Shibli. *Umar*. Makers of Islamic Civilization. London: I. B. Tauris, 2004.

Olster, David M. *Roman Defeat, Christian Response, and the Literary Construction of the Jews*. Philadelphia: University of Pennsylvania Press, 1994.

Omari, Racha el-. "The Muᶜtazilite Movement (I): The Origins of the Muᶜtazila." In *The Oxford Handbook of Islamic Theology*. Edited by Sabine Schmidtke, 130–141. Oxford: Oxford University Press, 2016.

O'Sullivan, Shaun. "Anti-Jewish Polemic and Early Islam." In *The Bible in Arab Christianity*. Edited by David Thomas, 49–68. Leiden: Brill, 2007.

Ouardi, Hela. *Les califes maudits: la déchirure*. Paris: Albin Michel, 2019.

Ouardi, Hela. *Les derniers jours de Muhammad*. Paris: Albin Michel, 2016.

Parry, Kenneth. *Depicting the Word: Byzantine Iconophile Thought of the Eighth and Ninth Centuries*. Leiden: Brill, 1996.

Patton, Walter M. *Aḥmed Ibn Ḥanbal and the Miḥna: A Contribution to a Biography of the Imam and the History of the Mohammedan Inquisition Called the Miḥna, 218–234 A.H.* Leiden: Brill, 1897.

Payne, Richard E. "Christianity and Iranian Society in Late Antiquity, ca. 500–700 C.E." PhD dissertation, Princeton University, 2010.

Perlmann, Moshe. "The Medieval Polemics between Islam and Judaism." In *Religion in a Religious Age*. Edited by Shlomo Dov Goitein, 103–138. Cambridge, MA: Association for Jewish Studies, 1974.

Perlmann, Moshe. "Muslim-Jewish Polemics." In *The Encyclopedia of Religion*. 16 vols. Edited by Mircea Eliade et al., 11:396–402. New York: Macmillan, 1987.

Perlmann, Moshe. "A Study of Muslim Polemics Directed against Jews." PhD dissertation, University of London, 1940.

Peters, F. E. *Muhammad and the Origins of Islam*. New York: State University of New York Press, 1994.

Peters, F. E. *The Muslim Pilgrimage to Mecca and the Holy Places*. Princeton, NJ: Princeton University Press, 1996.

Petersen, Erling Ladewig. *ᶜAlī and Muᶜāwiya in Early Arabic Tradition: Studies on the Genesis and Growth of Islamic Historical Writing until the End of the Ninth Century*. Translated by P. Lampe Christensen. Copenhagen: Aarhuus Stiftsbogtrykkerie, 1964.

Pfander, C. G. *Mīzān al-Ḥaqq*. London: Church Missionary House, Salisbury Square, 1866.

Powell, Avril Ann. *Muslims and Missionaries in Pre-mutiny India*. London: Taylor & Francis, 2013.

Powers, David S. *Muḥammad Is Not the Father of Any of Your Men: The Making of the Last Prophet*. Philadelphia: University of Pennsylvania Press, 2011.

Powers, David S. "Review of Sean W. Anthony's Muhammad and the Empires of Faith." *Al-Abḥāth* no. 69 (2021): 244–267.

Powers, David S. *Zayd*. Philadelphia: University of Pennsylvania Press, 2014.

Qādirī, ᶜAbdallāh ibn Aḥmad al-. *Al-Jihād fī sabīl Allāh: Ḥaqīqatuh wa-ghāyatuh*. 2 vols. Jeddah: Dār al-manāra, 1413/1992.

Qarībī, Ibrāhīm. *Marwiyyāt ghazwat Ḥunayn wa-ḥiṣār al-Ṭā'if*. Medina: al-Jāmiᶜa al-Islāmiyya, 1412/1991.

Qimanī, Sayyid Maḥmūd al-. *Al-Ḥizb al-hāshimī wa-ta'sīs al-dawla al-Islāmiyya*. Cairo: Maktabat Madbūlī al-ṣaghīr, 1996. Reprint.

Qimanī, Sayyid Maḥmūd al-. *Ḥurūb dawlat al-rasūl*, 2nd edition. 2 vols. Cairo: Maktabat Madbūlī al-ṣaghīr, 1996.

Rahemtulla, Shadaab. *Qur'an of the Oppressed: Liberation Theology and Gender Justice in Islam*. Oxford: Oxford University Press, 2017.

Rahlfs, Alfred. "Verzeichnis der Schriften Julius Wellhausens." In *Studien zur semitischen Philologie und Religionsgeschichte: Julius Wellhausen zum siebzigsten Geburtstag am 17. Mai 1914 gewidmet von Freunden und Schülern*. Edited by Karl Marti. Berlin: De Gruyter, 2019 [originally by Verlag von Alfred Töpelmann, Giessen, 1914].

Raḥmān, ᶜĀ'isha ᶜAbd al-. *Nisā' al-nabī*. Beirut: Dār al-hilāl, 1391/1971.

Raḥmān, ᶜAbd al-Hādī ᶜAbd al-. *Al-Tārīkh wa-l-usṭūra*. Cairo: Dār al-Ṭalīᶜa, 1994.

Raḥmān, ᶜAbd al-Hādī ᶜAbd al-. *Judhūr al-quwwa al-Islāmiyya*. Beirut: Dār al-Ṭalīᶜa li-l-Ṭibāᶜa wa-l-nashr, 1988.

Ramadan, Hisham M. *Understanding Islamic Law: From Classical to Contemporary*. Lanham, MD: AltaMira Press, 2006.

Reinink, Gerrit J. "The Beginnings of Syriac Apologetic Literature in Response to Islam." *Oriens Christianus* 77 (1993): 165–187.

Reinink, G. J., and Bernard H. Stolte, eds. *The Reign of Heraclius (610–641): Crisis and Confrontation*. Leuven: Peeters, 2002.

Renard, John, ed. *Islamic Theological Themes: A Primary Source Reader*. Oakland: University of California Press, 2014.

Reynolds, Gabriel Said. *Allah: God in the Qur'ān*. New Haven, CT: Yale University Press, 2020.

Reynolds, Gabriel Said. *The Emergence of Islam: Classical Traditions in Contemporary Perspective*. Minneapolis: Fortress, 2012.

Reynolds, Gabriel Said. *A Muslim Theologian in the Sectarian Milieu: ᶜAbd Al-Jabbār and the Critique of Christian Origins*. Leiden: Brill, 2004.

Reynolds, Gabriel Said. *The Qur'ān and Its Biblical Subtext*. London: Routledge, 2010.

Reynolds, Gabriel Said, ed. *The Qur'ān in Its Historical Context*. London: Routledge, 2008.

Riḍā, Muḥammad Rashīd. *Tafsīr al-manār*, 2nd edition. 12 vols. Cairo: Dār al-manār, 1366/1947.

Ridgeon, Lloyd. *Jawanmardi: A Sufi Code of Honour*. Edinburgh: Edinburgh University Press, 2011.

Rifāᶜī, Aḥmad Farīd. *ᶜAṣr al-Ma'mūn*. 2 vols. Cairo: Maktabat Dār al-Kutub al-Miṣriyya, 1346/1927.

Rippin, Andrew. "The Function of '*Asbāb al-Nuzūl*' in Qur'ānic Exegesis." *Bulletin of the School of Oriental and African Studies* 51, no. 1 (1988): 1–20.

Rippin, Andrew L. "Literary Analysis of Qurān, Tafsīr and Sīra: The Methodologies of John Wansborough." In *Approaches to Islam in Religious Studies*. Edited by Richard C. Martin, 151–163. Tucson: University of Arizona Press, 1985.

Roberts, Joseph Bradin. "Early Islamic Historiography: Ideology and Methodology (the Battle of the Camel)." PhD dissertation, The Ohio State University, 1986.

Robinson, Chase F. *Empire and Elites after the Muslim Conquest*. Cambridge: Cambridge University Press, 2000.

Robinson, Chase F. "Ibn al-Azraq, His *Ta'rīkh Mayyāfāriqīn*, and Early Islam." *Journal of the Royal Asiatic Society*, 3rd series, 6, no. 1 (April 1996): 7–27.

Robinson, Chase F. *Islamic Historiography*. Cambridge: Cambridge University Press, 2003.

Robinson, Chase F. "A Local Historian's Debt to al-Ṭabarī: The Case of al-Azdī's *Ta'rīkh al-Mawṣil*." *Journal of the American Oriental Society* 126 (2006): 521–536.

Robinson, Chase F. "Neck-Sealing in Early Islam." *Journal of the Economic and Social History of the Orient* 48, no. 3 (2005): 401–441.

Rodinson, Maxime. *Mohammad*. Translated by Anne Carter. New York: Penguin Books, 1971.

Roohi, Ehsan. "A Form-Critical Analysis of the al-Rajīᶜ and Bi'r Maᶜūna Stories: Tribal, Ideological, and Legal Incentives behind the Transmission of the Prophet's Biography." *Al-ᶜUṣūr al-Wusṭā* 30 (2022): 267–338.

Roohi, Ehsan. "Between History and Ancestral Lore: A Literary Approach to the *Sīra*'s Narratives of Political Assassinations." *Der Islam* 98, no. 2 (2021): 425–472.

Roohi, Ehsan. "Muḥammad's Disruptive Measures against the Meccan Trade: A Historiographical Reassessment." *Der Islam* 100, no. 1 (2023): 40–80.

Roohi, Ehsan. "The Murder of the Jewish Chieftain Kaᶜb b. al-Ashraf: A Re-examination." *JRAS*, series 3 (2020): 1–20.

Rosenthal, Franz. *A History of Muslim Historiography*, 2nd edition. Leiden: Brill, 1968.

Rosenthal, Franz. "The Influence of Biblical Tradition on Muslim Historiography." In *Historians of the Middle East*. Edited by Bernard Lewis and P. M. Holt, 35–45. London: Oxford University Press, 1962.

Rosenthal, Franz. *Man versus Society in Medieval Islam*. Edited by Dimitri Gutas. Leiden: Brill, 2014.

Rosenthal, Franz. "Review of *ᶜAlī and Muᶜāwiya in Early Arabic Tradition* by Erling Ladewign Petersen." *Speculum* 40, no. 3 (1965): 537–538.

Rubin, Uri. *The Eye of the Beholder: The Life of Muḥammad as Viewed by the Early Muslims*. Princeton, NJ: Darwin Press, 1995.

Rubin, Uri. "Prophets and Progenitors in the Early Shīᶜa Tradition." *Jerusalem Studies in Arabic and Islam* no. 1 (1979): 41–65.

Rubin, Uri. "Quraysh and Their Winter and Summer Journey: On the Interpretation of Sura 106." In *Muḥammad the Prophet and Arabia, Variorum Collected Studies Series*. Variorum 13. Edited by Uri Rubin, 1–32. Farnham: Ashgate, 2011.

Ruṣāfī, Maᶜrūf al-. *Al-Shakhṣiyya al-Muḥammadiyya*. Cologne: Al-Kamel Verlag (Manshūrāt al-jamal), 2002 [1933].

Saad, Salma. "The Legal and Social Status of Women in the Hadith Literature." PhD thesis, University of Leeds, 1990.

Ṣaᶜīdī, ᶜAbd al-Mutaᶜāl al-. *Al-Ḥurriyya al-dīniyya fī al-Islām*. Cairo: Dār al-kitāb al-Miṣrī, 1433/2012 [1375/1955].

Ṣaᶜīdī, ᶜAbd al-Mutaᶜāl al-. *Al-Siyāsa al-Islāmiyya fī ᶜahd al-khulafā' al-Rāshidīn*. Cairo: Dār al-fikr al-ᶜArabī, 1381/1962.

Ṣaᶜīdī, ᶜAbd al-Mutaᶜāl al-. *Dirāsāt Islāmiyya*. Cairo: Dār al-fikr al-ᶜArabī, 1961.

Ṣaᶜīdī, ᶜAbd al-Mutaᶜāl al-. *Tārīkh al-ᶜArab fī al-jāhiliyya wa-ṣadr al-Islām*. Cairo: Maṭbaᶜat al-ᶜulūm, 1352/1933.

Ṣāliḥ, Muḥammad Adīb al-. *Al-Yahūd fī al-Qur'ān wa-l-sunna*. Riyadh: Dār al-hudā li-l-nashr 1413/1993.

Ṣāliḥ, Salwā Balḥāj. *Daththirīnī yā Khadīja*. Beirut: Dār al-Ṭalīᶜa, 1999.

Ṣallābī, ᶜAlī Muḥammad al-. *Al-Dawla al-umawiyya*. 2 vols. Beirut: Dār al-maᶜrifa, 1429/2008.

Ṣallābī, ᶜAlī Muḥammad al-. *Al-Sīra al-nabawiyya: ᶜArḍ waqā'iᶜ wa-taḥlīl aḥdāth*. Beirut: Dār al-maᶜrifa, 1429/2008.

Ṣallābī, ᶜAlī Muḥammad al-. *ᶜAṣr al-dawlatayn al-umawiyya wa-l-ᶜabbāsiyya wa-ẓuhūr fikr al-khawārij*. Amman: Dār al-bayāriq, 1997.

Ṣallābī, ᶜAlī Muḥammad al-. *Ghazawāt al-Rasūl: Durūs wa-ᶜibar wa-fawā'id*. Cairo: Mu'assasat iqra', 2007.

Ṣallābī, ᶜAlī Muḥammad al-. *Sīrat amīr al-mu'minīn ᶜUmar ibn al-Khaṭṭāb*. Cairo: Mu'assasat iqra', 2005.

Samir, Samir Khalil. "The Earliest Arab Apology for Christianity (c. 750)." In *Christian Arabic Apologetics during the Abbasid Period (750–1258)*. Numen Book Series 63. Edited by Samir Khalil Samir and Jorgen Nielsen, 57–114. Leiden: Brill, 1994.

Ṣaqr, Shiḥāta Muḥammad. *Muᶜāwiya ibn Abī Sufyān, amīr al-mu'minīn wa-kātib waḥy al-nabī al-amīn*. Cairo: Dār al-khulafā' al-rāshidīn, n.d.

Savant, Sarah Bowen. *The New Muslims of Post-conquest Iran: Tradition, Memory, and Conversion*. Cambridge: Cambridge University Press, 2013.

Sawwāḥ, Firās al-. *Al-Usṭūra wa-l-maᶜnā*. Damascus: Dār ᶜAlā' al-Dīn, 2001.

Sawwāḥ, Firās al-. *Dīn al-insān*. Damascus: Dār ᶜAlā' al-Dīn, 2002.

Sayeed, Asma. *Women and the Transmission of Religious Knowledge in Islam*. Cambridge: Cambridge University Press, 2013.

Sayyid, Nāṣir al-. *Yahūd Yathrib wa-Khaybar*. Beirut: al-maktaba al-thaqāfiyya, 1412/1992.

Schacht, Joseph. "On Mūsā b. ᶜUqba's *Kitāb al-Maghāzī*." *Acta Orientalia* 21 (1953): 288–300.

Schick, Robert. *The Christian Communities of Palestine from Byzantine to Islamic Rule: A Historical and Archaeological Study*. Princeton, NJ: Darwin Press, 1995.

Schoeler, Gregor. *The Biography of Muḥammad: Nature and Authenticity*. Edited by James E. Montgomery. Translated by Uwe Vagelpohl. New York: Routledge, 2010.

Schoeler, Gregor. "Character and Authenticity of the Muslim Tradition on the Life of the Prophet." *Arabica* 48 (2002): 360–366.

Schoeler, Gregor. *Charakter und Authentie der muslimischen Überlieferung über das Leben Mohammeds*. Berlin: Walter de Gruyter, 1996.

Schoeler, Gregor. *Écrire et transmettre dans les débuts de l'islam*. Paris: Presses universitaires de France, 2002.

Schoeler, Gregor. *The Genesis of Literature in Islam: From the Aural to the Read*. Translated by Shawkat M. Toorawa. Edinburgh: Edinburgh University Press, 2009.

Schoeler, Gregor. "Mūsā b. ᶜUqba's *Maghāzī*." In *The Biography of Muḥammad*. Edited by Herald Motzki, 67–97. Leiden: Brill, 2000.

Schoeler, Gregor. *The Oral and the Written in Early Islam*. Edited by James E. Montgomery. Translated by Uwe Vagelpohl. New York: Routledge, 2006.

Sellheim, Rudolf. "Prophet, Chalif Und Geschichte. Die Muhammed-Biographie Des Ibn Isḥāq." *Oriens* 18/19 (1965): 33–91.

Sezgin, Fuat. *Ta'rīkh al-turāth al-ᶜArabī*. 10 vols. Edited by ᶜArafa Muṣṭafā and Saᶜīd ᶜAbd al-Raḥīm. Translated by Maḥmūd Fahmī Ḥijāzī. Riyadh: Imam Muhammad ibn Saud Islamic University, 1411/1991.

Sfar, Mondher. *In Search of the Original Koran: The True History of the Revealed Text*. Amherst, NY: Prometheus Books, 2008.

Shaᶜrāwī, Muḥammad Mitwallī al-. *Khawāṭirī ḥawl al-Qur'ān al-karīm: tafsīr al-Shaᶜrāwī*. 24 vols. Cairo: Akhbār al-yūm, 1991.

Shahid, Irfan. *Byzantium and the Arabs in the Sixth Century*. Volume 2, Part 2. Washington, DC: Dumbarton Oaks Research Library and Collection, 2009.

Shalabī, Khayrī. *Muḥākamat Ṭāhā Ḥusayn*. Cairo; Beirut: al-Mustaqbal, 1993.

Shams al-Dīn, Ibrāhīm. *Majmūᶜ ayyām al-ᶜArab fī al-jāhiliyya wa-l-Islām*. Beirut: Dār al-kutub al-ᶜilmiyya, 1422/2002.

Shamsy, Ahmed el-. *The Canonization of Islamic Law: A Social and Intellectual History*. Cambridge: Cambridge University Press, 2013.

Sharīf, Aḥmad Ibrāhīm al-. *Makka wa-l-Madīna fī al-jāhiliyya wa-ᶜahd al-Rasūl*. Cairo: Dār al-fikr al-ᶜArabī, 1985.

Shaw, Stanford J. "Bibliography of Hamilton A. R. Gibb." In *Arabic and Islamic Studies in Honor of Hamilton A. R. Gibb*. Edited by George Makdisi, 1–20. Leiden: Brill, 1965.

Shepard, Jonathan, ed. *The Cambridge History of the Byzantine Empire c. 500–1492*. Cambridge: Cambridge University Press, 2019.

Shoemaker, Stephen J. *The Apocalypse of Empire*. Philadelphia: University of Pennsylvania Press, 2018.

Shoemaker, Stephen J. *Creating the Qur'an: A Historical-Critical Study*. Berkeley: University of California Press, 2022.

Shoemaker, Stephen J. *The Death of a Prophet: The End of Muhammad's Life and the Beginnings of Islam*. Philadelphia: University of Pennsylvania Press, 2012.

Shoemaker, Stephen J. "In Search of ᶜUrwa's *Sīra*: Some Methodological Issues in the Quest for 'Authenticity' in the Life of Muhammad." *Der Islam* 85, no. 2 (2011): 257–344.

Shoshan, Boaz. *The Arabic Historical Tradition and the Early Islamic Conquests: Folklore, Tribal Lore, Holy War*. London: Routledge, 2016.

Shoshan, Boaz. *Poetics of Islamic Historiography: Deconstructing Ṭabarī's History*. Leiden: Brill, 2004.

Shukr, Mulḥim. *Al-Zandaqa fī dār al-Islām fī al-qarn al-thānī li-l-hijra*. Beirut: Manshūrāt al-jamal, 2016.

Shurrāb, Muḥammad. *Al-Maᶜālim al-athīra fī al-sunna wa-l-sīra*. Damascus: Dār al-qalam, 1411/1991.

Siddiqi, Mazheruddin. "Review of Islam and Christianity Today by W. Montgomery Watt." *Islamic Studies* 23, no. 4 (Winter 1984): 446–450.

Simon, Robert. *Ignać Goldziher: His Life and Scholarship as Reflected in His Works and Correspondence*. Leiden: Library of the Hungarian Academy of Sciences, 1986.

Sinai, Nicolai. *The Qur'an: A Historical-Critical Introduction*. Edinburgh: Edinburgh University Press, 2017.

Sinai, Nicolai. *Rain-Giver, Bone-Breaker, Score-Settler: Allāh in Pre-Quranic Poetry*. New Haven, CT: American Oriental Society, 2019.

Sinai, Nicolai. "The Unknown Known: Some Groundwork for Interpreting the Medinan Qur'an." *Mélanges de l'Université Saint-Joseph* 66 (2015–2016): 47–96.

Sirry, Mun'im. "Muqātil b. Sulaymān and Anthropomorphism." *Studia Islamica* 107, no. 1 (2012): 38–64.

Sirry, Mun'im A. *Scriptural Polemics: The Qur'ān and Other Religions*. Oxford: Oxford University Press, 2014.

Sizgorich, Thomas. "Narrative and Community in Islamic Late Antiquity." *Past and Present* 285 (November 2004): 9–42.

Sluglett, Peter, and Marion Farouk-Sluglett. "Albert Habib Hourani 1915–1993." *British Journal of Middle Eastern Studies* 20, no. 1 (1993): 139–141.

Smend, Rudolf. *Julius Wellhausen: ein Bahnbrecher in drei Disziplinen*. Munich: Carl Friedrich von Siemens Stiftung, 2006.

Smend, Rudolf. "Julius Wellhausen, 1844–1918." In *From Astruc to Zimmerli: Old Testament Scholarship in Three Centuries*. Edited by Rudolf Smend, 91–102. Tübingen: Mohr Siebeck, 2007.

Smend, Rudolf, et al., eds. *Julius Wellhausen: Briefe*. Tübingen: Mohr Siebeck, 2013.

Smith, Charles Daniel. *Islam and the Search for Social Order in Modern Egypt: A Biography of Muhammad Husayn Haykal*. New York: State University of New York Press, 1983.

Smith, Charles Daniel. *Muhammad Husayn Haykal: An Intellectual and Political Biography*. Ann Arbor: University of Michigan Press, 1968.

Sowell, Thomas. *Black Rednecks and White Liberals*. San Francisco: Encounter Books, 2006.

Sowell, Thomas. *The Thomas Sowell Reader*. New York: Basic Books, 2011.

Spellberg, Denise A. *Politics, Gender, and the Islamic Past: The Legacy of ʿĀ'isha Bint Abī Bakr*. New York: Columbia University Press, 1996.

Spiegel, Gabrielle M. "Forging the Past: The Language of Historical Truth in Middle Ages." *The History Teacher* 17, no. 2 (February 1984): 267–283.

Spiegel, Gabrielle M. "Form and Function in Medieval Historical Narrative." *History and Theory* 22, no. 1 (February 1983): 43–53.

Spiegel, Gabrielle M. "History, Historicism, and the Social Logic of the Text in the Middle Ages." *Speculum* 65, no. 1 (January 1990): 59–86.

Spiegel, Gabrielle M. "Memory and History: Liturgical Time and Historical Time." *History and Theory* 41, no. 2 (May 2002): 149–162.

Spiegel, Gabrielle M. "Political Utility in Medieval Historiography: A Sketch." *History and Theory* 14, no. 3 (October 1975): 314–325.

Spiegel, Gabrielle M. "Revising the Past / Revisiting the Present: How Change Happens in Historiography." *History and Theory* 46, no. 4 (December 2007): 1–19.

Spiegel, Gabrielle M. "The Task of the Historian." *The American Historical Review* 114, no. 1 (February 2009): 1–15.

Sprenger, Aloys. *The Life of Mohammad from Original Sources*. Allahabad: Presbyterian Mission Press, 1851.

Steinbock, Bernd. *Social Memory in Athenian Public Discourse: Uses and Meanings of the Past*. Ann Arbor: University of Michigan Press, 2012.

Stillman, Norman A. *The Jews of Arab Lands: A History and Source Book*. Philadelphia: Jewish Publication Society of America, 1979.

Stroumsa, Sarah. "The Beginning of the Muʿtazila Reconsidered." *Jerusalem Studies in Arabic and Islam* 13 (1990): 265–293.

Stroumsa, Sarah. "On Jewish Intellectuals Who Converted to Islam in the Early Middle Ages." In *The Jews of Medieval Islam: Community, Society, and Identity*. Edited by Daniel Frank, 179–197. Leiden: Brill, 1995.

Stroumsa, Sarah. "The Signs of Prophecy: The Emergence and Early Development of a Theme in Arabic Theological Literature." *Harvard Theological Review* 78, no. 1/2 (January–April 1985): 101–114.

Subḥānī, Ja^c^far al-. *Kulliyyāt fī ^c^ilm al-rijāl*. Qum: Mu'assasat al-nashr al-Islāmī, 1408/1987.

Ṭabāṭabā'ī, Muḥammad Ḥusayn al-. *Al-Mīzān fī tafsīr al-Qur'ān*. 22 vols. Edited by Ḥusayn al-A^c^lamī. Beirut: Mu'assasat al-A^c^lamī, 1997.

Tannous, Jack. *The Making of the Medieval Middle East: Religion, Society, and Simple Believers*. Princeton, NJ: Princeton University Press, 2018.

Tannous, Jack. "Review of Fred Donner's *Muhammad and the Believers*." *Expositions* 5, 2 (2011): 126–141.

Ṭaqqūsh, Muḥammad Suhayl. *Ta'rīkh al-^c^Arab qabla al-Islām*. Beirut: Dār al-nafā'is, 1430/2009.

Ṭaqqūsh, Muḥammad Suhayl. *Ta'rīkh al-khulafā' al-Rāshidīn: al-Futūḥāt wa-l-injāzāt al-siyāsiyya*. Amman: Dār al-nafā'is, 1424/2003.

Thompson, Alexs. "Re-reading al-Ṭabarī: Towards a Narratological Interpretation of the '*History*.'" PhD disseration, The University of Chicago, 2014.

Tobi, Joseph. *The Jews of Yemen: Studies in Their History and Culture*. Leiden: Brill, 1999.

Tolan, John. *Faces of Muhammad: Western Perceptions of the Prophet of Islam from the Middle Ages to Today*. Princeton, NJ: Princeton University Press, 2019.

Tolan, John. "The Prophet Muhammad: A Model of Monotheistic Reform for Nineteenth-Century Ashkenaz." *Common Knowledge* 24 (2018): 256–279.

Toral-Niehoff, Isabel. "Writing for the Caliphate: *The Unique Necklace* by Ibn ^c^Abd Rabbih." *Al-^c^Uṣūr al-Wusṭā* 26 (2018): 80–95.

Treadgold, Warren T. *A History of the Byzantine State and Society*. Redwood City: Stanford University Press, 1997.

Turán, Tamás. *Ignaz Goldziher as a Jewish Orientalist: Traditional Learning, Critical Scholarship, and Personal Piety*. Berlin: De Gruyter, 2023.

^c^Umarī, Akram Ḍiyā' al-. *Al-Mujtama^c^ al-madanī fī ^c^ahd al-nubuwwa*. Medina: Islamic University, 1403/1983.

^c^Umarī, Akram Ḍiyā' al-. *Al-Risāla wa-l-rasūl*. Medina: n.p., 1410/1990.

^c^Umarī, Akram Ḍiyā' al-. *Al-Sīra al-nabawiyya al-ṣaḥīḥa*. 6th ed. Medina: Maktabat al-^c^ulūm wa-l-ḥikam, 1415/1994.

^c^Umarī, Akram Ḍiyā' al-. *^c^Aṣr al-khilāfa al-rāshida*. Riyadh: Maktabat al-^c^Ubaykān, n.d.

^c^Umarī, Akram Ḍiyā' al-. *Buḥūth fī tārīkh al-sunna al-musharrafa*. 5th ed. Medina: Maktabat al-^c^ulūm wa-l-ḥikam, 1405/1984 [1387/1967].

Urban, Elizabeth. "The Early Islamic *Mawālī*: A Window onto Processes of Identity Construction and Social Change." PhD dissertation, University of Chicago, 2012.

Urban, Elizabeth. "The Identity Crisis of Abū Bakra: *Mawlā* of the Prophet, or Polemical Tool." In *The Lineaments of Islam: Studies in Honor of Fred McGraw Donner*. Edited by Paul Cobb, 121–150. Leiden: Brill, 2012.

Ūzūn, Zakariyyā. *Jināyat al-Bukhārī*. Beirut: Riad el-Rayyes Books, 2004.

Ūzūn, Zakariyyā. *Laffaq al-muslimūn idh qālū*. Beirut: Riad el-Rayyes Books, 2008.

van Ess, Josef. *The Flowering of Muslim Theology*. Translated by Jane Marie Todd. Cambridge, MA: Harvard University Press, 2006.

van Ess, Josef. *Theology and Society in the Second and Third Centuries of the Hijra: A History of Religious Thought in Early Islam*. 5 vols. Translated by John O'Kane. Leiden: Brill, 2017.

van Ess, Josef. "From Wellhausen to Becker: The Emergence of Kulturgeschichte." In *Islamic Studies: A Tradition and Its Problems*. Edited by Malcolm H. Kerr, 27–51. Malibu, CA: Undena Publication, 1980.

van Ess, Josef. *Zwischen Hadit und Theologie: Studien zum Entstehen prädestinatianischer Überlieferung*. Berlin: De Gruyter, 1975.

von Kremer, Alfred. "Introduction." In Al-Wāqidī's *Kitāb al-maghāzī*. Edited by Alfred von Kremer, 1–12. Calcutta, 1855.

Waardenburg, Jacques, ed. *Muslim Perceptions of Other Religions: A Historical Survey*. Oxford: Oxford University Press, 1999.

Walker, John. *A Catalogue of the Arab-Byzantine and Post-reform Umaiyad Coins*. London: Trustees of the British Museum, 1956.

Wansbrough, John E. *Qur'ānic Studies: Sources and Methods of Scriptural Interpretation*. Oxford: Oxford University Press, 1977.

Wansbrough, John. "Review of Marshall Hodgson's The Venture of Islam." *Bulletin of the School of Oriental and African Studies* 40, no. 1 (1977): 169–170.

Wansbrough, John E. *The Sectarian Milieu: Content and Composition of Islamic Salvation History*. Oxford: Oxford University Press, 1978.

Wardī, ᶜAlī al-. *Wuᶜᶜāẓ al-salāṭīn*. London: Dār kūfān, 1995 [1954].

Watt, William Montgomery. *The Influence of Islam on Medieval Europe*. Edinburgh: Edinburgh University Press, 1994.

Watt, William Montgomery. "Islamic Conceptions of the Holy War." In *The Holy War*. Edited by T. P. Murphy, 141–156. Columbus: Ohio State University Press, 1974.

Watt, William Montgomery. *Islamic Philosophy and Theology*, 2nd edition. Edinburgh: Edinburgh University Press, 1985.

Watt, William Montgomery. *Muḥammad: Prophet and Statesman*. Oxford: Oxford University Press, 1961.

Watt, William Montgomery. *Muḥammad at Mecca*. Oxford: Oxford University Press, 1953.

Watt, William Montgomery. *Muḥammad at Medina*. Oxford: Clarendon Press, 1956.

Webb, Peter. "Pre-Islamic al-Shām in Classical Arabic Literature: Spatial Narratives and History-Telling." *Studia Islamica* 110 (2015): 135–164.

Webb, Peter. *Imagining the Arabs: Arab Identity and the Rise of Islam*. Edinburgh: Edinburgh University Press, 2016.

Wehr, Hans. *A Dictionary of Modern Written Arabic*. Edited by J. Milton Cowan, 3rd edition. Ithaca, NY: Spoken Languages Services, 1976.

Weil, Gustav. *Geschichte der Chalifen*. 5 vols. Mannheim: F. Bassermann, 1846–1862.

Weil, Gustav. *Historisch-kritische Einleiting in den Koran*, 2nd edition. Bielefeld: Velhagen and Klasing, 1878.

Weil, Gustav. *A History of the Islamic Peoples*. Translated by Khuda Bukhsh. Calcutta: University of Calcutta, 1925.

Weil, Gustav. "An Introduction to the Quran." Translated by Frank K. Sanders and Harry W. Dunning, *The Biblical World* 6, no. 2 (August 1895): 181–191.

Weil, Gustav. *Mohammed der Prophet, sein Leben und seine Lehre: Aus handschriftlichen Quellen und dem Koran geschöpft und dargestellt*. Stuttgart: 1843.

Wellhausen, Julius. *The Arab Kingdom and Its Fall*. Translated by Margaret Graham Weir. Calcutta: University of Calcutta, 1927.

Wellhausen, Julius. *Das arabische Reich*. Berlin: Georg Reimer, 1902.

Wellhausen, Julius. *Medina vor dem Islam, Skizzen und Vorarbeiten*. Berlin, 1889.

Wellhausen, Julius. *Reste Arabischen Heidentums*. Berlin: De Gruyter, 1897.

Wensinck, Arent Jan. *Mohammed en de joden te Medina*. Leiden: Brill, 1928.

Wessels, Antonie. *A Modern Arabic Biography of Muḥammad: A Critical Study of Muḥammad Ḥusayn Haykal's* Ḥayāt Muḥammad. Leiden: Brill, 1972.

Whitby, Mary. "George of Pisidia's Presentation of the Emperor Heraclius and His Campaigns: Variety and Development." In *The Reign of Heraclius (610–641): Crisis and Confrontation*. Edited by Gerrit J. Reinink and Bernard H. Stolte, 157–173. Leuven: Peeters, 2002.

White, Hayden. "The Value of Narrativity in the Representation of Reality." *Critical Inquiry* 7, no. 1 (1980): 5–27.

Widengren, Geo. *Tor Andrae*. Uppsala: Lundequistska Bokhandeln, 1947.

Wilde, Clare Elena. *Approaches to the Qur'ān in Early Christian Arabic Texts: 750–1258 CE*. London and Washington, DC: Academica Press, 2014.

Willis, John Ralph, ed. *Slaves and Slavery in Africa: Islam and the Ideology of Enslavement*, Volume 1. New York: Routledge, 2014 (1986).

Wolfensohn, Israel. *Ta'rīkh al-Yahūd fī bilād al-ᶜArab fī al-jāhiliyya wa-ṣadr al-Islām*. Cairo: Maṭbaᶜat al-Iᶜtimād, 1345/1927.

Wurayyimī, Nājiya al-. *Fī al-I'tilāf wa-l-ikhtilāf: thunā'iyyat al-sā'id wa-l-muhammash fī al-fikr al-Islāmī al-qadīm*. Damascus: Dār al-Madā, 2004.

Wurayyimī, Nājiya al-. *Ḥafriyyāt fī al-khiṭāb al-khaldūnī: al-uṣūl al-salafiyya wa-wahm al-ḥadātha al-ᶜArabiyya*. Damascus: Dār Petra li-l-nashr wa-l-tawzīᶜ, 2008.

Yarbrough, Luke. "Did ᶜUmar b. ᶜAbd al-ᶜAzīz Issue an Edict Concerning Non-Muslim Officials?" In *Christians and Others in the Umayyad State*. Edited by Antoine Borrut and Fred McGraw Donner, 173–205. Chicago: The Oriental Institute of the University of Chicago, 2016.

Yarbrough, Luke. "'I'll Not Accept Aid from a *mushrik*': Rural Space, Persuasive Authority, and Religious Difference in Three Prophetic *ḥadiths*." In *Authority and Control in the Countryside: From Antiquity to Islam in the Mediterranean and Near East (6th–10th Century)*. Edited by Alain Delattre, Marie Legendre, and Petra Sijpesteijn, 44–95. Leiden: Brill, 2018.

Yāsīn, ᶜAbd al-Jawwād. *Al-Sulṭa fī al-Islām*. Beirut: al-Markaz al-thaqāfī al-ᶜArabī, 1998.

Yitzhak, Ronen. "Muhammad's Jewish Wives: Rayhana bint Zayd and Safiya bint Huyayy in the Classic Islamic Tradition." *Journal of Religion & Society* 9 (2007): 1–14.

Zahniser, Alison Howard Mathias. "The *ᶜUthmānīya* of al-Jāḥiẓ: An Analysis of Content, Method and Sources." PhD dissertation, The Johns Hopkins University, 1973.

Zaman, Muhammad Qasim, ed. *Princeton Readings in Islamist Thought: Texts and Contexts from Al-Banna to Bin Laden*. Princeton, NJ: Princeton University Press, 2009.

Zaydān, Jūrjī. *Ta'rīkh al-tamaddun al-Islāmī*. 5 vols. Beirut: Manshūrāt dār maktabat al-ḥayāt, 1902–1906.

Ziriklī, Khayr al-Dīn al-. *Al-Aᶜlām*. 8 vols. Beirut: Dār al-ᶜilm li-l-malāyīn, 2002. Reprint.

Index

For the benefit of digital users, indexed terms that span two pages (e.g., 52–53) may, on occasion, appear on only one of those pages.

ᶜAbbāsids
ᶜAlids and, 63n.15
Arab Bedouin raids, 260–61
claims of legitimacy, 63–64n.17
conquest of Mecca, 140–41, 185, 188–91, 194–95
historical writings of, 4–5, 35–36, 51n.282, 53–55, 72n.64, 114–16
Jews and, 220–22
ᶜAbd al-Karīm, Khalīl, 17–18, 135–36
ᶜAbdullāh ibn Aḥmad al-Qādirī, 14–15
ᶜAbdullāh ibn Jaḥsh, 90–102
ᶜAbdullāh ibn Rawāḥa, 286–88, 292–93
ᶜAbdullāh ibn Ubayy ibn Salūl, 127–28, 130–31, 147–48, 206–9, 312–13
Abou El Fadl, Khaled, 17–18
Abū al-Qāsim ibn ᶜAbd al-Ḥakam, 7–8
Abū ᶜAfak, assassination of, 209–14
Abū Ḥanīfa Dīnawarī, 7–8
Abū Māyla, Birayk, 16–17
Abū Sufyān ibn Ḥarb, 51–53, 71–73, 104–8, 116–19, 122–26, 143–45, 151, 184–93
aḥādīth (traditions, sayings), 168–69
Akram al-ᶜUmarī/Akram Ḍiyā al-ᶜUmarī, 15–17, 236
Akyol, Mustafa, 20–21
al-ᶜAbbās ibn ᶜAbd al-Muṭṭalib, 114–16, 260–61
al-Abwā village raid, 79–90
al-ashhur al-ḥurum (sacred or protected months), 90–102
al-Ḥakam ibn Kaysān, 93–95
ᶜAlids, 62–64, 63n.15, 162–63, 186–87, 194–95
ᶜAlī Muḥammad al-Ṣallābī, 16–17
Allah. *See also maghāzī rasūl Allāh* (expeditions of Allah's messenger)
allegiance under the tree, 163–64
apostle as warrior, 105–7
Arab Bedouin raids and, 251–53, 257–61, 263–64, 267–69, 272–76, 278–79
Battle of Badr and, 110–14
Byzantine expeditions and, 280, 286–309, 312–13, 316–22
divine command of, 61
divine intervention by, 108–10, 117–20, 131–33, 136
fighting against Allah's enemies, 92–93, 96–102, 114
fī sabīl Allāh (fighting in Allah's path), 14–16, 60, 69–70, 113, 263–64, 289–91, 311–12, 322, 325
heavenly power of, 13–14
Jews and, 208–9, 210–11, 214, 224n.123, 227–31, 239–40, 242–44
jihād and, 60, 61, 88–89, 119–20, 239–40, 242, 286–87, 299–300, 301–5
military campaigns as worship of, 17–18
military intervention by, 9–10, 127–30, 140–43, 147–48, 151–53, 154–55, 157–60, 205–6
Muhammad as messenger of, 189
in the name of, 166–67
portrayal at work, 75–77
religious concessions and, 166–67
sharraᶜ (Allah prescribed) *jihād*, 24–25, 88–89
al-Ṭā'if raid, 59, 247–48, 254–55, 259–60, 269–79, 299–300, 310–11, 328–29
al-Wāqidī, Umar, 5–6

ᶜ*ām al-wufūd* (year of delegations), 247–48, 278–79, 328–29
ᶜAmr ibn al-ᶜĀṣ, 171–73
ᶜAmr ibn al-Ḥaḍramī, 95–96
ᶜAmr ibn Hishām (Abū Jahl), 67, 116–17
ᶜAmr ibn Umayya al-Ḍamrī, 218–20
Andræ, Tor Julius Efraim, 40–41
anti-Umayyad inclinations, 51–53, 123–24, 186n.240, 188n.254, 190–91, 260–61
ᶜAqqād, ᶜAbbās Maḥmūd al, 13
Arab Bedouin pagans, 59, 153, 155–57, 243–44, 247–48
Arab Bedouin raids
  al-Ṭā'if raid, 269–79
  Banū Jadhīma raid, 247–54
  Battle of Ḥunayn, 59, 247–48, 254–69, 277–79, 328–29
  introduction to, 247–48
  overview, 328–29
  Qur'ān and, 257–58, 267–69, 275, 278–79
Arabic Christianity, 24–25, 180–81, 280–81, 284–85, 286–87
Arnold, Thomas, 41–42
aṣḥāb al-ḥadīth (traditionists), 73–75, 310–11, 313–15
ᶜAṣmā', assassination of, 209–14

baᶜtha (task force or mission), 9–10
Badr, battle of, 7–8, 58–59, 65–67, 103–21, 126–27, 138–39, 202–4, 271–72, 325
Banū al-Naḍīr tribe, 59, 114n.69, 139–40, 143–47, 151, 201–2, 212, 215–25, 240–41, 327–28
Banū Jadhīma raid, 247–54
Banū Qaynuqāᶜ tribe, 59, 143–45, 201–15, 223–25, 327–28
Banū Qurayẓa tribe, 20–21, 30–31, 59, 139–40, 146–51, 198, 201–2, 204–5, 206–7, 215–16, 223–38, 239–40, 326–28
Battle (and treaty) of Ḥudaybiyya, 58–59, 138–39, 153, 154–78
Battle of Badr, 7–8, 58–59, 65–67, 103–21, 126–27, 138–39, 202–4, 271–72, 325
Battle of Ḥunayn, 59, 247–48, 254–69, 277–79, 328–29
Battle of Mothous, 297–98
Battle of Mu'ta, 59, 180–81, 278–79, 280–99
Battle of the Trench, 58–59, 136–37, 138–53, 165, 173–74, 325–26
Battle of Uḥud, 12–13, 58–59, 62–64, 103–4, 117–18, 121–37, 138–39, 148, 207–8, 215–16
Becker, Carl Heinrich, 36–37
Buwāṭ raid, 81–82
Byzantine expeditions
  Battle of Mu'ta, 59, 180–81, 278–79, 280–99
  incursion into Syria, 316–22
  introduction to, 280–81
  jihād and, 286–87, 299–300, 301–2, 303–5, 309–10, 311–12, 322
  overview of, 329–30
  Qur'ān and, 281, 299–308, 311–13, 315–16, 320–21
  Tabūk raid, 59, 278–79, 280–81, 299–316, 329–30
  Usama's expedition against, 59

Caetani, Leone, 37–40
charitable preaching, 1, 13
Chirágh Ali, Moulavi, 31–32
Christian Byzantine Empire, 180–81, 245–46, 247–48, 278–79, 281–84, 293–94, 298–99, 329–30, 333
civil rights, 31–32
conquest of Mecca. *See* Mecca, conquest of
conversion to Islam, 171–73, 179–80, 189–96, 204–5, 254–55, 259–60, 263–64, 275, 323–24, 328–29
Cook, Michael, 44–46
Crone, Patricia, 44–46, 49, 67n.37

death of Muhammad, 318–22, 330
diyyat al-qatīl (bloodmoney), 218–20
Djait, Hichem, 20–21, 49–50, 173, 310–11
Donner, Fred, 100–2

early expeditions
  ᶜAbdullāh ibn Jaḥsh expedition, 90–102
  al-Abwā raid, 79–81
  Buwāṭ raid, 81–82
  Dhū al-ᶜUshayra raid, 84–85
  Ḥamza ibn ᶜAbd al-Muṭṭalib expedition, 62–70

introduction to, 60–62
Kurz ibn Jābir al-Fihrī, raid against, 82–84
Qur'ān and, 96–97, 100–2
Saᶜd ibn Abī Waqqāṣ expedition, 73–75, 76–79
ᶜUbayda ibn al-Ḥārith expedition, 70–76

Fadak raid, 59, 201–2, 238–46, 327–28
fatḥ (conquest), 9–10, 178–97, 193n.282
fī sabīl Allāh (fighting in Allah's path), 14–16, 60, 69–70, 113, 263–64, 289–91, 311–12, 322, 325
fī sabīl al-salām (for the sake of peace), 12–13

Gabriel (angel), 110, 227, 313–15
Geiger, Abraham, 25–28
ghazwa (raid or expedition), 9–10
ghazwat Dhū al-ᶜUshayra, 84–85
Gibb, Hamilton Alexander Roskeen, 41–43
Goldziher, Ignaz, 34–35, 39–40
Griffith, Sidney H., 24–25

ḥadīth traditions, 34–35, 37–39, 57–58, 73–75, 88–89, 110, 168–69, 310–11, 313–15
Ḥamrā' al-Asad raid, 142–43
Ḥamza ibn ᶜAbd al-Muṭṭalib expedition, 62–70
Hardy, Peter, 31–32
Hawāzin raid, 247–48
Hawting, Gerald, 50–51
Haykal, Muḥammad Ḥusayn, 12–13, 132–33
heavenly power of Allah, 13–14
Heilgeschichte, 49
hijra (emigration), 6, 58, 60–64, 78–79, 84–85, 90–91, 104–5, 216–17, 238–39, 278–79, 280–84, 325
historical memory, 9–10, 51–53
Hodgson, Marshall Goodwin Simms, 43–46
Horovitz, Josef, 35–36
Hourani, Albert Habib, 42
Hoyland, Robert, 44–46, 55n.305
Ḥubāb ibn al-Mundhir, 108–10
Ḥunayn, battle of, 59, 247–48, 254–69, 277–79, 328–29
Ḥusayn, Ṭāhā, 13–14
Ḥuyayy ibn Akhṭab, 151

Ibn Abī Khaythama, 7–8
Ibn ᶜUmar al-Wāqidī, 51–53
Ibn Ḥazm, 313–15
Ibn Hishām, 216–17
Ibn Hishām, Abd al-Malik, 6
Ibn Khaldūn, 51–53
Ibn Qutayba al-Dīnawarī, 7–8
Ibn Shihāb al-Zuhrī, 51–55, 198, 216–17
Ibn Wāḍiḥ al-Yaᶜqūbī, 221–22, 261–62
Ibn Yaḥyā al-Balādhurī, 7–8
idol worshippers, 24–25, 198–200
ilāf, defined, 87–88
Imām Bukhārī, 198
irenic approach in Islamic studies, 37–40
Islamic common law, 31–32
Islamic State, 11–12, 290n.46
Islam is truth, and everything else is false, 1, 15–16
Isrāfīl (angel), 110

Jaᶜfar ibn Abī Ṭālib, 285–86
Jews, confrontations with
Banū al-Naḍīr tribe, 59, 114n.69, 139–40, 143–47, 151, 201–2, 212, 215–25, 240–41, 327–28
Banū Qaynuqāᶜ tribe, 59, 143–45, 201–15, 223–25, 327–28
Banū Qurayẓa tribe, 20–21, 30–31, 59, 139–40, 146–51, 198, 201–2, 204–5, 206–7, 215–16, 223–38, 239–40, 326–28
Fadak raid, 59, 201–2, 238–46, 327–28
introduction to, 198–202
Khaybar raid, 7–8, 59, 201–2, 225, 238–46, 281–84, 320–21, 327–28
Medinan Jews, 12–13, 59, 143–46, 151, 171–73, 198–200, 203–6, 203–4n.23, 208–9, 215, 217–18, 227–28, 230n.152, 236–39, 247–48, 280–81, 327–29, 333
overview of, 327–28
Qur'ān and, 198, 200–1, 202–5, 208–9, 214, 223–25, 227–30, 236

Jews of Banū al-Naḍīr. *See* Banū al-Naḍīr tribe
Jews of Banū Qurayẓa. *See* Banū Qurayẓa tribe
Jews of Medina. *See* Medinan Jews
jihād
  Allah and, 60, 61, 88–89, 119–20, 239–40, 242, 286–87, 299–300, 301–5
  Byzantine expeditions, 286–87, 299–300, 301–2, 303–5, 309–10, 311–12, 322
  fī sabīl Allāh (fighting in Allah's path), 14–16, 60, 69–70, 113, 263–64, 289–91, 311–12, 322, 325
  maghāzī rasūl Allāh (expeditions of Allah's messenger), 60
  religious motivations for, 12–17, 22–23, 31–32, 309–10, 328–30
  *sharra*ᶜ (Allah prescribed) *jihād*, 24–25, 88–89

Kaᶜb ibn al-Ashraf, 143–45, 209–10, 212–14, 221–22, 223–25
Khālid ibn al-Walīd, 127–28, 171–73, 247–54, 256–57, 270–71, 294–97
Khalīfa ibn Khayyāṭ, 7–8
Khalīl ᶜAbd al-Karīm, 18n.92, 100–2
Khan, Sayyid Ahmad, 32–33
Khaybar raid, 7–8, 59, 201–2, 225, 238–46, 281–84, 320–21, 327–28
King of the Hijaz, 2–3, 177–78, 239–40, 244–45
Kitāb al-maghāzī (the Book of Expeditions), 5–6, 33–34, 57–58
kuffār (infidels/unbelievers), 208–9, 214, 300–1
Kurz ibn Jābir al-Fihrī, raid against, 82–84

Lammens, Henri, 37–39
Lapidus, Ira, 48–49
The Life of Mahomet: From Original Sources (Muir), 28–29
The Life of Mohammad (Sprenger), 28–29

maghāzī rasūl Allāh (expeditions of Allah's messenger)
  classical Muslims on, 4–11
  historiographical methodology and approach, 46–57
  introduction to, 1–3, 60–62, 324–25
  jihād and, 60
  modern and contemporary Muslims on, 11–24
  non-Muslim interactions, 24–46, 88–89
  overview of, 57–59, 324–25
maghzā (campaign), 9–10
Mālik ibn ᶜAwf al-Naṣrī, 255–57, 277–78
Margoliouth, David Samuel, 37–39
Mawdūdī, Sayyid Abū al-Aᶜlā, 14–15
Mecca, confrontations with pagans
  Battle of Badr, 7–8, 58–59, 65–67, 103–21, 126–27, 138–39, 202–4, 271–72, 325
  Battle of Uḥud, 12–13, 58–59, 62–64, 103–4, 117–18, 121–37, 138–39, 148, 207–8, 215–16
  introduction to, 103–4
  Meccan pagans, 58–59, 60–61, 69–71, 78–79, 82–83, 87–88
  overview of, 325–26
  Qur'ān and, 113, 117–18, 124–26
Mecca, conquest of
  Battle (and treaty) of Ḥudaybiyya, 58–59, 138–39, 153, 154–78
  Battle of the Trench, 58–59, 136–37, 138–53, 165, 173–74, 325–26
  introduction to, 58–59, 138–39
  overview of, 173–74n.185, 178–97, 325–26
  Qur'ān and, 140–41, 150–51, 152–53, 154–55, 163–64, 170–71, 178–79, 193–94
Meccan pagans, 58–59, 60–61, 69–71, 78–79, 82–83, 87–88
Medieval Syriac texts, 24–25
Medinan Jews, 12–13, 59, 143–46, 151, 171–73, 198–200, 203–6, 203–4n.23, 208–9, 215, 217–18, 227–28, 230n.152, 236–39, 247–48, 280–81, 327–29, 333
Medinan Muslims *(anṣār)*, 58–59, 64–65, 70–71, 77–78, 91–92, 108–10, 136–37, 206–7, 264–66, 285–86, 302–4, 315–16, 325–26

Messenger of God, 103, 110, 124–26, 156n.87, 166–67, 170–71, 186–91, 204–5, 217–18, 221–22, 229–30, 244–45, 261–62
Michael (angel), 110
Mīzān al-ḥaqq (*The Balance of Truth*) (Pfander), 30–31
Mohammadan Common Law, 31–32
mu'allafa qulūbuhum, 195–96, 264–66, 277–78
muhājirūn (Meccan emigrants), 64–65, 70–78, 91–92, 97–98, 155–56, 302–3, 317–18, 325
Muḥammad ibn Isḥāq, 6
Muḥammad ibn Maslama, 306–8
Muḥammad ibn Saᶜd, 7–8
Muir, William, 28–30
munāfiq/munāfiqūn (hypocrite), 124–26, 207–8, 303–4
Munᶜim Sirry, 198
Muqātil ibn Sulaymān, 4–5
Mūsā ibn ᶜUqba, 53–55
mushrikūn (polytheists, associaters), 4–5, 16–17, 156n.88, *See also* polytheism/polytheists
Muslim historiography, 48–49
Mu'ta, battle of, 59, 180–81, 278–79, 280–84, 289–91, 299

Nagel, Tilman, 48–49
Nawfal ibn ᶜAbdullāh ibn al-Mughīra, 93–95
non-Muslim interactions with Muhammad's *maghāzī*, 24–46

pagan Arabs. *See* Arab Bedouin pagans
Petersen, Erling, 51–53
Pfander, Karl Gottlieb, 29–32
poison narrative, 244–46
polytheism/polytheists, 4–5, 16–17, 60, 73–75, 114–16, 124–26, 159–60, 185, 186–87, 202–3, 255–56, 260–61, 264–67, 269, 287–88, 294–96. *See also* *mushrikūn*

Qarqarat al-Kudr expedition, 121–23
Qur'ān
  al-ashhur al-ḥurum (sacred or protected months), 90–102
  as an inspired scripture, 24–25
  Arab Bedouin raids, 257–58, 267–69, 275, 278–79
  Byzantine expeditions and, 281, 299–308, 311–13, 315–16, 320–21
  Chirágh Ali, Moulavi on, 31–32
  depictions of Jewish people, 200–1, 208–9, 214, 227–30
  early expeditions and, 96–97, 100–2
  Jews, confrontations with, 198, 200–1, 202–5, 208–9, 214, 223–25, 227–30, 236
  on married women, 267–69
  Mecca, confrontations with pagans, 113, 117–18, 124–26
  Mecca, conquest of, 140–41, 150–51, 152–53, 154–55, 163–64, 170–71, 178–79, 193–94
  mixed messages about violence, 17–18
  Muir, William on, 29–30
  Muslim commentaries on, 4–5, 20
  passages relating to battle, 152–53
  tafsīr traditions and, 44–46
  Wansbrough, John on, 44–46

Raid to Fadak, 59, 201–2, 238–46, 327–28
Raid to Khaybar, 7–8, 59, 201–2, 225, 238–46, 281–84, 320–21, 327–28
religious liberty, 31–32
Rightly Guided Caliphs, 162–63
Rippin, Andrew, 44–46, 49
Robinson, Chase, 49, 53–55
Rodinson, Maxime, 42–43

Saᶜd ibn Abī Waqqāṣ, 73–75, 76–79
Saᶜd ibn Muᶜādh, 229–32
Sachau, Eduard, 35–36
Ṣafī al-Raḥmān al-Mubārakpūrī, 14–15
Ṣafwān b. Umayyah, 255–56
Ṣāliḥ, Salwā Balḥāj, 49–50
Sallām ibn Abī al-Ḥuqayq, 213–14
Salmān the Persian, 140–41, 146–48
sariyya (incursion), 9–10, 61, 62–65, 69–78, 92–93, 98–99, 209–10, 281–84, 291
Savant, Sarah, 53–55
Sayyid al-Qimanī/Sayyid Maḥmūd al-Qimanī, 19, 79–81

self-defense campaigns, 1, 13, 19, 75–76, 89–90, 118–19, 174–75
*sharra*ᶜ (Allah prescribed) *jihād*, 24–25, 88–89
Shīᶜite Muslims
ᶜAbbāsids and, 221–22
accounts of assassination attempts on Muhammad, 312–16
accounts of poison narrative, 320–21, 330
Arab Bedouin raids, 251–53, 261–62
Byzantine expeditions and, 312–16
Ibn Wāḍiḥ al-Yaᶜqūbī and, 261–62, 300–1
Khālid ibn al-Walīd and, 251–53, 297
Muḥammad ibn Maslama and, 306–8
Muhammad's campaigns and, 7–8, 51–53, 60, 330
rejection of *aṣḥāb al-ḥadīth*, 73–75
rejection of Umayyads, 187–88, 190–91
Shuraḥbīl ibn ᶜAmr al-Ghassānī, 284–85
slaves/slavery, 16–17, 16n.80, 120n.104, 227, 232–34, 240–42, 266–67, 281–84
Snouck Hurgronje, Christiaan Snouck, 35–36
Sprenger, Aloys, 28–29
Sunnī Muslims
accounts of assassination attempts on Muhammad, 312–16
accounts of poison narrative, 320–21, 330
Arab Bedouin raids, 252–53, 273–74
Birayk Abū Māyla and, 211–12
Byzantine expeditions and, 294–96, 312–16
ᶜAbbāsids and, 186–87, 304–5, 318–19
Khālid ibn al-Walīd and, 252–53, 294–96, 297
ᶜUthmān ibn ᶜAbdullāh ibn al-Mughīra and, 162–63, 273–74
Sūrat al-Mā'ida, 198
Syrian incursion by Muhammad, 316–22

Ṭabarī, Ibn Jarīr al, 7–8, 53–55, 57–58, 64–65, 79–81, 84–85, 92–93, 94–95, 97, 100, 103, 104–21, 124–28, 132–35, 155–58, 163–66, 171–73, 182–84, 194–95, 202–3, 204–5, 216–20, 225, 244–45, 281–84
Tabūk raid, 59, 278–79, 280–81, 299–316, 329–30
tafsīr traditions, 44–46
Ṭaqqūsh, Muḥammad Suhayl, 16–17, 165–67
taṣawwur islāmī, 49–50
Thaqīf tribe raid, 247–48
Tolan, John, 25–28
Trench, battle of the, 58–59, 136–37, 138–53, 165, 173–74, 325–26
ṭulaqā', 194–96

ᶜUbāda ibn al-Ṣāmit, 206–7, 208–9
ᶜUbayda ibn al-Ḥārith expedition, 70–76
Uḥud, battle of, 12–13, 58–59, 62–64, 103–4, 117–18, 121–37, 138–39, 148, 207–8, 215–16
ᶜUmar ibn al-Khaṭṭāb, 162–63
Umayyads
ᶜAbbāsids against, 140–41
anti-Umayyad inclinations, 51–53, 123–24, 186n.240, 188n.254, 190–91, 260–61
Arab Bedouin raids, 247, 260–61, 276–77
conquest of Mecca, 140–41, 162–63, 185–91, 194–96
early expeditions, 62–64, 71–75, 90–91, 95–97
Jews, confrontations with, 216–17, 220–22, 223–25
Mecca, confrontations with pagans, 104–5, 114–16, 122–24
Mecca, conquest of, 140–41, 162–63, 185–91, 194–96
Shīᶜite rejection of, 187–88, 190–91
Umayya ibn Khalaf, 81–82
umma (Muslim community), 69–70
universal wisdom, 1, 20
Usāma bin Zayd, 280–81, 316–22, 330
ᶜUthmān ibn ᶜAbdullāh ibn al-Mughīra, 93–95, 162–64

Von Kremer, Alfred, 33–34

Wansbrough, John, 44–46, 100–2
Wāqidī, Abū ᶜAbdullāh ibn ᶜUmar al, 5–8, 33–36, 51–55, 57–58, 97, 103, 104–5,

113, 126–27, 131–32, 135–36, 159–60, 190–91, 202–3, 216–17, 233–34, 280, 293–94, 322
Watt, William Montgomery, 42–43, 100–2, 237–38
Weil, Gustav, 25–28
Wellhausen, Julius, 33–35
Yaᶜqūb al-Fasawī, 7–8
Yaḥyā ibn Maᶜīn, 7–8
Year of Delegations, 59, 247–48, 280–81, 328–29

Zayd ibn Ḥāritha, 123–24, 281–84, 285–86
Zaynab bint al-Ḥārith, 244–45, 320–21

www.ingramcontent.com/pod-product-compliance
Lightning Source LLC
Chambersburg PA
CBHW071433160325
23508CB00014B/128

* 9 7 8 0 1 9 7 7 6 9 1 7 1 *